June 18, 1987

Christy – On your "golden birthday", this is to remind you that you're not the only Irish Catholic girl in the class of '87! Happy eighteenth! – Love,

Laura H

THE ILLUSTRATED
HISTORY OF
IRELAND

THE ILLUSTRATED HISTORY OF IRELAND

FROM EARLY TIMES
400 AD – 1800 AD

by

C. F. CUSACK

"The Nun of Kenmare"

With Historical Illustrations by

HENRY DOYLE

CRESCENT BOOKS

NEW YORK

This edition published 1987 by Crescent Books
Distributed by Crown Publishers, Inc.
225 Park Avenue South
New York, New York 10003

Copyright © 1987

ISBN 0-517-62914-3

Printed and bound in Great Britain
h g f e d c b a

TO THE

RIGHT HONORABLE JUDGE O'HAGAN,

AND TO

HIS SISTER MARY,

FOUNDRESS AND ABBESS OF SAINT CLARE'S CONVENT,
KENMARE,

THIS VOLUME

IS AFFECTIONATELY AND RESPECTFULLY
DEDICATED

BY

The Author.

List of Full-Page Illustrations

ETC.

	PAGE
THE EMIGRANTS' FAREWELL,	32
SPECIMENS OF ANCIENT IRISH MANUSCRIPTS,	44
ST. PATRICK GOING TO TARA,	120
KING BRIAN BOROIMHE KILLED BY THE VIKING,	217
MARRIAGE OF EVA AND STRONGBOW,	264
INTERVIEW BETWEEN MACMURROUGH AND THE OFFICERS OF RICHARD II.,	367
INTERVIEW BETWEEN ESSEX AND O'NEILL,	456
MASSACRE AT DROGHEDA,	501
IRETON CONDEMNING THE BISHOP OF LIMERICK,	507
GRATTAN'S DEMAND FOR IRISH INDEPENDENCE,	590
O'CONNELL REFUSING TO TAKE THE OATH,	647
IRELAND AND AMERICA,	654

PREFACE

TO THE SECOND EDITION.

A DEMAND for a Second Edition of the "Illustrated History of Ireland," within three months from the date of the publication of the First, consisting of 2,000 copies, is a matter of no little gratification to the writer, both personally and relatively. It is a triumphant proof that Irishmen are not indifferent to Irish history—a fault of which they have been too frequently accused; and as many of the clergy have been most earnest and generous in their efforts to promote the circulation of the work, it is gratifying to be able to adduce this fact also in reply to the imputations, even lately cast upon the ecclesiastics of Ireland, of deficiency in cultivated tastes, and of utter neglect of literature.

Nor, as a Catholic and a religious, can I fail to express my respectful gratitude and thankfulness for the warm approbation which the work has received from so many distinguished prelates. A few of these approbations will be found at the commencement of the volume—it was impossible to find space for all. It may be, however, well to observe, that several of the English Catholic bishops have not been less kind and earnest in their commendations, though I have not asked their permission to publish their communications Some extracts are given from the reviews, which also are necessarily condensed and limited; and, as the Most Rev. Dr. Derry has observed, the press has been most favorable in its criticisms. Even those who differed from the present writer *toto cœlo,* both in religion and politics, have not been less commendatory, and, in some instances, have shown the writer more than ordinary courtesy.

Nor should I omit to acknowledge the encouragement which so many gentlemen, both English and Irish, have given to the work, and the assistance they have afforded in promoting its circulation. In a circular, quite recently published in London, and addressed to the members of a society for the republication of English mediæval literature, gentlemen are called on by the secretary, even at the risk, as he himself admits, of "boring them, by asking them to canvass for orders, like a bookseller's traveller," to assist in obtaining additional subscribers to the series, and he requests every subscriber "to get another at once." I am happy to say that, without such solicitation on our part, many Irish gentlemen have done us this kindness, and have obtained not one, but many orders from their friends. I confidently hope that many more will exert themselves in a similar manner, for the still wider dissemination of the Second Edition. It is a time, beyond all others, when Irish history should be thoroughly known and carefully studied. It is a disgrace to Irishmen not to know their history perfectly, and this with no mere outline view, but completely and in detail. It is very much to be regretted that Irish history is not made a distinct study in schools and colleges, both in England and Ireland. What should be thought of a school where English history was not taught? and is Irish history of less importance? I have had very serious letters complaining of this deficiency from the heads of several colleges, where our history has been introduced as a class-book.*

---

* The Rev. U. Burke, of St. Jarlath's College, Tuam, has a note on this subject, in a work which he is at this moment passing through the press, and which he kindly permits me to publish. He says: "This book [the "Illustrated History of Ireland"] ought to be in the hands of every young student and of every young Irish maiden attending the convent schools. Oh, for ten thousand Irish ladies knowing the history of Ireland! How few know anything of it! The present volume, by Sister Francis Clare, is an atoning sacrifice for this sin of neglect."

I am aware that the price of the "Illustrated History of Ireland," even in its present form, although it is offered at a sacrifice which no bookseller would make, is an obstacle to its extensive use as a school history. We purpose,

There are some few Irish Catholics who appear to think that Irishmen should not study their history—some because they imagine that our history is a painful subject; others, because they imagine that its record of wrongs cannot fail to excite violent feelings, which may lead to violent deeds. I cannot for one moment admit that our history is either so very sorrowful, or that we have cause to do anything but rejoice in it. If we consider temporal prosperity to be the *summum bonum* of our existence, no doubt we may say with truth, like the Apostle, that of all peoples we are "most miserable;" but we have again and again renounced temporal advantages, and discarded temporal prosperity, to secure eternal gain; and we have the promise of the Eternal Truth that we shall attain all that we have desired. Our history, then, far from being a history of failures, has been a history of the most triumphant success—of the most brilliant victories. I believe the Irish are the only nation on earth of whom it can be truly said that they have never apostatized nationally. Even the most Catholic countries of the Continent have had their periods of religious revolution, however temporary. Ireland has been deluged with blood again and again; she has been defeated in a temporal point of view again and again; but spiritually— NEVER! Is this a history to be ashamed of? Is this a history to regret? Is this a history to lament? Is it not rather a history over which the angels in heaven rejoice, and of which the best, the holiest, and the noblest of the human race may justly be proud?

On the second count, I shall briefly say that if Irish history were taught in our Irish colleges and schools to children while still young, and while the teacher could impress on his charge the duty of forgiveness of enemies, of patient endurance, of

however, before long, to publish a history for the use of schools, at a very low price, and yet of a size to admit of sufficient expansion for the purpose. Our countrymen must, however, remember that only a very large number of orders can enable the work to be published as cheaply as it should be. It would save immense trouble and expense, if priests, managers of schools, and the heads of colleges, would send orders for a certain number of copies at once. If every priest, convent, and college, ordered twelve copies for their schools, the work could be put in hands immediately.

the mighty power of moral force, which has effected even for
Ireland at times what more violent measures have failed to
accomplish, then there could be no danger in the study.   Perhaps the greatest human preservative of the faith, for those
whose lot may be cast hereafter in other lands, would be to
inculcate a great reverence for our history, and a *true* appreciation of its value.   The taunt of belonging to a despised
nation, has led many a youth of brilliant promise to feel
ashamed of his country, and almost inevitably to feel ashamed
of his faith.   A properly directed study of Irish history would
tend much to remove this danger.   During the debate on the
Irish Church question, Mr. Maguire, M.P. for Cork, significantly
remarked on the effect produced by the " deliberate exclusion"
of any instruction in Irish history from National schools.   It
does seem curious that national history should be a forbidden
subject in National schools, and this fact makes the appellation
of " National " seem rather a misnomer.   The result of this
deliberate exclusion was graphically described by the honorable member.   The youth comes forth educated, and at a
most impressible age he reads for the first time the history
of his country, and burns with indignant desire to avenge
her many wrongs.   The consequences are patent to all.   It is,
then, for the advantage of England, as well as of Ireland, that
Irish history should be made the earliest study of Irish youth;
nor is it of less importance that Irish history should be
thoroughly known by Englishmen.   It is the duty of every
Englishman who has a vote to give, to make himself acquainted
with the subjects on which his representative will give, in his
name, that final decision which makes his political opinion the
law of the land.   I suppose no one will deny that the Irish
Question is the question of the day.   The prosperity of England, as well as the prosperity of Ireland, is involved in it.
No educated man, however humble his station, has a right to
assist in returning a member to Parliament without clearly
comprehending the principles of his representative.   But unless
he has some comprehension of the principles themselves, it is of
little use for him to record his vote.   I do not say that every
English voter is bound to study Irish history in detail, but 1
do say that, at the present day, he is bound to know what the

Irish themselves demand from England; and if he considers their demands reasonable, he should record his vote only for those who will do their utmost to obtain the concessions demanded. A man is unworthy of the privilege of voting, if he is deficient either in the intellect or the inclination to understand the subject on which he votes.

But it is of still more importance that members of Parliament should read—and not only read, but carefully study—the history of Ireland. Irishmen have a right to *demand* that they shall do so. If they undertake to legislate for us, they are bound in conscience and in honour to know what we require, to know our past and our present state. Englishmen pride themselves on their honour; but it is neither honorable to undertake to govern without a thorough knowledge of the governed, or to misrepresent their circumstances to others whose influence may decide their future.

It was manifest from the speech of her Majesty's minister, on the night of the all-important division on the Irish Church question, that he either had not studied Irish history, or that he had forgotten its details. If his statements are correctly reported by the press, they are inconceivably wild. It may be said that the circumstances in which he found himself obliged him to speak as he did, but is this an excuse worthy of such an honorable position? The Normans, he is reported to have said, conquered the land in Ireland, but in England they conquered completely. The most cursory acquaintance with Irish history would have informed the right honorable gentleman, that the Normans did *not* conquer the land in Ireland—no man has as yet been rash enough to assert that they conquered the people. The Normans obtained possession of a small portion, a very small portion of Irish land; and if the reader will glance at the map of the Pale, which will be appended to this edition, at the proper place, he will see precisely what extent of country the English held for a few hundred years. Even that portion they could scarcely have been said to have conquered, for they barely held it from day to day at the point of the sword. Morally Ireland was never conquered, for he would be a bold man who dared to say that the Irish people ever submitted nationally to the English Church

established by law.   In fact, so rash does the attempt seem
even to those who most desire to make it, that they are fain
to find refuge and consolation in the supposed introduction of
Protestantism into Ireland by St. Patrick, a thousand years
and more before that modern phase of religious thought
appeared to divide the Christian world.

But I deny that Ireland has ever been really conquered; and
even should the most sanguinary suggestions proposed in a nine-
teenth-century serial be carried out, I am certain she could not
be.   Ireland has never been permanently subdued by Dane or
Norman, Dutchman or Saxon; nor has she ever been *really*
united to England.   A man is surely not united to a jailer because he is bound to him by an iron chain which his jailer has
forged for his safe keeping.   This is not union; and the term
"United Kingdom" is in fact a most miserable misnomer. Unity
requires something more than a mere material approximation.
I believe it to be *possible* that England and Ireland may become
united; and if ever this should be accomplished, let no man forget that the first link in the golden chain issued from the hands
of the right honorable member for South Lancashire, when he
proposed equality of government on religious questions—the
first step towards that equality of government which alone can
effect a moral union of the two countries.   It might be treasonable to hint that some noble-hearted men, who loved their
country not wisely but too well, and who are paying in lifelong
anguish the penalty of their patriotism, had anything to do
with the formation of this golden chain—so I shall not hint it.

I believe the Fenian movement, at one time scouted as a
mere ebullition, at another time treated as a dangerous and
terrible rebellion, has done at least this one good to England—
it has compelled honest and honorable men to inquire each
for himself what are the grievances of Ireland, and why she
continues disaffected to English rule.   For men who are
honest and honorable to make such inquiries, is the first step,
and a certain step, towards their remedy; and as I glanced down
the list of the *ayes* in the division, I could see the names of men
who, in England, have been distinguished during years for their
private and public virtues, and who have been lavish in their cha-
rities whenever their own countrymen required their assistance.

There can be little doubt that a new era has dawned upon old Erinn's shores. It remains to be proved if her sons shall be as faithful in prosperity as they have been in adversity. It remains to be proved, if opportunities are afforded us of obtaining higher intellectual culture without the danger of the moral deterioration which might have attended that culture under other circumstances, whether we shall avail ourselves of them to the full. May we not hope that Ireland will become once more famous both for learning and sanctity. The future of our nation is in the hands of the Irish hierarchy. No government dare refuse anything which they may demand perseveringly and unitedly. The people who have been guided by them, and saved by them for so many centuries, will follow as they lead. If their tone of intellectual culture is elevated, the people will become elevated also ; and we shall hear no more of those reproaches, which are a disgrace to those who utter them, rather than to those of whom they are uttered. Let our people be taught to appreciate something higher than a mere ephemeral literature ; let them be taught to take an interest in the antiquities and the glorious past of their nation ; and then let them learn the history of other peoples and of other races. A high ecclesiastical authority has declared recently that " ecclesiastics do not cease to be citizens," and that they do not consider anything which affects the common weal of their country is remote from their duty. The clergy of the diocese of Limerick, headed by their Dean, and, it must be presumed, with the sanction of their Bishop, have given a tangible proof that they coincide in opinion with his Grace the Archbishop of Westminster. The letter addressed to Earl Grey by that prelate, should be in the hands of every Irishman; and it is with no ordinary gratification that we acknowledge the kindness and condescension of his Grace in favouring us with an early copy of it.

This letter treats of the two great questions of the day with admirable discretion. As I hope that every one who reads these pages possesses a copy of the pamphlet, I shall merely draw attention to two paragraphs in it : one in which Fenianism is treated of in that rational spirit which appears to have been completely lost sight of in the storm of angry discussion which it has excited. On this subject his Grace writes: "It would be blindness not to see, and madness to deny, that we have entered into another crisis in the relation of England and Ireland, of which '98, '28, and '48 were precursors;" and he argues with clearness and authority, that when Englishmen once have granted justice to Ireland, Ireland will cease to accuse England of injustice.

To one other paragraph in this remarkable letter, I shall briefly allude: "I do not think Englishmen are enough aware of the harm some among us do by a contemptuous, satirical, disrespectful, defiant, language in speaking of Ireland and the Irish people." From peculiar circumstances, the present writer has had more than ordinary opportunities of verifying the truth of this statement. The wound caused by a sarcastic expression may often fester far longer than the wound caused by a hasty blow. The evil caused by such language is by no means confined entirely to Protestants. There are, indeed, but few English Catholics who speak contemptuously of Ireland, of its people, or of its history; but, if I am to credit statements which have been made to me on unquestionable authority, there are some who are not free from this injustice. A half-commiserating tone of patronage is quite as offensive as open contempt; and yet there have been instances where English Catholic writers, while obliged to show some deference to Ireland and the Irish, in order to secure the patronage and support of that country for their publications, have at the same time, when they dared, thrown out insinuations against peculiarities of Irish character, and made efforts to discredit Irish historical documents.

I had intended, in preparing the Second Edition of the "Illustrated History of Ireland," to omit the original Preface, in order to leave more space for the historical portion of the work. When this intention was mentioned, several laymen and ecclesiastics expostulated so earnestly against it, that I have been obliged to yield to their request. I am aware that some few persons objected to my remarks on the state of land laws in Ireland, or rather on the want of proper land laws; but the opinion of those interested in maintaining an evil, will always be averse to its exposure; and I cannot conceive how any one who desires an injustice to be removed, can object to a fair and impartial discussion of the subject. An English writer, also, has made some childish remarks about the materials for Irish history not being yet complete, and inferred that in consequence an Irish history could not yet be written. His observations are too puerile to need refutation. I have been informed also that some objection has been made to a "political preface;" and that one gentleman, whose name I have not had the honour of hearing, has designated the work as a "political pamphlet." Even were not Irish history exceptional, I confess myself perplexed to understand how history and politics can be severed. An author may certainly write a perfectly colourless history, but he must state the opinions of different parties, and the acts consequent on those opinions, even should he do so without any observation of his own. I never for a moment entertained the intention of writing such a history, though I freely confess I have exercised considerable self-restraint as to the expression of my own opinion when writing some portions of the present work. You might as well attempt to write an ecclesiastical history without the slightest reference to different religious opinions, as attempt to write the history of any nation, and, above all, of Ireland, without special and distinct reference to the present and past political opinions of the different sections of which the nation is composed. Such suggestions are only worthy of those who, when facts are painful, try to avert the wound they cause by turning on the framer of the weapon which has driven these facts a little deeper than usual into their intellectual conception; or of those uneducated, or low-minded, even if educated persons, who consider that a woman cannot write a history, and would confine her literary efforts to sensation novels and childish tales. I am thankful, and I hope I am not unduly proud, that men of the highest intellectual culture, both in England and Ireland, on the Continent of Europe, and in America, have pronounced a very different judgment on the present work, and on the desire of the writer to raise her countrywomen to higher mental efforts than are required by the almost exclusive perusal of works of fiction. If women may excel as painters and sculptors, why may not a woman attempt to excel as an historian? Men of cultivated intellect, far from wishing to depreciate such efforts, will be the first to encourage them with more than ordinary warmth; the opinions of other persons, whatever may be their position, are of little value.

On the Irish Church question I feel it unnecessary to say more than a word of congratulation to my countrymen, and of hearty thanks for the noble conduct of so many Englishmen at this important crisis. Irish Protestants have been quite as national as Irish Catholics; and now that the fatal bane of religious dissension has been removed, we may hope that Irishmen, of all classes and creeds, will work together harmoniously for the good of their common country: and thus one great means of Irish prosperity will be opened. The Irish are eminently a justice-loving people. Let justice once be granted to them, and there is that in their national character which will make them accept as a boon what others might accept as a right.

In concluding the Preface to this Edition, I cannot omit to express my grateful thanks to Sir William Wilde, and other members of the Royal Irish Academy, through whose kindness I obtained the special favour of being permitted to copy some of the most valuable illustrations of Irish antiquities contained in their Catalogue, and which has enabled the reader, for the first time, to have an Irish history illustrated with Irish antiquities—a favour which it is hoped an increase of cultivated taste amongst our people will enable them to appreciate more and more. To John O'Hagan, Esq., Q.C., I owe a debt of gratitude which cannot easily be repaid, for the time he bestowed on the correction of the proofs of the First Edition, and for many kind suggestions, and much valuable advice. I am indebted, also, to M. J. Rhodes, Esq., of Hoddersfield, for a liberal use of his library, perhaps one of the most valuable private libraries in Ireland, and for permitting me to retain, for a year and more, some of its most costly treasures. The same kindness was also granted by the Rev. D. M'Carthy, Professor of Sacred Scripture and Hebrew at Maynooth, who is himself doing so much for its ecclesiastical students by his valuable literary labours, and who was one of the first to urge me to undertake this work. In preparing the Second Edition, I am not a little indebted to the Rev. James Gaffney, C.C., M.R.I.A., of Clontarf, who, even during the heavy pressure of Lenten parochial duties, has found time to give me the benefit of many important suggestions, and to show his love of Ireland by deeming no effort too great to further a knowledge of her glorious history. I am also indebted to the Rev. John Shearman, C.C., M.R.I.A., of Howth, for the valuable paper read before the R.I.A., on the "Inscribed Stones at Killeen Cormac;" and to many other authors who have presented me with their works; amongst the number, none were more acceptable than the poems of Dr. Ferguson, and the beautiful and gracefully written *Irish before the Conquest*, of Mrs. Ferguson, whose gifts are all the more treasured for the peculiar kindness with which they were presented.

To my old friend, Denis Florence MacCarthy, Esq., M.R.I.A., who should be the laureate of Ireland—and why should not Ireland, that land of song, have her laureate ?—I can only offer my affectionate thanks, for his kindnesses are too numerous to record, and are so frequent that they would scarcely bear enumeration. At this moment, Roderick O'Flanagan, Esq., M.R.I.A., has found, or rather made, leisure, amongst his many professional and literary occupations, to prepare the valuable and important map of Irish families, which will be given *gratis* to all subscribers, and in which W. H. Hennessy, Esq., M.R.I.A., at present employed by Government on the important work of publishing ancient Irish MS., will also give his assistance.

To many of the gentlemen in Cork, and principally to Nicholas Murphy, Esq., of Norwood, and Eugene M'Sweeny, Esq., I cannot fail to offer my best thanks, for the generous help they have given in promoting the sale of the First Edition, and for over-payments of subscriptions, made unasked, and with the most considerate kindness, when they found the heavy cost of the First Edition was likely to prove a loss to the convent, in consequence of expenses which could scarcely be foreseen in the increased size of the work, and the high class of engravings used, which demanded an immense outlay in their production.   The subscribers to the Second Edition are indebted to not a few of the subscribers to the First, many of them priests with limited incomes, for the generosity which has enabled them to obtain this new issue on such favourable terms.   It is with feelings of no ordinary pleasure that I add also the names of the Superioresses of nearly all the convents of the order of Our Lady of Mercy and of the order of the Presentation, to the list of our benefactors.   With the exception of, perhaps, two or three convents of each order, they have been unanimous in their generous efforts to assist the circulation of the Irish History, and of all our publications; and this kindness has been felt by us all the more deeply, because from our own poverty, and the poverty of the district in which we live, we have been unable to make them any return, or to assist them even by the sale of tickets for their bazaars.   Such disinterested charity is, indeed, rare; and the efforts made by these religious—the true centres of civilization in Ireland—to promote the education and to improve the moral and intellectual tone of the lower and middle classes, are beyond all praise, combined, as these efforts are, with never-ceasing labour for the spiritual and temporal good of the poor in their respective districts.   Nor should I omit a word for the friends across the wide Atlantic, to whom the very name of Ireland is so precious, and to whom Irish history is so dear.   The Most Rev. Dr. Purcell, Archbishop of Cincinnati, has pronounced the work to be the only Irish history worthy of the name.   John Mitchel has proclaimed, in the *Irish Citizen*, that a woman has accomplished what men have failed to do; and Alderman Ternan, at a banquet in New York, has uttered the same verdict, and declares that there, at least, no other history can compete with ours, although Moore and D'Arcy Magee have preceded us in their efforts to promote the knowledge of what Ireland has been, and the hope of what Ireland may yet become.

M. F. C.

St. Clare's Convent, Kenmare, Co. Kerry,
       May 8th, 1868.

PREFACE

TO THE FIRST EDITION.

THE history of the different races who form an integral portion of the British Empire, should be one of the most carefully cultivated studies of every member of that nation. To be ignorant of our own history, is a disgrace; to be ignorant of the history of those whom we govern, is an injustice. We can neither govern ourselves nor others without a thorough knowledge of peculiarities of disposition which may require restraint, and of peculiarities of temperament which may require development. We must know that water can extinguish fire, before it occurs to us to put out a fire by the use of water. We must know that fire, when properly used, is a beneficent element of nature, and one which can be used to our advantage when properly controlled, before we shall attempt to avail ourselves of it for a general or a particular benefit. I believe a time has come when the Irish are more than ever anxious to study their national history. I believe a time has come when the English nation, or at least a majority of the English nation, are willing to read that history without prejudice, and to consider it with impartiality.

When first I proposed to write a History of Ireland, at the earnest request of persons to whose opinion I felt bound to defer, I was assured by many that it was useless; that Irishmen did not support Irish literature; above all, that the Irish clergy were indifferent to it, and to literature in general. I have since ascertained, by personal experience, that this charge is utterly unfounded, though I am free to admit it was made on what appeared to be good authority. It is certainly to be wished that there was a more general love of reading cultivated amongst the Catholics of Ireland, but the deficiency is on a fair way to amendment. As a body, the Irish priesthood may not be devoted to literature; but as a body, unquestionably they are devoted—nobly devoted—to the spread of education amongst their people.

With regard to Englishmen, I cannot do better than quote the speech of an English member of Parliament, Alderman Salomons, who has just addressed his constituents at Greenwich in these words:—

" The state of Ireland will, doubtless, be a prominent subject of discussion next session. Any one who sympathizes with distressed nationalities in their struggles, must, when he hears of the existence of a conspiracy in Ireland, similar to those combinations which used to be instituted in Poland in opposition to Russian oppression, be deeply humiliated. Let the grievances of the Irish people be probed, and let them be remedied when their true nature is discovered. Fenianism is rife, not only in Ireland, but also in England, and an armed police required, which is an insult to our liberty. I did not know much of the Irish land question, but I know that measures have been over and over again brought into the House of Commons with a view to its settlement, and over and over again they have been cushioned or silently withdrawn. If the question can be satisfactorily settled, why let it be so, and let us conciliate the people of Ireland by wise and honorable means. The subject of the Irish Church must also be considered. I hold in my hand an extract from the report of the commissioner of the Dublin *Freeman's Journal,* who is now examining the question. It stated what will be to you almost incredible—namely, that the population of the united dioceses of Cashel, Emly, Waterford, and Lismore is 370,978, and that of those only 13,000 are members of the Established Church, while 340,000 are Roman Catholics. If you had read of this state of things existing in any other country, you would call out loudly against it. Such a condition of things, in which large revenues are devoted, not for the good of the many, but the few, if it does not justify Fenianism, certainly does justify a large measure of discontent. I am aware of the difficulties in the way of settling the question, owing to the fear of a collision between Protestants and Catholics ; but I think Parliament ought to have the power to make the Irish people contented."

This speech, I believe, affords a fair idea of the opinion of educated and unprejudiced Englishmen on the Irish question. They do not know much about Irish history; they have heard a great deal about Irish grievances, and they have a vague idea that there is something wrong about the landlords, and something wrong about the ecclesiastical arrangements of the country. I believe a careful study of Irish history is essential to the comprehension of the Irish question ; and it is obviously the moral duty of every man who has a voice in the government of the nation, to make himself master of the subject. I believe there are honest and honorable men in England, who would stand aghast with horror if they thoroughly understood the injustices to which Ireland has been and *still is* subject. The English, as a nation, profess the most ardent veneration for liberty. To be a patriot, to desire to free one's country, unless, indeed, that country happen to have some very close connexion with their own, is the surest way to obtain ovations and applause. It is said that circumstances alter cases ; they certainly alter opinions, but they do not alter facts. An Englishman applauds and assists insurrection in countries where they profess to have for their object the freedom of the individual or of the nation ; he imprisons and stifles it at home, where the motive is precisely similar, and the cause, in the eyes of the insurgents at least, incomparably more valid. But I do not wish to raise a vexed question, or to enter on political discussions ; my object in this Preface is simply to bring before the minds of Englishmen that they have a duty to perform towards Ireland—a duty which they cannot cast aside on others—a duty which it may be for their interest,

as well as for their honour, to fulfil. I wish to draw the
attention of Englishmen to those Irish grievances which are
generally admitted to exist, and which can only be fully
understood by a careful and unprejudiced perusal of Irish
history, past and present. Until grievances are thoroughly
understood, they are not likely to be thoroughly remedied.
While they continue to exist, there can be no real peace in
Ireland, and English prosperity must suffer in a degree from
Irish disaffection.

It is generally admitted by all, except those who are specially
interested in the denial, that the Land question and the Church
question are the two great subjects which lie at the bottom of
the Irish difficulty. The difficulties of the Land question commenced in the reign of Henry II.; the difficulties of the Church
question commenced in the reign of Henry VIII. I shall request your attention briefly to the standpoints in Irish history
from which we may take a clear view of these subjects. I shall
commence with the Land question, because I believe it to be
the more important of the two, and because I hope to show
that the Church question is intimately connected with it.

In the reign of Henry II., certain Anglo-Norman nobles
came to Ireland, and, partly by force and partly by intermarriages, obtained estates in that country. Their tenure was
the tenure of the sword. By the sword they expelled persons
whose families had possessed those lands for centuries; and by
the sword they compelled these persons, through poverty, consequent on loss of property, to take the position of inferiors
where they had been masters. You will observe that this first
English settlement in Ireland was simply a colonization on a very
small scale. Under such circumstances, if the native population are averse to the colonization, and if the new and the old
races do not amalgamate, a settled feeling of aversion, more or
less strong, is established on both sides. The natives hate the
colonist, because he has done them a grievous injury by taking
possession of their lands; the colonist hates the natives, because
they are in his way; and, if he be possessed of "land hunger,"
they are an impediment to the gratification of his desires. It
should be observed that there is a wide difference between
colonization and conquest. The Saxons conquered what we

may presume to have been the aboriginal inhabitants of England; the Normans conquered the Saxon : the conquest in both cases was sufficiently complete to amalgamate the races—the interest of the different nationalities became one. The Norman lord scorned the Saxon churl quite as contemptuously as he scorned the Irish Celt; but there was this very important difference—the interests of the noble and the churl soon became one; they worked for the prosperity of their common country. In Ireland, on the contrary, the interests were opposite. The Norman noble hated the Celt as a people whom he could not subdue, but desired most ardently to dispossess; the Celt hated the invader as a man most naturally will hate the individual who is just strong enough to keep a wound open by his struggles, and not strong enough to end the suffering by killing the victim.

The land question commenced when Strongbow set his foot on Irish soil; the land question will remain a disgrace to England, and a source of misery to Ireland, until the whole system inaugurated by Strongbow has been reversed. "At the commencement of the connexion between England and Ireland," says Mr. Goldwin Smith, "the foundation was inevitably laid for the fatal system of ascendency—a system under which the dominant party were paid for their services in keeping down rebels by a monopoly of power and emolument, and thereby strongly tempted to take care that there should always be rebels to keep down." There is a fallacy or two in this statement; but let it pass. The Irish were not rebels then, certainly, for they were not under English dominion; but it is something to find English writers expatiating on Irish wrongs; and if they would only act as generously and as boldly as they speak, the Irish question would receive an early and a most happy settlement.

For centuries Ireland was left to the mercy and the selfishness of colonists. Thus, with each succeeding generation, the feeling of hatred towards the English was intensified with each new act of injustice, and such acts were part of the normal rule of the invaders. A lord deputy was sent after a time to rule the country. Perhaps a more unfortunate form of government could not have been selected for Ireland. The lord deputy

knew that he was subject to recall at any moment; he had
neither a personal nor a hereditary interest in the country.
He came to make his fortune there, or to increase it. He
came to rule for his own benefit, or for the benefit of his nation.
The worst of kings has, at least, an hereditary interest in the
country which he governs; the best of lord deputies might
say that, if he did not oppress and plunder for himself, other
men would do it for themselves: why, then, should he be the
loser, when the people would not be gainers by his loss?

When parliaments began to be held, and when laws were
enacted, every possible arrangement was made to keep the two
nations at variance, and to intensify the hostility which already
existed. The clergy were set at variance. Irish priests were forbidden to enter certain monasteries, which were reserved for the
use of their English brethren; Irish ecclesiastics were refused
admission to certain Church properties in Ireland, that English
ecclesiastics might have the benefit of them. Lionel, Duke of
Clarence, when Viceroy of Ireland, issued a proclamation, forbidding the "Irish by birth" even to come near his army, until
he found that he could not do without soldiers, even should
they have the misfortune to be Irish. The Irish and English
were forbidden to intermarry several centuries before the same
bar was placed against the union of Catholics and Protestants.
The last and not the least of the fearful series of injustices
enacted, in the name of justice, at the Parliament of Kilkenny,
was the statute which denied, which positively refused, the
benefit of English law to Irishmen, and equally forbid them to
use the Brehon law, which is even now the admiration of
jurists, and which had been the law of the land for many
centuries.

If law could be said to enact that there should be no law,
this was precisely what was done at the memorable Parliament
of Kilkenny. If Irishmen had done this, it would have been
laughed at as a Hibernicism, or scorned as the basest villany;
but it was the work of Englishmen, and the Irish nation were
treated as rebels if they attempted to resist. The confiscation
of Church property in the reign of Henry VIII., added a new
sting to the land grievance, and introduced a new feature in
its injustice. Church property had been used for the benefit of

the poor far more than for the benefit of its possessors. It is generally admitted that the monks of the middle ages were the best and most considerate landlords. Thousands of families were now cast upon the mercy of the new proprietors, whose will was their only law ; and a considerable number of persons were deprived of the alms which these religious so freely distributed to the sick and the aged. Poverty multiplied fearfully, and discontent in proportion. You will see, by a careful perusal of this history, that the descendants of the very men who had driven out the original proprietors of Irish estates, were in turn driven out themselves by the next set of colonists. It was a just retribution, but it was none the less terrible. Banishments and confiscations were the rule by which Irish property was administered. Can you be surprised that the Irish looked on English adventurers as little better than robbers, and treated them as such? If the English Government had made just and equitable land laws for Ireland at or immediately after the Union, all the miseries which have occurred since then might have been prevented. Unfortunately, the men who had to legislate for Ireland are interested in the maintenance of the unjust system ; and there is an old proverb, as true as it is old, about the blindness of those who do not wish to see. Irish landlords, or at least a considerable number of Irish landlords, are quite willing to admit that the existence of the Established Church is a grievance. Irish Protestant clergymen, who are not possessed by an anti-Popery crochet—and, thank God, there are few afflicted with that unfortunate disease now—are quite free to admit that it is a grievance for a tenant to be subject to ejection by his landlord, *even if he pays his rent punctually*.

I believe the majority of Englishmen have not the faintest idea of the way in which the Irish tenant is oppressed, *not by individuals*, for there are many landlords in Ireland devoted to their tenantry, but by a system. There are, however, it cannot be denied, cases of individual oppression, which, if they occurred in any part of Great Britain, and were publicly known, would raise a storm, from the Land's End to John o' Groat's House, that would take something more than revolvers to settle. As one of the great objects of studying the history of our own country, is to enable us to understand and to enact such regulations as shall be best suited to the genius of each race and their peculiar circumstances, I believe it to be my duty as an historian, on however humble a scale, not only to show how our present history is affected by the past, but also to give you such a knowledge of our present history as may enable you to judge how much the country is still suffering from *present grievances*, occasioned by past maladministration. Englishmen are quite aware that thousands of Irishmen leave their homes every year for a foreign country; but they have little idea of the cause of this emigration. Englishmen are quite aware that from time to time insurrections break out in Ireland, which seem to them very absurd, if not very wicked; but they do not know how much grave cause there is for discontent in Ireland. The very able and valuable pamphlets which have been written on these subjects by Mr. Butt and Mr. Levey, and on the Church question by Mr. De Vere, do not reach the English middle classes, or probably even the upper classes, unless their attention is directed to them individually. The details of the sufferings and ejectments of the Irish peasantry, which are given from time to time in the Irish papers, and principally in the Irish *local* papers, are never even known across the Channel. How, then, can the condition of Ireland, or of the Irish people, be estimated as it should? I believe there is a love of fair play and manly justice in the English nation, which only needs to be excited in order to be brought to act.

But ignorance on this subject is not wholly confined to the English. I fear there are many persons, even in Ireland, who are but imperfectly acquainted with the working of their own land laws, if, indeed, what sanctions injustice deserves the name of law. To avoid prolixity, I shall state very briefly the position of an Irish tenant at the present day, and I shall show (1) how this position leads to misery, (2) how misery leads to emigration, and (3) how this injustice recoils upon the heads of the perpetrators by leading to rebellion. First, the position of an Irish tenant is simply this: he is rather worse off than a slave. I speak advisedly. In Russia, the proprietors of large estates worked by slaves, are obliged to feed and clothe their slaves; in Ireland, it quite depends on the will of the proprietor whether he will let his lands to his tenants on terms which will enable them to feed their families on the coarsest food, and to clothe them in the coarsest raiment. If a famine occurs—and in some parts of Ireland famines are of annual occurrence—the landlord is not obliged to do anything for his tenant, but the tenant *must* pay his rent. I admit there are humane landlords in Ireland; but these are questions of fact, not of feeling. It is a most flagrant injustice that Irish landlords should have the power of dispossessing their tenants if they pay their rents. But this is not all; although the penal laws have been repealed, the power of the landlord over the conscience of his tenant is unlimited. It is true he cannot apply bodily torture, except, indeed, the torture of starvation, but he can apply mental torture. It is in the power of an Irish landlord to eject his tenant if he does not vote according to his wishes. A man who has no conscience, has no moral right to vote; a man who tyrannizes over the conscience of another, should have no legal right. But there is yet a deeper depth. I believe you will be lost in amazement at what is yet to come, and will say, as Mr. Young said of penal laws in the last century, that they were more "fitted for the meridian of Barbary." You have heard, no doubt, of wholesale evictions; they are of frequent occurrence in Ireland—sometimes from political motives, because the poor man will not vote with his landlord; sometimes from religious motives, because the poor man will not worship God according to his landlord's conscience; sometimes from selfish motives, because his landlord wishes to enlarge his domain, or to graze more cattle. The motive does not matter much to the poor victim. He is flung out upon the roadside; if he is very poor, he may die there, or he may go to the workhouse, but he must not be taken in, even for a time, by any other family on the estate. The Irish Celt, with his warm heart and generous impulses, would, at all risks to himself, take in the poor outcasts, and share his poverty with them; but the landlord could not allow this. The commission of one evil deed necessitates the commission of another. An Irish gentleman, who has no personal interest in land, and is therefore able to look calmly on the question, has been at the pains to collect instances of this tyranny, in his

Plea for the Celtic Race. I shall only mention one as a sample. In the year 1851, on an estate which was at the time supposed to be one of the most fairly treated in Ireland, "the agent of the property had given public notice to the tenantry that expulsion from their farms would be the penalty inflicted on them, if they harboured *any one* not resident on the estate. The penalty was enforced against a widow, for giving food and shelter *to a destitute grandson of twelve years old.* The child's mother at one time held a little dwelling, from which she was expelled; his father was dead. He found a refuge with his grandmother, who was ejected from her farm for harbouring the poor boy." When such things can occur, we should not hear anything more about the Irish having only "sentimental grievances." The poor child was eventually driven from house to house. He stole a shilling and a hen—poor fellow!—what else could he be expected to do? He wandered about, looking in vain for shelter from those who dared not give it. He was expelled with circumstances of peculiar cruelty from one cabin. He was found next morning, cold, stiff, and dead, on the ground outside. The poor people who had refused him shelter, were tried for their lives. They were found guilty of manslaughter *only*, in consideration of the agent's order. The agent was not found guilty of anything, nor even tried. The landlord was supposed to be a model landlord, and his estates were held up at the very time as models; yet evictions had been fearfully and constantly carried out on them. Mr. Butt has well observed : "The rules of the estate are often the most arbitrary and the most sternly enforced upon great estates, the property of men of the highest station, upon which rents are moderate, and no harshness practised to the tenantry, who implicitly submit." Such landlords generally consider emigration the great remedy for the evils of Ireland. They point to their own well-regulated and well-weeded estates ; but they do not tell you all the human suffering it cost to exile those who were turned out to make room for large dairy farms, or all the quiet tyranny exercised over those who still remain. Neither does it occur to them that their successors may raise these moderate rents at a moment's notice; and if their demands are not complied with, he may eject these "comfortable farmers" without one farthing of compensation for all their improvements and their years of labour.

I have shown how the serfdom of the Irish tenant leads to misery. But the subject is one which would require a volume. No one can understand the depth of Irish misery who has not lived in Ireland, and taken pains to become acquainted with the habits and manner of life of the lower orders. The tenant who is kept at starvation point to pay his landlord's rent, has no means of providing for his family. He cannot encourage trade; his sons cannot get work to do, if they are taught trades. Emigration or the workhouse is the only resource. I think the efforts which are made by the poor in Ireland to get work are absolutely unexampled, and it is a cruel thing that a man who is willing to work should not be able to get it. I know an instance in which a girl belonging to a comparatively respectable family was taken into service, and it was discovered that for years her only food, and the only food of her family, was dry bread, and, as an occasional luxury, weak tea. So accustomed had she become to this wretched fare, that she actually could not even eat an egg. She and her family have gone to America; and I have no doubt, after a few years, that the weakened organs will recover their proper tone, with the gradual use of proper food.

There is another ingredient in Irish misery which has not met with the consideration it deserves. If the landlord happens to be humane, he may interest himself in the welfare of the *families* of his tenantry. He may also send a few pounds to them for coals at Christmas, or for clothing; but such instances are unhappily rare, and the alms given is *comparatively* nothing. In England the case is precisely the reverse. On this subject I speak from personal knowledge. There is scarcely a little village in England, however poor, where there is not a committee of ladies, assisted by the neighbouring gentry, who distribute coals, blankets, and clothing in winter; and at all times, where there is distress, give bread, tea, and meat. Well may the poor Irish come home discontented after they have been to work in England, and see how differently the poor are treated there. I admit, and I repeat it again, that there are instances in which the landlord takes an interest in his tenantry, but those instances are exceptions. Many of these gentlemen, who possess the largest tracts of land in Ireland, have also large estates in England, and they seldom, sometimes *never*, visit their Irish estates. They leave it to their agent. Every application for relief is referred to the agent. The agent, however humane, cannot be expected to have the same interest in the people as a landlord *ought* to have. The agent is the instrument used to draw out the last farthing from the poor; he is constantly in collision with them. They naturally dislike him; and he, not unnaturally, dislikes them.

The burden, therefore, of giving that relief to the poor, which they always require in times of sickness, and when they cannot get work, falls almost exclusively upon the priests and the convents. Were it not for the exertions made by the priests and nuns throughout Ireland for the support of the poor, and to obtain work for them, and the immense sums of money sent to Ireland by emigrants, for the support of aged fathers and mothers, I believe the destitution would be something appalling, and that landlords would find it even more difficult than at present to get the high rents which they demand. Yet, some of these same landlords, getting perhaps £20,000 or £40,000 a-year from their Irish estates, will not give the slightest help to establish industrial schools in connexion with convents, or to assist them when they are established, though they are the means of helping their own tenants to pay their rent. There are in Ireland about two hundred conventual establishments. Nearly all of these convents have poor schools, where the poor are taught, either at a most trifling expense, or altogether without charge. The majority of these convents feed and clothe a considerable number of poor children, and many of them have established industrial schools, where a few girls at least can earn what will almost support a whole family in comfort. I give the statistics of one convent as a sample of others. I believe there are a few, but perhaps only a very few other places, where the statistics would rise higher; but there are many convents where the children are fed and clothed, and where work is done on a smaller scale. If such institutions were encouraged by the landlords, much more could be done. The convent to which I allude was founded at the close of the year 1861. There was a national school in the little town (in England it would be called a village), with an attendance of about forty children. The numbers rose rapidly year by year, after the arrival of the nuns, and at present the average daily attendance is just 400. It would be very much higher, were it not for the steady decrease in the population, caused by emigration. The emigration would have been very much greater, had not the parish priest given employment to a considerable number of men, by building a new church, convent, and convent schools. The poorest of the children, and, in Ireland, none but the very poorest will accept such alms, get a breakfast of Indian meal and milk all the year round. The comfort of this hot meal to them, when they come in half-clad and starving of a winter morning, can only be estimated by those who have seen the children partake of it, and heard the cries of delight of the babies of a year old, and the quiet expression of thankfulness of the elder children. Before they go home they get a piece of dry bread, and this is their dinner—a dinner the poorest English child would almost refuse. The number of meals given at present is 350 per diem. The totals of meals given per annum since 1862 are as follows :—

During the year	1862	. . . . . .	36,400
,,	,,	1863	45,800
,,	,,	1864	46,700
,,	,,	1865	49,000
,,	,,	1866	70,000
,,	,,	1867	73,000
	Making a total of		320,900

There were also 1,035 *suits* of clothing given.

The Industrial School was established in 1863. It has been principally supported by English ladies and Protestants. The little town where the convent is situated, is visited by tourists during the summer months; and many who have visited the convent have been so much struck by the good they saw done there, that they have actually devoted themselves to selling work amongst their English friends for the poor children. The returns of work sold in the Industrial School are as follows:—

		£	s.	d.
Work sold in 1863		70	3	6½
„ „ 1864		109	18	5
„ „ 1865		276	1	3½
„ „ 1866		421	16	3
„ „ 1867		350	2	4½
Making a total of	£1,228	1	10½	

The falling off in 1867 has been accounted for partly from the Fenian panic, which prevented tourists visiting Ireland as numerously as in other years, and partly from the attraction of the French Exhibition having drawn tourists in that direction. I have been exact in giving these details, because they form an important subject for consideration in regard to the present history of Ireland. They show at once the poverty of the people, their love of industry, and their eagerness to do work when they can get it. In this, and in other convent schools throughout Ireland, the youngest children are trained to habits of industry. They are paid even for their first imperfect attempts, to encourage them to go on; and they treasure up the few weekly pence they earn as a lady would her jewels. One child had in this way nearly saved up enough to buy herself a pair of shoes—a luxury she had not as yet possessed; but before the whole amount was procured she went to her eternal home, where there is no want, and her last words were a message of love and gratitude to the nuns who had taught her.

The causes of emigration, as one should think, are patent to all. Landlords do not deny that they are anxious to see the people leave the country. They give them every assistance to do so. Their object is to get more land into their own hands, but the policy will eventually prove suicidal. A revolutionary spirit is spreading fast through Europe. Already the standing subject of public addresses to the people in England, is the injustice of certain individuals being allowed to hold such immense tracts of country in their possession. We all know what came of the selfish policy of the landowners in France before the Revolution, which consigned them by hundreds to the guillotine. A little self-sacrifice, which, in the end, would have been for their own benefit, might have saved all this. The attempt to depopulate Ireland has been tried over and over again, and has failed signally. It is not more likely to succeed in the nineteenth century than at any preceding period. Even were it possible that wholesale emigration could benefit any country, it is quite clear that Irish emigration cannot benefit England. It is a plan to get rid of a temporary difficulty at a terrific future cost. Emigration has ceased to be confined to paupers. Respectable farmers are emigrating, and taking with them to America bitter memories of the cruel injustice which has compelled them to leave their native land.

Second, *How misery leads to emigration.* The poor are leaving the country, because they have no employment. The more respectable classes are leaving the country, because they prefer living in a free land, where they can feel sure that their hard earnings will be their own, and not their landlord's, and where they are not subject to the miserable political and religious tyranny which reigns supreme in Ireland. In the evidence given before the Land Tenure Committee of 1864, we find the following statements made by Dr. Keane, the Roman Catholic Bishop of Cloyne. His Lordship is a man of more than ordinary intelligence, and of more than ordinary patriotism. He has made the subject of emigration his special study, partly from a deep devotion to all that concerns the welfare of his country, and partly from the circumstance of his residence being at Queenstown, the port from which Irishmen leave their native shores, and the place where wails of the emigrants continually resound. I subjoin a few of his replies to the questions proposed :—

" I attribute emigration principally to the want of employment."

"A man who has only ten or twelve acres, and who is a tenant-at-will, finding that the land requires improvement, is afraid to waste it [his money], and he goes away.   I see many of these poor people in Queenstown every day."

" I have made inquiries over and over again in Queenstown and elsewhere, and I never yet heard that a single farmer emigrated and left the country who had a lease."

Well might Mr. Heron say, in a paper read before the Irish Statistical Society, in May, 1864: "Under the present laws, no Irish peasant able to read and write ought to remain in Ireland.   If Ireland were an independent country, in the present state of things there would be a bloody insurrection in every county, and the peasantry would ultimately obtain the property in land, *as they have obtained it in Switzerland and in France.*"   That the Irish people will eventually become the masters of the Irish property, from which every effort has been made to dispossess them, by fair means and by foul, since the Norman invasion of Ireland, I have not the slightest doubt.   The only doubt is whether the matter will be settled by the law or by the sword.   But I have hope that the settlement will be peaceful, when I find English members of Parliament treating thus of the subject, and ministers declaring, at least when they are out of office, that something should be done for Ireland.

Mr. Stuart Mill writes : " The land of Ireland, the land of every country, belongs to the people of that country.   The individuals called landowners have no right, in morality or justice, to anything but the rent, or compensation for its saleable value.   When the inhabitants of a country quit the country *en masse*, because the Government will not make it a place fit for them to live in, the Government is judged and condemned. It is the duty of Parliament to reform the landed tenure of Ireland."

More than twenty years ago Mr. Disraeli said : " He wished to see a public man come forward and say what the Irish question was.   Let them consider Ireland as they would any other country similarly circumstanced.   They had a starving population, an absentee aristocracy, an alien Church, and, in addition, the weakest executive in the world.   This was the Irish question.   What would gentlemen say on hearing of a country in such a position ?   They would say at once, in such case, the remedy is revolution—not the suspension of the Habeas Corpus Act. But the connexion with England prevented it: therefore England was logically in the active position of being the cause of all the misery of Ireland. What, then, was the duty of an English minister? To effect by policy all the changes which a revolution would do by force." If these words had been acted upon in 1848, we should not have had a Fenian insurrection in 1867. If a peaceful revolution is to be accomplished a few persons must suffer, though, in truth, it is difficult to see what Irish landlords could lose by a fair land law, except the power to exercise a tyrannical control over their tenants. I believe, if many English absentee landlords had even the slightest idea of the evil deeds done in their names by their agents, that they would not tolerate it for a day. If a complaint is made to the landlord, he refers it to his agent. It is pretty much as if you required the man who inflicted the injury to be the judge of his own conduct. The agent easily excuses himself to the landlord; but the unfortunate man who had presumed to lift up his voice, is henceforth a marked object of vengeance; and he is made an example to his fellows, that they may not dare to imitate him. The truth is, that the real state of Ireland, and the real feelings of the Irish people, can only be known by personal intercourse with the lower orders. Gentlemen making a hurried tour through the country, may see a good deal of misery, if they have not come for the purpose of not seeing it; but they can never know the real wretchedness of the Irish poor unless they remain stationary in some district long enough to win the confidence of the people, and to let them feel that they can tell their sorrows and their wrongs without fear that they shall be increased by the disclosure.

Third, one brief word of how this injustice recoils upon the heads of the perpetrators, and I shall have ended. It recoils upon them indirectly, by causing a feeling of hostility between the governors and the governed. A man cannot be expected to revere and love his landlord, when he finds that his only object is to get all he can from him—when he finds him utterly reckless of his misery, and still more indifferent to his feelings. A gentleman considers himself a model of humanity if he pays the emigration expenses of the family whom he wishes to

eject from the holding which their ancestors have possessed
for centuries.   He is amazed at the fearful ingratitude of the
poor man, who cannot feel overwhelmed with joy at his benevolent offer.   But the gentleman considers he has done his
duty, and consoles himself with the reflection that the Irish are
an ungrateful race.   Of all the peoples on the face of the globe,
the Irish Celts are the most attached to their families and to
their lands.   God only knows the broken hearts that go over
the ocean strangers to a strange land.   The young girls who
leave their aged mothers, the noble, brave young fellows who
leave their old fathers, act not from a selfish wish to better
themselves, but from the hope, soon to be realized, that they
may be able to earn in another land what they cannot earn in
their own.   I saw a lad once parting from his aged father.   I
wish I had not seen it.   I heard the agonized cries of the old
man: "My God! he's gone! he's gone!"   I wish I had not heard
it.   I heard the wild wailing cry with which the Celt mourns
for his dead, and glanced impulsively to the window.   It was
not death, but departure that prompts that agony of grief.
A car was driving off rapidly on the mountain road which
led to the nearest port.   The car was soon out of sight.   The
father and the son had looked their last look into each other's
eyes—had clasped the last clasp of each other's hands.   An
hour had passed, and still the old man lay upon the ground,
where he had flung himself in his heart's bitter anguish ; and
still the wail rung out from time to time : " My God! he's gone !
he's gone !"

Those who have seen the departure of emigrants at the Irish
seaports, are not surprised at Irish disaffection—are not surprised that the expatriated youth joins the first wild scheme
which promises to release his country from such cruel scenes,
and shares his money equally between his starving relatives
at home, and the men who, sometimes as deceivers, and sometimes with a patriotism like his own, live only for one object—
to obtain for Ireland by the sword, the justice which is denied
to her by the law.

I conclude with statistics which are undeniable proofs of
Irish misery.   The emigration *at present* amounts to 100,000
per annum.

The Emigrants' Farewell.

From the 1st of May, 1851, to the 31st of December, 1865, 1,630,722 persons emigrated. As the emigrants generally leave their young children after them for a time, and as aged and imbecile persons do not emigrate, the consequence is, that, from 1851 to 1861, the number of deaf and dumb increased from 5,180 to 5,653; the number of blind, from 5,787 to 6,879; and the number of lunatics and idiots, from 9,980 to 14,098. In 1841, the estimated value of crops in Ireland was £50,000,000; in 1851, it was reduced to £43,000,000; and in 1861, to £35,000,000. The number of gentlemen engaged in the learned professions is steadily decreasing; the traffic on Irish railways and the returns are steadily decreasing; the live stock in cattle, which was to have supplied and compensated for the live stock in men, is fearfully decreasing; the imports and exports are steadily decreasing. The decrease in cultivated lands, from 1862 to 1863, amounted to 138,841 acres.

While the Preface to the Second Edition was passing through the press, my attention was called to an article, in the *Pall Mall Gazette*, on the Right Rev. Dr. Manning's Letter to Earl Grey. The writer of this article strongly recommends his Grace to publish a new edition of his Letter, omitting the last sixteen pages. We have been advised, also, to issue a new edition of our HISTORY, to omit the Preface, and any remarks or facts that might tend to show that the Irish tenant was not the happiest and most contented being in God's creation.

The *Pall Mall Gazette* argues—if, indeed, mere assertion can be called argument—first, "that Dr. Manning has obviously never examined the subject for himself, but takes his ideas and beliefs from the universal statements of angry and ignorant sufferers whom he has met in England, or from intemperate and utterly untrustworthy party speeches and pamphlets, whose assertions he receives as gospel;" yet Dr. Manning has given statements of facts, and the writer has not attempted to disprove them. Second, he says: "Dr. Manning echoes the thoughtless complaints of those who cry out against emigration as a great evil and a grievous wrong, when he might have known, if he had thought or inquired at all about the matter, not only that this emigration has been the greatest conceivable blessing to the emigrants, but was an absolutely indispensable step towards improving the condition of those who remained at home ;" and then the old calumnies are resuscitated about the Irish being "obstinately idle and wilfully improvident," as if it had not been proved again and again that the only ground on which such appellations can be applied to them in Ireland is, that their obstinacy consists in objecting to work without fair remuneration for their labour, and their improvidence in declining to labour for the benefit of their masters. It is the old story, "you are idle, you are idle,"—it is the old demand, "make bricks without straw,"—and then, by way of climax, we are assured that these "poor creatures" are assisted to emigrate with the tenderest consideration, and that, in fact, emigration is a boon for which they are grateful.

It is quite true that many landlords pay their tenants to emigrate, and send persons to see them safe out of the country; but it is absolutely false that the people emigrate willingly. No one who has witnessed the departure of emigrants dare make such an assertion. They are offered their choice between starvation and emigration, and they emigrate. If a man were offered his choice between penal servitude and hanging, it is probable he would prefer penal servitude, but that would not make him appreciate the joys of prison life. The Irish parish priest alone can tell what the Irish suffer at home, and how unwillingly they go abroad. A pamphlet has just been published on this very subject, by the Very Rev. P. Malone, P.P., V.F., of Belmullet, co. Mayo, and in this he says : "I have *seen* the son, standing upon the deck of the emigrant ship, divest himself of his only coat, and place it upon his father's shoulders, saying, 'Father, take you this ; I will soon earn the price of a coat in the land I am going to.'" Such instances, which might be recorded by the hundred, and the amount of money sent to Ireland by emigrants for the support of aged parents, and to pay the passage out of younger members of the family, are the best refutation of the old falsehood that Irishmen are either idle or improvident.

AN

ILLUSTRATED HISTORY OF IRELAND.

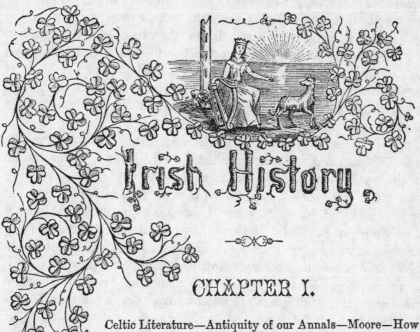

Irish History

CHAPTER I.

Celtic Literature—Antiquity of our Annals—Moore—How
we should estimate Tradition—The Materials for Irish
History—List of the Lost Books—The Cuilmenn—The
Saltair of Tara, &c.—The Saltair of Cashel—Important
MSS. preserved in Trinity College—By the Royal Irish
Academy—In Belgium.

HE study of Celtic literature, which is daily becoming of increased importance to the philologist,
has proved a matter of no inconsiderable value to
the Irish historian.   When Moore visited O'Curry,
and found him surrounded with such works as the
Books of Ballymote and Lecain, the *Speckled Book*,
the *Annals of the Four Masters*, and other treasures
of Gaedhilic lore, he turned to Dr. Petrie, and
exclaimed : " These large tomes could not have
been written by fools or for any foolish purpose.
I never knew anything about them before, and I
had no right to have undertaken the *History of
Ireland*." His publishers, who had less scruples,
or more utilitarian views, insisted on the completion of his task.   Whatever their motives may
have been, we may thank them for the result.   Though Moore's
history cannot now be quoted as an authority, it accomplished its

work for the time, and promoted an interest in the history of
one of the most ancient nations of the human race.

There are two sources from whence the early history of a nation
may be safely derived: the first internal—the self-consciousness
of the individual; the second external—the knowledge of its
existence by others—the *ego sum* and the *tu es;* and our acceptance
of the statements of each on *matters of fact,* should depend on their
mutual agreement.

The first question, then, for the historian should be, What accounts
does this nation give of its early history? the second, What account
of this nation's early history can be obtained *ab extra?* By stating
and comparing these accounts with such critical acumen as the
writer may be able to command, we may obtain something approaching to authentic history. The history of ancient peoples
must have its basis on tradition. The name tradition unfortunately
gives an *à priori* impression of untruthfulness, and hence the difficulty of accepting tradition as an element of truth in historic
research. But tradition is not necessarily either a pure myth or a
falsified account of facts. The traditions of a nation are like an
aged man's recollection of his childhood, and should be treated as
such. If we would know his early history, we let him tell the
tale in his own fashion. It may be he will dwell long upon
occurrences interesting to himself, and apart from the object of
our inquiries; it may be he will equivocate unintentionally if cross-
·examined in detail; but truth will underlie his garrulous story, and
by patient analysis we may sift it out, and obtain the information
we desire.

A nation does not begin to write its history at the first moment
of its existence. Hence, when the chronicle is compiled which
first embodies its story, tradition forms the basis. None but an
inspired historian can commence *In principio.* The nation has passed
through several generations, the people already begin to talk of " old
times;" but as they are nearer these " old times" by some thousands
of years than we are, they are only burdened with the traditions of
a few centuries at the most; and unless there is evidence of a wilful
object or intent to falsify their chronicles, we may in the main
depend on their accuracy. Let us see how this applies to Gaedhilic
history. The labours of the late lamented Eugene O'Curry have
made this an easy task. He took to his work a critical acumen
not often attained by the self-educated, and a noble patriotism not

often maintained by the gifted scions of a country whose people and whose literature have been alike trodden down and despised for centuries. The result of his researches is embodied in a work[1] which should be in the hands of every student of Irish history, and of every Irishman who can afford to procure it. This volume proves that the *early* history of Ireland has yet to be written; that it should be a work of magnitude, and undertaken by one gifted with special qualifications, which the present writer certainly does not possess; and that it will probably require many years of patient labour from the "host of Erinn's sons," before the necessary materials for such a history can be prepared.

The manuscript materials for ancient Irish history may be divided into two classes : the historical, which purports to be a narrative of facts, in which we include books of laws, genealogies, and pedigrees ; and the legendary, comprising tales, poems, and legends. The latter, though not necessarily true, are generally founded on fact, and contain a mass of most important information regarding the ancient customs and manner of life among our ancestors. For the present we must devote our attention to the historical documents. These, again, may be divided into two classes—the lost books and those which still remain. Of the former class the principal are the CUILMENN, *i.e.*, the great book written on skins ; the SALTAIR OF TARA ; the BOOK OF THE UACHONGBHAIL (pron. " ooa cong-wall "); the CIN DROMA SNECHTA ; and the SALTAIR OF CASHEL. Besides these, a host of works are lost, of lesser importance as far as we can now judge, which, if preserved, might have thrown a flood of light not only upon our annals, but also on the social, historical, and ethnographic condition of other countries. The principal works which have been preserved are : the ANNALS OF TIGHERNACH (pron. "Teernagh"); the ANNALS OF ULSTER ; the ANNALS OF INIS MAC NERINN ; the ANNALS OF INNISFALLEN ; the ANNALS OF BOYLE ; the CHRONICUM SCOTORUM,

---

Work.—*Lectures on the MS. Materials of Ancient Irish History.* This work was published at the sole cost of the Catholic University of Ireland, and will be an eternal monument of their patriotism and devotion to literature. A chair of Irish History and Archæology was also founded at the very commencement of the University ; and yet the " Queen's Colleges " are discarding this study, while an English professor in Oxford is warmly advocating its promotion. Is the value of a chair to be estimated by the number of pupils who surround it, or by the contributions to science of the professor who holds it?

so ably edited by Mr. Hennessy; the world-famous ANNALS OF
THE FOUR MASTERS; the BOOK OF LEINSTER; the BOOK OF LAWS
(the Brehon Laws), now edited by Dr. Todd, and many books of
genealogies and pedigrees.

For the present it must suffice to say, that these documents
have been examined by the ordinary rules of literary criticism,
perhaps with more than ordinary care, and that the result has been
to place their authenticity and their antiquity beyond cavil.

Let us see, then, what statements we can find which may throw
light on our early history, first in the fragments that remain of the
lost books, and then in those which are still preserved.

The CUILMENN is the first of the lost books which we mentioned.
It is thus referred to in the Book of Leinster :[2] "The *filés* [bards]
of Erinn were now called together by *Senchan Torpéist* [about A.D.
580], to know if they remembered the *Táin bó Chuailgné* in full;
and they said that they knew of it but fragments only. Senchan
then spoke to his pupils to know which of them would go into the
countries of *Letha* to learn the *Táin* which the *Sai* had taken ' east-
wards' after the *Cuilmenn*. Eminé, the grandson of Nininé, and
Muirgen, Senchan's own son, set out to go to the East."

Here we have simply an indication of the existence of this ancient
work, and of the fact that in the earliest, if not in pre-Christian
times, Irish manuscripts travelled to the Continent with Irish
scholars—Letha being the name by which Italy, and especially
what are now called the Papal States, was then designated by
Irish writers.

The SALTAIR OF TARA next claims our attention; and we may
safely affirm, merely judging from the fragments which remain,
that a nation which could produce such a work had attained no
ordinary pitch of civilization and literary culture. The Book of
Ballymote,[3] and the Yellow Book of Lecan,[4] attribute this work
to Cormac Mac Art : " A noble work was performed by Cormac at
that time, namely, the compilation of Cormac's Saltair, which was
composed by him and the Seanchaidhe [Historians] of Erinn, including Fintan, son of Bochra, and Fithil, the poet and judge. And
their synchronisms and genealogies, the succession of their kings

---

2 *Leinster.*—Book of Leinster, H. 2. 18, T.C.D. See O'Curry, p. 8.
3 *Ballymote.*—Library R.I.A., at fol. 145, a. a.
4 *Lecan.*—Trinity College, Dublin, classed H. 2. 16.

and monarchs, their battles, their contests, and their antiquities, from the world's beginning down to that time, were written ; and this is the Saltair of Temair [pron. "Tara," almost as it is called now], which is the origin and fountain of the Historians of Erinn from that period down to this time. This is taken from the Book of the Uachongbhail."[5]

As we shall speak of Cormac's reign and noble qualities in detail at a later period, it is only necessary to record here that his panegyric, as king, warrior, judge, and philosopher, has been pronounced by almost contemporary writers, as well as by those of later date. The name *Saltair* has been objected to as more likely to denote a composition of Christian times. This objection, however, is easily removed : first, the name was probably applied after the appellation had been introduced in Christian times ; second, we have no reason to suppose that King Cormac designated his noble work by this name ; and third, even could this be proven, the much maligned Keating removes any difficulty by the simple and obvious remark, that " it is because of its having been written in poetic metre, the chief book which was in the custody of the *Ollamh* of the King of Erinn, was called the *Saltair of Temair;* and the Chronicle of holy Cormac Mac Cullinan, *Saltair of Cashel;* and the Chronicle of Aengus *Ceilé Dé* [the Culdee], *Saltair-na-Rann* [that is, Saltair of the Poems or Verses], because a Salm and a Poem are the same, and therefore a *Salterium* and a *Duanairé* [book of poems] are the same."[6]

The oldest reference to this famous compilation is found in a

SITE OF TARA.

poem on the site of ancient Tara, by Cuan O'Lochain, a distinguished

[5] *Uachongbhail.*—O'Curry's *MS. Materials,* p. 11.
[6] *Same.*—Ibid. p. 12. The Psalms derived their name from the musical

scholar, and native of Westmeath, who died in the year 1024. The
quotation given below is taken from the Book of Ballymote, a magnificent volume, compiled in the year 1391, now in possession of the
Royal Irish Academy :—

> Temair, choicest of hills,
> For [possession of] which Erinn is now devastated,[7]
> The noble city of Cormac, son of Art,
> Who was the son of great Conn of the hundred battles :
> Cormac, the prudent and good,
> Was a sage, a filé [poet], a prince :
> Was a righteous judge of the Fené-men,[8]
> Was a good friend and companion.
> Cormac gained fifty battles :
> He compiled the Saltair of Temur.
> In that Saltair is contained
> The best summary of history ;
> It is that Saltair which assigns
> Seven chief kings to Erinn of harbours ;
> They consisted of the five kings of the provinces,—
> The Monarch of Erinn and his Deputy.
> In it are (written) on either side,
> What each provincial king is entitled to,
> From the king of each great musical province.
> The synchronisms and chronology of all,
> The kings, with each other [one with another] all ;
> The boundaries of each brave province,
> From a cantred up to a great chieftaincy.

From this valuable extract we obtain a clear idea of the importance and the subject of the famous Saltair, and a not less clear
knowledge of the admirable legal and social institutions by which
Erinn was then governed.

The CIN OF DROM SNECHTA is quoted in the Book of Ballymote,
in support of the ancient legend of the antediluvian occupation of

instrument to which they were sung. This was called in Hebrew *nebel*. It
obtained the name from its resemblance to a bottle or flagon. Psaltery is the
Greek translation, and hence the name psalm.

[7] *Devastated.*—This was probably written in the year 1001, when Brian
Boroimhé had deposed Malachy.

[8] *Fené-men.* — The farmers, who were not Fenians then certainly, for
" Cormac was a righteous judge of the *Agraria Lex* of the Gaels."

Erinn by the Lady *Banbha*, called in other books Cesair (pron. "kesar"). The Book of Lecan quotes it for the same purpose, and also for the genealogies of the chieftains of the ancient Rudrician race of Ulster. Keating gives the descent of the Milesian colonists from Magog, the son of Japhet, on the authority of the Cin of Drom Snechta, which, he states, was compiled before St. Patrick's mission to Erinn.[9] We must conclude this part of our subject with a curious extract from the same work, taken from the Book of Leinster : "From the Cin of Drom Snechta, this below. Historians say that there were exiles of Hebrew women in Erinn at the coming of the sons of Milesius, who had been driven by a sea tempest into the ocean by the Tirrén Sea. They were in Erinn before the sons of Milesius. They said, however, to the sons of Milesius [who, it would appear, pressed marriage on them], that they preferred their own country, and that they would not abandon it without receiving dowry for alliance with them. It is from this circumstance that it is the men that purchase wives in Erinn for ever, whilst it is the husbands that are purchased by the wives throughout the world besides."[1]

---

[9] *Erinn.*—Keating says: "We will set down here the branching off of the races of Magog, according to the Book of Invasions (of Ireland), which was called the Cin of Drom Snechta ; and it was before the coming of Patrick to Ireland the author of that book existed."—See Keating, page 109, in O'Connor's translation. It is most unfortunate that this devoted priest and ardent lover of his country did not bring the critical acumen to his work which would have made its veracity unquestionable. He tells us that it is "the business of his history to be particular," and speaks of having "faithfully collected and transcribed." But until recent investigations manifested the real antiquity and value of the MS. Materials of Ancient Irish History, his work was looked on as a mere collection of legends. The quotation at present under consideration is a case in point. He must have had a copy of the Cin of Drom Snechta in his possession, and he must have known who was the author of the original, as he states so distinctly the time of its compilation. Keating's accuracy in matters of fact and transcription, however, is daily becoming more apparent. This statement might have been considered a mere conjecture of his own, had not Mr. O'Curry discovered the name of the author in a partially effaced memorandum in the Book of Leinster, which he reads thus : "[Ernín, son of] Duach [that is], son of the King of Connacht, an *Ollamh*, and a prophet, and a professor in history, and a professor in wisdom : it was he that collected the Genealogies and Histories of the men of Erinn in one book, that is, the *Cin Droma Snechta*." Duach was the son of Brian, son of the monarch *Eochaidh*, who died A.D. 365.

[1] *Besides.*—O'Curry, page 16.

The SALTAIR OF CASHEL was compiled by Cormac Mac Cullinan King of Munster, and Archbishop of Cashel. He was killed in the' year 903. This loss of the work is most painful to the student of the early history of Erinn. It is believed that the ancient compilation known as Cormac's Glossary, was compiled from the interlined gloss to the Saltair ; and the references therein to our ancient history, laws, mythology, and social customs, are such as to indicate the richness of the mine of ancient lore. A copy was in existence in 1454, as there is in the Bodleian Library in Oxford (Laud, 610) a copy of such portions as could be deciphered at the time. This copy was made by Shane O'Clery for Mac Richard Butler.

The subjoined list of the lost books is taken from O'Curry's *MS. Materials*, page 20. It may be useful to the philologist and interesting to our own people, as a proof of the devotion to learning so early manifested in Erinn :—

" In the first place must be enumerated again the *Cuilmenn;* the Saltair of Tara ; the *Cin Droma Snechta;* the Book of St. Mochta ; the Book of *Cuana;* the Book of *Dubhdaleithe;* and the Saltair of Cashel. Besides these we find mention of the *Leabhar buidhe Sláine* or Yellow Book of Slane ; the original *Leabhar na h-Uidhre;* the Books of *Eochaidh O'Flannagain;* a certain book known as the Book eaten by the poor people in the desert ; the Book of *Inis an Duin;* the Short Book of St. Buithe's Monastery (or Monasterboice); the Books of Flann of the same Monastery ; the Book of Flann of *Dungeimhin* (Dungiven, co. Derry); the Book of *Dun da Leth Ghlas* (or Downpatrick); the Book of *Doiré* (Derry) ; the Book of *Sabhall Phatraic* (or Saull, co. Down) ; the Book of the *Uachongbhail* (Navan, probably); the *Leabhar dubh Molaga*, or Black Book of St. Molaga ; the *Leabhar buidhe Moling*, or Yellow Book of St. Moling; the *Leabhar buidhe Mhic Murchadha*, or Yellow Book of Mac Murrach ; the *Leabhar Arda Macha*, or Book of Armagh (quoted by Keating); the *Leabhar ruadh Mhic Aedhagain*, or Red Book of Mac Aegan ; the *Leabhar breac Mhic Aedhagain*, or Speckled Book of Mac Aegan ; the *Leabhar fada Leithghlinne*, or Long Book of Leithghlinn, or Leithlin ; the Books of O'Scoba of *Cluain Mic Nois* (or Clonmacnois); the *Duil Droma Ceata*, or Book of Drom Ceat; and the Book of Clonsost (in Leix, in the Queen's County)."

Happily, however, a valuable collection of ancient MSS. are still preserved, despite the " drowning " of the Danes, and the " burn-

ella ge

hige iacob iuca hige iiii

Omnes ergogenerationes im

ababriichum usq' acldaniel

generationes xiiii ctaclauiel

usquatrans migraone babii

in generaciones xiiii ctrans

imqii anne babilonis usq' ucl

iiiii cii gnerationes iiiii iiii

iiiii

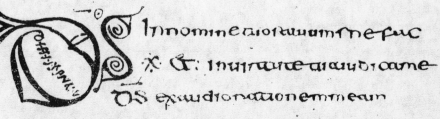

Innominediorxuuimmefac

X G: inuirardedialluidioame

os exaudiorationemmeam

aurubur pencipeuerbaourmei

Quomamulienimiimgexpoir aduenmime

ing" of the Saxon. The researches of continental scholars are
adding daily to our store; and the hundreds of Celtic MSS., so long
entombed in the libraries of Belgium and Italy, will, when published,
throw additional light upon the brightness of the past, and, it may
be, enhance the glories of the future, which we must believe are
still in reserve for the island of saints and sages.[2]

The list of works given above are supposed by O'Curry to
have existed anterior to the year 1100. Of the books which
Keating refers to in his History, written about 1630, only one
is known to be extant—the *Saltair-na-Rann*, written by Aengus
Céile Dé.

The principal Celtic MSS. which are still preserved to us, may be
consulted in the Library of Trinity College, Dublin, and in the Library
of the Royal Irish Academy. The latter, though founded at a much
later period, is by far the more extensive, if not the more important,
collection. Perhaps, few countries have been so happy as to possess a body of men so devoted to its archæology, so ardent in their
preservation of all that can be found to illustrate it, and so capable of
elucidating its history by their erudition, which, severally and collectively, they have brought to bear on every department of its ethno-
logy. The collection in Trinity College consists of more than 140
volumes, several of them are vellum,[3] dating from the early part of the
twelfth to the middle of the last century. The collection of the Royal
Irish Academy also contains several works written on vellum, with
treatises of history, science, laws, and commerce; there are also
many theological and ecclesiastical compositions, which have been
pronounced by competent authorities to be written in the purest
style that the ancient Gaedhilic language ever attained. There are
also a considerable number of translations from Greek, Latin, and
other languages. These are of considerable importance, as they
enable the critical student of our language to determine the meaning of many obscure or obsolete words or phrases, by reference to

[2] *Sages.*—M. Nigra, the Italian Ambassador at Paris, is at this moment
engaged in publishing continental MSS.

[3] *Vellum.*—The use of vellum is an indication that the MSS. must be of some
antiquity. The word " paper" is derived from *papyrus*, the most ancient material for writing, if we except the rocks used for runes, or the wood for oghams.
Papyrus, the pith of a reed, was used until the discovery of parchment, about
190 B.C. A MS. of the *Antiquities of Josephus* on papyrus, was among the
treasures seized by Buonaparte in Italy.

the originals; nor are they of less value as indicating the high state of literary culture which prevailed in Ireland during the early Christian and the Middle Ages. Poetry, mythology, history, and the classic literature of Greece and Rome, may be found amongst these translations; so that, as O'Curry well remarks, " any one well read in the comparatively few existing fragments of our Gaedhilic literature, and whose education had been confined solely to this source, would find that there are but very few, indeed, of the great events in the history of the world with which he was not acquainted."[4]   He then mentions, by way of illustration of classical subjects, Celtic versions of the Argonautic Expedition, the Siege of Troy, the Life of Alexander the Great; and of such subjects as cannot be classed under this head, the Destruction of Jerusalem; the Wars of Charlemagne, including the History of Roland the Brave; the History of the Lombards, and the almost contemporary translation of the Travels of Marco Polo.

There is also a large collection of MSS. in the British Museum, a few volumes in the Bodleian Library at Oxford, besides the well-known, though inaccessible, Stowe collection.[5]

The treasures of Celtic literature still preserved on the Continent, can only be briefly mentioned here. It is probable that the active researches of philologists will exhume many more of these long-hidden volumes, and obtain for our race the place it has always deserved in the history of nations.

The Louvain collection, formed chiefly by Fathers Hugh Ward, John Colgan, and Michael O'Clery, between the years 1620 and 1640, was widely scattered at the French Revolution. The most valuable portion is in the College of St. Isidore in Rome. The Burgundian Library at Brussels also possesses many of these treasures. A valuable resumé of the MSS. which are preserved there was given by Mr. Bindon, and printed in the Proceedings of the Royal Irish Academy in the year 1847. There are also many Latin MSS. with Irish glosses, which have been largely used by Zeuss in his world-famed *Grammatica Celtica*. The date of one of these—a codex

---

[4] *Acquainted.*—O'Curry's *MS. Materials*, page 24.

[5] *Collection.*—A recent writer in the *Cornhill* says that Lord Ashburnham refuses access to this collection, now in his possession, fearing that its contents may be depreciated so as to lessen its value at a future sale. We should hope this statement can scarcely be accurate. Unhappily, it is at least certain that access to the MSS. is denied, from whatever motive.

containing some of Venerable Bede's works—is fixed by an entry of the death of Aed, King of Ireland, in the year 817. This most important work belonged to the Irish monastery of Reichenau, and is now preserved at Carlsruhe. A codex is also preserved at Cambray, which contains a fragment of an Irish sermon, and the canons of an Irish council held A.D. 684.

DOORWAY OF CLONMACNOIS.

CLONMACNOIS.

CHAPTER II.

Tighernach and his Annals—Erudition and Research of our Early Writers—The Chronicum Scotorum—Duald Mac Firbis—Murdered, and his Murderer is protected by the Penal Laws—The Annals of the Four Masters—Michael O'Clery—His Devotion to his Country—Ward—Colgan—Dedication of the Annals—The Book of Invasions—Proofs of our Early Colonization.

OUR illustration can give but a faint idea of the magnificence and extent of the ancient abbey of Clonmacnois, the home of our famous annalist, Tighernach. It has been well observed, that no more ancient chronicler can be produced by the northern nations. Nestor, the father of Russian history, died in 1113; Snorro, the father of Icelandic history, did not appear until a century later; Kadlubeck, the first historian of Poland, died in 1223; and Stierman could not discover a scrap of writing in all Sweden older than 1159. Indeed, he may be compared favourably even with the British historians, who can by no means boast of such ancient pedigrees as the genealogists of Erinn.[6] Tighernach was of the Murray-race of

---

[6] *Erinn.*—O'Curry, page 57. It has also been remarked, that there is no nation in possession of such ancient chronicles written in what is still the language of its people.

Connacht ; of his personal history little is known.   His death is noted in the *Chronicum Scotorum*, where he is styled successor (*comharba*) of St. Ciaran and St. Coman.   The Annals of Innisfallen state that he was interred at Clonmacnois.   Perhaps his body was borne to its burial through the very doorway which still remains, of which we gave an illustration at the end of the last chapter.

The writers of history and genealogy in early ages, usually commenced with the sons of Noah, if not with the first man of the human race.   The Celtic historians are no exceptions to the general rule ; and long before Tighernach wrote, the custom had obtained in Erinn.   His chronicle was necessarily compiled from more ancient sources, but its fame rests upon the extraordinary erudition which he brought to bear upon every subject.   Flann, who was contemporary with Tighernach, and a professor of St. Buithé's monastery (Monasterboice), is also famous for his Synchronisms, which form an admirable abridgment of universal history.   He appears to have devoted himself specially to genealogies and pedigrees, while Tighernach took a wider range of literary research.   His learning was undoubtedly most extensive.   He quotes Eusebius, Orosius, Africanus, Bede, Josephus, Saint Jerome, and many other historical writers, and sometimes compares their statements on points in which they exhibit discrepancies, and afterwards endeavours to reconcile their conflicting testimony, and to correct the chronological errors of the writers by comparison with the dates given by others.   He also collates the Hebrew text with the Septuagint version of the Scriptures.   He uses the common era, though we have no reason to believe that this was done by the writers who immediately preceded him.   He also mentions the lunar cycle, and uses the dominical letter with the kalends of several years.[7]

Another writer, *Gilla Caemhain*, was also contemporary with Flann and Tighernach.   He gives the "annals of all time," from the beginning of the world to his own period ; and computes the second period from the Creation to the Deluge ; from the Deluge to Abraham ; from Abraham to David ; from David to the Babylonian Captivity, &c.   He also synchronizes the eastern monarchs with each other, and afterwards with the Firbolgs and

---

[7] *Years.*—See O'Curry, *passim.*

Tuatha Dé Danann of Erinn,[8] and subsequently with the Milesians. Flann synchronizes the chiefs of various lines of the children of Adam in the East, and points out what monarchs of the Assyrians, Medes, Persians, and Greeks, and what Roman emperors were contemporary with the kings of Erinn, and the leaders of its various early colonies. He begins with Ninus, son of Belus, and comes down to Julius Cæsar, who was contemporary with *Eochaidh Feidhlech*, an Irish king, who died more than half a century before the Christian era. The synchronism is then continued from Julius Cæsar and *Eochaidh* to the Roman emperors Theodosius the Third and Leo the Third; they were contemporaries with the Irish monarch Ferghal, who was killed A.D. 718.

The ANNALS and MSS. which serve to illustrate our history, are so numerous, that it would be impossible, with one or two exceptions, to do more than indicate their existence, and to draw attention to the weight which such an accumulation of authority must give to the authenticity of our early history. But there are two of these works which we cannot pass unnoticed: the CHRONICUM SCOTORUM and the ANNALS OF THE FOUR MASTERS.

The Chronicum Scotorum was compiled by Duald Mac Firbis. He was of royal race, and descended from *Dathi*, the last pagan monarch of Erinn. His family were professional and hereditary historians, genealogists, and poets,[9] and held an ancestral property at Lecain Mac Firbis, in the county Sligo, until Cromwell and his troopers desolated Celtic homes, and murdered the Celtic dwellers, often in cold blood. The young Mac Firbis was educated for his profession in a school of law and history taught by the Mac Egans of Lecain, in Ormonde. He also studied (about A.D. 1595) at Burren, in the county Clare, in the literary and legal school of the O'Davorens. His pedigrees of the ancient Irish and the Anglo-Norman families,

---

[8] *Erinn.—Eire* is the correct form for the nominative. Erinn is the genitive, but too long in use to admit of alteration. The ordinary name of Ireland, in the oldest Irish MSS., is (h)Erin, gen. (h)Erenn, dat. (h)Erinn; but the initial *h* is often omitted. See Max Müller's Lectures for an interesting note on this subject, to which we shall again refer.

[9] *Poets.*—The *Book of Lecain* was written in 1416, by an ancestor of Mac Firbis. Usher had it for some time in his possession; James II. carried it to Paris, and deposited it in the Irish College in the presence of a notary and witnesses. In 1787, the Chevalier O'Reilly procured its restoration to Ireland; and it passed eventually from Vallancey to the Royal Irish Academy, where it is now carefully preserved.

was compiled at the College of St. Nicholas, in Galway, in the year 1650. It may interest some of our readers to peruse the title of this work, although its length would certainly horrify a modern publisher :—

"The Branches of Relationship and the Genealogical Ramifications of every Colony that took possession of Erinn, traced from this time up to Adam (excepting only those of the Fomorians, Lochlanns, and Saxon-Gaels, of whom we, however, treat, as they have settled in our country); together with a Sanctilogium, and a Catalogue of the Monarchs of Erinn ; and, finally, an Index, which comprises, in alphabetical order, the surnames and the remarkable places mentioned in this work, which was compiled by *Dubhaltach Mac Firbhisigh* of Lecain, 1650." He also gives, as was then usual, the " place, time, author, and cause of writing the work." The " cause" was " to increase the glory of God, and for the information of the people in general ;" a beautiful and most true epitome of the motives which inspired the penmen of Erinn from the first introduction of Christianity, and produced the " countless host " of her noble historiographers.

Mac Firbis was murdered[1] in the year 1670, at an advanced age; and thus departed the last and not the least distinguished of our long line of poet-historians. Mac Firbis was a voluminous writer. Unfortunately some of his treatises have been lost ;[2] but the CHRONICUM SCOTORUM is more than sufficient to establish his literary reputation.

The ANNALS OF THE FOUR MASTERS demand a larger notice, as unquestionably one of the most remarkable works on record. It forms the last link between the ancient and modern history of Ireland ; a link worthy of the past, and, we dare add, it shall be

---

[1] *Murdered.*—The circumstances of the murder are unhappily characteristic of the times. The Celtic race was under the ban of penal laws for adherence to the faith of their fathers. The murderer was free. As the old historian travelled to Dublin, he rested at a shop in Dunflin. A young man came in and took liberties with the young woman who had care of the shop. She tried to check him, by saying that he would be seen by the gentleman in the next room. In a moment he seized a knife from the counter, and plunged it into the breast of Mac Firbis. There was no "justice for Ireland" then, and, of course, the miscreant escaped the punishment he too well deserved.

[2] *Lost.*—He was also employed by Sir James Ware to translate for him, and appears to have resided in his house in Castle-street, Dublin, just before his death.

also worthy of the future. It is a proof of what great and noble deeds may be accomplished under the most adverse circumstances, and one of the many, if not one of the most, triumphant denials of the often-repeated charges of indolence made against the mendicant orders, and of aversion to learning made against religious orders in general. Nor is it a less brilliant proof that intellectual gifts may be cultivated and are fostered in the cloister; and that a patriot's heart may burn as ardently, and love of country prove as powerful a motive, beneath the cowl or the veil, as beneath the helmet or the coif.

Michael O'Clery, the chief of the Four Masters, was a friar of the order of St. Francis. He was born at Kilbarron, near Ballyshannon, county Donegal, in the year 1580, and was educated principally in the south of Ireland, which was then more celebrated for its academies than the north. The date of his entrance into the Franciscan order is not known, neither is it known why he,

> " Once the heir of bardic honours,"

became a simple lay-brother. In the year 1627 he travelled through Ireland collecting materials for Father Hugh Ward, also a Franciscan friar, and Guardian of the convent of St. Antony at Louvain, who was preparing a series of Lives of Irish Saints. When Father Ward died, the project was taken up and partially carried out by Father John Colgan. His first work, the *Trias Thaumaturgus*, contains the lives of St. Patrick, St. Brigid, and St. Columba. The second volume contains the lives of Irish saints whose festivals occur from the 1st of January to the 31st of March; and here, unfortunately alike for the hagiographer and the antiquarian, the work ceased. It is probable that the idea of saving—

> " The old memorials
> Of the noble and the holy,
> Of the chiefs of ancient lineage,
> Of the saints of wondrous virtues ;
> Of the Ollamhs and the Brehons,
> Of the bards and of the betaghs,"[3]

occurred to him while he was collecting materials for Father Ward. His own account is grand in its simplicity, and beautiful as indi-

---

[3] *Betaghs.*—Poems, by D. F. Mac Carthy.

cating that the deep passion for country and for literature had but enhanced the yet deeper passion which found its culminating point in the dedication of his life to God in the poor order of St. Francis. In the troubled and disturbed state of Ireland, he had some difficulty in securing a patron. At last one was found who could appreciate intellect, love of country, and true religion. Although it is almost apart from our immediate subject, we cannot refrain giving an extract from the dedication to this prince, whose name should be immortalized with that of the friar patriot and historian :—

"I, Michael *O'Clerigh*, a poor friar of the Order of St. Francis (after having been for ten years transcribing every old material that I found concerning the saints of Ireland, observing obedience to each provincial that was in Ireland successively), have come before you, O noble *Fearghal* O'Gara. I have calculated on your honour that it seemed to you a cause of pity and regret, grief and sorrow (for the glory of God and the honour of Ireland), how much the race of Gaedhil, the son of Niul, have passed under a cloud and darkness, without a knowledge or record of the obit of saint or virgin, archbishop, bishop, abbot, or other noble dignitary of the Church, or king or of prince, of lord or of chieftain, [or] of the synchronism of connexion of the one with the other." He then explains how he collected the materials for his work, adding, alas ! most truly, that should it not be accomplished then, "they would not again be found to be put on record to the end of the world." He thanks the prince for giving "the reward of their labour to the chroniclers," and simply observes, that "it was the friars of the convent of Donegal who supplied them with food and attendance." With characteristic humility he gives his patron the credit of all the "good which will result from this book, in giving light to all in general ;" and concludes thus :—

"On the twenty-second day of the month of January, A.D. 1632, this book was commenced in the convent of Dun-na-ngall, and it was finished in the same convent on the tenth day of August, 1636, the eleventh year of the reign of our king Charles over England, France, Alba, and over *Eiré*."

There were "giants in those days ;" and one scarcely knows whether to admire most the liberality of the prince, the devotion of the friars of Donegal, who "gave food and attendance" to their literary brother, and thus had their share in perpetuating their country's fame, or the gentle humility of the great Brother Michael.

It is unnecessary to make any observation on the value and importance of the Annals of the Four Masters. The work has been edited with extraordinary care and erudition by Dr. O'Donovan, and published by an Irish house. We must now return to the object for which this brief mention of the MS. materials of Irish history has been made, by showing on what points other historians coincide in their accounts of our first colonists, of their language, customs, and laws ; and secondly, how far the accounts which may be obtained *ab extra* agree with the statements of our own annalists. The *Book of Invasions*, which was rewritten and " purified " by brother Michael O'Clery, gives us in a few brief lines an epitome of our history as recorded by the ancient chroniclers of Erinn :—

"The sum of the matters to be found in the following book, is the taking of Erinn by [the Lady] *Ceasair ;* the taking by *Partholan ;* the taking by *Nemedh ;* the taking by the Firbolgs ; the taking by the *Tuatha Dé Danann ;* the taking by the sons of *Miledh* [or Miletius] ; and their succession down to the monarch *Melsheachlainn,* or Malachy the Great [who died in 1022]." Here we have six distinct "takings," invasions, or colonizations of Ireland in pre-Christian times.

It may startle some of our readers to find any mention of Irish history " before the Flood," but we think the burden of proof, to use a logical term, lies rather with those who doubt the possibility, than with those who accept as tradition, and as *possibly* true, the statements which have been transmitted for centuries by careful hands. There can be no doubt that a high degree of cultivation, and considerable advancement in science, had been attained by the more immediate descendants of our first parents. Navigation and commerce existed, and Ireland may have been colonized. The sons of Noah must have remembered and preserved the traditions of their ancestors, and transmitted them to their descendants. Hence, it depended on the relative anxiety of these descendants to preserve the history of the world before the Flood, how much posterity should know of it. MacFirbis thus answers the objections of those who, even in his day, questioned the possibility of preserving such records :—" If there be any one who shall ask who preserved the history [*Seanchus*], let him know that they were very ancient and long-lived old men, recording elders of great age, whom God permitted to preserve and hand down the history of Erinn, in books, in succession, one after another, from the Deluge to the time of St. Patrick."

The artificial state of society in our own age, has probably acted disadvantageously on our literary researches, if not on our moral character. Civilization is a relative arbitrary term ; and the ancestors whom we are pleased to term uncivilized, may have possessed as high a degree of mental culture as ourselves, though it unquestionably differed in kind. Job wrote his epic poem in a state of society which we should probably term uncultivated ; and when Lamech gave utterance to the most ancient and the saddest of human lyrics, the world was in its infancy, and it would appear as if the first artificer in " brass and iron " had only helped to make homicide more easy. We can scarce deny that murder, cruel injustice, and the worst forms of inhumanity, are but too common in countries which boast of no ordinary refinement ; and we should hesitate ere we condemn any state of society as uncivilized, simply because we find such crimes in the pages of their history.

The question of the early, if not pre-Noahacian colonization of Ireland, though distinctly asserted in our annals, has been met with the ready scepticism which men so freely use to cover ignorance or indifference. It has been taken for granted that the dispersion, after the confusion of tongues at Babel, was the first dispersion of the human race; but it has been overlooked that, on the lowest computation, a number of centuries equal, if not exceeding, those of the Christian era, elapsed between the Creation of man and the Flood ; that men had " multiplied exceedingly upon the earth ;" and that the age of stone had already given place to that of brass and iron, which, no doubt, facilitated commerce and colonization, even at this early period of the world's history. The discovery of works of art, of however primitive a character, in the drifts of France and England, indicates an early colonization. The rudely-fashioned harpoon of deer's horn found beside the gigantic whale, in the alluvium of the carse near the base of Dummyat, twenty feet above the highest tide of the nearest estuary, and the tusk of the mastodon lying alongside fragments of pottery in a deposit of the peat and sands of the post-pliocene beds in South Carolina, are by no means solitary examples. Like the night torch of the gentle Guanahané savage, which Columbus saw as he gazed wearily from his vessel, looking, even after sunset, for the long hoped-for shore, and which told him that his desire was at last consummated, those indications of man, associated with the gigantic animals of a geological age, of whose antiquity there can be no question, speak to our hearts strange tales of the long past, and of the early dispersion and progressive distribution of a race created to "increase and multiply."

The question of transit has also been raised as a difficulty by those who doubt our early colonization. But this would seem easily removed. It is more than probable that, at the period of which we write, Britain, if not Ireland, formed part of the European continent ; but were it not so, we have proof, even in the present day, that screw propellers and iron cast vessels are not necessary for safety in distant voyages, since the present aboriginal vessels of the Pacific will weather a storm in which a *Great Eastern* or a *London* might founder hopelessly.

Let us conclude an apology for our antiquity, if not a proof of it, in the words of our last poet historian :—

"We believe that henceforth no wise person will be found who will not acknowledge that it is possible to bring the genealogies of the Gaedhils to their origin, to Noah and to Adam ; and if he does not believe that, may he not believe that he himself is the son of his own father. For there is no error in the genealogical history, but as it was left from father to son in succession, one after another.

"Surely every one believes the Divine Scriptures, which give a similar genealogy to the men of the world, from Adam down to Noah ;[4] and the genealogy of Christ and of the holy fathers, as may be seen in the Church [writings]. Let him believe this, or let him deny God. And if he does believe this, why should he not believe another history, of which there has been truthful preservation, like the history of Erinn ? I say truthful preservation, for it is not only that they [the preservers of it] were very numerous, as we said, preserving the same, but there was an order and a law with them and upon them, out of which they could not, without great injury, tell lies or falsehoods, as may be seen in the Books of *Fenechas* [Law], of *Fodhla* [Erinn], and in the degrees of the poets themselves, their order, and their laws."[5]

---

[4] *Noah.*—This is a clear argument. The names of pre-Noahacian patriarchs must have been preserved by tradition, with their date of succession and history. Why should not other genealogies have been preserved in a similar manner, and *even the names of individuals* transmitted to posterity ?

[5] *Laws.*—MacFirbis. Apud O'Curry, p. 219.

BEREHAVEN.

CHAPTER III.

First Colonists—The Landing of Ceasair, before the Flood—Landing of Partholan, after the Flood, at Inver Scene—Arrival of Nemedh—The Fomorians—Emigration of the Nemenians—The Firbolgs—Division of Ireland
by the Firbolg Chiefs—The Tuatha Dé Dananns—Their Skill as Artificers—
Nuada of the Silver Hand—The Warriors Sreng and Breas—The Satire of
Cairbré—Termination of the Fomorian Dynasty.

[A.M. 1599.]

E shall, then, commence our history with such
accounts as we can find in our annals of the pre-
Christian colonization of Erinn. The legends of
the discovery and inhabitation of Ireland before
the Flood, are too purely mythical to demand serious notice. But as the most ancient MSS. agree
in their account of this immigration, we may not
pass it over without brief mention.

The account in the *Chronicum Scotorum* runs
thus :—

"Kal. v. f. l. 10. Anno mundi 1599.

"In this year the daughter of one of the Greeks
came to Hibernia, whose name was h-Erui, or
Berba, or Cesar, and fifty maidens and three men
with her. Ladhra was their conductor, who was
the first that was buried in Hibernia."[6] The Cin of Drom Snechta

---

[6] *Hibernia.*—Chronicum Scotorum, p. 3.

is quoted in the Book of Ballymote as authority for the same tradition.[7] The Book of Invasions also mentions this account as
derived from ancient sources. MacFirbis, in the Book of Genealogies, says : " I shall devote the first book to Partholan, who first
took possession of Erinn after the Deluge, devoting the beginning
of it to the coming of the Lady Ceasair," &c. And the Annals of
the Four Masters : " Forty days before the Deluge, Ceasair came to
Ireland with fifty girls and three men—Bith, Ladhra, and Fintain
their names."[8] All authorities agree that Partholan was the first
who colonized Ireland after the Flood. His arrival is stated in the
Chronicum Scotorum to have taken place " in the sixtieth year of
the age of Abraham."[9] The Four Masters say : " The age of the
world, when Partholan came into Ireland, 2520 years."[1]

Partholan landed at Inver[2] Scene, now the Kenmare river, accompanied by his sons, their wives, and a thousand followers. His
antecedents are by no means the most creditable ; and we may,
perhaps, feel some satisfaction, that a colony thus founded should
have been totally swept away by pestilence a few hundred years
after its establishment.

The Chronicum Scotorum gives the date of his landing thus :
" On a Monday, the 14th of May, he arrived, his companions being
eight in number, viz., four men and four women." If the kingdom
of Desmond were as rich then as now in natural beauty, a scene
of no ordinary splendour must have greeted the eyes and glad-
dened the hearts of its first inhabitants. They had voyaged past
the fair and sunny isles of that " tideless sea," the home of the
Phœnician race from the earliest ages. They had escaped the dangers of the rough Spanish coast, and gazed upon the spot where
the Pillars of Hercules were the beacons of the early mariners.
For many days they had lost sight of land, and, we may believe,

---

[7] Tradition.—O'Curry, p. 13.

[8] Names.—Four Masters, O'Donovan, p. 3.

[9] Abraham.—Chronicum Scotorum, p. 5.

[1] Years.—Four Masters, p. 5.

[2] Inver.—Inver and Aber have been used as test words in discriminating
between the Gaedhilic and Cymric Celts. The etymology and meaning is the
same—a meeting of waters. Inver, the Erse and Gaedhilic form, is common
in Ireland, and in those parts of Scotland where the Gael encroached on the
Cymry. See Words and Places, p. 259, for interesting observations on this
subject.

had well-nigh despaired of finding a home in that far isle, to which some strange impulse had attracted them, or some old tradition— for the world even then was old enough for legends of the past— had won their thoughts. But there was a cry of land. The billows dashed in wildly, then as now, from the coasts of an undiscovered world, and left the same line of white foam upon Eiré's western coast. The magnificent *Inver* rolled its tide of beauty between gentle hills and sunny slopes, till it reached what now is appropriately called Kenmare. The distant Reeks showed their clear summits in sharp outline, pointing to the summer sky. The long-backed Mangerton and quaintly-crested Carn Tual were there also ; and, perchance, the Roughty and the Finihé sent their little streams to swell the noble river bay. But it was no time for dreams, though the Celt in all ages has proved the sweetest of dreamers, the truest of bards. These men have rough work to do, and, it may be, gave but scant thought to the beauties of the western isle, and scant thanks to their gods for escape from peril. Plains were to be cleared, forests cut down, and the red deer and giant elk driven to deeper recesses in the well-wooded country.

Several lakes are said to have sprung forth at that period ; but it is more probable that they already existed, and were then for the first time seen by human eye. The plains which Partholan's people cleared are also mentioned, and then we find the ever-returning obituary :—

"The age of the world 2550, Partholan died on Sean Mhagh-Ealta-Edair in this year."[3]

The name of Tallaght still remains, like the peak of a submerged world, to indicate this colonization, and its fatal termination. Some very ancient tumuli may still be seen there. The name signifies a place where a number of persons who died of the plague were interred together; and here the Annals of the Four Masters tells us that nine thousand of Partholan's people died in one week, after they had been three hundred years in Ireland.[4]

The third "taking" of Ireland was that of Nemedh. He came, according to the Annals,[5] A.M. 2859, and erected forts and cleared plains, as his predecessors had done. His people were also afflicted by plague, and appeared to have had occupation enough to bury their dead, and to fight with the "Fomorians in general," an

---

[3] *Year.*—Annals, p. 7.   [4] *Ireland.*—Ib. p. 9.   [5] *Annals.*—Ib. I. p. 9.

unpleasantly pugilistic race, who, according to the Annals of Clonmacnois, " were a sept descended from Cham, the sonne of Noeh,
and lived by pyracie and spoile of other nations, and were in those
days very troublesome to the whole world."[6] The few Nemedians
who escaped alive after their great battle with the Fomorians, fled
into the interior of the island.   Three bands were said to have emigrated with their respective captains.   One party wandered into
the north of Europe, and are believed to have been the progenitors
of the Tuatha Dé Dananns ; others made their way to Greece,
where they were enslaved, and obtained the name of Firbolgs, or
bagmen, from the leathern bags which they were compelled to
carry ; and the third section sought refuge in the north of England,
which is said to have obtained its name of Briton from their leader,
Briotan Maol.[7]

The fourth immigration is that of the Firbolgs ; and it is remarkable how early the love of country is manifested in the Irish race,
since we find those who once inhabited its green plains still anxious
to return, whether their emigration proved prosperous, as to the
Tuatha Dé Dananns, or painful, as to the Firbolgs.

According to the *Annals of Clonmacnois, Keating,* and the
Leabhar-Gabhala, the Firbolgs divided the island into five provinces,
governed by five brothers, the sons of Dela Mac Loich :—" Slane,
the eldest brother, had the province of Leynster for his part, which
containeth from Inver Colpe, that is to say, where the river Boyne
entereth into the sea, now called in Irish Drogheda, to the meeting
of the three waters, by Waterford, where the three rivers, Suyre,
Ffeoir, and Barrow, do meet and run together into the sea.
Gann, the second brother's part, was South Munster, which is a
province extending from that place to Bealagh-Conglaissey.   Sean-
gann, the third brother's part, was from Bealagh-Conglaissey to
Rossedahaileagh, now called Limbriche, which is in the province of
North Munster.   Geanaun, the fourth brother, had the province of
Connacht, containing from Limerick to Easroe.   Rorye, the fifth

[6] *World.*—See Conell MacGeoghegan's Translation of the Annals of Clonmacnois, quoted by O'Donovan, p. 11.

[7] *Maol.*—The Teutonic languages afford no explanation of the name of
Britain, though it is inhabited by a Teutonic race. It is probable, therefore,
that they adopted an ethnic appellation of the former inhabitants. This may
have been patronymic, or, perhaps, a Celtic prefix with the Euskarian suffix
etan, a district or country. See *Words and Places,* p. 60.

brother, and youngest, had from Easroe aforesaid to Inver Colpe, which is in the province of Ulster.'[8]

The Firbolg chiefs had landed in different parts of the island, but they soon met at the once famous Tara, where they united their forces. To this place they gave the name of *Druim Cain*, or the Beautiful Eminence.

The fifth, or Tuatha Dé Danann "taking" of Ireland, occurred in the reign of Eochaidh, son of Erc, A.M. 3303. The Firbolgian dynasty was terminated at the battle of *Magh Tuireadh*. Eochaidh fled from the battle, and was killed on the strand of Traigh Eothailé, near Ballysadare, co. Sligo. The cave where he was interred still exists, and there is a curious tradition that the tide can never cover it.

The Tuatha Dé Danann king, Nuada, lost his hand in this battle, and obtained the name of Nuada of the Silver Hand,[9] his artificer, Credne Cert, having made a silver hand for him with joints. It is probable the latter acquisition was the work of Mioch, the son of Diancecht, Nuada's physician, as there is a tradition that he "took off the hand and infused feeling and motion into every joint and finger of it, as if it were a natural hand." We may doubt the "feeling," but it was probably suggested by the "motion," and the fact that, in those ages, every act of more than ordinary skill was attributed to supernatural causes, though effected through human agents. Perhaps even, in the enlightened nineteenth century, we might not be much the worse for the pious belief, less the pagan cause to which it was attributed. It should be observed here, that the Brehon Laws were probably then in force ; for the "blemish" of the monarch appears to have deprived him of his dignity, at least until the silver hand could satisfy for the defective limb. The Four Masters tell us briefly that the Tuatha Dé Dananns gave the sovereignty to Breas, son of Ealathan, "while the hand of Nuada was under cure," and mentions that Breas resigned the kingdom to him in the seventh year after the cure of his hand.

A more detailed account of this affair may be found in one of our ancient historic tales, of the class called *Catha* or *Battles*, which

Professor O'Curry pronounces to be " almost the earliest event upon the record of which we may place sure reliance."[1]   It would appear that there were two battles between the Firbolgs and Tuatha Dé Dananns, and that, in the last of these, Nuada was

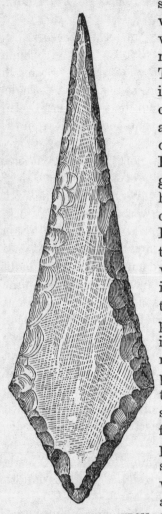

slain.   According to this ancient tract, when the Firbolg king heard of the arrival of the invaders, he sent a warrior named Sreng to reconnoitre their camp. The Tuatha Dé Dananns were as skilled in war as in magic; they had sentinels carefully posted, and their *videttes* were as much on the alert as a Wellington or a Napier could desire.   The champion Breas was sent forward to meet the stranger.   As they approached, each raised his shield, and cautiously surveyed his opponent from above the protecting ægis. Breas was the first to speak.   The mother-tongue was as dear then as now, and Sreng was charmed to hear himself addressed in his own language, which, equally dear to the exiled Nemedian chiefs, had been preserved by them in their long wanderings through northern Europe.   An examination of each others armour next took place.   Sreng was armed with " two heavy, thick, pointless, but sharply rounded spears;" while Breas carried " two beautifully shaped, thin, slender, long, sharp-pointed spears."[2]   Perhaps the one bore a spear of the same class of heavy flint weapons of which we give an illustration, and the other the lighter and more graceful sword, of which many specimens may be seen in the collection of the Royal Irish Academy.   Breas then proposed that they

FLINT SPEAR-HEAD, FROM THE COLLECTION OF THE R.I.A.

should divide the island between the two parties; and after exchanging spears and promises of mutual friendship, each returned to his own camp.

---

[1] *Reliance.*—O'Curry, p. 243.   [2] *Spears.*—O'Curry, p. 245.

The Firbolg king, however, objected to this arrangement; and it was decided, in a council of war, to give battle to the invaders. The Tuatha Dé Dananns were prepared for this from the account which Breas gave of the Firbolg warriors: they, therefore, abandoned their camp, and took up a strong position on Mount Belgadan, at the west end of *Magh Nia*, a site near the present village of Cong, co. Mayo.

The Firbolgs marched from Tara to meet them; but Nuada, anxious for pacific arrangements, opened new negociations with King Eochaidh through the medium of his bards. The battle which has been mentioned before then followed. The warrior Breas, who ruled during the disability of Nuada, was by no means popular. He was not hospitable, a *sine qua non* for king or chief from the earliest ages of Celtic being; he did not love the bards, for the same race ever cherished and honoured learning; and he attempted to enslave the nobles. Discontent came to a climax when the bard Cairbré, son of the poetess Etan, visited the royal court, and was sent to a dark chamber, without fire or bed, and, for all royal fare, served with three small cakes of bread. If we wish to know the true history of a people, to understand the causes of its sorrows and its joys, to estimate its worth, and to know how to rule it wisely and well, let us read such old-world tales carefully, and ponder them well. Even if prejudice or ignorance should induce us to undervalue their worth as authentic records of its ancient history, let us remember the undeniable fact, that they *are* authentic records of its deepest national feelings, and let them, at least, have their weight as such in our schemes of social economy, for the present and the future.

The poet left the court next morning, but not until he pronounced a bitter and withering satire on the king—the first satire that had ever been pronounced in Erinn. It was enough. Strange effects are attributed to the satire of a poet in those olden times; but probably they could, in all cases, bear the simple and obvious interpretation, that he on whom the satire was pronounced was thereby disgraced eternally before his people. For how slight a punishment would bodily suffering or deformity be, in comparison to the mental suffering of which a quick-souled people are eminently capable!

Breas was called on to resign. He did so with the worst possible grace, as might be expected from such a character. His father, Elatha, was a Fomorian sea-king or pirate, and he repaired to his court. His reception was not such as he had expected; he therefore went to Balor of the Evil Eye,[3] a Fomorian chief. The two warriors collected a vast army and navy, and formed a bridge of ships and boats from the Hebrides to the north-west coast of Erinn. Having landed their forces, they marched to a plain in the barony of Tirerrill (co. Sligo), where they waited an attack or surrender of the Tuatha Dé Danann army. But the magical skill, or, more correctly, the superior abilities of this people, proved them more than equal to the occasion. The chronicler gives a quaint and most interesting account of the Tuatha Dé Danann arrangements. Probably the Crimean campaign, despite our nineteenth century advancements in the art of war, was not prepared for more carefully, or carried out more efficiently.

Nuada called a "privy council," if we may use the modern term for the ancient act, and obtained the advice of the great Daghda; of Lug, the son of Cian, son of Diancecht, the famous physician; and of Ogma Grian-Aineach (of the sun-like face). But Daghda and Lug were evidently secretaries of state for the home and war departments, and arranged these intricate affairs with perhaps more honour to their master, and more credit to the nation, than many a modern and "civilized" statesman. They summoned to their presence the heads of each department necessary for carrying on the war. Each department was therefore carefully pre-organized, in such a manner as to make success almost certain, and to obtain every possible succour and help from those engaged in the combat, or those who had suffered from it. The "smiths" were prepared to make and to mend the swords, the surgeons to heal or staunch the wounds, the bards and druids to praise or blame; and each knew his work, and what was expected from the department which he headed before the battle, for the questions put to each, and their replies, are on record.

Pardon me. You will say I have written a romance, a legend, for the benefit of my country[4]—a history of what might have been,

---

[3] *Eye.*—There is a curious note by Dr. O'Donovan (Annals, p. 18) about this Balor. The tradition of his deeds and enchantments is still preserved in Tory Island, one of the many evidences of the value of tradition, and of the many proofs that it usually overlies a strata of facts.

[4] *Country.*—We find the following passages in a work purporting to be a history of Ireland, recently published: "It would be throwing away time to examine critically *fables* like those contained in the present and following chapter." The subjects of those chapters are the colonization of Partholan, of the Nemedians,

of what should be, at least in modern warfare, and, alas! often is not. Pardon me. The copy of the tracts from which I have compiled this meagre narrative, is in existence, and in the British Museum. It was written on vellum, about the year 1460, by Gilla-Riabhach O'Clery; but there is unquestionable authority for its having existed at a much earlier period. It is quoted by Cormac Mac Cullinan in his Glossary, in illustration of the word *Nes*, and Cormac was King of Munster in the year of grace 885, while his Glossary was compiled to explain words which had then become obsolete. This narrative must, therefore, be of great antiquity. If we cannot accept it as a picture of the period, in the main authentic, let us give up all ancient history as a myth; if we do accept it, let us acknowledge that a people who possessed such officials had attained a high state of intellectual culture, and that their memory demands at least the homage of our respect.

The plain on which this battle was fought, retains the name of the Plain of the Towers (or Pillars) of the Fomorians, and some very curious sepulchral monuments may still be seen on the ancient field.

Fomorians, Tuatha Dé Dananns, and Milesians, the building of the palace of Emania, the reign of Cairbré, Tuathal, and last, not least, the death of Dathi. And these are "fables"! The writer then calmly informs us that the period at which they were "invented, extended probably from the tenth to the twelfth century." Certainly, the "inventors" were men of no ordinary talent, and deserve some commendation for their inventive faculties. But on this subject we shall say more hereafter. At last the writer arrives at the "first ages of Christianity." We hoped that here at least he might have granted us a history; but he writes : "The history of early Christianity in Ireland is obscure and doubtful, precisely in proportion as it is unusually copious. If legends enter largely into the civil history of the country, they found their way tenfold into the history of the Church, because there the tendency to believe in them was much greater, as well as the inducement to invent and adopt them." The "inventors" of the pre-Christian history of Ireland, who accomplished their task "from the tenth to the twelfth century," are certainly complimented at the expense of the saints who Christianized Ireland. This writer seems to doubt the existence of St. Patrick, and has "many doubts" as to the authenticity of the life of St. Columba. We should not have noticed this work had we not reason to know that it has circulated largely amongst the middle and lower classes, who may be grievously misled by its very insidious statements. It is obviously written for the sake of making a book to sell; and the writer has the honesty to say plainly, that he merely gives the early history of Ireland, pagan and Christian, because he could not well write a history of Ireland and omit this portion of it !

In those days, as in the so-called middle ages, ladies exercised their skill in the healing art ; and we find honorable mention made of the Lady Ochtriuil, who assisted the chief physician (her father) and his sons in healing the wounds of the Tuatha Dé Danann heroes.   These warriors have also left many evidences of their existence in raths and monumental pillars.[5]   It is probable, also, that much that has been attributed to the Danes, of right belongs to the Dananns, and that a confusion of names has promoted a confusion of appropriation.   Before we turn to the Milesian immigration, the last colonization of the old country, let us inquire what was known and said of it, and of its people, by foreign writers.

[5] *Pillars.*—The monuments ascribed to the Tuatha Dé Danauns are principally situated in Meath, at Drogheda, Dowlet, Knowth, and New Grange. There are others at Cnoc-Ainè and Cnoc-Gréinè, co. Limerick, and on the Pap Mountains, co. Kerry.

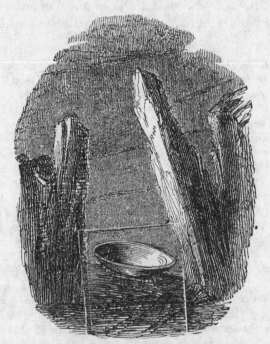

CAVITY, CONTAINING OVAL BASIN,
NEW GRANGE.

THE SEVEN CASTLES OF CLONMINES.

CHAPTER IV.

The Scythians Colonists—Testimony of Josephus—Magog and his Colony—
Statements of our Annals confirmed by a Jewish Writer—By Herodotus—
Nennius relates what is told by the "Most Learned of the Scoti"—
Phœnician Circumnavigation of Africa—Phœnician Colonization of Spain
—Iberus and Himerus—Traditions of Partholan—Early Geographical
Accounts of Ireland—Early Social Accounts of Ireland.

THE writer of the article on Ireland, in Rees' Cyclopædia, says : " It does not appear improbable, much
less absurd, to suppose that the Phœnicians might
have colonized Ireland at an early period, and introduced their laws, customs, and knowledge, with
a comparatively high state of civilization ; and that
these might have been gradually lost amidst the
disturbances of the country, and, at last, completely
destroyed by the irruptions of the Ostmen." Of
this assertion, which is now scarcely doubted, there
is abundant proof ; and it is remarkable that
Josephus[6] attributes to the Phœnicians a special
care in preserving their annals above that of other
civilized nations, and that this feeling has existed,
and still exists, more vividly in the Celtic race
than in any other European people.

[6] *Josephus.*—Con. Apionem, lib. i.

The Irish annalists claim a descent from the Scythians, who, they say, are descended from Magog, the son of Japhet, the son of Noah. Keating says : " We will set down here the branching off of the race of Magog, according to the Book of Invasions (of Ireland), which was called the Cin of Drom Snechta."[7] It will be remembered how curiously O'Curry verified Keating's statement as to the authorship of this work,[8] so that his testimony may be received with respect. In the Scripture genealogy, the sons of Magog are not enumerated ; but an historian, who cannot be suspected of any design of assisting the Celts to build up a pedigree, has happily supplied the deficiency. Josephus writes :[9] " Magog led out a colony, which from him were named Magoges, but by the Greeks called Scythians." But Keating specifies the precise title of Scythians, from which the Irish Celts are descended. He says they had established themselves in remote ages on the borders of the Red Sea, at the town of Chiroth ; that they were expelled by the grandson of that Pharaoh who had been drowned in the Red Sea ; and that he persecuted them because they had supplied the Israelites with provisions.

This statement is singularly and most conclusively confirmed by Rabbi Simon, who wrote two hundred years before the birth of Christ. He says that certain Canaanites near the Red Sea gave provisions to the Israelites ; " and because these Canaan ships gave Israel of their provisions, God would not destroy their ships, but with an east wind carried them down the Red Sea."[1] This colony settled in what was subsequently called Phœnicia ; and here again our traditions are confirmed ab extra, for Herodotus says: " The Phœnicians anciently dwelt, as they allege, on the borders of the Red Sea."[2]

It is not known at what time this ancient nation obtained the

---

[7] Snechta.—O'Curry, p. 14.

[8] Work.—See ante, p. 43.

[9] Writes.—Josephus, lib. i. c. 6. Most of the authorities in this chapter are taken from the Essay on the ancient history, religion, learning, arts, and government of Ireland, by the late W. D'Alton. The Essay obtained a prize of £80 and the Cunningham Gold Medal from the Royal Irish Academy. It is published in volume xvi. of the Transactions, and is a repertory of learning of immense value to the student of Irish history.

[1] Sea.—Lib. Zoar, p. 87, as cited by Vallancey, and Parson's Defence, &c., p. 205.

[2] Sea.—Herodotus, l. vii. c. 89.

specific appellation of Phœnician. The word is not found in Hebrew copies of the Scriptures, but is used in the Machabees, the original of which is in Greek, and in the New Testament. According to Grecian historians, it was derived from Phœnix, one of their kings, and brother of Cadmus, the inventor of letters. It is remarkable that our annals mention a king named Phenius, who devoted himself especially to the study of languages, and composed an alphabet and the elements of grammar. Our historians describe the wanderings of the Phœnicians, whom they still designate Scythians, much as they are described by other writers. The account of their route may differ in detail, but the main incidents coincide. Nennius, an English chronicler, who wrote in the seventh century, from the oral testimony of trustworthy Irish Celts, gives corroborative testimony. He writes thus : "If any one would be anxious to learn how long Ireland was uninhabited and deserted, he shall hear it, as the most learned of the Scots have related it to me.[3] When the children of Israel came to the Red Sea, the Egyptians pursued them and were drowned, as the Scripture records. In the time of Moses there was a Scythian noble who had been banished from his kingdom, and dwelt in Egypt with a large family. He was there when the Egyptians were drowned, but he did not join in the persecution of the Lord's people. Those who survived laid plans to banish him, lest he should assume the government, because their brethren were drowned in the Red Sea; so he was expelled. He wandered through Africa for forty-two years, and passed by the lake of Salinæ to the altars of the Philistines, and between Rusicada and the mountains Azure, and he came by the river Mulon, and by sea to the Pillars of Hercules, and through the Tuscan Sea, and he made for Spain, and dwelt there many years, and he increased and multiplied, and his people were multiplied."

Herodotus gives an account of the circumnavigation of Africa by the Phœnicians, which may have some coincidence with this narrative. His only reason for rejecting the tradition, which he relates at length, is that he could not conceive how these

[3] *Me.*—"Sic mihi peritissimi Scotorum nunciaverunt." The reader will remember that the Irish were called Scots, although the appellative of Ierins or Ierne continued to be given to the country from the days of Orpheus to those of Claudius. By Roman writers Ireland was more usually termed Hibernia. Juvenal calls it Juverna.

navigators could have seen the sun in a position contrary to that in which it is seen in Europe. The expression of his doubt is a strong confirmation of the truth of his narrative, which, however, is generally believed by modern writers.[4]

This navigation was performed about seven centuries before the Christian era, and is, at least, a proof that the maritime power of the Phœnicians was established at an early period, and that it was not impossible for them to have extended their enterprises to Ireland. The traditions of our people may also be confirmed from other sources. Solinus writes thus : "In the gulf of Boatica there is an island, distant some hundred paces from the mainland, which the Tyrians, who came from the Red Sea, called Erythrœa, and the Carthaginians, in their language, denominate Gadir, i.e., the enclosure."

Spanish historians add their testimony, and claim the Phœnicians as their principal colonizers. The *Hispania Illustrata*, a rare and valuable work, on which no less than sixty writers were engaged, fixes the date of the colonization of Spain by the Phœnicians at 764 A.C. De Bellegarde says : "The first of whom mention is made in history is Hercules, the Phœnician, by some called Melchant." It is alleged that he lived in the time of Moses, and that he retired into Spain when the Israelites entered the land of promise. This will be consistent with old accounts, if faith can be placed in the inscription of two columns, which were found in the province of Tingitane, at the time of the historian Procopius.[5] A Portuguese historian, Emanuel de Faria y Sousa, mentions the sailing of Gatelus from Egypt, with his whole family, and names his two sons, Iberus and Himerus, the first of whom, he says, "some will have to have sailed into Ireland, and given the name Hibernia to it."

---

[4] *Writers.*—The circumnavigation of Africa by a Phœnician ship, in the reign of Neco, about 610 B.C., is credited by Humboldt, Rennell, Heeren, Grote, and Rawlinson. Of their voyages to Cornwall for tin there is no question, and it is more than probable they sailed to the Baltic for amber. It has been even supposed that they anticipated Columbus in the discovery of America. Niebuhr connects the primitive astronomy of Europe with that of America, and, therefore, must suppose the latter country to have been discovered.—*Hist. of Rome*, vol. i. p. 281. This, however, is very vague ground of conjecture ; the tide of knowledge, as well as emigration, was more probably eastward.

[5] *Procopius.*—*Hist. Gen. d'Espagne*, vol. i. c. l. p. 4.

Indeed, so strong has been the concurrent testimony of a Phœnician colonization of Ireland from Spain, and this by independent authorities, who could not have had access to our bardic histories, and who had no motive, even had they known of their existence, to write in confirmation of them, that those who have maintained the theory of a Gaulish colonization of Ireland, have been obliged to make Spain the point of embarkation.

There is a curious treatise on the antiquities and origin of Cambridge, in which it is stated, that, in the year of the world 4321, a British prince, the son of Gulguntius, or Gurmund, having crossed over to Denmark, to enforce tribute from a Danish king, was returning victorious off the Orcades, when he encountered thirty ships, full of men and women. On his inquiring into the object of their voyage, their leader, *Partholyan*, made an appeal to his good-nature, and entreated from the prince some small portion of land in Britain, as his crew were weary of sailing over the ocean. Being informed that he came from Spain, the British prince received him under his protection, and assigned faithful guides to attend him into Ireland, which was then wholly uninhabited; and he granted it to them, subject to an annual tribute, and confirmed the appointment of Partholyan as their chief.[6]

This account was so firmly believed in England, that it is specially set forth in an Irish act (11th of Queen Elizabeth) among the " auncient and sundry strong authentique tytles for the kings of England to this land of Ireland." The tradition may have been obtained from Irish sources, and was probably " improved" and accommodated to fortify the Saxon claim, by the addition of the pretended grant; but it is certainly evidence of the early belief in the Milesian colonization of Ireland, and the name of their leader.

The earliest references to Ireland by foreign writers are, as might be expected, of a contradictory character. Plutarch affirms that Calypso was " an island five days' sail to the west of Britain," which, at least, indicates his knowledge of the existence of Erinn. Orpheus is the first writer who definitely names Ireland. In the imaginary route which he prescribes for Jason and the Argonauts, he names Ireland (Iernis), and describes its woody surface and its

---

[6] *Chief.—De Antiq. et Orig. Cantab.* See D'Alton's *Essay*, p. 24, for other authorities.

misty atmosphere.   All authorities are agreed that this poem[7] was
written five hundred years before Christ ; and all doubt as to
whether Iernis meant the present island of Ireland must be removed, at least to an unprejudiced inquirer, by a careful examination of the route which is described, and the position of the island
in that route.

The early history of a country which has been so long and so
cruelly oppressed, both civilly and morally, has naturally fallen
into disrepute.   We do not like to display the qualifications of one
whom we have deeply injured.   It is, at least, less disgraceful to
have forbidden a literature to a people who had none, than
to have banned and barred the use of a most ancient language,—to have destroyed the annals of a most ancient people.
In self-defence, the conqueror who knows not how to triumph
nobly will triumph basely, and the victims may, in time, almost
forget what it has been the policy of centuries to conceal from
them.   But ours is, in many respects, an age of historical justice,
and truth will triumph in the end.   It is no longer necessary
to England's present greatness to deny the facts of history ; and it
is one of its most patent facts that Albion was unknown, or, at
least, that her existence was unrecorded, at a time when Ireland is
mentioned with respect as the Sacred Isle, and the Ogygia[8] of the
Greeks.

As might be expected, descriptions of the social state of ancient
Erinn are of the most contradictory character ; but there is a
remarkable coincidence in all accounts of the physical geography
of the island.   The moist climate, the fertile soil, the richly-
wooded plains, the navigable rivers, and the abundance of its
fish,[9] are each and all mentioned by the early geographers.   The

[7] *Poem.*—There has been question of the author, but none as to the authenticity and the probable date of compilation.

[8] *Ogygia.*—Camden writes thus : " Nor can any one conceive why they
should call it Ogygia, unless, perhaps, from its antiquity ; for the Greeks
called nothing Ogygia unless what was extremely ancient."

[9] *Fish.*—And it still continues to be a national article of consumption and
export.   In a recent debate on the " Irish question," an honorable member
observes, that he regrets to say " fish" is the only thing which appears to be
flourishing in Ireland.   We fear, however, from the report of the Select Committee of the House of Commons on the question of Irish sea-coast fisheries,
that the poor fishermen are not prospering as well as the fish.   Mr. Hart
stated : " Fish was as plenty as ever ; but numbers of the fishermen had died
during the famine, others emigrated, and many of those who remained were

description given by Diodorus Siculus of a " certain large island a considerable distance out at sea, and in the direction of the west, many days' sail from Lybia," if it applies to Ireland, would make us suppose that the Erinn of pagan times was incomparably more prosperous than Erinn under Christian rule. He also specially mentions the fish, and adds : " The Phœnicians, from the very remotest times, made repeated voyages thither for purposes of commerce."[1]

The descriptions of our social state are by no means so flattering ; but it is remarkable, and, perhaps, explanatory, that the most unfavourable accounts are the more modern ones. All without the pale of Roman civilization were considered " barbarians," and the epithet was freely applied. Indeed, it is well known that, when Cicero had a special object in view, he could describe the Celtæ of Gaul as the vilest monsters, and the hereditary enemies of the gods, for whose wickedness extermination was the only remedy. As to the " gods " there is no doubt that the Druidic worship was opposed to the more sensual paganism of Greece and Rome, and,

unable, from want of means, to follow the pursuit." And yet these men are honest ; for it has been declared before the same committee, that they have scrupulously repaid the loans which were given them formerly ; and they are willing to work, for when they can get boats and nets, *they do work.* These are facts. Shakspeare has said that facts are "stubborn things ;" they are, certainly, sometimes very unpleasant things. Yet, we are told, the Irish have no real grievances. Of course, starvation from want of work is not a grievance !

Within the few months which have elapsed since the publication of the first edition of this History and the present moment, when I am engaged in preparing a second edition, a fact has occurred within my own personal knowledge relative to this very subject, and of too great importance to the history of Ireland in the present day to be omitted. A shoal of sprats arrived in the bay of ——, and the poor people crowded to the shore to witness the arrival and, alas ! the departure of the finny tribe. All their nets had been broken or sold in the famine year ; they had, therefore, no means of securing what would have been a valuable addition to their poor fare. The wealthy, whose tables are furnished daily with every luxury, can have but little idea how bitter such privations are to the poor. Had there been a resident landlord in the place, to interest himself in the welfare of his tenants, a few pounds would have procured all that was necessary, and the people, always grateful for kindness, would long have remembered the boon and the bestower of it.

[1] *Commerce.*— " Phœnices a vetustissimis inde temporibus frequenter crebras mercaturæ gratiâ navigationes instituerunt."—Diod. Sic. vers. Wesseling, t. i.

therefore, would be considered eminently irreligious by the votaries of the latter.

The most serious social charge against the Irish Celts, is that of
being anthropophagi ; and the statement of St. Jerome, that he
had seen two Scoti in Gaul feeding on a human carcass, has been
claimed as strong corroboration of the assertions of pagan writers.
As the good father was often vehement in his statements and impulsive in his opinions, he may possibly have been mistaken, or, perhaps,
purposely misled by those who wished to give him an unfavourable
impression of the Irish. It is scarcely possible that they could
have been cannibal as a nation, since St. Patrick never even alludes
to such a custom in his *Confessio*,[2] where it would, undoubtedly,
have been mentioned and reproved, had it existence.

---

[2] *Confessio.*—Dr. O'Donovan states, in an article in the *Ulster Archæological
Journal*, vol. viii. p. 249, that he had a letter from the late Dr. Prichard, who
stated that it was his belief the ancient Irish were not anthropophagi.   He
adds : "Whatever they may have been when their island was called *Insula
Sacra*, there are no people in Europe who are more squeamish in the use of meats
than the modern Irish peasantry, for they have a horror of every kind of
carrion ;" albeit he is obliged to confess that, though they abuse the French
for eating frogs, and the English for eating rooks, there is evidence to prove
that horseflesh was eaten in Ireland, even in the reign of Queen Elizabeth.

CROSS AT GLENDALOUGH, CO. WICKLOW.

CROMLECH AT DUNMORE, WATERFORD.

CHAPTER V.

Landing of the Milesians—Traditions of the Tuatha Dé Dananns in St. Patrick's time—The Lia Fail, or Stone of Destiny—The Milesians go back to sea "nine waves"—They conquer ultimately—Reign of Eremon—Landing of the Picts—Bede's Account of Ireland—Fame of its Fish and Goats—Difficulties of Irish Chronology—Importance and Authenticity of Irish Pedigrees—Qualifications of an Ollamh—Milesian Genealogies—Historical Value of Pedigrees—National Feelings should be respected—Historic Tales—Poems.

[A.M. 3500.]

THE last colonization of Ireland is thus related in the Annals of the Four Masters : " The age of the world 3500. The fleet of the sons of Milidh came to Ireland at the end of this year, to take it from the Tuatha Dé Dananns, and they fought the battle of Sliabh Mis with them on the third day after landing. In this battle fell Scota, the daughter of Pharaoh, wife of Milidh ; and the grave of Scota[3] is [to be seen] between Sliabh Mis and the sea. Therein also fell Fas, the wife of Un, son of Uige, from whom is [named] Gleann Faisi. After this the sons of Milidh fought a battle at Taillten[4] against the three kings of the Tuatha Dé Dananns, MacCuill, MacCeacht, and MacGriéné. The battle lasted for a long time, until MacCeacht fell by Eiremhon, MacCuill by Eimheur, and Mac

[3] *Scota.*—The grave is still pointed out in the valley of Gleann Scoithin, county Kerry.

[4] *Taillten*—Now Telltown, county Meath.

Griéné by Amhergen."[5] Thus the Tuatha Dé Danann dynasty passed away, but not without leaving many a quaint legend of magic and mystery, and many an impress of its more than ordinary skill in such arts as were then indications of national superiority. The real names of the last chiefs of this line, are said to have been respectively Ethur, Cethur, and Fethur. The first was called MacCuill, because he worshipped the hazel-tree, and, more probably, because he was devoted to some branch of literature which it symbolized; the second MacCeacht, because he worshipped the plough, *i.e.*, was devoted to agriculture; and the third obtained his appellation of MacGriéné because he worshipped the sun.

It appears from a very curious and ancient tract, written in the shape of a dialogue between St. Patrick and Caoilte MacRonain, that there were many places in Ireland where the Tuatha Dé Dananns were then supposed to live as sprites and fairies, with corporeal and material forms, but endued with immortality. The inference naturally to be drawn from these stories is, that the Tuatha Dé Dananns lingered in the country for many centuries after their subjugation by the Gaedhils, and that they lived in retired situations, where they practised abstruse arts, from which they obtained the reputation of being magicians.

The Tuatha Dé Dananns are also said to have brought the famous Lia Fail, or Stone of Destiny, to Ireland. It is said by some authorities that this stone was carried to Scotland when an Irish colony invaded North Britain, and that it was eventually brought to England by Edward I., in the year 1300, and deposited in Westminster Abbey. It is supposed to be identical with the large block of stone which may be seen there under the coronation chair. Dr. Petrie, however, controverts this statement, and believes it to be the present pillar stone over the Croppies' Grave in one of the raths of Tara.

A Danann prince, called Oghma, is said to have invented the occult form of writing called the Ogham Craove, which, like the round towers has proved so fertile a source of doubt and discussion to our antiquaries.

The Milesians, however, did not obtain a colonization in Ireland without some difficulty. According to the ancient accounts, they

---

[5] *Amhergen.*—Annals of the Four Masters, vol. i. p. 25.

landed at the mouth of the river Sláingé, or Slaney, in the present county of Wexford, unperceived by the Tuatha Dé Dananns. From thence they marched to Tara, the seat of government, and summoned the three kings to surrender. A curious legend is told of this summons and its results, which is probably true in the more important details. The Tuatha Dé Danann princes complained that they had been taken by surprise, and proposed to the invaders to re-embark, and to go out upon the sea " the distance of nine waves," stating that the country should be surrendered to them if they could then effect a landing by force. The Milesian chiefs assented; but when the original inhabitants found them fairly launched at sea, they raised a tempest by magical incantations, which entirely dispersed the fleet. One part of it was driven along the east coast of Erinn, to the north, under the command of Eremon, the youngest of the Milesian brothers; the remainder, under the command of Donn, the elder brother, was driven to the south-west of the island.

But the Milesians had druids also.[6] As soon as they suspected the agency which had caused the storm, they sent a man to the topmast of the ship to know " if the wind was blowing at that height over the surface of the sea." The man reported that it was not. The druids then commence practising counter arts of magic, in which they soon succeeded, but not until five of the eight brothers were lost. Four, including Donn, were drowned in the wild Atlantic, off the coast of Kerry. Colpa met his fate at the mouth of the river Boyne, called from him Inbhear Colpa. Eber Finn and Amergin, the survivors of the southern party, landed in Kerry, and here the battle of Sliabh Mis was fought, which has been already mentioned.

The battle of Taillten followed; and the Milesians having become masters of the country, the brothers Eber Finn and Eremon divided it between them; the former taking all the southern part, from the Boyne and the Shannon to Cape Clear, the latter taking all the part lying to the north of these rivers.

This arrangement, however, was not of long continuance. Each was desirous of unlimited sovereignty; and they met to decide their

---

[6] *Also.*—This tale bears a simple and obvious interpretation. The druids were the most learned and experienced in physical science of their respective nations; hence the advice they gave appeared magical to those who were less instructed.

claims by an appeal to arms at Géisill,[7] a place near the present
Tullamore, in the King's county. Eber and his chief leaders fell
in this engagement, and Eremon assumed the sole government of
the island.[8]

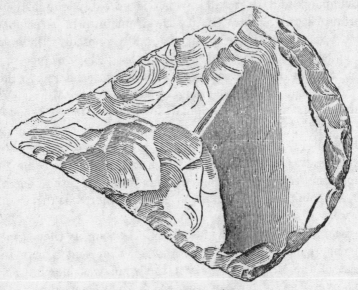

ANCIENT FLINT AXE.

He took up his residence in Leinster, and after a reign of fifteen
years died, and was buried at *Ráith Beóthaigh*, in *Argat Ross*. This

[7] *Géisill.*—The scene of the battle was at a place called *Tochar eter dhá
mhagh,* or "the causeway between two plains," and on the bank of the river
Bri damh, which runs through the town of Tullamore. The name of the
battle-field is still preserved in the name of the townland of Ballintogher, in
the parish and barony of *Géisill.* At the time of the composition of the
ancient topographical tract called the Dinnseanchus, the mounds and graves
of the slain were still to be seen.—See O'Curry, page 449. The author
of this tract, Amergin Mac Amalgaidh, wrote about the sixth century. A
copy of his work is preserved in the Book of Ballymote, which was compiled
in the year 1391. There is certainly evidence enough to prove the fact of the
mêlée, and that this was not a "legend invented from the tenth to the twelfth
centuries." It is almost amusing to hear the criticisms of persons utterly
ignorant of our literature, however well-educated in other respects. If the
treasures of ancient history which exist in Irish MSS. existed in Sanscrit, or
even in Greek or Latin, we should find scholars devoting their lives and best
intellectual energies to understand and proclaim their value and importance,
and warmly defending them against all impugners of their authenticity.

[8] *Island.*—The axe figured above is a remarkable weapon. The copy is
taken, by permission, from the collection of the Royal Irish Academy. Sir

ancient rath still exists, and is now called Rath Beagh. It is situated on the right bank of the river Nore, near the present village of Ballyragget, county Kilkenny. This is not narrated by the Four Masters, neither do they mention the coming of the Cruithneans or Picts into Ireland. These occurrences, however, are recorded in all the ancient copies of the Book of Invasions, and in the Dinnseanchus. The Cruithneans or Picts are said to have fled from the oppression of their king in Thrace, and to have passed into Gaul. There they founded the city of Poictiers. From thence they were again driven by an act of tyranny, and they proceeded first to Britain, and then to Ireland. Crimhthann Sciath-bél, one of King Eremon's leaders, was at Wexford when the new colony landed. He was occupied in extirpating a tribe of Britons who had settled in Fotharta,[9] and were unpleasantly distinguished for fighting with poisoned weapons. The Irish chieftain asked the assistance of the new comers. A battle was fought, and the Britons were defeated principally by the skill of the Pictish druid, who found an antidote for the poison of their weapons. According to the quaint account of Bede,[1] the Celtic chiefs gave good advice to their foreign allies in return for their good deeds, and recommended them to settle in North Britain, adding that they would come to their assistance should they find any difficulty or opposition from the inhabitants. The Picts took the advice, but soon found themselves in want of helpmates. They applied again to their neighbours, and were obligingly supplied with wives on the condition " that, when any difficulty should arise, they should choose a king from the female royal race rather than from the male." The Picts accepted the terms and the ladies ; " and the custom," says Bede, " as is well known, is observed among the Picts to this day."

Bede then continues to give a description of Ireland. His account, although of some length, and not in all points reliable, is too interesting to be omitted, being the opinion of an Englishman, and an author of reputation, as to the state of Ireland, socially and

W. Wilde describes the original thus in the Catalogue : "It is 3⅓ inches in its longest diameter, and at its thickest part measures about half-an-inch. It has been chipped all over with great care, and has a sharp edge all round. This peculiar style of tool or weapon reached perfection in this specimen, which, whether used as a knife, arrow, spike, or axe, was an implement of singular beauty of design, and exhibits great skill in the manufacture."

[9] *Fotharta.*—Now the barony of Forth, in Wexford.

[1] *Bede.*—*Ecclesiastical History,* Bohn's edition, p. 6.

physically, in the seventh century: "Ireland, in breadth and for wholesomeness and serenity of climate, far surpasses Britain; for the snow scarcely ever lies there above three days; no man makes hay in summer for winter's provision, or builds stables for his beasts of burden. No reptiles are found there; for, though often carried thither out of Britain, as soon as the ship comes near the shore, and the scent of the air reaches them, they die. On the contrary, almost all things in the island are good against poison. In short, we have known that when some persons have been bitten by serpents, the scrapings of leaves of books that were brought out of Ireland, being put into water and given them to drink, have immediately expelled the spreading poison, and assuaged the swelling. The island abounds in milk and honey;[2] nor is there any want of vines, fish,[3] and fowl; and it is remarkable for deer and goats."

The chronology of Irish pagan history is unquestionably one of its greatest difficulties. But the chronology of all ancient peoples is equally unmanageable. When Bunsen has settled Egyptian chronology to the satisfaction of other literati as well as to his own, and when Hindoo and Chinese accounts of their postdiluvian or antediluvian ancestors have been reconciled and synchronized, we may

---

[2] *Honey.*—Honey was an important edible to the ancients, and, therefore, likely to obtain special mention. Keating impugns the veracity of Solinus, who stated that there were no bees in Ireland, on the authority of Camden, who says: "Such is the quantity of bees, that they are found not only in hives, but even in the trunks of trees, and in holes in the ground." There is a curious legend anent the same useful insect, that may interest apiarians as well as hagiologists. It is said in the life of St. David, that when Modomnoc (or Dominic) was with St. David at Menevia, in Wales, he was charged with the care of the beehives, and that the bees became so attached to him that they followed him to Ireland. However, the Rule of St. Albans, who lived in the time of St. Patrick (in the early part of the fifth century), may be quoted to prove that bees existed in Ireland at an earlier period, although the saint may have been so devoted to his favourites as to have brought a special colony by miracle or otherwise to Ireland. The Rule of St. Alban says: "When they [the monks] sit down at table, let them be brought [served] beets or roots, washed with water, in clean baskets, also apples, beer, and honey from the hive." Certainly, habits of regularity and cleanliness are here plainly indicated as well as the existence of the bee.

[3] *Fish.*—It is to be presumed that fish are destined to prosper in Hibernia: of the ancient deer, more hereafter. The goats still flourish also, as visitors to Killarney can testify; though they will probably soon be relics of the past, as the goatherds are emigrating to more prosperous regions at a rapid rate.

hear some objections to "Irish pedigrees," and listen to a new "Irish question."

Pre-Christian Irish chronology has been arranged, like most ancient national chronologies, on the basis of the length of reign of certain kings. As we do not trace our descent from the "sun and moon," we are not necessitated to give our kings "a gross of centuries apiece," or to divide the assumed period of a reign between half-a-dozen monarchs;[4] and the difficulties are merely such as might be expected before chronology had become a science. The Four Masters have adopted the chronology of the Septuagint; but O'Flaherty took the system of Scaliger, and thus reduced the dates by many hundred years. The objection of hostile critics has been to the history rather than to the chronology of the history; but these objections are a mere *petitio principii*. They cannot understand how Ireland could have had a succession of kings and comparative civilization,—in fact, a national existence,—from 260 years before the building of Rome, when the Milesian colony arrived, according to the author of the *Ogygia*, at least a thousand years before the arrival of Cæsar in Britain, and his discovery that its inhabitants were half-naked savages. The real question is not what Cæsar said of the Britons, nor whether they had an ancient history before their subjugation by the victorious cohorts of Rome; but whether the annals which contained the pre-Christian history of Ireland may be accepted as, in the main, authentic.

We have already given some account of the principal works from which our annals may be compiled. Before we proceed to that portion of our history the authenticity of which cannot be questioned, it may, perhaps, be useful to give an idea of the authorities for the minor details of social life, the individual incidents of a nation's being, which, in fact, make up the harmonious whole. We shall find a remarkable coincidence between the materials for early Roman history, and those for the early history of that portion of the Celtic race which colonized Ireland.

We have no trace of any historical account of Roman history by a contemporary writer, native or foreign, before the war with Pyrrhus; yet we have a history of Rome for more than four hundred years previous offered to us by classical writers,[5] as a

---

[4] *Monarchs.*—See Bunsen's *Egypt, passim.*

[5] *Writers.*—The first ten books of Livy are extant, and bring Roman history to the consulship of Julius Maximus Gurges and Junius Brutus Scœne, in

trustworthy narrative of events. From whence did they derive their reliable information ? Unquestionably from works such as the *Origines* of Cato the Censor, and other writers, which were then extant, but which have since perished. And these writers, whence did they obtain their historical narratives ? If we may credit the theory of Niebuhr,[6] they were transmitted simply by bardic legends, composed in verse. Even Sir G. C. Lewis admits that " commemorative festivals and other periodical observances, may, in certain cases, have served to perpetuate a true tradition of some national event."[7] And how much more surely would the memory of such events be perpetuated by a people, to whom they had brought important political revolutions, who are eminently tenacious of their traditions, and who have preserved the memory of them intact for centuries in local names and monumental sites ! The sources from whence the first annalists, or writers of Irish history, may have compiled their narratives, would, therefore, be—1. The Books of Genealogies and Pedigrees. 2. The Historic Tales. 3. The Books of Laws. 4. The Imaginative Tales and Poems. 5. National Monuments, such as cromlechs and pillar stones, &c., which supplied the place of the brazen tablets of Roman history, the *libri lintei*,[8] or the chronological nail.[9]

The Books of Genealogies and Pedigrees form a most important element in Irish pagan history. For social and political reasons, the Irish Celt preserved his genealogical tree with scrupulous precision. The rights of property and the governing power were transmitted with patriarchal exactitude on strict claims of primogeniture, which claims could only be refused under certain conditions defined by law. Thus, pedigrees and genealogies

292 B.C. Dionysius published his history seven years before Christ. Five of Plutarch's Lives fall within the period before the war with Pyrrhus. There are many sources besides those of the works of historians from which general information is obtained.

[6] *Niebuhr.*—"Genuine or oral tradition has kept the story of Tarpeia for *five-and-twenty hundred years* in the mouths of the common people, who for many centuries have been total strangers to the names of Clœlia and Cornelia."—*Hist.* vol. i. p. 230.

[7] *Event.*—*Credibility of Early Roman History*, vol. i. p. 101.

[8] *Libri lintei.*—Registers written on linen, mentioned by Livy, under the year 444 B.C.

[9] *Nail.*—Livy quotes Cincius for the fact that a series of nails were extant in the temple of Hostia, at Volsinii, as a register of successive years. Quite as primitive an arrangement as the North American *quipus.*

became a family necessity; but since private claims might be doubted, and the question of authenticity involved such important results, a responsible public officer was appointed to keep the records, by which all claims were decided. Each king had his own recorder, who was obliged to keep a true account of his pedigree, and also of the pedigrees of the provincial kings and of their principal chieftains. The provincial kings had also their recorders (Ollamhs or Seanchaidhé[1]); and in obedience to an ancient law, established long before the introduction of Christianity, all the provincial records, as well as those of the various chieftains, were required to be furnished every third year to the convocation at Tara, where they were compared and corrected.

The compilers of these genealogies were persons who had been educated as Ollamhs—none others were admissible; and their "diplomas" were obtained after a collegiate course, which might well deter many a modern aspirant to professorial chairs. The education of the Ollamh lasted for twelve years; and in the course of these twelve years of "hard work," as the early books say, certain regular courses were completed, each of which gave the student an additional degree, with corresponding title, rank, and privileges.[2]

"In the Book of *Lecain* (fol. 168) there is an ancient tract, describing the laws upon this subject, and referring, with quotations, to the body of the *Brethibh Nimhedh*, or 'Brehon Laws.' According to this authority, the perfect Poet or *Ollamh* should know and practise the *Teinim Laegha*, the *Imas Forosnadh*, and the *Dichedal do chennaibh*. The first appears to have been a peculiar druidical verse, or incantation, believed to confer upon the druid or poet the power of understanding everything that it was proper for him to say or speak. The second is explained or translated, 'the illumination of much knowledge, as from the teacher to the pupil,' that is, that he should be able to explain and teach the four divisions of poetry or philosophy, 'and each division of them,' continues the authority quoted, 'is the chief teaching of three years of hard

---

[1] *Seanchaidhé* (pronounced "shanachy").—It means, in this case, strictly a historian; but the ancient historian was also a bard or poet.

[2] *Privileges.*—We can scarcely help requesting the special attention of the reader to these well-authenticated facts. A nation which had so high an appreciation of its annals, must have been many degrees removed from barbarism for centuries.

work.' The third qualification, or *Dichedal*, is explained, 'that he begins at once the head of his poem,' in short, to improvise extempore in correct verse. 'To the *Ollamh*,' says the ancient authority quoted in this passage in the Book of *Lecain*, 'belong synchronisms, together with the *laegha laidhibh*, or illuminating poems [incantations], and to him belong the pedigrees and etymologies of names, that is, he has the pedigrees of the men of Erinn with certainty, and the branching off of their various relationships.' Lastly, 'here are the four divisions of the knowledge of poetry (or philosophy),' says the tract I have referred to; 'genealogies, synchronisms, and the reciting of (historic) tales form the first division; knowledge of the seven kinds of verse, and how to measure them by letters and syllables, form another of them; judgment of the seven kinds of poetry, another of them; lastly, *Dichedal* [or improvisation], that is, to contemplate and recite the verses without ever thinking of them before.'"[3]

The pedigrees were collected and written into a single book, called the *Cin* or Book of Drom Snechta, by the son of Duach Galach, King of Connacht, an Ollamh in history and genealogies, &c., shortly before[4] the arrival of St. Patrick in Ireland, which happened about A.D. 432. It is obvious, therefore, that these genealogies must have existed for centuries prior to this period. Even if they were then committed to writing for the first time, they could have been handed down for many centuries orally by the Ollamhs; for no amount of literary effort could be supposed too great for a class of men so exclusively and laboriously devoted to learning.

As the Milesians were the last of the ancient colonists, and had subdued the races previously existing in Ireland, only their genealogies, with a few exceptions, have been preserved. The genealogical tree begins, therefore, with the brothers Eber and Eremon, the two surviving leaders of the expedition, whose ancestors are traced back to Magog, the son of Japhet. The great southern chieftains, such as the MacCarthys and O'Briens, claim descent from Eber; the northern families of O'Connor, O'Donnell, and O'Neill, claim Eremon as their head. There are also other families

[3] *Before.*—O'Curry, p. 240.
[4] *Before.*—This, of course, opens up the question as to whether the Irish Celts had a written literature before the arrival of St. Patrick. The subject will be fully entertained later on.

claiming descent from Emer, the son of Ir, brother to Eber and Eremon; as also from their cousin Lugaidh, the son of Ith. From these four sources the principal Celtic families of Ireland have sprung; and though they do not quite trace up the line to

"The grand old gardener and his wife,"

they have a pedigree which cannot be gainsaid, and which might be claimed with pride by many a monarch. MacFirbis' Book of Genealogies,[5] compiled in the year 1650, from lost records, is the most perfect work of this kind extant. But there are tracts in the Book of Leinster (compiled A.D. 1130), and in the Book of Ballymote (compiled A.D. 1391), which are of the highest authority. O'Curry is of opinion, that those in the Book of Leinster were copied from the Saltair of Cashel and other contemporaneous works.

The historical use of these genealogies is very great, not only because they give an authentic pedigree and approximate data for chronological calculation, but from the immense amount of correlative information which they contain. Every free-born man of the tribe was entitled by *blood*, should it come to his turn, to succeed to the chieftaincy: hence the exactitude with which each pedigree was kept; hence their importance in the estimation of each individual; hence the incidental matter they contain, by the mention of such historical events[6] as may have acted on different tribes and families, by which they lost their inheritance or independence, and consequently their claim, however remote, to the chieftaincy.

The ancient history of a people should always be studied with

[5] *Genealogies.*—There is a "distinction and a difference" between a genealogy and a pedigree. A genealogy embraces the descent of a family, and its relation to all the other families that descended from the same remote parent stock, and took a distinct tribe-name, as the Dalcassians. A pedigree traces up the line of descent to the individual from whom the name was derived.

[6] *Events.*—Arnold mentions "the *family traditions* and funeral orations out of which the oldest annalists [of Roman history] compiled their narratives."—vol. i. p. 371. Sir G. C. Lewis, however, thinks that the composition of national annals would precede the composition of any private history; but he adds that he judges from the "example of modern times." With all respect to such an authority, it seems rather an unphilosophical conclusion. Family pedigrees would depend on family pride, in which the Romans were by no means deficient; and on political considerations, which were all-important to the Irish Celt.

care and candour by those who, as a matter of interest or duty, wish to understand their social state, and the government best suited to that state. Many of the poorest families in Ireland are descendants of its ancient chiefs. The old habit—the habit which deepened and intensified itself during centuries—cannot be eradicated, though it may be ridiculed, and the peasant will still boast of his " blood :" it is all that he has left to him of the proud inheritance of his ancestors.

The second source of historical information may be found in the HISTORIC TALES. The reciting of historic tales was one of the principal duties of the Ollamh, and he was bound to preserve the truth of history " pure and unbroken to succeeding generations."

" According to several of the most ancient authorities, the *Ollamh*, or perfect Doctor, was bound to have (for recital at the public feasts and assemblies) at least Seven Fifties of these Historic narratives; and there appear to have been various degrees in the ranks of the poets, as they progressed in education towards the final degree, each of which was bound to be supplied with at least a certain number. Thus the *Anroth*, next in rank to an *Ollamh*, should have half the number of an *Ollamh ;* the *Cli*, one-third the number, according to some authorities, and eighty according to others ; and so on down to the *Fochlog*, who should have thirty ; and the *Driseg* (the lowest of all), who should have twenty of these tales."[7]

The Ollamhs, like the druids or learned men of other nations, were in the habit of teaching the facts of history to their pupils in verse,[8] probably that they might be more easily remembered.

---

[7] *Tales.*—O'Curry, p. 241.

[8] *Verse.*—See Niebuhr, *Hist.* vol. i. pp. 254-261. Arnold has adopted his theory, and Macaulay *has acted on it.* But the Roman poems were merely recited at public entertainments, and were by no means a national arrangement for the preservation of history, such as existed anciently in Ireland. These verses were sung by boys *more patrum* (Od. iv. 15), for the entertainment of guests. Ennius, who composed his *Annales* in hexameter verse, introducing, for the first time, the Greek metre into Roman literature, mentions the verses which the *Fauns*, or religious poets, used to chant. Scaliger thinks that the *Fauns* were a class of men who exercised in Latium, at a very remote period, the same functions as the Magians in Persia and *the Bards in Gaul.* Niebuhr supposes that the entire history of the Roman kings was formed from poems into a prose narrative.

A few of these tales have been published lately, such as the Battle of *Magh Rath*, the Battle of *Muighé Leana*, and the *Tochmarc Moméra*. Besides the tales of Battles (Catha), there are the tales of Longasa, or Voyages; the tales of Tóghla, or Destructions; of Slaughters, of Sieges, of Tragedies, of Voyages, and, not least memorable, of the Tána, or Cattle Spoils, and the Tochmarca, or Courtships. It should be remembered that numbers of these tales are in existence, offering historical materials of the highest value. The Books of Laws demand a special and more detailed notice, as well as the Historical Monuments. With a brief mention of the Imaginative Tales and Poems, we must conclude this portion of our subject.

Ancient writings, even of pure fiction, must always form an important historical element to the nation by which they have been produced. Unless they are founded on fact, so far as customs, localities, and mode of life are concerned, they would possess no interest; and their principal object is to interest. Without some degree of poetic improbabilities as to events, they could scarcely amuse; and their object is also to amuse. Hence, the element of truth is easily separated from the element of fiction, and each is available in its measure for historic research. The most ancient of this class of writings are the Fenian Poems and Tales, ascribed to Finn Mac Cumhaill, to his sons, Oisín and Fergus Finnbheoill (the Eloquent), and to his kinsman, Caeilité. There are also many tales and poems of more recent date. Mr. O'Curry estimates, that if all MSS. known to be in existence, and composed before the year 1000, were published, they would form at least 8,000 printed pages of the same size as O'Donovan's Annals of the Four Masters.

FROM SCULPTURES AT DEVENISH.

ROUND TOWER OF DYSART, NEAR CROOM, LIMERICK.

CHAPTER VI.

Tighearnmas—His Death—Introduces Colours as a Distinction of Rank—Silver
Shields and Chariots first used—Reign of Ugainé Môr—The Treachery of
Cobhthach—Romantic Tales—Queen Mab—Dispute which led to the
celebrated Cattle Spoil—The Story of the Táin bó Chuailgné—The
Romans feared to invade Ireland—Tacitus—Revolt of the Attacotti—
Reign of Tuathal—Origin of the Boromean Tribute.

[B.C. 1700.]

OUR annals afford but brief details from the time of
Eremon to that of *Ugainé Môr.* One hundred and
eighteen sovereigns are enumerated from the Milesian conquest of Ireland (according to the Four
Masters, B.C. 1700) to the time of St. Patrick,
A.D. 432. The principal events recorded are international deeds of arms, the clearing of woods, the
enactment of laws, and the erection of palaces.

Tighearnmas, one of these monarchs, is said to
have introduced the worship of idols into Ireland.
From this it would appear, that the more refined
Magian, or Sun-worship, had prevailed previously.
He died, with " three-fourths" of the men of Ireland about him, on the night of Samhain,[9] while
worshipping the idol called Crom Cruach, at

---

[9] *Samhain.*—Now All Hallows Eve. The peasantry still use the pagan
name. It is a compound word, signifying " summer" and " end."

Magh Slacht, in Breifné.[1] Tighearnmas reigned seventy-five years.
He is said to have been the first who attempted the smelting of
gold in Ireland; and the use of different colours,[2] as an indication
of rank, is also attributed to him.

Silver shields were now made (B.C. 1383) at Airget-Ros, by
Enna Airgtheach, and four-horse chariots were first used in the
time of Roitheachtaigh, who was killed by lightning near the
Giant's Causeway. Ollamh Fodhla (the wise or learned man)
distinguished himself still more by instituting triennial assemblies
at Tara. Even should the date given by the Four Masters (1317
B.C.) be called in question, there is no doubt of the fact, which
must have occurred some centuries before the Christian era; and
this would appear to be the earliest instance of a national convocation or parliament in any country. Ollamh Fodhla also appointed chieftains over every cantred or hundred, he constructed a
rath at Tara, and died there in the fortieth year of his reign.

At the reign of Cimbaoth (B.C. 716) we come to that period
which Tighernach considers the commencement of indisputably
authentic history. It is strange that he should have selected a
provincial chief, and a period in no way remarkable except for
the building of the palace of Emania.[3] But the student of Irish
pre-Christian annals may be content to commence with solid
foundation as early as seven centuries before Christ. The era was
an important one in universal history. The Greeks had then
counted sixteen Olympiads, and crowned Pythagoras the victor.
Hippomenes was archon at Athens. Romulus had been succeeded
by Numa Pompilius, and the foundations of imperial Rome were
laid in blood by barbarian hordes. The Chaldeans had just
taken the palm in astronomical observations, and recorded for the
first time a lunar eclipse; while the baffled Assyrian hosts relin-

[1] *Breifné.*—In the present county Cavan. We shall refer again to this
subject, when mentioning St. Patrick's destruction of the idols.

[2] *Colours.*—Keating says that a slave was permitted only one colour, a
peasant two, a soldier three, a public victualler five. The Ollamh ranked
with royalty, and was permitted six—another of the many proofs of extraordinary veneration for learning in pre-Christian Erinn. The Four Masters,
however, ascribe the origin of this distinction to Eochaidh Eadghadhach. It
is supposed that this is the origin of the Scotch plaid. The ancient Britons
dyed their *bodies* blue. The Cymric Celts were famous for their colours.

[3] *Emania.*—The legend of the building of this palace will be given in a
future chapter.

quished the siege of Tyre, unhappily reserved for the cruel destruction accomplished by Alexander, a few centuries later. The prophecies of Isaiah were still resounding in the ears of an ungrateful people. He had spoken of the coming Christ and His all-peaceful mission in mystic imagery, and had given miraculous evidences of his predictions. But suffering should be the precursor of that marvellous advent. The Assyrian dashed in resistless torrent upon the fold. Israel was led captive. Hosea was in chains. Samaria and the kingdom of Israel were added to the conquests of Sennacherib; and the kingdom of Judah, harassed but not destroyed, waited the accomplishment of prophecy, and the measure of her crimes, ere the most ancient of peoples should for ever cease to be a nation.

Ugainé Môr is the next monarch who demands notice. His obituary record is thus given by the Four Masters :—" At the end of this year, A.M. 4606, Ugainé Môr, after he had been full forty years King of Ireland, and of the whole of the west of Europe, as far as Muir-Toirrian, was slain by Badhbhchad at Tealach-an-Choisgair, in Bregia. This Ugainé was he who exacted oaths by all the elements, visible and invisible, from the men of Ireland in general, that they would never contend for the sovereignty of Ireland with his children or his race."

Ugainé was succeeded by his son, Laeghairé Lorc, who was cruelly and treacherously killed by his brother, Cobhthach Cael. Indeed, few monarchs lived out their time in peace during this and the succeeding centuries. The day is darkest before the dawn, in the social and political as well as in the physical world. The Eternal Light was already at hand ; the powers of darkness were aroused for the coming conflict; and deeds of evil were being accomplished, which make men shudder as they read. The assassination of Laeghairé was another manifestation of the old-world story of envy. The treacherous Cobhthach feigned sickness, which he knew would obtain a visit from his brother. When the monarch stooped to embrace him, he plunged a dagger into his heart. His next act was to kill his nephew, Ailill Ainé ; and his ill-treatment of Ainé's son, Maen, was the consummation of his cruelty. The fratricide was at last slain by this very youth, who had now obtained the appellation of Labhraidh-Loingseach, or Lowry of the Ships. We have special evidence here of the importance of our Historic Tales, and also that the blending of fiction and fact by no means deteriorates from their value.

Love affairs form a staple ground for fiction, with a very substantial under-strata of facts, even in the nineteenth century; and the annals of pre-Christian Erinn are by no means deficient in the same fertile source of human interest. The History of the Exile is still preserved in the Leabhar Buidhé Lecain, now in the Library of Trinity College, Dublin. It is a highly romantic story, but evidently founded on fact, and full of interest as descriptive of public and private life in the fifth century before Christ. It tells how Maen, though supposed to be deaf and dumb, was, nevertheless, given in charge of two officers of the court to be educated; that he recovered or rather obtained speech suddenly, in a quarrel with another youth; and that he was as symmetrical of form and noble of bearing as all heroes of romance are bound to be. His uncle expelled him from the kingdom, and he took refuge at the court of King Scoriath. King Scoriath had a daughter, who was beautiful; and Maen, of course, acted as a knight was bound to do under such circumstances, and fell desperately in love with the princess. The Lady Moriath's beauty had bewildered more heads than that of the knight-errant; but the Lady Moriath's father and mother were determined their daughter should not marry.

The harper Craftiné came to the rescue, and at last, by his all-entrancing skill, so ravished the whole party of knights and nobles, that the lovers were able to enjoy a tête-a-tête, and pledged mutual vows. As usual, the parents yielded when they found it was useless to resist; and, no doubt, the poet Craftiné, who, poet and all as he was, nearly lost his head in the adventure, was the most welcome of all welcome guests at the nuptial feast. Indeed, he appears to have been retained as comptroller of the house and confidential adviser long after; for when Labhraidh Maen was obliged to fly the country, he confided his wife to the care of Craftiné. On his return from France,[4] he obtained possession of the kingdom, to which he was the rightful heir, and reigned over the men of Erinn for eighteen years.

Another Historic Tale gives an account of the destruction of the court of Dá Derga, but we have not space for details. The Four Masters merely relate the fact in the following entry :—

[4] *France.*—It is said that foreigners who came with him from Gaul were armed with broad-headed lances (called in Irish *laighne*), whence the province of Leinster has derived its name. Another derivation of the name, from *coige*, a fifth part, is attributed to the Firbolgs.

"Conairé, the son of Ederscél, after having been seventy years in the sovereignty of Erinn, was slain at Bruighean Dá Dhearga by insurgents." Another prince, Eochaidh Feidhlech, was famous for sighing. He rescinded the division of Ireland into twenty-five parts, which had been made by Ugainé Môr, and divided the island into five provinces, over each of which he appointed a provincial king, under his obedience. The famous Meadhbh, or Mab, was his daughter; and though unquestionably a lady of rather strong physical and mental capabilities, the lapse of ages has thrown an obscuring halo of romance round her belligerent qualifications, and metamorphosed her into the gentle "Faery Queen" of the poet Spenser. One of Méav's exploits is recorded in the famous Táin bó Chuailgné, which is to Celtic history what the Argonautic Expedition, or the Seven against Thebes, is to Grecian. Méav was married first to Conor, the celebrated provincial king of Ulster; but the marriage was not a happy one, and was dissolved, in modern parlance, on the ground of incompatibility. In the meanwhile, Méav's three brothers had rebelled against their father; and though his arms were victorious, the victory did not secure peace. The men of Connacht revolted against him, and to retain their allegiance he made his daughter Queen of Connacht, and gave her in marriage to Ailill, a powerful chief of that province. This prince, however, died soon after; and Méav, determined for once, at least, to choose a husband for herself, made a royal progress to Leinster, where Ross Ruadh held his court at Naas. She selected the younger son of this monarch, who bore the same name as her former husband, and they lived together happily as queen and king consort for many years. On one occasion, however, a dispute arose about their respective treasures, and this dispute led to a comparison of their property. The account of this, and the subsequent comparison, is given at length in the *Táin*, and is a valuable repertory of archæological information. They counted their vessels, metal and wooden; they counted their finger rings, their clasps, their thumb rings, their diadems, and their gorgets of gold. They examined their many-coloured garments of crimson and blue, of black and green, yellow and mottled, white and streaked. All were equal. They then inspected their flocks and herds, swine from the forests, sheep from the pasture lands, and cows—here the first difference arose. It was one to excite Méav's haughty temper. There

was a young bull found among Ailill's bovine wealth : it had been
calved by one of Méav's cows; but "not deeming it honorable to be
under a woman's control," it had attached itself to Ailill's herds.
Méav was not a lady who could remain quiet under such provocation. She summoned her chief courier, and asked him could he
find a match for Finnbheannach
(the white-horned). The courier
declared that he could find even a
superior animal; and at once set
forth on his mission, suitably attended. Méav had offered the
most liberal rewards for the prize
she so much coveted ; and the
courier soon arranged with Daré,
a noble of large estates, who
possessed one of the valuable
breed. A drunken quarrel, however, disarranged his plans. One
of the men boasted that if Daré
had not given the bull for payment,
he should have been compelled to
give it by force. Daré's steward
heard the ill-timed and uncour-
teous boast. He flung down the
meat and drink which he had
brought for their entertainment,
and went to tell his master the
contemptuous speech. The result
may be anticipated. Daré refused the much-coveted animal,
and Méav proceeded to make

FLINT SPEAR-HEAD, FROM THE
COLLECTION OF THE R.I.A.

good her claim by force of arms. But this is only the prologue of
the drama ;. the details would fill a volume. It must suffice to
say, that the bulls had a battle of their own. Finnbheannach and
Donn Chuailgné (the Leinster bull) engaged in deadly combat,
which is described with the wildest flights of poetic diction.[5] The

[5] *Diction.*—This tract contains a description of arms and ornaments which
might well pass for a poetic flight of fancy, had we not articles of such exquisite workmanship in the Royal Irish Academy, which prove incontrovertibly
the skill of the ancient artists of Erinn. This is the description of a cham-

poor "white horn" was killed, and Donn Chuailgné, who had lashed himself to madness, dashed out his brains.[6]

Méav lived to the venerable age of a hundred. According to Tighernach, she died A.D. 70, but the chronology of the Four Masters places her demise a hundred years earlier. This difference of calculation also makes it questionable what monarch reigned in Ireland at the birth of Christ. The following passage is from the Book of Ballymote, and is supposed to be taken from the synchronisms of Flann of Monasterboice : " In the fourteenth year of the reign of Conairé and of Conchobar, Mary was born; and in the fourth year after the birth of Mary, the expedition of the Táin bó Chuailgné took place. Eight years after the expedition of the Táin, Christ was born."

The Four Masters have the following entry after the age of the world 5194 :—

THE AGE OF CHRIST.

" The first year of the age of Christ, and the eighth year of the reign of Crimhthann Niadhnair." Under the heading of the age

pion's attire :—" A red and white cloak flutters about him ; a golden brooch in that cloak, at his breast ; a shirt of white, kingly linen, with gold embroidery at his skin ; a white shield, with gold fastenings at his shoulder ; a gold-hilted long sword at his left side ; a long, sharp, dark green spear, together with a short, sharp spear, with a rich band and carved silver rivets in his hand."—O'Curry, p. 38. We give an illustration on previous page of a flint weapon of a ruder kind.

[6] *Brains.*—My friend, Denis Florence MacCarthy, Esq., M.R.I.A., our poet *par excellence*, is occupied at this moment in versifying some portions of this romantic story. I believe he has some intention of publishing the work in America, as American publishers are urgent in their applications to him for a complete and uniform edition of his poems, including his exquisite translations from the dramatic and ballad literature of Spain. We hope Irish publishers and the Irish people will not disgrace their country by allowing such a work to be published abroad. We are too often and too justly accused of deficiency in cultivated taste, which unfortunately makes trashy poems, and verbose and weakly-written prose, more acceptable to the majority than works produced by highly-educated minds. Irishmen are by no means inferior to Englishmen in natural gifts, yet, in many instances, unquestionably they have not or do not cultivate the same taste for reading, and have not the same appreciation of works of a higher class than the lightest literature. Much of the fault, no doubt, lies in the present system of education : however, as some of the professors in our schools and colleges appear to be aware of the deficiency, we may hope for better things.

of Christ 9, there is an account of a wonderful expedition of this monarch, and of all the treasures he acquired thereby. His "adventures" is among the list of Historic Tales in the Book or Leinster, but unfortunately there is no copy of this tract in existence. It was probably about this time that a recreant Irish chieftain tried to induce Agricola to invade Ireland. But the Irish Celts had extended the fame of their military prowess even to distant lands,[7] and the Roman general thought it better policy to keep what he had than to risk its loss, and, perhaps, obtain no compensation. Previous to Cæsar's conquest of Britain, the Irish had fitted out several expeditions for the plunder of that country, and they do not appear to have suffered from retaliation until the reign of Egbert. It is evident, however, that the Britons did not consider them their worst enemies, for we find mention of several colonies flying to the Irish shores to escape Roman tyranny, and these colonies were hospitably received.[8] The passage in Tacitus which refers to the proposed invasion of Ireland by the Roman forces, is too full of interest to be omitted :—" In the fifth year of these expeditions, Agricola, passing over in the first ship, subdued in frequent victories nations hitherto unknown. He stationed troops along that part of Britain which looks to Ireland, more on account of hope than fear,[9] since Ireland, from its situation between Britain and Spain, and opening to the Gallic Sea, might well connect the most powerful parts of the empire with reciprocal advantage. Its extent, compared with Britain, is narrower, but exceeds that of any islands of our sea. The genius and habits of the people, and the soil and climate, do not differ much from those of Britain. Its channels and ports are better known to commerce and to merchants.[1] Agricola gave his protection to one of its petty kings, who had been expelled by faction ; and with a show of friendship, he retained him for his own purposes. I often heard

[7] *Lands.*—Lhuid asserts that the names of the principal commanders in Gaul and Britain who opposed Cæsar, are Irish Latinized.

[8] *Received.*—" They are said to have fled into Ireland, some for the sake of ease and quietness, others to keep their eyes untainted by Roman insolence." —See Harris' Ware. The Brigantes of Waterford, Tipperary, and Kilkenny, are supposed to have been emigrants, and to have come from the colony of that name in Yorkshire.

[9] *Fear.*—" In spem magis quam ob formidinem."

[1] *Merchants.*—" Melius aditus portusque per commercia et negotiatores cognitis."

him say, that Ireland could be conquered and taken with one legion and a small reserve ; and such a measure would have its advantages even as regards Britain, if Roman power were extended on every side, and liberty taken away as it were from the view of the latter island."[2]

We request special attention to the observation, that the Irish ports were better known to commerce and merchants. Such a statement by such an authority must go far to remove any doubt as to the accounts given on this subject by our own annalists. The proper name of the recreant "regulus" has not been discovered, so that his infamy is transmitted anonymously to posterity. Sir John Davies has well observed, with regard to the boast of subduing Ireland so easily, "that if Agricola had attempted the conquest thereof with a far greater army, he would have found himself deceived in his conjecture." William of Neuburg has also remarked, that though the Romans harassed the Britons for three centuries after this event, Ireland never was invaded by them, even when they held dominion of the Orkney Islands, and that it yielded to no foreign power until the year[3] 1171. Indeed, the Scots and Picts gave their legions quite sufficient occupation defending the ramparts of Adrian and Antoninus, to deter them from attempting to obtain more, when they could so hardly hold what they already possessed.

The insurrection of the Aitheach Tuatha,[4] or Attacotti, is the next event of importance in Irish history. Their plans were deeply and wisely laid, and promised the success they obtained. It is one of the lessons of history which rulers in all ages would do well to study. There is a degree of oppression which even the most degraded will refuse to endure ; there is a time when the injured will seek revenge, even should they know that this revenge may bring on themselves yet deeper wrongs. The leaders of the revolt were surely men of some

---

[2] *Island.*— *Vita Julii Agric.* c. 24.

[3] *Year.*—*Hist. Rer. Angl.* lib. ii. c. 26.

[4] *Aitheach Tuatha.*—The word means rentpayers, or rentpaying tribes or people. It is probably used as a term of reproach, and in contradiction to the free men. It has been said that this people were the remnants of the inhabitants of Ireland before the Milesians colonized it. Mr. O'Curry denies this statement, and maintains that they were Milesians, but of the lower classes, who had been cruelly oppressed by the magnates of the land.

judgment; and both they and those who acted under them possessed the two great qualities needed for such an enterprise. They were silent, for their plans were not even suspected until they were accomplished; they were patient, for these plans were three years in preparation. During three years the helots saved their scanty earnings to prepare a sumptuous death-feast for their unsuspecting victims. This feast was held at a place since called *Magh Cru*, in Connaught. The monarch, Fiacha Finnolaidh, the provincial kings and chiefs, were all invited, and accepted the invitation. But while the enjoyment was at its height, when men had drank deeply, and were soothed by the sweet strains of the harp, the insurgents did their bloody work. Three ladies alone escaped. They fled to Britain, and there each gave birth to a son—heirs to their respective husbands who had been slain.

After the massacre, the Attacotti elected their leader, Cairbré Cinn-Cait (or the Cat-head), to the royal dignity, for they still desired to live under a " limited monarchy." But revolutions, even when successful, and we had almost said necessary, are eminently productive of evil. The social state of a people when once disorganized, does not admit of a speedy or safe return to its former condition. The mass of mankind, who think more of present evils, however trifling, than of past grievances, however oppressive, begin to connect present evils with present rule, and having lost, in some degree, the memory of their ancient wrongs, desire to recall a dynasty which, thus viewed, bears a not unfavourable comparison with their present state.[5]

Cairbré died after five years of most unprosperous royalty, and his son, the wise and prudent Morann,[6] showed his wisdom and prudence by refusing to succeed him. He advised that the rightful heirs should be recalled. His advice was accepted. Fear-

---

[5] *State.*—" Evil was the state of Ireland during his reign: fruitless the corn, for there used to be but one grain on the stalk; fruitless her rivers; milkless her cattle; plentiless her fruit, for there used to be but one acorn on the oak." —Four Masters, p. 97.

[6] *Morann.*—Morann was the inventor of the famous "collar of gold." The new monarch appointed him his chief Brehon or judge, and it is said that this collar closed round the necks of those who were guilty, but expanded to the ground when the wearer was innocent. This collar or chain is mentioned in several of the commentaries on the Brehon Laws, as one of the ordeals of the ancient Irish. The Four Masters style him "the very intelligent Morann."

adhach Finnfeachteach was invited to assume the reins of government. " Good was Ireland during this his time. The seasons were right tranquil ; the earth brought forth its fruit ; fishful its river-mouths ; milkful the kine ; heavy-headed the woods."[7]

Another revolt of the Attacotti took place in the reign of Fiacha of the White Cattle. He was killed by the provincial kings, at the slaughter of Magh Bolg.[8] Elim, one of the perpetrators of this outrage, obtained the crown, but his reign was singularly unprosperous ; and Ireland was without corn, without milk, without fruit, without fish, and without any other great advantage, since the Aitheach Tuatha had killed Fiacha Finnolaidh in the slaughter of Magh Bolg, till the time of Tuathal Teachtmar."[9]

Tuathal was the son of a former legitimate monarch, and had been invited to Ireland by a powerful party. He was perpetually at war with the Attacotti, but at last established himself firmly on the throne, by exacting an oath from the people, " by the sun, moon, and elements," that his posterity should not be deprived of the sovereignty. This oath was taken at Tara, where he had convened a general assembly, as had been customary with his predecessors at the commencement of each reign ; but it was held by him with more than usual state. His next act was to take a small portion of land from each of the four provinces, forming what is now the present county of Meath, and retaining it as the mensal portion of the Ard-Righ, or supreme monarch. On each of these portions he erected a palace for the king of every province, details of which will be given when we come to that period of our history which refers to the destruction of Tara. Tuathal had at this time two beautiful and marriageable daughters, named Fithir and Dairiné. Eochaidh Aincheann, King of Leinster, sought and obtained the hand of the younger daughter, Dairiné, and after her nuptials carried her to his palace at Naas, in Leinster. Some time after, his people pursuaded him that he had made a bad selection, and that the elder was the better of the two sisters ; upon which Eochaidh determined by

---

[7] *Woods.*—Four Masters, p. 97.

[8] *Magh Bolg.*—Now Moybolgue, a parish in the county Cavan.

[9] *Teachtmar*, *i.e.*, the legitimate, Four Masters, p. 99.—The history of the revolt of the Attacotti is contained in one of the ancient tracts called Histories. It is termed " The Origin of the Boromean Tribute." There is a copy of this most valuable work in the Book of Leinster, which, it will be remembered, was compiled in the twelfth century. The details which follow above concerning the Boromean Tribute, are taken from the same source.

stratagem to obtain the other daughter also. For this purpose he shut the young queen up in a secret apartment of his palace, and gave out a report that she was dead. He then repaired, apparently in great grief, to Tara, informed the monarch that his daughter was dead, and demanded her sister in marriage. Tuathal gave his consent, and the false king returned home with his new bride. Soon after her arrival at Naas, her sister escaped from her confinement, and suddenly and unexpectedly encountered the prince and Fithir. In a moment she divined the truth, and had the additional anguish of seeing her sister, who was struck with horror and shame, fall dead before her face. The death of the unhappy princess, and the treachery of her husband, was too much for the young queen; she returned to her solitary chamber, and in a very short time died of a broken heart.

The insult offered to his daughters, and their untimely death, roused the indignation of the pagan monarch, and was soon bitterly avenged. At the head of a powerful force, he burned and ravaged Leinster to its utmost boundary, and then compelled its humbled and terror-stricken people to bind themselves and their descendants for ever to the payment of a triennial tribute to the monarch of Erinn, which, from the great number of cows exacted by it, obtained the name of the "Boromean Tribute"—*bo* being the Gaedhilic for a cow.

The tribute is thus described in the old annals:

> " The men of Leinster were obliged to pay
> To Tuathal, and all the monarchs after him,
> Three-score hundred of the fairest cows,
> And three-score hundred ounces of pure silver,
> And three-score hundred mantles richly woven,
> And three-score hundred of the fattest hogs,
> And three-score hundred of the largest sheep,
> And three-score hundred cauldrons strong and polished."[1]

It is elsewhere described as consisting of five thousand ounces of silver, five thousand mantles, five thousand fat cows, five thousand fat hogs, five thousand wethers, and five thousand vessels of brass or bronze for the king's laving, with men and maidens for his service.

The levying of the tribute was the cause of periodical and

---

[1] *Polished.*—Keating, p. 264.

sanguinary wars, from the time of Tuathal until the reign of
Finnachta the Festive. About the year 680 it was abolished by
him, at the entreaty of St. Moling, of Tigh Moling (now St.
Mullen's, in the county Carlow). It is said by Keating, that he
a ailed himself of a pious ruse for this purpose,—asking the king
to pledge himself not to exact the tribute until after Monday, and
then, when his request was complied with, declaring that the
Monday he intended was the Monday after Doomsday. The tribute
was again revived and levied by Brian, the son of Cinneidigh, at
the beginning of the eleventh century, as a punishment on the
Leinster men for their adherence to the Danish cause. It was
from this circumstance that Brian obtained the surname of *Boroimhé*.

LOUGH HYNE.

ORATORY AT GALLARUS, CO. KERRY.

CHAPTER VII.

Tuathal—Conn " of the Hundred Battles "—The Five Great Roads of Ancient Erinn—Conn's Half—Conairé II.—The Three Cairbrés—Cormac Mac Airt —His Wise Decision—Collects Laws—His Personal Appearance—The Saltair of Tara written in Cormac's Reign—Finn Mac Cumhaill—His Courtship with the Princess Ailbhé—The Pursuit of Diarmaid and Grainné—Nial " of the Nine Hostages "—Dathi.

UATHAL reigned for thirty years, and is said to have fought no less than 133 battles with the Attacotti. He was at last slain himself by his successor, Nial, who, in his turn, was killed by Tuathal's son. Conn " of the Hundred Battles " is the next Irish monarch who claims more than a passing notice. His exploits are a famous theme with the bards, and a poem on his " Birth " forms part of the *Liber Flavus Fergusorum*, a MS. volume of the fifteenth century. His reign is also remarkable for the mention of five great roads[2] which were then discovered or completed. One of these highways, the Eiscir Riada, extended from the declivity on which Dublin Castle now stands, to the peninsula of Marey, at the head of Galway Bay.

[2] *Roads.*—Those roads were Slighe Asail, Slighe Midhluachra, Slighe Cualann, Slighe Dala, and Slighe Môr. Slighe Môr was the Eiscir Riada, and division line of Erinn into two parts, between Conn and Eóghan Môr. These five roads led to the fort of Teamair (Tara), and it is said that they were " discovered" on the birthnight of the former monarch. We shall refer to the subject again in a chapter on the civilization of the early Irish. There is no doubt of the existence of these roads, and this fact, combined with the care with which they were kept, is significant.

It divided Conn's half of Ireland from the half possessed by Eóghan Môr, with whom he lived in the usual state of internecine feud which characterized the reigns of this early period. One of the principal quarrels between these monarchs, was caused by a complaint which Eóghan made of the shipping arrangements in Dublin. Conn's half (the northern side) was preferred, and Eóghan demanded a fair division. They had to decide their claims at the battle of Magh Lena.[3] Eóghan was assisted by a Spanish chief, whose sister he had married. But the Iberian and his Celtic brother-in-law were both slain, and the mounds are still shown which cover their remains.

Conn was succeeded by Conairé II., the father of the three Cairbrés, who were progenitors of important tribes. Cairbré Musc gave his name to six districts in Munster; the territory of Corcabaiscinn, in Clare, was named after Cairbré Bascain; and the Dalriada of Antrim were descended from Cairbré Riada. He is also mentioned by Bede under the name of Reuda,[4] as the leader of the Scots who came from Hibernia to Alba. Three centuries later, a fresh colony of Dalriadans laid the foundation of the Scottish monarchy under Fergus, the son of Erc. Mac Con was the next Ard-Righ or chief monarch of Ireland. He obtained the royal power after a battle at Magh Mucruimhé, near Athenry, where Art the Melancholy, son of Con of the Hundred Battles, and the seven sons of Oilioll Oluim, were slain.

The reign of Cormac Mac Airt is unquestionably the most celebrated of all our pagan monarchs. During his early years he had been compelled to conceal himself among his mother's friends in Connaught; but the severe rule of the usurper Mac Con excited a desire for his removal, and the friends of the young prince were not slow to avail themselves of the popular feeling. He, therefore, appeared unexpectedly at Tara, and happened to arrive when the monarch was giving judgment in an important case, which is thus related: Some sheep, the property of a widow, residing at Tara, had strayed into the queen's private lawn, and eaten the grass. They were captured, and the case was brought before the king. He decided that the trespassers should be forfeited; but Cormac

---

[3] *Magh Lena.*—The present parish of Moylana, or Kilbride, Tullamore, King's county.

[4] *Reuda.*—Bede, *Eccl. Hist.* p. 7.

exclaimed that his sentence was unjust, and declared that as the sheep had only eaten the fleece of the land, they should only forfeit their own fleece. The *vox populi* applauded the decision. Mac Con started from his seat, and exclaimed : "That is the judgment of a king." At the same moment he recognized the prince, and commanded that he should be seized ; but he had already escaped. The people now recognized their rightful king, and revolted against the usurper, who was driven into Munster. Cormac assumed the reins of government at Tara, and thus entered upon his brilliant and important career, A.D. 227.

Cormac commenced his government with acts of severity, which were, perhaps, necessary to consolidate his power. This being once firmly established, he devoted himself ardently to literary pursuits, and to regulate and civilize his dominions. He collected the national laws, and formed a code which remained in force until the English invasion, and was observed for many centuries after outside the Pale. The bards dwell with manifest unction on the "fruit and fatness" of the land in his time, and describe him as the noblest and most bountiful of all princes. Indeed, we can scarcely omit their account, since it cannot be denied that it pictures the costume of royalty in Ireland at that period, however poetically the details may be given. This, then, is the bardic photograph :—

"His hair was slightly curled, and of golden colour : a scarlet shield with engraved devices, and golden hooks, and clasps of silver : a wide-folding purple cloak on him, with a gem-set gold brooch over his breast ; a gold torque around his neck ; a white-collared shirt, embroidered with gold, upon him ; a girdle with golden buckles, and studded with precious stones, around him ; two golden net-work sandals with golden buckles upon him ; two spears with golden sockets, and many red bronze rivets in his hand ; while he stood in the full glow of beauty, without defect or blemish. You would think it was a shower of pearls that were set in his mouth ; his lips were rubies ; his symmetrical body was as white as snow ; his cheek was like the mountain ash-berry ; his eyes were like the sloe ; his brows and eye-lashes were like the sheen of a blue-black lance."[5]

[5] *Lance.*—O'Curry, p. 45. This quotation is translâted by Mr. O'Curry, and is taken from the Book of Ballymote. This book, however, quotes it from the *Uachongbhail*, a much older authority.

The compilation of the Saltair of Tara, as we mentioned previously, is attributed to this monarch. Even in Christian times his praises are loudly proclaimed. The poet Maelmura, who lived in the eighth century, styles him Ceolach, or the Musical, and Kenneth O'Hartigan, who died A.D. 973, gives a glowing account of his magnificence and of his royal palace at Tara. O'Flaherty quotes a poem, which he says contains an account of three schools, instituted by Cormac at Tara; one for military discipline, one for history, and the third for jurisprudence. The Four Masters say : "It was this Cormac, son of Art, also, that collected the chronicles of Ireland to Teamhair [Tara], and ordered them to write[6] the chronicles of Ireland in one book, which was named the Saltair of Teamhair. In that book were [entered] the coeval exploits and synchronisms of the kings of Ireland with the kings and emperors of the world, and of the kings of the provinces with the monarchs of Ireland. In it was also written what the monarchs of Ireland were entitled to [receive] from the provincial kings, and the rents and dues of the provincial kings from their subjects, from the noble to the sub-altern. In it, also, were [described] the boundaries and mears of Ireland from shore to shore, from the provinces to the cantred, from the cantred to the townland, from the townland to the traighedh of land."[7] Although the Saltair of Tara has disappeared from our national records, a law tract, called the Book of Acaill, is still in existence, which is attributed to this king. It is always found annexed to a Law Treatise by Cennfaelad the Learned, who died A.D. 677. In an ancient MS. in Trinity College, Dublin (Class H. L. 15, p. 149), it is stated that it was the custom, at the inauguration

---

[6] *Write.*—Professor O'Curry well observes, that "such a man could scarcely have carried out the numerous provisions of his comprehensive enactments without some written medium. And it is no unwarrantable presumption to suppose, that, either by his own hand, or, at least, in his own time, by his command, his laws were committed to writing ; and when we possess very ancient testimony to this effect, I can see no reason for rejecting it, or for casting a doubt upon the statement."—*MS. Materials*, p: 47. Mr. Petrie writes, if possible, more strongly. He says : "It is difficult, if not impossible, to conceive how the minute and apparently accurate accounts found in the various MSS. of the names and localities of the Attacottic tribes of Ireland in the first century, could have been preserved, without coming to the conclusion that they had been preserved in writing in some work."—*Essay on Tara Hill*, p. 46. Elsewhere, however, he speaks more doubtfully.

[7] *Land.*—Four Masters, p. 117.

of Irish chiefs, to read the Instructions of the Kings (a work ascribed to Cormac) and his Laws.

There is a tradition that Cormac became a Christian before his death. In the thirty-ninth year of his reign, one of his eyes was thrust out by a spear, and he retired in consequence to one of those peaceful abodes of learning which were so carefully fostered in ancient Erinn. The high-minded nobility of this people is manifest notably in the law which required that the king should have no personal blemish; and in obedience to this law, Cormac vacated the throne. He died A.D. 266, at Cleiteach, near Stackallen Bridge, on the south bank of the Boyne. It is said that he was choked by a salmon bone, and that this happened through the contrivances of the druids, who wished to avenge themselves on him for his rejection of their superstitions.

This reign was made more remarkable by the exploits of his son-in-law, the famous Finn Mac Cumhaill (pronounced "coole"). Finn was famous both as a poet and warrior. Indeed, poetical qualifications were considered essential to obtain a place in the select militia of which he was the last commander. The courtship of the poet-warrior with the Princess Ailbhé, Cormac's daughter, is related in one of the ancient historic tales called *Tochmarca*, or Courtships. The lady is said to have been the wisest woman of her time, and the wooing is described in the form of conversations, which savour more of a trial of skill in ability and knowledge, than of the soft utterances which distinguish such narratives in modern days. It is supposed that the Fenian corps which he commanded was modelled after the fashion of the Roman legions; but its loyalty is more questionable, for it was eventually disbanded for insubordination, although the exploits of its heroes are a favourite topic with the bards. The Fenian poems, on which Macpherson founded his celebrated forgery, are ascribed to Finn's sons, Oísin and Fergus the Eloquent, and to his kinsman Caeilté, as well as to himself. Five poems only are ascribed to him, but these are found in MSS. of considerable antiquity. The poems of Oísin were selected by the Scotch writer for his grand experiment. He gave a highly poetical translation of what purported to be some ancient and genuine composition, but, unfortunately for his veracity, he could not produce the original. Some of the real compositions of the Fenian hero are, however, still extant in the Book of Leinster, as well as other valuable Fenian poems. There are also some Fenian tales in prose, of which the most remarkable is that of the Pursuit of Diarmaid and Grainné—a legend which has left its impress in every portion of the island to the present day. Finn, in his old age, asked the hand of Grainné, the daughter of Cormac Mac Airt; but the lady being young, preferred a younger lover. To effect her purpose, she drugged the guest-cup so effectually, that Finn, and all the guests invited with him, were plunged into a profound slumber after they had partaken of it. Oísin and Diarmaid alone escaped, and to them the Lady Grainné confided her grief. As true knights they were bound to rescue her from the dilemma. Oísin could scarcely dare to brave his father's vengeance, but Diarmaid at once fled with the lady. A pursuit followed, which extended all over Ireland, during which the young couple always escaped. So deeply is the tradition engraven in the popular mind, that the cromlechs are still called the "Beds of Diarmaid and Grainné," and shown as the resting-places of the fugitive lovers.

There are many other tales of a purely imaginative character, which, for interest, might well rival the world-famous Arabian Nights' Entertainments; and, for importance of details, illustrative of manners, customs, dress, weapons, and localities, are, perhaps, unequalled.

Nial of the Nine Hostages and Dathi are the last pagan monarchs who demand special notice. In the year 322, Fiacha Sraibhtine was slain by the three Collas,[8] and a few short-lived monarchs succeeded. In 378, Crimhthann was poisoned by his sister, who hoped that her eldest son, Brian, might obtain the royal power. Her attempt failed, although she sacrificed herself for its accomplishment, by taking the poisoned cup to remove her brother's suspicions; and Nial of the Nine Hostages, the son of her husband by a former wife, succeeded to the coveted dignity. This monarch distinguished himself by predatory warfare against Albion and Gaul. The "groans"[9] of the Britons testify to his success in that quarter, which eventually obliged them to become an Anglo-Saxon nation; and the Latin poet, Claudian, gives evidence that troops were sent by Stilicho, the general of Theodosius the Great, to repel his suc-

---

[8] *Collas.*—They were sons of Eochaidh Domlen, who made themselves famous by their warlike exploits, and infamous by their destruction of the palace of Emania.

[9] *Groans.*—Bede, *Eccl. Hist.* c. 12.

cessful forays. His successor, Dathi, was killed by lightning at the foot of the Alps, and the possibility of this occurrence is also strangely verified from extrinsic sources.[1]

[1] *Sources.*—The Abbé M'Geoghegan says that there is a very ancient registry in the archives of the house of Sales, which mentions that the King of Ireland remained some time in the Castle of Sales. See his *History*, p. 94.

GAP OF DUNLOE, KILLARNEY.

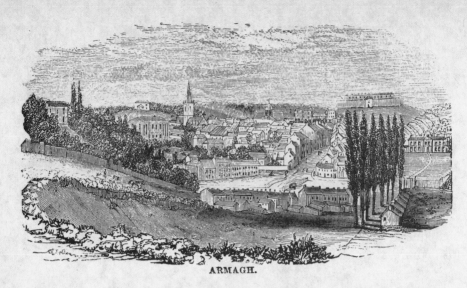

ARMAGH.

CHAPTER VIII.

St. Patrick—How Ireland was first Christianized—Pagan Rome used providentially to promote the Faith—The Mission of St. Palladius—Innocent I. claims authority to found Churches and condemn Heresy—Disputes concerning St. Patrick's Birthplace—Ireland receives the Faith generously—Victoricus—St. Patrick's Vision—His Roman Mission clearly proved—Subterfuges of those who deny it—Ancient Lives of the Saint—St. Patrick's Canons—His Devotion and Submission to the Holy See.

[A.D. 378—432.]

IT has been conjectured that the great Apostle of Ireland, St. Patrick, was carried captive to the land of his adoption, in one of the plundering expeditions of the monarch Nial—an eminent instance of the overruling power of Providence, and of the mighty effects produced by causes the most insignificant and unconscious. As we are not writing an ecclesiastical history of Ireland, and as we have a work of that nature in contemplation, we shall only make brief mention of the events connected with the life and mission of the saint at present; but the Christianizing of any country must always form an important epoch, politically and socially, and, as such, demands the careful consideration of the historian. How and when the seed of faith was sown in ancient Erinn before the time of the great Apostle, cannot now be ascertained. We know the silent rapidity with which that faith spread, from its first promulgation by the shores of the Galilean lake, until it became the recognized religion of earth's mightiest empire. We know, also, that, by a noticeable providence, Rome was chosen from the beginning as the source from whence the light should emanate. We know how pagan Rome, which had. subdued and crushed material empires, and scattered nations and national customs as chaff before the wind, failed utterly to subdue or crush this religion, though promulgated by the feeblest of its plebeians. We know how the material prosperity of that mighty people was overruled for the furtherance of eternal designs ; and as the invincible legions continually added to the geographical extent of the empire, they also added to the number of those to whom the gospel of peace should be proclaimed.

The first Christian mission to Ireland, for which we have definite and reliable data, was that of St. Palladius. St. Prosper, who held a high position in the Roman Church, published a chronicle in the year 433, in which we find the following register : "Palladius was consecrated by Pope Celestine, and sent as the first Bishop to the Irish believing in Christ."[2] This mission was unsuccessful. Palladius was repulsed by the inhabitants of Wicklow,[3] where he landed. He then sailed northward, and was at last driven by stress of weather towards the Orkneys, finding harbour, eventually, on the shores of Kincardineshire. Several ancient tracts give the details of his mission, its failure, and his subsequent career. The first of those authorities is the Life of St. Patrick in the Book of Armagh ; and in this it is stated that he died in the "land of the Britons." The second Life of St. Patrick, in Colgan's collection, has changed Britons into "Picts." In the "Annotations of Tierchan," also preserved in the Book of Armagh,[4] it is said that Palladius was also called Patricius,[5] and that he suffered martyrdom among the Scots, "as ancient saints relate."

---

[2] *Christ.*—"Ad Scotos in Christum credentes ordinatur a papa Cælestino Palladius et primus episcopus mittitur."—*Vet. Lat. Scrip. Chron. Roncallius*, Padua, 1787.

[3] *Wicklow.*—Probably on the spot where the town of Wicklow now stands. It was then called the region of Hy-Garchon. It is also designated *Fortreatha Laighen* by the Scholiast on Fiacc's Hymn. The district, probably, received this name from the family of *Eoichaidh Finn Fothart*, a brother of Conn of the Hundred Battles.

[4] *Armagh.*—Fol. 16, a.a.

[5] *Patricius.*—This name was but an indication of rank. In the later years of

Prosper also informs us, that Palladius was a deacon[6] of the Roman Church, and that he received a commission from the Holy See to send Germanus, Bishop of Auxerre, to root out heresy,[7] and convert the Britons to the Catholic faith. Thus we find the Church, even in the earliest ages, occupied in her twofold mission, of converting the heathen, and preserving the faithful from error. St. Innocent I., writing to Decentius, in the year 402, refers thus to this important fact: "Is it not known to all that the things which have been delivered to the Roman Church by Peter, the Prince of the Apostles, and preserved ever since, should be observed by all; and that nothing is to be introduced devoid of authority, or borrowed elsewhere? Especially, as it is manifest that no one has founded churches for all Italy, the Gauls, Spain, Africa, and the interjacent islands, except such as were appointed priests by the venerable Peter and his successors."

Palladius was accompanied by four companions: Sylvester and Solinus, who remained after him in Ireland; and Augustinus and Benedictus, who followed him[8] to Britain, but returned to their own country after his death. The *Vita Secunda* mentions that he brought relics of the blessed Peter and Paul, and other saints, to Ireland, as well as copies of the Old and New Testament, all of which were given to him by Pope Celestine.

The birthplace of the great Apostle of Ireland has long been, and still continues, a subject of controversy. St. Fiacc states that he was born at Nemthur,[9] and the Scholiast on St. Fiacc's Hymn identifies this with Alcuith, now Dumbarton, on the Firth of Clyde. The most reliable authority unquestionably is St. Patrick's own statements, in his *Confessio*. He there says (1) that his father had a farm or villa at Bonavem Taberniæ, from whence he was taken

the Roman Empire, Gibbon says, "the meanest subjects of the Roman Empire [5th century] assumed the illustrious name of Patricius."—*Decline and Fall*, vol. viii. p. 300. Hence the confusion that arose amongst Celtic hagiographers, and the interchanging of the acts of several saints who bore the same name.

6 *Deacon.*—This was an important office in the early Roman Church.

7 *Heresy.*—The Pelagian.

8 *Followed him.*—The Four Masters imply, however, that they remained in Ireland. They also name the three wooden churches which he erected. Cels-fine, which has not been identified; Teach-na-Romhan, House of the Romans, probably Tigroni; and Domhnach-Arta, probably the present Dunard.—*Annals*, p. 129.

9 *Nemthur.*—The *n* is merely a prefix; it should read Em-tur.

captive. It does not follow necessarily from this, that St. Patrick was born there; but it would appear probable that this was a paternal estate. (2) The saint speaks of Britanniæ as his country. The difficulty lies in the identification of these places. In the *Vita Secunda*, Nemthur and Campus Taberniæ are identified. Probus writes, that he had ascertained as a matter of certainty, that the *Vicus Bannave Taburniæ regionis* was situated in Neustria. The Life supposed to be by St. Eleran, states that the parents of the saint were of Strats-Cludi (Strath-Clyde), but that he was born in Nemthur—" Quod oppidum in Campo Taburniæ est ;" thus indicating an early belief that France was the land of his nativity. St. Patrick's mention of Britanniæ, however, appears to be conclusive. There was a tribe called Brittani in northern France, mentioned by Pliny, and the Welsh Triads distinctly declare that the Britons of Great Britain came from thence.

There can be no doubt, however, that St. Patrick was intimately connected with Gaul. His mother, Conchessa, was either a sister or niece of the great St. Martin of Tours ; and it was undoubtedly from Gaul that the saint was carried captive to Ireland.

Patrick was not the baptismal name of the saint ; it was given him by St. Celestine[1] as indicative of rank, or it may be with some prophetic intimation of his future greatness. He was baptized by the no less significant appellation of Succat—" brave in battle." But his warfare was not with a material foe. Erinn received the faith at his hands, with noble and unexampled generosity ; and one martyr, and only one, was sacrificed in preference of ancient pagan rites ; while we know that thousands have shed their blood, and it may be hundreds even in our own times have sacrificed their lives, to preserve the treasure so gladly accepted, so faithfully preserved.[2]

Moore, in his *History of Ireland*, exclaims, with the force of truth, and the eloquence of poetry : " While in all other countries the introduction of Christianity has been the slow work of time, has been resisted by either government or people, and seldom

---

[1] *Celestine.*—See the Scholiast on Fiacc's Hymn.

[2] *Preserved.*—It is much to be regretted that almost every circumstance in the life of St. Patrick has been made a field for polemics. Dr. Todd, of whom one might have hoped better things, has almost destroyed the interest of his otherwise valuable work by this fault. He cannot allow that St. Patrick's mother was a relative of St. Martin of Tours, obviously because St. Martin's

effected without lavish effusion of blood, in Ireland, on the contrary,
by the influence of one zealous missionary, and with but little previous preparation of the soil by other hands, Christianity burst
forth at the first ray of apostolic light, and, with the sudden ripe-
ness of a northern summer, at once covered the whole land.   Kings
and princes, when not themselves amongst the ranks of the converted, saw their sons and daughters joining in the train without a
murmur.   Chiefs, at variance in all else, agreed in meeting beneath
the Christian banner ; and the proud druid and bard laid their
superstitions meekly at the foot of the cross ; nor, by a singular
blessing of Providence—unexampled, indeed, in the whole history
of the Church—was there a single drop of blood shed on account
of religion through the entire course of this mild Christian revolution, by which, in the space of a few years, all Ireland was brought
tranquilly under the dominion of the Gospel."

It is probable that St. Patrick was born in 387, and that in 403
he was made captive and carried into Ireland.   Those who believe
Alcuith or Dumbarton to have been his birthplace, are obliged to
account for his capture in Gaul—which has never been questioned
—by supposing that he and his family had gone thither to visit
the friends of his mother, Conchessa.   He was sold as a slave, in
that part of Dalriada comprised in the county of Antrim, to four
men, one of whom, Milcho, bought up their right from the other
three, and employed him in feeding sheep or swine.   Exposed to
the severity of the weather day and night, a lonely slave in a
strange land, and probably as ignorant of the language as of the
customs of his master, his captivity, would, indeed, have been a
bitter one, had he not brought with him, from a holy home, the
elements of most fervent piety.   A hundred times in the day, and
a hundred times in the night, he lifted up the voice of prayer and
supplication to the Lord of the bondman and the free, and faithfully served the harsh, and at times cruel, master to whom Providence had assigned him.   Perhaps he may have offered his sufferings for those who were serving a master even more harsh and cruel.

Catholicity is incontrovertible. He wastes pages in a vain attempt to disprove
St. Patrick's Roman mission, for similar reasons ; and he cannot even admit
that the Irish received the faith as a nation, all despite the clearest evidence ;
yet so strong is the power of prejudice, that he accepts far less proof for other
questions.

After six years he was miraculously delivered. A voice, that was not of earth, addressed him in the stillness of the night, and commanded him to hasten to a certain port, where he would find a ship ready to take him to his own country. "And I came," says the saint, "in the power of the Lord, who directed my course towards a good end ; and I was under no apprehension until I arrived where the ship was. It was then clearing out, and I called for a passage. But the master of the vessel got angry, and said to me, 'Do not attempt to come with us.' On hearing this I retired, for the purpose of going to the cabin where I had been received as a guest. And, on my way thither, I began to pray; but before I had finished my prayer, I heard one of the men crying out with a loud voice after me, 'Come, quickly; for they are calling you,' and immediately I returned. And they said to me, 'Come, we receive thee on trust. Be our friend, just as it may be agreeable to you.' We then set sail, and after three days reached land." The two Breviaries of Rheims and Fiacc's Hymn agree in stating that the men with whom Patrick embarked were merchants from Gaul, and that they landed in a place called Treguir, in Brittany, some distance from his native place. Their charity, however, was amply repaid. Travelling through a desert country, they had surely perished with hunger, had not the prayers of the saint obtained them a miraculous supply of food.

It is said that St. Patrick suffered a second captivity, which, however, only lasted sixty days ; but of this little is known. Neither is the precise time certain, with respect to these captivities, at which the events occurred which we are about to relate. After a short residence at the famous monastery of St. Martin, near Tours, founded by his saintly relative, he placed himself (probably in his thirtieth year) under the direction of St. Germain of Auxerre.

It was about this period that he was favoured with the remarkable vision or dream relating to his Irish apostolate. He thus describes it in his *Confessio* :—

" I saw, in a nocturnal vision, a man named Victoricus[3] coming as

---

[3] *Victoricus.*—There were two saints, either of whom might have been the mysterious visitant who invited St. Patrick to Ireland. St. Victoricus was the great missionary of the Morini, at the end of the fourth century. There was also a St. Victoricus who suffered martyrdom at Amiens, A.D. 286. Those who do not believe that the saints were and are favoured with supernatural

if from Ireland, with a large parcel of letters, one of which he handed to me. On reading the beginning of it, I found it contained these words: 'The voice of the Irish;' and while reading it I thought I heard, at the same moment, the voice of a multitude of persons near the Wood of Foclut, which is near the western sea; and they cried out, as if with one voice, *We entreat thee, holy youth, to come and henceforth walk amongst us.* And I was greatly affected in my heart, and could read no longer; and then I awoke."

St. Patrick retired to Italy after this vision, and there spent many years. During this period he visited Lerins,[4] and other islands in the Mediterranean. Lerins was distinguished for its religious and learned establishments; and probably St. Germain,[5] under whose direction the saint still continued, had recommended him to study there. It was at this time that he received the celebrated staff, called the *Bachall Isu*, or Staff of Jesus.

St. Bernard mentions this *Bachall Isu*, in his life of St. Malachy, as one of those insignia of the see of Armagh, which were popularly believed to confer upon the possessor a title to be regarded and obeyed as the successor of St. Patrick. Indeed, the great antiquity of this long-treasured relic has never been questioned; nor is there any reason to suppose that it was not in some way a miraculous gift.

Frequent notices of this pastoral staff are found in ancient Irish history. St. Fiacc speaks of it as having been richly adorned by an ecclesiastic contemporary with the saint.

A curious MS. is still preserved in the Chapter House of Westminster Abbey, containing an examination of " Sir Gerald

communications, and whose honesty compels them to admit the genuineness of such documents as the Confession of St. Patrick, are put to sad straits to explain away what he writes.

[4] *Lerins.*—See *Monks of the West*, v. i. p. 463. It was then styled *insula beata*.

[5] *St. Germain.*—St. Fiacc, who, it will be remembered, was contemporary with St. Patrick, write thus in his Hymn:

> " The angel, Victor, sent Patrick over the Alps;
> Admirable was his journey—
> Until he took his abode with Germanus,
> Far away in the south of Letha.
> In the isles of the Tyrrhene sea he remained;
> In them he meditated;
> He read the canon with Germanus—
> This, histories make known."

Machshayne, knight, sworn 19th March, 1529, upon the Holie Mase-booke and the *great relicke of Erlonde, called Baculum Christi*, in the presence of the Kynge's Deputie, Chancellour, Tresoror, and Justice."

Perhaps it may be well to conclude the account of this interesting relic by a notice of its wanton destruction, as translated from the Annals of Loch Cè by Professor O'Curry :—

"The most miraculous image of Mary, which was at *Bailè Atha Truim* (Trim), and which the Irish people had all honoured for a long time before that, which used to heal the blind, the deaf, the lame, and every disease in like manner, was burned by the Saxons. And the Staff of Jesus, which was in Dublin, and which wrought many wonders and miracles in Erinn since the time of Patrick down to that time, and which was in the hand of Christ Himself, was burned by the Saxons in like manner. And not only that, but there was not a holy cross, nor an image of Mary, nor other cele-brated image in Erinn over which their power reached, that they did not burn. Nor was there one of the seven Orders which came under their power that they did not ruin. And the Pope and the Church in the East and at home were excommunicating the Saxons on that account, and they did not pay any attention or heed unto that, &c. And I am not certain whether it was not in the year preceding the above [A.D. 1537] that these relics were burned."

St. Patrick visited Rome about the year 431, accompanied by a priest named Segetius, who was sent with him by St. Germanus to vouch for the sanctity of his character, and his fitness for the Irish mission. Celestine received him favourably, and dismissed him with his benediction and approbation. St. Patrick then returned once more to his master, who was residing at Auxerre. From thence he went into the north of Gaul, and there receiving intelligence of the death of St. Palladius, and the failure of his mission, he was immediately consecrated bishop by the venerable Amato, a prelate of great sanctity, then residing in the neighbourhood of Ebovia. Auxilius, Isserninus, and other disciples of the saint, received holy orders at the same time. They were subsequently promoted to the episcopacy in the land of their adoption.

In the year 432 St. Patrick landed in Ireland. It was the first year of the pontificate of St. Sixtus III., the successor of Celestine ; the fourth year of the reign of Laeghairè, son of Nial of the Nine Hostages, King of Ireland. It is generally supposed that the saint

landed first at a place called Inbher De, believed to be the mouth
of the Bray river, in Wicklow. Here he was repulsed by the inhabitants,—a circumstance which can be easily accounted for from
its proximity to the territory of King Nathi, who had so lately
driven away his predecessor, Palladius.

St. Patrick returned to his ship, and sailing towards the north,
landed at the little island of Holm Patrick, near Skerries, off the
north coast of Dublin. After a brief stay he proceeded still farther
northward, and finally entering Strangford Lough, landed with
his companions in the district of Magh-Inis, in the present barony
of Lecale. Having penetrated some distance into the interior, they
were encountered by Dicho, the lord of the soil, who, hearing of
their embarkation, and supposing them to be pirates, had assembled
a formidable body of retainers to expel them from his shores. But
it is said that the moment he perceived Patrick, his apprehensions
vanished. After some brief converse, Dicho invited the saint and his
companions to his house, and soon after received himself the grace
of holy baptism. Dicho was St. Patrick's first convert, and the
first who erected a Christian church under his direction. The
memory of this event is still preserved in the name Saull, the
modern contraction of *Sabhall Padruic*, or Patrick's Barn. The
saint was especially attached to the scene of his first missionary
success, and frequently retired to the monastery which was established there later.

After a brief residence with the new converts, Patrick set out for
the habitation of his old master, Milcho, who lived near Slieve Mis,
in the present county of Antrim, then part of the territory
called Dalriada. It is said that when Milcho heard of the approach
of his former slave, he became so indignant, that, in a violent fit of
passion, he set fire to his house, and perished himself in the flames.
The saint returned to Saull, and from thence journeyed by water to
the mouth of the Boyne, where he landed at a small port called
Colp. Tara was his destination; but on his way thither he stayed
a night at the house of a man of property named Seschnan. This
man and his whole family were baptized, and one of his sons
received the name of Benignus from St. Patrick, on account of the
gentleness of his manner. The holy youth attached himself from
this moment to his master, and was his successor in the primatial
see of Armagh.

Those who are anxious, for obvious reasons, to deny the fact of

St. Patrick's mission from Rome, do so on two grounds : first, the absence of a distinct statement of this mission in one or two of the earliest lives of the saints ; and his not having mentioned it himself in his genuine writings. Second, by underrating the value of those documents which do mention this Roman mission. With regard to the first objection, it is obvious that a hymn which was written merely as a panegyric (the Hymn of St. Fiacc) was not the place for such details. But St. Fiacc *does* mention that Germanus was the saint's instructor, and that "he read his canons," *i.e.*, studied theology under him.

St. Patrick's Canons,[6] which even Usher admits to be genuine, contain the following passage. We give Usher's own translation, as beyond all controversy for correctness :—" Whenever any cause that is very difficult, and unknown unto all the judges of the Scottish nation, shall arise, it is rightly to be referred to the See of the Archbishop of the Irish (that is, of Patrick), and to the examination of the prelate thereof. But if there, by him and his wise men, a cause of this nature cannot easily be made up, we have decreed it shall be sent to the See Apostolic, that is to say, to the chair of the Apostle Peter, which hath the authority of the city of Rome." Usher's translation of St. Patrick's Canon is sufficiently plain, and evidently he found it inconveniently explicit, for he gives a " gloss " thereon, in which he apologizes for St. Patrick's Roman predilections, by suggesting that the saint was influenced by a "special regard for the Church of Rome." No doubt this was true ; it is the feeling of all good Catholics; but it requires something more than a " special regard " to inculcate such absolute submission ; and we can scarcely think even Usher himself could have gravely supposed, that a canon written to bind the whole Irish Church, should have inculcated a practice of such importance, merely because St. Patrick had a regard for the Holy See. This Canon was acted upon in the Synod of Magh-Lene, in 630, and St. Cummian attests the fact thus :—" In accordance with the canonical decree, that if questions of grave moment arise, they shall be referred to the head of

[6] *Canons.*—This Canon is found in the Book of Armagh, and in that part of that Book which was copied from *St. Patrick's own manuscript.* Even could it be proved that St. Patrick never wrote these Canons, the fact that they are in the Book of Armagh, which was compiled, according to O'Curry, before the year 727, and even at the latest before the year 807, is sufficient to prove the practice of the early Irish Church on this important subject.

cities, we sent such as we knew were wise and humble men to Rome." But there is yet another authority for St. Patrick's Roman mission. There is an important tract by Macutenius, in the Book of Armagh. The authenticity of the tract has not, and indeed could not, be questioned ; but a leaf is missing : happily, however, the titles of the chapters are preserved, so there can be no doubt as to what they contained. In these headings we find the following :—

"5. De ætate ejus quando iens videre Sedem Apostolicam voluit discere sapientiam."

"6. De inventione Sancti Germani in Galiis et ideo non exivit ultra."

Dr. Todd, by joining these two separate titles, with more ingenuity than fairness, has made it appear that "St. Patrick desired to visit the Apostolic See, and there to learn wisdom, but that meeting with St. Germanus in Gaul he went no further."[7] Even could the headings of two separate chapters be thus joined together, the real meaning of *et ideo non exivit ultra* would be, that St. Patrick never again left Germanus,—a meaning too obviously inadmissible to require further comment. But it is well known that the life of St. Patrick which bears the name of Probus, is founded almost verbally on the text of Macutenius, and this work supplies the missing chapters. They clearly relate not only the Roman mission of the saint, but also the saint's love of Rome, and his desire to obtain from thence "due authority" that he might "preach with confidence."

[7] *Further.—Life of St. Patrick*, p. 315.

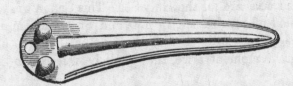

ANCIENT SWORD, FROM THE COLLECTION OF THE R.I.A., FOUND T HILLSWOOD, CO. GALWAY.

SCULPTURES AT DEVENISH.

CHAPTER IX.

St. Patrick visits Tara—Easter Sunday—St. Patrick's Hymn—Dubtach salute him—He overthrows the Idols at Magh Slecht—The Princesses Ethnea and Fethlimia—Their Conversion—Baptism of Aengus—St. Patrick travels through Ireland—His Success in Munster—He blesses the whole country from Cnoc Patrick—The First Irish Martyr—St. Patrick's Death—Pagan Prophecies—Conor Mac Nessa—Death of King Laeghairé—The Church did not and does not countenance Pagan Superstition—Oilioll Molt—Death of King Aengus—Foundation of the Kingdom of Scotland—St. Brigid—Shrines of the Three Saints—St. Patrick's Prayer for Ireland, and its Fulfilment.

[A.D. 432—543.]

ON Holy Saturday St. Patrick arrived at Slane, where he caused a tent to be erected, and lighted the paschal fire at nightfall, preparatory to the celebration of the Easter festival. The princes and chieftains of Meath were, at the same time, assembled at Tara, where King Laeghairé was holding a great pagan festival. The object of this meeting has been disputed, some authorities saying that it was convoked to celebrate the Beltinne, or fire of Bal or Baal ; others, that the king was commemorating his own birthday. On the festival of Beltinne it was forbidden to light any fire until a flame was visible from the top of Tara Hill. Laeghairé was indignant that this regulation should have been infringed ; and probably the representation of his druids regarding the mission of the great apostle, did not tend to allay his wrath. Determined to examine himself into the intention of these bold strangers, he set forth, accompanied by his bards and attendants, to the place where the sacred fire had been kindled, and ordered the apostle to be brought before him, strictly commanding, at the same time, that no respect should be shown to him.

Notwithstanding the king's command, Erc, the son of Dego, rose up to salute him, obtained the grace of conversion, and was subsequently promoted to the episcopate. The result of this interview was the appointment of a public discussion, to take place the next day at Tara, between St. Patrick and the pagan bards.

It was Easter Sunday—a day ever memorable for this event in the annals of Erinn. Laeghairé and his court sat in state to receive the ambassador of the Eternal King. Treacherous preparations had been made, and it was anticipated that Patrick and his companions would scarcely reach Tara alive. The saint was aware of the machinations of his enemies ; but life was of no value to him, save as a means of performing the great work assigned him, and the success of that work was in the safe keeping of Another. The old writers love to dwell on the meek dignity of the apostle during this day of trial and triumph. He set forth with his companions, from where he had encamped, in solemn procession, singing a hymn of invocation which he had composed, in the Irish tongue, for the occasion, and which is still preserved, and well authenticated.[8] He

8 *Authenticated.*—A copy of this ancient hymn, with a Latin and English translation, may be found in Petrie's *Essay on Tara*, p. 57, in Dr. Todd's *Life of St. Patrick*, and in Mr. Whitley Stokes' *Goidilica*. We regret exceedingly that our limited space will not permit us to give this and other most valuable and interesting documents. There is a remarkable coincidence of thought and expression between some portions of this hymn and the well-known prayer of St. Ignatius of Loyola, *Corpus Christi, salve me.* Such coincidences are remarkable and beautiful evidences of the oneness of faith, which manifests itself so frequently in similarity of language as well as in unity of belief. The Hymn of St. Patrick, written in the fifth century, is as purely Catholic as the Prayer of St. Ignatius, written in the sixteenth. St. Patrick places the virtue or power of the saints between him and evil, and declares his hope of merit for his good work with the same simple trust which all the saints have manifested from the earliest ages. This hymn is written in the *Bearla Feine,* or most ancient Gaedhilic dialect. Dr. O'Donovan well observes, that it bears internal evidence of its authenticity in its allusion to pagan customs. Tirechan, who wrote in the seventh century, says that there were four honours paid to St. Patrick in *all monasteries and churches throughout the whole of Ireland.* First, the festival of St. Patrick was honoured for three days and nights with all

St. Patrick going to Tara.

was clothed, as usual, in white robes; but he wore his mitre, and carried in his hand the Staff of Jesus. Eight priests attended him, robed also in white, and his youthful convert, Benignus, the son of Seschnan.

Thus, great in the arms of meekness and prayer, did the Christian hosts calmly face the array of pagan pomp and pride. Again the monarch had commanded that no honour should be paid to the saint, and again he was disobeyed. His own chief poet and druid, Dubtach, rose up instantly on the entrance of the strangers, and saluted the venerable apostle with affection and respect. The Christian doctrine was then explained by St. Patrick to his wondering audience, and such impression made, that although Laeghairé lived and died an obstinate pagan, he nevertheless permitted the saint to preach where and when he would, and to receive all who might come to him for instruction or holy baptism.

On the following day St. Patrick repaired to Taillten, where the public games were commencing; and there he remained for a week, preaching to an immense concourse of people. Here his life was threatened by Cairbré, a brother of King Laeghairé; but the saint was defended by another of the royal brothers, named Conall Creevan, who was shortly after converted. The church of Donough Patrick, in Meath, was founded by his desire. It is said that all the Irish churches which begin with the name Donough were founded by the saint, the foundation being always marked out by him on a Sunday, for which Domhnach is the Gaedhilic term.

Having preached for some time in the western part of the territory of Meath, the saint proceeded as far as Magh Slecht, where the great idol of the nation, Ceann [or Crom] Cruach was solemnly worshipped. The legend of its destruction, as given in the oldest annals, is singularly interesting. We give a brief extract from Professor O'Curry's translation: "When Patrick saw the idol from the water, which is named *Guthard* [loud voice] (*i.e.*, he elevated his voice); and when he approached near the idol, he raised his arm to lay the Staff of Jesus on him, and it did not reach him; he bent

good cheer, except flesh meat [which the Church did not allow then to be used in Lent]. Second, there was a proper preface for him in the Mass. Third, his hymn was sung for the whole time. Fourth, his Scotic hymn was sung always. As we intend publishing a metrical translation of his hymn suitable for general use, we hope it will be "said and sung" by thousands of his own faithful people on his festival for all time to come.

back from the attempt upon his right side, for it was to the south his face was; and the mark of the staff lies in his left side still, although the staff did not leave Patrick's hand; and the earth swallowed the other twelve idols to their heads; and they are in that condition in commemoration of the miracle. And he called upon all the people *cum rege Laeghuire;* they it was that adored the idol. And all the people saw him (*i.e.*, the demon), and they dreaded their dying if Patrick had not sent him to hell."[9]

After this glorious termination of Easter week, the saint made two other important converts. He set out for Connaught; and when near Rath Cruaghan, met the daughters of King Laeghairé, the princesses Ethnea and Fethlimia, who were coming, in patriarchal fashion, to bathe in a neighbouring well. These ladies were under the tuition of certain druids, or magi; but they willingly listened to the instruction of the saint, and were converted and baptized.

The interview took place at daybreak. The royal sisters heard the distant chant of the priests, who were reciting matins as they walked along; and when they approached and beheld them in their white garments, singing, with books in their hands, it was naturally supposed that they were not beings of earth.

"Who are ye?" they inquired of the saint and his companions. "Are ye of the sea, the heavens, or the earth?"

St. Patrick explained to them such of the Christian mysteries as were most necessary at the moment, and spoke of the one only true God.

"But where," they asked, "does your God dwell? Is it in the sun or on earth, in mountains or in valleys, in the sea or in rivers?"

Then the apostle told them of his God,—the Eternal, the Invisible,—and how He had indeed dwelt on earth as man, but only to suffer and die for their salvation. And as the maidens listened to his words, their hearts were kindled with heavenly love, and they inquired further what they could do to show their gratitude to this great King. In that same hour they were baptized; and in a short time they consecrated themselves to Him, the story of whose surpassing charity had so moved their young hearts.

---

[9] *Hell.*—O'Curry, p. 539. This is translated from the Tripartite Life of St. Patrick.

Their brother also obtained the grace of conversion; and an old Irish custom of killing a sheep on St. Michael's Day, and distributing it amongst the poor, is said to date from a miracle performed by St. Patrick for this royal convert.

Nor is the story of Aengus, another royal convert, less interesting. About the year 445, the saint, after passing through Ossory, and converting a great number of people, entered the kingdom of Munster. His destination was Cashel, from whence King Aengus, the son of Natfraech, came forth to meet him with the utmost reverence.

This prince had already obtained some knowledge of Christianity, and demanded the grace of holy baptism.

The saint willingly complied with his request. His courtiers assembled with royal state to assist at the ceremony. St. Patrick carried in his hand, as usual, the Bachall Isu; at the end of this crozier there was a sharp iron spike, by which he could plant it firmly in the ground beside him while preaching, or exercising his episcopal functions. On this occasion, however, he stuck it down into the king's foot, and did not perceive his mistake until—

"The royal foot transfixed, the gushing blood
Enrich'd the pavement with a noble flood."

The ceremony had concluded, and the prince had neither moved nor complained of the severe suffering he had endured. When the saint expressed his deep regret for such an occurrence, Aengus merely replied that he believed it to be a part of the ceremony, and did not appear to consider any suffering of consequence at such a moment.[1]

When such was the spirit of the old kings of Erinn who received the faith of Christ from Patrick, we can scarcely marvel that their descendants have adhered to it with such unexampled fidelity.

After the conversion of the princesses Ethnea and Fethlimia, the daughters of King Laeghairé, St. Patrick traversed almost every part of Connaught, and, as our divine Lord promised to those whom He commissioned to teach all nations, proved his mission by the exercise of miraculous powers. Some of his early biographers have been charged with an excess of credulity on this point. But were this the place or time for such a discussion, it might easily be shown

[1] *Moment.*—Keating, vol. ii. p. 15.

that miracles were to be expected when a nation was first evangelized, and that their absence should be rather a matter of surprise
than their frequency or marvellousness. He who alone could give
the commission to preach, had promised that "greater things" than
He Himself did should be done by those thus commissioned. And,
after all, what greater miracle could there be than that one who
had been enslaved, and harshly, if not cruelly treated, should
become the deliverer of his enslavers from spiritual bondage, and
should sacrifice all earthly pleasures for their eternal gain ? Nor is
the conversion of the vast multitude who listened to the preaching
of the saint, less marvellous than those events which we usually term
the most supernatural.

The saint's greatest success was in the land[2] of Tirawley, near the
town of Foclut, from whence he had heard the voice of the Irish
even in his native land. As he approached this district, he
learned that the seven sons of King Amalgaidh were celebrating a
great festival. Their father had but lately died, and it was said
these youths exceeded all the princes of the land in martial courage
and skill in combat. St. Patrick advanced in solemn procession
even into the very midst of the assembly, and for his reward obtained the conversion of the seven princes and twelve thousand of
their followers. It is said that his life was at this period in some
danger, but that Endeus, one of the converted princes, and his son
Conall, protected him.[3] After seven years spent in Connaught, he
passed into Ulster ; there many received the grace of holy baptism,
especially in that district now comprised in the county Monaghan.

It was probably about this time that the saint returned to
Meath, and appointed his nephew, St. Secundinus or Sechnal, who
was bishop of the place already mentioned as Domhnach Sechnail,
to preside over the northern churches during his own absence in
the southern part of Ireland.

The saint then visited those parts of Leinster which had been
already evangelized by Palladius, and laid the foundation of many
new churches. He placed one of his companions, Bishop Auxilius,
at Killossy, near Naas, and another, Isserninus, at Kilcullen, both
in the present county of Kildare. At Leix, in the Queen's county,
he obtained a great many disciples, and from thence he proceeded

---

[2] *Land.*—Near the present town of Killala, co. Mayo.
[3] *Protected him.*—Book of Armagh and Vit. Trip.

to visit his friend, the poet Dubtach, who, it will be remembered, paid him special honour at Tara, despite the royal prohibition to the contrary. Dubtach lived in that part of the country called Hy-Kinsallagh, now the county Carlow. It was here the poet Fiacc was first introduced to the saint, whom he afterwards so faithfully followed. Fiacc had been a disciple of Dubtach, and was by profession a bard, and a member of an illustrious house. He was the first Leinster man raised to episcopal dignity. It was probably at this period that St. Patrick visited Munster, and the touching incident already related occurred at the baptism of Aengus. This prince was singularly devoted to religion, as indeed his conduct during the administration of the sacrament of regeneration could not fail to indicate.

The saint's mission in Munster was eminently successful. Lonan, the chief of the district of Ormonde, entertained him with great hospitality, and thousands embraced the faith. Many of the inhabitants of Corca Baiscin crossed the Shannon in their hide-covered boats (curaghs) when the saint was on the southern side, in Hy-Figeinte, and were baptized by him in the waters of their magnificent river. At their earnest entreaty, St. Patrick ascended a hill which commanded a view of the country of the Dalcassians, and gave his benediction to the whole territory. This hill is called Findine in the ancient lives of the saint ; but this name is now obsolete. Local tradition and antiquarian investigation make it probable that the favoured spot is that now called Cnoc Patrick, near Foynes Island.

The saint's next journey was in the direction of Kerry, where he prophesied that "St. Brendan, of the race of Hua Alta, the great patriarch of monks and star of the western world, would be born, and that his birth would take place some years after his own death."[4]

We have now to record the obituary of the only Irish martyr who suffered for the faith while Ireland was being evangelized. While the saint was visiting Ui-Failghe, a territory now comprised in the King's county, a pagan chieftain, named Berraidhe, formed a plan for murdering the apostle. His wicked design came in some way to the knowledge of Odran, the saint's charioteer, who so

---

[4] *Death.*—Vit. Trip. It was probably at this time St. Patrick wrote his celebrated letter to Caroticus.

arranged matters as to take his master's place, and thus received the fatal blow intended for him.

The See of Armagh was founded about the year 455, towards the close of the great apostle's life. The royal palace of Emania, in the immediate neighbourhood, was then the residence of the kings of Ulster. A wealthy chief, by name Daire,[5] gave the saint a portion of land for the erection of his cathedral, on an eminence called *Druim-Sailech*, the Hill of Sallows. This high ground is now occupied by the city of Armagh (Ard-Macha). Religious houses for both sexes were established near the church, and soon were filled with ardent and devoted subjects.

The saint's labours were now drawing to a close, and the time of eternal rest was at hand. He retired to his favourite retreat at Saull, and there probably wrote his *Confessio*.[6] It is said that he wished to die in the ecclesiastical metropolis of Ireland, and for this purpose, when he felt his end approaching, desired to be conveyed thither; but even as he was on his journey an angel appeared to him, and desired him to return to Saull. Here he breathed his last, on Wednesday, the 17th of March, in the year of our Lord 492. The holy viaticum and last anointing were administered to him by St. Tussach.[7]

The saint's age at the time of his death, as also the length of his mission in Ireland, has been put at a much longer period by some authors, but modern research and correction of chronology have all but verified the statement given above.

The intelligence of the death of St. Patrick spread rapidly through the country; prelates and priests flocked from all parts to honour the mortal remains of their glorious father. As each arrived at Saull, he proceeded to offer the adorable sacrifice according to his rank. At night the plain resounded with the chanting of psalms; and the darkness was banished by the light of such innumerable torches, that it seemed even as if day had hastened to dawn brightly on the beloved remains. St. Fiacc, in his often-quoted Hymn,

---

[5] *Daire.*—Book of Armagh, fol. 6, b.a.

[6] *Confessio.*—This most remarkable and interesting document will be translated and noticed at length in the *Life of St. Patrick*, which we are now preparing for the press.

[7] *St. Tussach.*—All this Dr. Todd omits. The Four Masters enter the obituary of St. Patrick under the year 457. It is obvious that some uncertainty must exist in the chronology of this early period.

compares it to the long day caused by the standing of the sun at the command of Joshua, when he fought against the Gabaonites.

It is said that the pagan Irish were not without some intimation of the coming of their great apostle. Whether these prophecies were true or false is a question we cannot pretend to determine; but their existence and undoubted antiquity demand that they should have at least a passing notice. Might not the Gaedhilic druid, as well as the Pythian priestess, have received even from the powers of darkness, though despite their will, an oracle[8] which prophesied truth?

There is a strange, wild old legend preserved in the Book of Leinster, which indicates that even in ancient Erinn the awful throes of nature were felt which were manifested in so many places, and in such various ways, during those dark hours when the Son of God hung upon the accursed tree for the redemption of His guilty creatures.

This tale or legend is called the *Aideadh Chonchobair*. It is one of that class of narratives known under the generic title of Historical Tragedies, or Deaths. The hero, Conor Mac Nessa, was King of Ulster at the period of the Incarnation of our Lord. His succession to the throne was rather a fortuity than the result of hereditary claim. Fergus Mac Nessa was rightfully king at the time; but Cónor's father having died while he was yet an infant, Fergus, then the reigning monarch, proposed marriage to his mother when the youth was about fifteen, and only obtained the consent of the celebrated beauty on the strange condition that he should hand over the sovereignty of Ulster to her son for a year. The

---

[8] *Oracle.*—It is said that, three years before St. Patrick's apostolic visit to Ireland, the druids of King Laeghairé predicted the event to their master as an impending calamity. The names of the druids were Lochra and Luchat Mael; their prophecy runs thus :—

> "A *Tailcenn* will come over the raging sea,
> With his perforated garment, his crook-headed staff,
> With his table at the east end of his house,
> And all his people will answer 'Amen, Amen.'"

The allusions to the priestly vestments, the altar at the east end of the church, and the pastoral staff, are sufficiently obvious, and easily explained. The prophecy is quoted by Macutenius, and quoted again from him by Probus; but the original is in one of the most ancient and authentic Irish MSS., the Book of Armagh.

monarch complied, glad to secure the object of his affections on any terms.   Conor, young as he was, governed with such wisdom and discretion as to win all hearts ; and when the assigned period had arrived, the Ulster men positively refused to permit Fergus to resume his rightful dignity.   After much contention the matter was settled definitely in favour of the young monarch, and Fergus satisfied himself with still retaining the wife for whose sake he had willingly made such sacrifices.   Conor continued to give ample proofs of the wisdom of his people's decision.   Under his government the noble Knights of the Royal Branch sprang up in Ulster, and made themselves famous both in field and court.

It was usual in those barbarous times, whenever a distinguished enemy was killed in battle, to cleave open his head, and to make a ball of the brains by mixing them with lime, which was then dried, and preserved as a trophy of the warrior's valour.   Some of these balls were preserved in the royal palace at Emania.   One, that was specially prized, passed accidentally into the hands of a famous Connaught champion, who found a treacherous opportunity of throwing it at Conor, while he was displaying himself, according to the custom of the times, to the ladies of an opposing army, who had followed their lords to the scene of action.   The ball lodged in the king's skull, and his physicians declared that an attempt to extract it would prove fatal.   Conor was carried home ; he soon recovered, but he was strictly forbidden to use any violent exercise, and required to avoid all excitement or anger.   The king enjoyed his usual health by observing those directions, until the very day of the Crucifixion.   But the fearful phenomena which then occurred diverted his attention, and he inquired if *Bacrach*, his druid, could divine the cause.

The druid consulted his oracles, and informed the king that Jesus Christ, the Son of the living God, was, even at that moment, suffering death at the hands of the Jews.   " What crime has He committed ?" said Conor.   " None," replied the druid.   " Then are they slaying Him innocently ?" said Conor.   " They are," replied the druid.

It was too great a sorrow for the noble prince ; he could not bear that his God should die unmourned ; and rushing wildly from where he sat to a neighbouring forest, he began to hew the young trees down, exclaiming : " Thus would I destroy those who were around my King at putting Him to death."   The excitement proved fatal; and the brave and good King Conor Mac Nessa died[9] avenging, in his own wild pagan fashion, the death of his Creator.

The secular history of Ireland, during the mission of St. Patrick, affords but few events of interest or importance. King Laeghairé died, according to the Four Masters, A.D. 458. The popular opinion attributed his demise to the violation of his oath to the Leinster men. It is doubtful whether he died a Christian, but the account of his burial[1] has been taken to prove the contrary. It is much to be regretted that persons entirely ignorant of the Catholic faith, whether that ignorance be wilful or invincible, should attempt to write lives of Catholic saints, or histories of Catholic countries. Such persons, no doubt unintentionally, make the most serious mistakes, which a well-educated Catholic child could easily rectify. We find a remarkable instance of this in the following passage, taken from a work already mentioned : "Perhaps this [King Laeghairé's oath] may not be considered an absolute proof of the king's paganism. To swear by the sun and moon was apparently, no doubt, paganism. But is it not also paganism to represent the rain and wind as taking vengeance ? . . . . for this is the language copied by all the monastic annalists, and even by the Four Masters, Franciscan friars, writing in the seventeenth century." The passage is improved by a "note," in which the author mentions this as a proof that such superstitions would not have been necessarily regarded two centuries ago as inconsistent with orthodoxy. Now, in the first place, the Catholic Church has always[2] condemned superstition of every kind. It is true that as there are good as well as bad Christians in her fold, there are also superstitious as well as believing Christians ; but the Church is not answerable for the sins of her children. She is answerable for the doctrine which she teaches;

---

[9] *Died.*—O'Curry, p. 273.

[1] *Burial.*—"The body of Laeghairé was brought afterwards from the south, and interred with his armour of championship in the south-east of the outer rampart of the royal rath of Laeghairé, at Tara, with his face turned southwards upon the men of Leinster, as fighting with them, for he was the enemy of the Leinster men in his lifetime."—Translated from the *Leabhar na Nuidhre.* Petrie's *Tara*, p. 170.

[2] *Always.*—National customs and prejudices have always been respected by the Church : hence she has frequently been supposed to sanction what she was obliged to tolerate. A long residence in Devonshire, and an intimate acquaintance with its peasantry, has convinced us that there is incalculably

and no one can point to any place or time in which the Church taught such superstitions. Secondly, the writers of history are obliged to relate facts as they are. The Franciscan fathers do this, and had they not done it carefully, and with an amount of labour which few indeed have equalled, their admirable Annals would have been utterly useless. They do mention the pagan opinion that it was "the sun and wind that killed him [Laeghairé], because he had violated them ;" but they do not say that they believed this pagan superstition, and no one could infer it who read the passage with ordinary candour.

It is probable that Oilioll Molt, who succeeded King Laeghairé, A.D. 459, lived and died a pagan. He was slain, after a reign of twenty years, by Laeghairé's son, Lughaidh, who reigned next. The good king Aengus[3] died about this time. He was the first Christian King of Munster, and is the common ancestor of the MacCarthys, O'Sullivans, O'Keeffes, and O'Callahans. The foundation of the kingdom of Scotland by an Irish colony, is generally referred to the year 503.[4] It has already been mentioned that Cairbré Riada was the leader of an expedition thither in the reign of Conairé II. The Irish held their ground without assistance from the mother country until this period, when the Picts obtained a decisive victory, and drove them from the country. A new colony of the Dalriada

---

more superstitions believed and *practised* there of the *grossest kind*, than in any county in Ireland. Yet we should be sorry to charge the Established Church or its clergy, some of whom are most earnest and hard-working men, with the sins of their parishioners. The following extract from St. Columba's magnificent Hymn, will show what the early Irish saints thought of pagan superstitions :

> "I adore not the voice of birds,
>   Nor sneezing, nor lots in this world,
>   Nor a boy, nor chance, nor woman :
>   My Druid is Christ, the Son of God ;
>   Christ, Son of Mary, the great Abbot,
>   The Father, the Son, and the Holy Ghost.'

[3] *Aengus.*—

> "Died the branch, the spreading tree of gold,
>   Aenghus the laudable."

—Four Masters, p. 153. The branches of this tree have indeed spread far and wide, and the four great families mentioned above have increased and multiplied in all parts of the world.

[4] *Year* 503.—The Four Masters give the date 498, which O'Donovan corrects both in the text and in a note.

now went out under the leadership of Loarn, Aengus, and Fergus, the sons of Erc. They were encouraged and assisted in their undertaking by their relative Mortagh, the then King of Ireland. It is said they took the celebrated *Lia Fail* to Scotland, that Fergus might be crowned thereon. The present royal family of England have their claim to the crown through the Stuarts, who were descendants of the Irish Dalriada. Scotland now obtained the name of Scotia, from the colony of Scots. Hence, for some time, Ireland was designated Scotia Magna, to distinguish it from the country which so obtained, and has since preserved, the name of the old race.

Muircheartach, A.D. 504, was the first Christian King of Ireland; but he was constantly engaged in war with the Leinster men about the most unjust Boromean tribute. He belonged to the northern race of Hy-Nial, being descended from Nial of the Nine Hostages. On his death, the crown reverted to the southern Hy-Nials in the person of their representative, Tuathal Maelgarbh.

It would appear from a stanza in the Four Masters, that St. Brigid had some prophetic intimation or knowledge of one of the battles fought by Muircheartach. Her name is scarcely less famous for miracles than that of the great apostle. Broccan's Hymn[5] contains allusions to a very great number of these supernatural favours. Many of these marvels are of a similar nature to those which the saints have been permitted to perform in all ages of the Church's history.

Brigid belonged to an illustrious family, who were lineally descended from Eochad, a brother of Conn of the Hundred Battles. She was born at Fochard, near Dundalk, about the year 453, where her parents happened to be staying at the time; but Kildare was their usual place of residence, and there the holy virgin began her saintly career. In her sixteenth year she received the white cloak and religious veil, which was then the distinctive garment of those who were specially dedicated to Christ, from the hands of St. Macaille, the Bishop of Usneach, in Westmeath. Eight young maidens of noble birth took the veil with her. Their first residence was at a place in the King's county, still called Brigidstown. The fame of her sanctity now extended far and wide, and she was earnestly solicited from various parts of the country to found similar

---

[5] *Broccan's Hymn.*—This Hymn was written about A.D. 510. See the translation in Mr. Whitley Stokes' *Goidilica*, Calcutta, 1866. Privately printed.

establishments.   Her first mission was to Munster, at the request
of Erc, the holy Bishop of Slane, who had a singular respect for her
virtue.   Soon after, she founded a house of her order in the plain
of Cliach, near Limerick; but the people of Leinster at last became
fearful of losing their treasure, and sent a deputation requesting
her return, and offering land for the foundation of a large nunnery.
Thus was established, in 483, the famous Monastery of Kildare, or
the Church of the Oak.

At the request of the saint, a bishop was appointed to take
charge of this important work; and under the guidance of Con-
laeth, who heretofore had been a humble anchorite, it soon became
distinguished for its sanctity and usefulness.   The concourse of
strangers and pilgrims was immense; and in the once solitary
plain one of the largest cities of the time soon made its appearance.   It is singular and interesting to remark, how the call to a
life of virginity was felt and corresponded with in the newly
Christianized country, even as it had been in the Roman Empire,
when it also received the faith.   Nor is it less noticeable how the
same safeguards and episcopal rule preserved the foundations of
each land in purity and peace, and have transmitted even to our
own days, in the same Church, and in it only, that privileged life.

The Four Masters give her obituary under the year 525.   According to Cogitosus, one of her biographers, her remains were
interred in her own church.   Some authorities assert that her
relics were removed to Down, when Kildare was ravaged by the
Danes, about the year 824.

It has been doubted whether Downpatrick could lay claim to the
honour of being the burial-place of Ireland's three great saints,[6]
but there are good arguments in its favour.   An old prophecy
of St. Columba regarding his interment runs thus :—

> "My prosperity in guiltless Hy,
> And my soul in Derry,
> And my body under the flag
> Beneath which are Patrick and Brigid."

The relics of the three saints escaped the fury of the Danes, who
burned the town and pillaged the cathedral six or seven times,
between the years 940 and 1111.   In 1177, John de Courcy

---

[6] *Saints.*—St. Patrick, St. Columba, and St. Brigid.   See Reeves' *Ecc. Anti.
of Down and Connor*, p. 225, and Giraldus Cambrensis, d. 3, cap. 18.

took possession of the town, and founded a church attached to a house of Secular Canons, under the invocation of the Blessed Trinity. In 1183 they were replaced by a community of Benedictine monks, from St. Wirburgh's Abbey, at Chester. Malachy, who was then bishop, granted the church to the English monks and prior, and changed the name to that of the Church of St. Patrick. This prelate was extremely anxious to discover the relics of the saints, which a constant tradition averred were there concealed. It is said, that one day, as he prayed in the church, his attention was directed miraculously to an obscure part of it; or, according to another and more probable account, to a particular spot in the abbey-yard, where, when the earth was removed, their remains were found in a triple cave,—Patrick in the middle, Columba and Brigid on either side.

At the request of De Courcy, delegates were despatched to Rome by the bishop to acquaint Urban III. of the discovery of the bodies. His Holiness immediately sent Cardinal Vivian to preside at the translation of the relics. The ceremony took place on the 9th of June, 1186, that day being the feast of St. Columba. The relics of the three saints were deposited in the same monument at the right side of the high altar. The right hand of St. Patrick was enshrined and placed on the high altar. In 1315, Edward Bruce invaded Ulster, marched to Downpatrick, destroyed the abbey, and carried off the enshrined hand. In 1538, Lord Grey, who marched into Lecale to establish the supremacy of his master, Henry VIII., by fire and sword, " effaced the statues of the three patron saints, and burned the cathedral, for which act, along with many others equally laudable, he was beheaded three years afterwards." The restoration of the old abbey-church was undertaken of late years, and preceded by an act of desecration, which is still remembered with horror. The church had been surrounded by a burying-ground, where many had wished to repose, that they might, even in death, be near the relics of the three great patron saints of Erinn. But the graves were exhumed without mercy, and many were obliged to carry away the bones of their relatives, and deposit them where they could. The "great tomb," in which it was believed that "Patrick, Brigid, and Columkille" had slept for more than six centuries, was not spared ; the remains were flung out into the churchyard, and only saved from further desecration by the piety of a faithful people.

The shrine of St. Patrick's hand was in possession of the late Catholic Bishop of Belfast. The relic itself has long disappeared; but the shrine, after it was carried off by Bruce, passed from one trustworthy guardian to another, until it came into his hands. One of these was a Protestant, who, with noble generosity, handed it over to a Catholic as a more fitting custodian. One Catholic family, into whose care it passed at a later period, refused the most tempting offers for it, though pressed by poverty, lest it should fall into the hands of those who might value it rather as a curiosity than as an object of devotion.

This beautiful reliquary consists of a silver case in the shape of the hand and arm, cut off a little below the elbow. It is considerably thicker than the hand and arm of an ordinary man, as if it were intended to enclose these members without pressing upon them too closely. The fingers are bent, so as to represent the hand in the attitude of benediction.

But there is another relic of St. Patrick and his times of scarcely less interest. The *Domhnach Airgid*[7] contains a copy of the Four Gospels, which, there is every reason to believe, were used by the great apostle of Ireland. The relic consists of two parts—the shrine or case and the manuscript. The shrine is an oblong box, nine inches by seven, and five inches in height. It is composed of three distinct covers, in the ages of which there is obviously a great difference. The inner or first cover is of wood, apparently yew, and may be coeval with the manuscript it is intended to preserve. The second, which is of copper plated with silver, is assigned to a period between the sixth and twelfth centuries, from the style of its scroll or interlaced ornaments. The figures in relief, and letters on the third cover, which is of silver plated with gold, leave no doubt of its being the work of the fourteenth century.

The last or external cover is of great interest as a specimen of the skill and taste in art of its time in Ireland, and also for the highly finished representations of ancient costume which it preserves. The ornaments on the top consist principally of a large figure of the

---

[7] *Domhnach Airgid.*—See O'Curry, *MS. Materials*, p. 321, for a complete verification of the authenticity of this relic. The Tripartite Life of St. Patrick mentions the gift of this relic by the saint to *St. MacCarthainn.* Dr. Petrie concludes that the copy of the Gospels contained therein, was undoubtedly the one which was used by our apostle. We give a fac-simile of the first page, which cannot fail to interest the antiquarian.

Saviour in *alto-relievo* in the centre, and eleven figures of saints in *basso-relievo* on each side in four oblong compartments. There is a small square reliquary over the head of our divine Lord, covered with a crystal, which probably contained a piece of the holy cross. The smaller figures in relief are, Columba, Brigid, and Patrick; those in the second compartment, the Apostles James, Peter, and Paul; in the third, the Archangel Michael, and the Virgin and Child; in the fourth compartment a bishop presents a *cumdach*, or cover, to an ecclesiastic. This, probably, has a historical relation to the reliquary itself.

One prayer uttered by St. Patrick has been singularly fulfilled. "May my Lord grant," he exclaims, "that I may never lose His people, which He has acquired in the ends of the earth!" From hill and dale, from camp and cottage, from plebeian and noble, there rang out a grand "Amen." The strain was caught by Secundinus and Benignus, by Columba and Columbanus, by Brigid and Brendan. It floated away from Lindisfarne and Iona, to Iceland and Tarentum. It was heard on the sunny banks of the Rhine, at Antwerp and Cologne, in Oxford, in Pavia, and in Paris. And still the old echo is breathing its holy prayer. By the priest, who toils in cold and storm to the "station" on the mountain side, far from his humble home. By the confessor, who spends hour after hour, in the heat of summer and the cold of winter, absolving the penitent children of Patrick. By the monk in his cloister. By noble and true-hearted men, faithful through centuries of persecution. And loudly and nobly, though it be but faint to human ears, is that echo uttered also by the aged woman who lies down by the wayside to die in the famine years,[8] because she prefers the bread of heaven to the bread of earth, and the faith taught by Patrick to the tempter's gold. By the emigrant, who, with

[8] *Famine years.*—During the famous, or rather infamous, Partry evictions, an old man of eighty and a woman of seventy-four were amongst the number of those who suffered for their ancient faith. They were driven from the home which their parents and grandfathers had occupied, in a pitiless storm of sleet and snow. The aged woman utters some slight complaint; but her noble-hearted aged husband consoles her with this answer: "The sufferings and death of Jesus Christ were bitterer still." Sixty-nine souls were cast out of doors that day. Well might the *Times* say: "These evictions are a hideous scandal; and the bishop should rather die than be guilty of such a crime." Yet, who can count up all the evictions, massacres, tortures, and punishments which this people has endured?

broken heart bids a long farewell to the dear island home, to the old father, to the grey-haired mother, because his adherence to his faith tends not to further his temporal interest, and he must starve or go beyond the sea for bread. Thus ever and ever that echo is gushing up into the ear of God, and never will it cease until it shall have merged into the eternal alleluia which the often-martyred and ever-faithful children of the saint shall shout with him in rapturous voice before the Eternal Throne.

ST. PATRICK'S BELL.

CROMLECH, AT CASTLE MARY, CLOYNE.

CHAPTER X.

The Religion of Ancient Erinn—The Druids and their Teaching—The Irish were probably Fire-worshippers—The Customs of Ancient Erinn—Similarity between Eastern and Irish Customs—Beal Fires—Hunting the Wren —"Jacks," a Grecian game—"Keen," an Eastern Custom—Superstitions— The Meaning of the Word—What Customs are Superstitious and what are not—Holy Wells—The Laws of Ancient Erinn—Different kinds of Laws —The Lex non Scripta and the Lex Scripta—Christianity necessitated the Revision of Ancient Codes—The Compilation of the Brehon Laws—Proofs that St. Patrick assisted thereat—Law of Distress—Law of Succession— The Language of Ancient Erinn—Writing in pre-Christian Erinn— Ogham Writing—Antiquities of pre-Christian Erinn—Round Towers— Cromlechs—Raths—Crannoges.

EASTERN customs and eastern superstitions, which undoubtedly are a strong confirmatory proof of our eastern origin, abounded in ancient Erinn. Druidism was the religion of the Celts, and druidism was probably one of the least corrupt forms of paganism. The purity of the divinely-taught patriarchal worship, became more and more corrupted as it passed through defiled channels. Yet, in all pagan mythologies, we find traces of the eternal verity in an obvious prominence of cultus offered to one god above the rest; and obvious, though grossly misapplied, glimpses of divine attributes, in the many deified objects which seemed to symbolize his power and his omnipotence.

The Celtic druids probably taught the same doctrine as the Greek philosophers. The metempsychosis, a prominent article of this creed, may have been derived from the Pythagoreans, but more probably it was one of the many relics of patriarchal belief which were engrafted on all pagan religions. They also taught that the universe would never be entirely destroyed, supposing that it would be purified by fire and water from time to time. This opinion may have been derived from the same source. The druids had a *pontifex maximus*, to whom they yielded entire obedience,—an obvious imitation of the Jewish custom. The nation was entirely governed by its priests, though after a time, when the kingly power developed itself, the priestly power gave place to the regal. Gaul was the head-quarters of druidism ; and thither we find the Britons, and even the Romans, sending their children for instruction. Eventually, Mona became a chief centre for Britain. The Gaedhilic druids, though probably quite as learned as their continental brethren, were more isolated ; and hence we cannot learn so much of their customs from external sources. There is no doubt that the druids of Gaul and Britain offered human sacrifices ; it appears almost certain the Irish druids did not.

Our principal and most reliable information about this religion, is derived from Cæsar. His account of the learning of its druids, of their knowledge of astronomy, physical science, mechanics, arithmetic, and medicine, however highly coloured, is amply corroborated by the casual statements of other authors.[9] He expressly states that they used the Greek character in their writings, and mentions tables found in the camp of the Helvetii written in these characters, containing an account of all the men capable of bearing arms.

It is probable that Irish druidical rites manifested themselves principally in Sun-worship. The name of Bel, still retained in the Celtic Beltinne, indicates its Phœnician origin ; Baal being the name under which they adored that luminary. It is also remarkable that Grian, which signifies the sun in Irish, resembles an epithet of Apollo given by Virgil,[1] who sometimes styles him Grynæus. St. Patrick also confirms this conjecture, by condemning Sun-worship in his Confession, when he says : " All those who adore it shall descend into misery and punishment." If the well-known passage of Diodorus Siculus may be referred to Ireland, it affords another

---

[9] *Authors.*—Strabo, 1. iv. p. 197 ; Suetonius, *V. Cla. ;* Pliny, *Hist. Nat.* 1. xxv. c. 9. Pliny mentions having seen the serpent's egg, and describes it.

[1] *Virgil.—Ec.* 6, v. 73.

confirmation. Indeed, it appears difficult to conceive how any other place but Ireland could be intended by the "island in the ocean over against Gaul, to the north, and not inferior in size to Sicily, the *soil of which is so fruitful* that they mow there twice in the year."[2] In this most remarkable passage, he mentions the skill of their harpers, their sacred groves and *singular temple of round form*, their attachment to the Greeks by a singular affection from *old times*, and their tradition of having been visited by the Greeks, who left offerings which were noted in *Greek letters*.

Toland and Carte assume that this passage refers to the Hebrides, Rowlands applies it to the island of Anglesea; but these conjectures are not worth regarding. We can scarcely imagine an unprejudiced person deciding against Ireland; but where prejudice exists, no amount of proof will satisfy. It has been suggested that the Irish pagan priests were not druids properly so called, but magi;[3] and that the Irish word which is taken to mean druid, is only used to denote persons specially gifted with wisdom. Druidism probably sprung from magism, which was a purer kind of worship, though it would be difficult now to define the *precise* limits which separated these forms of paganism. If the original pagan religion of ancient Erinn was magism, introduced by its Phœnician colonizers, it is probable that it had gradually degenerated to the comparatively grosser rites of the druid before the advent of St. Patrick. His destruction of the idols at Magh Slecht is unquestionable evidence that idol worship[4] was then practised, though probably in a very limited degree.

The folklore of a people is perhaps, next to their language, the best guide to their origin. The editor of Bohn's edition of the Chronicle of Richard of Cirencester remarks, that "many points of coincidence have been remarked in comparing the religion of the Hindoos with that of the ancient Britons; and in the language of these two people some striking similarities occur in those proverbs

[2] *Year.*—Dio. Sic. tom. i. p. 158.

[3] *Magi.*—Magi is always used in Latin as the equivalent for the Irish word which signifies druid. See the *Vitæ S. Columbæ*, p. 73; see also Reeves' note to this word.

[4] *Worship.*—In the Chronicle of Richard of Cirencester, ch. 4, certain Roman deities are mentioned as worshipped by the British druids; but it is probable the account is merely borrowed from Cæsar's description of the Gauls.

and modes of expression which are derived from national customs
and religious ceremonies."[5]   We are not aware of any British customs or proverbs which bear upon this subject, nor does the writer
mention any in proof of his assertion: if, however, for Britons we
read Irish, his observations may be amply verified.

The kindly " God save you !" and " God bless all here !" of the
Irish peasant, finds its counterpart in the eastern " God be gracious
to thee, my son !"   The partiality, if not reverence, for the number
seven, is indicated in our churches.   The warm-hearted hospitality
of the very poorest peasant, is a practical and never-failing illustration of the Hindoo proverb, " The tree does not withdraw its shade
even from the woodcutter."

The celebration of St. John's Eve by watchfires, is undoubtedly
a remnant of paganism, still practised in many parts of Ireland, as
we can aver from personal knowledge ; but the custom of passing
cattle through the fire has been long discontinued, and those
who kindle the fires have little idea of its origin, and merely
continue it as an amusement.   Kelly mentions, in his *Folklore*,
that a calf was sacrificed in Northamptonshire during the present century, in one of these fires, to " stop the murrain."   The
superstitious use of fire still continues in England and Scotland,
though we believe the Beltinne on St. John's Eve is peculiar to
Ireland.   The hunting of the wren[6] on St. Stephen's Day, in this
country, is said, by Vallancey, to have been originated by the first
Christian missionaries, to counteract the superstitious reverence
with which this bird was regarded by the druids.   Classic readers
will remember the origin of the respect paid to this bird in pagan
times.   The peasantry in Ireland, who have never read either Pliny
or Aristotle, are equally conversant with the legend.

The common and undignified game of " jacks " also lays claim to

---

[5] *Ceremonies.*—Bohn's edition, p. 431.

[6] *Wren.*—In Scotland the wren is an object of reverence : hence the
rhyme—

> "Malisons, malisons, more than ten,
> That harry the Ladye of Heaven's hen."

But it is probable the idea and the verse were originally imported from
France, where the bird is treated with special respect.   There is a very interesting paper in the *Ulster Archæological Journal*, vol. vii. p. 334, on the remarkable correspondence of Irish, Greek, and Oriental legends, where the tale
of Labhradh Loinseach is compared with that of Midas.   Both had asses' ears,
and both were victims to the loquacious propensities of their barbers.

a noble ancestry. In Mr. St. John's work on *The Manners and Customs of Ancient Greece*, he informs us that the game was a classical one, and called *pentalitha*. It was played with five *astragals*—knuckle-bones, pebbles, or little balls—which were thrown up into the air, and then attempted to be caught when falling on the back of the hand. Another Irish game, "pricking the loop," in Greece is called *himantiliginos*, pricking the garter. Hemestertius supposes the Gordian Knot to have been nothing but a variety of the himantiliginos. The game consists in winding a thong in such an intricate manner, that when a peg is inserted in the right ring, it is caught, and the game is won; if the mark is missed, the thong unwinds without entangling the peg.

The Irish keen [*caoine*] may still be heard in Algeria and Upper Egypt, even as Herodotus heard it chanted by Lybian women. This wailing for the deceased is a most ancient custom; and if antiquity imparts dignity, it can hardly be termed barbarous. The Romans employed keeners at their funerals, an idea which they probably borrowed from the Etruscans,[7] with many others incomparably more valuable, but carefully self-appropriated. Our *wakes* also may have had an identity of origin with the funeral feasts of the Greeks, Etruscans, and Romans, whose customs were all probably derived from a common source.

The fasting of the creditor on the debtor is still practised in India, and will be noticed in connexion with the Brehon Laws. There is, however, a class of customs which have obtained the generic term of superstitions, which may not quite be omitted, and which are, for many reasons, difficult to estimate rightly. In treating of this subject, we encounter, *primâ facie*, the difficulty of giving a definition of superstition. The Irish are supposed to be preeminently a superstitious people. Those who make this an accusation, understand by superstition the belief in anything supernatural; and they consider as equally superstitious, veneration of a relic, belief in a miracle, a story of a banshee, or a legend of Finn Mac Cumhaill. Probably, if the Celts did not venerate relics, and believe in the possibility of miracles, we should hear far less of their superstitions. Superstition of the grossest kind is prevalent

---

[7] *Etruscans.*—See *Cities and Cemeteries of Etruria*, vol. i. p. 295, where the bas-reliefs are described which represent the *præficæ*, or hired mourners, wailing over the corpse.

among the lower orders in every part of England, and yet the nation prides itself on its rejection of this weakness. But according to another acceptation of the term, only such heathen customs as refer to the worship of false gods, are superstitions. These customs remain, unfortunately, in many countries, but in some they have been Christianized. Those who use the term superstition generically, still call the custom superstitious, from a latent and, perhaps, in some cases, unconscious impression that there is no supernatural. Such persons commence with denying all miraculous interventions except those which are recorded in holy Scripture; and unhappily, in some cases, end by denying the miracles of Scripture.

To salute a person who sneezed with some form of benediction, was a pagan custom. It is said to have originated through an opinion of the danger attending it; and the exclamation used was: " Jupiter help me !" In Ireland, the pagan custom still remains, but it has been Christianized, and " God bless you !" is substituted for the pagan form. Yet we have known persons who considered the use of this aspiration superstitious, and are pleased to assert that the Irish use the exclamation as a protection against evil spirits, meaning thereby fairies. When a motive is persistently attributed which does not exist, argument is useless.

Devotion to certain places, pilgrimages, even fasting and other bodily macerations, were pagan customs. These, also, have been Christianized. Buildings once consecrated to the worship of pagan gods, are now used as Christian temples : what should we think of the person who should assert that because pagan gods were once adored in these churches, therefore the worship now offered in them was offered to pagan deities ? The temples, like the customs, are Christianized.

The author of a very interesting article in the *Ulster Archæological Journal* (vol. ix. p. 256), brings forward a number of Irish customs for which he finds counterparts in India. But he forgets that in Ireland the customs are Christianized, while in India they remain pagan; and like most persons who consider the Irish preeminently superstitious, he appears ignorant of the teaching of that Church which Christianized the world. The special " superstition " of this article is the devotion to holy wells. The custom still exists in Hindostan; people flock to them for cure of their diseases, and leave " rags " on the bushes as " scapegoats," *ex votos,* so to say, of cures, or prayers for cures. In India, the prayer is made to a heathen deity; in Ireland, the people happen to believe that God hears the prayers of saints more readily than their own; and acting on the principle which induced persons, in apostolic times, to use "handkerchiefs and aprons" which had touched the person of St. Paul as mediums of cure, because of his virgin sanctity, in preference to "handkerchiefs and aprons" of their own, they apply to the saints and obtain cures. But they do not believe the saints can give what God refuses, or that the saints are more merciful than God. They know that the saints are His special friends, and we give to a friend what we might refuse to one less dear. *Lege totum, si vis scire totum*, is a motto which writers on national customs should not forget.

Customs were probably the origin of laws. Law, in its most comprehensive sense, signifies a rule of action laid down[8] by a superior. Divine law is manifested (1) by the law of nature, and (2) by revelation. The law of nations is an arbitrary arrangement, founded on the law of nature and the law of revelation : its perfection depends obviously on its correspondence with the divine law. Hence, by common consent, the greatest praise is given to those laws of ancient nations which approximate most closely to the law of nature, though when such laws came to be revised by those who had received the law of revelation, they were necessarily amended or altered in conformity therewith. No government can exist without law; but as hereditary succession preceded the law of hereditary succession, which was at first established by custom, so the *lex non scripta*, or national custom, preceded the *lex scripta*, or statute law. The intellectual condition of a nation may be well and safely estimated by its laws. A code of laws that were observed for centuries before the Christian era, and for centuries after the Christian era, and which can bear the most critical tests of forensic acumen in the nineteenth century, evidence that the framers of the code were possessed of no slight degree of mental culture. Such are the Brehon laws, by which pagan and Christian Erinn was governed for centuries.

The sixth century was a marked period of legal reform. The Emperor Justinian, by closing the schools of Athens, gave a death-

---

[8] *Laid down.*—Law, Saxon, *lagu, lah;* from *lecgan* = Goth. *lagjan*, to lay, to place; Gael. *lagh*, a law; *leag*, to lie down; Latin, *lex*, from Gr. *lego*, to lay.

blow to Grecian philosophy and jurisprudence. But Grecian influence had already acted on the formation of Roman law, and probably much of the Athenian code was embodied therein. The origin of Roman law is involved in the same obscurity as the origin of the Brehon code. In both cases, the mist of ages lies like a light, but impenetrable veil, over all that could give certainty to conjecture. Before the era of the Twelve Tables, mention is made of laws enacted by Romulus respecting what we should now call civil liabilities. Laws concerning religion are ascribed to Numa, and laws of contract to Servius Tullius, who is supposed to have collected the regulations made by his predecessors. The Twelve Tables were notably formed on the legal enactments of Greece. The cruel severity of the law for insolvent debtors, forms a marked contrast to the milder and more equitable arrangements of the Brehon code. By the Roman enactments, the person of the debtor was at the mercy of his creditor, who might sell him for a slave beyond the Tiber. The Celt allowed only the seizure of goods, and even this was under regulations most favourable to the debtor. The legal establishment of Christianity by Constantine, or we should rather say the existence of Christianity, necessitated a complete revision of all ancient laws : hence we find the compilation of the Theodosian code almost synchronizing with the revision of the Brehon laws. The spread of Christianity, and the new modes of thought and action which obtained thereby, necessitated the reconstruction of ancient jurisprudence in lands as widely distant geographically, and as entirely separated politically, as Italy and Ireland.

Those who have studied the subject most carefully, and who are therefore most competent to give an opinion, accept the popular account of the revision of our laws.

The Four Masters thus record this important event :—" The age of Christ 438. The tenth year of Laeghairé. The Feinchus of Ireland were purified and written, the writings and old works of Ireland having been collected [and brought] to one place at the request of St. Patrick. Those were the nine supporting props by whom this was done : Laeghairé, *i.e.*, King of Ireland, Corc, and Daire, the three kings ; Patrick, Benen, and Cairneach, the three saints ; Ross, Dubhthach, and Fearghus, the three antiquaries." Dr. O'Donovan, in his note, shelters himself under an extract from Petrie's *Tara ;* but it is to be supposed that he coin-

cides in the opinion of that gentleman. Dr. Petrie thinks that
"little doubt can be entertained that such a work was compiled
within a short period after the introduction of Christianity in the
country, and that St. Patrick may have laid the foundations of it ;"[9]
though he gives no satisfactory reason why that saint should not
have assisted at the compilation, and why the statements of our
annalists should be refused on this subject, when they are accepted
on others. A list of the "family" [household] of Patrick is given
immediately after, which Dr. O'Donovan has taken great pains to
verify, and with which he appears satisfied. If the one statement
is true, why should the other be false ? Mr. O'Curry, whose
opinion on such subjects is admittedly worthy of the highest consideration, expresses himself strongly in favour of receiving the
statements of our annalists, and thinks that both Dr. Petrie and
Dr. Lanigan are mistaken in supposing that the compilation was
not effected by those to whom it has been attributed. As to the
antiquity of these laws, he observes that Cormac Mac Cullinan
quotes passages from them in his Glossary, which was written not
later than the ninth century, and then the language of the Seanchus[1] Mor was so ancient that it had become obsolete. To these
laws, he well observes, the language of Moore, on the MSS. in the
Royal Irish Academy, may be applied : " They were not written by
a foolish people, nor for any foolish purpose ;" and these were the
"laws and institutions which regulated the political and social system
of a people the most remarkable in Europe, from a period almost
lost in the dark mazes of antiquity, down to about within two
hundred years of our own time, and whose spirit and traditions
influence the feelings and actions of the native Irish even to this
day."[2]

But we can adduce further testimony. The able editor and
translator of the *Seanchus Mor*, which forms so important a portion
of our ancient code, has, in his admirable Preface, fully removed all
doubt on this question. He shows the groundlessness of the objec-

---

[9] *It.*—Four Masters, vol. i. p. 133. The Seanchus Mor was sometimes
called *Cain Phadruig*, or Patrick's Law.

[1] *Seanchus.*—From the old Celtic root *sen*, old, which has direct cognates,
not merely in the Indo-European, but also in the Semitic ; Arabic, *sen*, old,
ancient—*sunnah*, institution, regulation ; Persian, *san*, law, right ; *sanna*.
Phœnicibus idem fuit quod Arabibus *summa*, lex, doctrina jux canonicum.—
Bochart, *Geo. Sœ.* l. ii. c. 17. See Petrie's *Tara*, p. 79.

[2] *Day.*—O'Curry, page 201.

tions (principally chronological) which had been made regarding those who are asserted to have been its compilers. He also makes it evident that it was a work in which St. Patrick should have been expected to engage : (1) because, being a Roman citizen, and one who had travelled much, he was probably well aware of the Christian modifications which had already been introduced into the Roman code. (2) That he was eminently a judicious missionary, and such a revision of national laws would obviously be no slight support to the advancement of national Christianity. It is also remarked, that St. Patrick may not necessarily have assisted personally in writing the MS.; his confirmation of what was compiled by others would be sufficient. St. Benignus, who is known to be the author of other works,[3] probably acted as his amanuensis.

The subject-matter of the portions of the Seanchus Mor which have been translated, is the law of distress. Two points are noticeable in this : First, the careful and accurate administration of justice which is indicated by the details of these legal enactments; second, the custom therein sanctioned of the creditor fasting upon the debtor, a custom which still exists in Hindostan. Hence, in some cases, the creditor fasts on the debtor until he is compelled to pay his debt, lest his creditor should die at the door; in other cases, the creditor not only fasts himself, but also compels his debtor to fast, by stopping his supplies. Elphinstone describes this as used even against princes, and especially by troops to procure payment of arrears.[4]

One of the most noticeable peculiarities of the Brehon law is the compensation for murder, called *eric*. This, however, was common to other nations. Its origin is ascribed to the Germans, but the institution was probably far more ancient. We find it forbidden[5] in the oldest code of laws in existence ; and hence the *eric* must have been in being at an early period of the world's civil history.

The law of succession, called *tanaisteacht*, or tanistry, is one of the most peculiar of the Brehon laws. The eldest son succeeded the father to the exclusion of all collateral claimants, unless he was

---

[3] *Works.*—He appears to have been the author of the original Book of Rights, and " commenced and composed the Psalter of Caiseal, in which are described the acts, *laws*," &c.—See Preface to Seanchus Mor, p. 17.

[4] *Arrears.*—Elphinstone's *India*, vol. i. p. 372.

[5] *Forbidden.*—" You shall not take money of him that is guilty of blood, but he shall die forthwith."—Numbers, xxxv. 31.

disqualified by deformity, imbecility, or crime. In after ages, by a compact between parents or mutual agreement, the succession was sometimes made alternate in two or more families. The eldest son, being recognized as presumptive heir, was denominated *tanaiste*, that is, minor or second; while the other sons, or persons eligible in case of failure, were termed *righdhamhua*, which literally means king-material, or king-makings. The *tanaiste* had a separate establishment and distinct privileges. The primitive intention was, that the "best man" should reign; but practically it ended in might being taken for right, and often for less important qualifications.

The possession and inheritance of landed property was regulated by the law called gavelkind (gavail-kinne), an ancient Celtic institution, but common to Britons, Anglo-Saxons, and others. By this law, inherited or other property was divided equally between the sons, to the exclusion of the daughters (unless, indeed, in default of heirs male, when females were permitted a life interest). The *tanaiste*, however, was allotted the dwelling-house and other privileges.

The tenure of land was a tribe or family right; and, indeed, the whole system of government and legislation was far more patriarchal than Teutonic—another indication of an eastern origin. All the members of a tribe or family had an equal right to their proportionate share of the land occupied by the whole. This system created a mutual independence and self-consciousness of personal right and importance, strongly at variance with the subjugation of the Germanic and Anglo-Norman vassal.

The compilation of the Brehon laws originated in a question that arose as to how the murderer of Odran, Patrick's charioteer, should be punished. The saint was allowed to select whatever Brehon he pleased to give judgment. He chose Dubhthach; and the result of his decision was the compilation of these laws, as it was at once seen that a purely pagan code would not suit Christian teaching.

The Celtic language is now admittedly one of the most ancient in existence. Its affinity with Sanscrit, the eldest daughter of the undiscoverable mother-tongue, has been amply proved,[6] and the study of the once utterly despised Irish promises to be one which

---

[6] *Proved.*—See Pictet's *Origines Indo-Européennes.* He mentions his surprise at finding a genuine Sanscrit word in Irish, which, like a geological boulder, had been transported from one extremity of the Aryan world to the other. Pictet considers that the first wave of Aryan emigration occurred 3,000 years before the Christian Era.

will abundantly repay the philologist. It is to be regretted that we
are indebted to German students for the verification of these statements; but the Germans are manifestly born philologists, and they
have opportunities of leisure, and encouragement for the prosecution
of such studies, denied to the poorer Celt. It is probable that Celtic
will yet be found to have been one of the most important of the
Indo-European tongues. Its influence on the formation of the
Romance languages has yet to be studied in the light of our continually increasing knowledge of its more ancient forms; and
perhaps the conjectures of Betham will, by the close of this century, receive as much respect as the once equally ridiculed history
of Keating.

It is almost impossible to doubt that the Irish nation had letters
and some form of writing before the arrival of St. Patrick. There
are so many references to the existence of writings in the most
ancient MSS., that it appears more rash to deny their statements
than to accept them.

The three principal arguments against a pre-Christian alphabet

RUNES FROM THE RUNIC
CROSS AT RUTHWELL.

appears to be : (1) The absence of any MS.
of such writing. (2) The use of the Roman
character in all MSS. extant. (3) The universal opinion, scarcely yet exploded, that
the Irish Celts were barbarians. In reply
to the first objection, we may observe that
St. Patrick is said to have destroyed all the
remnants of pagan writing.[7] Cæsar mentions that the druids of Gaul used Greek
characters. It appears impossible that the
Irish druids, who were at least their
equals in culture, should have been destitute
of any kind of written character. The ancient form of Welsh letters were somewhat
similar to the runes of which we give a
specimen, and this alphabet was called the
"alphabet of the bards," in contradistinction to which is placed

---

[7] *Writing.*—"Finally, Dudley Firbisse, hereditary professor of the antiquities
of his country, mentions in a letter [to me] a fact collected from the monuments of his ancestors, that one hundred and eighty tracts [tractatus] of the
doctrine of the druids or magi, were condemned to the flames in the time of
St. Patrick."—*Ogygia*, iii. 30, p. 219. A writer in the *Ulster Arch. Journal*

the "alphabet of the monks," or Roman alphabet. The alphabet of the Irish bard may have been the Beith-luis-nion, represented by the Ogham character, of which more hereafter.

The difficulty arising from the fact of St. Patrick's having given *abgitorium*, or alphabets, to his converts, appears to us purely chimerical. Latin was from the first the language of the Church, and being such, whether the Irish converts had or had not a form of writing, one of the earliest duties of a Christian missionary was to teach those preparing for the priesthood the language in which they were to administer the sacraments. The alphabet given by the saint was simply the common Roman letter then in use. The Celtic characteristic veneration for antiquity and religion, has still preserved it; and strange to say, the Irish of the nineteenth century alone use the letters which were common to the entire Roman Empire in the fifth. The early influence of ecclesiastical authority, and the circumstance that the priests of the Catholic Church were at once the instructors in and the preservers of letters, will account for the immediate disuse of whatever alphabet the druids may have had. The third objection is a mere *argumentum ad ignorantiam*.

It is to be regretted that the subject of Ogham writing has not been taken up by a careful and competent hand.[8] There are few people who have not found out some method of recording their history, and there are few subjects of deeper interest than the study of the efforts of the human mind to perpetuate itself in written characters. The Easterns had their cuneiform or arrow-headed symbols, and the Western world

CUNEIFORM CHARACTERS.

has even yet its quipus, and tells its history by the number of its knots.

mentions a "Cosmography," printed at "Lipsiæ, 1854." It appears to be a Latin version or epitome of a Greek work. The writer of this Cosmography was born in 103. He mentions having "examined the volumes" of the Irish, whom he visited. If this authority is reliable, it would at once settle the question.—See *Ulster Arch. Journal*, vol. ii. p. 281.

[8] *Hand.*—A work on this subject has long been promised by Dr. Graves, and is anxiously expected by paleographists. We regret to learn that there is no immediate prospect of its publication.

The peasant girl still knots her handkerchief as her *memoria technica*, and the lady changes her ring from its accustomed finger.

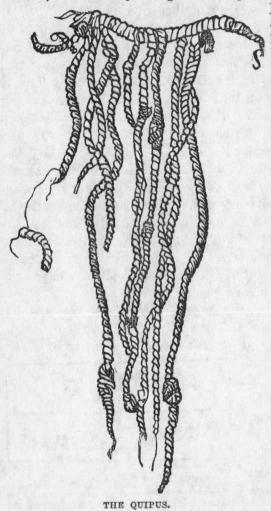

Each practice is quite as primitive an effort of nature as the Ogham of the Celtic bard. He used a stone pillar or a wooden stick for his notches,—a more permanent record than the knot or the Indian quipus.[9] The use of a stick as a vehicle for recording ideas by conventional marks, appears very ancient; and this in itself forms a good argument for the antiquity of Ogham writing. Mr. O'Curry has given it expressly as his opinion, " that the pre-Christian Gaedhils possessed and practised a system of writing and keeping records quite different from and independent of the Greek and Roman form and characters, which gained currency in the country after the introduction of Christianity." He then gives in evidence passages from our ancient writings which are preserved, in which the use of the Ogham character is distinctly mentioned. One instance is the

THE QUIPUS.

[9] *Quipus.*—Quipus signifies a knot. The cords were of different colours. Yellow denoted gold and all the allied ideas; white, silver, or peace; red, war, or soldiers. Each quipus was in the care of a quiper-carnayoe, or keeper. Acorta mentions that he saw a woman with a handful of these strings, which she said contained a confession of her life. See Wilson's *Pre-Historic Man* for most interesting details on the subject of symbolic characters and early writing.

relation in the *Táin bó Chuailgné* of directions having been left on wands or hoops written in Ogham by Cuchulainn for Méav. When these were found, they were read for her by Fergus, who understood the character. We have not space for further details, but Professor O'Curry devotes some pages to the subject, where fuller information may be found. In conclusion, he expresses an

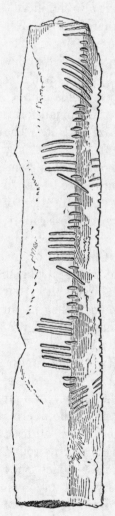

opinion that the original copies of the ancient books, such as the Cuilmenn and the Saltair of Tara, were not written in Ogham. He supposes that the druids or poets, who, it is well known, constantly travelled for educational purposes, brought home an alphabet, probably the Roman then in use. "It is, at all events, quite certain that the Irish druids had writen books before the coming of St. Patrick, in 432 ; since we find the statement in the Tripartite Life of the saint, as well as in the Annotations of Tirechan, preserved in the Book of Armagh, which were taken by him from the lips and books of his tutor, St. Mochta, who was the pupil and disciple of St. Patrick himself."

We give two illustrations of Ogham writing. The pillar-stone is from the collection of the Royal Irish Academy. It is about four and a-half feet high, and averages eleven inches across. It was found, with three others similarly inscribed, built into the walls of a dwelling-house in the county Kerry, to which it is believed they had been removed from the interior of a neighbouring rath. The bilingual Ogham was found at St. Dogmael's, near Cardiganshire. The Ogham alphabet is called *beithluisnion*, from the name of its two first letters, *beith*, which signifies

SAGRANI FILI CVNOTAMI.

a birch-tree, and *luis*, the mountain-ash. If this kind of writing had been introduced in Christian times, it is quite unlikely that such names would have been chosen. They are manifestly referable to a time when a tree had some significance beyond the useful or the ornamental. It has been supposed that the names of the letters were given to the trees, and not the names of the trees to the letters. It is at least certain that the names of the trees and the letters coincide, and that the trees are all indigenous to Ireland. The names of the letters in the Hebrew alphabet are also significant, but appear to be chosen indiscriminately, while there is a manifest and evidently arbitrary selection in the Celtic appellations. The number of letters also indicate antiquity. The ancient Irish alphabet had but sixteen characters, thus numerically corresponding with the alphabet brought into Greece by Cadmus. This number was gradually increased with the introduction of the Roman form, and the arrangement was also altered to harmonize with it. The Ogham alphabet consists of lines, which represent letters. They are arranged in an arbitrary manner to the right or left of a stem-line, or on the edge of the material on which they are traced. Even the names of those letters, *fleasg* (a tree), seem an indication of their origin. A cross has been found, sculptured more or less rudely, upon many of these ancient monuments; and this has been supposed by some antiquarians to indicate their Christian origin. Doubtless the practice of erecting pillar-stones, and writing Oghams thereon, was continued after the introduction of Christianity; but this by no means indicates their origin. Like many other pagan monuments, they may have been consecrated by having the sign of the cross engraven on them hundreds of years after their erection.

During the few months which have elapsed between the appearance of the first edition and the preparation of the second edition, my attention has been called to this portion of the history by four or five eminent members of the Royal Irish Academy, who express their regret that I should appear to have adopted, or at least favoured, Mr. D'Alton's view of the Christian origin of the round towers. I cannot but feel gratified at the interest which they manifested, and not less so at their kind anxiety that my own views should accord with those of the majority. I am quite aware that my opinion on such a subject could have little weight. To form a decided opinion on this subject, would require many years' study; but when one of these gentlemen, the Earl of Dunraven, distinguished for his devotion to archæology, writes to me that both Irish, English, and Continental scholars are all but unanimous in ascribing a Christian origin to these remarkable buildings, I cannot but feel that I am bound to accept this opinion, thus supported by an overwhelming weight of authority. It may, however, be interesting to some persons to retain an account of the opposing theories, and for this reason I still insert page 115 of the original edition, only making such modifications as my change of opinion make necessary.

The theories which have been advanced on this subject may be classified under seven heads—

(1) That the Phœnicians erected them for fire temples.

(2) That the Christians built them for bell towers.

(3) That the Magians used them for astronomical purposes.

(4) That they were for Christian anchorites to shut themselves up in.

(5) That they were penitentiaries.

(6) That the Druids used them to proclaim their festivals.

(7) That the Christians used them to keep their church plate and treasures.

Contradictory as these statements appear, they may easily be ranged into two separate theories of pagan or Christian origin. Dr. Petrie has been the great supporter of the latter opinion, now almost generally received. He founds his opinion: (1) On the assumption that the Irish did not know the use of lime mortar before the time of St. Patrick. For this assumption, however, he gives no evidence. (2) On the presence of certain Christian emblems on some of these towers, notably at Donaghmore and Antrim. But the presence of Christian emblems, like the cross on the Ogham stones, may merely indicate that Christians wished to consecrate them to Christian use. (3) On the assumption that they were used as keeps or monastic castles, in which church plate was concealed, or wherein the clergy could shelter themselves from the fury of Danes, or other invaders. But it is obvious that towers would have been built in a different fashion had such been the object of those who erected them. The late Mr. D'Alton has been the most moderate and judicious advocate of their pagan origin. He rests his theory (1) on certain statements in our annals, which, if true, must at once decide the dispute. The Annals of Ulster mention the destruction of fifty-seven of them in consequence

URN AND ITS CONTENTS FOUND IN A CROMLECH IN THE PHŒNIX PARK,
DUBLIN.

of a severe earthquake, A.D. 448. He adduces the testimony of Giraldus Cambrensis, who confirms the account of the origin of Lough Neagh by an inundation, A.D. 65, and adds : " It is no improbable testimony to this event, that the fishermen beheld the religious towers (*turres ecclesiasticas*), which, according to the custom of the country, are narrow, lofty, and round, immersed under the waters; and they frequently show them to strangers passing over them, and wondering at their purposes " (*reique causas admirantibus*). This is all the better evidence of their then acknowledged antiquity, because the subject of the writer was the formation of the lough, and not the origin of the towers. Mr. D'Alton's (2) second argument is, that it was improbable the Christians would have erected churches of wood and bell towers of stone, or have bestowed incomparably more care and skill on the erection of these towers, no matter for what use they may have been intended, than on the churches, which should surely be their first care.[1]

The cromlechs next claim our notice. There has been no question of their pagan origin ; and, indeed, this method of honouring or interring the dead, seems an almost universal custom of ancient peoples.[2] Cremation does not appear to have been the rule as to the mode of interment in ancient Erinn, as many remains of skeletons have been found ; and even those antiquarians who are pleased entirely to deny the truth of the *historical* accounts of our early annalists, accept their statements as to customs of the most ancient date. When the dead were interred without cremation, the body was placed either in a horizontal, sitting, or recumbent posture. When the remains were burned, a fictile vessel was used to contain the ashes. These urns are of various forms and sizes. The style of decoration also differs widely, some being but rudely ornamented,

[1] *Care.*—Annals of Boyle, vol. ii. p. 22. *Essay*, p. 82.

[2] *Peoples.*—See *Cities and Cemeteries of Etruria*, vol. ii. p. 314, where the writer describes tombs sunk beneath a tumulus, about twenty-five or thirty feet in diameter, and also tombs exactly resembling the Irish cromlech, the covering slab of enormous size, being inclined " apparently to carry off the rain." In his account of the geographical sites of these remains, he precisely, though most unconsciously, marks out the line of route which has been assigned by Irish annalists as that which led our early colonizers to Ireland. He says they are found in the presidency of Madras, among the mountains of the Caucasus, on the steppes of Tartary, in northern Africa, " *on the shores of the Mediterranean they are particularly abundant,*" and in Spain.

while others bear indications of artistic skill which could not have
been exercised by a rude or uncultivated people.

We give a full-page illustration of an urn and its contents, at
present in the collection of the Royal Irish Academy. This urn
was found in a tumulus, which was opened in the Phœnix Park,
near Dublin, in the year 1838. The tumulus was about 120
feet in diameter at the base, and fifteen feet high. Four sepulchral
vases, containing burnt ashes, were found within the tomb. It also
enclosed two perfect male skeletons, the tops of the femora of
another, and a bone of some animal. A number of shells[3] were
found under the head of each skeleton, of the kind known to
conchologists as the *Nerita littoralis*. The urn which we have
figured is the largest and most perfect. and manifestly the earliest of

the set. It is six inches high, rudely carved, yet not without some
attempt at ornament. The bone pin was probably used for the
hair, and the shells are obviously strung for a necklace. We give
above a specimen of the highest class of cinerary urns. It stands
unrivalled, both in design and execution, among all the specimens
found in the British isles. This valuable remain was discovered
in the cutting of a railway, in a small stone chamber, at Knockne-
conra, near Bagnalstown, county Carlow. Burned bones of an
infant, or very young child, were found in it, and it was inclosed
in a much larger and ruder urn, containing the bones of an adult.

[3] *Shells.*— Cat. Ant. R. I. A. ; Stone Mat. p. 180. The ethnographic phases
of conchology might form a study in itself. Shells appear to be the earliest
form of ornament in use. The North American Indians have their shell neck-
laces buried with them also. See Wilson's *Pre-Historic Man.*

Possibly, suggests Sir W. Wilde, they may have been the remains of mother and child.[4]

The collection of antiquities in the Royal Irish Academy, furnishes abundant evidence that the pagan Irish were well skilled in the higher arts of working in metals. If the arbitrary division of the ages of stone, bronze, and iron, can be made to hold good, we must either suppose that the Irish Celt was possessed of extraordinary mental powers, by which he developed the mechanical

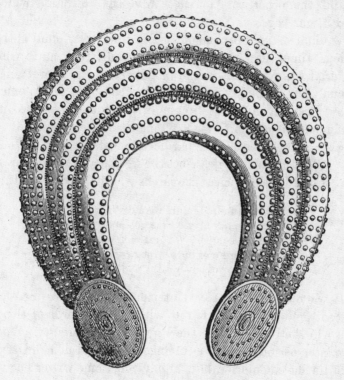

GOLD HEAD-DRESS, R.I.A.

arts gradually, or that, with successive immigrations, he obtained an increase of knowledge from exterior sources. The bardic annals indicate the latter theory. We have already given several illustra-

[4] *Child.*—Mr. Wilson gives a most interesting description of an interment of a mother and child in an ancient Peruvian grave. The mother had an unfinished piece of weaving beside her, with its colours still bright. The infant was tenderly wrapped in soft black woollen cloth, to which was fastened a pair of little sandals, 2½ inches long ; around its neck was a green cord, attached to a small shell.—*Pre-Historic Man*, vol. i. p. 234.

tions of the ruder weapons. The illustration appended here may
give some idea of the skill obtained by our pagan ancestors in
working gold. This ornament, which is quite complete, though
fractured in two places, stands 11½ inches high. It weighs 16 oz.
10 dwts. 13 grs. The gold of which it is formed is very red. It
was procured with the Sirr Collection, and is said to have been found
in the county Clare.[5] Our readers are indebted to the kindness of
the Council of the Royal Irish Academy, for the permission to depict
these and the other rare articles from the collection which are
inserted in our pages.

The amount of gold ornaments which have been found in Ireland
at various times, has occasioned much conjecture as to whether
the material was found in Ireland or imported. It is probable that
auriferous veins existed, which were worked out, or that some may
even now exist which are at present unknown. The discovery of
gold ornaments is one of the many remarkable confirmations of the
glowing accounts given by our bardic annalists of Erinn's ancient
glories. O'Hartigan thus describes the wealth and splendour of the
plate possessed by the ancient monarchs who held court at Tara :—

> " Three hundred cupbearers distributed
> Three times fifty choice goblets
> Before each party of great numbers,
> Which were of pure strong carbuncle,[6]
> Or gold or of silver all."

Dr. Petrie observes that this statement is amply verified by the
magnificent gold ornaments, found within a few yards of this very
spot, now in the possession of the Royal Irish Academy. We shall
see, at a later period, when the cursing of Tara will demand a special
notice of its ancient glories, how amply the same writer has vindi-
cated the veracity of Celtic annalists on this ground also.

A remarkable resemblance has been noticed between the pagan
military architecture of Ireland, and the early Pelasgian monuments in Greece. They consist of enclosures, generally circular,
of massive clay walls, built of small loose stones, from six to
sixteen feet thick. These forts or fortresses are usually entered by

---

[5] *Clare.*—In 1855, in digging for a railway-cutting in the county Clare,
gold ornaments were found worth £2,000 as bullion.

[6] *Carbuncle.*—This word was used to denote any shining stone of a red
colour, such as garnet, a production of the country.

a narrow doorway, wider at the bottom than at the top, and are of Cyclopean architecture. Indeed, some of the remains in Ireland can only be compared to the pyramids of Egypt, so massive are the blocks of stone used in their construction. As this stone is frequently of a kind not to be found in the immediate neighbourhood, the means used for their transportation are as much a matter of surprise and conjecture, as those by which they were placed in the position in which they are found. The most remarkable of these forts may still be seen in the Isles of Arran, on the west coast of Galway; there are others in Donegal, Mayo, and in Kerry. Some of these erections have chambers in their massive walls, and in others stairs are found round the interior of the wall; these lead to narrow platforms, varying from eight to forty-three feet in length, on which the warriors or defenders stood. The fort of Dunmohr, in the middle island of Arran, is supposed to be at least 2,000 years old. Besides these forts, there was the private house, a stone habitation, called a *clochann*, in which an individual or family resided; the large circular dome-roofed buildings, in which probably a community lived; and the rath, intrenched and stockaded.

But stone was not the only material used for places of defence or domestic dwellings; the most curious and interesting of ancient Irish habitations is the *crannoge*, a name whose precise etymology is uncertain, though there is little doubt that it refers in some way to the peculiar nature of the structure.

The crannoges were formed on small islets or shallows of clay or marl in the centre of a lake, which were probably dry in summer, but submerged in winter. These little islands, or mounds, were used as a foundation for this singular habitation. Piles of wood, or heaps of stone and bones driven into or heaped on the soil, formed the support of the crannoge. They were used as places of retreat or concealment, and are usually found near the ruins of such old forts or castles as are in the vicinity of lakes or marshes. Sometimes they are connected with the mainland by a causeway, but usually there is no appearance of any; and a small canoe has been, with but very few exceptions, discovered in or near each crannoge.

Since the investigation of these erections in Ireland, others have been discovered in the Swiss lakes of a similar kind, and containing, or rather formed on, the same extraordinary amount of bones heaped up between the wooden piles.

The peculiar objects called celts, and the weapons and domestic utensils of this or an earlier period, are a subject of scarcely less interest. The use of the celt has fairly perplexed all antiquarian research. Its name is derived not, as might be supposed, from the nation to whom this distinctive appellation was given, but from the Latin word *celtis*, a chisel. It is not known whether these celts, or the round, flat, sharp-edged chisels, were called *Lia Miledh*, "warriors' stones." In the record of the battle of the Ford of Comar, Westmeath, the use of this instrument is thus described :—

"There came not a man of Lohar's people without a broad green spear, nor without a dazzling shield, nor without a *Liagh-lamha-laich* (a champion's hand stone), stowed away in the hollow cavity of his shield . . . . And Lohar carried his stone like each of his men ; and seeing the monarch his father standing in the ford with Ceat, son of Magach, at one side, and Connall Cearnach at the other, to guard him, he grasped his battle-stone quickly and dexterously, and threw it with all his strength, and with unerring aim, at the king his father ; and the massive stone passed with a swift rotatory motion towards the king, and despite the efforts of his two brave guardians, it struck him on the breast, and laid him prostrate in the ford. The king, however, recovered from the shock, arose, and placing his foot upon the formidable stone, pressed it into the earth, where it remains to this day, with a third part of it over ground, and the print of the king's foot visible upon it."

Flint proper, or chalk flint, is found but in few places in Ireland ; these are principally in the counties of Antrim, Down, and Derry. In the absence of a knowledge of the harder metals, flint and such-like substances were invaluable as the only material that could be fashioned into weapons of defence, and used to shape such rude clothing as was then employed. The scarcity of flint must have rendered these weapons of great value in other districts. Splitting, chipping, and polishing, and this with tools as rude as the material worked on, were the only means of manufacturing such articles ; and yet such was the perfection, and, if the expression be applicable, the amount of artistic skill attained, that it seems probable flint-chipping was a special trade, and doubtless a profitable one to those engaged in it.

When flints were used as arrows, either in battle or in the chase, a bow was easily manufactured from the oak and birch trees with which the island was thickly wooded. It was bent by a leathern thong, or the twisted intestine of some animal. The handles of the lance or javelin—formidable weapons, if we may judge from the specimens in the Museum of the Royal Irish Academy—were also formed of wood; but these have perished in the lapse of ages, and left only the strangely and skilfully formed implement of destruction.

Among primitive nations, the tool and the weapon differed but little. The hatchet which served to fell the tree, was as readily used to cleave open the head of an enemy. The knife, whether of stone or hard wood, carved the hunter's prey, or gave a death-stroke to his enemy. Such weapons or implements have, however, frequently been found with metal articles, under circumstances which leave little doubt that the use of the former was continued long after the discovery of the superior value of the latter. Probably, even while the Tuatha Dé Danann artificers were framing their more refined weapons for the use of nobles and knights, the rude fashioner of flint-arrows and spear-heads still continued to exercise the craft he had learned from his forefathers, for the benefit of poorer or less fastidious warriors.

CROMLECH IN THE PHŒNIX PARK.

The urn and necklace, figured at page 154, were found in this tomb.

CLONDALKIN ROUND TOWER.

CHAPTER XI.

Pestilence of the *Blefed*—The Cursing of Tara by St. Rodanus—Extent and Importance of Ancient Tara—The First Mill in Ireland—The *Lia Fail*—Cormac's House—The Rath of the Synods—The Banqueting Hall—Chariots and Swords—St. Columba—St. Brendan and his Voyages—Pre-Columbian Discovery of America—The Plague again—St. Columba and St. Columbanus —Irish Saints and Irish Schools—Aengus the Culdee.

[A.D. 543—693.]

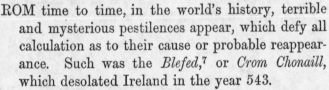

ROM time to time, in the world's history, terrible and mysterious pestilences appear, which defy all calculation as to their cause or probable reappearance. Such was the *Blefed*,[7] or *Crom Chonaill*, which desolated Ireland in the year 543.

The plague, whatever its nature may have been, appears to have been general throughout Europe. It originated in the East; and in Ireland was preceded by famine, and followed by leprosy. St. Berchan of Glasnevin and St. Finnen of Clonard were amongst its first victims.

Diarmaid, son of Fergus Keval, of the southern Hy-Nial race, was Ard-Righ during this period. In his reign Tara was cursed by St. Rodanus of Lothra, in Tipperary, in punishment for violation of sanctuary;[8] and so complete was its subse-

---

[7] *Blefed.*—The name *Crom Chonaill* indicates a sickness which produced a yellow colour in the skin.

[8] *Sanctuary.*—This may appear a severe punishment, but the right of sanctuary was in these ages the great means of protection against lawless force, and its violation was regarded as one of the worst of sacrileges.

quent desertion, that in 975 it was described as a desert overgrown with grass and weeds.

But enough still remains to give ample evidence of its former magnificence. An inspection of the site must convince the beholder of the vast extent of its ancient palaces ; nor can we, for a moment, coincide with those who are pleased to consider that these palaces consisted merely of a few planks of wood, rudely plastered over, or of hollow mounds of earth. It is true that, from an association of ideas, the cause of so many fallacies, we naturally connect " halls" with marble pavements, magnificently carved pillars, and tesselated floors ; but the harp that once resounded through Tara's halls, may have had as appreciating, if not as critical, an audience as any which now exists, and the " halls" may have been none the less stately, because their floor was strewn with sand, or the trophies which adorned them fastened to walls of oak.[9]

According to Celtic tradition, as embodied in our annals, Tara became the chief residence of the Irish kings on the first establishment of a monarchical government under Slainge :—

" Slaine of the Firbolgs was he by whom Temair was first raised."

One hundred and fifty monarchs reigned there from this period until its destruction, in 563. The *Fes*, or triennial assembly, was instituted by Ollamh Fodhla. The nature of these meetings is explained in a poem, which Keating ascribes to O'Flynn, who died A.D. 984. It is clear that what was then considered crime was punished in a very peremptory manner ; for—

> " Gold was not received as retribution from him,
> But his soul in one hour."[1]

In the reign of Tuathal a portion of land was separated from each of the four provinces, which met together at a certain place : this portion was considered a distinct part of the country from the provinces. It was situated in the present county of Meath.

In the tract separated from Munster, Tuathal[2] built the royal seat of Tlachtga, where the fire of Tlachtga was ordained to be

---

[9] *Oak.*—Dr. Petrie mentions that there were stones still at Tara which probably formed a portion of one of the original buildings. It was probably of the Pelasgian or Cyclopean kind.

[1] *Hour.*—Petrie's *Tara*, p. 31.

[2] *Tuathal.*—Very ancient authorities are found for this in the *Leabhar Gabhala*, or Book of Conquests.

kindled. On the night of All Saints, the druids assembled here to offer sacrifices, and it was established, under heavy penalties, that no fire should be kindled on that night throughout the kingdom, so that the fire which was used afterwards might be procured from it. To obtain this privilege, the people were obliged to pay a scraball, or about three-pence, yearly, to the King of Munster.

On the 1st of May a convocation was held in the royal palace of the King of Connaught. He obtained subsidies in horses and arms from those who came to this assembly. On this occasion two fires were lit, between which cattle were driven as a preventative or charm against the murrain and other pestilential distempers. From this custom the feast of St. Philip and St. James was anciently called Beltinne, or the Day of Bel's Fire.

The third palace, erected by Tuathal, was on the portion of land taken from the province of Ulster. Here the celebrated fair of Tailtean was held, and contracts of marriage were frequently made. The royal tribute was raised by exacting an ounce of silver from every couple who were contracted and married at that time. The fair of Tailtean had been instituted some years before, in honour of Tailte, who was buried here. This fair, says Keating, was then kept upon the day known in the Irish language as La Lughnasa, or the day ordained by Lughaidh, and is called in English Lammas-day.

The fourth and the most important of the royal seats was the palace of Temair, or Tara: here, with the greatest state and ceremony, the affairs of the nation were discussed and decided. On these occasions, in order to preserve the deliberations from the public, the most strict secrecy was observed, and women were entirely excluded.

The Dinnseanchus, a topographical work, compiled in the twelfth century from ancient MSS., is the principal source of information on this subject. Dr. Petrie, in his famous Essay, has given both the original and translation of this tract, and of other documents on the same subject; and he remarks how exactly the accounts given by the poet historians coincide with the remains which even now exist. In fact, each site has been ascertained with precise accuracy—an accuracy which should very much enhance our appreciation of the value of our ancient histories.

The well Neamhnach was first identified. Tradition asserts that the first mill[3] erected in Ireland was turned by the stream which flowed from it, and even at the present day a mill is still worked there. The situation of the *Rath-na-Riogh* was then easily ascertained. This is the most important of these ancient sites, but it is now, unfortunately, nearly levelled to the ground. This rath is oval, and measures about 853 feet from north to south; it contains the ruins of the *Forradh* and of *Teach Cormac* (the House of Cormac). A pillar-stone was removed in 1798 to the centre of the mound of the Forradh. It formerly stood by the side of a small mound lying within the enclosure of Rath-Riogh. This stone Dr. Petrie considers identical[4] with the famous *Lia Fail*, or Stone of Destiny, which other authorities suppose to have been removed to Scotland, and subsequently to Westminster. The *Rath-na-Riogh* is identical with Teamur, and is, in fact, *the* ancient Tara, or royal residence, around which other scarcely less important buildings were gradually erected. It was also called *Cathair Crofinn*. The name of *Cathair* was exclusively applied to circular stone fortifications built without cement; and stones still remain which probably formed a portion of the original building. In ancient Irish poems this fortification is sometimes called the Strong Tower of Teamur, an appellation never applied to a rath, but constantly to a *Cathair*, or circular stone fort.

The Rath of the Synods obtained its name at a comparatively

[3] *Mill.*—"Cormac, the grandson of Con, brought a millwright over the great sea." It is clear from the Brehon laws that mills were common in Ireland at an early period. It is probable that Cormac brought the "miller and his men" from Scotland. Whittaker shows that a water-mill was erected by the Romans at every stationary city in Roman Britain. The origin of mills is attributed to Mithridates, King of Cappadocia, about seventy years B.C. The present miller claims to be a descendant of the original miller.

[4] *Identical.*—First, "because the *Lia Fail* is spoken of by all ancient Irish writers in such a manner as to leave no doubt that it remained in its original situation at the time they wrote." Second, "because no Irish account of its removal to Scotland is found earlier than Keating, and he quotes Boetius, who obviously wished to sustain the claims of the Stuarts." The pillar-stone is composed of granular limestone, but no stone of this description is found in the vicinity. As may be supposed, there are all kinds of curious traditions about this stone. One of these asserts that it was the pillar on which Jacob reposed when he saw the vision of angels. Josephus states that the descendants of Seth invented astronomy, and that they *engraved their discoveries on a pillar of brick and a pillar of stone*. These pillars remained, in the historian's time, in the land of Siris.—*Ant. Jud.* 1. 2, § 3.

recent period. The situation is distinctly pointed out both in the prose and verse accounts. Here was held the Synod of Patrick, the Synod of Ruadhan and Brendan, and lastly, the Synod of Adamnan. The next existing monument which has been identified with certainty, is the *Teach-Miodhchuarta*, or Banqueting Hall, so famous in Irish history and bardic tradition. This was also the great house of the thousand soldiers, and the place where the *Fes* or triennial assemblies were held. It had fourteen doors— seven to the east and seven to the west. Its length, taken from the road, is 759 feet, and its breadth was probably about 90 feet. Kenneth O'Hartigan is the great, and indeed almost the only, authority for the magnificence and state with which the royal banquets were held herein. As his descriptions are written in a strain of eloquent and imaginative verse, his account has been too readily supposed to be purely fictitious. But we have already shown that his description of the gold vessels which were used, is amply corroborated by the discovery of similar articles. His account of the extent, if not of the exterior magnificence, of the building, has also been fully verified; and there remains no reason to doubt that a "thousand soldiers" may have attended their lord at his feasts, or that "three times fifty stout cooks" may have supplied the viands. There was also the "House of the Women," a term savouring strangely of eastern customs and ideas; and the "House of the Fians," or commons soldiers.

Two poems are still preserved which contain ground-plans of the different compartments of the house, showing the position allotted to different ranks and occupations, and the special portion which was to be assigned to each. The numerous distinctions of rank, and the special honours paid to the learned, are subjects worthy of particular notice. The "*saoi* of literature" and the "royal chief" are classed in the same category, and were entitled to a *primchrochait*, or steak; nor was the Irish method of cooking barbarous, for we find express mention of a spit for roasting meat, and of the skill of an artificer who contrived a machine by which thirty spits could be turned at once.[5] The five great Celtic roads[6] have already been mentioned. Indistinct traces of them are still found at Tara.

---

[5] *At once.*—See Petrie's *Tara*, p. 213.

[6] *Roads.*—See Napoleon's *Julius Cæsar*, vol. ii. p. 22, for mention of the Celtic roads in Gaul.

The *Slighe Môr* struck off from the Slope of the Chariots,[7] at the northern head of the hill, and joined the Eiscir Riada, or great Connaught road, from Dublin *via* Trim. Dr. Petrie concludes his Essay on Tara thus : "But though the houses were unquestionably. of these materials [wood and clay, with the exception of the Tuatha DéDanann Cathair], it must not be inferred that they were altogether of a barbarous structure. It is not probable that they were unlike or inferior to those of the ancient Germans, of which Tacitus speaks in terms of praise, and which he describes as being overlaid with an earth so pure and splendid, that they resembled painting." And the historian Moore, writing on the same subject, observes : "That these structures were in wood is by no means conclusive either against the elegance of their structure, or the civilization, to a certain extent, of those who erected them. It was in wood that the graceful forms of Grecian architecture first unfolded their beauties ; and there is reason to believe that, at the time when Xerxes invaded Greece, most of her temples were still of this perishable material."

But the cursing of Tara was by no means the only misfortune of Diarmaid's reign. His unaccountable hostility to St. Columba involved him in many troubles ; and, in addition to these, despite famine and pestilence, the country was afflicted with domestic wars. It is said that his war with Guaire, King of Connaught, was undertaken as a chastisement for an injustice committed by that monarch, who, according to an old chronicle, had deprived a woman, who had vowed herself to a religious life, of a cow, which was her only means of support. It is more probable, however, that the motive was not quite so chivalric, and that extortion of a tribute to which he had no right was the real cause. The high character for probity unanimously attributed to Guaire, makes it extremely unlikely that he should have committed any deliberate act of injustice.

The first great convention of the Irish states, after the abandonment of Tara, was held in Drumceat, in 573, in the reign of Hugh, son of Ainmire. St. Columba and the leading members of the Irish

---

[7] *Chariots.*—St. Patrick visited most parts of Ireland in a chariot, according to the Tripartite Life. *Carbad* or chariots are mentioned in the oldest Celtic tales and romances, and it is distinctly stated in the life of St. Patrick preserved in the Book of Armagh, that the pagan Irish had chariots. Different kinds of roads are expressly mentioned, and also the duty of road-mending, and those upon whom this duty devolved. See Introduction to the Book of Rights, p. 56.

clergy attended. Precedence was given to the saint by the prelates of North Britain, to honour his capacity of apostle or founder of the Church in that country.

Two important subjects were discussed on this occasion, and on each the opinion of St. Columba was accepted as definitive. The first referred to the long-vexed question whether the Scottish colony of Alba should still be considered dependent on the mother country. The saint, foreseeing the annoyances to which a continuance of this dependence must give rise, advised that it should be henceforth respected as an independent state. The second question was one of less importance in the abstract, but far more difficult to settle satisfactorily. The bards, or more probably persons who wished to enjoy their immunities and privileges without submitting to the ancient laws which obliged them to undergo a long and severe course of study before becoming licentiates, if we may use the expression, of that honorable calling, had become so numerous and troublesome, that loud demands were made for their entire suppression. The king, who probably suffered from their insolence as much as any of his subjects, was inclined to comply with the popular wish, but yielded so far to the representations of St. Columba, as merely to diminish their numbers, and place them under stricter rules.

Hugh Ainmire was killed while endeavouring to exact the Boromean Tribute. The place of his death was called Dunbolg, or the Fort of the Bags. The Leinster king, Bran Dubh, had recourse to a stratagem, from whence the name was derived. Finding himself unable to cope with the powerful army of his opponent, he entered his camp disguised as a leper, and spread a report that the Leinster men were preparing to submit.

In the evening a number of bullocks, laden with leathern bags, were seen approaching the royal camp. The drivers, when challenged by the sentinels, said that they were bringing provisions; and this so tallied with the leper's tale, that they were permitted to deposit their burdens without further inquiry. In the night, however, an armed man sprang from each bag, and headed by their king, whose disguise was no longer needed, slaughtered the royal army without mercy, Hugh himself falling a victim to the personal bravery of Bran Dubh.

The deaths of several Irish saints, whose lives are of more than ordinary interest, are recorded about this period. Amongst them,

St. Brendan of Clonfert demands more than a passing notice. His early youth was passed under the care of St. Ita, a lady of the princely family of the Desii. By divine command she established the Convent of *Cluain Credhuil*, in the present county of Limerick, and there, it would appear, she devoted herself specially to the care of youth. When Brendan had attained his fifth year, he was placed under the protection of Bishop Ercus, from whom he received such instruction as befitted his advancing years. But Brendan's tenderest affection clung to the gentle nurse of his infancy; and to her, in after years, he frequently returned, to give or receive counsel and sympathy.

The legend of his western voyage, if not the most important, is at least the most interesting part of his history. Kerry was the native home of the enterprising saint; and as he stood on its bold and beautiful shores, his naturally contemplative mind was led to inquire what boundaries chained that vast ocean, whose grand waters rolled in mighty waves beneath his feet. His thoughtful piety suggested that where there might be a country there might be life—human life and human souls dying day by day, and hour by hour, and knowing of no other existence than that which at best is full of sadness and decay.

Traditions of a far-away land had long existed on the western coast of ancient Erinn. The brave Tuatha Dé Dananns were singularly expert in naval affairs, and their descendants were by no means unwilling to impart information to the saint.

The venerable St. Enda, the first Abbot of Arran, was then living, and thither St. Brendan journeyed for counsel. Probably he was encouraged in his design by the holy abbot; for he proceeded along the coast of Mayo, inquiring as he went for traditions of the western continent. On his return to Kerry, he decided to set out on the important expedition. St. Brendan's Hill still bears his name; and from the bay at the foot of this lofty eminence he sailed for the " far west." Directing his course towards the south-west, with a few faithful companions, in a well-provisioned bark, he came, after some rough and dangerous navigation, to calm seas, where, without aid of oar or sail, he was borne along for many weeks. It is probable that he had entered the great Gulf Stream, which brought his vessel ashore somewhere on the Virginian coasts. He landed with his companions, and penetrated into the interior, until he came to a large river flowing from east to west, supposed to be that now known as the Ohio. Here, according to the legend, he was accosted by a man of venerable bearing, who told him that he had gone far enough ; that further discoveries were reserved for other men, who would in due time come and christianize that pleasant land.

After an absence of seven years, the saint returned once more to Ireland, and lived not only to tell of the marvels he had seen, but even to found a college of three thousand monks at Clonfert. This voyage took place in the year 545, according to Colgan ; but as St. Brendan must have been at that time at least sixty years old, an earlier date has been suggested as more probable.[8]

The northern and southern Hy-Nials had long held rule in Ireland ; but while the northern tribe were ever distinguished, not only for their valour, but for their chivalry in field or court, the southern race fell daily lower in the estimation of their countrymen. Their disgrace was completed when two kings, who ruled Erinn jointly, were treacherously slain by Conall Guthvin. For this crime the family were excluded from regal honours for several generations.

Home dissensions led to fatal appeals for foreign aid, and this frequently from the oppressing party. Thus, Congal Caech, who killed the reigning sovereign in 623, fled to Britain, and after

---

[8] *Probable.*—The legend of St. Brendan was widely diffused in the Middle Ages. In the *Bibliothéque Impériale*, at Paris, there are no less than eleven MSS. of the original Latin legend, the dates of which vary from the eleventh to the fourteenth century. In the old French and Romance dialects there are abundant copies in most public libraries in France ; while versions in Irish, Dutch, German, Italian, Spanish, and Portuguese, abound in all parts of the Continent. Traces of ante-Columbian voyages to America are continually cropping up. But the appearance, in 1837, of the *Antiquitates Americanæ sive ita Scriptores Septentrionales rerum ante-Columbiarum*, in America, edited by Professor Rafu, at Copenhagen, has given final and conclusive evidence on this interesting subject. America owes its name to an accidental landing. Nor is it at all improbable that the Phœnicians, in their voyage across the stormy Bay of Biscay, or the wild Gulf of Guinea, may have been driven far out of their course to western lands. Even in 1833 a Japanese junk was wrecked upon the coast of Oregon. Humboldt believes that the Canary Isles were known, not only to the Phœnicians, but " perhaps even to the Etruscans." There is a map in the Library of St. Mark, at Venice, made in the year 1436, where an island is delineated and named Antillia. See Trans. R.I.A. vol. xiv. A distinguished modern poet of Ireland has made the voyage of St. Brendan the subject of one of the most beautiful of his poems.

remaining there nine years, returned with foreign troops, by whose assistance he hoped to attain the honours unlawfully coveted. The famous battle of Magh-Rath,[9] in which the auxiliaries were utterly routed, and the false Congal slain, unfortunately did not deter his countrymen from again and again attempting the same suicidal course.

In 656 the country was once more visited by the fatal *Crom Chonaill*, and again holy prelates and sainted religious were foremost amongst its victims. Many orphans were of necessity thrown on the mercy of those to whom charity was their only claim. Nor was the call unheeded. The venerable Bishop of Ardbraccan, St. Ultan, whom we may perhaps term the St. Vincent of Ireland, gathered these hapless little ones into a safe asylum, and there, with a thoughtfulness which in such an age could scarcely have been expected, sought to supply by artificial means for the natural nourishment of which they had been deprived.

Venerable Bede mentions this pestilence, and gives honorable testimony to the charity of the Irish, not only to their own people, but even to strangers. He says : " This pestilence did no less harm in the island of Ireland. Many of the nobility and of the lower ranks of the English nation were there at that time, who, in the days of Bishop Finan and Colman, forsaking their native land, retired thither, either for the sake of divine studies, or for a more continent life. The Scots willingly received them all, and took care to supply them with food, as also to furnish them with books to read and their teaching gratis."[1]

In 673 Finnachta Fleadhach, or the Hospitable, began his reign. He yielded to the entreaties of St. Moling, and remitted the Boromean Tribute, after he had forced it from the Leinster men in a bloody battle. In 687 he abdicated, and showed his respect for religion still further by embracing the monastic state himself. In 684 the Irish coasts were devastated, and even the churches pillaged, by the soldiers of Egfrid, the Saxon King of Northumbria. Venerable Bede attributes his subsequent defeat and death, when fighting against the Picts, to the judgment of God, justly merited

---

[9] *Magh-Rath.*—Now Moira, in the county Down. The Chronicum Scotorum gives the date 636, and the Annals of Tighernach at 637, which Dr. O'Donovan considers to be the true date.

[1] *Gratis.*—Ven. Bede, cap. xxviii.

by these unprovoked outrages on a nation which had always been most friendly to the English (*nationi Anglorum semper amicissimam*).

It has been supposed that revenge may have influenced Egfrid's conduct: this, however, does not make it more justifiable in a Christian king. Ireland was not merely the refuge of men of learning in that age; it afforded shelter to more than one prince driven unjustly from his paternal home. Alfred, the brother of the Northumbrian monarch, had fled thither from his treachery, and found a generous welcome on its ever-hospitable shores. He succeeded his brother in the royal dignity; and when St. Adamnan visited his court to obtain the release of the Irish captives whom Egfrid's troops had torn from their native land, he received him with the utmost kindness, and at once acceded to his request.

St. Adamnan, whose fame as the biographer of St. Columba has added even more to the lustre of his name than his long and saintly rule over the Monastery of Iona, was of the race of the northern Hy-Nials. He was born in the territory of Tir-Connell, about the year 627. Little is known of his early history; it is generally supposed that he was educated at Iona, and that, having embraced the monastic rule, he returned to his own country to extend its observance there. He presided over the great Abbey of Raphoe, of which he was the founder, until the year 679, when he was raised to the government of his order, and from that period he usually resided at Iona. The fact of his having been chosen to such an important office, is a sufficient testimony to his virtues, and of the veneration and respect in which he was held by his contemporaries.

St. Adamnan paid more than one visit to his friend the Northumbrian monarch (*regem Alfridem amicum*). On the second occasion he went with the Abbot Ceolfrid, and after some conversation with him and other learned ecclesiastics, he adopted the Roman paschal computation. Yet, with all his influence and eloquence, he was unable to induce his monks to accept it; and it was not until the year 716 that they yielded to the persuasions of Egbert, a Northumbrian monk. Adamnan was more successful in his own country In 697 he visited Ireland, and took an important part in a legislative council held at Tara. On this occasion he procured the enactment of a law, which was called the Canon of Adamnan, or the Law of the Innocents, and sometimes "the law not to kill women." We have already referred to the martial tendencies of the ladies of ancient Erinn—a tendency, however, which was by no means peculiar at that period of the world's history. The propensity for military engagements was not confined to queens and princesses—women of all ranks usually followed their lords to the field of battle; but as the former are generally represented as having fallen victims to each other's prowess in the fight, it appears probable that they had their own separate line of battle, or perhaps fought out the field in a common *mêlée* of feminine forces.

Had we not the abundant testimony of foreign writers to prove the influence and importance of the missions undertaken by Irish saints at this period of her history, it might be supposed that the statements of her annalists were tinged with that poetic fancy in which she has ever been so singularly prolific, and that they rather wrote of what might have been than of what was. But the testimony of Venerable Bede (to go no further) is most ample on this subject.

Irish missionary zeal was inaugurated in the person of St. Columba, although its extension to continental Europe was commenced by another, who, from similarity of name, has been frequently confounded with the national apostle.

St. Columbanus was born about the year 539. The care of his education was confided to the venerable Senile, who was eminent for his sanctity and knowledge of the Holy Scriptures. It was probably through his influence that the young man resolved to devote himself to the monastic life. For this purpose he placed himself under the direction of St. Comgall, who then governed the great Monastery of Bangor (Banchorr).

It was not until he entered his fiftieth year that he decided on quitting his native land, so that there can be no reason to doubt that his high intellectual attainments were acquired and perfected in Ireland.

With the blessing of his superior, and the companionship of twelve faithful monks, he set forth on his arduous mission; and arduous truly it proved to be. The half-barbarous Franks, then ruled by Thierry or Theodoric, lived more a pagan than a Christian life, and could ill brook the stern lessons of morality which they heard from, and saw practised by, their new teacher. The saint did not spare the demoralized court, and the Queen-Dowager Brunehalt became his bitterest foe. He had already established two monasteries: one at Luxovium, or Luxeuil, in a forest at the foot of the Vosges; the other, on account of its numerous springs, was called Ad-fontanas (Fontaines). Here the strict discipline of the Irish monks was rigidly observed, and the coarsest fare the only refection permitted to the religious.

For a time they were allowed to continue their daily routine of prayer and penance without molestation; but the relentless Brunehalt, who, from the basest motives, had encouraged the young king in every vice, could no longer brave either the silent preaching of the cloister or the bold denunciations of the saint. As Columbanus found that his distant remonstrances had no effect on the misguided monarch, for whose eternal welfare he felt the deep interest of true sanctity, he determined to try a personal interview. For a brief space his admonitions were heard with respect, and even the haughty queen seemed less bent on her career of impiety and deceit; but the apparent conversion passed away as a summer breeze, and once more the saint denounced and threatened in vain.

Strict enclosure had been established in the monasteries professing the Columbanian rule;[2] and this afforded a pretext for the royal vengeance. Theodoric attempted to violate the sanctuary in person; but though he was surrounded by soldiers, he had to encounter one whose powers were of another and more invincible character. The saint remained in the sanctuary, and when the king approached addressed him sternly:

"If thou, sire," he exclaimed, "art come hither to violate the discipline already established, or to destroy the dwellings of the servants of God, know that in heaven there is a just and avenging power; thy kingdom shall be taken from thee, and both thou and thy royal race shall be cut off and destroyed on the earth."

The undaunted bearing of Columbanus, and, perhaps, some lingering light of conscience, not yet altogether extinguished, had its effect upon the angry monarch. He withdrew; but he left to others the task he dared not attempt in person. The saint was compelled by armed men to leave his monastery, and only his Irish and British subjects were permitted to bear him company. They

---

[2] *Rule.*—"The light which St. Columbanus disseminated, by his knowledge and doctrine, wherever he presented himself, caused a contemporary writer to compare him to the sun in his course from east to west; and he continued after his death to shine forth in numerous disciples whom he had trained in learning and piety."—*Benedictine Hist. Litt. de la France.*

departed in deep grief, not for the cruel treatment they suffered, but for their brethren from whom they were thus rudely torn. As the monks who were left behind clung weeping to their father, he consoled them with these memorable words : " God will be to you a Father, and reward you with mansions where the workers of sacrilege can never enter."

Nantes was the destination of the exiled religious. Here they were put on board a vessel bound for Ireland ; but scarcely had they reached the open sea, when a violent storm arose, by which the vessel was driven back and stranded on the shore, where it lay all night. The captain attributed the misfortune to his travelling companions, and refused to carry them any farther. Columbanus, perceiving in this accident an indication of the will of heaven in their regard, determined to seek a settlement in some other part of the Continent. In the third year after his expulsion from Luxeuil, he arrived at Milan, where he was hospitably received by the Lombard king, A.D. 612. On his journey thither he had evangelized Austrasia, then governed by Theodebert. This prince, though a brother of the monarch by whom he had been expelled, entertained him with the utmost courtesy. At Mentz, the bishop vainly endeavoured to detain him. Zeal for the conversion of souls led the saint to desire a less cultivated field of labour. As he passed along the Lake of Zurich, and in the Canton of Zug, he reaped a rich harvest; from thence he directed his course to Bregentz, then inhabited by an idolatrous people.

Here he was repulsed by those who most needed his apostolic labours; but, undaunted, he retired to the neighbouring county, where he secured a band of zealous converts. Surrounded by these, and attended by his faithful monks, he once more entered the idolatrous city, and proceeded boldly to the temple where their false gods were enshrined. Here he invoked the Holy Name, and by its power the idols were miraculously overthrown, and a multitude of the people were converted, including in their number some of the principal inhabitants of Bregentz.

The theological controversy, known as that of the " Three Chapters," was now prevalent in northern Italy. A letter is still extant which St. Columbanus addressed to Pope Boniface on this subject, in which, while he uses the privilege of free discussion on questions not defined by the Church, he is remarkably, and perhaps for some inconveniently, explicit as to his belief in papal supremacy. A brief

extract from this important document will show that the faith for
which Ireland has suffered, and still suffers so much, was the same
in the "early ages" as it is now. He writes thus to the Holy
Father :—

"For we Irish [Scoti] are disciples of St. Peter and St. Paul, and
of all the divinely inspired canonical writers, adhering constantly
to the evangelical and apostolical doctrine. Amongst us neither
Jew, heretic, nor schismatic can be found ; but the Catholic faith,
entire and unshaken, precisely as we have received it from you,
who are the successors of the holy Apostles. For, as I have already
said, we are attached to the chair of St. Peter ; and although Rome
is great and renowned, yet with us it is great and distinguished
only on account of that apostolic chair. Through the two Apostles
of Christ you are almost celestial, and Rome is the head of the
churches of the world."[3]

In the year 613 St. Columbanus founded the world-famed Monastery of Bovium, or Bobbio,[4] in a magnificently romantic site on
the Apennines. Near his church was an oratory dedicated to the
Mother of God, who, as we shall presently see, was as devoutly
worshipped in ancient as in modern Erinn.

Agilulph, the Lombardian monarch, was ever a warm patron of
the monks. Clothaire had now ascended the French throne. He
earnestly pressed the saint to return to Luxeuil, but Columbanus
excused himself on the plea of age and infirmities. He did not fail,

---

[3] *World.*—See Herring's *Collectanea* and the *Bibliotheca Patrum*, tom. xii.

[4] *Bobbio.*—My learned friend, the Rev. J. P. Gaffney, of Clontarf, has in his
possession a printed copy of the celebrated *Bobbio Missal*. It is contained in a
work entitled "MUSEUM ITALICUM, seu collectio Veterum Scriptorum ex Biblio-
thesis Italicis," eruta a D. J. Mabillon et D. M. Germain, presbyteris et mona-
chis, Benedictinæ, Cong. S. Mauré. This work was published at Paris in 1687.
The original Missal was discovered by Mabillon two hundred years ago, and is
at present preserved in the Ambrosian Library at Milan. It dates from the
seventh century, and is no doubt the identical Missal or Mass-book used by the
saint. As my friend has allowed me to retain the treasure for a time, I intend
to give full details on the subject in my Ecclesiastical History. For further
information at present, I refer the reader to the Rev. J. P. Gaffney's *Religion of the Ancient Irish Church* p. 43, and to Dr. Moran's learned *Essays*,
p. 287. I especially request the superiors of religious orders to afford me
any information in their possession concerning the history of their respective
orders in Ireland, and also of their several houses. Details of re-erections of
religious houses on old sites are particularly desired. All books or documents
which may be forwarded to me shall be carefully returned.

however, to send advice for the government of the monasteries which he had founded, where his rule had continued to be observed with the utmost fervour.

St. Columbanus died at Bobbio, on the 21st of November, 615, at the age of seventy-two years. His name is still preserved in the town of St. Columbano. His memory has been ever venerated in France and Italy.

While the saint was evangelizing in Switzerland, one of his disciples became seriously ill, and was unable to travel farther. It was a providential sickness for the Helvetians. The monk was an eloquent preacher, and well acquainted with their language, which was a dialect of that of the Franks. He evangelized the country, and the town of St. Gall still bears the name of the holy Irishman, while his abbey contains many precious relics of the literature and piety of his native land. St. Gall died on the 16th October, 645, at a very advanced age. The monastery was not erected until after his decease, and it was not till the year 1798 that the abbey lands were aggregated to the Swiss Confederation as one of the cantons.

Another Irish saint, who evangelized in France, was St. Fiacre. He erected a monastery to the Blessed Virgin in a forest near Meaux. The fame of his sanctity became so great, and the pilgrimage to his tomb so popular, that the French hackney coaches (*fiacre*) obtained their name from their constant employment in journeys to his shrine.

About the same period, St. Fursey founded a monastery near Burgh Castle, in Suffolk, where he was kindly received by Sigbert, King of the East Angles. From thence he proceeded to Lagny, in France, where his missionary zeal was long remembered. His brothers, St. Foillan and St. Altan, were his constant companions. St. Fursey died on the 16th January, 650, at Macerius. His remains were subsequently translated to Peronne, in Picardy. The evangelic labours of many of his Irish disciples, are matter of history in the Gallic Church. It is said that the fame of the Irish for their skill in music, was so well known on the Continent at this period, that St. Gertrude, daughter of King Pepin, and Abbess of Nivelle, in Brabant, invited the brothers of St. Fursey to instruct her community in sacred music. They complied with her request, and soon after erected a monastery at Fosse, near Nivelle. Nor were the Scoti without their missionary martyrs, amongst whom the great St. Kilian holds a distinguished place. The spirit of devotion to

the Holy See seems almost to be an heirloom in the little island
of the western sea.   True to the instincts of his native land, the
martyr-saint would not undertake his mission in Franconia, great
as was its necessity, until he knelt at the feet of the Vicar of Christ
to obtain his permission and blessing.   Thus fortified, he commenced his glorious race, so happily crowned with the martyr's
palm.   His bold rebuke of the open scandal given by the conduct
of the ruling prince, was the immediate cause of his obtaining this
favour.   St. Kilian was assassinated at midnight, while singing the
Divine Office, with two of his faithful companions.   Their remains
were interred in the church of Wurtzberg, where St. Kilian is still
revered as its patron and apostle.

We can but name St. Mailduf, from whom Malmsbury has been
named ; St. Livin, who converted the inhabitants of Flanders and
Brabant ; St. Cataldus and his brother, St. Donatus, the former
patron of the metropolitan see of Tarentum, and whose name is
still preserved in the little town of *San Cataldo*, the latter Bishop
of Lecce, in the kingdom of Naples, and both famous for miracles
and sanctity of life ; St. Virgilius, called in the ancient annals
" Ferghil the Geometer," and by Latin writers Solivagus,[5] or the
" solitary wanderer," who died Bishop of Saltzburg, distinguished
for literary fame ; St. Fridolin, " the traveller," son of an Irish
king, who evangelized Thuringia, and was appointed by the Pope
Bishop of Buraburgh, near Fritzlar, in the year 741 ; St. Sedulius
the younger, who wrote commentaries on Holy Scripture, and assisted at a council held in Rome, in the year 721, under Gregory II.
It is noticeable that this saint was consecrated Bishop of Oreto,
in Spain, while in Rome.   When he entered on the mission thus
confided to him, he wrote a treatise to prove that, being Irish,
he was of Spanish descent ; thus showing that at this period the
idea of a Milesian origin was common to men of learning in
Ireland.[6]

But if Ireland gave saints and martyrs to foreign lands, her
charity was in some measure repaid in kind.   True, she needed not
the evangelic labours of other missionaries, for the gospel-seed had
taken deep root, and borne a rich harvest on her happy shores ;

<hr/>

[5] *Solivagus.*—Four Masters, p. 391.

[6] *Ireland.*—The elder Sedulius, whose hymns are even now used by the
Church, lived in the fifth century.   The hymn, *A solis ortis cardine*, and
many others, are attributed to him.

still, as the prayers of saints are the very life and joy of the Church, she could not choose but rejoice in the hundreds of pure and saintly soulswho gathered round her altars at home, who crowded her monasteries, or listened devoutly to the teachers of her distinguished schools. In the Litany of Aengus the Culdee[7] we find hundreds of foreign saints invoked, each grouped according to their nation. "The oldest tract, or collection of the pedigrees of the saints of Erinn," says Professor O'Curry, "of which we have now any recognizable copy remaining, is that which is ascribed to Aengus Ceilé Dé, commonly called Aengus the Culdee. The genuineness of this composition is admitted by all writers of modern times, Protestant and Catholic, by Usher and Ware as well as by Colgan."

Aengus wrote about the year 798. He was descended from the illustrious chieftains of Dalriada, and completed his education in the Monastery of Cluain Eidhneach, in the present Queen's county. The remains of a church he founded at Disert Aengusa, near Ballingarry, in the county of Limerick, may still be seen.

The Monastery of Tamhlacht (Tallaght), near Dublin, was founded in the year 769, by St. Maelruain, on a site offered "to God, to Michael the Archangel, and to Maelruain," by Donnach, the pious and illustrious King of Leinster. St. Aengus presented himself at this monastery as a poor man seeking for service, and was employed for some time in charge of the mill or kiln, the ruins of which have but lately yielded to "the improving hand of modern progress." Here he remained hidden for many years, until, by some happy accident, his humility and his learning were at once discovered.

Aengus composed his "Festology" in the reign of Hugh Oirdnidhe (the Legislator), who was Monarch of Ireland from the year 793 to the year 817. Hugh commenced his reign by attaching the province of Leinster, and then marched to the confines of Meath.

---

[7] *Culdee.*—There was much dispute at one time as to the origin and true character of the Culdees. The question, however, has been quite set at rest by the researches of recent Irish scholars. Professor O'Curry traces them up to the time of St. Patrick. He thinks they were originally mendicant monks, and that they had no communities until the end of the eighth century, when St. Maelruain of Tallaght drew up a rule for them. This rule is still extant. Mr. Haverty (*Irish History*, p. 110) has well observed, they probably resembled the Tertiaries, or Third Orders, which belong to the Orders of St. Dominic and St. Francis at the present day. See also Dr. Reeves' *Life of St. Columba*, for some clear and valuable remarks on this subject.

The Archbishop of Armagh and all his clergy were commanded to attend this expedition, for such had hitherto been the custom. The ecclesiastics, however, protested against the summons, and complained to the king of the injustice and inconsistency of demanding their presence on such occasions. Hugh referred the matter to Fothadh, his poet and adviser. The learning and piety of the bard were well known; and a decision favourable to the clergy was the result. This decision was given in a short poem of four quatrains, which is preserved in the preface to the "Martyrology" of Aengus. The following is a literal translation :—

> "The Church of the living God,
> Touch her not, nor waste;
> Let her rights be reserved,
> As best ever they were.

> "Every true monk who is
> Possessed of a pious conscience,
> To the church to which it is due
> Let him act as any servant.

> "Every faithful servant from that out,
> Who is not bound by vows of obedience,
> Has liberty to join in the battles
> Of Aedh (Hugh) the Great, son of Nial.

> "This is the proper rule,
> Certain it is not more, not less :
> Let every one serve his lot,
> Without defect, and without refusal."

This decision obtained the name of a canon, and henceforth its author was distinguished as *Fothadh na Canoiné,* or Fothadh of the Canons.

At the time of the promulgation of this canon, Aengus was residing at his church of Disert Bethech, near the present town of Monasterevan, not far from where the Irish monarch had pitched his camp.

The poet visited Aengus, and showed him the canon before presenting it to the king. An intimacy was thus commenced, which must have proved one of singular pleasure to both parties. Aengus hadjust finished his "Festology," and showed it for the first time to his brother poet, who expressed the warmest approbation of the work.

This composition consists of three parts. The first part is a poem of five quatrains, invoking the grace and sanctification of Christ for the poet and his undertaking :—

> "Sanctify, O Christ ! my words :
> O Lord of the seven heavens !
> Grant me the gift of wisdom,
> O Sovereign of the bright sun !

> " O bright Sun, who dost illuminate
> The heavens with all Thy holiness !
> O King, who governest the angels !
> O Lord of all the people !

> "O Lord of the people !
> O King, all righteous and good !
> May I receive the full benefit
> Of praising Thy royal hosts.

> " Thy royal hosts I praise,
> Because Thou art my sovereign ;
> I have disposed my mind
> To be constantly beseeching Thee.

> "I beseech a favour from Thee,
> That I be purified from my sins,
> Through the peaceful bright-shining flock,
> The royal host whom I celebrate."

Then follows a metrical preface, consisting of eighty stanzas. These verses are in the same measure[8] as the invocation, Englished by modern Gaedhilic scholars as " chain-verse ;" that is, an arrangement of metre by which the first words of every succeeding quatrain are identical with the last words of the preceding one.

[8] *Measure.*—The subject of Irish poetical composition would demand a considerable space if thoroughly entertained. Zeuss has done admirable justice to the subject in his *Grammatica Celtica*, where he shows that the word rhyme [*rimum*] is of Irish origin. The Very Rev. U. Burke has also devoted some pages to this interesting investigation, in his *College Irish Grammar*. He observes that the phonetic framework in which the poetry of a people is usually fashioned, differs in each of the great national families, even as their language and genius differ. He also shows that the earliest Latin ecclesiastical poets were Irish, and formed their hymns upon the rules of Irish versification ; thus quite controverting the theory that rhyme was introduced by the Saracens in the ninth century.

After the invocation follows a preface, the second part of this remarkable poem.   In this there is a glowing account of the tortures
and sufferings of the early Christian martyrs ; it tells " how the
names of the persecutors are forgotten, while the names of their
victims are remembered with honour, veneration, and affection ;
how Pilate's wife is forgotten, while the Blessed Virgin Mary is
remembered and honoured from the uttermost bounds of the earth
to its centre."   The martyrology proper, or festology, comes next,
and consists of 365 quatrains, or a stanza for each day in the
year.

It commences with the feast of the Circumcision :—

> " At the head of the congregated saints
> Let the King take the front place ;
> Unto the noble dispensation did submit
> Christ—on the kalends of January."

St. Patrick is commemorated thus, on the 17th of March :—

> " The blaze of a splendid sun,
> The apostle of stainless Erinn,
> Patrick, with his countless thousands,
> May he shelter our wretchedness."

On the 13th of April, Bishop Tussach, one of the favourite companions of the great saint, is also mentioned as—

> " The kingly bishop Tussach,
> Who administered, on his arrival,
> The Body of Christ, the truly powerful King,
> And the Communion to Patrick."

It will be remembered it was from this saint that the great
apostle received the holy viaticum.   In the third division of his
great work, Aengus explains its use, and directs the people how to
read it.

It will be manifest from these poems that the religious principles
of the Culdees and of the Irish ecclesiastics generally, were those of
the Universal Church at this period.   We find the rights of the
Church respected and advocated ; the monarchs submitting to the
decision of the clergy ; invocation of the saints ; the practice of
administering the holy viaticum ; and the commemoration of the
saints on the days devoted to their honour.

Usher observes, that the saints of this period might be grouped into a fourth order.[9] Bede says : " That many of the Scots [Irish] came daily into Britain, and with great devotion preached the word and administered baptism. . . . . . The English, great and small, were by their Scottish [Irish] masters instructed in the rules and observances of regular discipline."[1] Eric of Auxerre writes thus to Charles the Bald : " What shall I say of Ireland, which, despising the dangers of the deep, is migrating with her whole train of philosophers to our coast ?" Rency, after describing the poetry and literature of ancient Erinn as perhaps the most cultivated of all Western Europe, adds, that Ireland " counted a host of saints and learned men, venerated in England[2] and Gaul ; for no country had furnished more Christian missionaries." It is said that three thousand students, collected from all parts of Europe, attended the schools of Armagh ; and, indeed, the regulations which were made for preserving scholastic discipline, are almost sufficient evidence on this subject.

The discussions of the Irish and English ecclesiastics on the time of keeping of Easter, with their subsequent decision, and all details concerning domestic regulations as to succession to office and church lands, are more properly matters for elucidation in a Church History, for which we reserve their consideration.

[9] *Order.*—This refers to the vision in which St. Patrick is said to have seen three orders of saints, who should succeed each other in Ireland.

[1] *Discipline.*—Bede, lib. iii. cap. 3. We have used Bohn's translation, as above all suspicion.

[2] *England.*—Camden says : " At that age the Anglo-Saxons repaired on all sides to Ireland as to a general mart of learning, whence we read, in our writers, of holy men, that they went to study in Ireland"—*Amandatus est ad disciplinam in Hiberniam.*

ANCIENT ADZE, FROM THE COLLECTION OF THE ROYAL IRISH ACADEMY.

CROSS AT FINGLAS.

CHAPTER XII.

Christianity improves the Social State of Ireland—A Saxon Invasion of Ireland—Domestic Wars—The English come to Ireland for Instruction—A Famine and Tempests—The First Danish Invasion—Cruelty of the Danes—The Black and White Gentiles—King Cormac Mac Cullinan—Cashel—Amlaff the Dane—Plunder of the Towns—Arrival of Sitric—Death of Nial Glundubh—The Circuit of Ireland—Malachy the Second—Entries in the Annals.

[A.D. 693—926.]

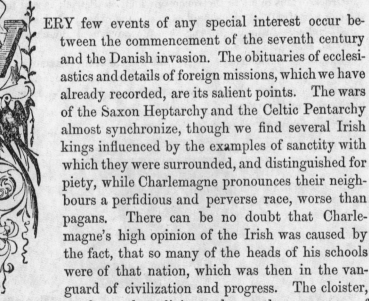

ERY few events of any special interest occur between the commencement of the seventh century and the Danish invasion. The obituaries of ecclesiastics and details of foreign missions, which we have already recorded, are its salient points. The wars of the Saxon Heptarchy and the Celtic Pentarchy almost synchronize, though we find several Irish kings influenced by the examples of sanctity with which they were surrounded, and distinguished for piety, while Charlemagne pronounces their neighbours a perfidious and perverse race, worse than pagans. There can be no doubt that Charlemagne's high opinion of the Irish was caused by the fact, that so many of the heads of his schools were of that nation, which was then in the vanguard of civilization and progress. The cloister, always the nursery of art, the religious, always the promoters of learning, were pre-eminent in this age for their devotion to literary pursuits. In the present work it is impossible to give details of their MSS. still preserved, of their wonderful skill in caligraphy, still the admiration of the most gifted, and of the perfection to which they brought the science of music; but I turn from this attractive subject with less regret, from the hope of being soon able to produce an Ecclesiastical History of Ireland, in which such details will find their proper place, and will be amply expanded.[3] The revolution of social feeling which was effected in Ireland by the introduction of Christianity, is strongly marked. Before the advent of St. Patrick, few Irish monarchs died a natural death—ambition or treachery proved a sufficient motive for murder and assassination; while of six kings who reigned during the eighth and ninth centuries, only one died a violent death, and that death was an exception, which evidently proved the rule, for Nial was drowned in a generous effort to save the life of one of his own servants.

The fatal pestilence, already recorded, did not appear again after its severe visitation, which terminated in 667. In 693 Finnachta Fleadhach (the Hospitable) commenced his reign. He remitted the Boromean Tribute at the request of St. Moling, and eventually abdicated, and embraced a religious life. In the year 684, Egfrid, the Saxon King of Northumberland, sent an army to Ireland, which spared neither churches nor monasteries, and carried off a great number of the inhabitants as slaves. Bede denounces and laments this barbarous invasion, attributing the defeat and death of King Egfrid, which took place in the following year, to the vengeance of heaven.[4] St. Adamnan was sent to Northumbria, after the death of this prince, to obtain the release of the captives. His mission was successful, and he was honoured there as the worker of many miracles.

[3] *Expanded.*—I take this opportunity of requesting from laymen or ecclesiastics who may read this announcement, the favour of any information they may consider valuable.

[4] *Heaven.*—*Ec. Hist.* lib. iv. c. 26. " From that time the hopes and strength of the English crown began to waver and retrograde, for the Picts recovered their own lands," &c. The Annals of the Four Masters mention a mortality among cattle throughout the whole world, and a severe frost, which followed this invasion : "The sea between Ireland and Scotland was frozen, so that there was a communication between them on the ice."—vol. ii. p. 291. They also mention the mission of Adamnan to " Saxon land."

The generosity of Finnachta failed in settling the vexed question
of tribute.   Comgal, who died in 708, ravaged Leinster as fiercely
as his predecessors, and Fearghal, his successor, invaded it " five
times in one year."   Three wonderful showers are said to have
fallen in the eighth year of his reign (A.D. 716 according to the
Four Masters)—a shower of silver, a shower of honey, and a shower
of blood.   These were, of course, considered portents of the awful
Danish invasions.   Fearghal was killed at the battle of Almhain
(Allen, near Kildare), in 718.   In this engagement, the Leinster
men only numbered nine thousand, while their opponents numbered twenty-one thousand.   The Leinster men, however, made up
for numbers by their valour ; and it is said that the intervention
of a hermit, who reproached Fearghal with breaking the pacific
promise of his predecessor, contributed to the defeat of the northern forces.   Another battle took place in 733, when Hugh Allan,
King of Ireland, and Hugh, son of Colgan, King of Leinster, engaged
in single combat.   The latter was slain, and the Leinster men
"were killed, slaughtered, cut off, and dreadfully exterminated."
In fact, the Leinster men endured so many " dreadful extermina-
tions," that one almost marvels how any of their brave fellows
were left for future feats of arms.   The " northerns were joyous
after this victory, for they had wreaked their vengeance and their
animosity upon the Leinster men," nine thousand of whom were
slain.   St. Samhthann, a holy nun, who died in the following year,
is said to have predicted the fate of Aedh, Comgal's son, if the
two Aedhs (Hughs) met.   Aedh Allan commemorated her virtues
in verse, and concludes thus :—

"In the bosom of the Lord, with a pure death, Samhthann passed from her
sufferings."

Indeed, the Irish kings of this period manifested their admiration
of peaceful living, and their desire for holy deaths, in a more practical way than by poetic encomiums on others.   In 704 Beg Boirche
"took a pilgrim's staff, and died on his pilgrimage."   In 729 Flahertach renounced his regal honours, and retired to Armagh,
where he died.   In 758 Donal died on a pilgrimage at Iona, after
a reign of twenty years ; and in 765 his successor, Nial Frassagh,
abdicated the throne, and became a monk at Iona.   Here he died
in 778, and was buried in the tomb of the Irish kings in that
island.

An Irish poet, who died in 742, is said to have played a clever trick on the " foreigners" of Dublin. He composed a poem for them, and then requested payment for his literary labours. The *Galls*,[5] who were probably Saxons, refused to meet his demand, but Rumrann said he would be content with two *pinguins* (pennies) from every good man, and one from each bad one. The result may be anticipated. Rumrann is described as " an adept in wisdom, chronology, and poetry ;" we might perhaps add, and in knowledge of human nature. In the Book of Ballymote he is called the Virgil of Ireland. A considerable number of Saxons were now in the country ; and it is said that a British king, named Constantine, who had become a monk, was at that time Abbot of Rahen, in the King's county, and that at Cell-Belaigh there were seven streets[6] of those foreigners. Gallen, in the King's county, was called Galin of the Britons, and Mayo was called Mayo of the Saxons, from the number of monasteries therein, founded by members of these nations.

The entries during the long reign of Domhnall contain little save obituaries of abbots and saints. The first year of the reign of Nial Frassagh is distinguished by a shower of silver, a shower of wheat, and a shower of honey. The Annals of Clonmacnois say that there was a most severe famine throughout the whole kingdom during the early part of his reign, so much that the king himself had very little to live upon. Then the king prayed very fervently to God, being in company with seven holy bishops ; and he asked that he might die rather than see so many of his faithful subjects perishing, while he was helpless to relieve them. At the conclusion of his prayer, the " three showers " fell from heaven ; and then the king and the seven bishops gave great thanks to the Lord.

But a more terrible calamity than famine was even then impending, and, if we may believe the old chroniclers, not without marvellous prognostications of its approach. In the year 767 there occurred a most fearful storm of thunder and lightning, with "terrific

---

[5] *Galls.*—Gall was a generic name for foreigners. The Danes were Finn Galls, or White Foreigners, and Dubh Galls, or Black Foreigners. The former were supposed to have been the inhabitants of Norway; the latter, of Jutland. In Irish, *gaill* is the nom., and *gall*, gen.

[6] *Streets.*—In Armagh the buildings were formed into streets and wards, for the better preservation of monastic discipline. Armagh was divided into three parts—*trian-more*, the town proper ; *trian-Patrick*, the cathedral close ; and *trian-Sassenagh*, the home of the foreign students.

and horrible signs." It would appear that the storm took place while a fair was going on, which obtained the name of the "Fair of the clapping of hands." Fear and horror seized the men of Ireland, so that their religious seniors ordered them to make two fasts, together with fervent prayer, and one meal between them, to protect and save them from a pestilence, precisely at Michaelmas.[7]

The first raid of the Danish pirates is recorded thus : "The age of Christ 790 [*recte* 795]. The twenty-fifth year of Donnchadh. The burning of Reachrainn[8] by plunderers ; and its shrines were broken and plundered." They had already attacked the English coasts, "whilst the pious King Bertric was reigning over its western division." Their arrival was sudden and so unexpected, that the king's officer took them for merchants, paying with his life for the mistake.[9] A Welsh chronicle, known by the name of *Brut y Tywysogion*, or the Chronicle of the Chieftains, has a corresponding record under the year 790 : "Ten years with fourscore and seven hundred was the age of Christ when the pagans went to Ireland." Three MSS. add, "and destroyed Rechren." Another chronicle mentions, that the black pagans, who were the first of their nation to land in Ireland, had previously been defeated in Glamorganshire, and after their defeat they had invaded Ireland, and devastated Rechru.

If by bravery we understand utter recklessness of life, and utter recklessness in inflicting cruelties on others, then the Vikings may be termed brave. The heroism of patient endurance was a bravery but little understood at that period. If the heathen Viking was brave when he plundered and burned monastic shrines—when he massacred the defenceless with wanton cruelty—when he flung

---

[7] *Michaelmas.*—Annals, p. 371. Another fearful thunderstorm is recorded in the Annals for 799. This happened on the eve of St. Patrick's Day. It is said that a thousand and ten persons were killed on the coast of Clare. The island of Fitha (now Mutton Island) was partly submerged, and divided into three parts. There was also a storm in 783—"thunder, lightning, and wind-storms"—by which the Monastery of Clonbroney was destroyed.

[8] *Reachrainn.*—Rechru appears to be the correct form. It has not yet been ascertained whether this refers to Lambay, near Dublin, or the island of Rathlinn. See note, p. 32, to the "Introduction" to the *Wars of the Gaedhil with the Gall.*

[9] *Mistake.*—*Ethel. Chron. Pro.* book iii.

little children on the points of spears, and gloated over their dying
agonies; perhaps we may also admit those who endured such
torments, either in their own persons, or in the persons of those
who were dear to them, and yet returned again and again to restore
the shrine so rudely destroyed, have also their claim to be termed
brave, and may demand some commendation for that virtue from
posterity

As plunder was the sole object of these barbarians, they naturally
sought it first where it could be obtained most easily and surely.
The islands on the Irish coast were studded with monasteries.
Their position was chosen as one which seemed peculiarly suitable
for a life of retreat from worldly turmoil, and contemplation of
heavenly things.   They were richly endowed, for ancient piety
deemed it could never give enough to God.   The shrines were
adorned with jewels, purchased with the wealth which the monks
had renounced for their own use ; the sacred vessels were costly,
the gifts of generous hearts.   The Danes commenced their work of
plunder and devastation in the year 795.   Three years after, A.D.
798, they ravaged Inis-patrick of Man and the Hebrides.   In 802
they burned " Hi-Coluim-Cille."   In 806 they attacked the island
again, and killed sixty-eight of the laity and clergy.   In 807 they
became emboldened by success, and for the first time marched in-
land ; and after burning Inishmurray, they attacked Roscommon.
During the years 812 and 813 they made raids in Connaught and
Munster, but not without encountering stout resistance from the
native forces.   After this predatory and internecine warfare had
continued for about thirty years, Turgesius, a Norwegian prince,
established himself as sovereign of the Vikings, and made Armagh
his head-quarters, A.D. 830.   If the Irish chieftains had united
their forces, and acted in concert, the result would have been the
expulsion of the intruders ; but, unhappily, this unity of purpose
in matters political has never existed.   The Danes made and broke
alliances with the provincial kings at their own convenience, while
these princes gladly availed themselves of even temporary assistance
from their cruel foes, while engaged in domestic wars, which should
never have been undertaken.   Still the Northmen were more than
once driven from the country by the bravery of the native commanders, and they often paid dearly for the cruel wrongs they
inflicted on their hapless victims.   Sometimes the Danish chiefs
mustered all their forces, and left the island for a brief period, to

ravage the shores of England or Scotland; but they soon returned to inflict new barbarities on the unfortunate Irish.[1]

Burning churches or destroying monasteries was a favourite pastime of these pirates, wherever they could obtain a landing on Christian shores; and the number of religious houses in Ireland afforded them abundant means of gratifying their barbarous inclinations. But when they became so far masters as to have obtained some permanent settlement, this mode of proceeding was considered either more troublesome or less profitable than that of appropriating to themselves the abbeys and churches. Turgesius, it is said, placed an abbot of his own in every monastery; and as he had already conferred ecclesiastical offices on himself and on his lady, we may presume he was not very particular in his selections. The villages, too, were placed under the rule of a Danish captain; and each family was obliged to maintain a soldier of that nation, who made himself master of the house, using and wasting the food for lack of which the starving children of the lawful owner were often dying of hunger.

All education was strictly forbidden; books and manuscripts were burned and *drowned;* and the poets, historians, and musicians imprisoned and driven to the woods and mountains. Martial sports were interdicted, from the lowest to the highest rank. Even nobles and princes were forbidden to wear their usual habiliments, the cast-off clothes of the Danes being considered sufficiently good for slaves.

The clergy, who had been driven from their monasteries, concealed themselves as best they could, continuing still their prayers and fasts, and the fervent recital of the Divine Office. The Irish,

---

[1] *Irish.*—The history of the two hundred years during which these northern pirates desolated the island, has been preserved in a MS. of venerable age and undoubted authenticity. It is entitled *Cogadh Gaedhil re Gallaibh* (the Wars of the Gaedhil with the Gall). It was quoted by Keating, known to Colgan, and used by the Four Masters; but for many years it was supposed to have been completely lost, until it was discovered, in 1840, by Mr. O'Curry, among the Seabright MSS. The work is now edited, with a translation and most valuable notes, by Dr. Todd. Several other copies have been discovered since, notably one by the Franciscan Brother, Michael O'Clery, which is at present in the Burgundian Library at Brussels. From internal evidence, it is presumed that the author was a contemporary of King Brian Boroimhé. Dr. O'Connor refers the authorship to Mac Liag, who was chief poet to that monarch, and died in 1016, two years after his master. Dr. Todd evidently inclines to this opinion, though he distinctly states that there is no authority for it.

true to their faith in every trial, were not slow to attribute their deliverance to the prayers of these holy men.

In 831 Nial Caille led an army against them, and defeated them at Derry ; but in the meanwhile, Felim, King of Cashel, with contemptible selfishness, marched into Leinster to claim tribute, and plundered every one, except the Danes, who should have been alone considered as enemies at such a time. Even the churches were not spared by him, for he laid waste the termon-lands of Clonmacnois, "up to the church door." After his death,[2] A.D. 843, a brave and good king came to the rescue of his unfortunate country. While still King of Meath, Meloughlin had freed the nation from Turgesius, one of its worst tyrants, by drowning him in Lough Owel. His death was a signal for a general onslaught on the Danes. The people rose simultaneously, and either massacred their enemies, or drove them to their ships. In 846 Meloughlin met their forces at Skreen, where they were defeated ; they also suffered a reverse at Kildare.

The Danes themselves were now divided into two parties—the Dubh Galls, or Black Gentiles ; and the Finn Galls, or White Gentiles. A fierce conflict took place between them in the year 850, in which the Dubh Galls conquered.[3] In the following year, however, both parties submitted to Amlaff, son of the Norwegian king ; and thus their power was once more consolidated. Amlaff remained in Dublin ; his brothers, Sitric and Ivar, stationed themselves in Waterford and Limerick. A great meeting was now convened by the ecclesiastics of Ireland at Rathugh, for the purpose

[2] *Death.*—It appears doubtful whether he really died at this time. It is said that he repented of his sins of sacrilege, and ended his days in penance and religious retirement. See Four Masters, p. 472.

[3] *Conquered.*—Duald Mac Firbis gives a curious account of these contests in his *Fragments of Annals.* The White Galls, or Norwegians, had long been masters of the situation. The Black Galls fought with them for three days and nights, and were finally victorious. They take the ships they have captured to Dublin, and deprive the Lochlanns (Black Galls) of all the spoil they had so cruelly and unjustly acquired from the " shrines and sanctuaries of the saints of Erinn ;" which the annalist naturally considers a judgment on them for their sins. They make another struggle, and gain the victory. But the Danish general, Horm, advises his men to put themselves under the protection of St. Patrick, and to promise the saint " honorable alms for gaining victory and triumph " over enemies who had plundered his churches. They comply with this advice; and though greatly inferior in numbers, they gain the victory, " on account of the tutelage of St. Patrick."

of establishing peace and concord amongst the native princes. The northern Hy-Nials alone remained belligerent; and to defend themselves, pursued the usual suicidal course of entering into an alliance with the Danes. Upon the death of the Irish monarch, the northern chief, Hugh Finnlaith, succeeded to the royal power; broke his treaty with Amlaff, which had been only one of convenience; and turned his arms vigorously against the foreigners. This prince was married to a daughter of Kenneth M'Alpine, the first sole Monarch of Scotland. After the death of the Irish prince, his wife married his successor, Flann, who, according to the alternate plan of succession, came of the southern Hy-Nial family, and was a son of Meloughlin, once the formidable opponent of the lady's former husband. During the reign of Flann, Cormac Mac Cullinan, a prelate distinguished for his learning and sanctity, was obliged to unite the office of priest and king. This unusual combination, however, was not altogether without precedent. The archbishopric of Cashel owes its origin remotely to this great man; as from the circumstance of the city of Cashel having been the seat of royalty in the south, and the residence of the kings of Munster, it was exalted, in the twelfth century, to the dignity of an archiepiscopal see.

Of Cormac, however interesting his history, we can only give a passing word. His reign commenced peaceably; and so wise— perhaps we should rather say, so holy—was his rule, that his kingdom once more enjoyed comparative tranquillity, and religion and learning flourished again as it had done in happier times.

But the kingdom which he had been compelled to rule, was threatened by the very person who should have protected it most carefully; and Cormac, after every effort to procure peace, was obliged to defend his people against the attacks of Flann. Even then a treaty might have been made with the belligerent monarch; but Cormac, unfortunately for his people and himself, was guided by an abbot, named Flahertach, who was by no means so peaceably disposed as his good master. This unruly ecclesiastic urged war on those who were already too willing to undertake it; and then made such representations to the bishop-king, as to induce him to yield a reluctant consent. It is said that Cormac had an intimation of his approaching end. It is at least certain, that he made preparations for death, as if he believed it to be imminent.

On the eve of the fatal engagement he made his confession, and added some articles to his will, in which he left large bounties to many of the religious houses throughout the kingdom. To Lismore he bequeathed a golden chalice and some rich vestments; to Armagh, twenty-four ounces of gold and silver; to his own church of Cashel, a golden and a silver chalice, with the famous Saltair. Then he retired to a private place for prayer, desiring the few persons whom he had informed of his approaching fate to keep their information secret, as he knew well the effect such intelligence would have on his army, were it generally known.

Though the king had no doubt that he would perish on the field, he still showed the utmost bravery, and made every effort to cheer and encourage his troops; but the men lost spirit in

ROCK OF CASHEL.

the very onset of the battle, and probably were terrified at the numerical strength of their opponents. Six thousand Munster men were slain, with many of their princes and chieftains. Cormac was killed by falling under his horse, which missed its footing on a bank slippery with the blood of the slain. A common soldier, who recognized the body, cut off his head, and brought it as a trophy to Flann; but the monarch bewailed the death of the good and great prince, and reproved the indignity with which his remains had been treated. This battle was fought at a place called Bealagh Mughna, now Ballaghmoon, in the county of Kildare, a few miles from the town of Carlow.[4]

---

[4] *Carlow.*—The site of the battle is still shown there, and even the stone on which the soldier decapitated Cormac. Cormac's death is thus described in a

Flahertach survived the battle, and, after some years spent in penance, became once more minister, and ultimately King of Munster. As he advanced in years, he learned to love peace, and his once irascible temper became calm and equable.

The Rock of Cashel, and the ruins of a small but once beautiful chapel, still preserve the memory of the bishop-king. His literary fame also has its memorials. His Rule is contained in a poem of fourteen stanzas, written in the most pure and ancient style of Gaedhilic, of which, as well as of many other languages, the illustrious Cormac was so profound a master. This Rule is general in several of its inculcations; but it appears to have been written particularly as an instruction to a priest, for the moral and spiritual direction of himself and his flock. He was also skilled in the Ogham writings, as may be gathered from a poem written by a contemporary, who, in paying compliments to many of the Irish kings and chiefs, addresses the following stanza to Cormac :—

> "Cormac of Cashel, with his champions,
> Munster is his,—may he long enjoy it !
> Around the King of *Raith-Bicli* are cultivated
> The letters and the trees."

The death of Cormac is thus pathetically deplored by Dallan, son of Môr :—

> "The bishop, the soul's director, the renowned, illustrious doctor,
> King of Caiseal, King of Farnumha : O God ! alas for Cormac ! "

Flann's last years were disturbed by domestic dissensions. His sons, Donough and Conor, both rebelled against him ; but Nial Glundubh (of the black knee), a northern Hy-Nial chief, led an army against them, and compelled them to give hostages to their father. Flann died the following year, A.D. 914, and was succeeded by the prince who had so ably defended him. Meanwhile, the Danes

---

MS. in the Burgundian Library : "The hind feet of his horse slipped on the slippery road in the track of that blood ; the horse fell backwards, and broke his [Cormac's] back and his neck in twain ; and he said, when falling, *In manus tuas commendo spiritum meum*, and he gives up his spirit ; and the impious sons of malediction come and thrust spears into his body, and sever his head from his body." Keating gives a curious account of this battle, from an ancient tract not known at present.

were not idle. Amlaff[5] has signalized his advent by drowning Conchobhar, " heir apparent of Tara ;" by slaying all the chieftains of the Deisi at Cluain-Daimh ; by killing the son of Clennfaeladh, King of Muscraighe Breoghain ; by smothering Machdaighren in a cave, and by the destruction of Caitill Find (Ketill the White) and his whole garrison. Oisill is the next chief of importance ; and he " succeeded in plundering the greatest part of Ireland." It is not recorded how long he was occupied in performing this exploit, but he was eventually slain, and his army cut off, by the men of Erinn. The deaths of several Danish chieftains occured about this period, and are referred to the vengeance of certain saints, whose shrines they had desecrated. In A.D. 864 according to the Four Masters, 867 according to O'Flaherty, the Danes were defeated at Lough Foyle, by Hugh Finnliath, King of Ireland. Soon after, Leinster and Munster were plundered by a Scandinavian chief, named Baraid, who advanced as far as *Ciarraighe* (Kerry) : "And they left not a cave under ground that they did not explore ; and they left nothing, from Limerick to Cork, that they did not ravish." What treasures the antiquarian of the nineteenth century must have lost by this marauder ! How great must have been the wealth of the kings and princes of ancient Erinn, when so much remains after so much was taken ! In 877 the Black Gentiles took refuge in Scotland, after suffering a defeat in an engagement with the White Gentiles. They were, however, consoled by a victory over the men of Alba, in which Constantine, son of Kenneth, was slain, and many others with him. Their success proved beneficial to Ireland, for we are told that a period of "rest to the men of Erinn" ensued. The Danes still held their own in Dublin and at Limerick, occasionally plundered the churches, and now and then had a skirmish with the "men of Erinn ;" but for forty years the country was free from the foreign fleets, and, therefore, enjoyed a time of comparative quiet.

In the year 913 new fleets arrived. They landed in the harbour of Waterford, where they had a settlement formerly ; but though they obtained assistance here, they were defeated by the native Irish, both in Kerry and in Tipperary. Sitric came with another

---

[5] *Amlaff.*—Dr. Todd identifies Amlaff with Olaf Huita (the white), of Scandinavian history, who was usually styled King of Dublin, and was the leader of the Northmen in Ireland for many years. See "Introduction" to the *Wars of the Gaedhil,* p. 69.

fleet in 915, and settled at Cenn-Fuait.[6]   Here he was attacked by
the Irish army, but they were repulsed with great slaughter.   Two
years after they received another disastrous defeat at Cill-Mosanhog,
near Rathfarnham.   A large cromlech, still in that neighbourhood,
probably marks the graves of the heroes slain in that engagement.
Twelve kings fell in this battle.   Their names are given in the
Wars of the Gaedhil, and by other authorities, though in some
places the number is increased.   Nial Glundubh was amongst the
slain.   He is celebrated in pathetic verse by the bards.   Of the
battle was said :—

> " Fierce and hard was the Wednesday
>   On which hosts were strewn under the fall of shields ;
>   It shall be called, till judgment's day,
>   The destructive burning of Ath-cliath."

The lamentation of Nial was, moreover, said :—

> " Sorrowful this day is sacred Ireland,
>   Without a valiant chief of hostage reign !
>   It is to see the heavens without a sun,
>   To view Magh-Neill[7] without a Nial."

> " There is no cheerfulness in the happiness of men ;
>   There is no peace or joy among the hosts ;
>   No fair can be celebrated
>   Since the sorrow of sorrow died."

Donough, son of Flann Sinna, succeeded, and passed his reign in
obscurity, with the exception of a victory over the Danes at Bregia.
Two great chieftains, however, compensated by their prowess for
his indifference ; these were Muircheartach, son of the brave Nial
Glundubh, the next heir to the throne, and Callaghan of Cashel,
King of Munster.   The northern prince was a true patriot, willing
to sacrifice every personal feeling for the good of his country: consequently, he proved a most formidable foe to the Danish invader.
Callaghan of Cashel was, perhaps, as brave, but his name cannot
be held up to the admiration of posterity.   The personal advancement of the southern Hy-Nials was more to him than the political
advancement of his country ; and he disgraced his name and his

---

[6] *Cenn-Fuait.*—Fuat Head.   The site has not been accurately identified.

[7] *Magh-Neill, i.e.*, the Plain of Nial, a bardic name for Ireland.—Four
Masters, vol. ii. p. 595.

nation by leaguing with the invaders. In the year 934 he pillaged Clonmacnois. Three years later he invaded Meath and Ossory, in conjunction with the Danes. Muircheartach was several times on the eve of engagements with the feeble monarch who nominally ruled the country, but he yielded for the sake of peace, or, as the chroniclers quaintly say, " God pacified them." After one of these pacifications, they joined forces, and laid " siege to the foreigners of Ath-cliath, so that they spoiled and plundered all that was under the dominion of the foreigners, from Ath-cliath to Ath-Truisten."[8]

In the twenty-second year of Donough, Muircheartach determined on a grand expedition for the subjugation of the Danes. He had already conducted a fleet to the Hebrides, from whence he returned flushed with victory. His first care was to assemble a body of troops of special valour ; and he soon found himself at the head of a thousand heroes, and in a position to commence "his circuit of Ireland." The Danish chief, Sitric, was first seized as a hostage. He then carried off Lorcan, King of Leinster. He next went to the Munster men, who were also prepared for battle ; but they too yielded, and gave up their monarch also, " and a fetter was put on him by Muircheartach." He afterwards proceeded into Connaught, where Conchobhar, son of Tadhg, came to meet him, "but no gyve or lock was put upon him." He then returned to Oileach, carrying these kings with him as hostages. Here he feasted them for five months with knightly courtesy, and then sent them to the Monarch Donough.

After these exploits we cannot be surprised that Muircheartach should be styled the Hector of the west of Europe. But he soon finds his place in the never-ceasing obituary. In two years after his justly famous exploit, he was slain by " Blacaire, son of Godfrey, lord of the foreigners." This event occurred on the 26th of March, A.D. 941, according to the chronology of the Four Masters. The true year, however, is 943. The chroniclers briefly observe, that "Ard-Macha was plundered by the same foreigners, on the day after the killing of Muircheartach."[9]

Donough died in 942, after a reign of twenty-five years. He was

8 *Ath-Truisten.*—From Dublin to a ford on the river Green, near Mullaghmast, co. Kildare.

9 *Muircheartach.*—This prince obtained the soubriquet of Muircheartach of the Leathern Cloaks. The origin of this appellation has not been precisely ascertained.

succeeded by Congallach, who was killed by the Danes, A.D. 954.
Donnell O'Neill, a son of the brave Muircheartach, now obtained
the royal power, such as it was; and at his death the throne reverted to Maelseachlainn, or Malachy II., the last of his race who
ever held the undisputed sovereignty of Ireland. But it must not
be supposed that murders and massacres are the staple commodities of our annals during this eventful period. Every noteworthy
event is briefly and succinctly recorded. We find, from time to
time, mention of strange portents, such as double suns, and other
celestial phenomena of a more or less remarkable character. Fearful
storms are also chronicled, which appear to have occurred at certain
intervals, and hard frosts, which proved almost as trying to the
"men of Erinn" as the wars of the Gentiles, black or white. But
the obituaries of abbots or monks, with the quaint remarks appended thereto, and epitomes of a lifetime in a sentence, are by no
means the least interesting portion of those ancient tomes. In one
page we may find record of the Lord of Aileach, who takes a pilgrim's staff; in another, we have mention of the Abbot Muireadhach
and others, who were "destroyed in the refectory" of Druim-
Mesclainn by Congallach; and we read in the lamentation of Muireadhach, that he was "the lamp of every choir." Then we are told
simply how a nobleman "died in religion," as if that were praise
enough for him; though another noble, Domhnall, is said to have
"died in religion, after a good life." Of some abbots and bishops
there is nothing more than the death record; but in the age of
Christ 926, when Celedabhaill, son of Scannal, went to Rome on
his pilgrimage from the abbacy of Beannchair, we are given in full
the four quatrains which he composed at his departure,—a composition which speaks highly for the poetic powers and the true piety
of the author. He commences thus :—

Time for me to prepare to pass from the shelter of a habitation,
To journey as a pilgrim over the surface of the noble lively sea;
Time to depart from the snares of the flesh, with all its guilt;
Time now to ruminate how I may find the great Son of Mary;
Time to seek virtue, to trample upon the will with sorrow;
Time to reject vices, and to renounce the demon.

. . . .

Time to barter the transitory things for the country of the King of heaven;
Time to defy the ease of the little earthly world of a hundred pleasures;
Time to work at prayer in adoration of the high King of angels."

The obituary notices, however, were not always complimentary. We find the following entry in the Annals of Clonmacnois:— "Tomhair Mac Alchi, King of Denmark, is reported to go [to have gone] to hell with his pains, as he deserved."

GREY MAN'S PATH, GIANT'S CAUSEWAY.

RATH AT LEIGHLIN, CARLOW.

CHAPTER XIII.

The Battle of Dundalk—The Danes supposed to be Christianized—Brian Boroimhé and his Brother Mahoun—The Dalcassians fight the Danes—Mahoun is assassinated—Brian revenges his Brother's Murder—Malachy's Exploits against the Danes—Malachy and Brian form a Treaty and fight the Danes—Malachy wins "the Collar of Gold"—Brian's "Happy Family" at Kincora—He usurps the Supreme Power, and becomes Monarch of Ireland—Remote Causes of the Battle of Clontarf—Gormflaith is "grim" with Brian—Blockade of Dublin—The Danes prepare for a Fierce Conflict—Brian prepares also—The Battle of Clontarf—Disposition of the Forces—Brian's Death—Defeat of the Danes.

[A.D. 926—1022.]

MANY of the sea-coast towns were now in possession of the Danes. They had founded Limerick, and, indeed, Wexford and Waterford almost owe them the debt of parentage. Obviously, the ports were their grand securities—a ready refuge if driven by native valour to embark in their fleets; convenient head-quarters when marauding expeditions to England or Scotland were in preparation. But the Danes never obtained the same power in Ireland as in the sister country. The domestic dissensions of the men of Erinn, ruinous as they were to the nation, gave it at least the advantage of having a brave and resolute body of men always in arms, and ready to face the foe at a moment's notice, when no selfish policy interfered. In 937 Athelstane gained his famous victory over the

Danes at Brunanbriegh in Northumberland, and came triumphantly to reclaim the dagger[1] which he had left at the shrine of St. John of Beverley. After his death, in 941, Amlaff returned to Northumberland, and once more restored the Danish sway. From this time, until the accession of the Danish King Canute, England was more or less under the dominion of these ruthless tyrants.[2]

" The Danes of Ireland, at this period, were ruled by Sitric, son of Turgesius, whose name was sufficient to inspire the Irish with terror. Through policy he professed willingness to enter into a treaty of peace with Callaghan, King of Munster ; and, as proof of his sincerity, offered him his sister, the Princess Royal of Denmark, in marriage. The Irish king had fallen in love with this amiable and beautiful princess, and he readily consented to the fair and liberal measures proposed. He sent word to Sitric he would visit him ; and, attended by a royal retinue, to be followed in a little time by his guards, as escort for his future queen, proceeded to meet his royal bride.

" Sitric's project of inveigling the King of Munster into his district, in order to make him prisoner, under the expectation of being married to the Princess of Denmark, having been disclosed to his wife, who was of Irish birth, she determined to warn the intended victim of the meditated treachery, and accordingly she disguised herself, and placed herself in a pass which Callaghan should traverse, and met him. Here she informed him who she was, the design of Sitric against him, and warned him to return as fast as possible. This was not practicable. Sitric had barred the way with armed men ; and Callaghan and his escort, little prepared for an encounter, found themselves hemmed in by an overwhelming Danish force. To submit without a struggle was never the way with the Momonians. They formed a rampart round the person of their king, and cut

---

[1] *Dagger.*—The king visited the shrine on his way to battle, and hanging up his dagger, the then symbol of knightly valour, vowed to release it with a kingly ransom if God gave him the victory. He obtained his desire, and nobly fulfilled his vow.

[2] *Tyrants.*—J. Roderick O'Flanagan, Esq., M.R.I.A., has permitted me to extract the account of the battle of Dundalk from his valuable and interesting *History of Dundalk and its Environs.* Dublin: Hodges and Smith, 1864. This gentleman has devoted himself specially to elucidating the subject, and with a kindness which I cannot easily forget, permits me to avail myself, not only of his literary labours, but even to transfer to the pages of this work several complete pages from his own.

through the Danish ranks.   Fresh foes met them on every side;
and, after a bloody struggle, the men of Munster were conquered.
Callaghan, the king, and Prince Duncan, son of Kennedy, were
brought captives to Dublin.   Then the royal prisoners were removed
to Armagh, and their safe keeping entrusted to nine Danish earls,
who had a strong military force at their orders to guard them.

"The news of this insidious act rapidly fanned the ardour of the
Munster troops to be revenged for the imprisonment of their beloved king.   Kennedy, the Prince of Munster, father of Duncan,
was appointed regent, with ample powers to govern the country in
the king's absence.   The first step was to collect an army to cope
with the Danes.   To assemble a sufficient body of troops on land
was easy; but the great strength of the northern rovers lay in their
swift-sailing ships.   'It must strike the humblest comprehension
with astonishment,' says Marmion, 'that the Irish, although possessed of an island abounding with forests of the finest oak, and
other suitable materials for ship-building—enjoying also the most
splendid rivers, loughs, and harbours, so admirably adapted to the
accommodation of extensive fleets, should, notwithstanding, for so
many centuries, allow the piratical ravages of the Danes, and subsequently the more dangerous subversion of their independence by
the Anglo-Normans, without an effort to build a navy that could
cope with those invaders on that element from which they could
alone expect invasion from a foreign foe.'   This neglect has also
been noticed by the distinguished Irish writer—Wilde—who, in
his admirably executed *Catalogue of the Antiquities in the Royal Irish
Academy*, observes :—'Little attention has been paid to the subject
of the early naval architecture of this country.   So far as we yet
know, two kinds of boats appear to have been in use in very early
times in the British Isles—the canoe and the corragh; the one
formed of a single piece of wood, the other composed of wicker-
work, covered with hides.'   Larger vessels there must have been;
though, from the length of time which has since elapsed, we have no
traces of them now.   Kennedy not only collected a formidable army
by land, but 'he fitted out a fleet of ships, and manned it with
able seamen, that he might make sure of his revenge, and attack
the enemy by sea and land.'   The command of the fleet was conferred on an admiral perfectly skilled in maritime affairs, Failbhe
Fion, King of Desmond.

"When the army of Munster arrived near Armagh, they learnt the prisoners had been removed thence by Sitric, and placed on board ship. Enraged at this disappointment, they gave no quarter to the Danes, and advanced rapidly to Dundalk, where the fleet lay, with the king and young prince on board. Sitric, unable to withstand the opposing army on shore, ordered his troops to embark, and resolved to avoid the encounter through means of his ships. While the baffled Irish army were chafing at this unexpected delay to their hoped for vengeance, they espied, from the shore of Dundalk, where they encamped, a sail of ships, in regular order, steering with a favourable gale towards the Danish fleet moored in Dundalk bay. Joy instantly filled their hearts ; for they recognized the fleet of Munster, with the admiral's vessel in the van, and the rest ranged in line of battle. The Danes were taken by surprise; they beheld an enemy approach from a side where they rather expected the raven flag of their country floating on the ships. The Munster admiral gave them no time to form. He steered straight to Sitric's vessel, and, with his hardy crew, sprang on board. Here a sight met his gaze which filled his heart with rage ; he saw his beloved monarch, Callaghan, and the young prince, tied with cords to the main-mast. Having, with his men, fought through the Danish troops to the side of the king and prince, he cut the cords and set them free. He then put a sword into the hands of the rescued king, and they fought side by side: Meanwhile Sitric, and his brothers, Tor and Magnus, did all they could to retrieve the fortunes of the day. At the head of a chosen band they attacked the Irish admiral, and he fell, covered with wounds. His head, exposed by Sitric on a pole, fired the Danes with hope—the Irish with tenfold rage. Fingal, next in rank to Failbhe Fion, took the command, and determined to avenge his admiral. Meeting the Danish ruler in the combat, he seized Sitric round the neck, and flung himself with his foe into the sea, where both perished. Seagdor and Connall, two captains of Irish ships, imitated this example—threw themselves upon Tor and Magnus, Sitric's brothers, and jumped with them overboard, when all were drowned. These desperate deeds paralysed the energy of the Danes, and the Irish gained a complete victory in Dundalk bay.

" The Irish fleet having thus expelled the pirates from their coast, came into harbour, where they were received with acclamations of joy by all who witnessed their bravery. Such is a summary of Keating's poetic account of this day's achievements ; and there are

extant fuller accounts in various pieces of native poetry, especially
one entitled 'The Pursuit after Callaghan of Cashel, by the Chief
of Munster, after he had been entrapped by the Danes.'"

The year 948 has generally been assigned as that of the conversion of the Danes to Christianity ; but, whatever the precise period
may have been, the conversion was rather of a doubtful character,
as we hear of their burning churches, plundering shrines, and
slaughtering ecclesiastics with apparently as little remorse as ever.
In the very year in which the Danes of Dublin are said to have
been converted, they burned the belfry of Slane while filled with
religious who had sought refuge there.   Meanwhile the Irish mo-
narchies were daily weakened by divisions and domestic wars.
Connaught was divided between two or three independent princes,
and Munster into two kingdoms.

The ancient division of the country into five provinces no longer
held good ; and the Ard-Righ, or chief monarch, was such only in
name.   Even the great northern Hy-Nials, long the bravest and
most united of the Irish clans, were now divided into two portions,
the Cinel-Connaill and Cinel-Owen ; the former of whom had been
for some time excluded from the alternate accession of sovereignty,
which was still maintained between the two great families of the
race of Nial.   But, though this arrangement was persevered in
with tolerable regularity, it tended little to the promotion of peace,
as the northern princes were ever ready to take advantage of the
weakness of the Meath men, who were their inferiors both in numbers and in valour.

The sovereignty of Munster had also been settled on the alternate principle, between the great tribe of Dalcassians, or north
Munster race, and the Eoghanists, or southeners.   This plan of
succession, as may be supposed, failed to work peaceably ; and,
in 942, Kennedy, the father of the famous Brian Boroimhé,
contested the sovereignty with the Eoghanist prince, Callaghan
Cashel, but yielded in a chivalrous spirit, not very common
under such circumstances, and joined his former opponent in his
contests with the Danes.   The author of the *Wars of the Gaedhil
with the Gall* gives a glowing account of the genealogy of Brian
and his eldest brother, Mathgamhain.   They are described as "two
fierce, magnificent heroes, the two stout, able, valiant pillars,"
who then governed the Dalcassian tribes ; Mathgamhain (Mahoun) being the actual chieftain, Brian the heir apparent.   A

guerilla war was carried on for some time in the woods of Thomond, in which no quarter was given on either side, and wherein it was "woe to either party to meet the other." Mahoun at last proposed a truce, but Brian refused to consent to this arrangement. He continued the war until he found his army reduced to fifteen men. Mahoun then sent for him. An interview took place, which is described in the form of a poetic dialogue, between the two brothers. Brian reproached Mahoun with cowardice; Mahoun reproached Brian with imprudence. Brian hints broadly that Mahoun had interested motives in making this truce, and declares that neither Kennedy, their father, nor Lorcan, their grandfather, would have been so quiescent towards the foreigners for the sake of wealth, nor would they have given them even as much time as would have sufficed to play a game of chess[3] on the green of Magh Adhair. Mahoun kept his temper, and contented himself with reproaching Brian for his recklessness, in sacrificing the lives of so many of his faithful followers to no purpose. Brian replied that he would never abandon his inheritance, without a contest, to "such foreigners as Black Grim Gentiles."

The result was a conference of the tribe, who voted for war, and marched into the country of the Eoghanists (the present co. Kerry), who at once joined the standard of the Dalcassians. The Danes suffered severely in Munster. This aroused the Limerick Danes; and their chieftain, Ivar, attacked the territory of Dal-Cais, an exploit in which he was joined, to their eternal shame, by several native princes and tribes, amongst whom were Maolmuadh (Molloy), son of Braun, King of Desmond, and Donabhan (Donovan), son of Cathal, King of Ui Cairbhri. The result was a fierce battle at Sulcoit, near Tipperary, wherein the Danes were gloriously defeated. The action was commenced by the Northmen. It continued from sunrise till mid-day, and terminated in the rout of the foreigners, who fled "to the ditches, and to the valleys, and to the solitudes of the great sweet flower plain," where they were followed by the conquerors, and massacred without mercy.

The Dalcassians now obtained possession of Limerick, with immense spoils of jewels, gold and silver, foreign saddles, " soft,

[3] *Chess.*—Flann Sionna, Monarch of Ireland, had encamped on this plain, and ostentatiously commenced a game of chess as a mark of contempt for the chieftains whose country he had invaded. His folly met its just punishment, for he was ignominiously defeated. See *Wars of the Gaedhil*, p. 113, note.

youthful, bright girls, blooming silk-clad women, and active, well-formed boys." The active boys were soon disposed of, for we find that they collected the prisoners on the hillocks of Saingel, where "every one that was fit for war was put to death, and every one that was fit for a slave was enslaved." This event is dated A.D. 968.

Mahoun was now firmly established on the throne, but his success procured him many enemies. A conspiracy was formed against him under the auspices of Ivar of Limerick and his son, Dubhcenn. The Eoghanist clans basely withdrew their allegiance from their lawful sovereign, allied themselves with the Danes, and became principals in the plot of assassination. Their motive was as simple as their conduct was vile. The two Eoghanist families were represented by Donovan and Molloy. They were descendants of Oilioll Oluim, from whom Mahoun was also descended, but his family were Dalcassians. Hitherto the Eoghanists had succeeded in depriving the tribes of Dal-Cais of their fair share of alternate succession to the throne of Munster; they became alarmed at and jealous of the advancement of the younger tribe, and determined to do by treachery what they could not do by force. With the usual headlong eagerness of traitors, they seem to have forgotten Brian, and quite overlooked the retribution they might expect at his hands for their crime. There are two different accounts of the murder, which do not coincide in detail. The main facts, however, are reliable: Mahoun was entrapped in some way to the house of Donovan, and there he was basely murdered, in violation of the rights of hospitality, and in defiance of the safe-conduct of the bishop, which he secured before his visit.

The traitors gained nothing by their treachery except the contempt of posterity. Brian was not slow in avenging his brother. "He was not a stone in place of an egg, nor a wisp of hay in place of a club; but he was a hero in place of a hero, and valour after valour."[4]

Public opinion was not mistaken in its estimate of his character. Two years after the death of Mahoun, Brian invaded Donovan's territory, drove off his cattle, took the fortress of Cathair Cuan, and slew Donovan and his Danish ally, Harolt. He next proceeded to settle accounts with Molloy. Cogarán is sent to the

---

[4] *Valour.—Wars of the Gaedhil*, p. 101.

whole tribe of Ui Eachach, to know " the reason why" they killed Mahoun, and to declare that no *cumhal* or fine would be received, either in the shape of hostages, gold, or cattle, but that Molloy must himself be given up. Messages were also sent to Molloy, both general and particular—the general message challenged him to battle at Belach-Lechta; the particular message, which in truth he hardly deserved, was a challenge to meet Murrough, Brian's son, in single combat. The result was the battle of Belach-Lechta,[5] where Molloy was slain, with twelve hundred of his troops, both native and foreign. Brian remained master of the field and of the kingdom, A.D. 978.

Brian was now undisputed King of Munster. In 984 he was acknowledged Monarch of Leth Mogha, the southern half of Ireland. Meanwhile Malachy, who governed Leth Cuinn, or the northern half of Ireland, had not been idle. He fought a battle with the Danes in 979, near Tara, in which he defeated their forces, and slew Raguall, son of Amlaibh, King of Dublin. Amlaibh felt the defeat so severely, that he retired to Iona, where he died of a broken heart. Donough O'Neill, son of Muircheartach, died this year, and Malachy obtained the regal dignity. Emboldened by his success at Tara, he resolved to attack the foreigners in Dublin; he therefore laid siege to that city, and compelled it to surrender after three days, liberated two thousand prisoners, including the King of Leinster, and took abundant spoils. At the same time he issued a proclamation, freeing every Irishman then in bondage to the Danes, and stipulating that the race of Nial should henceforth be free from tribute to the foreigners.

It is probable that Brian had already formed designs for obtaining the royal power. The country resounded with the fame of his exploits, and Malachy became aware at last that he should either have him for an ally or an enemy. He prudently chose the former alternative, and in the nineteenth year of his reign (997 according to the Four Masters) he made arrangements with Brian for a great campaign against the common enemy. Malachy surrendered all hostages to Brian, and Brian agreed to recognize Malachy as sole monarch of northern Erinn, " without war or trespass." This treaty was absolutely necessary, in order to offer effective resistance

---

[5] *Belach-Lechta.*—The site has not been definitely ascertained. Some authorities place it near Macroom, co. Cork.

to the Danes. The conduct of the two kings towards each other, had not been of a conciliatory nature previously. In 981 Malachy had invaded the territory of the Dalcassians, and uprooted the great oak-tree of Magh Adair, under which its kings were crowned —an insult which could not fail to excite bitter feelings both in prince and people. In 989 the monarch occupied himself fighting the Danes in Dublin, to whom he laid siege for twenty nights, reducing the garrison to such straits that they were obliged to drink the salt water when the tide rose in the river. Brian then made reprisals on Malachy, by sending boats up the Shannon, burning the royal rath of Dun Sciath. Malachy, in his turn, recrossed the Shannon, burned Nenagh, plundered Ormonde, and defeated Brian himself in battle. He then marched again to Dublin, and once more attacked "the proud invader." It was on this occasion that he obtained the "collar of gold," which Moore has immortalized in his world-famous "Melodies."

When the kings had united their forces, they obtained another important victory at Glen-Mama.[6] Harolt, son of Olaf Cuaran, the then Danish king, was slain, and four thousand of his followers perished with him. The victorious army marched at once to Dublin. Here they obtained spoils of great value, and made many slaves and captives. According to some accounts, Brian remained in Dublin until the feast of St. Brigid (February 1st); other annalists say he only remained from Great Christmas to Little Christmas. Meanwhile there can be but little doubt that Brian had in view the acquisition of the right to be called sole monarch of Ireland. It is a blot on an otherwise noble character—an ugly spot in a picture of more than ordinary interest. Sitric, another son of Olaf's, fled for protection to Aedh and Eochaidh, two northern chieftains; but they gave him up, from motives of fear or policy to Brian's soldiers, and after due submission he was restored to his former position. Brian then gave his daughter in marriage to Sitric, and completed the family alliance by espousing Sitric's mother, Gormflaith, a lady of rather remarkable character, who had

---

[6] *Glen-Mama*,—The Glen of the Gap, near Dunlavin. This was the ancient stronghold of the kings of Leinster in Wicklow. There is a long and very interesting note on the locality, by the Rev. J. F. Shearman, R.C.C., in the "Introduction" to the *Wars of the Gaedhil*. He mentions that pits have been discovered even recently, containing the remains of the slain.

been divorced from her second husband, Malachy.   Brian now proceeded to depose Malachy.   The account of this important transaction is given in so varied a manner by different writers, that it seems almost impossible to ascertain the truth.   The southern annalists are loud in their assertions of the incapacity of the reigning monarch, and would have it believed that Brian only yielded to the urgent entreaties of his countrymen in accepting the proffered crown.   But the warlike exploits of Malachy have been too faithfully recorded to leave any doubt as to his prowess in the field ; and we may probably class the regret of his opponent in accepting his position, with similar protestations made under circumstances in which such regret was as little likely to be real.

The poet Moore, with evident partiality for the subject of his song, declares that the magnanimous character of Malachy was the real ground of peace under such provocation, and that he submitted to the encroachments of his rival rather from motives of disinterested desire for his country's welfare, than from any reluctance or inability to fight his own battle.

But Brian had other chieftains to deal with, of less amiable or more warlike propensities : the proud Hy-Nials of the north were long in yielding to his claims ; but even these he at length subdued, compelling the Cinel-Eoghain to give him hostages, and carrying off the Lord of Cinel-Connaill bodily to his fortress at Kincora.   Here he had assembled a sort of " happy family," consisting of refractory princes and knights, who, refusing hostages to keep the peace with each other, were obliged to submit to the royal will and pleasure, and at least to appear outwardly in harmony.

These precautionary measures, however summary, and the energetic determination of Brian to have peace kept either by sword or law, have given rise to the romantic ballad of the lady perambulating Erinn with a gold ring and white wand, and passing unmolested through its once belligerent kingdoms.

Brian now turned his attention to the state of religion and literature, restoring the churches and monasteries which had been plundered and burnt by the Danes.   He is said also to have founded the churches of Killaloe and Iniscealtra, and to have built the round tower of Tomgrany, in the present county Clare.   A gift of twenty ounces of gold to the church of Armagh,—a large donation for that period,—is also recorded amongst his good deeds.[7]

There is some question as to the precise year in which Brian obtained or usurped the authority and position of Ard-Righ : A.D. 1002, however, is the date most usually accepted. He was probably about sixty-one years of age, and Malachy was then about fifty-three.[8]

It will be remembered that Brian had married the Lady Gormflaith. Her brother, Maelmordha, was King of Leinster, and he had obtained his throne through the assistance of the Danes. Brian was Gormflaith's third husband. In the words of the Annals, she had made three leaps—" jumps which a woman should never jump "—a hint that her matrimonial arrangements had not the sanction of canon law. She was remarkable for her beauty, but her temper was proud and vindictive. This was probably the reason why she was repudiated both by Malachy and Brian. There can be no doubt that she and her brother, Maelmordha, were the remote causes of the famous battle of Clontarf. The story is told thus : Maelmordha came to Brian with an offering of three large pine-trees to make masts for shipping. These were probably a tribute which he was bound to pay to his liege lord. The trees had been cut in the great forest of Leinster, called Fidh-Gaibhli.[9] Some other tribes were bringing their tree-tributes at the same time ; and as they all journeyed over the mountains together, there was a dispute for precedence. Maelmordha decided the question by assisting to carry the tree of the Ui-Faelain. He had on a tunic of silk which Brian had given[1] him, with a border

---

[7] *Deeds.*—The origin of surnames is also attributed to Brian Boroimhé, from a fragment in the Library of Trinity College, Dublin, supposed to be a portion of a life of that monarch written by his poet Mac Liag. Surnames were generally introduced throughout Europe in the tenth and twelfth centuries. The Irish gave their names to their lands. In other countries patronymics were usually taken from the names of the hereditary possessions.

[8] *Fifty-three.*—See Dr. O'Donovan's note to Annals, p. 747.

[9] *Fidh-Gaibhli.*—Now Feegile, near Portarlington.

[1] *Given.*—The Book of Rights mentions, that one of the rights to which the King of Leinster was entitled from the King of Ireland, was " fine textured clothes at Tara," as well as " sevenscore suits of clothes of good colour, for the use of the sons of the great chieftain."—Book of Rights, p. 251. From the conduct of Gormflaith, as related above, it is evident that the tunic was some token of vassalage.

of gold round it and silver buttons. One of the buttons came off
as he lifted the tree. On his arrival at Kincora, he asked his
sister, Gormflaith, to replace it for him ; but she at once flung the
garment into the fire, and then bitterly reproached her brother with
having accepted this token of vassalage. The Sagas say she was
" grim" against Brian, which was undoubtedly true. This excited
Maelmordha's temper. An opportunity soon offered for a quarrel.
Brian's eldest son, Murrough,[2] was playing a game of chess with
his cousin, Conoing ; Maelmordha was looking on, and suggested a
move by which Murrough lost the game. The young prince exclaimed : " That was like the advice you gave the Danes, which
lost them Glen-Mama." " I will give them advice now, and they
shall not be defeated," replied the other. " Then you had better
remind them to prepare a yew-tree[3] for your reception," answered
Murrough.

Early the next morning Maelmordha left the place, "without
permission and without taking leave." Brian sent a messenger
after him to pacify him, but the angry chief, for all reply, " broke
all the bones in his head." He now proceeded to organize a revolt
against Brian, and succeeded. Several of the Irish princes flocked
to his standard. An encounter took place in Meath, where they
slew Malachy's grandson, Domhnall, who should have been heir
if the usual rule of succession had been observed. Malachy
marched to the rescue, and defeated the assailants with great
slaughter, A.D. 1013. Fierce reprisals now took place on each
side. Sanctuary was disregarded, and Malachy called on Brian to
assist him. Brian at once complied. After successfully ravaging
Ossory he marched to Dublin, where he was joined by Murrough,
who had devastated Wicklow, burning, destroying, and carrying
off captives, until he reached *Cill Maighnenn* (Kilmainham). They
now blockaded Dublin, where they remained from St. Ciaran's in
harvest (Sept. 9th) until Christmas Day. Brian was then obliged
to raise the siege and return home for want of provisions.

The storm was now gathering in earnest, and the most active preparations were made on both sides for a mighty and decisive conflict.

[2] *Murrough.*—He was eldest son by Brian's first wife, Môr. He had three
sons by this lady, who were all slain at Clontarf.

[3] *Yew-tree.*—This was a sharp insult. After the battle of Glen-Mama,
Maelmordha had hidden himself in a yew-tree, where he was discovered and
taken prisoner by Murrough.

The Danes had already obtained possession of England, a country
which had always been united in its resistance to their power,
a country numerically superior to Ireland : why should they not
hope to conquer, with at least equal facility, a people who had
so many opposing interests, and who rarely sacrificed these interests
to the common good ? Still they must have had some fear of the
result, if we may judge by the magnitude of their preparations.
They despatched ambassadors in all directions to obtain reinforcements. Brodir, the earl, and Amlaibh, son of the King of
Lochlann, " the two Earls of Cair, and of all the north of Saxon
land,"[4] came at the head of 2,000 men ; "and there was not one
villain of that 2,000 who had not polished, strong, triple-plated
armour of refined iron, or of cooling, uncorroding brass, encasing
their sides and bodies from head to foot." Moreover, the said
villains " had no reverence, veneration, or respect, or mercy for God
or man, for church or for sanctuary ; they were cruel, ferocious,
plundering, hard-hearted, wonderful Dannarbrians, selling and
hiring themselves for gold and silver, and other treasure as well."
Gormflaith was evidently " head centre " on the occasion ; for we
find wonderful accounts of her zeal and efforts in collecting forces.
" Other treasure " may possibly be referred to that lady's heart
and hand, of which she appears to have been very liberal on this
occasion. She despatched her son, Sitric, to Siguard, Earl of the
Orkneys, who promised his assistance, but he required the hand of
Gormflaith as payment for his services, and that he should be
made King of Ireland. Sitric gave the required promise, and
found, on his return to Dublin, that it met with his mother's entire
approbation. She then despatched him to the Isle of Man, where
there were two Vikings, who had thirty ships, and she desired
him to obtain their co-operation " at any price." They were the
brothers Ospak and Brodir. The latter demanded the same conditions as the Earl Siguard, which were promised quite as readily
by Sitric, only he charged the Viking to keep the agreement secret,
and above all not to mention it to Siguard.

Brodir,[5] according to the Saga, was an apostate Christian, who

---

[4] *Land.—Wars of the Gaedhil*, p. 151.

[5] *Brodir.*—It has been suggested that this was not his real name. He was
Ospak's *brother*, and Brodir may have been mistaken for a proper name.
There was a Danish Viking named Gutring, who was an apostate deacon, and
who may have been the Brodir of Irish history.

had "thrown off his faith, and become God's dastard." He was both tall and strong, and had such long black hair that he tucked it under his belt; he had also the reputation of being a magician. The Viking Ospak refused to fight against "the good King Brian," and, touched by some prodigies, became a convert to Christianity, joined the Irish monarch at Kincora, on the Shannon, and received holy baptism.[6] The author of the *Wars of the Gaedhil* gives a formidable list of the other auxiliaries who were invited by the Dublin Danes. The Annals of Loch Cé also give an account of the fleet he assembled, and its "chosen braves." Maelmordha had mustered a large army also; indeed, he was too near the restless and revengeful Lady Gormflaith to have taken matters quietly, even had he been so inclined.

Meanwhile Brian had been scarcely less successful, and probably not less active. He now marched towards Dublin, "with all that obeyed him of the men of Ireland." These were the provincial troops of Munster and Connaught and the men of Meath. His march is thus described in the *Wars of the Gaedhil*:—" Brian looked out behind him, and beheld the battle phalanx—compact, huge, disciplined, moving in silence, mutely, bravely, haughtily, unitedly, with one mind, traversing the plain towards them; threescore and ten banners over them—of red, and of yellow, and of green, and of all kinds of colours; together with the everlasting, variegated, lucky, fortunate banner, that had gained the victory in every battle, and in every conflict, and in every combat."[7] The portion of the narrative containing this account is believed to be an interpolation, but the description may not be the less accurate. Brian plundered and destroyed as usual on his way to Dublin. When he had encamped near that city, the Danes came out to give him battle on the plain of Magh-n-Ealta.[8] The king then held a council of war, and the result, apparently, was a determination to give battle in the morning. It is said that the Northmen pretended flight in order to delay the engagement. The Njal Saga says the Viking Brodir had found out by his sorcery, "that if the fight were on Good Friday, King Brian would fall, but win the day; but if they fought before, they would all fall who were against him." Some authorities also

[6] *Baptism.—Burnt Njal*, ii. 332.

[7] *Combat.—Wars of the Gaedhil*, p. 157.

[8] *Magh-n-Ealta.*—The Plain of the Flocks, lying between Howth and Tallaght, so called from Eder, a chieftain who perished before the Christian era.

mention a traitor in Brian's camp, who had informed the Danes that his forces had been weakened by the absence of his son Donough, whom he had sent to devastate Leinster. Malachy has the credit of this piece of treachery, with other imputations scarcely less disreputable.

The site of the battle has been accurately defined. It took place on the plain of Clontarf,[9] and is called the Battle of the Fishing Weir of Clontarf. The weir was at the mouth of the river Tolka, where the bridge of Ballybough now stands. The Danish line was extended along the coast, and protected at sea by their fleets. It was disposed in three divisions, and comprised about 21,000 men, the Leinster forces being included in the number. The first division or left wing was the nearest to Dublin. It was composed of the Danes of Dublin, and headed by Sitric, who was supported by the thousand mail-clad Norwegians, commanded by Carlus and Anrud. In the centre were the Lagennians, under the command of Maelmordha. The right wing comprised the foreign auxiliaries, under the command of Brodir and Siguard.[1]

Brian's army was also disposed in three divisions. The first was composed of his brave Dalcassians, and commanded by his son Murrough, assisted by his four brothers, Teigue, Donough, Connor, and Flann, and his youthful heir, Turlough, who perished on the field. The second division or centre was composed of troops from Munster, and was commanded by Mothla, grandson of the King of the Deisi, of Waterford, assisted by many native princes. The

[9] *Clontarf.*—There is curious evidence that the account of the battle of Clontarf must have been written by an eye-witness, or by one who had obtained his information from an eye-witness. The author states that "the foreigners came out to fight the battle in the morning at the full tide," and that the tide came in again in the evening at the same place. The Danes suffered severely from this, "for the tide had carried away their ships from them." Consequently, hundreds perished in the waves.—*Wars of the Gaedhil*, p. 191. Dr. Todd mentions that he asked the Rev. S. Haughton, of Trinity College, Dublin, to calculate for him "what was the hour of high water at the shore of Clontarf, in Dublin Bay, on the 23rd of April, 1014." The result was a full confirmation of the account given by the author of the *Wars of the Gaedhil*—the Rev. S. Haughton having calculated that the morning tide was full in at 5.30 a.m., the evening tide being full at 55.5 p.m.

[1] *Siguard.*—Various accounts are given of the disposition of forces on each side, so that it is impossible to speak with accuracy on the subject. We know how difficult it is to obtain correct particulars on such occasions, even with the assistance of "own correspondents" and electric telegraphs.

third battalion was commanded by Maelruanaidh (Mulrooney of the Paternosters) and Teigue O'Kelly, with all the nobles of Connaught. Brian's army numbered about twenty thousand men. The accounts which relate the position of Malachy, and his conduct on this occasion, are hopelessly conflicting. It appears quite impossible to decide whether he was a victim to prejudice, or whether Brian was a victim to his not unnatural hostility.

On the eve of the battle, one of the Danish chiefs, Plait, son of King Lochlainn, sent a challenge to Domhnall, son of Emhin, High Steward of Mar. The battle commenced at daybreak. Plait came forth and exclaimed three times, *"Faras Domhnall?"* (Where is Domhnall?) Domhnall replied : " Here, thou reptile." A terrible hand-to-hand combat ensued. They fell dead at the same moment, the sword of each through the heart of the other, and the hair of each in the clenched hand of the other. And the combat of those two was the first combat of the battle.

Before the engagement Brian harangued his troops, with the crucifix in one hand and a sword in the other. He reminded them of all they had suffered from their enemies, of their tyranny, their sacrilege, their innumerable perfidies ; and then, holding the crucifix aloft, he exclaimed : " The great God has at length looked down upon our sufferings, and endued you with the power and the courage this day to destroy for ever the tyranny of the Danes, and thus to punish them for their innumerable crimes and sacrileges by the avenging power of the sword. Was it not on this day that Christ Himself suffered death for you ?"

He was then compelled to retire to the rear, and await the result of the conflict ; but Murrough performed prodigies of valour. Even the Danish historians admit that he fought his way to their standard, and cut down two successive bearers of it.

The mailed armour of the Danes seems to have been a source of no little dread to their opponents. But the Irish battle-axe might well have set even more secure protection at defiance. It was wielded with such skill and force, that frequently a limb was lopped off with a single blow, despite the mail in which it was encased ; while the short lances, darts, and slinging-stones proved a speedy means of decapitating or stunning a fallen enemy.

The Dalcassians surpassed themselves in feats of arms. They hastened from time to time to refresh their thirst and cool their hands in a neighbouring brook ; but the Danes soon filled it up, and

deprived them of this resource. It was a conflict of heroes—a
hand-to-hand fight. Bravery was not wanting on either side, and
for a time the result seemed doubtful. Towards the afternoon, as
many of the Danish leaders were cut down, their followers began
to give way, and the Irish forces prepared for a final effort. At
this moment the Norwegian prince, Anrud, encountered Murrough,
whose arms were paralyzed from fatigue; he had still physical
strength enough to seize his enemy, fling him on the ground, and
plunge his sword into the body of his prostrate foe. But even as
he inflicted the death-wound, he received a mortal blow from the
dagger of the Dane, and the two chiefs fell together.

The *mêlée* was too general for an individual incident, however
important in itself, to have much effect. The Northmen and their
allies were flying hard and fast, the one towards their ships, the
others towards the city. But as they fled across the Tolka, they
forgot that it was now swollen with the incoming tide, and thousands
perished by water who had escaped the sword. The body of
Brian's grandson, the boy Turlough, was found in the river after the
battle, with his hands entangled in the hair of two Danish warriors,
whom he had held down until they were drowned. Sitric and
his wife had watched the combat from the battlements of Dublin.
It will be remembered that this lady was the daughter of King
Brian, and her interests were naturally with the Irish troops.
Some rough words passed between her and her lord, which ended
in his giving her so rude a blow, that he knocked out one of her
teeth. But we have yet to record the crowning tragedy of the day.
Brian had retired to his tent to pray, at the commencement of the
conflict. When the forces met, he began his devotions, and said
to his attendant : "Watch thou the battle and the combats,
whilst I say the psalms." After he had recited fifty psalms, fifty
collects, and fifty paternosters, he desired the man to look out and
inform him how the battle went, and the position of Murrough's
standard. He replied the strife was close and vigorous, and the
noise was as if seven battalions were cutting down Tomar's wood ;
but the standard was safe. Brian then said fifty more psalms, and
made the same inquiry. The attendant replied that all was in confusion, but that Murrough's standard still stood erect, and moved
westwards towards Dublin. "As long as that standard remains
erect," replied Brian, "it shall go well with the men of Erinn."
The aged king betook himself to his prayers once more, saying again

King Brian Boroimhe killed by the Viking.

fifty psalms[2] and collects; then, for the last time, he asked intelligence of the field. Latean replied : " They appear as if Tomar's wood was on fire, and its brushwood all burned down ;" meaning that the private soldiers of both armies were nearly all slain, and only a few of the chiefs had escaped ; adding the most grievous intelligence of all, that Murrough's standard had fallen. " Alas !" replied Brian, " Erinn has fallen with it : why should I survive such losses, even should I attain the sovereignty of the world?" His attendant then urged him to fly, but Brian replied that flight was useless, for he had been warned of his fate by Aibinn (the banshee of his family), and that he knew his death was at hand. He then gave directions about his will and his funeral, leaving 240 cows to the " successor of Patrick." Even at this moment the danger was impending. A party of Danes approached, headed by Brodir. The king sprang up from the cushion where he had been kneeling, and unsheathed his sword. At first Brodir did not know him, and thought he was a priest from finding him at prayer ; but one of his followers informed him that it was the Monarch of Ireland. In a moment the fierce Dane had opened his head with his battle-axe. It is said that Brian had time to inflict a wound on the Viking, but the details of this event are so varied that it is impossible to decide which account is most reliable. The Saga states that Brodir knew Brian,[3] and, proud of his exploit, held up the monarch's reeking head, exclaiming, " Let it be told from man to man that Brodir felled Brian." All accounts agree in stating that the Viking was slain immediately, if not cruelly, by Brian's guards, who thus revenged their own neglect of their master. Had Brian survived this conflict, and had he been but a few years younger, how different might have been the political and social state of Ireland even at the present day ! The Danish power was overthrown, and never again obtained an ascendency in the country. It needed but one strong will, one wise head, one brave arm, to consolidate the nation, and to establish a regular monarchy ; for there was mettle enough in the Celt, if only united, to resist foreign invasion for all time to come.

On Easter Monday the survivors were employed in burying the

[2] *Psalms.*—To recite the Psalter in this way was a special devotional practice of the middle ages.

[3] *Brian.—Burnt Njal*, ii. 337. If this account be reliable, Brian did not live to receive the last sacraments, as other authorities state.

dead and attending to the wounded. The remains of more than thirty chieftains were borne off to their respective territorial churches for interment. But even on that very night dissension arose in the camp. The chieftains of Desmond, seeing the broken condition of the Dalcassian force, renewed their claim to the alternate succession. When they had reached Rath Maisten (Mullaghmast, near Athy) they claimed the sovereignty of Munster, by demanding hostages. A battle ensued, in which even the wounded Dalcassians joined. Their leader desired them to be placed in the fort of Maisten, but they insisted on being fastened to stakes, firmly planted in the ground to support them, and stuffing their wounds with moss, they awaited the charge of the enemy. The men of Ossory, intimidated by their bravery, feared to give battle. But many of the wounded men perished from exhaustion—a hundred and fifty swooned away, and never recovered consciousness again. The majority were buried where they stood; a few of the more noble were carried to their ancestral resting-places. " And thus far the wars of the Gall with the Gaedhil, and the battle of Clontarf."

The Annals state that both Brian and his son, Murrough, lived to receive the rites of the Church, and that their remains were conveyed by the monks to Swords, and from thence, through Duleek and Louth, to Armagh, by Archbishop Maelmuire, the " successor of St. Patrick." Their obsequies were celebrated with great splendour, for twelve days and nights, by the clergy ; after which the body of Brian was deposited in a stone coffin, on the north side of the high altar, in the cathedral. Murrough was buried on the south side. Turlough was interred in the old churchyard of Kilmainham, where the shaft of an ancient cross still marks the site.

Malachy once more assumed the reins of government by common consent, and proved himself fully equal to the task. A month before his death he gained an important victory over the Danes at Athboy, A.D. 1022. An interregnum of twenty years followed his death, during which the country was governed by two wise men, Cuan O'Lochlann, a poet, and Corcran Cleireach, an anchoret. The circumstances attending Malachy's death are thus related by the Four Masters :—" The age of Christ 1022. Maelseachlainn Môr, pillar of the dignity and nobility of the west of the world, died in Croinis Locha-Aininn, in the seventy-third year of his age,

on the 4th of the nones of September, on Sunday precisely, after
intense penance for his sins and transgressions, after receiving the
body of Christ and His blood, after being anointed by the hands
of Amhalgaidh, successor of Patrick, for he and the successor of
Colum-Cille, and the successors of Ciaran, and most of the seniors
of Ireland were present [at his death], and they sung masses,
hymns, psalms, and canticles for the welfare of his soul."

COVER OF ST. PATRICK'S BELL.

DESMOND CASTLE AND RATH, LIMERICK.

CHAPTER XIV.

Distinguished Irish Scholars and Religious—Domestic Feuds—O'Brien's Illness caused by Fright—Pestilence and Severe Winters—Contentions between the Northerns and Southerns—Murtough's Circuit of Ireland—The Danes attempt an Invasion—An Irish King sent to the Isle of Man—Destruction of Kincora—St. Celsus makes Peace—The Synod of Fidh Aengussa—Subjects considered by the Synod: (1) The Regulation of the Number of Dioceses, (2) the Sacrament of Matrimony, (3) the Consecration of Bishops, (4) Ceremonies at Baptism—St. Malachy—The Traitor Dermod—Synod at Mellifont Abbey—St. Laurence O'Toole.

[A.D. 1022—1167.]

DOMESTIC wars were, as usual, productive of the worst consequences, as regards the social state of the country. The schools and colleges, which had been founded and richly endowed by the converted Irish, were now, without exception, plundered of their wealth, and, in many cases, deprived of those who had dispensed that wealth for the common good. It has been already shown that men lived holy lives, and died peaceful deaths, during the two hundred years of Danish oppression; we shall now find that schools were revived, monasteries repeopled, and missionaries sent to convert and instruct in foreign lands. A few monks from Ireland settled in Glastonbury early in the tenth century, where they devoted themselves to the instruction of youth. St. Dunstan, who was famous for his skill in music, was one of their most illustrious pupils : he was a scholar, an artist, and a musician. But English writers, who give him the credit of having brought "Englishmen to care once more for learning, after they had quite lost the taste for it, and had sunk back into ignorance and barbarism," forget to mention who were his instructors.

St. Maccallin, another Irishman, was teaching in France at the same period ; and Duncan, who governed the Monastery of St. Remigius, at Rheims, was writing books of instruction for his students, which are still extant. Marianus Scotus, whose chronicles are considered the most perfect compositions of their times, was teaching at Cologne. St. Fingen, who succeeded St. Cadroe as Abbot of the Monastery of St. Felix at Metz, was invested with the government of the Monastery of St. Symphorian in that city.[4] It was then ordered by the bishop, that none but Irish monks should be received into his house, unless their supply failed. In 975 the Monastery of St. Martin, near Cologne, was made over to the Irish monks in perpetuity. Happily, however, Ireland still retained many of her pious and gifted sons. We have mentioned elsewhere the Annals of Tighernach, and the remarkable erudition they evince. The name of Cormac Mac Cullinan may also be added to the list of literary men of the period. The poems of Kenneth O'Hartigan are still extant, as well as those of Eochd O'Flynn. The authorship of the *Wars of the Gaedhil and the Gall*, has been attributed to Brian Boroimhé's secretary, Mac Liag ; it is, at least, tolerably certain that it was written by one who witnessed the events described. The obituaries of several saints also occur at the close of the tenth and commencement of the eleventh centuries. Amongst these we find St. Duncheadh, Abbot of Clonmacnois, who is said to have been the last Irish saint who raised the dead. St. Aedh (Hugh) died in the year 1004, "after a good life, at Ard-Macha, with great honour and veneration." And in the year 1018, we have the mortuary record of St. Gormgal, of Ardvilean, "the remains of whose humble oratory and cloghan cell are still to be seen on that rocky island, amid the surges of the Atlantic, off the coast of Connemara."[5]

[4] *City.*—Some Irish religious are also said to have lived in amity with Greek monks, who were established at Tours, in France; and it is said that the Irish joined them in the performance of the ecclesiastical offices in their own language.

[5] *Connemara.*—Haverty's *History of Ireland*, p. 156. See also an interesting note on this subject in the Chronicum Scotorum.

Dr. Todd has well observed, in his admirably written " Introduction " to the *Wars of the Gaedhil and the Gall*, that from the
death of Malachy to the days of Strongbow, the history of Ireland
is little more than a history of the struggles for ascendency between
the great clans or families of O'Neill, O'Connor, O'Brien, and the
chieftains of Leinster.

After the death of Brian Boroimhé, his son Donough obtained
the undisputed sovereignty of Munster. He defeated the Des-
monians, and instigated the murder of his brother Teigue. His next
step was to claim the title of King of Ireland, but he had a formidable opponent in Dermod Mac Mael-na-mbo, King of Leinster.
Strange to say, though he had the guilt of fratricide on his
conscience, he assembled the clergy and chieftains of Munster at
Killaloe, in the year 1050, to pass laws for the protection of life
and property—a famine, which occurred at this time, making such
precautions of the first necessity. In 1063, his nephew, Turlough,
avenged the death of Teigue, in a battle, wherein Donough was
defeated. After his reverse he went on a pilgrimage to Rome,
where he died in the following year, after doing penance for his
brother's murder. The Annals say that " he died under the victory
of penance, in the Monastery of Stephen the Martyr."[6] Dermod
Mac Mael-na-mbo was killed in battle by the King of Meath, A.D.
1072, and Turlough O'Brien, consequently, was regarded as his
successor to the monarchy of Ireland. Turlough, as usual,
commenced by taking hostages, but he found serious opposition
from the northern Hy-Nials. His principal opponents were the
Mac Loughlins of Aileach, and the O'Melaghlins of Meath. In 1079
O'Brien invaded the territory of Roderic O'Connor, King of Connaught, expelled him from his kingdom, and plundered it as far as
Croagh Patrick. Next year he led an army to Dublin, and received
the submission of the men of Meath, appointing his son Murtough
lord of the Danes of Dublin. The Annals of the Four Masters give
a curious account of O'Brien's death. They say that the head of

---

[6] *Martyr.*—Page 887. The famine in the preceding year is also recorded,
as well as the cholic and "lumps," which prevailed in Leinster, and also
spread throughout Ireland. Donough was married to an English princess,
Driella, the daughter of the English Earl Godwin, and sister of Harold, afterwards King of England. During the rebellion of Godwin and his sons against
Edward the Confessor, Harold was obliged to take refuge in Ireland, and
remained there "all the winter on the king's security."

Connor O'Melaghlin, King of Meath, was taken from the church of Clonmacnois, and brought to Thomond, by his order. When the king took the head in his hand, a mouse ran out of it, and the shock was so great that "he fell ill of a sore disease by the miracles (intervention) of St. Ciaran." This happened on the night of Good Friday. The day of the resurrection (Easter Sunday) the head was restored, with two rings of gold as a peace-offering. But Turlough never recovered from the effects of his fright, and lingered on in bad health until the year 1086, when he died. He is called the "modest Turlough" in the Annals, for what special reason does not appear. It is also recorded that he performed "intense penance for his sins"—a grace which the kings and princes of Ireland seem often to have needed, and, if we may believe the Annals, always to have obtained.

A period of anarchy ensued, during which several princes contended for royal honours. This compliment was finally awarded to Mac Loughlin, King of Aileach, and a temporary peace ensued. Its continuance was brief. In 1095 there was a pestilence all over Europe, "and some say that the fourth part of the men of Ireland died of the malady." A long list is given of its victims, lay and ecclesiastical. Several severe winters are recorded as having preceded this fatal event; probably they were its remote cause. In the year 1096, the festival of St. John Baptist fell on Friday. This event caused general consternation, in consequence of some old prophecy. A resolution "of the clergy of Ireland, with the successor of St. Patrick[7] at their head," enjoined a general abstinence from Wednesday to Sunday every month, with other penitential observances ; and "the men of Ireland were saved for that time from the fire of vengeance."[8]

But the most important event of the period was the contention between the northern and southern Hy-Nials. Murtough was planning, with great military ability, to obtain the supreme rule. The Archbishop of Armagh and the clergy strove twice to avert hostilities, but their interference was almost ineffectual. "A year's peace" was all they could obtain. In the year 1100, Murtough

---

[7] *St. Patrick.*—It is observable all through the Annals, how the name and spiritual authority of St. Patrick is revered. This expression occurs regularly from the earliest period, wherever the Primate of Ireland is mentioned.

[8] *Vengeance.*—See O'Curry, *passim*, for curious traditions or so-called prophecies about St. John Baptist's Day.

brought a Danish fleet against the northerns, but they were cut off
by O'Loughlin, "by killing or drowning." He also assembled an
army at Assaroe, near Ballyshannon, "with the choice part of the
men of Ireland," but the Cinel-Connaill defended their country
bravely, and compelled him to retire "without booty, without
hostages, without pledges." In 1101, when the twelvemonths' truce
obtained by the clergy had expired, Murtough collected a powerful
army, and devastated the north, without opposition. He demolished the palace of the Hy-Nials, called the Grianan of Aileach.[9]
This was an act of revenge for a similar raid, committed a few years
before, on the stronghold of the O'Briens, at Kincora, by O'Loughlin.
So determined was he on devastation, that he commanded a stone
to be carried away from the building in each of the sacks which
had contained provisions for the army. He then took hostages of
Ulidia, and returned to the south, having completed the circuit of
Ireland in six weeks. The expedition was called the "circuitous
hosting." His rather original method of razing a palace, is commemorated in the following quatrain :—

> " I never heard of the billeting of grit stones,
>   Though I heard [sic] of the billeting of companies,
>   Until the stones of Aileach was billeted
>   On the horses of the king of the west."[1]

Murtough appears to have been a not unusual compound of piety
and profanity. We read in one place of his reckless exploits in
burning churches and desecrating shrines, and in others of his
liberal endowments of the same.

The Danes had now settled quietly in the mercantile towns
which they had mainly contributed to form, and expended all
their energies on commerce instead of war; but the new generation
of Northmen, who had not yet visited Ireland, could not so easily
relinquish the old project of conquering it. About the year 1101,
Magnus planned an expedition to effect this purpose. He arrived
in Dublin the following year; a "hosting of the men of Ireland
came to oppose him;"[2] but they made peace with him for one
year, and Murtough gave his daughter in marriage to his son Sitric,
"with many jewels and gifts." The year 1103 was distinguished for

---

[9] *Aileach.*—The remains of this fortress are still visible near Londonderry,
and are called Grianan-Elagh.

[1] *West.*—Annals, vol. ii. p. 969.   [2] *Him.*—*Ib.* p. 973.

sanguinary conflicts. Murdhadh Drun was killed on a predatory excursion in Magh Cobha. Raghnall Ua h-Ocain,[3] lawgiver of Felach Og, was slain by the men of Magh Itha. There was a "great war" between the Cinel-Eoghain and the Ulidians; and Murtough O'Brien, with the men of Munster, Leinster, and Ossory, the chiefs of Connaught, and the men of Meath and their kings, proceeded to Magh Cobha (Donaghmore, co. Down) to relieve the Ulidians. When the men of Munster "were wearied," Murtough proceeded to Ard-Macha, and left eight ounces of gold upon the altar, and promised eightscore cows. The northern Hy-Nials then attacked the camp of the Leinster men, and a spirited battle was fought. The Cinel-Eoghain and Cinel-Connaill returned victoriously and triumphantly to their forts, with valuable jewels and much wealth, together with the royal tent, the standard, and jewels.

Magnus, King of Lochlann and the Isles, was slain by the Ulidians this year.

It is noticeable that, in the Annals of the Four Masters, obituaries of saints or good men always occupy the first place. The Annals of this year are of unusual length; but they commence with the obituary of Murchadh O'Flanaghan, Arrchinneach of Ardbo, a paragon of wisdom and instruction, who died on his pilgrimage at Ard-Macha. A priest of Kildare is also mentioned, and the Tanist-Abbot of Clonmacnois, a prosperous and affluent man.

It would appear that the Irish were sufficiently occupied with domestic wars to prevent their offering assistance elsewhere. This, however, was not the case. When Harold returned to England, his brother-in-law, Donough, lent him nine ships; and we find the Irish affording assistance in several other feuds of the Anglo-Saxons of this period. A deputation of the nobles of Man and other islands visited Dublin, and waited on Murtough O'Brien to solicit a king. He sent his nephew, Donnell; but he was soon expelled on account of his tyranny. Another Donnell O'Brien, his cousin, was, at the same time, lord of the Danes in Dublin. In 1114 Murtough O'Brien was obliged to resign the crown in consequence of ill-health; the Annals say that he became a living skeleton. His brother, Dermod, took advantage of this circumstance to declare

---

[3] *Ua h-Ocain.*—Now anglicised O'Hagan. This family had the special privilege of crowning the O'Neills, and were their hereditary Brehons. The Right Honorable Judge O'Hagan is, we believe, the present head of the family.

himself King of Munster. This obliged Murtough to resume the reins of government, and put himself at the head of his army. He succeeded in making Dermod prisoner, but eventually he was obliged to resign the kingdom to him, and retired into the Monastery of Lismore, where he died in 1119. The Annals call him the prop of the glory and magnificence of the western world. In the same year Nial Mac Lochlann, royal heir of Aileach and of Ireland, fell by the Cinel-Moain, in the twenty-eighth year of his age. He was the "paragon of Ireland, for personal form, sense, hospitality, and learning." The Chief Ollamh of Ireland, Cucollchoille ua Biagh-eallain, was killed by the men of Lug and Tuatha-ratha (Tooragh, co. Fermanagh), with his wife, "two very good sons," and five-and-thirty persons in one house, on the Saturday before Little Easter. The cause of this outrage is not mentioned. The Annals of the Four Masters and the Annals of Ulster record the same event, and mention that he was distinguished for charity, hospitality, and universal benevolence.

Donnell O'Loughlin died in 1121, in the Monastery of St. Columba, at Derry. He is styled King of Ireland, although the power of his southern rival preponderated during the greater part of his reign. In 1118 Rory O'Connor died in the Monastery of Clonmacnois. He had been blinded some years previously by the O'Flaherties. This cruel custom was sometimes practised to prevent the succession of an obnoxious person, as freedom from every blemish was a *sine qua non* in Erinn for a candidate to royal honours. Teigue Mac Carthy, King of Desmond, died, "after penance," at Cashel, A.D. 1124. From the time of Murtough O'Brien's illness, Turlough O'Connor, son of the prince who had been blinded, comes prominently forward in Irish history. His object was to exalt the Eoghanists or Desmonian family, who had been virtually excluded from the succession since the time of Brian Boroimhé. In 1116 he plundered Thomond as far as Limerick. In 1118 he led an army as far as Glanmire (co. Cork), and divided Munster, giving Desmond to Mac Carthy, and Thomond to the sons of Dermod O'Brien. He then marched to Dublin, and took hostages from the Danes, releasing Donnell, son of the King of Meath, whom they had in captivity. The following year he sailed down the Shannon with a fleet, and destroyed the royal palace of Kincora, hurling its stones and timber beams into the river. He then devoted himself to wholesale plundering, and expelled his late ally and father-in-law from Meath, ravaging the country from Traigh Li (Tralee) to the sanctuary lands of Lismore. In 1126 he bestowed the kingdom of Dublin on his son Cormac. In 1127 he drove Cormac Mac Carthy from his kingdom, and divided Munster in three parts. In fact, there was such a storm of war throughout the whole country, that St. Celsus was obliged to interfere. He spent a month and a year trying to establish peace, and promulgating rules and good customs in every district, among the laity and clergy. His efforts to teach " good rules and manners " seem to have been scarcely effectual, for we find an immediate entry of the decapitation of Ruaidhri, after he had made a " treacherous prey " in Aictheara. In the year 1128 the good Archbishop succeeded in making a year's truce between the Connaught men and the men of Munster. The following year the saint died at Ardpatrick, where he was making a visitation. He was only fifty years of age, but anxiety and care had worn him old. St. Celsus was buried at Lismore, and interred in the cemetery of the bishops.

We must now give a brief glance at the ecclesiastical history of Ireland, before narrating the events which immediately preceded the English invasion.

In the year 1111 a synod was convened at Fidh Aengussa, or Aengus Grove, near the Hill of Uisneach, in Westmeath. It was attended by fifty bishops, 300 priests, and 3,000 religious. Murtough O'Brien was also permitted to be present, and some of the nobles of his province. The object of the synod was to institute rules of life and manners for the clergy and people. St. Celsus, the Archbishop of Armagh, and Maelmuire[4] or Marianus O'Dunain, Archbishop of Cashel, were present. Attention had already been directed to certain abuses in ecclesiastical discipline. Such abuses must always arise from time to time in the Church, through the frailty of her members ; but these abuses are always carefully reprehended as they arise, so that she is no longer responsible for them. It is remarkable that men of more than ordinary sanctity have usually been given to the Church at such periods. Some have withheld heretical emperors from deeds of evil, and some have braved the fury of heretical princes. In Ireland, happily, the rulers needed not such opposition ; but when the country

[4] *Maelmuire.*—" The servant of Mary." Devotion to the Mother of God, which is still a special characteristic of the Irish nation, was early manifested by the adoption of this name.

had been again and again devastated by war, whether from foreign
or domestic sources, the intervention of saintly men was especially
needed to restore peace, and to repair, as far as might be, the
grievous injury which war always inflicts on the social state of those
who have suffered from its devastations.

Lanfranc, the great Archbishop of Canterbury, had already
noticed the state of the Irish Church.   He was in constant communication with the Danish bishops, who had received consecration
from him ; and their accounts were probably true in the main,
however coloured by prejudice.   He wrote an earnest epistle to
Turlough O'Brien, whom he addresses respectfully as King of
Ireland, and whose virtues as a Christian prince he highly commends.   His principal object appears to have been to draw the
king's attention to an abuse, of which the Danes had informed him,
with regard to the sacrament of matrimony.   This subject shall be
noticed again.   Pope Gregory VII. also wrote to Turlough, but
principally on the temporal authority of the Holy See.

The synod had four special subjects for consideration : (1) First,
to regulate the number of bishops—an excessive and undue multiplication of episcopal dignity having arisen from the custom of creating
chorepiscopi or rural bishops.   It was now decided that there should
be but twenty-four dioceses—twelve for the northern and twelve
for the southern half of Ireland.   Cashel was also recognized as an
archiepiscopal see, and the successor of St. Jarlath was sometimes
called Archbishop of Connaught.   The custom of lay appropriations,
which had obtained in some places, was also firmly denounced.
This was an intolerable abuse.   St. Celsus, the Archbishop of
Armagh, though himself a member of the family who had usurped
this office, made a special provision in his will that he should
be succeeded by St. Malachy.   This saint obtained a final victory
over the sacrilegious innovators, but not without much personal
suffering.[5]

The (2) second abuse which was now noticed, referred to the
sacrament of matrimony.   The Irish were accused of abandoning
their lawful wives and taking others, of marrying within the degrees

---

[5] *Suffering.*—This abuse was not peculiar to the Irish Church.   A canon of
the Council of London, A.D. 1125, was framed to prevent similar lay appropriations.   In the time of Cambrensis there were lay (so called) abbots, who
took the property of the Church into their own hands, and made their children
receive holy orders that they might enjoy the revenues.

of consanguinity, and it was said that in Dublin wives were even exchanged. Usher, in commenting on the passage in Lanfranc's letter which refers to these gross abuses, observes that the custom of discarding wives was prevalent among the Anglo-Saxons and in Scotland. This, however, was no excuse for the Irish. The custom was a remnant of pagan contempt of the female sex,—a contempt from which women were never fully released, until Christianity restored the fallen, and the obedience of the second Eve had atoned for the disobedience of the first. It appears, however, that these immoralities were almost confined to the half-Christianized Danes, who still retained many of their heathen customs. The canons of St. Patrick, which were always respected by the native Irish, forbid such practices ; and the synod, therefore, had only to call on the people to observe the laws of the Church more strictly.

Two other subjects, (3) one regarding the consecration of bishops, the other (4) referring to the ceremonies of baptism, were merely questions of ecclesiastical discipline, and as such were easily arranged by competent authority. In St. Anselm's correspondence with the prelates of the south of Ireland, he passes a high eulogium on their zeal and piety, while he deplores certain relaxations of discipline, which they were as anxious to reform as he could desire.

We have already mentioned that St. Celsus appointed St. Malachy his successor in the Archiepiscopal See of Armagh. Malachy had been educated by the Abbot Imar O'Hagan, who presided over the great schools of that city; and the account given of his early training, sufficiently manifests the ability of his gifted instructor, and the high state of intellectual culture which existed in Ireland. While still young, St. Malachy undertook the restoration of the famous Abbey of Bangor. Here he erected small oratory of wood, and joined himself to a few devoted men ardent for the perfection of a religious life. He was soon after elected Bishop of Connor. With the assistance of some of his faithful monks, he restored what war and rapine had destroyed; and was proceeding peacefully and successfully in his noble work, when he was driven from his diocese by a hostile prince. He now fled to Cormac Mac Carthy, King of Desmond ;[6] but he was not

---

[6] *Desmond.*—See the commencement of this chapter, for an illustration of the ruins of its ancient rath and the more modern castle. These remains are among the most interesting in Ireland.

permitted to remain here long. The See of Armagh was vacated by the death of St. Celsus, and Malachy was obliged to commence another arduous mission. It is said that it almost required threats of excommunication to induce him to undertake the charge. Bishop Gilbert of Limerick, the Apostolic-Delegate, and Bishop Malchus of Lismore, with other bishops and several chieftains, visited him in the monastery which he had erected at Ibrach,[7] and at last obtained compliance by promising him permission to retire when he had restored order in his new diocese.

BANGOR CASTLE.

St. Malachy found his mission as painful as he had anticipated. The lay intruders were making a last attempt to keep up their evil custom; and, after the death of the usurper who made this false claim, another person attempted to continue it; but popular feeling was so strong against the wretched man, that he was obliged to fly. Ecclesiastical discipline was soon restored; and after Malachy had made a partition of the diocese, he was permitted to resign in favour of Gelasius, then Abbot of the great Columbian Monastery of Derry.

[7] *Ibrach.*—Supposed to be Ivragh, in Kerry, which was part of Cormac Mac Carthy's kingdom.

But peace was not yet established in Ireland. I shall return again to the narrative of domestic feuds, which made it a "trembling sod," the O'Loughlins of Tyrone being the chief aggressors; for the present we must follow the course of ecclesiastical history briefly. St. Malachy was now appointed Bishop of Down, to which his old see of Connor was united. He had long a desire to visit Rome—a devotional pilgrimage of the men of Erinn from the earliest period. He was specially anxious to obtain a formal recognition of the archiepiscopal sees in Ireland, by the granting of palliums. On his way to the Holy City he visited St. Bernard at Clairvaux, and thus commenced and cemented the friendship which forms so interesting a feature in the lives of the French and Irish saints. It is probable that his account of the state of the Irish Church took a tinge of gloom from the heavy trials he had endured in his efforts to remove its temporary abuses. St. Bernard's ardent and impetuous character, even his very affectionateness, would lead him also to look darkly on the picture : hence the somewhat over-coloured accounts he has given of its state at that eventful period. St. Malachy returned to Ireland after an interview with the reigning Pontiff, Pope Innocent II. His Holiness had received him with open arms, and appointed him Apostolic Legate ; but he declined to give the palliums, until they were formally demanded by the Irish prelates.

In virtue of his legatine power, the saint assembled local synods in several places. He rebuilt and restored many churches ; and in 1142 he erected the famous Cistercian Abbey of Mellifont, near Drogheda. This monastery was liberally endowed by O'Carroll, King of Oriel, and was peopled by Irish monks, whom St. Malachy had sent to Clairvaux, to be trained in the Benedictine rule and observances. But his great act was the convocation of the Synod of Inis Padraig. It was held in the year 1148. St. Malachy presided as Legate of the Holy See; fifteen bishops, two hundred priests, and some religious were present at the deliberations, which lasted for four days. The members of the synod were unwilling that Malachy should leave Ireland again; but Eugene III., who had been a Cistercian monk, was visiting Clairvaux, and it was hoped he might grant the favour there. The Pope had left the abbey when the saint arrived, who, in a few days after, was seized with mortal sickness, and died on the 2nd November, 1148. His remains were interred at Clairvaux. His feast was changed from the 2nd of

November, All Souls, to the 3rd, by " the seniors," that he might be the more easily revered and honoured.

In 1151 Cardinal Paparo arrived in Ireland with the palliums which had been solicited by St. Malachy. The insignia of dignity were conferred the following year, at the Council of Kells. Tithes were then introduced for the first time in Ireland, but they were not enforced until after the English invasion.

It will be remembered that we turned to ecclesiastical history, after mentioning the year's truce (A.D. 1128) which had been made, through the intervention of St. Celsus, between the men of Munster and Connaught. In 1129 the great Church of Clonmacnois was robbed[8] of some of its greatest treasures. Amongst these was a model of Solomon's Temple, presented by a prince of Meath, and a silver chalice burnished with gold, which had been engraved by a sister of King Turlough O'Connor—an evidence that the ladies of Ireland were by no means behind the age in taste and refinement.

After the death of Donnell O'Loughlin, Turlough had full scope for the exercise of his ambitious projects; but in 1131 he found serious opposition from Connor O'Brien, who had succeeded his father, Dermod, on the throne of Munster. Connor now carried off hostages from Leinster and Meath, and defeated the cavalry of Connaught. The following year he sent a fleet to the western coast of Ireland. Eventually Turlough O'Connor was glad to make a truce with his opponents. In 1184 the consecration of a church at Cashel was celebrated. This is still known as Cormac's Chapel, and was long supposed to have been erected by the more ancient monarch of that name. But the good king was soon after treacherously slain in his own house, by Turlough O'Connor and the two sons of the O'Connor of Kerry. Turlough was unquestionably somewhat Spartan in his severities, if not Draconian in his administration of justice. In 1106 he put out the eyes of his own son, Hugh, and in the same year he imprisoned another son, named Roderic. The nature of their offences is not manifest; but Roderic

---

8 *Robbed.*—In MacGeoghegan's translation of the Annals of Clonmacnois he says :—" The clergy of Clone made incessant prayer to God and St. Keyran, to be a means for the revelation of the party that took away the said jewels." The " party " was a Dane. He was discovered, and hung in 1130. It is said that he entered several ships to leave the country, but they could get no wind, while other vessels sailed off freely.—Annals of the Four Masters, vol. ii. p. 1035.

was liberated through the interference of the clergy. Seven years after he was again imprisoned, " in violation of the most solemn pledges and guarantees." The clergy again interfered ; from which we may infer that he was a favourite. They even held a public feast at Rathbrendan on his behalf; but he was not released until the following year. In the year 1136 we find the obituary of the chief keeper of the calendar of Ard-Macha, on the night of Good Friday. He is also mentioned as its chief antiquary and librarian, an evidence that the old custom was kept up to the very eve of the English invasion. The obituary of Donnell O'Duffy, Archbishop of Connaught, is also given. He died after Mass and celebration; according to the Annals of Clonmacnois, he had celebrated Mass by himself, at Clonfert, on St. Patrick's Day, and died immediately after. About the same time the Breinemen behaved " so exceedingly outrageous," that they irreverently stript O'Daly, arch-poet of Ireland, " of all his clothes."

In the meantime domestic wars multiplied with extraordinary rapidity. Dermod Mac Murrough, the infamous King of Leinster, now appears for the first time in the history of that country which he mainly contributed to bring under the English yoke. He commenced his career of perfidy by carrying off the Abbess of Kildare from her cloister, killing 170 of the people of Kildare, who interfered to prevent this wanton and sacrilegious outrage. In 1141 he endeavoured to crush the opposers of his atrocious tyranny by a barbarous onslaught, in which he killed two nobles, put out the eyes of another, and blinded[9] seventeen chieftains of inferior rank. A fitting commencement of his career of treachery towards his unfortunate country ! In 1148 a temporary peace was made by the Primate of Armagh between the northern princes, who had carried on a deadly feud ; but its duration, as usual, was brief. Turlough O'Brien was deposed by Teigue in 1151. He was assisted by Turlough O'Connor and the infamous Dermod. The united armies plundered as far as Moin Môr,[1] where they encountered

[9] *Blinded.*—In 1165 Henry II. gratified his irritation against the Welsh by laying hands upon the hostages of their noblest families, and commanding that the eyes of the males should be rooted out, and the ears and noses of the females cut off; and yet Henry is said to have been liberal to the poor, and though passionately devoted to the chase, he did not inflict either death or mutilation on the intruders in the royal forests.

[1] *Moin Môr.*—Now Moanmore, county Tipperary.

the Dalcassian forces returning from the plunder of Desmond. A sanguinary combat ensued, and the men of north Munster suffered a dreadful slaughter, leaving 7,000 dead upon the field of battle. This terrible sacrifice of life is attributed to the mistaken valour of the Dal-Cais, who would neither fly nor ask quarter.

In 1157 a synod was held in the Abbey of Mellifont, attended by the Bishop of Lismore, Legate of the Holy See, the Primate, and seventeen other bishops. Murtough O'Loughlin, the Monarch of Ireland, and several other kings, were also present. The principal object of this meeting was the consecration of the abbey church and the excommunication of Donough O'Melaghlin, who had become the common pest of the country. He was, as might be expected, the particular friend and ally of Dermod Mac Murrough. His last exploit was the murder of a neighbouring chief, despite the most solemn pledges. In an old translation of the Annals of Ulster, he is termed, with more force than elegance, " a cursed atheist." After his excommunication, his brother Dermod was made King of Meath, in his place.

At this synod several rich gifts were made to the abbey. O'Carroll, Prince of Oriel, presented sixty ounces of gold. O'Loughlin made a grant of lands, gave one hundred and forty cows and sixty ounces of gold. The Lady Dervorgil gave the same donation in gold, together with a golden chalice for the altar of Mary, with gifts for each of the other nine altars of the church. Dervorgil was the wife of Tiernan O'Rourke, Lord of Breffni, who had been dispossessed of his territories in 1152; at the same time she was carried off by Dermod Mac Murrough. Her abduction seems to have been effected with her own consent, as she carried off the cattle which had formed her dowry. Her husband, it would appear, had treated her harshly. Eventually she retired to the Monastery of Mellifont, where she endeavoured to atone for her past misconduct by a life of penance.

Another synod was held in the year 1158, at Trim. Derry was then erected into an episcopal see, and Flahertach O'Brolchain, Abbot of St. Columba's Monastery, was consecrated its first bishop. The bishops of Connaught were intercepted and plundered by Dermod's soldiers; they therefore returned and held a provincial synod in Roscommon.

In 1162 St. Laurence O'Toole was chosen to succeed Greine, or Gregory, the Danish Archbishop of Dublin. He belonged to one of the most noble ancient families of Leinster. His father was chieftain of the district of Hy-Muirahy, a portion of the present county Kildare. St. Laurence had chosen the ecclesiastical state early in life; at the age of twenty-five he was chosen Abbot of St. Kevin's Monastery, at Glendalough. The Danish Bishop of Dublin had been consecrated by the Archbishop of Canterbury, but the saint received the episcopal office from the successor of St. Patrick. A synod was held at Clane the year of his consecration; it was attended by twenty-six prelates and many other ecclesiastics. The college of Armagh was then virtually raised to the rank of a university, as it was decreed that no one, who had not been an alumnus of Armagh, should be appointed lector or professor of theology in any of the diocesan schools in Ireland. Indeed, the clergy at this period were most active in promoting the interests of religion, and most successful in their efforts, little anticipating the storm which was then impending over their country.

In 1166 the Irish Monarch, O'Loughlin, committed a fearful outrage on Dunlevy, Prince of Dalriada. A peace had been ratified between them, but, from some unknown cause, O'Loughlin suddenly became again the aggressor, and attacked the northern chief, when he was unprepared, put out his eyes, and killed three of his leading officers. This cruel treachery so provoked the princes who had guaranteed the treaty, that they mustered an army at once and proceeded northwards. The result was a sanguinary engagement, in which the Cinel-Eoghan were defeated, and the Monarch, O'Loughlin, was slain. Roderick O'Connor immediately assumed the reins of government, and was inaugurated in Dublin with more pomp than had ever been manifested on such an occasion. It was the last glittering flicker of the expiring lamp. Submission was made to him on every side; and had he only possessed the ability or the patriotism to unite the forces under his command, he might well have set all his enemies at defiance. An assembly of the clergy and chieftains of Ireland was convened in 1167, which is said to have emulated, if it did not rival, the triennial *Fes* of ancient Tara. It was but the last gleam of sunlight, which indicates the coming of darkness and gloom. The traitor already had his plans prepared, and was flying from a country which scorned his meanness, to another country where that meanness was made the tool of political purposes, while the unhappy traitor was probably quite as heartily despised.

ARDMORE ROUND TOWER.

CHAPTER XV.

Social Life previous to the English Invasion—Domestic Habitations—Forts—Granard and Staigue—Crannoges and Log-houses—Interior of the Houses—The Hall—Food and Cooking Utensils—Regulations about Food—The Kind of Food used—Animal Food—Fish—Game—Drink and Drinking Vessels—Whisky—Heath Beer—Mead—Animal Produce—Butter and Cheese—Fire—Candles—Occupations and Amusements—Chess—Music—Dress—Silk—Linen—Ancient Woollen Garments—Gold Ornaments—Trade—General Description of the Fauna and Flora of the Country.

USTOMS which illustrate the social life of our ancestors, are scarcely the least interesting or important elements of history. Before we enter upon that portion of our annals which commences with the English invasion, under the auspices of Henry II., we shall give a brief account of the habitations, manners, customs, dress, food, and amusements of the people of Ireland. Happily there is abundant and authentic information on this subject, though we may be obliged to delve beneath the tertiary deposits of historical strata in order to obtain all that is required. English society and English social life were more or less influenced by Ireland from the fifth to the twelfth century. The monks who had emigrated to "Saxon land" were men of considerable intellectual culture, and, as such, had a preponderating influence, creditable alike to themselves and to those who bowed to its sway. From the twelfth to the sixteenth century, English manners and customs were introduced in Ireland within the Pale. The object of the present chapter is to show the social state of the country before the English invasion—a condition of society which continued for some centuries later in the western and southern parts of the island.

The pagan architecture of public erections has already been as fully considered as our limits would permit. Let us turn from pillar-stones, cromlechs, and cairns, to the domestic habitations which preceded Christianity, and continued in use, with gradual improvements, until the period when English influence introduced the comparative refinements which it had but lately received from Norman sources. The raths, mounds, and forts, whose remains still exist throughout the country, preceded the castellated edifices, many of which were erected in the twelfth and thirteenth centuries, principally by English settlers. The rath was probably used for the protection and enclosure of cattle; and as the wealth of the country consisted principally in its herds, it was an important object. Its form is circular, having an internal diameter averaging from forty to two hundred feet, encompassed by a mound and outer fosse or ditch. In some localities, where stone is abundant and the soil shallow, rude walls have been formed: the raths, however, are principally earthwork alone. Forts were erected for defence, and the surrounding fosse was filled with water. They were, in fact, the prototypes of the more modern castle and moat. These forts were sometimes of considerable size, and in such cases were surrounded by several fosses and outworks. They were approached by a winding inclined plane, which at once facilitated the entrance of friends, and exposed comers with hostile intentions to the concentrated attacks of the garrison. The fort at Granard is a good example of this kind of building. It is probably of considerable antiquity, though it has been improved and rebuilt in some portions at a more modern period. The interior of it evidences the existence of several different apartments. An approach internally has been exposed on one side, and exhibits a wide, flat arch of common masonry, springing from the top of two side walls, the whole well-constructed.

Forts of dry-wall masonry, which are, undoubtedly, the more ancient, are very numerous in the south-west of Ireland. It is probable that similar erections existed throughout the country at a

former period, and that their preservation is attributable to the
remoteness of the district.   The most perfect of these ancient habitations is that of Staigue Fort, near Derryquin Castle, Kenmare.
This fort has an internal diameter of eighty-eight feet.   The
masonry is composed of flat-bedded stones of the slate rock of the
country, which show every appearance of being quarried, or carefully broken from larger blocks.   There is no appearance of dressed
work in the construction ; but the slate would not admit of this,
as it splinters away under the slightest blow.   Still the building
is an admirable example of constructive masonry ; it is almost
impossible to dislodge any fragment from off the filling stones
from the face of the wall.   A competent authority has pronounced
that these structures cannot be equalled by any dry masonry elsewhere met with in the country, nor by any masonry of the kind
erected in the present day.[2]   Some small stone buildings are also
extant in this part of Ireland, but it is doubtful whether they
were used for ecclesiastical or domestic purposes.   The crannoge
was another kind of habitation, and one evidently much used, and
evincing no ordinary skill in its construction.   From the remains
found in these island habitations, we may form a clear idea of the
customs and civilization of their inmates : their food is indicated
by the animal remains, which consist of several varieties of oxen,
deer, goats, and sheep ; the implements of cookery remain, even
to the knife, and the blocks of stone blackened from long use as
fire-places ; the arrows, which served for war or chase, are found
in abundance ; the personal ornaments evidence the taste of the
wearers, and the skill of the artist ; while the canoe, usually of solid
oak, and carefully hidden away, tells its own tale how entrance
and exit were effected.   One of the earliest crannoges which was
discovered and examined in modern times, was that of Lagere,
near Dunshaughlin, county Meath.   It is remarkable that Loch Ga-
bhair is said to have been one of the nine lakes which burst forth in
Ireland, A.M. 3581.   The destruction of this crannoge is recorded by
the Four Masters, A.D. 933, giving evidence that it was occupied
up to that period.   In 1246 there is a record of the escape of
Turlough O'Connor from a crannoge, after he had drowned his
keepers ; from which it would appear such structures might be used
for prisons, and, probably, would be specially convenient for the

[2] Day.—Wilkinson's *Geology and Architecture of Ireland*, p. 59.

detention of hostages. In 1560 we read that Teigue O'Rourke was drowned as he was going across a lake to sleep in a crannoge; and even so late as the sixteenth century, crannoges were declared to be the universal system of defence in the north of Ireland.

Log-houses were also used, and were constructed of beams and planks of timber, something like the Swiss *chalet*. One of these ancient structures was discovered in Drumhalin bog, county Donegal, in 1833. The house consisted of a square structure, twelve feet wide and nine feet high: it was formed of rough planks and blocks of timber; the mortises were very roughly cut—a stone celt,[3] which was found lying upon the floor, was, probably, the instrument used to form them. The logs were most likely formed by a stone axe.[4] The roof was flat, and the house consisted of two compartments, one over the other, each four feet high. A paved causeway led from the house to the fire-place, on which was a quantity of ashes, charred wood, half-burnt turf, and hazle-nuts. So ancient was this habitation, that twenty-six feet of bog had grown up around and over it. It is sup-

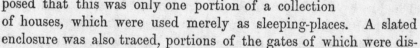

CELT.

posed that this was only one portion of a collection of houses, which were used merely as sleeping-places. A slated enclosure was also traced, portions of the gates of which were discovered. A piece of a leathern sandal, an arrow-headed flint, and a wooden sword, were also found in the same locality.

It is probable that wattles and clay formed the staple commodity for building material in ancient Erinn. Planks and beams, with rough blocks of wood or stone, were most likely reserved for

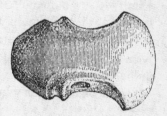

STONE AXE.

the dwelling-place of chieftains. Such were the material used also for the royal residence in Thorney Island, a swampy morass in the

---

[3] *Celt.*—Catalogue of R. I. A. p. 43. This celt is the largest discovered in Ireland, and is formed of coarse clay-slate. It is 22 inches long, 1 inch thick, and 3¾ broad at the widest part. It was found in the bed of the river Blackwater, two miles below Charlemont, county Armagh.

[4] *Axe.*—Catalogue of R. I. A. p. 80. Sir W. Wilde pronounces this to be

Thames, secured by its insular position, where the early English
kings administered justice ; and such, probably, were the material of
the original *Palais de Justice*, where the kings of Gaul entrenched
themselves in a *pal-lis*, or impaled fort.

From the description which Wright[5] gives of Anglo-Saxon domestic architecture, it appears to have differed but little from that which
was in use at the same period in Ireland.   The hall[6] was the most important part of the building, and halls of stone are alluded to in a
religious poem at the beginning of the Exeter Book : " Yet, in the
earlier period at least, there can be little doubt that the materials
of building were chiefly wood."   The hall, both in Erinn and
Saxon land, was the place of general meeting for all domestic purposes.   Food was cooked and eaten in the same apartment ; the
chief and his followers eat at the same time and in the same place.
On the subject of food we have ample details scattered incidentally
through our annals.   Boiling was probably the principal method of
preparing meat, and for this purpose the Irish were amply provided
with vessels.   A brazen cauldron is lithographed in the *Ulster Archæological Journal*, which is a most interesting specimen of its kind.
It was found in a turf bog in the county Down, at a depth of five feet
from the surface ; and as this bog has been used from time immemorial for supplying the neighbourhood with fuel, and is remembered to have been forty feet above its present level by a generation
now living, the antiquity of the vessel is unquestionable.   As a
specimen of superior workmanship, the cauldron has been greatly
admired.   It is made of sheets of gold-coloured bronze, evidently
formed by hammering : the rim is of much thicker metal than the
rest, and is rendered stiffer by corrugation—a process which has
been patented in England within the last dozen years, as a new and
valuable discovery.[7]

Cauldrons are constantly mentioned in the Book of Rights, in a

one of the most beautiful specimens of the stone battle-axe which has been
found in Ireland, both for design and execution.   It is composed of fine-
grained remblendic sylicite, and is highly polished all over.   It was found in
the river at Athlone.

   [5] *Wright.—History of Domestic Manners and Sentiments*, p. 11.

   [6] *Hall.*—Hence the term "hall" is still used to denote mansions of more
than ordinary importance.   The hall was the principal part of the ancient
Saxon house, and the term used for the part was easily transferred to the
whole.

   [7] *Discovery.—Ulster Arch. Journal*, vol. v. p. 83.

manner which shows that these vessels were in constant use. It was one of the tributes to be presented in due form by the King of Cashel to the King of Tara; and in the will of Cahir Môr, Monarch of Ireland in the second century, fifty copper cauldrons are amongst the items bequeathed to his family. Probably the poorer classes, who could not afford such costly vessels, may have contented themselves with roasting their food exclusively, unless, indeed, they employed the primitive method of casting red hot stones into water when they wished it boiled.

The exact precision which characterizes every legal enactment in ancient Erinn, and which could not have existed in a state of barbarism, is manifested even in the regulations about food. Each member of the chieftain's family had his appointed portion, and there is certainly a quaintness in the parts selected for each. The *saoi* of literature and the king were to share alike, as we observed when briefly alluding to this subject in the chapter on ancient Tara: their portion was a prime steak. Cooks and trumpeters were specially to be supplied with " cheering mead," it is to be supposed because their occupations required more than ordinary libations; the historian was to have a crooked bone; the hunter, a pig's shoulder: in fact, each person and each office had its special portion assigned[8] to it, and the distinction of ranks and trades affords matter of the greatest interest and of the highest importance to the antiquarian. There can be but little doubt that the custom of Tara was the custom of all the other kings and chieftains, and that it was observed throughout the country in every family rich enough to have dependents. This division of food was continued in the Highlands of Scotland until a late period. Dr. Johnson mentions it, in his *Tour in the Hebrides*, as then existing. He observes that he had not ascertained the details, except that the smith[9] had the head.

The allowance for each day is also specified. Two cows, and two *tinnés*,[1] and two pigs was the quantity for dinner. This allowance

[8] *Assigned.*—Petrie's *Tara*, p. 200.

[9] *Smith.*—The animals were brought to the smith, who knocked them down with his big hammer: hence, probably, the name of Smithfield for a cattle market. He was an important personage in the olden time. In the Odyssey, as armourer, he ranks with the bard and physician.

[1] *Tinnés.*—Dr. Petrie does not give the meaning of this word, but Dr. O'Donovan supplies the deficiency in the Book of Rights, where he explains it to mean a salted pig, or in plain English, bacon.

was for a hundred men. The places which the household were to occupy were also specified ; so that while all sat at a common table,[2] there was, nevertheless, a certain distinction of rank. At Tara there were different apartments, called *imdas*, a word now used in the north of Ireland to denote a couch or bed. The name probably originated in the custom of sleeping in those halls, on the benches which surrounded them, or on the floor near the fire-place. In the ground plan of the banqueting hall at Tara, the house is shown as divided into five parts, which are again divided into others. Each of the two divisions extending along the side wall, is shown as subdivided into twelve *imdas*, which here mean seats ; the central division is represented as containing three fires at equal distances, a vat, and a chandelier.

Benches were the seats used, even by persons of rank, until a late period. In the French Carlovingian romances, even princes and great barons sat on them. Chairs were comparatively rare, and only used on state occasions, as late as the twelfth century. Wright gives some curious woodcuts of persons conversing together, who are seated on settles, or on seats formed in the walls round the room ; such as may still be seen in monastic cloisters and the chapter houses of our old cathedrals. Food which had been roasted was probably handed round to the guests on the spit on which it had been cooked.[3] Such at least was the Anglo-Saxon fashion ; and as the Irish had spits, and as forks were an unknown luxury for centuries later, we may presume they were served in a similar manner. The food was varied and abundant, probably none the less wholesome for being free from the Anglo-Norman refinements of cookery, introduced at a later period. For animal diet there were fat beeves, dainty venison, pork, fresh and salted, evidently as favourite a dish

---

[2] *Table.*—In the earliest ages of Tara's existence, the household may have been served as they sat on the benches round the hall. The table was at first simply a board : hence we retain the term a hospitable board ; a board-room, a room where a board was placed for writing on. The board was carried away after dinner, and the trestles on which it stood, so as to leave room for the evening's amusements.

[3] *Cooked.*—Wright's *Domestic Manners*, p. 87. The knights in this engraving are using their shields as a substitute for a table. At p. 147 there is an illustration of the method of cooking on a spit ; this is turned by a boy. The Irish appear to have had a mechanical arrangement for this purpose some centuries earlier. Bellows, which are now so commonly used in Ireland, and so rare in England, appear to have been a Saxon invention.

with the ancients as with the moderns—except, alas! that in the good old times it was more procurable. Sheep and goats also varied the fare, with "smaller game," easily procured by chase, or shot down with arrows or sling stones. The land abounded in " milk and honey." Wheat was planted at an early period; and after the introduction of Christianity, every monastic establishment had its mill. There were " good old times" in Ireland unquestionably. Even an English prince mentions "the honey and wheat, the gold and silver," which he found in " fair Innis-fail." It is probable that land was cultivated then which now lies arid and unreclaimed, for a writer in the *Ulster Archæological Journal* mentions having found traces of tillage, when laying out drains in remote unproductive districts, several feet beneath the peaty soil. Dr. O'Donovan also writes in the same journal : " I believe the Irish have had wheat in the more fertile valleys and plains from a most remote period. It is mentioned constantly in the Brehon laws and in our most ancient poems."[4] Nor should we omit to mention fish in the list of edibles. During the summer months, fishing was a favourite and lucrative occupation; and if we are to believe a legend quoted in the *Transactions of the Ossianic Society*, the Fenians enjoyed a monopoly in the trade, for no man dare take a salmon, " dead or alive," excepting a man in the Fenian ranks ; and piscatory squabbles seem to have extended themselves into downright battles between the Northmen and the natives, when there was question of the possession of a weir.[5]

Drinking vessels, of various shapes and materials, are constantly mentioned in the Book of Rights. There were drinking-horns with handsome handles, carved drinking-horns, variegated drinking-horns, drinking-horns of various colours, and drinking-horns of gold.[6] Even in pagan times, cups or goblets were placed beside

---

[4] *Poems.—Ulster Arch. Journal*, vol. i. p. 108. It would appear as if corn had been eaten raw, or perhaps partly scorched, at an early period, as was customary in eastern countries. Teeth have been found in crania taken from our ancient tombs, quite worn down by some such process of mastication.

[5] *Weir.*—Salt appears to have been used also at a very ancient period, though it cannot now be ascertained how it was procured. Perhaps it was obtained from native sources now unknown.

[6] *Gold.*—Book of Rights, pp. 145, 209, &c. The King of Cashel was entitled to a hundred drinking horns.—p. 33.

the public wells ; and it is related that, in the reign of Conn of the Hundred Battles, Ireland was so prosperous, so wealthy, and so civilized (*circa* A.D. 123) that those cups were made of silver. Brian revived this custom nearly a thousand years later. The Danes probably carried off most of these valuables, as there are no remains of them at present. We are able, however, to give an illustration of a stone drinking-cup, which is considered a very beautiful speci-

STONE DRINKING-CUP.

men of its kind. This great rarity was found in the Shannon excavations. We give a specimen below of a celt, and on page 246 of a celt mould, for which we have also to acknowledge our grateful obligations to the Council of the Royal Irish Academy.

Drink was usually served to the guests after meals. Among the seven prerogatives for the King of Teamhair (Tara) we find :

> "The fruits of Manann, a fine present ;
> And the heath fruit of Brigh Leithe ;
> The venison of Nas ; the fish of the Boinn ;
> The cresses of the kindly Brosnach."

Dr. O'Donovan suggests that the "heath fruit" may have been bilberries or whortleberries, and adds that some of the old Irish suppose that this, and not the heath, was the shrub from which the Danes brewed their beer.[7] It would appear that the Celts were not in the habit of excessive drinking until a comparatively recent period. In the year 1405 we read of the death of a chieftain who died of "a surfeit in drinking ;" but previous to this entry we may safely assert that the Irish were compara-

PALSTAVE CELT.

tively a sober race. The origin of the drink called whisky in modern parlance, is involved in considerable obscurity. Some authorities consider that the word is derived from the first part of the term usquebaugh ; others suppose it to be derived from the name of a place, the Basque provinces, where some such

---

[7] *Beer.*—Book of Rights, p. 9.

compound was concocted in the fourteenth century. In More-
wood's *History of Inebriating Liquors*, he gives a list of the ingredients
used in the composition of usquebaugh, and none of these are Irish
productions.

There is a nice distinction between aqua vitæ and aqua vini in
the Red Book of Ossory, which was rescued by Dr. Graves from
a heap of rubbish, the result of a fire in Kilkenny Castle in 1839
MacGeoghegan, in his annotations on the death of the chieftain
above-mentioned, observes that the drink was not *aqua vitæ* to him,
but rather *aqua mortis;* and he further remarks, that this is the first
notice of the use of *aqua vitæ*, usquebaugh, or whisky, in the Irish
annals. Mead was made from honey, and beer from malt; and
these were, probably, the principal liquors at the early period[8] of
which we are now writing. As to the heath beer of Scandinavian
fame, it is probable that the heather was merely used as a tonic
or aromatic ingredient, although the author of a work, published
in London in 1596, entitled *Sundrie Newe and Artificial Remedies
against Famine,* does suggest the use of heath tops to make a
"pleasing and cheap drink for Poor Men, when Malt is extream
Deare;" much, we suppose, on the same principle that shamrocks
and grass were used as a substitute for potatoes in the famine year,
when the starving Irish had no money to buy Indian corn. But
famine years were happily rare in Ireland in the times of which we
write; and it will be remembered that on one such occasion the
Irish king prayed to God that he might die, rather than live to
witness the misery he could not relieve.

---

[8] *Period.*—Accounts will be given later of the use of *aqua vitæ*, or whisky,
after the English invasion. The English appear to have appreciated this
drink, for we find, in 1585, that the Mayor of Waterford sent Lord Burleigh a
"rundell of *aqua vitæ;* and in another letter, in the State Paper Office, dated
October 14, 1622, the Lord Justice Coke sends a "runlett of milde Irish
uskebach," from his daughter Peggie (heaven save the mark!) to the "good
Lady Coventry," because the said Peggie "was so much bound to her lady-
ship for her great goodness." However, the said Lord Justice strongly
recommends the *uskebach* to his lordship, assuring him that "if it please his
lordship next his heart in the morning to drinke a little of this Irish *uskebach*,
it will help to digest all raw humours, expell wynde, and keep his inward
parte warm all the day after." A poor half-starved Irishman in the present
century, could scarcely have brought forward more extenuating circumstances
for his use of the favourite beverage; and he might have added that *he* had
nothing else to "keep him warm."

It would appear that butter was also a plentiful product then as now. Specimens of bog butter are still preserved, and may be found in the collection of the Royal Irish Academy. The butter was thus entombed either for safety, or to give it that peculiar flavour which makes it resemble the old dry Stilton cheese, so much admired by the modern *bon vivant*. A writer in the *Ulster Archæological Journal* mentions that he found a quantity of red cows' hair mixed with this butter, when boring a hole in it with a gouge. It would appear from this as if the butter had been made in a cow-skin, a fashion still in use among the Arabs. A visitor to the Museum (Mr. Wilmot Chetwode) asked to see the butter from Abbeyleix. He remarked that some cows' heads had been discovered in that neighbourhood, which belonged to the old Irish long-faced breed of cattle ; the skin and hair remained on one head, and that was red. An analysis of the butter proved that it was probably made in the same way as the celebrated Devonshire cream, from which the butter in that part of England is generally prepared. The Arabs and Syrians make their butter now in a similar manner. There is a curious account of Irish butter in the *Irish Hudibras*, by William Moffat, London, 1755, from which it appears that bog butter was then well known :—

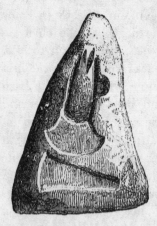

MOULD FOR CASTING BRONZE CELTS.

> " But let his faith be good or bad,
> He in his house great plenty had
> Of burnt oat bread, and butter found,
> With garlick mixt, in boggy ground ;
> So strong, a dog, with help of wind,
> By scenting out, with ease might find."

A lump of butter was found, twelve feet deep, in a bog at Gortgole, county Antrim, rolled up in a coarse cloth. It still retains visibly the marks of the finger and thumb of the ancient dame who pressed it into its present shape.

Specimens of cheese of great antiquity have also been discovered.

It was generally made in the shape of bricks,[9] probably for greater convenience of carriage and pressure in making. Wax has also been discovered, which is evidently very ancient. A specimen may be seen in the collection of the Royal Irish Academy. According to the Book of Rights, the use of wax candles was a royal prerogative :—

> " A hero who possesses five prerogatives,
> Is the King of Laighlin of the fort of Labhraidh :
> The fruit of Almhain [to be brought to him] to his house ;
> And the deer of Gleann Searraigh ;
> To drink by [the light of] fair wax candles,
> At Din Riogh, is very customary to the king."[1]

In this matter, at least, the Irish kings and princes were considerably in advance of their Anglo-Saxon neighbours. Wright informs us[2] that their candle was a mere mass of fat, plastered round a wick, and stuck upon an upright stick : hence the name candlestick.

It is probable that fire-light was, however, the principal means of assisting the visual organs after dark in both countries. Until comparatively recent times, fires were generally made on square, flat stones, and these could be placed, as appears to have been the case at Tara, in different parts of any large hall or apartment. There was sometimes a " back stone " to support the pile of wood and turf. The smoke got out how best it might, unless where there was a special provision made for its exit, in the shape of a round hole in the roof. At a later period a " brace " was sometimes made for conducting it. The brace was formed of upright stakes, interlaced with twigs, and plastered over, inside and outside, with prepared clay—the earliest idea of the modern chimney.

Macaulay[3] gives us a picture of an ancient Roman fire-side, and the occupations of those who sat round it. We can, perhaps, form a more accurate and reliable idea of the dress, amusements, and occupations of those who surrounded the hall-fires of ancient Tara, or the humble, domestic hearths of the crannoges or wattled houses.

---

[9] *Bricks.*—In an ancient life of St. Kevin of Glendalough, there is mention made of certain brick-cheeses, which the saint converted into real bricks, in punishment to a woman for telling a lie.

[1] *King.*—Book of Rights, p. 15.

[2] *Informs us.*—Domestic Manners, p. 43.

[3] *Macaulay.*—Lays of Ancient Rome.—Horatius.

The amusements of the pre-Christian Celt were, undeniably, intellectual. Chess has already been mentioned more than once in this work as a constant occupation of princes and chieftains. Indeed, they appear to have sat down to a game with all the zest of a modern amateur. A few specimens of chessmen have been discovered : a king, elaborately carved, is figured in the Introduction to the Book of Rights. It belonged to Dr. Petrie, and was found, with some others, in a bog in the county Meath. The chessmen of ancient times appear to have been rather formidable as weapons. In the *Táin bó Chuailgné*, Cuchullain is represented as having killed a messenger, who told him a lie, with a chessman, "which pierced him to the centre of his brain." English writers speak of the use of chess immediately after the Conquest, and say that the Saxons learned the game from the Danes. The Irish were certainly acquainted with it at a much earlier period ; if we are to credit the Annals, it was well known long before the introduction of Christianity. Wright gives an engraving of a Quarrel at Chess, in which Charles, the son of the Emperor Charlemagne, is represented knocking out the brains of his adversary with a chessboard. The illustration is ludicrously graphic, and the unfortunate man appears to submit to his doom with a touching grace of helpless resignation.

We may then suppose that chess was a favourite evening amusement of the Celt. Chessboards at least were plentiful, for they are frequently mentioned among the rights of our ancient kings. But music was the Irish amusement *par excellence ;* and it is one of the few arts for which they are credited. The principal Irish instruments were the harp, the trumpet, and the bagpipe. The harp in the Museum of Trinity College, Dublin, usually known as Brian Boroimhé's harp, is supposed, by Dr. Petrie, to be the oldest instrument of the kind now remaining in Europe. It had but one row of strings, thirty in number ; the upright pillar is of oak, and the sound-board of red sallow. The minute and beautiful carving on all parts of the instrument, attests a high state of artistic skill at whatever period it was executed. As the harp is only thirty-two inches high, it is supposed that it was used by ecclesiastics in the church services. Cambrensis[4] mentions this custom ; and there is

---

[4] *Cambrensis.*—" Hinc accidit, ut Episcopi et Abbates, et Sancti in Hiberniâ viri cytharas circumferre et in eis modulando pié delectari consueverunt."— *Cam. Des.* p. 739.

evidence of its having existed from the first introduction of Christianity.   Harps of this description are figured on the knees of ecclesiastics on several of our ancient stone crosses.

The subject of Irish music would require a volume, and we cannot but regret that it must be dismissed so briefly.   The form of the harp has been incorrectly represented on our coins.   It was first assumed in the national arms about the year 1540.   When figured on the coins of Henry VIII., the artist seems to have taken the Italian harp of twenty-four strings for his model ; but in the national arms sketched on the map of Ireland in the State Papers, executed in the year 1567, the form is more correct.   That the Irish possessed this musical instrument in pre-Christian times, cannot be doubted.   The ornamental cover of an Irish MS., which Mr. Ferguson considers to date prior to A.D. 1064, contains five examples of the harp of that period.   This, and the sculptured harp at Nieg, in Rosshire, are believed to be the earliest delineations of the perfect harp.   Dr. Bunting gives a sketch of a harp and harper, taken from one of the compartments of a sculptured cross at Ullard, county Kilkenny.   This is a remarkable example.   The cross is supposed to be older than that of Monasterboice, which was erected A.D. 830, and this is believed to be the first specimen of a harp without a fore pillar that has been discovered out of Egypt. If the Irish harp be really a variety of the cithara, derived through an Egyptian channel, it would form another important link in the chain of evidence, which leads us back to colonization from Egypt through Scythia.   Captain Wilford observes,[5] that there may be a clue to the Celtic word bard in the Hindoo *bárdátri ;* but the Irish appellation appears to be of comparatively modern use.   It is, however, a noticeable fact, that the farther we extend our inquiries, the more forcibly we are directed to the East as the cradle of our music.   Several recent travellers have mentioned the remarkable similarity between Celtic airs and those which they heard in different parts of Asia.[6]   Sir W. Ouseley observed, at the close of the last century, that many Hindoo melodies possessed the plaintive simplicity of the Scotch and Irish.

A German scholar has written a work, to prove that the pentatonic scale was brought over by the Celts from Asia, and that it

[5] *Observes.—Asiatic Researches,* vol. ix. p. 76.

[6] *Asia.*—See Carl Eugen's valuable work on the *Music of Ancient Nations passim.*

was preserved longer in Scotland than elsewhere, on account of the isolated position of that country.[7] The Phœnicians are supposed to have invented the *kinnor*, *trigonon*, and several other of the most remarkable instruments of antiquity. Their skill as harpists, and their love of music, are indicated by the prophetic denunciation in Ezechiel, where the ceasing of songs and the sound of the harp are threatened as a calamity they were likely specially to feel.

We give at least one evidence that the Irish monks practised the choral performance of rhythmical hymns. Colgan supplies the proof, which we select from one of the Latin hymns of St. Columba :—

> "Protegat nos altissimus,
> De suis sanctis sedibus,
> Dum ibi hymnos canimus,
> Decem statutis vicibus."

Mr. O'Curry gives the names of all the ancient Irish musical instruments as follows :—*Cruit*, a harp ; *Timpan*, a drum, or tambourine ; *Corn*, a trumpet ; *Stoc*, a clarion ; *Pipai*, the pipes ; *Fidil*, the fiddle. He adds: " All those are mentioned in an ancient poem in the Book of Leinster, a MS. of about the year 1150, now in the Library of Trinity College. The first four are found in various old tales and descriptions of battles."

We shall find how powerful was the influence of Irish music on the Irish race at a later period of our history, when the subject of political ballads will be mentioned.

The dress of the rich and the poor probably varied as much in the century of which we write as at the present day. We have fortunately remains of almost every description of texture in which the Irish Celt was clad ; so that, as Sir W. Wilde has well observed, we are not left to conjecture, or forced to draw analogies from the habits of half-civilized man in other countries at the present day.

In the year 1821 the body of a male adult was found in a bog on the lands of Gallagh, near Castleblakeney, county Galway, clad in its

---

[7] *Country.*—*Erste Wanderung der ältesten Tonkunst,* von G. W. Fruh, Essen, 1831. In Conran's *National Music of Ireland,* he attributes this to the influence of ecclesiastical music. But an article by Mr. Darmey, in the *Journal of the Royal Asiatic Society,* takes a much more probable view. The Ambrosian chant, introduced about A.D. 600, could not have influenced national music which existed for centuries before that period.

antique garb of deerskin. A few fragments of the dress are preserved, and may be seen in the collection of the Royal Irish Academy. Portions of the seams still remain, and are creditable specimens of early needlework. The material employed in sewing was fine gut of three strands, and the regularity and closeness of the stitching cannot fail to excite admiration. It is another of the many proofs that, even in the earliest ages, the Celt was gifted with more than ordinary skill in the execution of whatever works he took in hand. After all, the skin of animals is one of the most costly and appreciated adornments of the human race, even at the present day; and our ancestors differ less from us in the kind of clothes they wore, than in the refinements by which they are fashioned to modern use. It is stated in the old bardic tale of the *Táin bó Chuailgné*, that the charioteer of the hero was clothed in a tunic of deerskin. This statement, taken in connexion with the fact above-mentioned, is another evidence that increased knowledge is daily producing increased respect for the veracity of those who transmitted the accounts of our ancestral life, which, at one time, were supposed to be purely mythical. Skin or leather garments were in use certainly until the tenth century, in the form of cloaks. It is supposed that Muircheartach obtained the soubriquet " of the leathern cloaks," from the care which he took in providing his soldiers with them; and it is said that, in consequence of this precaution, there was not a single man lost in this campaign.

ANCIENT BOOT.

We give a specimen of an ancient shoe and boot, from the collection of the Royal Irish Academy. It would appear as if the Celt was rather in advance of the Saxon in the art of shoemaking; for

Mr. Fairholt has been obliged to give an illustration selected from
Irish remains, in his history, although it is exclusively devoted to
British costume.   In illustrating the subject of gold ornaments, he
has also made a selection from the same source.   Some curious
specimens of shoes joined together, and therefore perfectly useless
for ordinary wear, have also been discovered.   Sir W. Wilde conjectures they may have been used by chieftains as inauguration
shoes.[8]

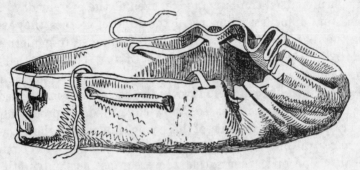

ANCIENT SHOE.

Saffron was a favourite colour, though it does not appear evident
how the dye was procured.   There is no doubt the Irish possessed
the art of dyeing from an early period.   Its introduction is attributed to King Tighearnmas, who reigned from A.M. 3580 to 3664.
It is probable the Phœnicians imparted this knowledge to our
ancestors.   Although our old illuminations are not as rich in figures
as those from which English historians have obtained such ample
information regarding the early costume of that country, we have
still some valuable illustrations of this interesting subject.   These
representations also are found to correspond faithfully, even in the
details of colour, with the remains which have been discovered from
time to time.   Our ancient crosses give immense scope for antiquarian research, though the costumes are principally ecclesiastical,
and hence are not of so much general interest.

---

[8] *Shoes.*—The use of inauguration shoes appears to have been very ancient
in Ireland.   It will be remembered how early and how frequently the shoe is
mentioned in Scripture in connexion with legal arrangements.   It was obviously an important object in Eastern business transactions.

But the Book of Rights[9] affords ample information, as far as mere description, of the clothing of a higher class. While the peasant was covered with a garment of untanned skin or fur, however artistically sown together, the bards, the chieftains, and the monarchs had their tunics [*imar*] of golden borders, their mantles [*leanna*] or shirts of white wool or deep purple, their fair beautiful matals, and their cloaks of every colour. If we add to this costume the magnificent ornaments which still remain to attest the truth of the bardic accounts of Erinn's ancient greatness, we may form a correct picture of the Celtic noble as he stood in Tara's ancient palace; and we must coincide in the opinion of the learned editor of the Catalogue of the Royal Irish Academy, that "the variegated and glowing colours, as well as the gorgeous decorations of the different articles of dress enumerated in the Book of Rights, added to the brilliancy of the arms, must have rendered the Irish costume of the eighth and ninth centuries very attractive."

With a passing glance at our ancient *Fauna* and *Flora*, and the physical state of the country at this period, we must conclude briefly.

It is probable that the province of Ulster, which was styled by statute, in Queen Elizabeth's time, "the most perilous place in all the isle," was much in the same state as to its physical characteristics in the century of which we write. It was densely wooded, and strong in fortresses, mostly placed on lakes, natural or artificial. Two great roads led to this part of Ireland—the "Gap of the North," by Carrickmacross, and the historically famous pass by Magh-Rath. From the former place to Belturbet the country was nearly impassable, from its network of bogs, lakes, and mountains. We shall find at a later period what trouble these natural defences gave to the English settlers.

Munster so abounded in woods, that it was proposed, in 1579, to employ 4,000 soldiers for the sole purpose of hewing them down. Indeed, its five great forests were the strongholds of the Earls of

---

[9] *Book of Rights.*—The great antiquity and perfect authenticity of this most valuable work, should be remembered. It is admitted that the original Book of Rights was compiled by St. Benignus, the disciple of St. Patrick. Dr. O'Donovan thinks there is every reason to believe that this work was in existence in the time of Cormac, the bishop-king of Cashel, A.D. 900. It is probable that the present Book of Rights was compiled about this period, from the more ancient volume of the same name.

Desmond; and enough evidence still remains at Glengariff and Killarney, to manifest the value of their sylvan possessions. The cold and withering blasts of the great Atlantic, appear to have stunted or hindered the growth of trees in Connaught. In 1210 the Four Masters mention the wilderness of Cinel-Dorfa, its principal forest; but it was amply provided with other resources for the protection of native princes. In 1529 Chief Baron Finglas gave a list of dangerous passes, with the recommendation that the "Lord Deputy be eight days in every summer cutting passes into the woods next adjoining the king's subjects."

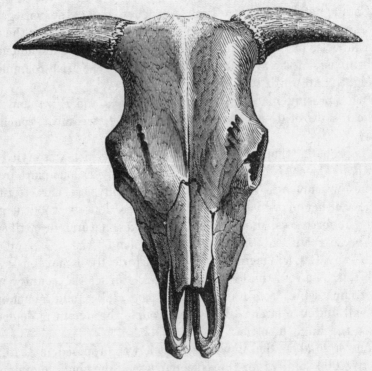

HEAD OF OX.

In Leinster the forests had been cleared at an earlier period; and the country being less mountainous, was more easily cultivated. But this portion of Ireland contained the well-known Curragh of Kildare, which has its history also, and a more ancient one than its modern visitors are likely to suppose. The Curragh is mentioned for the first time in the *Liber Hymnorum*, in a hymn in praise of St. Brigid. The Scholiast in a contemporary gloss says: " *Currech*, *a cursu equorum dictus est.*" It is also mentioned in Cormac's Glossary, where the etymology is referred to running or racing. But the most important notice is contained in the historical tale of the destruction of the mansion of Dá Derga.[1] In this, Connairé Môr, who was killed A.D. 60, is represented as having gone to the games at the Curragh with four chariots. From this and other sources we may conclude, that chariot-races preceded horse-races in ancient Erinn, and that the Curragh has been used as a place of public amusement for the last 2,000 years. It would appear that every province in Ireland possessed an *Aenach* or "fair-green," where the men assembled to celebrate their games and festivals. In an old list of Irish Triads, the three great *Aenachs* of Ireland are said to have been *Aenach Crogan*, in Connaught; *Aenach Taillten*, in Meath ; and *Aenach Colmain*, the Curragh. The last would appear, however, to have been frequented by persons from all parts of Ireland ; and it is not a little strange that it should still be used in a similar manner as a place of public amusement. Ireland in the tenth century and Ireland in the nineteenth form a painful contrast, notwithstanding the boasted march of intellect. The ancient forests have been hewn down with little profit[2] to the spoiler, and to the injury in many ways of the native. The noble rivers are there

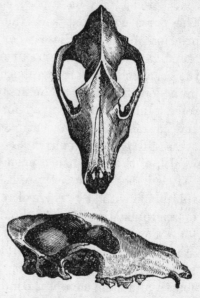

HEADS OF IRISH WOLF DOGS.

still, and the mountains look as beautiful in the sunsets of this year of grace as they did so many hundred years before ; but the country, which was in " God's keeping" then, has but little improved since

---

[1] *Dá Derga.*—See an interesting Essay on the Curragh of Kildare, by Mr. W. M. Hennessy, read before the R. I. A., February 26, 1866.

[2] *Profit.*—The trustees of the estates forfeited in 1688 notice this especially. Trees to the value of £20,000 were cut down and destroyed on the estate of Sir Valentine Brown, near Killarney, and to the value of £27,000 on the territory of the Earl of Clancarty. Some of these trees were sold for *sixpence a piece.*

it came into the keeping of man ; for the poor tenant, who may be here to-day, and to-morrow cast out on the wayside, has but substituted ill-fenced and ill-cultivated fields for wide tracts of heather and moorland, which had at least the recommendation of attractive scenery, and of not suggesting painful reflections.

The most formidable, if not the largest, of the carnivora in this island, was the brown bear. The wolf lingered on until the beginning of the last century ; and the Irish greyhound has passed with it also. The gigantic Irish elk, *Cervus megaseros*, belongs more to the palæontologist than to the historian, as it is supposed to have existed only in pre-historic times. A smaller variety has been found in peat overlaying the clay, from which it is inferred that some species may have been contemporary with the human race. The horse co-existed with the elephant. The red deer was the principal object of chase from an early period. The wild boar found abundant food from our noble oaks; and the hare, the rabbit, the goat, and the sheep supplied the wants of the Celt in ancient as in modern times. But the great wealth of Ireland consisted in her cows, which then, as now, formed a staple article of commerce. Indeed, most of the ancient feuds were simply cattle raids, and the successful party signalized his victory by bearing off the bovine wealth of the vanquished enemy.

It is impossible exactly to estimate the population of Ireland at this period with any degree of reliable exactitude. The only method of approximating thereto should be based on a calculation of the known or asserted number of men in arms at any given time. When Roderic and his allies invested the Normans in Dublin, he is said to have had 50,000 fighting men. Supposing this to include one-fourth of all the men of the military age in the country, and to bear the proportion of one-fifth to the total number of the inhabitants, it would give a population of about a million, which would probably be rather under than over the correct estimate.

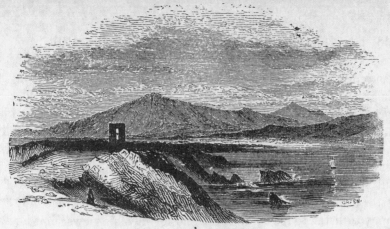

FERRITER'S CASTLE.

CHAPTER XVI.

The English Invasion—Dermod's Interview with Henry II.—Henry grants
Letters-patent—Dermod obtains the assistance of Strongbow, Earl de Clare—
He returns to Ireland—Arrival of English Forces under FitzStephen—
Fatal Indifference of Roderic, the Irish Monarch—He is at last roused to
action, but acknowledges Dermod's Authority almost without a Struggle—
Strongbow's Genealogy—He obtains a Tacit Permission to invade Ireland—
His Arrival in Ireland—Marriage of Strongbow and Eva—Death of Dermod
Mac Murrough—Strongbow proclaims himself King of Leinster—Difficulties
of his Position—Siege of Dublin—Strongbow's Retreat—He returns to
England.

[A.D. 1168—1171.]

NTIL this period (A.D. 1168) the most friendly
relations appear to have existed between England
and Ireland. Saxon nobles and princes had fled
for shelter, or had come for instruction to the
neighbouring shores. The assistance of Irish
troops had been sought and readily obtained by
them. Irish merchants[3] had taken their goods to
barter in English markets; but when the Norman
had won the Saxon crown, and crushed the Saxon
race under his iron heel, the restless spirit of the
old Viking race looked out for a new quarry, and
long before Dermod had betrayed his country, that
country's fate was sealed.

William Rufus is reported to have said, as he
stood on the rocks near St. David's, that he would
make a bridge with his ships from that spot to Ireland—a haughty boast, not quite so easily accomplished. His speech

---

[3] *Merchants.*—Wright says that "theft and unfair dealing" were fearfully

was repeated to the King of Leinster, who inquired "if the king, in his great threatening, had added, ' if it so please God' ?" The reporter answered in the negative. "Then," said he, " seeing this king putteth his trust only in man, and not in God, I fear not his coming."

When Dermod Mac Murrough was driven in disgrace from Ireland, he fled at once to Bristol. There he learned that Henry was still in Aquitaine, and thither, with a perseverance worthy of a better cause, he followed the English king. Henry was only too happy to listen to his complaints, and forward his views; but he was too much occupied with his personal affairs to attempt the conquest of a kingdom. Letters-patent were incomparably more convenient than men-at-arms, and with letters-patent the renegade was fain to be content. Dermod only asked help to recover the kingdom from which he had been expelled for his crimes; Henry pretended no more than to give the assistance asked, and for all reward only wished that Dermod should pay a vassal's homage to the English king. Henry may have known that his client was a villain, or he may not. Henry may have intended to annex Ireland to the British dominions (if he could), or he may merely have hoped for some temporary advantage from the new connexion. Whatever he knew or whatever he hoped, he received Dermod " into the bosom of his grace and benevolence," and he did but distantly insinuate his desires by proclaiming him his " faithful and liege subject." The royal letter ran thus :—" Henry, King of England, Duke of Normandy and Aquitaine, and Earl of Anjou, to all his liegemen, English, Norman, Welsh, and Scotch, and to all the nation under his dominion, sends greeting. As soon as the present letter shall

prevalent among the Anglo-Normans, and mentions, as an example, how some Irish merchants were robbed who came to Ely to sell their wares.—*Domestic Manners*, p. 78. It would appear that there was considerable slave-trade carried on with the British merchants. The Saxons, who treated their dependents with savage cruelty (see Wright, p. 56), sold even their children as slaves to the Irish. In 1102 this inhuman traffic was forbidden by the Council of London. Giraldus Cambrensis mentions that, at a synod held at Armagh, A.D. 1170, the Irish clergy, who had often forbidden this trade, pronounced the invasion of Ireland by Englishmen to be a just judgment on the Irish for their share in the sin, and commanded that all who had English slaves should at once set them free. Mr. Haverty remarks, that it was a curious and characteristic coincidence, that an Irish deliberative assembly should thus, by an act of humanity to Englishmen, have met the merciless aggressions which the latter had just then commenced against this country.—*Hist. of Ireland*, p. 169.

come to your hands, know that Dermod, Prince of Leinster, has been received into the bosom of our grace and benevolence : wherefore, whosoever, within the ample extent of our territories, shall be willing to lend aid towards this prince as our faithful and liege subject, let such person know that we do hereby grant to him for said purpose our licence and favour."

In this document there is not even the most remote reference to the Bull of Adrian, conferring the island of Ireland on Henry, although this Bull had been obtained some time before. In whatever light we may view this omission, it is certainly inexplicable.

For some time Dermod failed in his efforts to obtain assistance. After some fruitless negotiations with the needy and lawless adventurers who thronged the port of Bristol, he applied to the Earl of Pembroke, Richard de Clare. This nobleman had obtained the name of Strongbow, by which he is more generally known, from his skill in archery. Two other young men of rank joined the party ; they were sons of the beautiful and infamous Nesta,[4] once the mistress of Henry I., but now the wife of Gerald, Governor of Pembroke and Lord of Carew. The knights were Maurice FitzGerald and Robert FitzStephen. Dermod had promised them the city of Wexford and two cantreds of land as their reward. Strongbow was to succeed him on the throne of Leinster, and to receive the hand of his young and beautiful daughter, Eva, in marriage.

There is considerable uncertainty as to the real date and the precise circumstances of Dermod's arrival in Ireland. According to one account, he returned at the close of the year 1168, and concealed himself during the winter in a monastery of Augustinian Canons at Ferns, which he had founded. The two principal authorities are Giraldus Cambrensis and Maurice Regan ; the latter was Dermod Mac Murrough's secretary. According to his account, Robert Fitz-Stephen landed at Bannow, near Waterford, in May, 1169, with an army of three hundred archers, thirty knights, and sixty men-at-

---

[4] *Nesta.*—David Powell, in his notes to the *Itinerary of Cambria*, states that this lady was a daughter of Rufus, Prince of Demetia. She was distinguished for her beauty, and infamous for her gallantries. She had a daughter by Gerald of Windsor, called Augweth, who was mother to Giraldus Cambrensis. This relationship accounts for the absurd eulogiums which he has lavished on the Geraldines. Demetia is the district now called Pembrokeshire, where a colony of Normans established themselves after the Norman Conquest.—See Thierry's *Norman Conquest.*

arms.[5] A second detachment arrived the next day, headed by Maurice de Prendergast, a Welsh gentleman, with ten knights and sixty archers. Dermod at once assembled his men, and joined his allies. He could only muster five hundred followers; but with their united forces, such as they were, the outlawed king and the needy adventurers laid siege to the city of Wexford. The brave inhabitants of this mercantile town at once set forth to meet them; but, fearing the result if attacked in open field by well-disciplined troops, they fired the suburbs, and entrenched themselves in the

BARGY CASTLE.

town. Next morning the assaulting party prepared for a renewal of hostilities, but the clergy of Wexford advised an effort for peace: terms of capitulation were negotiated, and Dermod was obliged to pardon, when he would probably have preferred to massacre. It is said that FitzStephen burned his little fleet, to show his followers that they must conquer or die. Two cantreds of land, comprising the present baronies of Forth and Bargy,[6] were bestowed

[5] *Men-at-arms.—Hibernia Expugnata*, lib. i. c. 16.

[6] *Bargy.*—Our illustration gives a view of the remains of this ancient castle. It was formerly the residence of Bagenal Harvey, a Protestant gentleman, who suffered in the rebellion of 1798, for his adherence to the cause of Ireland.

on him ; and thus was established the first English colony in Ireland.
The Irish princes and chieftains appear to have regarded the whole
affair with silent contempt.   The Annals say they " set nothing by
the Flemings ;"[7] practically, they set nothing by any of the invaders.
Could they have foreseen, even for one moment, the consequences
of their indifference, we cannot doubt but that they would have
acted in a very different manner.   Roderic, the reigning monarch,
was not the man either to foresee danger, or to meet it when foreseen ; though we might pardon even a more sharp-sighted and
vigilant warrior, for overlooking the possible consequence of the invasion of a few mercenary troops, whose only object appeared to be
the reinstatement of a petty king.   Probably, the troops and their
captains were equally free from suspecting what would be the real
result of their proceedings.

The fair of Telltown was celebrated about this time ; and from the
accounts given by the Annals of the concourse of people, and the
number of horsemen who attended it, there can be little doubt that
Ireland was seldom in a better position to resist foreign invasion.
But unity of purpose and a competent leader were wanted then, as
they have been wanted but too often since.   Finding so little opposition to his plans, Mac Murrough determined to act on the offensive.
He was now at the head of 3,000 men.   With this force he marched
into the adjoining territory of Ossory, and made war on its chief,
Donough FitzPatrick ; and after a brave but unsuccessful resistance,
it submitted to his rule.[8]   The Irish monarch was at length aroused
to some degree of apprehension.   He summoned a hosting of the
men of Ireland at Tara ; and with the army thus collected, assisted
by the Lords of Meath, Oriel, Ulidia, Breffni, and some northern
chieftains, he at once proceeded to Dublin.   Dermod was alarmed,
and retired to Ferns.   Roderic pursued him thither.   But dissension

---

[7] *Flemings.*—Dr. O'Donovan mentions, in a note to the Four Masters, that he
was particularly struck with the difference between the personal appearance
of the inhabitants of the baronies where they settled.   The Cavanaghs and
Murphys are tall and slight ; the Flemings and Codds short and stout.   They
still retain some peculiarities of language.

[8] *Rule.*—What the rule of this ferocious monster may have been we can judge
from what is related of him by Cambrensis.   Three hundred heads of the slain
were piled up before him ; and as he leaped and danced with joy at the ghastly
sight, he recognized a man to whom he had a more than ordinary hatred.   He
seized the head by the ears, and gratified his demoniacal rage by biting off the
nose and lips of his dead enemy.

had already broken out in the Irish camp: the Ulster chiefs returned home ; the contingent was weakened ; and, either through fear, or from the natural indolence of his pacific disposition, he agreed to acknowledge Mac Murrough's authority. Mac Murrough gave his son Cormac as hostage for the fulfilment of the treaty. A private agreement was entered into between the two kings, in which Dermod pledged himself to dismiss his foreign allies as soon as possible, and to bring no more strangers into the country. It is more than probable that he had not the remotest idea of fulfilling his promise ; it is at least certain that he broke it the first moment it was his interest to do so. Dermod's object was simply to gain time, and in this he succeeded.

Maurice FitzGerald arrived at Wexford a few days after, and the recreant king at once proceeded to meet him ; and with this addition to his army, marched to attack Dublin. The Dano-Celts, who inhabited this city, had been so cruelly treated by him, that they dreaded a repetition of his former tyrannies. They had elected a governor for themselves ; but resistance was useless. After a brief struggle, they were obliged to sue for peace—a favour which probably would not have been granted without further massacres and burnings, had not Dermod wished to bring his arms to bear in another quarter.

Donnell O'Brien, Prince of Thomond, who had married a daughter of Dermod, had just rebelled against Roderic, and the former was but too willing to assist him in his attempt. Thus encouraged where he should have been treated with contempt, and hunted down with ignominy, his ambition became boundless. He played out the favourite game of traitors ; and no doubt hoped, when he had consolidated his own power, that he could easily expel his foreign allies. Strongbow had not yet arrived, though the winds had been long enough " at east and easterly."[9] His appearance was still delayed. The fact was, that the Earl was in a critical position. Henry and his barons were never on the most

---

[9] *Easterly.*—Cambrensis takes to himself the credit of having advised the despatch of a letter to Strongbow. He also gives us the letter, which probably was his own composition, as it is written in the same strain of bombast as his praises of his family.—*Hib. Expug.* lib. i. c. 12. It commences thus: "We have watched the storks and swallows ; the summer birds are come and gone," &c. We imagine that Dermod's style, if he had taken to epistolary correspondence, would have been rather a contrast.

amiable terms; and there were some very special reasons why Strongbow should prove no exception to the rule.

The first member of the Earl's family who had settled in England, was Richard, son of the Norman Earl Brien, a direct descendant of Robert "the Devil," Duke of Normandy, father of William the Conqueror. In return for services at the battle of Hastings, and general assistance in conquering the Saxon, this family obtained a large grant of land in England, and took the title of Earl of Clare from one of their ninety-five lordships in Suffolk.[1] The Strongbow family appears to have inherited a passion for making raids on neighbouring lands, from their Viking ancestors. Strongbow's father had obtained his title of Earl of Pembroke, and his property in the present county of that name, from his successful marauding expedition in Wales, in 1138. But as he revolted against Stephen, his lands were seized by that king; and after his death, in 1148, his son succeeded to his very numerous titles, without any property commensurate thereto. Richard was not in favour with his royal master, who probably was jealous of the Earl, despite his poverty; but as Strongbow did not wish to lose the little he had in England, or the chance of obtaining more in Ireland, he proceeded at once to the court, then held in Normandy, and asked permission for his new enterprise. Henry's reply was so carefully worded, he could declare afterwards that he either had or had not given the permission, whichever version of the interview might eventually prove most convenient to the royal interests. Strongbow took the interpretation which suited his own views, and proceeded to the scene of action with as little delay as possible. He arrived in Ireland, according to the most generally received account, on the vigil of St. Bartholomew, A.D. 1170, and landed at Dundonnell, near Waterford. His uncle, Hervey de Montmarisco, had already arrived, and established himself in a temporary fort, where he had been attacked by the brave citizens of Wexford. But the besieged maintained their position, killed five hundred men, and made prisoners of seventy of the principal citizens of Waterford. Large sums of money were offered for their ransom, but in vain. They were brutally murdered by the English soldiers, who first broke

---

[1] *Suffolk.*—See Gilbert's *Viceroys of Dublin, passim.* We recommend this work to our readers. It should be in the hands of every Irishman at least. It combines the attraction of romance with the accuracy of carefully written history.

their limbs, and then hurled them from a precipice into the sea. It was the first instalment of the utterly futile theory, so often put in practice since that day, of " striking terror into the Irish ;" and the experiment was quite as unsuccessful as all such experiments have ever been.[2]

While these cruelties were enacting, Strongbow had been collecting forces in South Wales; but, as he was on the very eve of departure, he received a peremptory order from Henry, forbidding him to leave the kingdom. After a brief hesitation, he determined to bid defiance to the royal mandate, and set sail for Ireland. The day after his arrival he laid siege to Waterford. The citizens behaved like heroes, and twice repulsed their assailants ; but their bravery could not save them in the face of overpowering numbers. A breach was made in the wall ; the besiegers poured in ; and a merciless massacre followed. Dermod arrived while the conflict was at its height, and for once he has the credit of interfering on the side of mercy. Reginald, a Danish lord, and O'Phelan, Prince of the Deisi, were about to be slain by their captors, but at his request they were spared, and the general carnage was suspended. For the sake of common humanity, one could wish to think that this was an act of mercy. But Mac Murrough had his daughter Eva with him; he wished to have her nuptials with Strongbow celebrated at once ; and he could scarcely accomplish his purpose while men were slaying their fellows in a cold-blooded massacre. The following day the nuptials were performed. The English Earl, a widower, and long past the prime of manhood, was wedded to the fair young Celtic maiden ; and the marriage procession passed lightly over the bleeding bodies of the dying and the dead. Thus commenced the union between Great Britain and Ireland : must those nuptials be for ever celebrated in tears and blood ?

Immediately after the ceremony, the army set out for Dublin. Roderic had collected a large force near Clondalkin, and Hosculf, the Danish governor of the city, encouraged by their presence, had again revolted against Dermod. The English army having learned that the woods and defiles between Wexford and Dublin were well guarded, had made forced marches along the mountains, and succeeded in reaching the capital long before they were expected.

[2] *Been.*—If we are to believe Cambrensis, Raymond argued against this cruelty, and Henry in favour of it.

Marriage of Eva and Strongbow.

Their decision and military skill alarmed the inhabitants—they might also have heard reports of the massacres at Wexford; be this as it may, they determined to negotiate for peace, and commissioned their illustrious Archbishop, St. Laurence O'Toole, to make terms with Dermod. While the discussion was pending, two of the English leaders, Raymond *le Gros* and Miles de Cogan, obtained an entrance into the city, and commenced a merciless butchery of the inhabitants. When the saint returned he heard cries of misery and groans of agony in all quarters, and it was not without difficulty that he succeeded in appeasing the fury of the soldiers, and the rage of the people, who had been so basely treated.

The Four Masters accuse the people of Dublin of having attempted to purchase their own safety at the expense of the national interests, and say that "a miracle was wrought against. them" as a judgment for their selfishness. Hosculf, the Danish governor, fled to the Orkneys, with some of the principal citizens, and Roderic withdrew his forces to Meath, to support O'Rourke, on whom he had bestowed a portion of that territory. Miles de Cogan was invested with the government of Dublin, and Dermod marched to Meath, to attack Roderic and O'Rourke, against whom he had an old grudge of the worst and bitterest kind. He had injured him by carrying off his wife, Dervorgil, and men generally hate most bitterly those whom they have injured most cruelly.

Meanwhile MacCarthy of Desmond had attacked and defeated the English garrison at Waterford, but without any advantageous results. Roderic's weakness now led him to perpetrate an act of cruelty, although it could scarcely be called unjust according to the ideas of the times. It will be remembered that he had received hostages from Dermod for the treaty of Ferns. That treaty had been openly violated, and the King sent ambassadors to him to demand its fulfilment, by the withdrawal of the English troops, threatening, in case of refusal, to put the hostages to death. Dermod laughed at the threat. Under any circumstances, he was not a man who would hesitate to sacrifice his own flesh and blood to his ambition. Roderic was as good as his word ; and the three royal hostages were put to death at Athlone.

An important synod was held at the close of this year (A.D. 1170), at Armagh. We have already mentioned one of its principal enactments, which deplored and condemned the practice of buying English slaves from the Bristol merchants. Other subjects shall be more fully entertained when we come to the Synod of Cashel, which was held two years later.

In 1171 Dermod MacMurrough, the author of so many miseries, and the object of so much just reprobation, died at Ferns, on the 4th of May. His miserable end was naturally considered a judgment for his evil life. His obituary is thus recorded : " Diarmaid Mac Murchadha, King of Leinster, by whom a trembling soil was made of all Ireland, after having brought over the Saxons, after having done extensive injuries to the Irish, after plundering and burning many churches, as Ceanannus, Cluain-Iraired, &c., died before the end of a year [after this plundering], of an insufferable and unknown disease ; for he became putrid while living, through the miracle of God, Colum-cille, and Finnen, and the other saints of Ireland, whose churches he had profaned and burned some time before ; and he died at Fearnamor, without [making] a will, without penance, without the body of Christ, without unction, as his evil deeds deserved."[3]

But the death of the traitor could not undo the traitor's work. Men's evil deeds live after them, however they may repent them on their deathbeds. Strongbow had himself at once proclaimed King of Leinster—his marriage with Eva was the ground of his claim ; but though such a mode of succession might hold good in Normandy, it was perfectly illegal in Ireland. The question, however, was not one of right but of might, and it was settled as all such questions invariably are. But Strongbow had a master at the other side of the Channel, who had his own views of these complications. His tenure, however, was somewhat precarious. His barons, always turbulent, had now a new ground for aggression, in the weakness to which he had exposed himself by his virtual sanction of the murder of St. Thomas of Canterbury, and he was fain to content himself with a strong injunction commanding all his English subjects then in Ireland to return immediately, and forbidding any further reinforcements to be sent to that country. Strongbow was alarmed, and at once despatched Raymond *le Gros* with apologies and explanations, offering the King all the lands he had acquired in Ireland. Henry does not appear to have taken the slightest notice of these

---

[3] *Deserved.*—The Annals of Clonmacnois give a similar account ; but in a paper MS. in Trinity College, Dublin, it is said that he died "after the victory of penance and unction." The old account is probably the more reliable, as it is the more consonant with his previous career.

communications, and the Earl determined to risk his displeasure, and remain in Ireland.

His prospects, however, were by no means promising. His Irish adherents forsook him on the death of Dermod; Dublin was besieged by a Scandinavian force, which Hosculf had collected in the Orkneys, and which was conveyed in sixty vessels, under the command of Johan *le Déve* (the Furious). Miles de Cogan repulsed this formidable attack successfully, and captured the leaders. Hosculf was put to death; but he appears to have brought his fate on himself by a proud and incautious boast.

At this period the thoughtful and disinterested Archbishop of Dublin saw a crisis in the history of his country on which much depended. He endeavoured to unite the national chieftains, and rally the national army. His words appear to have had some effect. Messengers were sent to ask assistance from Godfred, King of the Isle of Man, and other island warriors. Strongbow became aware of his danger, and threw himself into Dublin; but he soon found himself landlocked by an army, and enclosed at sea by a fleet. Roderic O'Connor commanded the national forces, supported by Tiernan O'Rourke and Murrough O'Carroll. St. Laurence O'Toole remained in the camp, and strove to animate the men by his exhortations and example. The Irish army contented themselves with a blockade, and the besieged were soon reduced to extremities from want of food. Strongbow offered terms of capitulation through the Archbishop, proposing to hold the kingdom of Leinster as Roderic's vassal; but the Irish monarch demanded the surrender of the towns of Dublin, Wexford, and Waterford, and required the English invaders to leave the country by a certain day.

While these negotiations were pending, Donnell Cavanagh, son of the late King of Leinster, got into the city in disguise, and informed Strongbow that FitzStephen was closely besieged in Wexford. It was then at once determined to force a passage through the Irish army. Raymond *le Gros* led the van, Miles de Cogan followed; Strongbow and Maurice FitzGerald, who had proposed the sortie, with the remainder of their force, brought up the rere. The Irish army was totally unprepared for this sudden move; they fled in panic, and Roderic, who was bathing in the Liffey, escaped with difficulty.[4]

---

[4] *Difficulty.*—The army was so well supplied, that the English got sufficient corn, meal, and pork to victual the city of Dublin for a whole year.—Harris' *Hibernæ*, p. 25.

Strongbow again committed the government of Dublin to Miles de Cogan, and set out for Wexford. On his way thither he was opposed by O'Regan, Prince of Idrone. An action ensued, which might have terminated fatally for the army, had not the Irish prince received his death-wound from an English archer. His troops took to flight, and Strongbow proceeded on his journey. But he arrived too late. Messengers met him on the way, to inform him that the fort of Carrig had fallen into the hands of the Irish, who are said to have practised an unjustifiable stratagem to obtain possession of the place. As usual, there are two versions of the story. One of these versions, which appears not improbable, is that the besieged had heard a false report of the affair in Dublin; and believing Strongbow and the English army to have been overthrown, they surrendered on the promise of being sent in safety to Dublin. On their surrender, the conditions were violated, FitzStephen was imprisoned, and some of his followers killed. The charge against the besiegers is that they invented the report as a stratagem to obtain their ends, and that the falsehood was confirmed in a solemn manner by the bishops of Wexford and Kildare.

As soon as the Wexford men had heard of Strongbow's approach, they set fire to the town, and fled to Beg-Erin, a stockaded island, at the same time sending him a message, that, if he attempted to approach, they would kill all their prisoners. The Earl withdrew to Waterford in consequence of this threat, and here he learned that his presence was indispensable in England; he therefore set off at once to plead his own cause with his royal master. A third attack had been made on Dublin, in the meantime, by the Lord of Breffni, but it was repulsed by Miles. With this exception, the Irish made no attempt against the common enemy, and domestic wars were as frequent as usual.

Henry had returned to England, and was now in Newenham, in Gloucestershire, making active preparations for his visit to Ireland. The odium into which he had fallen, after his complicity in the murder of St. Thomas of Canterbury, had rendered his position perilous in the extreme; and probably his Irish expedition would never have been undertaken, had he not required some such object to turn his thoughts and the thoughts of his subjects from the consequences of his crime.[5] He received Strongbow coldly, and at first refused

---

[5] *Crime.*—So fearful was the unfortunate monarch of a public excommunication and interdict, that he sent courtiers at once to Rome to announce his

him an interview. After a proper delay, he graciously accepted the Earl's offer of "all the lands he had won in Ireland"—a very questionable gift, considering that there was not an inch of ground there which he could securely call his own. Henry, however, was pleased to restore his English estates; but, with consummate hypocrisy and villany, he seized the castles of the Welsh lords, whom he hated for their vigorous and patriotic opposition, and punished them for allowing the expedition, which he had just sanctioned, to sail from their coasts unmolested.

submission. When he heard of the murder he shut himself up for three days, and refused all food, except "milk of almonds." See *Vita Quadrip.* p. 143. It would appear this was a favourite beverage, from the amount of almonds which were brought to Ireland for his special benefit. See p. 272.

THE LOGAN STONE, KILLARNEY.

ANCIENT IRISH BROOCH.[6]

CHAPTER XVII.

Arrival of Henry II.—Some of the Native Princes pay him Homage—His Character—Dublin in the time of Henry II.—His Winter Palace—Norman Luxuries—King Henry holds a Court—Adrian's Bull—Temporal Power of the Popes in the Middle Ages—Conduct of the Clergy—Irish Property given to English Settlers—Henry II. returns to England—The Account Cambrensis gives of the Injuries done to Ireland by his Countrymen—Raymond, Montmarisco, and Strongbow—The latter is defeated—He recalls Raymond from Wales—Treaty between Roderic and Henry—Death of Strongbow.

[A.D. 1171—1176.]

ENRY landed in Ireland on the 18th of October, 1171, at Crook, in the county of Waterford. He was accompanied by Strongbow, William Fitz-Aldelm, Humphrey de Bohun, Hugh de Lacy, Robert FitzBarnard, and many other lords. His whole force, which, according to the most authentic English accounts, was distributed in four hundred ships, consisted of 500 knights and 4,000 men-at-arms. It would appear the Irish had not the least idea that he intended to claim the kingdom as his own, and rather looked upon him as a powerful potentate who had come to assist the native administration of justice. Even had they suspected his real object, no opposition might have been made to it. The nation had suffered much from domestic dissension ; it had yet to learn that foreign oppression was an incomparable greater evil.

If a righteous king or a wise statesman had taken the affair in

[6] *Irish Brooch.*—The brooch figured above is of great antiquity. It was found in the Ardkillen crannoge, near Strokestown, county Roscommon. The original is in the Royal Irish Academy, and is considered the finest specimen of bronze workmanship in the collection.

hand, Ireland might have been made an integral and most valuable portion of the British Empire without a struggle. The nation would have bowed gratefully to an impartial government; they have not yet ceased to resent a partial and frequently unjust rule. From the very commencement, the aggrandizement of the individual, and not the advantage of the people, has been the rule of action. Such government is equally disgraceful to the rulers, and cruel to the governed.

MacCarthy of Desmond was the first Irish prince who paid homage to the English King. At Cashel, Donnell O'Brien, King of Thomond, swore fealty, and surrendered the city of Limerick. Other princes followed their example. The "pomp and circumstance" of the royal court, attracted the admiration of a people naturally deferential to authority; the condescension and apparent disinterestedness of the monarch, won the hearts of an impulsive and affectionate race. They had been accustomed to an Ard-Righ, a chief monarch, who, in name at least, ruled all the lesser potentates: why should not Henry be such to them? and why should they suppose that he would exercise a tyranny as yet unknown in the island?

The northern princes still held aloof; but Roderic had received Henry's ambassadors personally, and paid the usual deference which one king owed to another who was considered more powerful. Henry determined to spend his Christmas in Dublin, and resolved on a special display of royal state. It is to be presumed that he wished to make up for deficiency in stateliness of person by stateliness of presence; for, like most of the descendants of Duke Robert "the Devil" and the daughter of the Falaise tanner, his appearance was not calculated to inspire respect. His grey bloodshot eyes and tremulous voice, were neither knightly nor kingly qualifications; his savage and ungovernable temper, made him appear at times rather like a demon than a man. He was charged with having violated the most solemn oaths when it suited his convenience. A cardinal had pronounced him an audacious liar. Count Thiebault of Champagne had warned an archbishop not to rely on any of his promises, however sacredly made. He and his sons spent their time quarrelling with each other, when not occupied in quarrelling with their subjects. His eldest son, Richard, thus graphically sketched the family characteristics:—"The custom in our family is that the son shall hate the father; our destiny is to detest each other; from the devil we came, to the devil we shall go." And the head of this family had now come to reform the Irish, and to improve their condition—social, secular, and ecclesiastical!

A special residence was erected for the court on part of the ground now occupied by the southern side of Dame-street. The whole extent of Dublin at that time was, in length, from Corn Market to the Lower Castle Yard; and in breadth, from the Liffey, then covering Essex-street, to Little Sheep-street, now Ship-street, where a part of the town wall is yet standing.[7] The only edifices in existence on the southern side of Dame-street, even at the commencement of the seventeenth century, were the Church of St. Andrew and the King's Mills.[8] College-green was then quite in the country, and was known as the village of *Le Hogges*, a name that is apparently derived from the Teutonic word *Hoge*, which signifies a small hill or sepulchral mound. Here there was a nunnery called St. Mary le Hogges, which had been erected or endowed not many years before Henry's arrival, and a place called Hoggen's Butt, where the citizens exercised themselves in archery. Here, during the winter of 1171, the Celt, the Saxon, and the Norman, may have engaged in peaceful contests and pleasant trials of skill.

Henry's "winter palace" was extemporized with some artistic taste. It was formed of polished osiers. Preparations had been made on an extensive scale for the luxuries of the table—a matter in which the Normans had greatly the advantage of either Celt or Saxon. The use of crane's flesh was introduced into Ireland for the first time, as well as that of herons, peacocks,[9] swans, and wild

---

[7] *Standing.*—Four Masters, vol. iii. p. 5, note *m*.

[8] *Mills.*—Dame-street derived its name from a dam or mill-stream near it. There was also the gate of Blessed Mary del Dam. The original name was preserved until quite recently. In the reign of Charles I. the Master of the Rolls had a residence here, which is described as being "in a very wholesome air, with a good orchard and garden leading down to the water-side."— Gilbert's *Dublin*, vol. ii. p. 264. In fact, the residences here were similar to those pleasant places on the Thames, once the haunts of the nobility of London.

[9] *Peacocks.*—To serve a peacock with its feathers was one of the grandest exploits of mediæval cookery. It was sown up in its skin after it had been roasted, when it was allowed to cool a little. The bird then appeared at the last course as if alive. Cream of almonds was also a favourite dainty. Indeed, almonds were used in the composition of many dishes; to use as many and as various ingredients as possible seeming to be the acme of gastronomy. St. Bernard had

geese. Almonds had been supplied already by royal order in great abundance; wine was purchased in Waterford, even now famous for its trade with Spain in that commodity. Nor had the King's physician forgotten the King's health; for we find a special entry amongst the royal disbursements of the sum of £10 7s., paid to Josephus Medicus for spices and electuaries. Yet Henri-curt-mantel[1] was careful of his physical well-being, and partook but sparingly of these luxuries. Fearing his tendency to corpulency, he threw the short cloak of his native Anjou round him at an earlier hour in the morning than suited the tastes of his courtiers, and took exercise either on horseback or on foot, keeping in constant motion all day.

When the Christmas festivities had passed, Henry turned his attention to business, if, indeed, the same festivities had not also been a part of his diplomatic plans, for he was not deficient in kingcraft. In a synod at Cashel he attempted to settle ecclesiastical affairs. In a *Curia Regis*, held at Lismore, he imagined he had arranged temporal affairs. These are subjects which demand our best consideration. It is an historical fact, that the Popes claimed and exercised great temporal power in the middle ages; it is admitted also that they used this power in the main for the general good;[2] and that, as monks and friars were the preservers of literature, so popes and bishops were the protectors of the rights of nations, as far as was possible in such turbulent times. It does not belong to our present subject to theorize on the origin or the grounds[3] of this

already loudly condemned the *bon vivants* of the age. His indignation appears to have been especially excited by the various methods in which eggs were cooked. But even seculars condemned the excesses of Norman luxuries, and declared that the knights were loaded with wine instead of steel, and spits instead of lances.

[1] *Henri-curt-mantel.*—A soubriquet derived from the short mantle he constantly wore.

[2] *Good.*—Even the infidel Voltaire admitted that the Popes restrained princes, and protected the people. The Bull *In Cœna Domini* contained an excommunication against those who should levy new taxes upon their estates, or should increase those already existing beyond the bounds of right. For further information on this subject, see Balmez, *European Civilization, passim.* M. Guizot says: "She [the Church] alone resisted the system of castes; she alone maintained the principle of equality of competition; she alone called all legitimate superiors to the possession of power."—*Hist. Gen. de la Civilization en Europe,* Lect. 5.

[3] *Grounds.*—De Maistre and Fénélon both agree in grounding this power

power; it is sufficient to say that it had been exercised repeatedly both before and after Adrian granted the famous Bull, by which he conferred the kingdom of Ireland on Henry II. The Merovingian dynasty was changed on the decision of Pope Zachary. Pope Adrian threatened Frederick I., that if he did not renounce all pretensions to ecclesiastical property in Lombardy, he should forfeit the crown, "received from himself and through his unction." When Pope Innocent III. pronounced sentence of deposition against Lackland in 1211, and conferred the kingdom of England on Philip Augustus, the latter instantly prepared to assert his claim, though he had no manner of title, except the Papal grant.[4] In fact, at the very moment when Henry was claiming the Irish crown in right of Adrian's Bull, given some years previously, he was in no small trepidation at the possible prospect of losing his English dominions, as an excommunication and an interdict were even then hanging over his head. Political and polemical writers have taken strangely perverted views of the whole transaction. One writer,[5] with apparently the most genuine impartiality, accuses the Pope, the King, and the Irish prelates of the most scandalous hypocrisy. A cursory examination of the question might have served to prove the groundlessness of this assertion. The Irish clergy, he asserts— and his assertion is all the proof he gives—betrayed their country for the sake of tithes. But tithes had already been enacted, and the Irish clergy were very far from conceding Henry's claims in the manner which some historians are pleased to imagine.

It has been already shown that the possession of Ireland was coveted at an early period by the Norman rulers of Great Britain. When Henry II. ascended the throne in 1154, he probably intended to take the matter in hands at once. An Englishman, Adrian IV., filled the Papal chair. The English monarch would naturally find him favourable to his own country. John of Salisbury, then chaplain to the Archbishop of Canterbury, was commissioned to request the favour. No doubt he represented his master as very zealous for the interests of religion, and made it appear that his sole motive was the good, temporal and spiritual, of the barbarous Irish; at least this is plainly

on constitutional right; but the former also admitted a divine right.—De Maistre, *Du Pape*, lib. ii. p. 387.

[4] *Grant.*—See M. Gosselin's *Power of the Popes during the Middle Ages*, for further information on this subject.

[5] *Writer.—Ireland, Historical and Statistical.*

implied in Adrian's Bull.[6]   The Pope could have no motive except
that which he expressed in the document itself.   He had been led
to believe that the state of Ireland was deplorable ; he naturally
hoped that a wise and good government would restore what was
amiss.   There is no doubt that there was much which required
amendment, and no one was more conscious of this, or strove more
earnestly to effect it, than the saintly prelate who governed the
archiepiscopal see of Dublin.   The Irish clergy had already made
the most zealous efforts to remedy whatever needed correction ; but
it was an age of lawless violence.   Reform was quite as much wanted
both in England and in the Italian States; but Ireland had the
additional disadvantage of having undergone three centuries of
ruthless plunder and desecration of her churches and shrines, and
the result told fearfully on that land which had once been the home
of saints.

Henry's great object was to represent himself as one who had
come to redress grievances rather than to claim allegiance ; but
however he may have deceived princes and chieftains, he certainly
did not succeed in deceiving the clergy   The Synod of Cashel,
which he caused to be convened, was not attended as numerously
as he had expected, and the regulations made thereat were simply
a renewal of those which had been made previously.   The Primate
of Ireland was absent, and the prelates who assembled there, far
from having enslaved the State to Henry, avoided any interference
in politics either by word or act.   It has been well observed, that,
whether "piping or mourning," they are not destined to escape.
Their office was to promote peace.   So long as the permanent peace
and independence of the nation seemed likely to be forwarded by
resistance to foreign invasion, they counselled resistance ; when resistance was hopeless, they recommended acquiescence, not because

[6] *Bull.*—There can be no reasonable doubt of the authenticity of this document.   Baronius published it from the *Codex Vaticanus ;* John XXII. has
annexed it to his brief addresed to Edward II. ; and John of Salisbury states
distinctly, in his *Metalogicus*, that he obtained this Bull from Adrian.   He
grounds the right of donation on the supposed gift of the island by Constantine.
As the question is one of interest and importance, we subjoin the original : "Ad
preces meas illustri Regi Anglorum Henrico II. concessit (Adrianus) et dedit
Hiberniam jure hæreditario possidendam, sicut literæ ipsius testantur in
hodiernum diem.   Nam omnes insulæ de jure antiquo ex donatione Constan-
tini, qui eam fundavit et dotavit, dicuntur ad Romanam Ecclesiam pertinere."
—*Metalogicus*, i. 4.

they believed the usurpation less unjust, but because they considered submission the wisest course. But the Bull of Adrian had not yet been produced; and Henry's indifference about this document, or his reluctance to use it, shows of how little real importance it was considered at the time. One fearful evil followed from this Anglo-Norman invasion. The Irish clergy had hitherto been distinguished for the high tone of their moral conduct; the English clergy, unhappily, were not so rich in this virtue, and their evil communication had a most injurious effect upon the nation whom it was supposed they should be so eminently capable of benefiting.

Henry did not succeed much better with his administration of secular affairs. In his *Curia Regis*, at Lismore, he modelled Irish administration on Norman precedents, apparently forgetting that a kingdom and a province should be differently governed. Strongbow was appointed Earl Marshal; Hugh de Lacy, Lord Constable; Bertram de Verdun, Seneschal; Theobald Walter, Chief Butler; and De Wellesley, Royal Standard-bearer. It was also arranged that, on the demise of a Chief Governor, the Norman nobles were to elect a successor, who should have full authority, until the royal pleasure could be known. Henry did not then attempt to style himself King or Lord of Ireland; his object seems to have been simply to obtain authority in the country through his nobles, as Wales had been subdued in a similar manner. English laws and customs were also introduced for the benefit of English settlers; the native population still adhered to their own legal observances. Henry again forgot that laws must be suited to the nation for whom they are made, and that Saxon rules were as little likely to be acceptable to the Celt, as his Norman tongue to an English-speaking people.

Dublin was now made over to the inhabitants of Bristol. Hugh de Lacy, its governor, has been generally considered in point of fact the first Viceroy for Ireland. He was installed in the Norman fashion, and the sword and cap of maintenance were made the insignia of the dignity. Waterford and Wexford were also bestowed on royal favourites, or on such knights as were supposed most likely to hold them for the crown. Castles were erected throughout the country, which was portioned out among Henry's needy followers; and, for the first time in Ireland, a man was called a rebel if he presumed to consider his house or lands as his own property.

The winter had been so stormy that there was little communication with England; but early in spring the King received the portentous intelligence of the arrival of Papal Legates in Normandy, and learned that they threatened to place his dominions under an interdict, if he did not appear immediately to answer for his crime. Queen Eleanor and his sons were also plotting against him, and there were many who boldly declared that the murder of the Archbishop of Canterbury would yet be fearfully avenged. Henry determined at once to submit to the Holy See, and to avert his doom by a real or pretended penitence. He therefore sailed for England from Wexford Harbour, on Easter Monday, the 17th of April, 1172, and arrived the same day at Port Finnen, in Wales. We give the testimony of Cambrensis, no friend to Ireland, to prove that neither clergy nor laity benefited by the royal visit. He thus describes the inauguration of that selfish system of plunder and devastation, to which Ireland has been subjected for centuries—a system which prefers the interests of the few to the rights of the many, and then scoffs bitterly at the misery it has created: "The clergy are reduced to beggary in the island; the cathedral churches mourn, having been deprived, by the aforesaid persons [the leading adventurers], and others along with them, or who came over after them, of the lands and ample estates which had been formerly granted to them faithfully and devoutly. And thus the exalting of the Church has been changed into the despoiling or plundering of the Church." Nor is his account of the temporal state of the kingdom any better. He informs us that Dermod Mac Murrough, the originator of all those evils, " oppressed his nobles, exalted upstarts, was a calamity to his countrymen, hated by the strangers, and, in a word, at war with the world." Of the Anglo-Norman nobles, who, it will be remembered, were his own relatives, and of their work, he writes thus : " This new and bloody conquest was defiled by an enormous effusion of blood, and the slaughter of a Christian people." And again : " The lands even of the Irish who stood faithful to our cause, from the first descent of FitzStephen and the Earl, you have, in violation of a treaty, made over to your friends."[7] His character of Henry is, that he was more given to " hunting than to holiness."

The English monarch, however, could assume an appearance of most profound humility and the deepest piety, when it suited his convenience. He excelled himself in this department by his

[7] *Friends.—Hib. Expug.* lib. ii. c. 38.

submission to the Holy See, when he found that submission alone
could save his crown.

The Lord of Breffni had been one of Henry's favourite guests at
his Christmas festivities. He possessed the territory of East Meath,
and this territory Henry had coolly bestowed on Hugh de Lacy.[8]
The rightful owner was not quite so dazzled by the sunshine of
royal favour, as to be willing to resign his property without a
struggle. The Irish chieftain, whose name was Tiernan O'Rourke,
was persuaded to hold a conference with the English usurper at the
Hill of Tara, near Athboy. Both parties were attended by armed
men. A dispute ensued. The interpreter was killed by a blow
aimed at De Lacy, who fled precipitately ; O'Rourke was killed by
a spear-thrust as he mounted his horse, and vengeance was wreaked
on his dead body, for the crime of wishing to maintain his rights, by
subjecting it to decapitation. His head was impaled over the gate
of Dublin Castle, and afterwards sent as a present to Henry II.
His body was gibbeted, with the feet upwards, on the northern
side of the same building.[9] The Four Masters say that O'Rourke
was treacherously slain. From the account given by Cambrensis,
it would appear that there was a plot to destroy the aged chieftain,
but for want of clearer evidence we may give his enemies the benefit
of the doubt.

Strongbow was now employing himself by depredating the territories which had been conferred on him. He took an army of
1,000 horse and foot into Offaly, to lay waste O'Dempsey's territory,
that prince having also committed the crime of wishing to keep his
ancestral estates. He met with no opposition until he was about
to return with the spoils ; then, as he passed through a defile, the
chieftain set upon him in the rear, and slew several of his knights,
carrying off the Norman standard. Robert de Quincey, who had
just married a daughter of Strongbow's by a former marriage, was

---

[8] *Hugh de Lacy.*—In a charter executed at Waterford, Henry had styled
this nobleman "Bailli," a Norman term for a representative of royalty. The
territory bestowed on him covered 800,000 acres. This was something like
wholesale plunder.

[9] *Building.*—This was the Danish fortress of Dublin, which occupied the
greater part of the hill on which the present Castle of Dublin stands. See *note*,
Four Masters, vol. iii. p. 5. The Annals say this was a "spectacle of intense
pity to the Irish." It certainly could not have tended to increase their devotion to English rule.

amongst the slain.   The Earl had bestowed a large territory in Wexford on him.

Henry was at that time suffering from domestic troubles in Normandy ; he therefore summoned De Clare to attend him there.   It would appear that he performed good service for his royal master, for he received further grants of lands and castles, both in Normandy and in Ireland.   On his return to the latter country, he found that the spoilers had quarrelled over the spoil.   Raymond *le Gros* contrived to ingratiate himself with the soldiers, and they demanded that the command should be transferred from Hervey de Montmarisco, Strongbow's uncle, to the object of their predilection.   The Earl was obliged to comply.   Their object was simply to plunder. The new general gratified them ; and after a raid on the unfortunate inhabitants of Offaly and Munster, they collected their booty at Lismore, intending to convey it by water to Waterford.

The Ostmen of Cork attacked them by sea, but failed to conquer. By land the Irish suffered another defeat.   Raymond encountered MacCarthy of Desmond on his way to Cork, and plundered him, driving off a rich cattle spoil, in addition to his other ill-gotten goods.   Raymond now demanded the appointment of Constable of Leinster, and the hand of Strongbow's sister, Basilia.   But the Earl refused ; and the general, notwithstanding his successes, retired to Wales in disgust.

Hervey now resumed the command, A.D. 1174, and undertook an expedition against Donnell O'Brien, which proved disastrous to the English.   Roderic once more appears in the field.   The battle took place at Thurles, and seventeen hundred of the English were slain.   In consequence of this disaster, the Earl proceeded in sorrow to his house in Waterford.[1]   This great success was a signal for revolt amongst the native chieftains.   Donald Cavanagh claimed his father's territory, and Gillamochalmog and other Leinster chieftains rose up against their allies.   Roderic O'Connor at the same time invaded Meath, and drove the Anglo-Normans from their castles at Trim and Duleek.   Strongbow was obliged to despatch messengers at once to invite the return of Raymond *le Gros*, and to promise him the office he had demanded, and his sister's hand in marriage.

[1] *Waterford.*—The English and Irish accounts of this affair differ widely. The Annals of Innisfallen make the number of slain to be only seven hundred. MacGeoghegan agrees with the Four Masters.

Raymond came without a moment's delay, accompanied by a considerable force. His arrival was most opportune for the English cause. The Northmen of Waterford were preparing to massacre the invaders, and effected their purpose when the Earl left the town to join the new reinforcements at Wexford. The nuptials were celebrated at Wexford with great pomp ; but news was received, on the following morning, that Roderic had advanced almost to Dublin ; and the mantle and tunic of the nuptial feast were speedily exchanged for helmet and coat-of-mail.[2] Unfortunately Roderic's army was already disbanded. The English soon repaired the injuries which had been done to their fortresses ; and once more the Irish cause was lost, even in the moment of victory, for want of combination and a leader.

Henry now considered it time to produce the Papal Bulls, A.D. 1175. He therefore despatched the Prior of Wallingford and William FitzAldelm to Waterford, where a synod of the clergy was assembled to hear these important documents. The English monarch had contrived to impress the Holy See with wonderful ideas of his sanctity, by his penitential expiations of his share in the murder of St. Thomas à Becket. It was therefore easy for him to procure a confirmation of Adrian's Bull from the then reigning Pontiff, Alexander III. The Pope also wrote to Christian, the Legate, to the Irish archbishops, and to the King. Our historians have not informed us what was the result of this meeting. Had the Papal donation appeared a matter of national importance, there can be little doubt that it would have excited more attention.

Raymond now led an army to Limerick, to revenge himself on Donnell O'Brien, for his defeat at Thurles. He succeeded in his enterprise. Several engagements followed, in which the Anglo-Normans were always victorious. Roderic now sent ambassadors to Henry II. The persons chosen were Catholicus, Archbishop of Tuam ; Concors, Abbot of St. Brendan's, in Clonfert ; and St. Lau-

---

[2] *Coat-of-mail.*—Costly mantles were then fashionable. Strutt informs us that Henry I. had a mantle of fine cloth, lined with black sable, which cost £100 of the money of the time—about £1,500 of our money. Fairholt gives an illustration of the armour of the time (*History of Costume*, p. 74). It was either tegulated or formed of chains in rings. The nasal appendage to the helmet was soon after discarded, probably from the inconvenient hold it afforded the enemy of the wearer in battle. Face-guards were invented soon after.

rence O'Toole, styled quaintly, in the old Saxon manner, "Master Laurence." The King and Council received them at Windsor. The result of their conference was, that Roderic consented to pay homage to Henry, by giving him a hide from every tenth head of cattle ; Henry, on his part, bound himself to secure the sovereignty of Ireland to Roderic, excepting only Dublin, Meath, Leinster, Waterford, and Dungarvan. In fact, the English King managed to have the best share, made a favour of resigning what he never possessed, and of not keeping what he could never have held. This council took place on the octave of the feast of St. Michael, A.D. 1175. By this treaty Henry was simply acknowledged as a superior feudal sovereign ; and had Ireland been governed with ordinary justice, the arrangement might have been advantageous to both countries.

Roderic was still a king, both nominally and *ipso facto*. He had power to judge and depose the petty kings, and they were to pay their tribute to him for the English monarch. Any of the Irish who fled from the territories of the English barons, were to return ; but the King of Connaught might compel his own subjects to remain in his land. Thus the English simply possessed a colony in Ireland ; and this colony, in a few years, became still more limited, while throughout the rest of the country the Irish language, laws, and usages, prevailed as they had hitherto done.

Henry now appointed Augustin, an Irishman, to the vacant see of Waterford, and sent him, under the care of St. Laurence, to receive consecration from the Archbishop of Cashel, his metropolitan. For a century previous to this time, the Bishops of Waterford had been consecrated by the Norman Archbishops of Canterbury, with whom they claimed kindred.

St. Gelasius died in 1173, and was succeeded in the see of Armagh by Connor MacConcoille. This prelate proceeded to Rome very soon after his consecration, and was supposed to have died there. When the Most Rev. Dr. Dixon, the late Archbishop of Armagh, was visiting Rome, in 1854, he ascertained that Connor had died at the Monastery of St. Peter of Lemene, near Chambery, in 1176, where he fell ill on his homeward journey. His memory is still honoured there by an annual festival on the 4th of June; another of the many instances that, when the Irish Church was supposed to be in a state of general disorder, it had still many holy men to stem and subdue the torrent of evil. We shall find,

at a later period, that several Irish bishops assisted at the Council
of Lateran.

Dermod MacCarthy's son, Cormac, had rebelled against him, and
he was unwise enough to ask Raymond's assistance. As usual, the
Norman was successful; he reinstated the King of Desmond, and
received for his reward a district in Kerry, where his youngest son,
Maurice, became the founder of the family of FitzMaurice, and

RAM'S ISLAND, ARMAGH.

where his descendants, the Earls of Lansdowne, still possess immense
property.[3] The Irish princes were again engaging in disgraceful
domestic feuds. Roderic now interfered, and, marching into Munster, expelled Donnell O'Brien from Thomond.

While Raymond was still in Limerick, Strongbow died in Dublin.
As it was of the highest political importance that his death should
be concealed until some one was present to hold the reigns of govern-

---

[3] *Property.*—Maurice FitzGerald died at Wexford in 1179. He is the
common ancestor of the Earls of Desmond and Kildare, the Knights of Glynn,
of Kerry, and of all the Irish Geraldines.

ment, his sister, Basilia, sent an enigmatical letter[4] to her husband, which certainly does no small credit to her diplomatic skill. The messengers were not acquainted with the Earl's death; and such of the Anglo-Normans in Dublin as were aware of it, had too much prudence to betray the secret. Raymond at once set out on his journey. Immediately after his arrival, FitzGislebert, Earl de Clare, was interred in the Cathedral of the Holy Trinity, now called Christ's Church.

Strongbow has not obtained a flattering character, either from his friends or his enemies. Even Cambrensis admits that he was obliged to be guided by the plans of others, having neither originality to suggest, nor talent to carry out any important line of action.

The Irish annalists call him the greatest destroyer of the clergy and laity that came to Ireland since the times of Turgesius (Annals of Innisfallen). The Four Masters record his demise thus: "The English Earl [*i.e.*, Richard] died in Dublin, of an ulcer which had broken out in his foot, through the miracles of SS. Brigid and Colum-cille, and of all the other saints whose churches had been destroyed by him. He saw, he thought, St. Brigid in the act of killing him." Pembridge says he died on the 1st of May, and Cambrensis about the 1st of June. His personal appearance is not described in very flattering terms ;[5] and he has the credit of being more of a soldier than a statesman, and not very knightly in his manner or bearing.

The Earl de Clare left only one child, a daughter, as heir to his vast estates. She was afterwards married to William Marshal, Earl of Pembroke. Although Strongbow was a "destroyer" of the native clergy, he appears to have been impregnated with the mediæval devotion for establishing religious houses. He founded a priory at Kilmainham for the Knights of the Temple, with an alms-house and hospital. He was also a liberal benefactor to the Church of the Holy Trinity, where he was buried.[6]

[4] *Letter.*— "To Raymond, her most loving lord and husband, his own Basilia wishes health as to herself. Know you, my dear lord, that the great tooth in my jaw, which was wont to ache so much, is now fallen out ; wherefore, if you have any love or regard for me, or of yourself, you will delay not to hasten hither with all speed."—Gilbert's *Viceroys*, p. 40. It is said that this letter was read for Raymond by a cleric of his train, so it is presumable that reading and writing were not made a part of his education.

[5] *Terms.—Hib. Expug.* lib. i. cap. 27.

[6] *Buried.*—The early history of this church is involved in much obscurity.

An impression on green wax of his seal still exists, pendent from a charter in the possession of the Earl of Ormonde. The seal bears on the obverse a mounted knight, in a long surcoat, with a triangular shield, his head covered by a conical helmet, with a nasal. He has a broad, straight sword in his right hand. A foot soldier, with the legend, "Sigillum Ricardi, Filii Comitis Gilleberti," is on the reverse. The last word alone is now legible.

It probably owes its origin to the Danes. Cambrensis gives some interesting details about it, and mentions several miraculous occurrences which caused it to be held in great veneration in his days. He specially mentions the case of a young man in the train of Raymond *le Gros*, who had robbed him of his greaves, and who had taken a false oath before the cross of that church to clear himself. After a short absence in England he was compelled to return and confess his guilt, "as he felt the weight of the cross continually oppressing him." Strongbow's effigy was broken in 1562, but it was repaired in 1570, by Sir Henry Sidney. Until the middle of the last century, the Earl's tomb was a regularly appointed place for the payment of bonds, rents, and bills of exchange. A recumbent statue by his side is supposed to represent his son, whom he is said to have cut in two with his sword, for cowardice in flying from an engagement. A writer of the seventeenth century, however, corrects this error, and says that "Strongbow did no more than run his son through the belly, as appears by the monument and the chronicle."—Gilbert's *Dublin*, vol. i. p. 113.

KEIM-AN-EIGH.

CHAPTER XVIII.

FitzAldelm appointed Viceroy—De Courcy in Ulster—Arrival of Cardinal
Vivian—Henry II. confers the Title of King of Ireland on his son John—
Irish Bishops at the Council of Lateran—Death of St. Laurence O'Toole—
Henry's Rapacity—John Comyn appointed Archbishop of Dublin—John's
Visit to Ireland—Insolence of his Courtiers—De Lacy's Death—Death of
Henry II.—Accession of Richard I.—An English Archbishop tries to obtain
Justice for Ireland—John succeeds to the Crown—Cathal Crovderg—Mas-
sacres in Connaught—De Courcy's Disgrace and Downfall—His Death.

[A.D. 1176—1201.]

NEWS of the Earl's death soon reached Henry II., who
was then holding his court at Valognes, in Normandy.   He at once nominated his Seneschal, Fitz-
Aldelm de Burgo, Viceroy of Ireland, A.D. 1176.
The new governor was accompanied by John
de Courcy, Robert FitzEstevene, and Miles de
Cogan.   Raymond had assumed the reins of government after the death of Strongbow, but Henry
appears always to have regarded him with jealousy,
and gladly availed himself of every opportunity of
lessening the power of one who stood so high in
favour with the army.   The Viceroy was received
at Wexford by Raymond, who prudently made a
merit of necessity, and resigned his charge.   It
is said that FitzAldelm was much struck by his
retinue and numerous attendants, all of whom belonged to the

same family; and that he then and there vowed to effect their ruin. From this moment is dated the distrust so frequently manifested by the English Government towards the powerful and popular Geraldines.

The new Viceroy was not a favourite with the Anglo-Norman colonists. He was openly accused of partiality to the Irish, because he attempted to demand justice for them. It is not known whether this policy was the result of his own judgment, or a compliance with the wishes of his royal master. His conciliatory conduct, whatever may have been its motive, was unhappily counteracted by the violence of De Courcy. This nobleman asserted that he had obtained a grant of Ulster from Henry II., on what grounds it would be indeed difficult to ascertain. He proceeded to make good his claim; and, in defiance of the Viceroy's prohibition, set out for the north, with a small army of chosen knights and soldiers. His friend, Sir Almaric Tristram de Saint Lawrence, was of the number. He was De Courcy's brother-in-law, and they had made vows of eternal friendship in the famous Cathedral of Rouen. De Courcy is described as a man of extraordinary physical strength, of large proportions, shamefully penurious, rashly impetuous, and, despite a fair share in the vices of the age, full of reverence for the clergy, at least if they belonged to his own race. Cambrensis gives a glowing description of his valour, and says that " any one who had seen Jean de Courci wield his sword, lopping off heads and arms, might well have commended the might of this warrior."[7]

De Courcy arrived in Downpatrick in four days. The inhabitants were taken by surprise; and the sound of his bugles at daybreak was the first intimation they received of their danger. Cardinal Vivian, who had come as Legate from Alexander III., had but just arrived at the spot. He did his best to promote peace. But neither party would yield; and as the demands of the Norman knights were perfectly unreasonable, Vivian advised Dunlevy, the chieftain of Ulidia, to have recourse to arms. A sharp conflict ensued, in which the English gained the victory, principally through the personal bravery of their leader. This battle was fought about the beginning of February; another engagement took place on the 24th of June, in which the northerns were again defeated.[8]

---

[7] *Warrior.*—*Hib. Expug.* lib. ii. cap. 17.

[8] *Defeated.*—Giraldus gives a detailed account of these affairs.—*Hib. Expug.* lib. ii. cap. 17. He says the Irish forces under Dunlevy amounted to ten thousand warriors; but this statement cannot at all be credited. De Courcy

Cardinal Vivian now proceeded to Dublin, where he held a synod. The principal enactment referred to the right of sanctuary. During the Anglo-Norman wars, the Irish had secured their provisions in the churches ; and it is said that, in order to starve out the enemy, they even refused to sell at any price. It was now decreed that sanctuary might be violated to obtain food ; but a fair price was to be paid for whatever was taken. It is to be feared these conditions were seldom complied with. The Abbey of St. Thomas the Martyr was founded in Dublin about this time, by FitzAldelm, at the command of Henry II., one of his many acts of reparation. The site was the place now called Thomas Court. The Viceroy endowed it with a carnucate of land, in the presence of the Legate and St. Laurence O'Toole. After the settlement of these affairs, Cardinal Vivian passed over to Chester, on his way to Scotland.

One of Roderic O'Connor's sons, Murrough, having rebelled against him, Miles de Cogan went to his assistance,—a direct and flagrant violation of the treaty of Windsor. At Roscommon the English were joined by the unnatural rebel, who guided them through the province. The King was in Iar-Connaught, and the allies burned and plundered without mercy, as they passed along to Trim. Here they remained three nights ; but as the people had fled with their cattle and other moveable property into the fastnesses, they had not been able to procure any spoil on their march. Roderic soon appeared to give them battle ; but they were defeated without considerable loss. Murrough was taken prisoner by his father, and his eyes were put out as a punishment for his rebellion, and to prevent a repetition of his treachery.

Another violation of the treaty of Windsor was also perpetrated this year, A.D. 1177. Henry II. summoned a council of his prelates and barons at Oxford, and solemnly conferred the title of King of Ireland on his youngest son, John, then a mere child. A new grant of Meath to Hugh de Lacy was made immediately after, in the joint names of Henry II. and John. Desmond was also granted to Miles de Cogan, with the exception of the city of Cork, which the King reserved to himself. Thomond was offered to two English

took advantage of some old Irish prophecies to further his cause. They were attributed to St. Columbkille, and to the effect that a foreigner who would ride upon a white horse, and have little birds painted on his shield, should conquer the country. De Courcy did ride upon a white horse, and the birds were a part of his armorial bearings.

nobles, who declined the tempting but dangerous favour. It was then presented to Philip de Bresosa; but though the knight was no coward, he fled precipitately, when he discovered, on coming in sight of Limerick, that the inhabitants had set it on fire, so determined was their resistance to foreign rule. The territory of Waterford was granted to Roger le Poer; but, as usual, the city was reserved for the royal benefit. In fact, Sir John Davies well observed, that "all Ireland was by Henry II. cantonized among ten of the English nation; and though they did not gain possession of one-third of the kingdom, yet in title they were owners and lords of all, as nothing was left to be granted to the natives." He might have said with greater truth, that the natives were deprived of everything, as far as it was possible to do so, by those who had not the slightest right or title to their lands.

Meanwhile De Courcy was plundering the northern provinces. His wife, Affreca, was a daughter of Godfrey, King of Man, so that he could secure assistance by sea as well as by land. But the tide of fortune was not always in his favour. After he had plundered in Louth, he was attacked, in the vale of Newry[9] river, by O'Carroll of Oriel and Dunlevy of Ulidia. On this occasion he lost four hundred men, many of whom were drowned. Soon after he suffered another defeat in Antrim, from O'Flynn. The Four Masters say he fled to Dublin; Dr. O'Donovan thinks that we should read Downpatrick. The latter part of the name cannot be correctly ascertained, as the paper is worn away.

The Irish were, as usual, engaged in domestic dissensions, and the English acted as allies on whichever side promised to be most advantageous to themselves. The Annals record a great "windstorm" during this year, which prostrated oaks, especially at Derry-Columcille, which was famous for its forest. They also record the drying up of the river Galliv (Galway), "for a period of a natural day. All the articles that had been lost in it from the remotest times, as well as its fish, were collected by the inhabitants of the fortress, and by the people of the country in general."[1]

---

[9] *Newry.*—See an interesting note to the Annals (Four Masters), vol. iii. p. 40, which identifies the valley of Glenree with the vale of Newry. In an ancient map, the Newry river is called *Owen Glenree fluvius.*

[1] *General.*—This is mentioned also by O'Flaherty, who quotes from some other annals. See his account of Iar-Connaught, printed for the Archæological Society.

In 1179 Henry gave the office of Viceroy to De Lacy, and recalled FitzAldelm. The new governor employed himself actively in erecting castles and oppressing the unfortunate Irish. Cambrensis observes, that he "amply enriched himself and his followers by oppressing others with a strong hand." Yet he seems to have had some degree of popularity, even with the native Irish, for he married a daughter of Roderic O'Connor as his second wife. This alliance, for which he had not asked permission, and his popularity, excited the jealousy of the English King, who deprived him of his office. But he was soon reinstated, although the Bishop of Shrewsbury, with the name of counsellor, was set as a spy on his actions. These events occurred A.D. 1181. De Lacy's old companion, Hervey de Montmarisco, became a monk at Canterbury, after founding the Cistercian Monastery of Dunbrody, in the county of Wexford. He died in this house, in his seventy-fifth year.

In 1179 several Irish bishops were summoned by Alexander III. to attend the third General Council of Lateran. These prelates were, St. Laurence of Dublin, O'Duffy of Tuam, O'Brien of Killaloe, Felix of Lismore, Augustine of Waterford, and Brictius of Limerick. Usher says[2] several other bishops were summoned; it is probable they were unable to leave the country, and hence their names have not been given. The real state of the Irish Church was then made known to the Holy See; no living man could have described it more accurately and truthfully than the sainted prelate who had sacrificed himself for so many years for its good. Even as the bishops passed through England, the royal jealousy sought to fetter them with new restrictions; and they were obliged to take an oath that they would not sanction any infringements on Henry's prerogatives. St. Malachy was now appointed Legate by the Pope, with jurisdiction over the five suffragans, and the possessions attached to his see were confirmed to him. As the Bull was directed to Ireland, it would appear that he returned there; but his stay was brief, and the interval was occupied in endeavouring to repress the vices of the Anglo-Norman and Welsh clergy, many of whom were doing serious injury to the Irish Church by their immoral and dissolute lives.[3]

[2] Says.—Sylloge, ep. 48.

[3] Lives.—We give authority for this statement, as it manifests how completely the Holy See was deceived in supposing that any reform was likely to be effected in Ireland by English interference: "Ita ut quodam tempore

Henry now became jealous of the Archbishop, and perhaps was not overpleased at his efforts to reform these ecclesiastics. Roderic O'Connor had asked St. Laurence to undertake a mission on his behalf to the English court; but the King refused to listen to him, and forbid him to return to Ireland. After a few weeks' residence at the Monastery of Abingdon, in Berkshire, the saint set out for France. He fell ill on his journey, in a religious house at Eu, where his remains are still preserved. When on his deathbed, the monks asked him to make his will; but he exclaimed, "God knows that out of all my revenues I have not a single coin to bequeath." With the humility of true sanctity, he was heard frequently calling on God for mercy, and using the words of the Psalmist, so familiar to ecclesiastics, from their constant perusal of the Holy Scriptures. As he was near his end, he was heard exclaiming, in his own beautiful mother-tongue : "Foolish people, what will become of you? Who will relieve you? Who will heal you?" And well might his paternal heart ache for those who were soon to be left doubly orphans, and for the beloved nation whose sorrows he had so often striven to alleviate.

St. Laurence went to his eternal reward on the 14th of November, 1180. He died on the *feria sexta* at midnight.[4] His obsequies were celebrated with great pomp and solemnity, and attended by the Scotch Legate, Alexis, an immense concourse of clergy, and many knights and nobles. His remains were exposed for some days in the Church of Notre Dame, at Eu.

Henry immediately despatched his chaplain, Geoffrey de la Haye,

---

(quod dictu mirum est) centum et quadraginta presby. incontinentiæ convictos Romani miserit absolvendos."—Surius, t. vi. St. Laurence had faculties for absolving these persons, but for some reason—probably as a greater punishment—he sent them to Rome. English writers at this period also complain of the relaxed state of ecclesiastical discipline in that country. How completely all such evils were eradicated by the faithful sons of the Church, and the exertions of ecclesiastical superiors, is manifest from the fact, that no such charges could be brought against even a single priest at the time of the so-called Reformation.

[4] *Midnight.*—"Itaque cum sextæ feriæ terminus advenisset, in confinio sabbati subsequentis Spiritum Sancti viri requies æterna suscepit."—*Vita S. Laurentii,* cap. xxxiii. The saint's memory is still honoured at Eu. The church has been lately restored, and there is a little oratory on the hill near it to mark the spot where he exclaimed, *Hæc est requies mea,* as he approached the town where he knew he should die. Dr. Kelly (*Cambrensis Eversus,* vol. ii. p. 648) mentions in a note that the names of several Irishmen were inscribed there.

to Ireland, not with a royal message of consolation for the national calamity, but to sequester the revenues of the archiepiscopal see of Dublin. He took care to possess himself of them for a year before he would consent to name a successor to the deceased prelate. St. Laurence had happily left no funds in store for the royal rapacity; the orphan and the destitute had been his bankers. During a year of famine he is said to have relieved five hundred persons daily; he also established an orphanage, where a number of poor children were clothed and educated. The Annals of the Four Masters say he suffered martyrdom in England. The mistake arose in consequence of an attempt having been made on his life there by a fanatic, which happily did not prove fatal.[5]

The Archbishop of Dublin became an important functionary from this period. Henry obtained the election of John Comyn to this dignity, at the Monastery of Evesham, in Worcester, and the King granted the archiepiscopal estates to him " in barony," by which tenure he and his successors in the see were constituted parliamentary barons, and entitled to sit in the councils, and hold court in their lordships and manors. Comyn, after his election by the clergy of Dublin, proceeded to Rome, where he was ordained priest, and subsequently to Veletri, where Pope Lucius III. consecrated him archbishop. He then came to Dublin, A.D. 1184, where preparations were making for the reception of Henry's son, John, who, it will be remembered, he had appointed King of Ireland when a mere child.

In 1183 the unfortunate Irish monarch, Roderic, had retired to the Abbey of Cong, and left such empty titles as he possessed to his son, Connor. De Lacy and De Courcy had occupied themselves alternately in plundering and destroying the religious houses which had so long existed, and in founding new monasteries with a portion of their ill-gotten gains. It would appear that De Lacy built so far on his popularity with the Anglo-Normans, as to have aspired to the sovereignty of Ireland,—an aspiration which his master soon discovered, and speedily punished. He was supplanted by Philip of

---

[5] *Fatal.*—Dr. O'Donovan gives a long and most interesting note on the genealogy of St. Laurence O'Toole, in which he shows that his father was a chieftain of an important territory in the county Kildare, and that he was not a Wicklow prince, as has been incorrectly asserted. The family removed there after the death of St. Laurence, when they were driven from their property by an English adventurer.

Worcester, who excelled all his predecessors in rapacity and cruelty. Not satisfied with the miseries inflicted on Ulster by De Courcy, he levied contributions there by force of arms. One of his companions, Hugh Tyrrell, who " remained at Armagh, with his Englishmen, during six days and nights, in the middle of Lent," signalized himself by carrying off the property of the clergy of Armagh. Amongst other things, he possessed himself of a brewing-pan, which he was obliged to abandon on his way, he met so many calamities, which were naturally attributed to his sacrilegious conduct.[6]

John was now preparing for his visit to Ireland, and his singularly unfelicitous attempt at royalty. It would appear that the Prince wished to decline the honour and the expedition ; for, as he was on the eve of his departure, Eraclius, Patriarch of Jerusalem, arrived in England, to enjoin the fulfilment of the King's vow to undertake a crusade to Palestine. As Henry had got out of his difficulties, he declined to fulfil his solemn engagement, and refused permission to his son, John, who threw himself at his father's feet, and implored leave to be his substitute. Eraclius then poured forth his indignation upon Henry, with all the energetic freedom of the age. He informed him that God would punish his impieties—that he was worse than any Saracen ; and hinted that he might have inherited his wickedness from his grandmother, the Countess of Anjou, who was reported to be a witch, and of whom it was said that she had flown through the window during the most solemn part of Mass, though four squires attempted to hold her.

John sailed from Milford Haven on the evening of Easter Wednesday, 1185. He landed with his troops at Waterford, at noon, on the following day. His retinue is described as of unusual splendour, and, no doubt, was specially appointed to impress the " barbarous" Irish. Gerald Barry, the famous Cambrensis, who had arrived in Ireland some little time before, was appointed his tutor, in conjunction with Ranulf de Glanville. The bitter prejudice of the former against Ireland and the Irish is a matter of history, as well as the indefatigable zeal of the latter in pursuit of his own interests at the expense of justice.

---

[6] *Conduct.*—This is mentioned even by Cox, who, Dr. O'Donovan observes, was always anxious to hide the faults of the English, and vilify the Irish. He calls Hugh Tyrrell " a man of ill report," and says he returned to Dublin " loaden both with curses and extortions."—*Hib. Angl.* p. 38, ad an. 1184.

A retinue of profligate Normans completed the court, whom an English authority describes as "great quaffers, lourdens, proud, belly swains, fed with extortion and bribery." The Irish were looked upon by these worthies as a savage race, only created to be plundered and scoffed at. The Normans prided themselves on their style of dress, and, no doubt, the Irish costume surprised them. Common prudence, however, might have taught them, when the Leinster chieftains came to pay their respects to the young Prince, that they should not add insult to injury; for, not content with open ridicule, they proceeded to pull the beards of the chieftains, and to gibe their method of wearing their hair.

De Lacy has the credit of having done his utmost to render the Prince's visit a failure. But his efforts were not necessary. The insolence of the courtiers, and the folly of the youth himself, were quite sufficient to ruin more promising prospects. In addition to other outrages, the Irish had seen their few remaining estates bestowed on the new comers; and even the older Anglo-Norman and Welsh settlers were expelled to make room for the Prince's favourites—an instalment of the fatal policy which made them eventually "more Irish than the Irish." When the colony was on the verge of ruin, the young Prince returned to England. He threw the blame of his failure on Hugh de Lacy; but the Norman knight did not live long enough after to suffer from the accusation.[7] De Lacy was killed while inspecting a castle which he had just built on the site of St. Columbkille's Monastery at Durrow, in the Queen's county. He was accompanied by three Englishmen; as he was in the act of stooping, a youth of an ancient and noble family, named O'Meyey, gave him his deathblow, severed his head from his body, and then fled with such swiftness as to elude pursuit. It is said that he was instigated to perform this deed by Sumagh O'Caharnay (the Fox), with whom he now took refuge.

The Annals mention this as a "revenge of Colum-cille,"[8] they also

[7] *Accusation.*—There can be no doubt that De Lacy had ambitious designs. See Cambrensis, *Hib. Expug.* lib. ii. cap. 20. Henry II. heard of his death with considerable satisfaction.

[8] *Colum-cille.*—Dr. O'Donovan remarks that a similar disaster befell Lord Norbury. He was also assassinated by a hand still unknown, after having erected a castle on the same *site* as that of De Lacy, and preventing the burial of the dead in the ancient cemetery of Durrow.

say that "all Meath was full of his English castles, from the Shannon to the sea." Henry at once appointed his son, John, to the Irish Viceroyalty, but domestic troubles prevented his plans from being carried out. Archbishop Comyn held a synod in Dublin during this year, 1187; and on the 9th of June the relics of SS. Patrick, Columba, and Brigid were discovered, and solemnly entombed anew under the direction of Cardinal Vivian, who came to Ireland to perform this function. During the year 1188 the Irish continued their usual fatal and miserable dissensions; still they contrived to beat the common enemy, and O'Muldony drove De Courcy and his troops from Ballysadare. He was again attacked in crossing the Curlieu Mountains, and escaped to Leinster with considerable loss and difficulty.

In 1189 Henry II. died at Chinon, in Normandy. He expired launching anathemas against his sons, and especially against John, as he had just discovered that he had joined those who conspired ag inst him. In his last moments he was stripped of his garments and jewels, and left naked and neglected.

Richard I., who succeeded to the throne, was too much occupied about foreign affairs to attend to his own kingdom. He was a brave soldier, and as such merits our respect; but he can scarcely be credited as a wise king. Irish affairs were committed to the care of John, who does not appear to have profited by his former experience. He appointed Hugh de Lacy Lord Justice, to the no small disgust of John de Courcy; but it was little matter to whom the government of that unfortunate country was confided. There were nice distinctions made about titles; for John, even when King of England, did not attempt to write himself King of Ireland.[9] But there were no nice distinctions about property; for the rule seemed to be, that whoever could get it should have it, and whoever could keep it should possess it.

In 1189 Roderic's son, Connor Moinmoy, fell a victim to a conspiracy of his own chieftains,—a just retribution for his rebellion against his father. He had, however, the reputation of being brave and generous. At his death Connaught was once more plunged in

---

[9] *King of Ireland.*—During the reign of Richard all the public affairs of the Anglo-Norman colony were transacted in the name of "John, Lord of Ireland, Earl of Montague." Palgrave observes that John never claimed to be King of the Irish; like Edward, who wrote himself Lord of Scotland, and acknowledged Baliol to be King of the Scots.

civil war, and after some delay and difficulty Roderic resumed the government.

In 1192 the brave King of Thomond again attacked the English invaders. But after his death, in 1194, the Anglo-Normans had little to apprehend from native valour. His obituary is thus recorded : " Donnell, son of Turlough O'Brien, King of Munster, a burning lamp in peace and war, and the brilliant star of the hospitality and valour of the Momonians, and of all Leth-Mogha, died." Several other "lamps" went out about the same time ; one of these was Crunce O'Flynn, who had defeated De Courcy in 1178, and O'Carroll, Prince of Oriel, who had been hanged by the English the year before, after the very unnecessary cruelty of putting out his eyes.

The affairs of the English colony were not more prosperous. New Lords Justices followed each other in quick succession. One of these governors, Hamon de Valois, attempted to replenish his coffers from church property,—a proceeding which provoked the English Archbishop Comyn. As this ecclesiastic failed to obtain redress in Ireland, he proceeded to England with his complaints ; but he soon learned that justice could not be expected for Ireland. The difference between the conduct of ecclesiastics, who have no family but the Church, and no interests but the interests of religion, is very observable in all history. While English and Norman soldiers were recklessly destroying church property and domestic habitations in the country they had invaded, we find, with few exceptions, that the ecclesiastic, of whatever nation, is the friend and father of the people, wherever his lot may be cast. The English Archbishop resented the wrongs of the Irish Church as personal injuries, and devoted himself to its advancement as a personal interest. We are indebted to Archbishop Comyn for building St. Patrick's Cathedral in Dublin, as well as for his steady efforts to promote the welfare of the nation. After an appeal in person to King Richard and Prince John, he was placed in confinement in Normandy, and was only released by the interference of the Holy See ; Innocent III., who had probably by this time discovered that the English monarchs were not exactly the persons to reform the Irish nation, having addressed a letter from Perugia to the Earl of Montague (Prince John), reprimanding him for detaining " his venerable brother, the Archbishop of Dublin," in exile, and requiring him to repair the injuries done by his Viceroy, Hamon de

Valois, on the clergy of Leighlin. The said Hamon appears to have meddled with other property besides that belonging to the Church—a more unpardonable offence, it is to be feared, in the eyes of his master. On returning from office after two years vice-royalty, he was obliged to pay a thousand marks to obtain an acquittance from his accounts.[1]

John ascended the English throne in 1199. He appointed Meiller FitzHenri[2] Governor of Ireland. It has been conjectured that if John had not obtained the sovereignty, he and his descendants might have claimed the "Lordship of Ireland." There can be no doubt that he and they might have claimed it; but whether they could have held it is quite another consideration. It is generally worse than useless to speculate on what might have been. In this case, however, we may decide with positive certainty, that no such condition of things could have continued long. The English kings would have looked with jealousy even on the descendants of their ancestors, if they kept possession of the island; and the descendants would have become, as invariably happened, *Hibernicis ipsis Hibernior*, and therefore would have shared the fate of the "common enemy."

Meanwhile the O'Connors were fighting in Kerry. Cathal Carragh obtained the services of FitzAldelm, and expelled Cathal Crovderg. He, in his turn, sought the assistance of Hugh O'Neill, who had been distinguishing himself by his valour against De Courcy and the English. They marched into Connaught, but were obliged to retreat with great loss. The exiled Prince now sought English assistance, and easily prevailed on De Courcy and young De Lacy to help him. But misfortune still followed him. His army was again defeated; and as they fled to the peninsula of Rin-down, on Lough Ree, they were so closely hemmed in, that no way of escape remained, except to cross the lake in boats. In attempting to do this a great number were drowned. The Annals of Kilronan and Clonmacnois enter these events under the year 1200; the Four Masters under the year 1199. The former state that " Cahall Carragh was taken deceitfully by the English of Meath," and imprisoned until he paid a ransom; and that De Courcy, "after slaying of his people," returned to Ulster.

---

[1] *Accounts.*—Gilbert's *Viceroys*, p. 58.

[2] *FitzHenri.*—His father was an illegitimate son of Henry I. When a mere youth, FitzHenri came to Ireland with the Geraldines, and obtained large possessions.

Cathal Crovderg now obtained the assistance of the Lord Justice, who plundered Clonmacnois. He also purchased the services of FitzAldelm, and thus deprived his adversary of his best support. The English, like the mercenary troops of Switzerland and the Netherlands, appear to have changed sides with equal alacrity, when it suited their convenience; and so as they were well paid, it mattered little to them against whom they turned their arms. In 1201 Cathal Crovderg marched from Limerick to Roscommon, with his new ally and the sons of Donnell O'Brien and Florence Mac-Carthy. They took up their quarters at Boyle, and occupied themselves in wantonly desecrating the abbey. Meanwhile Cathal Carragh, King of Connaught, had assembled his forces, and came to give them battle. Some skirmishes ensued, in which he was slain, and thus the affair was ended. FitzAldelm, or De Burgo, as he is more generally called now, assisted by O'Flaherty of West Connaught, turned against Cathal when they arrived at Cong to spend the Easter. It would appear that the English were billeted on the Irish throughout the country; and when De Burgo demanded wages for them, the Connacians rushed upon them, and slew six hundred men. For once his rapacity was foiled, and he marched off to Munster with such of his soldiers as had escaped the massacre. Three years after he revenged himself by plundering the whole of Connaught, lay and ecclesiastical.

During this period Ulster was also desolated by civil war. Hugh O'Neill was deposed, and Connor O'Loughlin obtained rule; but the former was restored after a few years.

John de Courcy appears always to have been regarded with jealousy by the English court. His downfall was at hand, A.D. 1204; and to add to its bitterness, his old enemies, the De Lacys, were chosen to be the instruments of his disgrace. It is said that he had given mortal offence to John, by speaking openly of him as a usurper and the murderer of his nephew; but even had he not been guilty of this imprudence, the state he kept, and the large tract of country which he held, was cause enough for his ruin. He had established himself at Downpatrick, and was surrounded in almost regal state by a staff of officers, including his constable, seneschal, and chamberlain; he even coined money in his own name. Complaints of his exactions were carried to the King. The De Lacys accused him of disloyalty. In 1202 the then Viceroy, Hugh de Lacy, attempted to seize him treacherously, at a friendly meeting.

He failed to accomplish this base design; but his brother, Walter, succeeded afterwards in a similar attempt, and De Courcy was kept in durance until the devastations which his followers committed in revenge obliged his enemies to release him.

In 1204 he defeated the Viceroy in a battle at Down. He was aided in this by the O'Neills, and by soldiers from Man and the Isles. It will be remembered that he could always claim assistance from the latter, in consequence of his connexion by marriage. But this did not avail him. He was summoned before the Council in Dublin, and some of his possessions were forfeited. Later in the same year (A.D. 1204) he received a safe conduct to proceed to the King. It is probable that he was confined in the Tower of London for some time; but it is now certain that he revisited Ireland in 1210, if not earlier, in the service of John, who granted him an annual pension.[3] It is supposed that he died about 1219; for in that year Henry III. ordered his widow, Affreca, to be paid her dower out of the lands which her late husband had possessed in Ireland.

Cambrensis states that De Courcy had no children; but the Barons of Kinsale claim to be descended from him; and even so late as 1821 they exercised the privilege of appearing covered before George IV.—a favour said to have been granted to De Courcy by King John, after his recall from Ireland, as a reward for his prowess. Dr. Smith states, in his *History of Cork*, that Miles de Courcy was a hostage for his father during the time when he was permitted to leave the Tower to fight the French champion. In a pedigree of the MacCarthys of Cooraun Lough, county Kerry, a daughter of Sir

[3] *Pension.*—One hundred pounds per annum. Orders concerning it are still extant on the Close Rolls of England.—*Rot. Lit. Clau.* 1833, 144. It is curious, and should be carefully noted, how constantly proofs are appearing that the Irish bards and chroniclers, from the earliest to the latest period, were most careful as to the truth of their facts, though they may have sometimes coloured them highly. Dr. O'Donovan has devoted some pages in a note (Four Masters, vol. iii. p. 139) to the tales in the Book of Howth which record the exploits of De Courcy. He appears satisfied that they were "invented in the fifteenth or sixteenth century." Mr. Gilbert has ascertained that they were placed on record as early as 1360, in Pembridge's Annals. As they are merely accounts of personal valour, we do not reproduce them here. He also gives an extract from Hoveden's Annals, pars port, p. 823, which further supports the Irish account. Rapin gives the narrative as history. Indeed, there appears nothing very improbable about it. The Howth family were founded by Sir Almaric St. Lawrence, who married De Courcy's sister.

John de Courcy is mentioned. The Irish annalists, as may be supposed, were not slow to attribute his downfall to his crimes.

Another English settler died about this period, and received an equal share of reprobation ; this was FitzAldelm, more commonly known as Mac William Burke (De Burgo), and the ancestor of the Burke family in Ireland. Cambrensis describes him as a man addicted to many vices. The Four Masters declare that "God and the saints took vengeance on him ; for he died of a shameful disease." It could scarcely be expected that one who had treated the Irish with such unvarying cruelty, could obtain a better character, or a more pleasing obituary. Of his miserable end, without "shrive or unction," there appears to be no doubt.

STALACTITE CAVE, TIPPERARY.

KING JOHN'S CASTLE, LIMERICK.

CHAPTER XIX.

Quarrels of the English Barons—The Interdict—John crushes and starves an Archdeacon to Death—King John's Visit to Ireland—He starves the Wife and Son of Earl de Braose to Death—Henry de Londres—The Poet O'Daly—Obituaries of Good Men—Henry III.—Regulations about the Viceroy—The Scorch Villain—Scandalous Conduct of the Viceroys—Three Claimants for Connaught—Death of Hugh Crovderg—Felim O'Connor—Henry's Foreign Advisers—Plots against the Earl of Pembroke—He is wounded treacherously—His Pious Death—Misfortunes of the Early Settlers—De Marisco's Son is hanged for High Treason, and he dies miserably in Exile.

[A.D. 1201—1244.]

KING JOHN was now obliged to interfere between his English barons in Ireland, who appear to have been quite as much occupied with feuds among themselves as the native princes. In 1201 Philip of Worcester and William de Braose laid waste the greater part of Munster in their quarrels. John had sold the lands of the former and of Theobald Walter to the latter, for four thousand marks—Walter redeemed his property for five hundred marks; Philip obtained his at the point of the sword. De Braose had large property both in Normandy and in England. He had his chancellor, chancery, and seal, recognizances of all pleas, not even excepting those of the crown, with judgment of life and limb. His sons and daughters had married into powerful families. His wife, Matilda, was notable in domestic affairs, and a vigorous oppressor of the Welsh. A bloody war was waged about the same time between De Lacy, De Marisco, and the Lord Justice. Cathal Crovderg and O'Brien aided the latter in besieging Limerick, while some of the English fortified themselves in their castles and plundered indiscrimately.

In 1205 the Earldom of Ulster was granted to Hugh de Lacy. The grant is inscribed on the charter roll of the seventh year of King John, and is the earliest record now extant of the creation of an Anglo-Norman dignity in Ireland. England was placed under an interdict in 1207, in consequence of the violence and wickedness of its sovereign. He procured the election of John de Grey to the see of Canterbury, a royal favourite, and, if only for this reason, unworthy of the office. Another party who had a share in the election chose Reginald, the Sub-Prior of the monks of Canterbury. But when the choice was submitted to Pope Innocent III., he rejected both candidates, and fixed on an English Cardinal, Stephen Langton, who was at once elected, and received consecration from the Pope himself. John was highly indignant, as might be expected. He swore his favourite oath, " by God's teeth," that he would cut off the noses and pluck out the eyes of any priest who attempted to carry the Pope's decrees against him into England. But some of the bishops, true to their God and the Church, promulgated the interdict, and then fled to France to escape the royal vengeance. It was well for them they did so ; for Geoffrey, Archdeacon of Norwich, was seized, and enveloped, by the royal order, in a sacerdotal vestment of massive lead, and thus thrown into prison, where he was starved to death beneath the crushing weight. We sometimes hear of the cruelties of the Inquisition, of the barbarity of the Irish, of the tyranny of priestcraft ; but such cruelties, barbarities, and tyrannies, however highly painted, pale before the savage vengeance which English kings have exercised, on the slightest provocation, towards their unfortunate subjects. But we have not yet heard all the refinements of cruelty which this same monarch exercised. Soon after, John was excommunicated personally. When he found that Philip of France was prepared to seize his kingdom, and that his crimes had so alienated him from his own people that he could hope for little help from them, he cringed with the craven fear so usually found in cruel men, and made the most abject submission. In the interval between the proclamation

of the interdict and the fulmination of the sentence of excommunication (A.D. 1210), John visited Ireland. It may be supposed his
arrival could not excite much pleasure in the hearts of his Irish
subjects, though, no doubt, he thought it a mark of disloyalty that
he should not be welcomed with acclamations. A quarter of a
century had elapsed since he first set his foot on Irish ground. He
had grown grey in profligacy, but he had not grown wiser or better
with advancing years.

The year before his arrival, Dublin had been desolated by a
pestilence, and a number of people from Bristol had taken advantage
of the decrease in the population to establish themselves there. On
the Easter Monday after their arrival, when they had assembled to
amuse themselves in Cullen's Wood, the O'Byrnes and O'Tooles
rushed down upon them from the Wicklow Mountains, and took a
terrible vengeance for the many wrongs they had suffered, by a
massacre of some three hundred men. The citizens of Bristol sent
over new colonists ; but the anniversary of the day was long known
as Black Monday.

The English King obtained money for his travelling expenses by
extortion from the unfortunate Jews. He landed at Crook, near
Waterford, on the 20th June, 1210. His army was commanded by
the Earl of Salisbury, son to Henry I., by "Fair Rosamond," of
tragic memory. De Braose fled to England when he heard of the
King's movements. Here he endeavoured to make peace with his
master, but failing to do so, he carefully avoided putting himself in
his power, and took refuge in France. His wife was not so fortunate.
After John's return to England, Matilda and her son were seized
by his command, and imprisoned at Corfe Castle, in the isle of
Pembroke. Here they were shut up in a room, with a sheaf of
wheat and a piece of raw bacon for their only provision. When the
prison door was opened on the eleventh day, they were both found
dead.

De Lacy also fled before the King's visit ; John took Carrickfergus Castle from his people, and stationed a garrison of his own
there. Several Irish princes paid homage to him ; amongst others
we find the names of Cathal Crovderg and Hugh O'Neill. The
Norman lords were also obliged to swear fealty, and transcripts of
their oaths were placed in the Irish Exchequer. Arrangements
were also made for the military support of the colony, and certain
troops were to be furnished with forty days' ration by all who held

lands by "knight's service." The Irish princes who lived in the southern and western parts of Ireland, appear to have treated the King with silent indifference; they could afford to do so, as they were so far beyond the reach of his vengeance.

John remained only sixty days in Ireland. He returned to Wales on the 26th of August, 1210, after confiding the government of the colony to John de Grey, Bishop of Norwich, whose predilection for secular affairs had induced the Holy See to refuse his nomination to the Archbishopric of Canterbury. The most important act of his Viceroyalty was the erection of a bridge and castle at *Ath-Luain* (Athlone). He was succeeded, in 1213, by Henry de Londres, who had been appointed to the see of Dublin during the preceding year. This prelate was one of those who were the means of obtaining *Magna Charta*. His name appears second on the list of counsellors who advised the grant; and he stood by the King's side, at Runnymede, when the barons obtained the bulwark of English liberty. It is sometimes forgotten that the clergy were the foremost to demand it, and the most persevering in their efforts to obtain it.

The Archbishop was now sent to Rome by the King to plead his cause there, and to counteract, as best he might, the serious complaints made against him by all his subjects—A.D. 1215. In 1213 Walter de Lacy obtained the restoration of his father's property in Wales and England. Two years later he recovered his Irish lands; but the King retained his son, Gislebert, as hostage, and his Castle of *Droicead-Atha* (Drogheda).

The Irish chieftains made some stand for their rights at the close of this reign. Cormac O'Melaghlin wrested Delvin, in Meath, from the English. O'Neill and O'Donnell composed their difference *pro tem.*, and joined in attacking the invaders. In the south there was a war between Dermod and Connor Carthy, in which the Anglo-Normans joined, and, as usual, got the lion's share, obtaining such an increase of territory as enabled them to erect twenty new castles in Cork and Kerry.

The Four Masters give a curious story under the year 1213. O'Donnell More sent his steward to Connaught to collect his tribute. On his way he visited the poet Murray O'Daly, and began to wrangle with him, "although his lord had given him no instructions to do so." The poet's ire was excited. He killed him on the spot with a sharp axe—an unpleasant exhibition of literary justice—and then fled into Clanrickarde for safety. O'Donnell determined to revenge the insult, until Mac William (William de Burgo) submitted to him. But the poet had been sent to seek refuge in Thomond. The chief pursued him there also, and laid siege to Limerick.[4] The inhabitants at once expelled the murderer, who eventually fled to Dublin. After receiving tribute from the men of Connaught, O'Donnell marched to Dublin, and compelled the people to banish Murray to Scotland. Here he remained until he had composed three poems in praise of O'Donnell, imploring peace and forgiveness. He was then pardoned, and so far received into favour as to obtain a grant of land and other possessions.

The Irish bishops were, as usual, in constant intercourse with Rome. Several prelates attended the fourth General Council of Lateran, in 1215. The Annals give the obituaries of some saintly men, whose lives redeemed the age from the character for barbarity, which its secular literature would seem to justify. Amongst these we find the obituary of Catholicus O'Duffy, in 1201 ; of Uaireirghe, "one of the noble sages of Clonmacnois, a man full of the love of God and of every virtue ;" of Con O'Melly, Bishop of Annagh-down, "a transparently bright gem of the Church ;" of Donnell O'Brollaghan, "a prior, a noble senior, a sage, illustrious for his intelligence ;" and of many others. A great number of monasteries were also founded, especially by the Anglo-Normans, who appear to have had periodical fits of piety, after periodical temptations to replenish their coffers out of their neighbours' property. We may not quite judge their reparations as altogether insincere ; for surely some atonement for evil deeds is better than an utter recklessness of future punishment.

Henry III. succeeded his father, John, while only in his tenth year. William Marshal, Earl of Pembroke, was appointed protector of the kingdom and the King. The young monarch was hastily crowned at Bristol, with one of his mother's golden bracelets. Had the wise and good Earl lived to administer affairs for a longer period, it

---

[4] *Limerick.*—We give an illustration, at the head of this chapter, of King John's Castle, Limerick. Stanihurst says that King John " was so pleased with the agreeableness of the city, that he caused a very fine castle and bridge to be built there." This castle has endured for more than six centuries. Richard I. granted this city a charter to elect a Mayor before London had that privilege, and a century before it was granted to Dublin. M'Gregor says, in his *History of Limerick*, that the trade went down fearfully after the English invasion.— vol. ii. p. 53.

would have been a blessing to both countries. Geoffrey de Marisco still continued Governor of Ireland. Affairs in England were in an extremely critical position. The profligate Isabella had returned to her first husband, Hugh de Lusignan, whom she had before forsaken for King John. Gloucester, London, and Kent, were in the hands of the Dauphin of France. Some few acts of justice to Ireland were the result; but when justice is only awarded from motives of fear or interest, it becomes worse than worthless as a mode of conciliation. Such justice, however, as was granted, only benefited the Anglo-Norman settlers; the " mere Irish" were a race devoted to plunder and extermination.

In consequence of complaints from the English barons in Ireland, a modified form of Magna Charta was granted to them, and a general amnesty was proclaimed, with special promises of reparation to the nobles whom John had oppressed. Hugh de Lacy was also pardoned and recalled; but it was specially provided that the Irish should have no share in such favours; and the Viceroy was charged to see that no native of the country obtained cathedral preferment. This piece of injustice was annulled through the interference of Pope Honorius III.

In 1217 the young King, or rather his advisers, sent the Archbishop of Dublin to that city to levy a "tallage," or tax, for the royal benefit. The Archbishop and the Justiciary were directed to represent to the "Kings of Ireland," and the barons holding directly from the crown, that their liberality would not be forgotten; but neither the politeness of the address[5] nor the benevolence of the promises were practically appreciated, probably because neither were believed to be sincere, and the King's coffers were not much replenished.

Arrangements were now made defining the powers of the Viceroy or Justiciary. The earliest details on this subject are embodied in an agreement between Henry III. and Geoffrey de Marisco, sealed at Oxford, in March, 1220, in presence of the Papal Legate, the Archbishop of Dublin, and many of the nobility.

By these regulations the Justiciary was bound to account in the Exchequer of Dublin for all taxes and aids received in Ireland for the royal purse. He was to defray all expenses for the maintenance of the King's castles and lands out of the revenues. In fact, the

---

[5] *Address.*—Gilbert's *Viceroys*, p. 82, where the address may be seen *in extenso.*

people of the country were taxed, either directly or indirectly, for
the support of the invaders. The King's castles were to be kept
by loyal and proper constables, who were obliged to give hostages.
Indeed, so little faith had the English kings in the loyalty of their
own subjects, that the Justiciary himself was obliged to give a
hostage as security for his own behaviour. Neither does the same
Viceroy appear to have benefited trade, for he is accused of exacting wine, clothing, and victuals, without payment, from the merchants of Dublin.

In 1221 the Archbishop of Dublin, Henry de Londres, was made
Governor. He obtained the name of " Scorch Villain," from having
cast into the fire the leases of the tenants of his see, whom he had
cited to produce these documents in his court. The enraged land-
holders attacked the attendants, and laid hands on the Archbishop,
who was compelled to do them justice from fear of personal violence.
When such was the mode of government adopted by English
officials, we can scarcely wonder that the people of Ireland have not
inherited very ardent feelings of loyalty and devotion to the crown
and constitution of that country.

Such serious complaints were made of the unjust Governor, that
Henry was at last obliged to check his rapacity. Probably, he was
all the more willing to do so, in consequence of some encroachments
on the royal prerogative.

After the death of the Earl of Pembroke, who had obtained the
pardon of Hugh de Lacy, a feud arose between the latter and the son
of his former friend. In consequence of this quarrel, all Meath was
ravaged, Hugh O'Neill having joined De Lacy in the conflict.

Some of the Irish chieftains now tried to obtain protection from
the rapacity of the Anglo-Norman barons, by paying an annual
stipend to the crown; but the crown, though graciously pleased to
accept anything which might be offered, still held to its royal
prerogative of disposing of Irish property as appeared most convenient to royal interests. Though Cathal Crovderg had made
arrangements with Henry III., at an immense sacrifice, to secure
his property, that monarch accepted his money, but, nevertheless,
bestowed the whole province of Connaught shortly after on Richard
de Burgo.

Crovderg had retired into a Franciscan monastery at Knockmoy,
which he had founded, and there he was interred nobly and
honourably. After his death there were no less than three claim-

ants for his dignity. De Burgo claimed it in right of the royal
gift; Hugh Cathal claimed it as heir to his father, Crovderg;
Turlough claimed it for the love of fighting, inherent in the Celtic
race; and a general guerilla warfare was carried on by the three
parties, to the utter ruin of each individual. For the next ten
years the history of the country is the history of deadly feuds between the native princes, carefully fomented by the English settlers,
whose interest it was to make them exterminate each other.

The quarrel for the possession of Connaught began in the year
1225. The Anglo-Normans had a large army at Athlone, and
Hugh Cathal went to claim their assistance. The Lord Justice put
himself at the head of the army; they marched into Connaught, and
soon became masters of the situation. Roderic's sons at once submitted, but only to bide their time. During these hostilities the
English of Desmond, and O'Brien, a Thomond prince, assisted by
the Sheriff of Cork, invaded the southern part of Connaught for
the sake of plunder. In the previous year, 1224, " the corn remained unreaped until the festival of St. Brigid [1st Feb.], when
the ploughing was going on." A famine also occurred, and was followed by severe sickness. Well might the friar historian exclaim :
" Woeful was the misfortune which God permitted to fall upon the
west province in Ireland at that time; for the young warriors did
not spare each other, but preyed and plundered to the utmost of
their power. Women and children, the feeble and the lowly poor,
perished by cold and famine in this year."[6]

O'Neill had inaugurated Turlough at Carnfree.[7] He appears to
have been the most popular claimant. The northern chieftains
then returned home. As soon as the English left Connaught, Turlough again revolted. Hugh Cathal recalled his allies; and the
opposite party, finding their cause hopeless, joined him in such
numbers that Roderic's sons fled for refuge to Hugh O'Neill. The
Annals suggest that the English might well respond when called
on, " for their spirit was fresh, and their struggle trifling." Again
we find it recorded that the corn remained unreaped until after
the festival of St. Brigid. The wonder is, not that the harvest was
not gathered in, but that there was any harvest to gather.

[6] *Year.*—Four Masters, vol. iii. p. 227.

[7] *Carnfree.*—This place has been identified by Dr. O'Donovan. It is near
the village of Tulsk, co. Roscommon. It was the usual place of inauguration
for the O'Connors. See *note d*, Annals, vol. iii. p. 221.

Soon after these events, Hugh O'Connor was captured by his English allies, and would have been sacrificed to their vengeance on some pretence, had not Earl Marshal rescued him by force of arms. He escorted him out of the court, and brought him safely to Connaught; but his son and daughter remained in the hands of the English. Hugh soon found an opportunity of retaliating. A conference was appointed to take place near Athlone,[8] between him and William de Marisco, son of the Lord Justice. When in sight of the English knights, the Irish prince rushed on William, and seized him, while his followers captured his attendants, one of whom, the Constable of Athlone, was killed in the fray. Hugh then proceeded to plunder and burn the town, and to rescue his son and daughter, and some Connaught chieftains.

At the close of the year 1227, Turlough again took arms. The English had found it their convenience to change sides, and assisted him with all their forces. Probably they feared the brave Hugh, and were jealous of the very power they had helped him to obtain. Hugh Roderic attacked the northern districts, with Richard de Burgo. Turlough Roderic marched to the peninsula of Rindown, with the Viceroy. Hugh Crovderg had a narrow escape near the Curlieu Mountains, where his wife was captured by the English. The following year he appears to have been reconciled to the Lord Deputy, for he was killed in his house by an Englishman, in revenge for a liberty he had taken with a woman.[9]

---

[8] *Athlone.*—This was one of the most important of the English towns, and ranked next to Dublin at that period. We give an illustration of the Castle of Athlone at the beginning of Chapter XX. The building is now used for a barrack, which in truth is no great deviation from its original purpose. It stands on the direct road from Dublin to Galway, and protects the passage of the Shannon. There is a curious representation on a monument here of an unfortunate English monk, who apostatized and came to Ireland. He was sent to Athlone to superintend the erection of the bridge by Sir Henry Sidney; but, according to the legend, he was constantly pursued by a demon in the shape of a rat, which never left him for a single moment. On one occasion he attempted to preach, but the eyes of the animal glared on him with such fury that he could not continue. He then took a pistol and attempted to shoot it, but in an instant it had sprung on the weapon, giving him, at the same time, a bite which caused his death. It is to be presumed that this circumstance must have been well known, and generally believed at the time, or it would not have been made a subject for the sculptor.

[9] *Woman.*—There are several versions of this story. The Four Masters say he was killed " treacherously by the English." The Annals of Clonmacnois

As usual, on the death of Hugh O'Connor, the brothers who had fought against him now fought against each other. The Saxon certainly does not deserve the credit of all our national miseries. If there had been a little less home dissension, there would have been a great deal less foreign oppression. The English, however, helped to foment the discord. The Lord Justice took part with Hugh, the younger brother, who was supported by the majority of the Connaught men, although Turlough had already been inaugurated by O'Neill. A third competitor now started up; this was Felim brother to Hugh O'Connor. Some of the chieftains declared that they would not serve a prince who acknowledged English rule, and obliged Hugh to renounce his allegiance. But this question was settled with great promptitude. Richard de Burgo took the field, desolated the country—if, indeed, there was anything left to desolate—killed Donn Oge Mageraghty, their bravest champion, expelled Hugh, and proclaimed Felim.

The reign of this prince was of short duration. In 1231 he was taken prisoner at Meelick, despite the most solemn guarantees, by the very man who had so lately enthroned him. Hugh was reinstated, but before the end of the year Felim was released. He now assembled his forces again, and attacked Hugh, whom he killed, with several of his relations, and many English and Irish chieftains. His next exploit was to demolish the castles of Galway; Dunannon, on the river Suck, Roscommon; Hags' Castle, on Lough Mask; and Castle Rich, on Lough Corrib; all of which had been erected by Roderic's sons and their English allies. But the tide of fortune soon turned. The invincible De Burgo entered Connaught once more, and plundered without mercy. In a pitched battle the English gained the day, principally through the skill of their cavalry[1] and the protection of their coats-of-mail.

Felim fled to the north, and sought refuge with O'Donnell of Tir-Connell. O'Flaherty, who had always been hostile to Felim, joined the English, and, by the help of his boats, they were able to

---

say that "he came to an atonement with Geoffrey March, and was restored to his kingdom," and that he was afterwards treacherously killed by an Englishman, "for which cause the Deputy the next day hanged the Englishman that killed him, for that foul fact." The cause of the Englishman's crime was "meer jealousie," because O'Connor had kissed his wife.

[1] *Cavalry.*—Horse soldiery were introduced early into Britain, through the Romans, who were famous for their cavalry.

lay waste the islands of Clew Bay.   Nearly all the inhabitants were killed or carried off.   The victorious forces now laid siege to a castle[2] on the Rock of Lough Key, in Roscommon, which was held for O'Connor by Mac Dermod.   They succeeded in taking it, but soon lost their possession by the quick-witted cleverness of an Irish soldier, who closed the gates on them when they set out on a plundering expedition.   The fortress was at once demolished, that it might not fall into English hands again.

When William Pembroke died, A.D. 1231, he bequeathed his offices and large estates in England and Ireland to his brother, Richard, who is described by the chroniclers as a model of manly beauty.   Henry III. prohibited his admission to the inheritance, and charged him with treason.   The Earl escaped to Ireland, and took possession of the lands and castles of the family, waging war upon the King until his rights were acknowledged.   In 1232 Henry had granted the Justiciary of England and of Ireland, with other valuable privileges, to Hubert de Burgo.   Earl Richard supported him against the adventurers from Poitou and Bretagne, on whom the weak King had begun to lavish his favours.   The Parliament and the barons remonstrated, and threatened to dethrone Henry, if he persevered in being governed by foreigners.   And well they might; for one of these needy men, Pierre de Rivaulx, had obtained a grant for life of nearly every office and emolument in Ireland; amongst others, we find mention of " the vacant sees, and the Jews in Ireland."   Henry did his best to get his own views carried out; but Earl Richard leagued with the Welsh princes, and expelled the intruders from the towns and castles in that part of the country.

The King's foreign advisers determined to destroy their great enemy as speedily as possible.   Their plain was deeply laid.   They despatched letters to Ireland, signed by twelve privy counsellors, requiring the Viceroy and barons to seize his castles, bribing them with a promise of a share in his lands.   The wily Anglo-Normans demanded a charter, specifying which portion of his property each individual should have.   They obtained the document, signed with the royal seal, which had been purloined for the occasion from the Chancellor.   The Anglo-Normans acted with detestable dissimula-

---

[2] *Castle.*—The Annals of Boyle contain a wonderful account of the *pirrels* or engines constructed by the English for taking this fortress.

tion. Geoffrey de Marisco tried to worm himself into the confidence of the man on whose destruction he was bent. On the 1st of April, 1232, a conference was arranged to take place on the Curragh of Kildare. The Viceroy was accompanied by De Lacy, De Burgo, and a large number of soldiers and mercenaries. The Earl was attended by a few knights and the false De Marisco. He declined to comply with the demands of the barons, who refused to restore his castles. The treacherous De Marisco withdrew from him at this moment, and he suddenly found himself overpowered by numbers. With the thoughtfulness of true heroism, he ordered some of his attendants to hasten away with his young brother, Walter. Nearly all his retainers had been bribed to forsake him in the moment of danger; and now that the few who obeyed his last command were gone, he had to contend single-handed with the multitude. His personal bravery was not a little feared, and the coward barons, who were either afraid or ashamed to attack him individually, urged on their soldiers, until he was completely surrounded. The Earl laid prostrate six of his foes, clove one knight to the middle, and struck off the hands of another, before he was captured. At last the soldiers aimed at the feet of his spirited steed, until they were cut off, and by this piece of cruelty brought its rider to the ground. A treacherous stab from behind, with a long knife, plunged to the haft in his back, completed the bloody work.

The Earl was borne off, apparently lifeless, to one of his own castles, which had been seized by the Viceroy. It is said that even his surgeon was bribed to prevent his recovery. Before submitting his wounds to the necessary treatment, he prepared for death, and received the last sacraments. He died calmly and immediately, clasping a crucifix, on Palm Sunday, the sixteenth day after his treacherous capture. And thus expired the " flower of chivalry," and the grandson of Strongbow, the very man to whom England owed so much of her Irish possessions.

It could not fail to be remarked by the Irish annalists, that the first Anglo-Norman settlers had been singularly unfortunate. They can scarcely be blamed for supposing that these misfortunes were a judgment for their crimes. Before the middle of this century (the thirteenth) three of the most important families had become extinct. De Lacy, Lord of Meath, died in 1241, infirm and blind; his property was inherited by his grand-daughters, in default of a male heir. Hugh de Lacy died in 1240, and left only a daughter. The Earl of

Pembroke died from wounds received at a tournament. Walter, who succeeded him, also died without issue. The property came eventually to Anselm, a younger brother, who also died childless; and it was eventually portioned out among the females of the family.

It is said Henry III. expressed deep grief when he heard of Earl Richard's unfortunate end, and that he endeavoured to have restitution made to the family. Geoffrey de Marisco was banished. His son, William, conspired against the King, and even employed an assassin to kill him. The man would have probably accomplished his purpose, had he not been discovered accidentally by one of the Queen's maids, hid under the straw of the royal bed. The real traitor was eventually captured, drawn at horses' tails to London, and hanged with the usual barbarities.

His miserable father, who had been thrice Viceroy of Ireland, and a peer of that country and of England, died in exile, "pitifully, yet undeserving of pity, for his own treason against the unfortunate Earl Richard, and his son's treason against the King." Such were the men who governed Ireland in the thirteenth century.

Treachery seems to have been the recognized plan of capturing an enemy. In 1236 this method was attempted by the government in order to get Felim O'Connor into their power. He was invited to attend a meeting in Athlone, but, fortunately for himself, he discovered the designs of his enemies time enough to effect his escape. He was pursued to Sligo. From thence he fled to Tir-Connell, which appears to have been the Cave of Adullam in that era; though there were so many discontented persons, and it was so difficult to know which party any individual would espouse continuously, that the Adullamites were tolerably numerous. Turlough's son, Brian O'Connor, was now invested with the government of Connaught by the English, until some more promising candidate should appear. But even their support failed to enable him to keep the field. Felim[3] returned the following year, and after defeating the soldiers of the Lord Justice, made Brian's people take to flight so effectually, that none of Roderic's descendants ever again attempted even to possess their ancestral lands.

The Four Masters have the following graphic entry under the

---

[3] *Felim.*—The Four Masters say, when writing of the act of treachery mentioned above: "They all yearned to act treacherously towards Felim, although he was the gossip of the Lord Justice."—Annals, vol. iii. p. 285. He was sponsor or godfather to one of his children.

year 1236 : " Heavy rains, harsh weather, and much war prevailed in this year." The Annals of Kilronan also give a fearful account of the wars, the weather, and the crimes. They mention that Brian's people burned the church of Imlagh Brochada over the heads of O'Flynn's people, while it was full of women, children, and nuns, and had three priests in it. There were so many raids on cows, that the unfortunate animals must have had a miserable existence. How a single cow survived the amount of driving hither and thither they endured, considering their natural love of ease and contemplative habits, is certainly a mystery. In the year 1238, the Annals mention that the English erected castles in Connaught, principally in the territory from which the O'Flahertys had been expelled. This family, however, became very powerful in that part of the country in which they now settled.

As Connaught had been fairly depopulated, and its kings and princes nearly annihilated, the English turned their attention to Ulster, where they wished to play the same game. The Lord Justice and Hugh de Lacy led an army thither, and deposed Mac-Loughlin, giving the government to O'Neill's son; but MacLoughlin obtained rule again, after a battle fought the following year at Carnteel.

In 1240 the King of Connaught went to England to complain personally of De Burgo's oppressions and exactions ; but his mission, as might be expected, was fruitless, although he was received courteously, and the King wrote to the Lord Justice " to pluck out by the root that fruitless sycamore, De Burgo, which the Earl of Kent, in the insolence of his power, hath planted in these parts." However, we find that Henry was thankful to avail himself of the services of the "fruitless sycamore" only two years after, in an expedition against the King of France. He died on the voyage to Bourdeaux, and was succeeded by his son, Walter. In 1241 More O'Donnell, Lord of Tir-Connell, died in Assaroe, in the monastic habit. In 1244 Felim O'Connor and some Irish chieftains accompanied the then Viceroy, FitzGerald, to Wales, where Henry had requested their assistance.

The King was nearly starved out, the Irish reinforcements were long in coming over, and the delay was visited on the head of the unfortunate Justiciary, who was deprived of his office. John de Marisco was appointed in his place.

ATHLONE CASTLE.

CHAPTER XX.

The Age was not all Evil—Good Men in the World and in the Cloister—Religious Houses and their Founders—The Augustinians and Cistercians—Franciscans and Dominicans—Their close Friendship—Dominican Houses—St. Saviour's, Dublin—The Black Abbey, Kilkenny—Franciscan Houses—Youghal—Kilkenny—Multifarnham—Timoleague—Donegal—Carmelite Convents and Friars—Rising of the Connaught Men—A Plunderer of the English—Battle of Downpatrick—The MacCarthys defeat the Geraldines at Kenmare—War between De Burgo and FitzGerald.

[A.D. 1244—1271.]

ZEAL for founding religious houses was one of the characteristics of the age. Even the men who spent their lives in desolating the sanctuaries erected by others, and in butchering their fellow-creatures, appear to have had some thought of a future retribution—some idea that crime demanded atonement—with a lively faith in a future state, where a stern account would be demanded. If we contented ourselves with merely following the sanguinary careers of kings and chieftains, we should have as little idea of the real condition of the country, as we should obtain of the present social state of England by an exclusive study of the police reports in the *Times*. Perhaps, there was not much more crime committed then than now. Certainly there were atonements made for offending against God and man, which we do not hear of at the present day.

Even a cursory glance through the driest annals, will show that it was not all evil—that there was something besides crime and misery. On almost every page we find some incident which tells us that faith was not extinct. In the Annals of the Four Masters, the obituaries of good men are invariably placed before the records of the evil deeds of warriors or princes. Perhaps writers may have thought that such names would be recorded in another Book with a similar precedence. The feats of arms, the raids, and destructions occupy the largest space. Such deeds come most prominently before the eyes of the world, and therefore we are inclined to suppose that they were the most important. But though the Annals may devote pages to the exploits of De Lacy or De Burgo, and only say of Ainmie O'Coffey, Abbot of the Church of Derry-Columcille, that he was "a noble ecclesiastic, distinguished for his piety, meekness, charity, wisdom, and every other virtue;" or of MacGilluire, Coarb of St. Patrick, and Primate of Ireland, that "he died at Rome, after a well-spent life,"[4]—how much is enfolded in the brief obituary! How many, of whom men never have heard in this world, were influenced, advised, and counselled by the meek and noble ecclesiastic!

The influence of good men is like the circle we make when we cast a little stone into a great stream, and which extends wider and wider until it reaches the opposite bank. It is a noiseless influence, but not the less effective. It is a hidden influence, but not the less efficacious. The Coarb of St. Patrick, in his "well-spent life," may have influenced for good as many hundreds, as the bad example of some profligate adventurer influenced for evil; but we are quite sure to hear a great deal about the exploits of the latter, and equally certain that the good deeds of the former will not be so carefully chronicled.

Nor should we at all suppose that piety in this age was confined to ecclesiastics. The Earls of Pembroke stand conspicuously amongst their fellows as men of probity, and were none the less brave because they were sincerely religious. At times, even in the midst of the fiercest raids, men found time to pray, and to do deeds of mercy. On one Friday, in the year of grace 1235, the English knights, in the very midst of their success at Umallia, and after fearful devastations commanded "that no people shall be slain on that day, in

---

[4] *Life.*—Annals, vol. iii. p. 189.

honour of the crucifixion of Christ."[5]   It is true they "plundered
and devastated both by sea and land the very next day;" but even one
such public act of faith was something that we might wish to see
in our own times.   After the same raid, too, we find the "English
of Ireland" and the Lord Justice sparing and protecting Clarus, the
Archdeacon of Elphin, and the Canons of Trinity Island, in honour
of the Blessed Trinity—another act of faith ; and the "Lord Justice
himself and the chiefs of the English went to see that place, and to
kneel and pray there."   On another occasion the "English chiefs
were highly disgusted" when their soldiers broke into the sacristy
of Boyle Abbey, and "took away the chalices, vestments, and other
valuable things."   Their leaders "sent back everything they could
find, and paid for what they could not find."[6]   We must, however,
acknowledge regretfully that this species of "disgust" and reparation were equally rare.   To plunder monasteries which they
had not erected themselves, seems to have been as ordinary an
occupation as to found new ones with a portion of their unjust
spoils.

Although this is not an ecclesiastical history, some brief account
of the monks, and of the monasteries founded in Ireland about this
period, will be necessary.   The earliest foundations were houses of the
Cistercian Order and the Augustinians.   The Augustinian Order, as
its name implies, was originally founded by St. Augustine, the great
Archbishop of Hippo, in Africa.   His rule has been adopted and
adapted by the founders of several congregations of men and women.
The great Benedictine Order owes its origin to the Patriarch of the
West, so famous for his rejection of the nobility of earth, that he
might attain more securely to the ranks of the noble in heaven.
This Order was introduced into England at an early period.   It
became still more popular and distinguished when St. Bernard
preached under the mantle of Benedict, and showed how austerity
towards himself and tenderness towards others could be combined
in its highest perfection.

The twin Orders of St. Dominic and St. Francis, founded in the
early part of the thirteenth century—the one by a Spanish nobleman, the other by an Italian merchant—were established in Ireland
in the very lifetime of their founders.   Nothing now remains of the
glories of their ancient houses, on which the patrons had expended

---

[5] *Christ.*—Annals, vol. iii. p. 281.   [6] *Find.*—*Ib.* vol. iii. p. 275.

so much wealth, and the artist so much skill; but their memory still lives in the hearts of the people, and there are few places in the country without traditions which point out the spot where a Franciscan was martyred, or a Dominican taken in the act of administering to the spiritual necessities of the people.

The Abbey of Mellifont was founded A.D. 1142, for Cistercian monks, by Donough O'Carroll, King of Oriel. It was the most ancient monastery of the Order in this country, and was supplied with monks by St. Bernard, direct from Clairvaux, then in all its first fervour. We have already mentioned some of the offerings which were made to this monastery. The date of the erection of St. Mary's Abbey in Dublin has not been correctly ascertained, but it is quite certain that the Cistercians were established here in 1139, although it was probably built originally by the Danes. The abbots of this monastery, and of the monastery at Mellifont, sat as barons in Parliament. There were also houses at Bectiff, county Meath; Baltinglass, county Wicklow; Moray, county Limerick; Ordorney, county Kerry (quaintly and suggestively called *Kyrie Eleison*), at Newry, Fermoy, Boyle, Monasterevan, Ashro, and Jerpoint. The superiors of several of these houses sat in Parliament. Their remains attest their beauty and the cultivated tastes of their founders. The ruins of the Abbey of Holy Cross, county Tipperary, founded in 1182, by Donald O'Brien, are of unusual extent and magnificence. But the remains of Dunbrody, in the county of Wexford, are, perhaps, the largest and the most picturesque of any in the kingdom. It was also richly endowed. It should be remembered that these establishments were erected by the founders, not merely as an act of piety to God during their lifetime, but with the hope that prayers should be offered there for the repose of their souls after death. Those who confiscated these houses and lands to secular purposes, have therefore committed a double injustice, since they have robbed both God and the dead.

A great number of priories were also founded for the Canons Regular of St. Augustine. These establishments were of great use in supplying a number of zealous and devoted priests, who ministered to the spiritual wants of the people in their several districts. Tintern Abbey was founded in the year 1200, by the Earl of Pembroke. When in danger at sea, he made a vow that he would erect a monastery on whatever place he should first arrive in safety. He fulfilled his promise, and brought monks from Tintern, in Monmouthshire, who gave their new habitation the name of their old home.   In 1224 the Cistercians resigned the Monastery of St. Saviour, Dublin, which had been erected for them by the same Earl, to the Dominicans, on condition that they should offer a lighted taper, on the Feast of the Nativity, at the Abbey of St. Mary, as an acknowledgment of the grant.   The Mayor of Dublin, John Decer (A.D. 1380), repaired the church, and adorned it with a range of massive pillars.   The friars of this house were as distinguished for literature as the rest of their brethren ; and in 1421 they opened a school of philosophy and divinity on Usher's Island.[7]

The Dominican Convent of St. Mary Magdalene at Drogheda was founded, in 1224, by John Netterville, Archbishop of Armagh. Richard II. and Henry IV. were great benefactors to this house. Four general chapters were also held here.   The Black Abbey of Kilkenny was erected by the younger William, Earl of Pembroke. Four general chapters were also held here, and it was considered one of the first houses of the Order in Ireland.   We shall give details, at a later period, of the destruction and restoration of this and other monasteries.   The Dominicans had also houses at Waterford, Cork, Mullingar, Athenry, Cashel, Tralee, Sligo, Roscommon, and, in fact, in nearly all the principal towns in the country.

Nor were their Franciscan brethren less popular.   The Order of Friars Minor generally found a home near the Friars Preachers ; and so close was the friendship between them, that it was usual, on the festivals of their respective founders, for the Franciscan to preach the panegyric of St. Dominic, and the Dominican to preach the panegyric of St. Francis.   Youghal was the first place where a convent of this Order was erected.   The founder, Maurice FitzGerald, was Lord Justice in the year 1229, and again in 1232.   He was a patron of both Orders, and died in the Franciscan habit, on the 20th May, 1257.   Indeed, some of the English and Irish chieftains were so

---

[7] *Usher's Island.*—This was once a fashionable resort.   Moira House stood here.   It was ornamented so beautifully, that John Wesley observed, when visiting Lady Moira, that one of the rooms was more elegant than any he had seen in England.   Here, in 1777, Charles Fox was introduced to Grattan. Poor Pamela (Lady Edward FitzGerald) was at Moira House on the evening of her husband's arrest ; and here she heard the fatal news on the following morning, her friends having concealed it from her until then.   In 1826 it was converted into a mendicity institution, and all its ornamental portions removed.

devout to the two saints, that they appear to have had some difficulty in choosing which they would have for their special patron. In 1649 the famous Owen O'Neill was buried in a convent of the Order at Cavan. When dying he desired that he should be clothed in the Dominican habit, and buried in the Franciscan monastery.

Some curious particulars are related of the foundation at Youghal. The Earl was building a mansion for his family in the town, about the year 1231. While the workmen were engaged in laying the foundation, they begged some money, on the eve of a great feast, that they might drink to the health of their noble employer. Fitz-Gerald willingly complied with their request, and desired his eldest son to be the bearer of his bounty. The young nobleman, however, less generous than his father, not only refused to give them the money, but had angry words with the workmen. It is not mentioned whether the affair came to a more serious collision; but the Earl, highly incensed with the conduct of his son, ordered the workmen to erect a monastery instead of a castle, and bestowed the house upon the Franciscan fathers. The following year he took their habit, and lived in the convent until his death. This house was completely destroyed during the persecutions in the reign of Elizabeth.

The Convent of Kilkenny was founded immediately after. Its benefactor was the Earl of Pembroke, who was buried in the church. Here was a remarkable spring, dedicated to St. Francis, at which many miraculous cures are said to have been wrought. The site occupied by this building was very extensive; its ruins only remain to tell how spacious and beautiful its abbey and church must have been. It was also remarkable for the learned men who there pursued their literary toil, among whom we may mention the celebrated annalist, Clynn. He was at first Guardian of the Convent of Carrick-on-Suir; but, about 1338, he retired to Kilkenny, where he compiled the greater part of his Annals. It is probable that he died about 1350. His history commences with the Christian era, and is carried down to the year 1349. At this time the country was all but depopulated by a fearful pestilence. The good and learned brother seems to have had some forebodings of his impending fate, for his last written words run thus :—" And, lest the writing should perish with the writer, and the work should fail with the workman, I leave behind me parchment for continuing it ; if any man should have the good fortune to survive this calamity, or any one of the race of Adam should escape this pestilence, and live to continue what I have begun." This abbey was also one of the great literary schools of Ireland, and had its halls of philosophy and divinity, which were well attended for many years.

In Dublin the Franciscans were established by the munificence of their great patron, Henry III. Ralph le Porter granted a site of land in that part of the city where the street still retains the name of the founder of the Seraphic Order. In 1308 John le Decer proved a great benefactor to the friars, and erected a very beautiful chapel, dedicated to the Blessed Virgin, in which he was interred.

But the Convent of Multifarnham was the great glory of this century. It was erected, in 1236, by Lord Delemere; and from its retired situation, and the powerful protection of its noble patrons, escaped many of the calamities which befell other houses of the Order. The church and convent were built "in honour of God and St. Francis." The monastery itself was of unusual size, and had ample accommodation for a number of friars. Hence, in times of persecution, it was the usual refuge of the sick and infirm, who were driven from their less favoured homes. The church was remarkable for its beauty and the richness of its ornaments. Here were the tombs of its noble founders and patrons; and the south-eastern window was gorgeous with their heraldic devices. The convent was situated on Lake Derravaragh, and was endowed with many acres of rich land, through which flow the Inny and the Gaine. Such a position afforded opportunity for mills and agricultural labours, of which the friars were not slow to avail themselves.

The site, as we have remarked, was secluded, at some distance even from any village, and far from the more frequented roads. In process of time the family of the Nugents became lords of the manor, but they were not less friendly to the religious than the former proprietors. Indeed, so devoted were they to the Order, that, at the time of the dissolution of the monasteries, Multifarnham would have shared the common fate, had they not again and again repurchased it from those to whom it had been sold by Henry. Even during the reign of Elizabeth it was protected by the same family. But the day of suffering was even then approaching. In the October of the year 1601, a detachment of English soldiers was sent from Dublin by Lord Mountjoy, to destroy the convent which had been so long spared. The friars were seized and imprisoned, the monastery pillaged; and the soldiers, disappointed in

their hope of a rich booty, wreaked their vengeance by setting fire
to the sacred pile.

The Convent of Kilcrea was another sequestered spot. It was
founded in the fifteenth century, by the MacCarthys, under the invocation of St. Brigid. The richness and magnificence of the church,
its graceful bell-tower, carved windows, and marble ornaments,
showed both the generosity and the taste of the Lord Muskerry.
Cormac was interred here in 1495 ; and many noble families, having
made it their place of sepulture, protected the church for the sake
of their ancestral tombs.

Nor was the Monastery of Timoleague less celebrated. The
honour of its foundation is disputed, as well as the exact date ; but
as the tombs of the MacCarthys, the O'Donovans, O'Heas, and De
Courcys, are in its choir, we may suppose that all had a share in the
erection or adornment of this stately church. One of the De Courcy
family, Edmund, Bishop of Ross, himself a Franciscan friar, rebuilt
the bell-tower, which rises to a height of seventy feet, as well as the
dormitory, infirmary, and library. At his death, in 1548, he bequeathed many valuable books, altar-plate, &c., to his brethren.

The history of the establishment of the Order at Donegal is
amusing enough, and very characteristic of the customs of the age.
In the year 1474 the Franciscans were holding a general chapter in
their convent near Tuam. In the midst of their deliberations, however, they were unexpectedly interrupted by the arrival of the Lady
Nuala O'Connor, daughter of the noble O'Connor Faly, and wife of
the powerful chieftain, Hugh O'Donnell. She was attended by a
brilliant escort, and came for no other purpose than to present her
humble petition to the assembled fathers, for the establishment of
their Order in the principality of Tir-Connell. After some deliberation, the Provincial informed her that her request could not be complied with at present, but that at a future period the friars would
most willingly second her pious design. The Lady Nuala, however,
had a woman's will, and a spirit of religious fervour to animate it.
" What !" she exclaimed, " have I made this long and painful
journey only to meet with a refusal ? Beware of God's wrath ! for
to Him I will appeal, that He may charge you with all the souls
whom your delay may cause to perish." This was unanswerable.
The Lady Nuala journeyed home with a goodly band of Franciscans in her train ; and soon the establishment of the Monastery of
Donegal, situated at the head of the bay, showed that the piety of

the lady was generously seconded by her noble husband. Lady Nuala did not live to see the completion of her cherished design. Her mortal remains were interred under the high altar, and many and fervent were the prayers of the holy friars for the eternal repose of their benefactress.

The second wife of O'Donnell was not less devoted to the Order. This lady was a daughter of Connor O'Brien, King of Thomond. Her zeal in the good work was so great, that the monastery was soon completed, and the church dedicated in 1474. The ceremony was carried out with the utmost magnificence, and large benefactions bestowed on the religious. After the death of her husband, who had built a castle close to the monastery, and was buried within the sacred walls, the widowed princess retired to a small dwelling near the church, where she passed the remainder of her days in prayer and penance. Her son, Hugh Oge, followed the steps of his good father. So judicious and upright was his rule, that it was said, in his days, the people of Tir-Connell never closed their doors except to keep out the wind. In 1510 he set out on a pilgrimage to Rome. Here he spent two years, and was received everywhere as an independent prince, and treated with the greatest distinction. But neither the honours conferred on him, nor his knightly fame (for it is said he was never vanquished in the field or the lists), could satisfy the desires of his heart. After a brief enjoyment of his ancestral honours, he retired to the monastery which his father had erected, and found, with the poor children of St. Francis, that peace and contentment which the world cannot give.

In the county Kerry there were at least two convents of the Order—one at Ardfert, founded, probably, in the year 1389; the other, famous for the beauty of its ruins, and proximity to the far-famed Lakes of Killarney, demands a longer notice.

The Convent of Irrelagh, or, as it is now called, Muckross, was founded early in the fifteenth century, by a prince of the famous family of MacCarthy More, known afterwards as *Tadeige Manisti-reach*, or Teigue of the Monastery.

According to the tradition of the county, and a MS. description of Kerry, written about the year 1750, and now preserved in the Library of the Royal Irish Academy, the site on which the monastery was to be built was pointed out to MacCarthy More in a vision, which warned him not to erect his monastery in any situation except at a place called Carrig-an-Ceoil, *i.e.*, the rock of the music.

As no such place was known to him, he despatched some of his faithful followers to ascertain in what part of his principality it was situated. For some time they inquired in vain; but as they returned home in despair, the most exquisite music was heard to issue from a rock at Irrelagh. When the chief was made aware of this, he at once concluded it was the spot destined by Providence for his pious undertaking, which he immediately commenced.

It was finished by his son, Donnell (1440). The convent was dedicated to the Blessed Trinity. It is said there was a miraculous image of the Blessed Virgin here, which brought great crowds of pilgrims. The feast of the Porziuncula was kept here long after the abbey had fallen to ruins, and the friars dispersed, and was known as the Abbey Day. Until the last few years stations were held there regularly, on the 2nd of October.

Clonmel Monastery was founded, about 1269, by the Desmonds; Drogheda, in 1240, by the Plunkets.

Some convents of Carmelite friars were also founded in the thirteenth century, but as yet they have not been fortunate enough to obtain the services of a historian, so that we can only briefly indicate the sites. The Convent of Dublin, for White Friars, was founded by Sir Robert Bagot, in 1274. The date of the establishment of the house at Leighlin-bridge has not been ascertained; but it was probably erected by the Carews, at the end of the reign of Henry III. There were also convents at Ardee, Drogheda, Galway, Kildare, and Thurles. The Convent of Kildare was the general seminary for the Order in Ireland; and one of its friars, David O'Brege, is styled "the burning light, the mirror and ornament of his country."

In 1248 the young men of Connaught inaugurated the periodical rebellions, which a statesman of modern times has compared to the dancing manias of the middle ages. Unfortunately for his comparison, there was a cause for the one, and there was no cause for the other. They acted unwisely, because there was not the remotest possibility of success; and to rebel against an oppression which cannot be remedied, only forges closer chains for the oppressed. But it can scarcely be denied that their motive was a patriotic one. Felim's son, Hugh, was the leader of the youthful band. In 1249 Maurice FitzGerald arrived to crush the movement, or, in modern parlance, " to stamp it out "—not always a successful process; for sparks are generally left after the most careful stamping, which another method might effectually have quenched. Felim at once fled the country. The English made his nephew, Turlough, ruler in his place ; but the following year Felim made a bold swoop down from the Curlieus, expelled the intruder, and drove off a cattle prey. After this proof of his determination and valour, the English made peace with him, and permitted him to retain his own dominions without further molestation. Florence MacCarthy was killed this year, and Brian O'Neill, Lord of Tyrone, submitted to the Lord Justice—thereby freeing the invaders from two troublesome combatants. The next year, however, the English, who were not particular about treaties, invaded the north, and were repulsed with such loss as to induce them to treat the enemy with more respect for the time.

Under the year 1249 the Annals mention a defeat which the Irish suffered at Athenry, which they attribute to their refusal to desist from warfare on Lady Day, the English having asked a truce in honour of the Blessed Virgin. They also record the death of Donough O'Gillapatrick, and say that this was a retaliation due to the English ; for he had killed, burned, and destroyed many of them. He is characterized, evidently with a little honest pride, as the third greatest plunderer of the English. The names of the other two plunderers are also carefully chronicled ; they were Connor O'Melaghlin and Connor MacCoghlan. The "greatest plunderer" was in the habit of going about to reconnoitre the English towns in the disguise of pauper or poet, as best suited him for the time ; and he had a quatrain commemorating his exploits :—

> "He is a carpenter, he is a turner,
> My nursling is a bookman ;
> He is selling wine and hides,
> Where he sees a gathering."

The quatrain, if of no other value, gives us an idea of the commodities bartered, and the tradesmen who offered their goods at Irish fairs in English towns during the thirteenth century.

In 1257 there was a fierce conflict between the Irish, under Godfrey O'Donnell, and the English, commanded by Maurice Fitz-Gerald. The conflict took place at Creadrankille, near Sligo. The leaders engaged in single combat, and were both severely wounded : eventually the invaders were defeated and expelled from Lower Connaught. Godfrey's wound prevented him from following up his success, and soon after the two chieftains died. The circumstances of Maurice's death have been already recorded. The death of O'Donnell is a curious illustration of the feeling of the times. During his illness, Brian O'Neill sent to demand hostages from the Cinel-Connaill. The messengers fled the moment they had fulfilled their commission. For all reply, O'Donnell commanded his people to assemble, to place him on his bier, and to bear him forth at their head. And thus they met the enemy. The battle took place on the banks of the river Swilly, in Donegal. O'Donnell's army conquered. The hero's bier was laid down in the street of a little village at Connal, near Letterkenny, and there he died.

O'Neill again demanded hostages; but while the men deliberated what answer they should give, Donnell Oge returned from Scotland, and though he was but a youth of eighteen, he was elected chieftain. The same year the long-disused title of Monarch of Ireland was conferred on O'Neill by some of the Irish kings. After a conference at Caol Uisge, O'Neill and O'Connor turned their forces against the English, and a battle was fought near Downpatrick, where the Irish were defeated.[8] O'Neill was killed, with fifteen of the O'Kanes and many other chieftains, A.D. 1260. The English were commanded by the then Viceroy, Stephen Longespé, who was murdered soon after by his own people.

In the south the English suffered a severe reverse. The Geraldines were defeated by Connor O'Brien in Thomond, and again at Kilgarvan, near Kenmare, by Fineen MacCarthy. The Annals of Innisfallen give long details of this engagement, the sight of which is still pointed out by the country people. John FitzThomas, the founder of the Dominican Monastery at Tralee, was killed. The MacCarthys immediately proceeded to level all the castles which

---

[8] *Defeated.*—O'Neill's bard, MacNamee, wrote a lament for the chieftains who fell in this engagement. He states that the head of " O'Neill, King of Tara, was sent to London ;" and attributes the defeat of the Irish to the circumstance of their adversaries having fought in coats-of-mail, while they had only satin shirts :—

> " Unequal they entered the battle,
> The Galls and the Irish of Tara ;
> Fair satin shirts on the race of Conn,
> The Galls in one mass of iron."

He further deplores the removal of the chief's noble face from Down, lamenting that his resurrection should not be from amongst the limestone-covered graves of the fathers of his clan at Armagh.

had been erected by the English; they were very numerous in that district. Soon after the hero of the fight was killed himself by the De Courcys.

The Annals mention an instance of a man who had taken a bell from the Church of Ballysadare, and put it on his head when attacked by the enemy, hoping that he might escape with his prize and his life, from the respect always shown to everything consecrated to God's service; but he was killed notwithstanding. This incident is mentioned as characteristic of the age. After the defeat narrated above, Hanmer says, "the Geraldines dared not put a plough into the ground in Desmond." The next year, 1262, Mac William Burke marched with a great army as far as Elphin. He was joined by the Lord Justice and John de Verdun. They marked out a place for a castle at Roscommon, and plundered all that remained after Hugh O'Connor in Connaught. He, in his turn, counterburned and plundered so successfully, that the English were glad to ask for peace. The result was a conference at the ford of Doire-Chuire. A peace was concluded, after which "Hugh O'Connor and Mac William Burke slept together in the one bed, cheerfully and happily; and the English left the country on the next day, after bidding farewell to O'Connor."

After this fraternal demonstration, Burke led an army into Desmond, and an engagement took place with MacCarthy on the side of Mangerton Mountain, where both English and Irish suffered great losses. Gerald Roche, who is said to be the third best knight of his time in Ireland, was slain by MacCarthy.[9] Burke was soon after created Earl of Ulster.[1] He and FitzGerald waged war against each other in 1264, and desolated the country with their raids. The Lord Justice sided with FitzGerald, who succeeded in taking all Burke's castles in Connaught.

The quarrels of the invaders now became so general, that even the Lord Justice was seized at a conference by FitzMaurice Fitz-Gerald, and was detained prisoner, with several other nobles, for some time. During the wars between De Burgo (or Burke) and FitzGerald, the good people of Ross threatened to defend their town from all invaders; and to effect this purpose the council com-

---

[9] *MacCarthy.*—Four Masters, vol. iii. p. 389.

[1] *Ulster.*—The Annals of Innisfallen say he obtained this title in 1264, after his marriage with Maud, daughter of Hugh de Lacy the younger.

manded all the citizens to assist in erecting the necessary fortifications. Even the ladies[2] and clergy[3] took part in the works, which were soon and successfully completed.

An Anglo-Norman poet commemorated this event in verse, and celebrates the fame of Rose, a lady who contributed largely to the undertaking, both by her presence and her liberal donations. He informs us first of the reason for this undertaking. It was those two troublesome knights, "sire Morice e sire Wauter," who would not permit the world to be at peace. He assures us that the citizens of New Ross were most anxious for peace, because they were merchants, and had an extensive trade, which was quite true ; but he adds that they were determined to defend their rights if attacked, which was also true.

The poet also compliments the ladies, and thinks that the man would be happy who could have his choice of them. He also informs us they were to build a " Ladies' Gate," where there should be a prison in which all who gave offence to the fair sex should be confined at their pleasure. Of a surety, New Ross must have been the paradise of ladies in those days. We have not ascertained whether its fair citizens retain the same potent sway in the present century.

Felim O'Connor died in 1265. The Four Masters give his obituary thus : "Felim, son of Cathal Crovderg O'Connor, the defender and supporter of his own province, and of his friends on every side, the expeller and plunderer of his foes ; a man full of hospitality, prowess, and renown ; the exalter of the clerical orders and men of science ; a worthy materies [*sic*] of a King of Ireland for his nobility, personal shape, heroism, wisdom, clemency, and truth ; died, after the victory of unction and penance, in the monastery of the Dominican friars at Roscommon, which he had himself granted to God and that Order."

He was succeeded by his son, Hugh, " who committed his regal

---

2 *Ladies.*—" Tantz bele dames ne vi en fossée,
       Mult fu cil en bon sire née,
       Re purreit choisir à sa volonté.
3 *Clergy.*—" E les prestres, quant on chanté,
       Si vont ovrir au fossé,
       E travellent mut durement,
       Plus qe ne funt autre gent."

This ballad has been published, with a translation by W. Crofton Croker.

depredation in Offaly." It appears to have been considered a customary thing for a new sovereign to signalize himself, as soon as possible, by some display of this description. He succeeded so well in this same depredation, that the Lord Justice was alarmed, and came to assist De Burgo. The latter proposed a conference at Carrick-on-Shannon ; but Hugh O'Connor suspected treachery, and contrived to get the Earl's brother, William Oge, into his hands before the conference commenced. The Earl " passed the night in sadness and sorrow." At daybreak a fierce conflict ensued. Turlough O'Brien, who was coming to assist the Connacians, was met on his way, and slain in single combat by De Burgo. But his death was fearfully avenged ; great numbers of the English were slain, and immense spoils were taken from them. De Burgo died the following year, in Galway Castle, after a short illness, A.D. 1271.

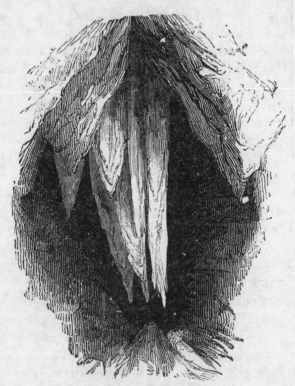

CURTAIN CAVE, TIPPERARY.

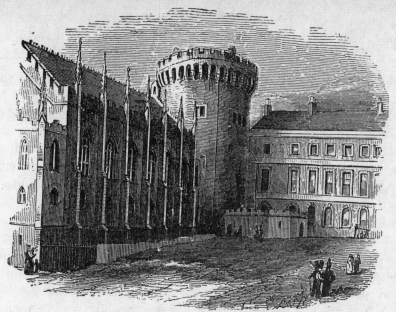

BERMINGHAM TOWER, DUBLIN CASTLE

CHAPTER XXI.

Reign of Edward I.—Social State of Ireland—English Treachery—Irish
Chieftains set at Variance—The Irish are refused the Benefit of English
Law—Feuds between the Cusacks and the Barretts—Death of Boy O'Neill—
The Burkes and the Geraldines—Quarrel between FitzGerald and De Vesci—
Possessions obtained by Force or Fraud—Why the Celt was not Loyal—
The Governors and the Governed—Royal Cities and their Charters—Dublin
Castle, its Officers, Law Courts—A Law Court in the Fourteenth Cen-
tury—Irish Soldiers help the English King—A Murder for which Justice is
refused—Exactions of the Nobles—Invasion of Bruce—Remonstrance to the
Pope—The Scotch Armies withdrawn from Ireland.

[A.D. 1271—1326.]

IT was now nearly a century since the Anglo-Normans
invaded Ireland. Henry III. died in 1272, after a
reign of fifty-six years. He was succeeded by his son,
Edward I., who was in the Holy Land at the time of
his father's death. In 1257 his father had made him
a grant of Ireland, with the express condition that it
should not be separated from England. It would
appear as if there had been some apprehensions of
such an event since the time of Prince John. The
English monarchs apparently wished the benefit of
English laws to be extended to the native population, but their desire was invariably frustrated by
such of their nobles as had obtained grants of land in
Ireland, and whose object appears to have been the

extermination and, if this were not possible, the depression of the Irish race.

Ireland was at this time convulsed by domestic dissensions. Sir Robert D'Ufford, the Justiciary, was accused of fomenting the discord ; but he appears to have considered that he only did his duty to his royal master. When sent for into England, to account for his conduct, he " satisfied the King that all was not true that he was charged withal ; and for further contentment yielded this reason, that in policy he thought it expedient to wink at one knave cutting off another, and that would save the King's coffers, and purchase peace to the land. Whereat the King smiled, and bid him return to Ireland." The saving was questionable ; for to prevent an insurrection by timely concessions, is incomparably less expensive than to suppress it when it has arisen. The " purchase of peace" was equally visionary ; for the Irish never appear to have been able to sit down quietly under unjust oppression, however hopeless resistance might be.

The Viceroys were allowed a handsome income ; therefore they were naturally anxious to keep their post. The first mention of salary is that granted to Geoffrey de Marisco. By letters-patent, dated at Westminster, July 4th, 1226, he was allowed an annual stipend of £580. This was a considerable sum for times when wheat was only 2s. a quarter, fat hogs 2s. each, and French wine 2s. a gallon.

Hugh O'Connor renewed hostilities in 1272, by destroying the English Castle of Roscommon. He died soon after, and his successor had but brief enjoyment of his dignity. In 1277 a horrible act of treachery took place, which the unfortunate Irish specially mention in their remonstrance to Pope John XXII., as a striking instance of the double-dealing of the English and the descendants of the Anglo-Normans then in Ireland. Thomas de Clare obtained a grant of Thomond from Edward I. It had already been secured to its rightful owners, the O'Briens, who probably paid, as was usual, an immense fine for liberty to keep their own property. The English Earl knew he could only obtain possession by treachery ; he therefore leagued with Roe O'Brien, " so that they entered into gossipred with each other, and took vows by bells and relics to retain mutual friendship ;" or, as the Annals of Clonmacnois have it, "they swore to each other all the oaths in Munster, as bells, relics of saints, and bachalls, to be true to each other for ever."

The unfortunate Irish prince little suspected all the false oaths his friend had taken, or all the villany he premeditated. There was another claimant for the crown as usual, Turlough O'Brien. He was defeated, but nevertheless the Earl turned to his side, got Brian Roe into his hands, and had him dragged to death between horses. The wretched perpetrator of this diabolical deed gained little by his crime,[4] for O'Brien's sons obtained a victory over him the following year. At one time he was so hard pressed as to be obliged to surrender at discretion, after living on horse-flesh for several days. In 1281 the unprincipled Earl tried the game of dissension, and set up Donough, the son of the man he had murdered, against Turlough, whom he had supported just before. But Donough was slain two years after, and Turlough continued master of Thomond until his death, in 1306. De Clare was slain by the O'Briens, in 1286.

In 1280 the Irish who lived near the Anglo-Norman settlers presented a petition to the English King, praying that they might be admitted to the privileges of the English law. Edward issued a writ to the then Lord Justice, D'Ufford, desiring him to assemble the lords spiritual and temporal of the "land of Ireland," to deliberate on the subject. But the writ was not attended to; and even if it had been, the lords "spiritual and temporal" appear to have decided long before that the Irish should not participate in the benefit of English laws, however much they might suffer from English oppression. A pagan nation pursued a more liberal policy, and found it eminently successful. The Roman Empire was held together for many centuries, quite as much by the fact of her having made all her dependencies to share in the benefits of her laws, as by the strong hand of her cohorts. She used her arms to conquer, and her laws to retain her conquests.

---

[4] *Crime.*—We really must enter a protest against the way in which Irish history is written by some English historians. In Wright's *History of Ireland* we find the following gratuitous assertion offered to excuse De Clare's crime: "Such a refinement of cruelty *must* have arisen from a suspicion of treachery, or from some other grievous offence with which we are not acquainted." If all the dark deeds of history are to be accounted for in this way, we may bid farewell to historical justice. And yet this work, which is written in the most prejudiced manner, has had a far larger circulation in Ireland than Mr. Haverty's truthful and well-written history. When Irishmen support such works, they must not blame their neighbours across the Channel for accepting them as truthful histories.

In 1281 a sanguinary engagement took place at Moyne, in the county Mayo, between the Cusacks and the Barretts. The latter were driven off the field. The Annals say : " There were assisting the Cusacks in this battle two of the Irish, namely, Taichleach O'Boyle and Taichleach O'Dowda, who surpassed all that were there in bravery and valour, and in agility and dexterity in shooting."[5] There was a battle this year also between the Cinel-Connáill and the Cinel-Owen, in which the former were defeated, and their chieftain, Oge O'Donnell, was slain. This encounter took place at Desertcreaght, in Tyrone.

Hugh Boy O'Neill was slain in 1283. He is styled " the head of the liberality and valour of the Irish ; the most distinguished in the north for bestowing jewels and riches; the most formidable and victorious of his tribe ; and the worthy heir to the throne of Ireland." The last sentence is observable, as it shows that the English monarch was not then considered King of Ireland. In 1285 Theobald Butler died at Berehaven. After his death a large army was collected by Lord Geoffrey Geneville, and some other English nobles. They marched into Offaly, where the Irish had just seized the Castle of Leix. Here they had a brief triumph, and seized upon a great prey of cows; but the native forces rallied immediately, and, with the aid of Carbry O'Melaghlin, routed the enemy completely. Theobald de Verdun lost both his men and his horses, and Gerald FitzMaurice was taken prisoner the day after the battle, it is said through the treachery of his own followers. The Four Masters do not mention this event, but it is recorded at length in the Annals of Clonmacnois. They add : "There was a great snow this year, which from Christmas to St. Brigid's day continued."

The two great families of De Burgo and Geraldine demand a special mention. The former, who were now represented by Richard de Burgo (the Red Earl), had become so powerful, that they took precedence even of the Lord Justice in official documents. In 1286 the Earl led a great army into Connaught, destroying the monasteries and churches, and " obtaining sway in every place through

---

[5] *Shooting.*—Four Masters, vol. iii. p. 435. These champions appear to have been very famous. They are mentioned in the Annals of Ulster and in the Annals of Clonmacnois, with special commendations for their skill. The following year O'Dowda was killed by Adam Cusack. It is hoped that he is not the same person as " the Cusack" whom he had assisted just before.

which he passed." This nobleman was the direct descendant of FitzAldelm de Burgo, who had married Isabella, a natural daughter of Richard Cœur de Lion, and widow of Llewellyn, Prince of Wales. Walter de Burgo became Earl of Ulster in right of his wife, Maud, daughter of the younger Hugh de Lacy. The Red Earl's grandson, William, who was murdered, in 1333, by the English of Ulster, and whose death was most cruelly revenged, was the third and last of the De Burgo Earls of Ulster. The Burkes of Connaught are descended from William, the younger brother of Walter, the first Earl.

John FitzThomas FitzGerald, Baron of Offaly, was the common ancestor of the two great branches of the Geraldines, whose history is an object of such peculiar interest to the Irish historian. One of his sons, John, was created Earl of Kildare; the other, Maurice, Earl of Desmond.

In 1286 De Burgo laid claim to that portion of Meath which Theobald de Verdun held in right of his mother, the daughter of Walter de Lacy. He besieged De Verdun in his Castle of Athlone, A.D. 1288, but the result has not been recorded. De Toleburne, Justiciary of Ireland, died this year; the King seized on all his property, to pay debts which he owed to the crown. It appears he was possessed of a considerable number of horses.[6]

Jean de Samford, Archbishop of Dublin, administered the affairs of the colony until 1290, when he was succeeded by Sir William de Vesci, a Yorkshire man, and a royal favourite.

In 1289 Carbry O'Melaghlin possessed a considerable amount of power in Meath, and was therefore extremely obnoxious to the English settlers. An army was collected to overthrow his government, headed by Richard Tuite (the Great Baron), and assisted by O'Connor, King of Connaught. They were defeated, and "Tuite, with his kinsmen, and Siccus O'Kelly, were slain."

Immediately after the arrival of the new Lord Justice, a quarrel sprung up between him and FitzGerald, Baron of Offaly. They both appeared before the Council; and if Hollinshed's account may be credited, they used language which would scarcely be

---

[6] *Horses.*—As votaries of the turf may be interested in knowing the appellations of equine favourites in the thirteenth century, we subjoin a sample of their names : Lynst, Jourdan, Feraunt de Trim, Blanchard de Londres, Connétable, Obin the Black, &c.

tolerated in Billingsgate. FitzGerald proposed an appeal to arms, which was accepted by his adversary. Edward summoned both parties to Westminster. FitzGerald came duly equipped for the encounter, but De Vesci had fled the country. He was, however, acquitted by Parliament, on the ground of informality, and the affair was referred to the royal decision. According to Hollinshed's account, the King observed, that "although de Vesci had conveyed his person to France, he had left his land behind him in Ireland;" and bestowed the lordships of Kildare and Rathangan on his adversary.

Wogan was Viceroy during the close of this century, and had ample occupation pacifying the Geraldines and Burkes—an occupation in which he was not always successful. Thomas FitzMaurice, "of the ape," father of the first Earl of Desmond, had preceded him in the office of Justiciary. This nobleman obtained his cognomen from the circumstances of having been carried, when a child, by a tame ape round the walls of a castle, and then restored to his cradle without the slightest injury.

The English possessions in Ireland at the close of this century consisted of the "Liberties" and ten counties—Dublin, Louth, Kildare, Waterford, Tipperary, Cork, Limerick, Kerry, Roscommon, and part of Connaught. The "Liberties" were those of Connaught and Ulster, under De Burgo; Meath, divided between De Mortimer and De Verdun; Wexford, Carlow, and Kilkenny, under the jurisdiction of the respective representatives of the Marshal heiresses; Thomond, claimed by De Clare; and Desmond, partly controlled by the FitzGeralds. Sir William Davies says: "These absolute palatines made barons and knights; did exercise high justice in all points within their territories; erected courts for criminal and civil cases, and for their own revenues, in the same forms as the King's courts were established at Dublin; made their own judges, sheriffs, coroners, and escheators, so as the King's writ did not run in these counties (which took up more than two parts of the English colonies), but only in the church-lands lying within the same, which were called the 'Cross,' wherein the King made a sheriff; and so in each of these counties-palatine there were two sheriffs, one of the Liberty, and another of the Cross. These undertakers were not tied to any form of plantation, but all was left to their discretion and pleasure; and although they builded castles and made freeholds, yet there were no tenures or services reserved to the crown, but the lords drew all the respect and dependency of the common people unto themselves." Hence the strong objection which the said lords had to the introduction of English law; for had this been accomplished, it would have proved a serious check to their own advancement for the present time, though, had they wisdom to have seen it, in the end it would have proved their best safeguard and consolidated their power. The fact was, these settlers aimed at living like the native princes, oblivious or ignorant of the circumstance, that these princes were as much amenable to law as the lowest of their subjects, and that they governed by a prescriptive right of centuries. If they made war, it was for the benefit of the tribe, not for their individual aggrandizement; if they condemned to death, the sentence should be in accordance with the Brehon law, which the people knew and revered. The settlers owned no law but their own will; and the unhappy people whom they governed could not fail to see that their sole object was their own benefit, and to obtain an increase of territorial possessions at any cost.

On the lands thus plundered many native septs existed, whom neither war nor famine could quite exterminate. Their feelings towards the new lord of the soil can easily be understood; it was a feeling of open hostility, of which they made no secret. They considered the usurper's claim unjust; and to deprive him of the possessions which he had obtained by force or fraud, was the dearest wish of their hearts.

This subject should be very carefully considered and thoroughly understood, for much, if not all, of the miseries which Ireland has endured, have arisen from the fatal policy pursued at this period. How could the Celt be loyal to the Anglo-Norman, who lived only to oppress him, to drive him from his ancestral home, and then to brand him with the foul name of rebel, if he dared resist? Had he not resisted, he would have been branded with a worse name—a coward.

Such portions of the country as lay outside the land of which the Anglo-Normans had possessed themselves, were called " marches." These were occupied by troops of natives, who continually resisted the aggressions of the invader, always anxious to add to his territory. These troops constantly made good reprisals for what had been taken, by successful raids on the castle or the garrison. Fleet-footed, and well aware of every spot which would afford concealment, these hardy Celts generally escaped scot-free. Thus occupied for several centuries, they acquired a taste for this roving life; and they can scarcely be reproached for not having advanced in civilization with the age, by those who placed such invincible obstacles to their progress.[7]

The most important royal castles, after Dublin, were those of Athlone, Roscommon, and Randown. They were governed by a constable, and supplied by a garrison paid out of the revenues of the colony. The object of these establishments was to keep down the natives, who were accordingly taxed to keep the garrisons. The people quite understood this, and it was not an additional motive for loyalty. The battlements of the castle were generally adorned with a grim array of ghastly skulls, the heads of those who had been slain in the warfare so constantly going on. But the attempt to strike terror into the Irish utterly failed, and new candidates passed into the ranks. How, indeed, could they die more gloriously than in the service of their country?

The royal cities held charters direct from the crown of England. These cities were Dublin, Waterford, Limerick, and Cork. Some idea has already been given of the streets and the size of Dublin. The Castle was the most important building, at least to the civil portion of the community. It contained within its walls a chapel, a jail, and a mill—characteristic of the age. The mill was styled the "King's Mill." The chaplains had each an annual salary of fifty shillings—not an insufficient provision, if we calculate that the penny then was nearly the same value as the shilling now; moreover, they had two shillings each for wax, and probably fees besides. The chapel was under the patronage of St. Thomas of Canterbury, who, when he had been martyred, sent to heaven, and could give no 'more inconvenient reproofs, stood very high in

---

[7] *Progress.*—The following passage is taken from a work published a few years ago. It is not a work of any importance, but it had some circulation in its day; and like many other works then published, was calculated to do immense mischief, by quoting the false statements of Cambrensis as authority, and by giving grotesque sketches of Irish character, which were equally untrue. The writer says: "They [the Irish chieftains] opposed the introduction of English law, because they had a direct interest in encouraging murder and theft." The fact was, as we have shown, that the Irish did their best to obtain the benefit of English law; but the English nobles who ruled Ireland would not permit it, unquestionably "because *they* had a direct interest encouraging murder and theft."

royal favour.   The Castle was partly encompassed by a moat, called the "Castlegripe;" the walls were fortified with bastions, and had various gates, towers, and narrow entrances, which were defended by strong doors and portcullises.   The chief communication with the city was by a drawbridge on the southern side of Castle-street. Rolls of the fourteenth century exhibit disbursements for repairs, ropes, bolts, and rings, from which we gather that everything was kept ready for immediate service.

The hostages which were exacted from the Anglo-Norman lords, as well as from the Irish chieftains, were kept in the Castle at their own expense.   They can hardly have found their position very pleasant, as at any moment they might be called on to submit to the operation of having their eyes put out, or to be hanged.   The judges and other officials held their courts in the Castle.   In the Court of Exchequer the primitive method of using counters for calculating[8] was still continued.   These were laid in rows upon the "chequered" cloth which covered the table.   Square hazel rods, notched[9] in a particular manner, styled tallies and counter-tallies, were employed as vouchers.

The Red Book of the Exchequer contains a curious sketch of "the Exchequer of the King of England in Dublin."   Six officers of the court are at the top; to the left, three judges; to the right, three suitors; a sheriff is seated at the bottom.   The crier is in the act of adjourning the court, exclaiming " à demain," showing that even in Ireland Norman-French was still the language of law, and probably of courtesy.   The officer to the left, supposed to be the Second Remembrancer, holds a parchment containing the words, " Preceptum fuit Vice-comiti, per breve hujus Scaccarii."   The Chief Remembrancer occupies himself with a pen and an Exchequer roll, commencing " Memorandum quod X° die Maij," &c. ; while the Clerk of the Pipe prepares a writ, placed on his left knee, his foot resting on the table.   The Marshal of the Exchequer addresses the usher, and holds a document inscribed, " Exiit breve Vice-comiti."   One of the judges exclaims, " Soient forfez ;" another, " Voyr dire."   On the

---

[8] *Calculating.*—We derived the word from *calculus*, a white stone, the Romans having used small white stones for arithmetical purposes.   Probably they taught this custom to the aboriginal English, whose descendants retained it long after.

[9] *Notched.*—Quite as primitive an arrangement as the *quipus*, and yet used in a condition of society called civilized.

chequered-covered table, before the judges, are the Red Book, a bag
with rolls, the counters used for computation, and a document commencing with the words, "*Ceo vous*," &c.   The sheriff sits at the
bottom, wearing the leathern cap used by such officers when their
accounts were under examination in the Exchequer.   Three suitors
stand at the right side of the picture.   One, with uplifted hand, says,
"*Oz de brie;*" another, extending his arm, cries, "*Chalange;*" the
third, with sword at his side, laced boots, and ample sleeves, holds
the thumb of his left hand between the fore and middle finger of
his right, and exclaims, "*Soite oughte.*"   Thus affording us an
interesting and truthful picture of a law court in the fourteenth
century.

The crown revenues and customs were frequently pawned out to
associations of Italian money-lenders; and the "Ricardi" of Lucca,
and "Frescobaldi" of Florence, had agents in the principal towns
in Ireland.   The royal treasure was deposited in the Castle, in a coffer
with three locks.   The keys were confided to different persons, and
no payment could be made unless the three were present;   still, as
might be expected from men, the sole object of whose lives appears
to have been to enrich themselves at the expense of others, the
accounts were not always satisfactory.   Even the Viceroys were accused of conniving at and sharing in frauds, notwithstanding the
salary of £500 per annum and their other emoluments, with the
permission to levy provisions of all kinds for "the king's price,"
which was far below the current value.

The Castle garrison consisted of archers and halberdiers; the
Constable, Warders, and Guardian of Works and Supplies, being
the principal officers.   The Constable was generally a nobleman of
high rank, and received an annual salary[1] of £18 5s.

It will be remembered that Sir John Wogan had been appointed
Viceroy at the close of the thirteenth century.   He brought about
a two years' truce between the Geraldines and Burkes (De Burgos),
and then summoned a Parliament at Kilkenny, A.D. 1295.   The roll
of this Parliament contains only twenty-seven names.   Richard,
Earl of Ulster, is the first on the list.   The principal Acts passed

---

[1] *Salary.*—The value may be estimated by the current price of provisions:
cows from 5s. to 13s. 4d. each; heifers, 3s. 4d. to 5s.; sheep, 8d. to 1s.; ordinary
horses, 13s. 4d. to 40s.; pigs, 1s. 6d. to 2s.; salmon, 6d. each; wheat, corn, and
malt varied with the produce of the season.   Most of the details given above
have been taken from Mr. Gilbert's *Viceroys.*

were : one for revising King John's division of the country into counties; another for providing a more strict guard over the marches, so as to "keep out the Irish." The Irish were not permitted to have any voice in the settlement of the affairs of their country, and it was a rebellious symptom if they demurred. Nevertheless, in 1303, King Edward was graciously pleased to accept the services of Irish soldiers, in his expedition against Scotland. It is said that, in 1299, his army was composed principally of Welsh and Irish, and that on this occasion they were royally feasted at Roxburgh Castle.

The O'Connors of Offaly were for nearly two centuries the most heroic, and therefore the most dangerous, of the "Irish enemies." Maurice O'Connor Faly and his brother, Calvagh, were the heads of the sept. The latter had obtained the soubriquet of "the Great Rebel," from his earnest efforts to free his country. He had defeated the English in a battle, in which Meiller de Exeter and several others were slain ; he had taken the Castle of Kildare ; therefore, as he could not be taken himself by fair means, treachery was employed.

The chiefs of Offaly were invited to dinner on Trinity Sunday, A.D. 1315, by Sir Pierce MacFeorais (Peter Bermingham). As they rose up from table they were cruelly massacred, one by one, with twenty-four of their followers. This black deed took place at Bermingham's own Castle of Carbury,[2] county Kildare. Bermingham was arraigned before King Edward, but no justice was ever obtained for this foul murder.

In the year 1308, Piers Gaveston, the unworthy favourite of Edward II., was appointed Viceroy. The English barons had long been disgusted by his insolence, and jealous of his influence. He was banished to France—or rather a decree to that effect was issued—but Ireland was substituted, for it was considered a banishment to be sent to that country. Gaveston, with his usual love of display, was attended by a magnificent suite, and commenced his Viceroyalty in high state. He was accompanied by his wife, Marguerite, who was closely connected with the royal family.

The Templars had been suppressed and plundered by royal command; but though this evil deed was accomplished without much trouble, there were Irish clans whose suppression was not so

---

[2] *Carbury.*—Extensive ruins still mark the site.

easily effected. The O'Tooles and O'Briens, styled by the Anglo-Normans "les Ototheyles et les Obrynnes," stood their ground so well, that they had put the late Viceroy to flight this very year, and promised some active employment for his successor.

Edward appears to have had apprehensions as to the kind of reception his favourite was likely to receive from the powerful Earl of Ulster ; he therefore wrote him a special letter, requesting his aid and counsel for the Viceroy. But De Burgo knew his own power too well; and instead of complying with the royal request, he marched off to Drogheda, and then to Trim, where he employed himself in giving sumptuous entertainments, and conferring the honour of knighthood on his adherents. The favourite was recalled to England at the end of a year. Edward had conducted him to Bristol, on his way to Ireland ; he now went to meet him at Chester, on his return. Three years later he paid the forfeit of his head for all these condescensions.

In 1309 De Wogan was again appointed Governor. The exactions of the nobles had risen to such a height, that some of their number began to fear the effects would recoil on themselves. High food rates and fearful poverty then existed, in consequence of the cruel exactions of the Anglo-Normans on their own dependents. They lived frequently in their houses, and quartered their soldiers and followers on them, without offering them the smallest remuneration. A statute was now made which pronounced these proceedings "open robbery," and accorded the right of suit in such cases to the crown. But this enactment could only be a dead letter. We have already seen how the crown dealt with the most serious complaints of the natives ; and even had justice been awarded to the complainant, the right of eviction was in the hands of the nearest noble, and the unfortunate tenant would have his choice between starvation in the woods or marauding on the highways, having neither the *dernier resort* of a workhouse or emigration in that age.

The Viceroy had abundant occupation suppressing the feuds both of the Irish and the colonists. Civil war raged in Thomond, but the quarrels between the Anglo-Norman settlers in the same province, appear to have been more extensive and less easily appeased. In a note to the Annals of Clonmacnois, MacGeoghegan observes, that " there reigned more dissentions, strife, warrs, and debates between the Englishmen themselves, in the beginning of the conquest of this kingdome, than between the Irishmen; as by perusing the warrs between the Lacies of Meath, John Coursey, Earle of Ulster, William Marshal, and the English of Meath and Munster, Mac Gerald, the Burke, Butler, and Cogan, may appear."

The famous invasion of Ireland by Bruce took place on the 16th of May, A.D. 1315. On that day Edward landed on the coast of Ulster, near Carrickfergus, with six thousand men. He was attended by the heroes of Bannockburn; and as a considerable number of native forces soon joined them, the contingent was formidable. Although a few of the Irish had assisted Edward II. in his war against Scotch independence, the sympathies of the nation were with the cause of freedom; and they gladly hailed the arrival of those who had delivered their own country, hoping they would also deliver Ireland. It was proposed that Edward Bruce should be made King of Ireland. The Irish chieftain, Donnell O'Neill, King of Ulster, in union with the other princes of the province, wrote a spirited but respectful remonstrance to the Holy See, on the part of the nation, explaining why they were anxious to transfer the kingdom to Bruce.

In this document the remonstrants first state, simply and clearly, that the Holy Father was deceived; that they were persuaded his intentions were pure and upright; and that his Holiness only knew the Irish through the misrepresentations of their enemies. They state their wish " to save their country from foul and false imputations," and to give a correct idea of their state. They speak, truthfully and mournfully, " of the sad remains of a kingdom, which has groaned so long beneath the tyranny of English kings, of their ministers and their barons;" and they add, " that some of the latter, though born in the island, continued to exercise the same extortions, rapine, and cruelties, as their ancestors inflicted." They remind the Pontiff that " it is to Milesian princes, and not to the English, that the Church is indebted for those lands and possessions of which it has been stripped by the sacrilegious cupidity of the English." They boldly assert " it was on the strength of false statements " that Adrian transferred the sovereignty of the country to Henry II., " the probable murderer of St. Thomas à Becket." Details are then given of English oppression, to some of which we have already referred. They state the people have been obliged to take refuge, " like beasts, in the mountains, in the woods, marshes, and caves. Even *there* we are not safe. They envy us these deso-

late abodes." They contrast the engagements made by Henry to
the Church, and his fair promises, with the grievous failure in their
fulfilment. They give clear details of the various enactments made
by the English, one of which merits special attention, as an eternal
refutation of the false and base charge against the Irish of having
refused to accept English laws, because they were a lawless race.
They state (1) "that no Irishman who is not a prelate can take the
law against an Englishman, but every Englishman may take the
law against an Irishman." (2) That any Englishman may kill an
Irishman, "falsely and perfidiously, *as often happened*, of whatsoever
rank, innocent or guilty, and yet he cannot be brought before the
English tribunals ; and further, that the English murderer can seize
the property of his victim." When such was the state of Ireland,
as described calmly in an important document still extant, we cannot
be surprised that the people eagerly sought the slightest hope of
redress, or the merest chance of deliverance from such oppression.[3]
In conclusion, the Irish princes inform his Holiness, "that in
order to obtain their object the more speedily and securely, they
had invited the gallant Edward Bruce, to whom, being descended
from their most noble ancestors, they had transferred, as they
justly might, their own right of royal domain."

A few years later Pope John wrote a letter to Edward III., in
which he declares that the object of Pope Adrian's Bull had been
entirely neglected, and that the "most unheard-of miseries and persecutions had been inflicted on the Irish." He recommends that
monarch to adopt a very different policy, and to remove the causes
of complaint, "lest it might be too late hereafter to apply a remedy,
when the spirit of revolt had grown stronger."

The accounts of Bruce's Irish campaign have not been very clearly
given. The Four Masters mention it briefly, notwithstanding its
importance ; the fullest account is contained in the Annals of Clonmacnois, which agree with the Annals of Connaught. Dundalk,
Ardee, and some other places in the north, were taken in rapid succession, and a good supply of victuals and wine was obtained from

---

[3] *Oppression.*—The original Latin is preserved by Fordun. Translations
may be found in the Abbé MacGeoghegan's *History of Ireland*, p. 323, and in
Plowden's *Historical Review*. We append one clause, in which these writers
complain of the corruption of manners produced by intercourse with the English settlers : "Quod sancta et columbina ejus simplicitas, ex eorum cohabita-
tione et exemplo reprobo, in serpentinam calliditatem mirabiliter est mutata."

the former place. The Viceroy, Sir Edmund le Botiller, marched to attack the enemy; but the proud Earl of Ulster refused his assistance, and probably the Justiciary feared to offend him by offering to remain. Meanwhile, Felim, King of Connaught, who had hitherto been an ally of the Red Earl, came over to the popular side; and the English forces suffered a defeat at Connor, in which William de Burgo and several knights were taken prisoners. This battle was fought on the 10th of September, according to Grace's Annals, and the battle of Dundalk on the 29th of July.

After the battle of Connor, the Earl of Ulster fled to Connaught, where he remained a year; the remainder of his forces shut themselves up in Carrickfergus. Bruce was proclaimed King of Ireland, and marched southward to pursue his conquests. The Earl of Moray was sent to Edinburgh to invite King Robert over, and the Scotch armies prepared to spend the winter with the De Lacys in Westmeath.

When the Christmas festivities were concluded, Bruce again took the field, and defeated the Viceroy at Ardscull, in the co. Kildare. In the month of February some of the chief nobles of the English colony met in Dublin, and signed a manifesto, in which they denounced the traitorous conduct of the Scotch enemy, in trying to wrest Ireland from their Lord, " Monsieur Edward," taking special care to herald forth their own praises for loyalty, and to hint at the compensation which might be required for the same.

But the Irish were again their own enemies; and to their miserable dissensions, though it can never justify the cruelties of their oppressors, must be attributed most justly nearly all their misfortunes. Had the Irish united against the invaders, there can be no doubt that, with the assistance of the Scotch army, they would have obtained a complete and glorious victory, though it may be doubtful whether any really beneficial results would have accrued to the country should disunion continue. When Felim O'Connor joined Bruce, Rory O'Connor and his clan commenced depredations on his territory. Felim returned to give him battle, and defeated him with terrible slaughter. Thus men and time were lost in useless and ignoble strife. Rory was slain in this engagement—a fate he richly merited; and Felim was once more free to fight for his country. He was joined by the O'Briens of Thomond, and they marched together to attack Athenry, which was defended by Burke and Bermingham. A fierce conflict ensued. The Irish fought with their usual valour ; but English coats-of-mail were proof against their attacks, and English cross-bows mowed down their ranks.

The brave young Felim was slain, with 11,000 of his followers ; and the Irish cause was irretrievably injured, perhaps more by the death of the leader than by the loss of the men. This disaster took place on the 10th of August, 1316.

Still the Irish were not daunted. The O'Tooles and O'Byrnes rose in Wicklow, the O'Mores in Leix. Robert Bruce came over to Ireland. The Franciscan friars, always devoted to their country, made themselves specially obnoxious by encouraging their countrymen to die in defence of their country. They were threatened and cajoled by turns, but with little effect.[4] Edward Bruce again appeared before Carrickfergus. The siege was protracted until September, when Robert Bruce arrived, and found the English so hard pressed, that they ate hides, and fed on the bodies of eight Scots whom they had made prisoners.[5] In the year 1317, the Scottish army was computed at 20,000 men, besides their Irish auxiliaries. After Shrovetide, King Robert and his brother crossed the Boyne, and marched to Castleknock, near Dublin, where they took Hugh Tyrrell prisoner, and obtained possession of the fortress. There was no little fear in Dublin Castle thereupon, for the Anglo-Normans distrusted each other. And well they might. The De Lacys had solemnly pledged their fidelity, yet they were now found under the standard of Bruce. Even De Burgo was suspected; for his daughter, Elizabeth, was the wife of the Scottish King. When the invading army approached Dublin, he was seized and confined in the Castle. It will be remembered that Dublin had been more than once peopled by the citizens of Bristol. They were naturally in the English interest, and disposed to offer every resistance. They fortified Dublin so strongly, even at the expense of burning the suburbs and pulling down churches, that Bruce deemed it more prudent to avoid an encounter, and withdrew towards the Salmon Leap ; from whence he led his forces southward as far as Limerick, without encountering any serious opposition.

[4] *Effect.*—See Theiner, *Vet. Mon. Hiber. et Scot.* p. 188, for the efforts made by the Holy See to procure peace. The Pope's letter to Edward III. will be found at p. 206. It is dated *Avinione*, iii. *Kal. Junii, Pontificatus nostri anno secundo.*

[5] *Prisoners.*—Gilbert's *Viceroys*, p. 138.

But a reverse was even then at hand. An Anglo-Irish army was formed, headed by the Earl of Kildare; famine added its dangers; and on the 1st of May Robert Bruce returned to Scotland, leaving his brother, Edward, with the Earl of Moray, to contend, as best they could, against the twofold enemy. In 1318 a good harvest relieved the country in some measure from one danger; two Cardinals were despatched from Rome to attempt to release it from the other. On the 14th October, in the same year, the question was finally decided. An engagement took place at Faughard, near Dundalk. On the one side was the Scotch army, headed by Bruce, and assisted (from what motive it is difficult to determine) by the De Lacys and other Anglo-Norman lords; on the other side, the English army, commanded by Lord John Bermingham. The numbers on each side have been differently estimated; but it is probable the death of Edward Bruce was the turning point of the conflict. He was slain by a knight named John Maupas, who paid for his valour with his life. Bermingham obtained the Earldom of Louth and the manor of Ardee as a reward for Bruce's head; and the unfortunate Irish were left to their usual state of chronic resistance to English oppression. The head of the Scottish chieftain was " salted in a chest," and placed unexpectedly, with other heads, at a banquet, before Edward II. The English King neither swooned nor expressed surprise; but the Scotch ambassadors, who were present, rushed horror-stricken from the apartment. The King, however, was "right blyth," and glad to be delivered so easily of a " felon foe." John de Lacy and Sir Robert de Coulragh, who had assisted the said "felon," paid dearly for their treason; and as they were Anglo-Normans, and subjects of the English crown, the term was justly applied to them, however cruel the sentence. They were starved to death in prison, " on three morsels of the worst bread, and three draughts of foul water on alternate days, until life became extinct."

Since this chapter was written, Mr. O'Flanagan has kindly presented me with his valuable *History of Dundalk*, from which I am permitted to make the following extracts, which throw much additional light upon the subject:—[6]

"'In the ninth year of King Edward's reign,' writes Hollinshed, 'Edward Bruce, brother to Robert Bruce, King of Scots, entered

[6] *Subject.*—*History of Dundalk*, pp. 46-58.

the north part of Ireland, with 6,000 men. There were with him divers captains of high renown among the Scottish nation, of whom were these :—The Earls of Murray and Monteith, the Lord John Stewart, the Lord John Campbell, the Lord Thomas Randolf, Fergus of Ardrossan, John Wood, and John Bisset. They landed near to Cragfergus, in Ulster, and joining with the Irish (a large force of whom was led out by Fellim, son of Hugh O'Conor). Thus assisted, he conquered the Earldom of Ulster, and gave the English there divers great overthrows, took the town of Dundalk, spoiled and burned it, with a great part of Orgiel. They burned churches and abbeys, with the people whom they found in the same, sparing neither man, woman, nor child. Then was the Lord Butler chosen Lord Justice, who made the Earl of Ulster and the Geraldines friends, and reconciled himself with Sir John Mandeville, thus seeking to preserve the residue of the realm which Edward Bruce meant wholly to conquer, having caused himself to be crowned King of Ireland.'

" Dundalk was heretofore the stronghold of the English power, and the head-quarters of the army for the defence of the Pale. At the north, as Barbour preserves in his metrical history of Robert Bruce :

> " ' At Kilsaggart Sir Edward lay,
> And wellsom he has heard say
> That at Dundalk was assembly
> Made of the lords of that country.'

It was not, however, within this town that the ceremony of Bruce's coronation took place, but, according to the best avouched tradition, on the hill of Knock-na-Melin, at half a mile's distance.

" Connaught the while was torn with dissensions and family feuds, of which availing himself, 'the Lord Justice' (to resume the narrative of Hollinshed) ' assembled a great power out of Munster and Leinster, and other parts thereabouts ; and the Earl of Ulster, with another army, came in unto him near unto Dundalk. There they consulted together how to deal in defending the country against the enemies ; but, hearing the Scots were withdrawn back, the Earl of Ulster followed them, and, fighting with them at " Coiners," he lost the field. There were many slain on both parts ; and William de Burgh, the Earl's brother, Sir John Mandeville, and Sir Alan FitzAlan were taken prisoners.' Bruce's adherents afterwards ravaged other parts of the Pale, Meath, Kildare, &c., but met with much resistance. At length 'Robert le Bruce, King of Scots, came over himself, landed at Cragfergus, to the aid of his brother, whose soldiers most wickedly entered into churches, spoiling and defacing the same of all such tombs, monuments, plate, copes, and other ornaments which they found and might lay hands on.' Ultimately 'the Lord John Bermingham, being general of the field, and having with him divers captains of worthy fame, namely—Sir Richard Tuiyte, Sir Miles Verdon, Sir John Cusack, Sirs Edmund, and William, and Walter Bermingham, the Primate of Armagh, Sir Walter de la Pulle, and John Maupas (with some choice soldiers from Drogheda), led forth the King's power to the number of 1,324 able men, against Edward Bruce, who had, with his adherents (the Lord Philip Moubray, the Lord Walter Soulis, the Lord Allan Stuart, with three brothers, Sir Walter Lacy, Sir Robert and Aumar Lacy, John Kermerelyn, Walter White, and about 3,000 others, writes Pembridge), encamped, not two miles from Dundalk, with 3,000 men, there abiding the Englishmen to fight with them if they came forward, which they did with all convenient speed, being as desirous to give battle as the Scots were to receive it. The Primate of Armagh, personally accompanying the English power, and blessing the enterprise, gave them such comfortable exhortation as he thought served the time ere they began to encounter, and herewith buckling together, at length the Scots fully and wholly were vanquished, and 2,000 of them slain, together with the Captain, Edward Bruce. Maupas, that pressed into the throng to encounter with Bruce hand to hand, was found, in the search, dead, aloft upon the slain body of Bruce. The victory thus obtained, upon St. Calixtus' day, made an end of the Scottish kingdom in Ireland; and Lord Bermingham, sending the head of Bruce into England, presented it to King Edward, who, in recompense, gave him and his heirs male the Earldom of Louth, and the Baronies of Ardee and Athenry to him and his heirs general for ever,' as hereafter noticed.

" 'Edward Bruce,' say the Four Masters, 'a man who spoiled Ireland generally, both English and Irish, was slain by the English, by force of battle and bravery, at Dundalk; and MacRory, Lord of the Hebrides, MacDonell, Lord of the Eastern Gael (in Antrim), and many others of the Albanian or Scottish chiefs were also slain; and no event occurred in Ireland for a long period from which so much benefit was derived as that, for a general famine prevailed in

the country during the three years and a half he had been in it, and
the people were almost reduced to the necessity of eating each
other.' Edward Bruce was, however, unquestionably a man of
great spirit, ambition, and bravery, but fiery, rash, and impetuous,
wanting that rare combination of wisdom and valour which so conspicuously marked the character of his illustrious brother.

"During the sojourn of Edward Bruce in this kingdom, he did
much to retard the spread of English rule. Having for allies many
of the northern Irish, whose chieftain, O'Neill, invited him to be
King over the Gael in Ireland, and whose neighbourhood to the
Scottish coast made them regard his followers as their fellow-
countrymen, he courted them on all occasions, and thus the Irish
customs of gossipred and fostering—preferring the Brehon laws to
statute law, whether enacted at Westminster or by the Parliaments
of the Pale—destroyed all traces of the rule which the English
wished to impose upon the province of Ulster. Many of the
English settlers—Hugh de Lacy, John Lord Bissett, Sir Hugh Bissett, and others—openly took part with Bruce.

"The eastern shores of Ulster, Spenser informs us, previous to
Bruce's arrival, bounded a well-inhabited and prosperous English
district, having therein the good towns of Knockfergus, Belfast,
Armagh, and Carlingford ; but in process of time became ' out-
bounds and abandoned places in the English Pale.' According to
the metrical history of Barbour, Edward Bruce was by no means
disposed to continue a subject, while his brother reigned King; and,
though Robert conferred his hereditary Earldom of Carrick upon
him, it by no means satisfied his ambitious projects :—

> " ' The Erle of Carrick, Schyr Eduward,
> That stouter was than a libbard,
> And had na will to be in pess,
> Thoucht that Scotland to litill was
> Till his brother and hym alsua,
> Therefor to purpose he gav ta
> That he of Irland wold be king.'

"Shortly after his landing at Carrickfergus he proceeded towards
the Pale. Dundalk, then the principal garrison within the Pale,
had all the Englishry of the country assembled in force to defend
it, when the Scots proceeded to the attack, ' with banners all dis-
playit.' The English sent out a reconnoitering party, who brought
back the cheering news, the Scots would be but ' half a dinner ' to

them. This dinner, however, was never eaten. The town was stormed with such vigour that the streets flowed with the blood of the defenders ; and such as could escape fled with the utmost precipitancy, leaving their foes profusion of victuals and great abundance of wine. This assault took place 29th June, 1315. It was upon this success the Scots crowned Edward Bruce King of Ireland, on the hill of Knocknamelan, near Dundalk, in the same simple national manner in which his brother had been inaugurated at Scone.

"The new monarch, however, was not disposed to rest inactive, and his troops had many skirmishes with Richard de Burgh, called the Red Earl of Ulster, who drove them as far as Coleraine. There they were in great distress ; and they would have suffered much from hunger and want, had not a famous pirate, Thomas of Down, or Thomas Don, sailed up the Bann and set them free. De Burgh's army were supplied with provisions from a distance ; and one of Bruce's famous leaders, named Randolph, Earl of Murray, who commanded the left wing at Bannockburn, having surprised the convoy on its way to De Burgh's camp, equipped his men in the clothes of the escort, advanced at dusk with his cavalry, and the banner of the English flaunting in the night wind. A large party of De Burgh's force, perceiving, as they thought, the approach of the expected provisions, advanced unguardedly to drive off the cattle, when they were vigorously assailed by the Scots, shouting their war-cry, and they were chased back with the loss of a thousand slain. De Burgh's army included all the chivalry of Ireland—that is, the English portion, viz. :—'The Butlers, earls two, of Kildare and Desmond ; Byrnhame (Bermingham), Widdan (Verdon), and FitzWaryne, and Schyr Paschall off Florentyne, a Knight of Lombardy ; with the Mandvillas, Bissetts, Logans, Savages, and Schyr Nycholl off Kilkenave.' *The Ulster Journal* thinks this list of Barbour's incorrect ; certainly Sir Edmond Butler was not among them, nor probably either of the Geraldine lords. Some lords of Munster, however, were present—Power, Baron of Donisle ; Sir George Lord Roche, and Sir Roger Hollywood, of county Meath.

"On the 10th September, A.D. 1315, De Burgh, being reinforced, marched to attack Bruce's position ; but the Scots, leaving their banners flying to deceive the Anglo-Irish, fell upon their flank and gained the victory. This gave them Coleraine ; and next day they bore off a great store of corn, flour, wax, and wine, to Carrick-fergus.

"This success gave to the Gael of the north an opportunity of declaring their exultation. Bruce, whose royal authority was pre-viously confined to his Scottish troops, was proclaimed King of Ireland, and addressed as such.

"He then sent the Earl of Murray to Edinburgh, where the King of Scotland kept his court, entreating him to join him in Ireland.

> " ' For war thai both in to that land
> Thai suld find nane culd thaim withstand.'

Robert gladly promised compliance, but was for some time pre-vented by the exigencies of his own kingdom. Murray returned with a small reinforcement, but 500 men, and landed at Dundalk, where Edward Bruce met him. This was in the December of 1315.

"In January, 1316, Edward Bruce led his forces into the county of Kildare, and was stoutly opposed by the Lord Justiciary, or Viceroy, Sir Edward Butler, who, backed by the Geraldines, under John Fitzgerald, first Earl of Kildare, bravely repulsed the inva-ders. They retreated with the loss of Sir Walter Murray and Sir Fergus of Ardrossan, with seventy men, as Clyn records. A new ally for the Palesmen arrived at this juncture—Mortimer, Lord of Meath, in right of his wife, Joan de Joinville. He assembled a large force, and endeavoured to intercept the Scots at Kells, but, on the eve of the onset, was deserted by the Lacys and others, who left him almost defenceless. The season and scarcity made war against the Scots, and vast numbers perished from hunger. Bruce was forced to retreat once more northward, where his chief adhe-rents lay. The citadel of Carrickfergus resisted the attacks of Bruce's army for a year. It was in this town that (probably in September, 1316) Robert, King of Scotland, with a strong force, came to his brother's help. Barbour gives the number who accom-panied Robert at 5,000. This was enough to make the Viceroy take heed for his government. He hasted, Barbour says :

> " ' To Dewellyne, in full gret hy,
> With othyr lordis that fled him by,
> And warnysit both castyls and towness
> That war in their possessionnys.'

" The stout defence of Dublin is already mentioned ; and, as on the fate of this metropolis the duration of English rule depended in Ireland, the public spirit and intrepidity of the citizens of Dublin ought, according to Lord Hailes, be held in perpetual remembrance. The citizens took the defence of the city into their own hands. The chief civic dignity was at that time most worthily borne by Robert Nottingham, who seems to have distanced the celebrated Sir Richard Whittington considerably, being *seventeen times* Mayor of Dublin. Knowing the close connexion between the Earl of Ulster and the Bruces (he was father of the Queen of Scots), the Mayor headed a strong band of citizens, and resolved to make him a hostage for the safety of the city. This was not effected without loss of life. The Mayor succeeded, and announced 'he would put the earl to death if the city was attacked.' This prompt step had the desired effect. Robert Bruce feared to risk his father-in-law's life, and, instead of entering the city, turned aside and encamped. Time was gained, of which the citizens promptly availed themselves. That night the blazing suburbs told they were ready to anticipate the fire of Moscow, rather than allow their invaders to possess their capital. They also worked so hard to strengthen the walls, that the Scots, seeing such determination, broke up their camp and retired. The value set upon the earl as a hostage was so great, that, although the King of England instantly wrote for his liberation, he was detained until the Scots left the kingdom.

" Disappointed in their efforts on Dublin, the Scots ravaged the Pale, burned Naas, plundered Castledermot, passed on to Gowran, and advanced to Callan ; thence they went to Limerick. Sir Edmond Butler followed with an army of 30,000 well-armed men ; but, at the express desire of Roger Mortimer, Earl of March, the Lord Deputy, who was himself desirous of having the command against the King of Scots, delayed the encounter.

" Mortimer did not accomplish this; for, shortly after, Robert hastened to his own kingdom, leaving a great number of his bravest knights to carry on the war for his brother. Edward continued in the north for several months, and once more proceeded south.

> " ' For he had not then in that land
> Of all men, I trow, two thousand,
> Owtane (except) the Kings of Irischery
> That in great route raid him by,
> Towart Dundalk he tuk the way.'

"When the Viceroy was aware of the advance of the Scots towards the Pale, he assembled a great army, said to amount to '20,000 trappit horse,' and an equal number of foot.

"The approach of this immensely superior force did not dishearten the brother of the lion-hearted King of Scotland. He declared he would fight were they sixfold more numerous.

"In vain his officers and allies counselled caution; in vain the Irish chiefs recommended him to avoid a pitched battle, and harass the enemy by skirmishing. Edward indignantly bade them 'draw aside, and look on.' which Barbour declares they did. A very interesting account of the battle on St. Callixtus' day is given in the *Ulster Archæological Journal*. The battle was on Sunday, 14th October, 1318. According to Barbour, Edward Bruce had a presentiment of his death, and would not use his usual coat-armour. The legend is, that having the idea the fall of King Edward Bruce would decide the battle, Sir John Bermingham, leader of the Anglo-Irish army, disguised himself as a friar, passed into the Scottish camp, and, being shown the king, who was hearing Mass, craved alms, so as to induce Bruce to look up from his prayer-book. This gave Bermingham the opportunity of marking well his face, in order to single him out in the fray. The king ordered relief to be given to the importunate friar; but the eager glance of the intrusive applicant so disquieted him—agitated, doubtless, from the idea of his small force being about to engage at such desperate odds—that he presently caused the attendants to look for the friar, but he was nowhere to be found. This caused him to array one Gib Harper in his armour, and appoint Lord Alan Stewart general of the field. The fight commenced with a rapid charge on the Scots by the Anglo-Irish under Bermingham. With him were divers lords and a great army. The force was chiefly composed, however, of yeomanry, or, as an ancient record says, 'the common people, with a powerful auxiliary *dextram Dei*.' Bermingham, believing Lord Stewart was Bruce, singled him out, and, after a terrible combat, slew him, whereon the Scots fled. According to the *Howth Chronicle*, few escaped, their loss being 1,230 men. Bruce's death is generally ascribed to John Mapas, one of the Drogheda contingent. The *Ulster Journal* states:—'There can be little doubt that the ancient Anglo-Irish family of "Mape," of Maperath, in the shire of Meath, was descended from this distinguished slayer of Edward Bruce.' The heiress of John Mapas, Esq., of Rochestown, county of Dublin, was married to the late Richard Wogan Talbot, Esq., of Malahide. After the defeat at Dundalk, the small remnant of the Scottish invaders yet alive fled northward, where they met a body of troops sent by King Robert as a reinforcement to his brother.   They could not make head against the victorious troops of Bermingham, so they made their way to the coast, burning and destroying the country through which they passed."

BUTLER'S TOMB, FRIARY CHURCH, CLONMEL.

CARRICKFERGUS.

CHAPTER XXII.

The Butlers—Quarrels of the Anglo-Norman Nobles—Treachery and its Con·
sequences—The Burkes proclaim themselves Irish—Opposition Parliaments—The Statute of Kilkenny and its Effects—Mistakes of English
Writers—Social Life in Ireland described by a French Knight—"Banishment" to Ireland—Richard II. visits Ireland.

[A.D. 1326—1402.]

RICHARD DE BURGO, the Red Earl, died in 1326.
He took leave of the nobles after a magnificent banquet at Kilkenny. When he had resigned his possessions to his grandson, William, he retired into
the Monastery of Athassel, where he expired soon
after. In the same year Edward II. attempted to
take refuge in Ireland, from the vengeance of his
people and his false Queen, the "she-wolf of
France." He failed in his attempt, and was murdered soon after—A.D. 1327.

The Butler family now appear prominently in
Irish history for the first time. It would appear
from Carte[7] that the name was originally Walter,
Butler being an addition distinctive of office. The
family was established in Ireland by Theobald
Walter (Gaultier), an Anglo-Norman of high rank,
who received extensive grants of land from Henry II., together with
the hereditary office of "Pincerna," Boteler, or Butler, in Ireland, to

---

[7] *Carte.*—See his *Life of the Duke of Ormonde*, folio edition, p. 7.

the Kings of England. In this capacity he and his successors were to attend these monarchs at their coronation, and present them with the first cup of wine. In return they obtained many privileges. On account of the quarrels between this family and the De Burgos, De Berminghams, Le Poers, and the southern Geraldines, royal letters were issued, commanding them, under pain of forfeiture, to desist from warring on each other. The result was a meeting of the factious peers in Dublin, at which they engaged to keep the "King's peace." On the following day they were entertained by the Earl of Ulster; the next day, at St. Patrick's, by Maurice FitzThomas; and the third day by the Viceroy and his fellow Knights Hospitallers, who had succeeded the Templars at Kilmainham. The Earldoms of Ormonde[8] and Desmond were now created. The heads of these families long occupied an important place in Irish affairs. Butler died on his return from a pilgrimage to Compostella, and was succeeded by his eldest son, Jacques—"a liberal, friendly, pleasant, and stately youth"—who was married this year to King Edward's cousin, Eleanor, daughter of the Earl of Essex. The Desmond peerage was created in 1329, when the County Palatine[9] of Kerry was given to that family.

The quarrels of these nobles seemed to have originated, or rather to have culminated, in an insulting speech made by Poer to Fitz-Gerald, whom he designated a "rhymer." The "King's peace" did not last long; and in 1330 the Lord Justice was obliged to imprison both Desmond and Ulster, that being the only method in which they could be "bound over to keep the peace." The following year Sir Anthony de Lucy was sent to Ireland, as he had a reputation for summary justice. He summoned a Parliament in Dublin; but as the barons did not condescend to attend, he adjourned it to Kilkenny. This arrangement also failed to procure their presence. He seized Desmond, who had been placed in the care of the Sheriff of Limerick, and conveyed him to Dublin Castle. Several other nobles were arrested at the same time. Sir William Bermingham was confined with his son in the Keep of Dublin Castle, which still

---

[8] *Ormonde.*—The name Ormonde is intended to represent the Irish appellative *Ur-Mhumhain*, or Eastern Munster. This part of the country was the inheritance of *Cairbré Musc*.

[9] *Palatine.*—The Lords-Palatine were endowed with extraordinary power, and were able to exercise a most oppressive tyranny over the people under their government.

bears his name. He was hanged there soon after. De Lucy was recalled to England, probably in consequence of the indignation which was excited by this execution.[1]

The years 1333 and 1334 were disgraced by fearful crimes, in which the English and Irish equally participated. In the former year the Earl of Ulster seized Walter de Burgo, and starved him to death in the Green Castle of Innishowen. The sister of the man thus cruelly murdered was married to Sir Richard Mandeville, and she urged her husband to avenge her brother's death. Mandeville took the opportunity of accompanying the Earl with some others to hear Mass at Carrickfergus,[2] and killed him as he was fording a stream. The young Earl's death was avenged by his followers, who slew 300 men. His wife, Maud, fled to England with her only child, a daughter, named Elizabeth,[3] who was a year old. The Burkes of Connaught, who were the junior branch of the family, fearing that she would soon marry again, and transfer the property to other hands, immediately seized the Connaught estates, declared themselves independent of English law, and renounced the English language and customs. They were too powerful to be resisted with impunity ; and while the ancestor of the Clanrickardes assumed the Irish title of MacWilliam *Oughter*, or the Upper, Edmund Burke, the progenitor of the Viscounts of Mayo, took the appellation of MacWilliam *Eighter*, or the Lower. This was not the last time when English settlers identified themselves, not merely from policy, but even from inclination, with the race whom they had once hated and oppressed.

In 1334 the English and Irish marched into Munster to attack MacNamara, and added the guilt of sacrilege to their other crimes, by burning a church, with 180 persons and two priests in it, none of whom were permitted to escape. Another outrage was committed by the settlers, who appear to have been quite as jealous of each

---

[1] *Execution.*—Bermingham was related to De Lucy, which perhaps induced him to deal more harshly with him. De Lucy's Viceroyalty might otherwise have been popular, as he had won the affections of the people by assisting them during a grievous famine. See page 329 for an illustration of the scene of this tragedy.

[2] *Carrickfergus.*—See illustration at the commencement of this chapter.

[3] *Elizabeth.*—This lady was married to Lionel, third son of Edward III., in 1352. This prince was created in her right Earl of Ulster. The title and estates remained in possession of different members of the royal family, until they became the special inheritance of the crown in the reign of Edward IV.

others property as the Irish clans ; for we find that one Edmund Burke drowned another of the same name in Lough Mask, and, as usual, a war ensued between the partisans of each family.   After a sanguinary struggle, Turlough O'Connor drove the murderer out of the province.   But this prince soon after ruined himself by his wickedness.   He married Burke's widow, and put away his own lawful wife ; from which it may be concluded that he had avenged the crime either from love of this woman, or from a desire to possess himself of her husband's property.   His immoral conduct alienated the other chieftains, and after three years' war he was deposed.

Edward had thrown out some hints of an intended visit to Ireland, probably to conceal his real purpose of marching to Scotland. Desmond was released on bail in 1333, after eighteen months' durance, and repaired with some troops to assist the King at Halidon Hill.   Soon after we find him fighting in Kerry, while the Earl of Kildare was similarly occupied in Leinster.   In 1339 twelve hundred Kerry men were slain in one battle.   The Anglo-Norman, FitzNicholas, was among the number of prisoners.   He died in prison soon after.   This gentleman, on one occasion, dashed into the assize court at Tralee, and killed Dermod, the heir of the Mac-Carthy More, as he sat with the judge on the bench.   As MacCarthy was Irish, the crime was suffered to pass without further notice.

In 1341 Edward took sweeping measures for a general reform of the Anglo-Norman lords, or, more probably, he hoped, by threats of such measures, to obtain subsidies for his continental wars.   The colonists, however, were in possession, and rather too powerful to brook such interference.   Sir John Morris was sent over to carry the royal plans into execution ; but though he took prompt and efficient measures, the affair turned out a complete failure.   The lords refused to attend his Parliament, and summoned one of their own, in which they threw the blame of maladministration on the English officials sent over from time to time to manage Irish affairs. They also protested strongly against the new arrangement, which proposed that all the offices then held in Ireland should be filled by Englishmen having no personal interest whatever in Ireland.   The certainty that they would have a personal interest in it the very moment there was a chance of bettering their fortunes thereby, appears to have been quite overlooked.   The settlers, therefore, were allowed to continue their career as before, and felt all the more secure for their effectual resistance of the royal interference.

In 1334 Sir Ralph Ufford, who had married Maud Plantagenet, the widow of the Earl of Ulster, was appointed Justiciary of Ireland. He commenced with a high hand, and endeavoured especially to humble the Desmonds. The Earl refused to attend the Parliament, and assembled one of his own at Callan; but the new Viceroy marched into Leinster with an armed force, seized his lands, farmed them out for the benefit of the crown, got possession of the strongholds of Castleisland and Inniskisty in Kerry, and hanged Sir Eustace Poer, Sir William Grant, and Sir John Cottrell, who commanded these places, on the charge of illegal exactions of coigne and livery.[4] The Viceroy also contrived to get the Earl of Kildare into his power; and it is probable that his harsh measures would have involved England in an open war with her colony and its English settlers, had not his sudden death put an end to his summary exercise of justice.

It is said that his wife, Maud, who could scarcely forget the murder of her first husband, urged him on to many of these violent acts; and it was remarked, that though she had maintained a queenly state on her first arrival in Ireland, she was obliged to steal away from that country, with Ufford's remains enclosed in a leaden coffin, in which her treasure was concealed. Her second husband was buried near her first, in the Convent of Poor Clares, at Camposey, near Ufford, in Suffolk.

The Black Death broke out in Ireland in the year 1348. The annalists give fearful accounts of this visitation. It appeared in Dublin first, and so fatal were its effects, that four thousand souls are said to have perished there from August to Christmas. It was remarked that this pestilence attacked the English specially, while the "Irish-born"—particularly those who lived in the mountainous parts of the country—escaped its ravages. We have already mentioned the account of this calamity given by Friar Clynn, who fell a victim to the plague himself, soon after he had recorded his mournful forebodings. Several other pestilences, more or less severe, visited the country at intervals during the next few years.

Lionel, the third son of Edward III., who, it will be remembered, was Earl of Ulster in right of his wife, Isabella, was now appointed

---

[4] *Coigne and livery.*—This was an exaction of money, food, and entertainment for the soldiers, and fodder for their horses. A tax of a similar kind existed among the ancient Irish; but it was part of the ordinary tribute paid to the chief, and therefore was not considered an exaction.

Viceroy. He landed in Dublin, on the 15th September, 1360, with an army of one thousand men. From the first moment of his arrival he exercised the most bitter hostility to the Irish, and enhanced the invidious distinction between the English by birth and the English by descent. Long before his arrival, the "mere Irishman" was excluded from the offices of mayor, bailiff, or officer in any town within the English dominions, as well as from all ecclesiastical promotion. Lionel carried matters still further, for he forbid any " Irish by birth to come near his army." But he soon found that he could not do without soldiers, even should they have the misfortune to be Irish; and as a hundred of his best men were killed soon after this insulting proclamation, he was graciously pleased to allow all the King's subjects to assist him in his war against the enemy. He soon found it advisable to make friends with the colonists, and obtained the very substantial offering of two years' revenue of their lands, as a return for his condescension.

In 1367 the Viceroy returned to England, but he was twice again intrusted with office in Ireland. During the last period of his administration, he held the memorable Parliament at Kilkenny, wherein the famous "Statute of Kilkenny" was enacted. This statute is another proof of the fatal policy pursued towards the Irish, and of the almost judicial blindness which appears to have prevented the framers of it, and the rulers of that unfortunate nation, from perceiving the folly or the wickedness of such enactments.

It was a continuance of the old policy. The natives of the country were to be trampled down, if they could not be trampled out; the English and Irish were to be kept for ever separate, and for ever at variance. How, then, could the Irish heart ever beat loyally towards the English sovereign? How could the Irish people ever become an integral portion of the British Empire? Pardon me for directing your attention specially to this statute. It will explain to you that the Irish were not allowed to be loyal; it will excuse them if they have sometimes resented such cruel oppressions by equally cruel massacres and burnings—if they still remembered these wrongs with that statute before them, and the unfortunate fact that its enactments were virtually continued for centuries.

This statute enacts (1) that any alliance with the Irish by marriage, nurture of infants, or gossipred [standing sponsors], should be punishable as high treason; (2) that any man of English race taking an Irish name, or using the Irish language, apparel, or customs, should forfeit all his lands ; (3) that to adopt or submit to the Brehon law was treason ; (4) that the English should not make war upon the natives without the permission of Government; (5) that the English should not permit the Irish to pasture or graze upon their lands, nor admit them to any ecclesiastical benefices or religious houses, nor entertain their minstrels or rhymers. (6) It was also forbidden to impose or cess any soldiers upon the *English* subjects against their will, under pain of felony; and some regulations were made to restrain the abuse of sanctuary, and to prevent the great lords from laying heavy burdens upon gentlemen and free-holders.

I shall ask you to consider these statutes carefully; to remember that they were compiled under the direction of a crown prince, and confirmed by the men who had the entire government of Ireland in their hands. The first was an open and gross insult to the natives, who were treated as too utterly beneath their English rulers to admit of their entering into social relations with them. The settlers who had lived some time in the country, were ascertaining every day that its inhabitants were not savages, and that they considered the ties of honour which bound them to those whom they "fostered," or for whom they stood sponsors, as of the most sacred description. Their own safety and interests, if not common feelings of humanity and affection, led them to form these connexions, which were now so ruthlessly denounced. But it led them also to treat the Irish with more respect, and placed them on some sort of social equality with themselves ; and this was clearly a crime in the eyes of those who governed the country. The second clause had a similar object, and insulted the deepest feelings of the Celt, by condemning his language, which he loved almost as his life, and his customs, which had been handed down to him by an ancestry which the Anglo-Norman nobles might themselves have envied. The third enactment was an outrage upon common justice. It has been already shown that the Irish were *refused* the benefit of the English law ; you will now see that their own law was forbidden. Some of these laws are at present open to public inspection, and show that the compilers, who wrote immediately after the introduction of Christianity into Ireland, and the original lawgivers, who existed many centuries before the Christian era, were by no means deficient in forensic abilities. Whatever feuds the Irish may have had between their clans, there is every reason to believe that justice was impartially administered long before the English settlement. That it was not so administered after that settlement, the preceding history, nay, even the very subject under discussion, sufficiently proves.

The fourth clause might have been beneficial to the Irish, if it had been strictly observed. The other enactments were observed; but this, which required the consent of the Government to make war on the natives, was allowed to remain a dead letter. In any case, the Government would seldom have refused any permission which might help to lessen the number of the "Irish enemy."

The last enactments, or series of enactments, were simply barbarous. The Irish were an agricultural nation; therefore they were not permitted to be agriculturists. Their wealth consisted solely in their flocks; therefore every obstacle should be placed to their increase. So much for the poor. The higher classes had formerly some hope of advancement if they chose to enter the English service in the army; to do so now they must renounce their Irish name, their language, and their customs. They might also have chosen the ecclesiastical state; from this now they are completely barred.

Most fatal, most unjust policy! Had it been devised for the express purpose of imbittering the feelings of the Irish Celt eternally against the Saxon ruler, it could not have succeeded more effectually. The laws of Draco were figuratively said to have been written in blood: how many bloody deeds, at which men have stood aghast in horror and dismay, were virtually enacted by the Statute of Kilkenny? The country-loving, generous-hearted Celt, who heard it read for the first time, must have been more or less than human, if he did not utter "curses, not loud, but deep," against the framers of such inhuman decrees. If Englishmen studied the history of Ireland carefully, and the character of the Celtic race, they would be less surprised at Irish discontent and disloyalty. An English writer on Irish history admits, that while "there is no room to doubt the wisdom of the policy which sought to prevent the English baron from sinking into the unenviable state of the persecuted Irish chieftain, still less is there an apology to be offered for the iniquity of the attempt to shut the great mass of the Irish people out from the pale of law, civilization, and religion. The cruelty of conquest never broached a principle more criminal, unsound, or

unsuccessful."[5]   It is to be regretted that a more recent and really
liberal writer should have attempted this apology, which his own
countryman and namesake pronounced impossible.   The author to
whom we allude grants " it sounds shocking that the killing of an
Irishman by an Englishman should have been no felony ;" but he
excuses it by stating, " nothing more is implied than that the Irish
were not under English jurisdiction, but under the native or Brehon
law."[6]   Unfortunately this assertion is purely gratuitous.   It was
made treason by this very same statute even to submit to the
Brehon law ; and the writer himself states that, in the reign of
Edward I., " a large body of the Irish petitioned for the English
law, and offered 8,000 marks as a fee for that favour."[7]   He states
that an Irishman who murdered an Englishman, would only have
been fined by his Brehon.   True, no doubt ; but if an Englishman
killed an Irishman, he escaped scot-free.   If, however, the Irishman was captured by the Englishman, he was executed according
to the English law.   If a regulation had been made that the Englishman should always be punished for his crimes by English law, and
the Irishman by Irish law,[8] and if this arrangement had been
carried out with even moderate impartiality, it would have been a
fair adjustment, however anomalous.

A little episode of domestic life, narrated by Froissart, is a sufficient proof that the social state of the Irish was neither so wild nor
so barbarous as many have supposed ; and that even a Frenchman
might become so attached to the country as to leave it with regret,

[5] *Unsuccessful.—Ireland, Historical and Statistical,* vol. i. p. 200.

[6] *Law.—Irish History and Irish Character,* p. 69.

[7] *Favour. —Ibid.* p. 70.

[8] *Irish law.*—A considerable amount of testimony might be produced to
prove that the Irish were and are peculiarly a law-loving people ; but, in the
words of the writer above-quoted, " a people cannot be expected to love and
reverence oppression, because it is consigned to a statute-book, and called
law."—p. 71.   The truth is, that it was and is obviously the interest of English
writers to induce themselves to believe that Irish discontent and rebellion were
caused by anything or everything but English oppression and injustice.   Even
in the present day the Irish are supposed to be naturally discontented and
rebellious, because they cannot submit silently to be expelled from their farms
without any compensation or any other means of support, either from political
or religious motives, and because they object to maintain a religion contrary
to their conscience, and which is admitted by its own members to be " clearly
a political evil."   See concluding remarks in Mr. Goldwin Smith's interesting
little volume.

though, at the same time, it was not a little difficult to find
an English Viceroy who would face the political complications
which the Statute of Kilkenny had made more troublesome than
ever.   Froissart's account runs thus : He was waiting in the royal
chamber at Eltham one Sunday, to present his treatise " On Loves"
to Henry II. ; and he takes care to tell us that the King had every
reason to be pleased with the present, for it was " handsomely
written and illuminated," bound in crimson velvet, decorated
with ten silver-gilt studs, and roses of the same.   While he was
awaiting his audience, he gossiped with Henry Crystède, whom he
describes as a very agreeable, prudent, and well-educated gentleman, who spoke French well, and had for his arms a chevron gules
on a field argent, with three besants gules, two above the chevron,
and one below.

Crystède gave him a sketch of his adventures in Ireland, which
we can but condense from the quaint and amusing original.   He
had been in the service of the Earl of Ormonde, who kept him
out of affection for his good horsemanship.   On one occasion he
was attending the Earl, mounted on one of his best horses, at a
" border foray" on the unfortunate Irish, with whom he kept up
constant warfare.   In the pursuit his horse took fright, and ran
away into the midst of the enemy, one of whom, by a wonderful
feat of agility, sprang up behind him, and bore him off to his own
house.   He calls the gentleman who effected the capture " Brian
Costeree," and says he was a very handsome man, and that he lived
in a strong house in a well barricaded city.

Crystède remained here for seven years, and married one of the
daughters of his host, by whom he had two children.   At the end
of this period his father-in-law was taken prisoner in an engagement with the Duke of Clarence, and Crystède's horse, which he
rode, was recognized.   Evidently the knight must have been a person of some distinction, for he states that the Duke of Clarence and
the English officers were so well pleased to hear of the " honorable
entertainment" he had received from " Brian Costeree," that they
at once proposed to set him at liberty, on condition that he should
send Crystède to the army with his wife and children.   At first
" he refused the offer, from his love to me, his daughter, and our
children."   Eventually the exchange was made.   Crystède settled at
Bristol.   His two daughters were then married.   One was settled
in Ireland.   He concluded the family history by stating that the

Irish language was as familiar to him as English, for he always spoke it to his wife, and tried to introduce it, " as much as possible," among his children.

On the retirement of the Duke of Clarence, in 1367, the Vice-royalty was accepted by Gerald, fourth Earl of Desmond, styled " the poet." He was one of the most learned men of the day, and thereby, as usual, obtained the reputation of practising magic. Yet this refined and educated nobleman wished to have his son fostered in an Irish family, and, despite the Statute of Kilkenny, obtained a special permission to that effect—another evidence that social life among the natives could not have been quite what the malice of Cambrensis, and others who wrote from hearsay reports, and not from personal knowledge, have represented it.

Sir Richard Pembridge refused the office of Viceroy in 1369. He was stripped of all his lands and offices held under the crown, as a punishment for his contumacy, but this appears to have had no effect upon his determination. It was decided legally, however, that the King could neither fine nor imprison him for this refusal, since no man could be condemned to go into exile. High prices were now offered to induce men to bear this intolerable punishment. Sir William de Windsor asked something over £11,000 per annum for his services, which Sir John Davis states exceeded the whole revenue of Ireland. The salary of a Lord Justice before this period was £500 per annum, and he was obliged to support a small standing army. The truth was, that the government of Ireland had become every day more difficult, and less lucrative. The natives were already despoiled of nearly all their possessions, and the settlement of the feuds of the Anglo-Norman nobles was neither a pleasant nor a profitable employment. In addition to this, Edward was levying immense subsidies in Ireland, to support his wars in France and Scotland. At last the clergy were obliged to interfere. The Archbishop of Cashel opposed these unreasonable demands, and solemnly excommunicated the King's collector, and all persons employed in raising the obnoxious taxes.

Richard II. succeeded his grandfather, A.D. 1377. As he was only in his eleventh year, the government was carried on by his uncles. The Earl of March was sent to Ireland as Justiciary, with extraordinary powers. He had married Philippa, daughter of Lionel, Duke of Clarence, by his first wife, and in her right became Earl of Ulster. One of the Irish princes who came to his court, was treacherously arrested and thrown into prison. The injustice was resented, or, perhaps, we should rather say, feared, by the English nobles, as well as the Irish chieftains, who took care to keep out of the way of such adventures, by absenting themselves from the Viceregal hospitalities. Roger Mortimer succeeded his father, and was followed by Philip de Courtenay, the King's cousin. He was granted the office for ten years, but, in the interval, was taken into custody by the Council of Regency, for his peculations.

There was war in Connaught between the O'Connors, in 1384, and fierce hostility continued for years after between the families of the O'Connor Don (Brown) and the O'Connor Roe (Red). Richard II. had his favourites as usual; and in a moment of wild folly he bestowed the sovereignty of Ireland on the Earl of Oxford, whom he also created Marquis of Dublin. His royal master accompanied him as far as Wales, and then, determining to keep the Earl near his person, despatched Sir John Sydney to the troublesome colony.

A royal visit was arranged and accomplished soon after; and on the 2nd October, A.D. 1394, Richard II. landed on the Irish shores. The country was in its normal state of partial insurrection and general discontent; but no attempt was made to remove the chronic cause of all this unnecessary misery. There was some show of submission from the Irish chieftains, who were overawed by the immense force which attended the King. Art MacMurrough, the heir of the ancient Leinster kings, was the most formidable of the native nobles; and from his prowess and success in several engagements, was somewhat feared by the invaders. He refused to defer to any one but Richard, and was only prevailed on to make terms when he found himself suddenly immured in Dublin Castle, during a friendly visit to the court.

The King's account of his reception shows that he had formed a tolerably just opinion of the political state of the country. He mentions in a letter from Dublin, that the people might be divided into three classes—the "wild Irish, or enemies," the Irish rebels, and the English subjects; and he had just discernment enough to see that the "rebels had been made such by wrongs, and by want of close attention to their grievances," though he had not the judgment or the justice to apply the necessary remedy. His next exploit was to persuade the principal Irish kings to receive knighthood in the English fashion. They submitted with the worst possible grace, having again and again repeated that they had already received the honour according to the custom of their own country. The dealings of the Anglo-Norman knights, with whom they already had intercourse, were not likely to have inspired them with very sublime ideas of the dignity. They might, indeed, have been chevaliers *sans peur*, but the latter part of the flattering appellation could not be applied.

The customs of the Irish nobles were again made a subject of ridicule, as they had been during the visit of Prince John; though one should have supposed that an increased knowledge of the world should have led to a wiser policy, if not to an avoidance of that ignorant criticism, which at once denounces everything foreign as inferior.[9] Richard returned to England in 1395, after nine months of vain display. He appointed Roger Mortimer his Viceroy. Scarcely had the King and his fleet sailed from the Irish shores, when the real nature of the proffered allegiance of seventy-two kings and chieftains became apparent. The O'Byrnes rose up in Wicklow, and were defeated by the Viceroy and the Earl of Ormonde; the MacCarthys rose up in Munster, and balanced affairs by gaining a victory over the English. The Earl of Kildare was captured by Calvagh O'Connor, of Offaly, in 1398; and, in the same year, the O'Briens and O'Tooles avenged their late defeat, by a great victory, at Kenlis, in Ossory.

In 1399 King Richard paid another visit to Ireland. His exactions and oppressions had made him very unpopular in England, and it is probable that this expedition was planned to divert the minds of his subjects. If this was his object, it failed signally; for the unfortunate monarch was deposed by Parliament the same year, and was obliged to perform the act of abdication with the best grace he could. His unhappy end belongs to English history. Richard again landed in state at Waterford, and soon after marched against

---

[9] *Inferior.*—While these sheets were passing through the press, we chanced to meet the following paragraph in an English paper. The article was headed "International Courtesy," apropos of the affair at Dinan:—"Prince John pulling the beards of the Irish chiefs is the aggravated type of a race which alienated half a continent by treating its people as colonial, and which gave India every benefit but civility, till Bengal showed that it was strong, and Bombay that it could be rich." And yet it would be quite as unjust to accuse a whole nation of habitual insolence to foreigners and dependents, as to blame every Englishman, in the reigns of John or Richard, for the insults offered to the Irish nation.

Interview between MacMurrough and the Officers of
Richard the Second.

the indomitable MacMurrough. His main object, indeed, appears to have been the subjugation of this "rebel," who contrived to keep the English settlers in continual alarm. A French chronicler again attended the court, and narrated its proceedings. He describes MacMurrough's stronghold in the woods, and says that they did not seem much appalled at the sight of the English army. A special notice is given of the chieftain's horse, which was worth 400 cows.[1] The chieftain's uncle and some others had made an abject submission to the English monarch, who naturally hoped that MacMurrough would follow their example. He, therefore, despatched an embassy to him, to repair the "wrongs" which he had inflicted on the settlers, for which he demanded reparation. The Leinster king, however, could neither be frightened nor persuaded into seeing matters in that light, and, probably, thought the term rebel would be more appropriately applied to those who resisted the native rulers of the country. He declared that for all the gold in the world he would not submit.

Richard's army was on the verge of starvation, so he was obliged to break up his camp, and march to Dublin. Upon his arrival there, MacMurrough made overtures for peace, which were gladly accepted, and the Earl of Gloucester proceeded at once to arrange terms with him. But no reconciliation could be effected, as both parties refused to yield. When Richard heard the result, " he flew into a violent passion, and swore by St. Edward he would not leave Ireland until he had MacMurrough in his hands, dead or alive." How little he imagined, when uttering the mighty boast, that his own fate was even then sealed ! Had he but the grace to have conciliated instead of threatened, a brave and loyal band of Irish chieftains would soon have surrounded him, and the next chapter of English history would have been less tragic. Disastrous accounts soon reached him from England, which at once annihilated his schemes of Irish conquest or revenge. His own people were up in arms, and the prescriptive right to grumble, which an Englishman is supposed to enjoy *par excellence*, had broken out into overt acts of violence. War was inaugurated between York and Lancaster, and for years England was deluged with blood.

---

[1] *Cows.*—" Un cheval ot sans sele ne arcon,
     Qui lui avint consté, ce disoit-on,
     Quatre cens vaches, tant estoil bel et bon."

BUTTS' CROSS, KILKENNY.

CHAPTER XXIII.

Henry IV.—A Viceroy's Difficulties—The Houses of York and Lancaster—
The Colony almost Bankrupt—Literary Ladies in Ireland—A Congress of
Literati—The Duke of York is made Viceroy—Affection of the Irish for
him—Popularity of the Yorkists in Ireland—A Book given for a Ransom—
Desolating Effects of the Wars of the Roses—Accession of Henry VII.—
Insurrection of the Yorkists—Simnel is crowned in Dublin—Warbeck's In-
surrection—Poyning's Parliament—Poyning's Law and its Effects—The
Earl of Kildare accused of Treason—His Defence and Pardon—His Quick-
witted Speeches—He is acquitted honorably—His Letter to the Gherardini—Ariosto.

[A.D. 1402—1509.]

SCION of royalty was again sent to administer law
—we cannot say truthfully to administer justice—
in Ireland. On the accession of Henry IV., his
second son, Thomas, Duke of Lancaster, was made
Viceroy, and landed at Bullock, near Dalkey, on
Sunday, November 13, 1402. As the youth was
but twelve years of age, a Council was appointed
to assist him. Soon after his arrival, the said
Council despatched a piteous document from "Le
Naas," in which they represent themselves and
their youthful ruler as on the very verge of starvation, in consequence of not having received remit-
tances from England. In conclusion, they gently
allude to the possibility—of course carefully depre-
cated—of "peril and disaster" befalling their lord,
if further delay should be permitted. The King,

however, was not in a position to tax his English subjects; and we find the prince himself writing to his royal father on the same matter, at the close of the year 1402. He mentions also that he had entertained the knights and squires with such cheer as could be procured under the circumstances, and adds : "I, by the advice of my Council, rode against the Irish, your enemies, and did my utmost to harass them."[2] Probably, had he shared the cheer with "the Irish his enemies," or even showed them some little kindness, he would not have been long placed in so unpleasant a position for want of supplies.

John Duke, the then Mayor of Dublin, obtained the privilege of having the sword borne before the chief magistrate of that city, as a reward for his services in routing the O'Byrnes of Wicklow. About the same time John Dowdall, Sheriff of Louth, was murdered in Dublin, by Sir Bartholomew Vernon and three other English gentlemen, who were outlawed for this and other crimes, but soon after received the royal pardon. In 1404 the English were defeated in Leix. In 1405 Art MacMurrough committed depredations at Wexford and elsewhere, and in 1406 the settlers suffered a severe reverse in Meath.

Sir Stephen Scroope had been appointed Deputy for the royal Viceroy, and he led an army against MacMurrough, who was defeated after a gallant resistance. Teigue O'Carroll was killed in another engagement soon after. This prince was celebrated for learning, and is styled in the Annals[3] "general patron of the literati of Ireland." A few years before his death he made a pilgrimage to Rome, and was honorably received on his return by Richard II., at Westminster. In 1412 the O'Neills desolated Ulster with their feuds, and about the same time the English merchants of Dublin and Drogheda armed to defend themselves against the Scotch merchants, who had committed several acts of piracy. Henry V. succeeded his father in 1413, and appointed Sir John Stanley Lord Deputy. He signalized himself by his exactions and cruelties, and, according to the Irish account, was "rhymed to death" by the poet Niall O'Higgin, of Usnagh, whom he had plundered in a foray. Sir John Talbot was the next Governor. He inaugurated his career by such martial exploits against the enemy, as

---

[2] *Them.*—Gilbert's *Viceroys*, p. 292.
[3] *Annals.*—Four Masters, vol. iv. p. 791.

to win golden opinions from the inhabitants of "the Pale." Probably the news of his success induced his royal master to recall him to England, that he might have his assistance in his French wars.

His departure was a general signal for "the enemy" to enact reprisals. O'Connor despoiled the Pale, and the invincible Art Mac-Murrough performed his last military exploit at Wexford (A.D. 1416), where he took 340 prisoners in one day. He died the following year, and Ireland lost one of the bravest and best of her sons. The Annals describe him as "a man who had defended his own province, against the English and Irish, from his sixteenth to his sixtieth year; a man full of hospitality, knowledge, and chivalry." It is said that he was poisoned by a woman at New Ross, but no motive is mentioned for the crime. His son, Donough, who has an equal reputation for valour, was made prisoner two years after by the Lord Deputy, and imprisoned in the Tower of London. O'Connor of Offaly, another chieftain who had also distinguished himself against the English, died about this time. He had entered the Franciscan Monastery of Killeigh a month before his death.

The Irish of English descent were made to feel their position painfully at the close of this reign, and this might have led the new settlers to reflect, if capable of reflection, that their descendants would soon find themselves in a similar condition. The commons presented a petition complaining of the extortions and injustices practised by the Deputies, some of whom had left enormous debts unpaid. They also represented the injustice of excluding Irish law students from the Inns of Court in London. A few years previous (A.D. 1417), the settlers had presented a petition to Parliament, praying that no Irishman should be admitted to any office or benefice in the Church, and that no bishop should be permitted to bring an Irish servant with him when he came to attend Parliament or Council. This petition was granted; and soon after an attempt was made to prosecute the Archbishop of Cashel, who had presumed to disregard some of its enactments.

Henry VI. succeeded to the English throne while still a mere infant, and, as usual, the "Irish question" was found to be one of the greatest difficulties of the new administration. The O'Neills had been carrying on a domestic feud in Ulster; but they had just united to attack the English, when Edward Mortimer, Earl of March, assumed the government of Ireland (A.D. 1425). He died of the plague the following year; but his successor in office, Lord

Furnival, contrived to capture a number of the northern chieftains, who were negotiating peace with Mortimer at the very time of his death. Owen O'Neill was ransomed, but the indignation excited by this act served only to arouse angry feelings; and the northerns united against their enemies, and soon recovered any territory they had lost.

Donough MacMurrough was released from the Tower in 1428, after nine years' captivity. It is said the Leinster men paid a heavy ransom for him. The young prince's compulsory residence in England did not lessen his disaffection, for he made war on the settlers as soon as he returned to his paternal dominions. The great family feud between the houses of York and Lancaster, had but little effect on the state of Ireland. Different members of the two great factions had held the office of Lord Justice in that country, but, with one exception, they did not obtain any personal influence there. Indeed, the Viceroy of those days, whether an honest man or a knave, was sure to be unpopular with some party.

The Yorkists and Lancastrians were descended directly from Edward III. The first Duke of York was Edward's fifth son, Edmund Plantagenet; the first Duke of Lancaster was John of Gaunt, the fourth son of the same monarch. Richard II. succeeded his grandfather, Edward III., as the son of Edward the Black Prince, so famed in English chivalry. His arrogance and extravagance soon made him unpopular; and, during his absence in Ireland, the Duke of Lancaster, whom he had banished, and treated most unjustly, returned to England, and inaugurated the fatal quarrel. The King was obliged to return immediately, and committed the government of the country to his cousin, Roger de Mortimer, who was next in succession to the English crown, in right of his mother, Philippa, the only child of the Duke of Clarence, third son of Edward III. The death of this nobleman opened the way for the intrusion of the Lancastrians, the Duke of Lancaster having obtained the crown during the lifetime of Richard, to the exclusion of the rightful heir-apparent, Edmund, Earl of March, son to the late Viceroy.

The feuds of the Earl of Ormonde and the Talbots in Ireland, proved nearly as great a calamity to that nation as the disputes about the English succession. A Parliament was held in Dublin ir 1441, in which Richard Talbot, the English Archbishop of Dublin proceeded to lay various requests before the King, the great object of which was the overthrow of the Earl, who, by the intermarrying of his kinsmen with the Irish, possessed great influence among the native septs contiguous to his own territory. The petitioners pray that the government may be committed to some "mighty English lord ;" and they moderately request that the said "mighty lord" may be permitted to create temporal peers. They hint at the Earl's age as an objection to his administration of justice, and assert that "the Lieutenant should be a mighty, courageous, and laborious man, to keep the field and make resistance against the enemy." But the great crime alleged against him, is that "he hath ordained and made Irishmen, and grooms and pages of his household, knights of the shire." These representations, however, had but little weight in the quarter to which they were addressed, for Ormonde was a stout Lancastrian ; and if he had sinned more than his predecessors, his guilt was covered by the ample cloak of royal partiality. However, some appearance of justice was observed. Sir Giles Thornton was sent over to Ireland to make a report, which was so very general that it charged no one in particular, but simply intimated that there was no justice to be had for any party, and that discord and division prevailed amongst all the King's officers. The system of appointing deputies for different offices was very properly condemned ; and the rather startling announcement made, that the annual expenses of the Viceroy and his officers exceeded all the revenues of Ireland for that year by £4,456. In fact, it could not be otherwise ; for every official, lay and ecclesiastical, English and Anglo-Irish, appear to have combined in one vast system of peculation, and, when it was possible, of wholesale robbery. Even the loyal burghers of Limerick, Cork, and Galway had refused to pay their debts to the crown, and the representatives of royalty were not in a position to enforce payment. The Talbot party seems to have shared the blame quite equally with the Ormondes, and the churchmen in power were just as rapacious as the seculars. After having ruined the "mere Irish," the plunderers themselves were on the verge of ruin ; and the Privy Council declared that unless an immediate remedy was applied, the law courts should be closed, and the royal castles abandoned. Further complaints were made in 1444 ; and Robert Maxwell, a groom of the royal chamber, was despatched to Ireland with a summons to Ormonde, commanding him to appear before the King and Council.

The Earl at once collected his followers and adherents in Drogheda, where they declared, in the presence of the King's messenger, as in duty bound, that their lord had never been guilty of the treasons and extortions with which he was charged, and that they were all thankful for "his good and gracious government :" furthermore, they hint that he had expended his means in defending the King's possessions. However, the Earl was obliged to clear himself personally of these charges in London, where he was acquitted with honour by his royal master.[4]

His enemy, Sir John Talbot, known better in English history as the Earl of Shrewsbury, succeeded him, in 1446. This nobleman had been justly famous for his valour in the wars with France, and it is said that even mothers frightened their children with his name. His success in Ireland was not at all commensurate with his fame in foreign warfare, for he only succeeded so far with the native princes as to compel O'Connor Faly to make peace with the English Government, to ransom his sons, and to supply some beeves for the King's kitchen. Talbot held a Parliament at Trim, in which, for the first time, an enactment was made about personal appearance, which widened the fatal breach still more between England and Ireland. This law declared that every man who did not shave[5] his upper lip, should be treated as an "Irish enemy ;" and the said shaving was to be performed once, at least, in every two weeks.

In the year 1447 Ireland was desolated by a fearful plague, in which seven hundred priests are said to have fallen victims, probably from their devoted attendance on the sufferers. In the same year Felim O'Reilly was taken prisoner treacherously by the Lord Deputy ; and Finola, the daughter of Calvagh O'Connor Faly, and wife of Hugh Boy O'Neill, "the most beautiful and stately, the most renowned and illustrious woman of all her time in Ireland, her own mother only excepted, retired from this transitory world,

---

[4] *Master.*—Gilbert's *Viceroys*, p. 347.

[5] *Shave.*—There are no monumental effigies of Henry VI. His remains were removed several times by Richard III., who was annoyed at the popular belief that he worked miracles ; but the costume of the period may be studied in an engraving by Strutt, from a scene depicted in the Royal M. S., 15E 6, which represents Talbot in the act of presenting a volume of romances to the King and Queen. Henry was notoriously plain in his dress, but his example was not followed by his court. Fairholt says : "It would appear as if the English nobility and gentry sought relief in the invention of all that was absurd in apparel, as a counter-excitement to the feverish spirit engendered by civil war."—*History of Costume*, p. 146.

to prepare for eternal life, and assumed the yoke of piety and devotion in the Monastery of Cill-Achaidh."

This lady's mother, Margaret O'Connor, was the daughter of O'Carroll, King of Ely, and well deserved the commendation bestowed on her. She was the great patroness of the *literati* of Ireland, whom she entertained at two memorable feasts. The first festival was held at Killeigh, in the King's county, on the Feast-day of *Da Sinchell* (St. Seanchan, March 26). All the chiefs, brehons, and bards of Ireland and Scotland were invited, and 2,700 guests are said to have answered the summons. The Lady Margaret received them clothed in cloth of gold, and seated in queenly state. She opened the "congress" by presenting two massive chalices of gold on the high altar of the church—an act of duty towards God; and then took two orphan children to rear and nurse—an act of charity to her neighbour. Her noble husband, who had already distinguished himself in the field on many occasions, remained on his charger outside the church, to welcome his visitors as they arrived. The second entertainment was given on the Feast of the Assumption, in the same year, and was intended to include all who had not been able to accept the first invitation. The chronicler concludes his account with a blessing on Lady Margaret, and a curse on the disease which deprived the world of so noble an example : " God's blessing, the blessing of all the saints, and every blessing, be upon her going to heaven; and blessed be he that will hear and read this, for blessing her soul."[6] It is recorded of her also, that she was indefatigable in building churches, erecting bridges, preparing highways, and providing mass-books. It is a bright picture on a dark page ; and though there may not have been many ladies so liberal or so devoted to learning at that period in Ireland, still the general state of female education could not have been neglected, or such an example could not have been found or appreciated. Felim O'Connor, her son, died in the same year as his mother ; he is described as "a man of great fame and renown." He had been ill of decline for a long time, and only one night intervened between the death of the mother and the son, A.D. 1451. Calvagh died in 1458, and was succeeded by his son, Con, who was not unworthy of his noble ancestry.

In 1449 the Duke of York was sent to undertake the Viceregal

---

[6] *Soul.*—Duald Mac Firbis.—*Annals.*

dignity and cares. His appointment is attributed to the all-powerful influence of Queen Margaret. The immortal Shakspeare, whose consummate art makes us read history in drama, and drama in history,[7] has commemorated this event, though not with his usual ability. The object of sending him to Ireland was to deprive the Yorkists of his powerful support and influence, and place the affairs of France, which he had managed with considerable ability, in other hands. In fact, the appointment was intended as an honorable exile. The Irish, with that natural veneration for lawful authority which is so eminently characteristic of the Celtic race, were ever ready to welcome a prince of the blood, each time hoping against hope that something like ordinary justice should be meted out from the fountain-head. For once, at least, they were not disappointed; and " noble York " is represented, by an English writer of the sixteenth century, as consoling himself " for every kinde of smart," with the recollection of the faithful love and devotion of the Irish people.[8]

The royal Duke arrived in Ireland on the 6th of July, 1447. He was accompanied by his wife, famous for her beauty, which had obtained her the appellation of the " Rose of Raby," and famous also as the mother of two English kings, Edward IV. and Richard III. This lady was the daughter of Neville, Earl of Westmoreland,

[7] *History.*—The scene is laid at the Abbey of Bury. A *Poste* enters and exclaims—

" *Poste.*—Great lords, from Ireland am I come amain,
　　　　To signify that rebels there are up,
　　　　And put the Englishmen unto the sword.
　　　　Send succours (lords), and stop the rage betime,
　　　　Before the wound do grow uncurable :
　　　　For being green, there is great hope of help."
　　　　　　　　　　　　—*King Henry VI. Part* ii. *Act* 3.

[8] *People.*—"I twise bore rule in Normandy and Fraunce,
　　　　And last lieutenant in Ireland, where my hart
　　　　Found remedy for every kinde of smart ;
　　　　For through the love my doings there did breede,
　　　　I had my helpe at all times in my neede."
　　　　　　　　　　　　—*Mirrour for Magistrates*, vol. ii. p. 189.

Hall, in his *Union of the Two Noble Houses* (1548), wrote that York " got him such love and favour of the country [Ireland] and the inhabitants, that their sincere love and friendly affection could never be separated from him and his lineage."

whose rather numerous family, consisting of twenty-two children, had all married amongst the highest families. The Duke was Earl of Ulster in right of Duke Lionel, from whom he was descended ; but instead of marching at once to claim his possessions, he adopted such conciliatory measures as secured him the services and affections of a large body of Irish chieftains, with whose assistance he soon subdued any who still remained refractory. His popularity increased daily. Presents were sent to him by the most powerful and independent of the native chieftains. Nor was his " fair ladye" forgotten, for Brian O'Byrne, in addition to an offering of four hundred beeves to the Duke, sent "two hobbies "[9] for the special use of the " Rose of Raby." Indeed, it was reported in England that " the wildest Irishman in Ireland would before twelve months be sworn English." Such were the fruits of a conciliatory policy, or rather of a fair administration of justice.

The cities of Cork, Kinsale, and Youghal, now sent in petitions to the Viceroy, complaining bitterly of the way in which the English noblemen " fall at variance among themselves," so that the whole country was desolated. The settlers of Waterford and Wexford made similar complaints against an Irish chieftain, O'Driscoll, whom they describe as " an Irish enemy to the King and to all his liege people of Ireland." The Duke pacified all parties, and succeeded in attaching the majority of the nation more and more to his person and his interests. His English friends, who looked on his residence in Ireland as equivalent to banishment and imprisonment, were actively employed in promoting his return. The disgraceful loss of the English possessions in France, and probably still more the haughty and unconciliatory policy adopted by the Queen, had strengthened the Yorkist party, and emboldened them to action. The Duke was requested to return to England, where the insurgents in Kent had already risen under the leadership of the famous Jack Cade, whose origin is involved in hopeless obscurity, and whose character has been so blackened by writers on the Lancastrian side that it is equally incomprehensible. He called himself John Mor-

---

[9] *Hobbies.*—Irish horses were famous from an early period of our history. They were considered presents worthy of kings. The name *hobbies* is a corruption of *hobilarius,* a horseman. It is probable the term is derived from the Spanish *caballo,* a horse. There were three different Irish appellations for different kinds of horses, *groidh, each,* and *gearran.* These words are still in use, but *capall* is the more common term.

timer, and asserted that he was cousin to the Viceroy. A proclamation, offering one thousand marks for his person, "quick or dead," described him as born in Ireland. In consequence of the nonpayment of the annuity which had been promised to the Duke during his Viceroyalty, he had been obliged to demand assistance from the Irish, who naturally resisted so unjust a tax. After useless appeals to the King and Parliament, he returned to England suddenly, in September, 1450, leaving Sir James Butler, the eldest son of the Earl of Ormonde, as his Deputy.

The history of the Wars of the Roses does not belong to our province ; it must, therefore, suffice to say, that when his party was defeated in England for a time, he fled to Ireland, where he was enthusiastically received, and exercised the office of Viceroy at the very time that an act of attainder was passed against him and his family. He soon returned again to his own country ; and there, after more than one brilliant victory, he was slain at the battle of Wakefield, on the 31st December, 1460. Three thousand of his followers are said to have perished with him, and among the number were several Irish chieftains from Meath and Ulster. The Geraldines sided with the House of York, and the Butlers with the Lancastrians : hence members of both families fell on this fatal field on opposite sides.

The Earl of Kildare was Lord Justice on the accession of Edward IV., who at once appointed his unfortunate brother, the Duke of Clarence, to that dignity. The Earls of Ormonde and Desmond were at war (A.D. 1462), and a pitched battle was fought between them at Pilltown, in the county Kilkenny, where the former was defeated with considerable loss. His kinsman, MacRichard Butler, was taken prisoner ; and we may judge of the value of a book,[1] and the respect for literature in Ireland at that period, from the curious fact that a manuscript was offered and accepted for his ransom.

---

[1] *Book*.—This ancient MS. is still in existence, in the Bodleian Library in Oxford (Laud, 610). It is a copy of such portions of the Psalter of Cashel as could then be deciphered, which was made for Butler, by Shane O'Clery, A.D. 1454. There is an interesting memorandum in it in Irish, made by MacButler himself : "A blessing on the soul of the Archbishop of Cashel, *i.e.*, Richard O'Hedigan, for it was by him the owner of this book was educated. This is the Sunday before Christmas ; and let all those who shall read this give a blessing on the souls of both."

The eighth Earl of Desmond, Thomas, was made Viceroy in 1462. He was a special favourite with the King. In 1466 he led an army of the English of Meath and Leinster against O'Connor Faly, but he was defeated and taken prisoner in the engagement. Teigue O'Connor, the Earl's brother-in-law, conducted the captives to Carbury Castle, in Kildare, where they were soon liberated by the people of Dublin. The Irish were very successful in their forays at this period. The men of Offaly devastated the country from Tara to Naas ; the men of Breffni and Oriel performed similar exploits in Meath. Teigue O'Brien plundered Desmond, and obliged the Burkes of Clanwilliam to acknowledge his authority, and only spared the city of Limerick for a consideration of sixty marks.

The Earl of Desmond appears to have exerted himself in every way for the national benefit. He founded a college in Youghal, with a warden, eight fellows, and eight choristers. He obtained an Act for the establishment of a university at Drogheda, which was to have similar privileges to that of Oxford. He is described by native annalists—almost as loud in their praises of learning as of valour—as well versed in literature, and a warm patron of antiquaries and poets. But his liberality proved his ruin. He was accused of making alliances and fosterage of the King's Irish enemies ; and perhaps he had also incurred the enmity of the Queen (Elizabeth Woodville), for it was hinted that she had some share in his condemnation. It is at least certain that he was beheaded at Drogheda, on the 15th of February, 1467, by the command of Typtoft, Earl of Worcester, who was sent to Ireland to take his place as Viceroy, and to execute the unjust sentence. The Earl of Kildare was condemned at the same time ; but he escaped to England, and pleaded his cause so well with the King and Parliament, that he obtained his own pardon, and a reversal of the attainder against the unfortunate Earl of Desmond.

During the reigns of Edward IV., Edward V., and the usurper Richard, there was probably more dissension in England than there ever had been at any time amongst the native Irish chieftains. Princes and nobles were sacrificed by each party as they obtained power, and regicide might almost be called common. The number of English slain in the Wars of the Roses was estimated at 100,000. Parliament made acts of attainder one day, and reversed them almost on the next. Neither life nor property was safe. Men armed themselves first in self-defence, and then in lawlessness ; and a thoughtful mind might trace to the evil state of morals, caused by a long period of desolating domestic warfare, that fatal indifference to religion which must have permeated the people, before they could have departed as a nation from the faith of their fathers, at the mere suggestion of a profligate monarch.

The English power in Ireland was reduced at this time to the lowest degree of weakness. This power had never been other than nominal beyond the Pale; within its precincts it was on the whole all-powerful. But now a few archers and spearmen were its only defence; and had the Irish combined under a competent leader, there can be little doubt that the result would have been fatal to the colony. It would appear as if Henry VII. hoped to propitiate the Yorkists in Ireland, as he allowed the Earl of Kildare to hold the office of Lord Deputy; his brother, Thomas FitzGerald, that of Chancellor; and his father-in-law, FitzEustace, that of Lord Treasurer. After a short time, however, he restored the Earl of Ormonde to the family honours and estates, and thus a Lancastrian influence was secured. The most important events of this reign, as far as Ireland is concerned, are the plots of Simnel and Perkin Warbeck, and the enactments of Poyning's Parliament. A contemporary Irish chronicler says: "The son of a Welshman, by whom the battle of Bosworth field was fought, was made King; and there lived not of the royal blood, at that time, but one youth, who came the next year (1486) in exile to Ireland."[2]

The native Irish appear not to have had the least doubt that Simnel was what he represented himself to be. The Anglo-Irish nobles were nearly all devoted to the House of York; but it is impossible now to determine whether they were really deceived, or if they only made the youth a pretext for rebellion. His appearance is admitted by all parties to have been in his favour; but the King asserted that the real Earl of Warwick was then confined in the Tower, and paraded him through London[3] as soon as the pseudo-

[2] *Ireland.—The Annals of Ulster*, compiled by Maguire, Canon of Armagh, who died A.D. 1498.

[3] *London.*—The Irish Yorkists declared that this youth was a counterfeit. The Earl of Lincoln, son of Elizabeth Plantagenet, sister of Richard III., saw and conversed with the boy at the court at Shene, and appeared to be convinced that he was not his real cousin, for he joined the movement in favour of Simnel immediately after the interview. Mr. Gilbert remarks in his *Viceroys*, p. 605, that the fact of all the documents referring to this period of Irish

noble was crowned in Ireland. Margaret, Dowager Duchess of
Burgundy, was the great promoter of the scheme. She despatched
Martin Swart, a famous soldier, of noble birth, to Ireland, with 2,000
men. The expedition was fitted out at her own expense. The English
Yorkists joined his party, and the little army landed at Dublin, in
May, 1487. On Whit-Sunday, the 24th of that month, Lambert
Simnel was crowned in the Cathedral of the Holy Trinity. After
the ceremony he was borne in state, on the shoulders of tall men,
to the Castle. One of his bearers, a gigantic Anglo-Irishman, was
called Great Darcy. Coins were now struck, proclamations issued,
and all the writs and public acts of the colony executed in the
name of Edward VI.

Soon after, Simnel's party conducted him to England, where
they were joined by a few desperate men of the Yorkist party. The
battle of Stoke, in Nottinghamshire, terminated the affair. The
youth and his tutor were captured, and the principal officers were
slain. According to one account, Simnel was made a turnspit in
the royal kitchen; according to another authority[4] he was imprisoned
in the Tower of London. It would appear as if Henry was afraid
to visit the Earl of Kildare too heavily for his transgressions, as he
retained him in the office of Lord Deputy.

The use of fire-arms appears to have become general in Ireland
about this period (1487), as the Annals mention that an O'Rourke
was slain by an O'Donnell, "with a ball from a gun;" and the following year the Earl of Kildare destroyed the Castle of Balrath, in
Westmeath, with ordnance. The early guns were termed hand-
cannons and hand-guns, to distinguish them from the original fire-
arms, which were not portable, though there were exceptions to
this rule; for some of the early cannons were so small, that the
cannonier held his gun in his hand, or supported it on his shoulder,
when firing it.[5]

---

history having been destroyed, has been quite overlooked. A special Act of
Poyning's Parliament commanded the destruction of all "records, processes,
ordinances, &c., done in the 'Laddes' name."

[4] *Authority.*—Gilbert's *Viceroys*, p. 605. The English Parliament attainted
those English gentlemen and nobles who had fought against the King at Stoke,
but they took no notice of the English in Ireland, who were the real promoters
of the rebellion. This is a curious and valuable illustration of the state of affairs
in that country.

[5] *Firing it.*—A valuable paper on this subject, by Sir S. R. Meyrick, will
be found in the *Archæologia*, vol. xxii. The people of Lucca are supposed to

In 1488 Sir Richard Edgecumbe was sent to Ireland to exact
new oaths of allegiance from the Anglo-Norman lords, whose fidelity
Henry appears to have doubted, and not without reason. The
commissioner took up his lodgings with the Dominican friars, who
appear to have been more devoted to the English interests than
their Franciscan brethren; but they did not entertain the knight
at their own expense, for he complains grievously of his "great
costs and charges." A Papal Bull had been procured, condemning
all who had rebelled against the King. This was published by the
Bishop of Meath, with a promise of absolution and royal pardon for
all who should repent. Edgecumbe appears to have been at his
wit's end to conciliate the "rebels," and informs us that he spent
the night in "devising as sure an oath as he could." The nobles
at last came to terms, and took the proffered pledge in the most
solemn manner, in presence of the Blessed Sacrament. This accomplished, the knight returned to England; and on his safe arrival,
after a stormy passage, made a pilgrimage to Saint Saviour's, in
Cornwall.

It is quite impossible now to judge whether these solemn oaths
were made to be broken, or whether the temptation to break them
proved stronger than the resolution to keep them. It is at least certain that they were broken, and that in a year or two after the Earl
of Kildare had received his pardon under the Great Seal. In May,
1492, the Warbeck plot was promulgated in Ireland, and an adventurer landed on the Irish shores, who declared himself to be
Richard, Duke of York, the second son of Edward IV., who was
supposed to have perished in the Tower. His stay in Ireland, however, was brief, although he was favourably received. The French
monarch entertained him with the honours due to a crowned head;
but this, probably, was merely for political purposes, as he was discarded as soon as peace had been made with England. He next
visited Margaret, the Dowager Duchess of Burgundy, who treated
him as if he were really her nephew.

Henry now became seriously alarmed at the state of affairs in
Ireland, and sent over Sir Edward Poyning, a privy counsellor and
a Knight of the Garter, to the troublesome colony. He was

have been the first to use hand-cannons, at the beginning of the fifteenth century. Cannon-balls were first made of stone, but at the battle of Cressy the
English "shot small balls of iron." For popular information on this subject,
see Fairholt, *History of Costume.*

attended by some eminent English lawyers, and what was of considerably greater importance, by a force of 1,000 men. But neither
the lawyers nor the men succeeded in their attempt, for nothing
was done to conciliate, and the old policy of force was the rule of
action, and failed as usual. The first step was to hunt out the
abettors of Warbeck's insurrection, who had taken refuge in the
north ; but the moment the Deputy marched against them, the
Earl of Kildare's brother rose in open rebellion, and seized Carlow
Castle. The Viceroy was, therefore, obliged to make peace with
O'Hanlon and Magennis, and to return south. After recovering ·
the fortress, he held a Parliament at Drogheda, in the month of
November, 1494. In this Parliament the celebrated statute was
enacted, which provided that henceforth no Parliament should be
held in Ireland until the Chief Governor and Council had first
certified to the King, under the Great Seal, as well the causes
and considerations as the Acts they designed to pass, and till the
same should be approved by the King and Council. This Act obtained the name of " Poyning's Law." It became a serious grievance when the whole of Ireland was brought under English
government ; but at the time of its enactment it could only affect
the inhabitants of the Pale, who formed a very small portion of
the population of that country; and the colonists regarded it rather
favourably, as a means of protecting them against the legislative
oppressions of the Viceroys.

The general object of the Act was nominally to reduce the people to
" whole and perfect obedience." The attempt to accomplish this desirable end had been continued for rather more than two hundred years,
and had not yet been attained. The Parliament of Drogheda did
not succeed, although the Viceroy returned to England afterwards
under the happy conviction that he had perfectly accomplished his
mission. Acts were also passed that ordnance[6] should not be kept
in fortresses without the Viceregal licence ; that the lords spiritual
and temporal were to appear in their robes in Parliament, for the
English lords of Ireland had, " through penuriousness, done away

---

[6] *Ordnance.*—In 1489 six hand-guns or musquets were sent from Germany
to the Earl of Kildare, which his guard bore while on sentry at Thomas Court,
his Dublin residence. The word " Pale " came to be applied to that part of
Ireland occupied by the English, in consequence of one of the enactments of
Poyning's Parliament, which required all the colonists to " pale " in or enclose
that portion of the country possessed by the English.

the said robes to their own great dishonour, and the rebuke of all the whole land;" that the "many damnable customs and uses," practised by the Anglo-Norman lords and gentlemen, under the names of "coigne, livery, and pay," should be reformed; that the inhabitants on the frontiers of the four shires should forthwith build and maintain a double-ditch, raised six feet above the ground on the side which "meared next unto the Irishmen," so that the said Irishmen should be kept out; that all subjects were to provide themselves with cuirasses and helmets, with English bows and sheaves of arrows; that every parish should be provided with a pair of butts,[7] and the constables were ordered to call the parishioners before them on holidays, to shoot at least two or three games.

The Irish war-cries[8] which had been adopted by the English lords were forbidden, and they were commanded to call upon St. George or the King of England. The Statutes of Kilkenny were confirmed, with the exception of the one which forbid the use of the Irish language. As nearly all the English settlers had adopted it, such an enactment could not possibly have been carried out. Three of the principal nobles of the country were absent from this assembly: Maurice, Earl of Desmond, was in arms on behalf of Warbeck; Gerald, Earl of Kildare, was charged with treason; and Thomas, Earl of Ormonde, was residing in England. The Earl of Kildare was sent to England to answer the charges of treason which were brought against him. Henry had discovered that Poyning's mission had not been as successful as he expected, and what, probably, influenced him still more, that it had proved very expensive.[9] He has the credit of being a wise king in many respects, notwithstanding his avariciousness; and he at once saw that Kildare would be more useful as a friend, and less expensive, if he ceased to be an enemy. The result was the pardon of the "rebel," his marriage

[7] *Butts.*—We give an illustration, at the head of this chapter, of the Butts' Cross, Kilkenny.

[8] *War-cries.*—That of the Geraldines of Kildare was *Cromadh-abu*, from Croom Castle, in Limerick; the war-cry of the Desmond Geraldines was *Seanaid-abu*, from Shannid Castle.

[9] *Expensive.*—English writers accuse Henry of miserable avariciousness. He is accused of having consented to the execution of Sir William Stanley, who had saved his life, for the sake of his enormous wealth.—Lingard's *History of England*, vol. v. p. 308. He is also accused, by a recent writer, of having seized the wealth of the Queen Dowager, because he chose to believe that she had assisted Simnel.—*Victoria History of England*, p. 223.

with the King's first cousin, Elizabeth St. John, and his restoration to the office of Deputy. His quick-witted speeches, when examined before the King, took the royal fancy. He was accused of having burned the Cathedral of Cashel, to revenge himself on the Archbishop, who had sided with his enemy, Sir James Ormonde. There was a great array of witnesses prepared to prove the fact; but the Earl excited shouts of laughter by exclaiming : " I would never have done it, had it not been told me the Archbishop was within."

The Archbishop was present, and one of his most active accusers. The King then gave him leave to choose his counsel, and time to prepare his defence. Kildare exclaimed that he doubted if he should be allowed to choose the good fellow whom he would select. Henry gave him his hand as an assurance of his good faith. "Marry," said the Earl, " I can see no better man in England than your Highness, and will choose no other." The affair ended by his accusers declaring that " all Ireland could not rule this Earl," to which Henry replied : " Then, in good faith, shall this Earl rule all Ireland."[1]

In August, 1489, Kildare was appointed Deputy to Prince Henry, who was made Viceroy. In 1498 he was authorized to convene a Parliament, which should not sit longer than half a year. This was the first Parliament held under Poyning's Act. Sundry regulations were made "for the increasing of English manners and conditions within the land, and for diminishing of Irish usage." In 1503 the Earl's son, Gerald, was appointed Treasurer for Ireland by the King, who expressed the highest approval of his father's administration. He married the daughter of Lord Zouch of Codnor during his visit to England, and then returned with his father to Ireland. Both father and son were treated with the utmost consideration at court, and the latter took an important part in the funeral ceremonies for the King's eldest son, Arthur. The Earl continued in office during the reign of Henry VII. An interesting letter, which he wrote in reply to an epistle from the Gherardini of Tuscany, is still extant. In this document he requests them to communicate anything they

---

[1] *Ireland.*—On one occasion, when the Earl and Sir James Ormonde had a quarrel, the latter retired into the chapter-house of St. Patrick's Cathedral, the door of which he closed and barricaded. The Earl requested him to come forth, and pledged his honour for his safety. As the knight still feared treachery, a hole was cut in the door, through which Kildare passed his hand ; and after this exploit, Ormonde came out, and they embraced each other,

can of the origin of their house, their numbers, and their ancestors. He informs them that it will give him the greatest pleasure to send them hawks, falcons, horses, or hounds, or anything that he can procure which they may desire. He concludes:

"God be with you; love us in return.

"GERALD, Chief in Ireland of the family of Gherardini, Earl of Kildare, Viceroy of the most serene Kings of England in Ireland."

Eight years after this letter was written, Ariosto writes thus of a brave old man, whose fame had passed long before to distant lands:

"Or guarda gl' Ibernisi : appresso il piano
Sono due squadre : e il Conte di Childera
Mena la pinna ; e il Conte di Desmonda,
Da fieri monti ha tratta la seconda."

ROUND TOWER, DONAGHMORE, CO. MEATH.

RUINS OF SELSKER ABBEY, WEXFORD.

CHAPTER XXIV.

The Reign of Henry VIII.—The Three Eras in Irish History : Military Violence, Legal Iniquity, and Religious Oppression—The Earl of Kildare—
Report on the State of Ireland—The Insurrection of Silken Thomas—His
Execution with his five Uncles—First Attempt to introduce the Reformation
in Ireland—Real Cause of the English Schism—The King acts as Head of
the Church—The New Religion enacted by Law, and enforced by the
Sword—How the Act was opposed by the Clergy, and how the Clergy were
disposed of—Dr. Browne's Letter to Henry—The Era of Religious Persecution—Massacre of a Prelate, Priest, and Friars—Wholesale Plunder of
Religious Property.

[A.D. 1509—1540.]

WE have now approached one of the most important
standpoints in Irish history. An English writer
has divided its annals into three eras, which he
characterizes thus: first, the era of military violence ; second, the era of legal iniquity ; third, the
era of religious persecution.[2] We may mark out
roughly certain lines which divide these periods,
but unhappily the miseries of the two former
blended eventually with the yet more cruel wrongs
of the latter. Still, until the reign of Henry
VIII., the element of religious contention did
not exist; and its importance as an increased
source of discord, may be easily estimated by a
careful consideration of its subsequent effects.
Nevertheless, I believe that Irish history has not
been fairly represented by a considerable number

[2] *Persecution.*—Smith's *Ireland Hist. and Statis.* vol. i. p. 327.

of writers, who are pleased to attribute all the sufferings and wrongs endured by the people of that country to religious grounds.

Ireland was in a chronic state of discontent and rebellion, in the eras of military violence and legal iniquity, which existed some centuries before the era of religious persecution; but, unquestionably, all the evils of the former period were enhanced and intensified, when the power which had so long oppressed and plundered, sought to add to bodily suffering the still keener anguish of mental torture.

In the era of military violence, a man was driven from his ancestral home by force of arms; in the era of legal iniquity, he was treated as a rebel if he complained; but in the era of religious persecution, his free will, the noblest gift of God to man—the gift which God Himself will not shackle—was demanded from him; and if he dared act according to the dictates of his conscience, a cruel death or a cruel confiscation was his portion. And this was done in the name of liberty of conscience! While England was Catholic, it showed no mercy to Catholic Ireland; I doubt much, if Ireland had become Protestant to a man, when England had become Protestant as a nation, that she would have shown more consideration for the Celtic race. But the additional cruelties with which the Irish were visited, for refusing to discard their faith at the bidding of a profligate king, are simply matters of history.

Henry succeeded his father in the year 1509. The Earl of Kildare was continued in his office as Deputy; but the King's minister, Wolsey, virtually ruled the nation, until the youthful monarch had attained his majority; and he appears to have devoted himself with considerable zeal to Irish affairs. He attempted to attach some of the Irish chieftains to the English interest, and seems in some degree to have succeeded. Hugh O'Donnell, Lord of Tir-Connell, was hospitably entertained at Windsor, as he passed through England on his pilgrimage to Rome. It is said that O'Donnell subsequently prevented James IV. of Scotland from undertaking his intended expedition to Ireland; and, in 1521, we find him described by the then Lord Deputy as the best disposed of all the Irish chieftains " to fall into English order."

Gerald, the ninth and last Catholic Earl of Kildare, succeeded his father as Lord Deputy in 1513. But the hereditary foes of his family were soon actively employed in working his ruin; and even his sister, who had married into that family, proved not the least formidable of his enemies. He was summoned to London; but either the charges against him could not be proved, or it was deemed expedient to defer them, for we find him attending Henry for four years, and forming one of his retinue at the Field of the Cloth of Gold. Kildare was permitted to return to Dublin again in 1523, but he was tracked by Wolsey's implacable hatred to his doom.[3] In 1533 he was confined in the Tower for the third time. The charges against him were warmly urged by his enemies. Two of his sisters were married to native chieftains; and he was accused of playing fast and loose with the English as a baron of the Pale— with the Irish as a warm ally.[4] Two English nobles had been appointed to assist him, or rather to act the spy upon his movements, at different times. One of these, Sir Thomas Skeffington, became his most dangerous enemy.

In 1515 an elaborate report on the state of Ireland was prepared by the royal command. It gives a tolerably clear idea of the military and political condition of the country. According to this account, the only counties really subject to English rule, were Louth, Meath, Dublin, Kildare, and Wexford. Even the residents near the boundaries of these districts, were obliged to pay " black mail " to the neighbouring Irish chieftains. The King's writs were not executed beyond the bounds described; and within thirty miles of Dublin, the Brehon law was in full force. This document, which is printed in the first volume of the " State Papers" relating to Ireland, contains a list of the petty rulers of sixty different states or " regions," some of which " are as big as a shire; some more, some less." The writer then gives various opinions as to the plans which might be adopted for improving the state of Ireland, which he appears to have taken principally from a curious old book, called *Salus Populi*.[5] Both writers were of opinion that war to the knife was the only remedy for Ireland's grievances. It was at least clear that if dead men could tell no tales, neither could dead men rebel against oppression; and the writer of the report concludes, " that

---

[3] *Doom.*—See *The Earls of Kildare*, vol. i. p. 106, for Wolsey's reasons for not removing him from the Viceroyalty, notwithstanding his dislike.

[4] *Ally.*—He was charged with having written a letter to O'Carroll of Ely, in which he advised him to keep peace with the Pale until a Deputy should come over, and then to make war on the English. The object of this advice is not very clear.

[5] *Salus Populi.*—There is a copy of this book in MS. in the British Museum. The name of the author is not known.

if the King were as wise as Solomon the Sage, he shall never subdue the wild Irish to his obedience without dread of the sword." Even this he admits may fail; for he adds, " so long as they may resist and save their lives, they will never obey the King." He then quotes the *Salus Populi*, to show the advantages which England might derive if the Irish united with her in her wars on foreign countries, and observes, " that if this land were put once in order as aforesaid, it would be none other but a very paradise, delicious of all pleasaunce, in respect and regard of any other land in this world; inasmuch as there never was stranger nor alien person, great or small, that would leave it willingly, notwithstanding the said misorder, if he had the means to dwell therein honestly."

It cannot now be ascertained whether Kildare had incited the Irish chieftains to rebellion or not. In 1520, during one of his periods of detention in London, the Earl of Surrey was sent over as Deputy with a large force. It would appear as if a general rising were contemplated at that time, and it was then the Earl wrote the letter[6] already mentioned to O'Carroll. The new Viceroy was entirely ignorant of the state of Ireland, and imagined he had nothing to do but conquer. Several successful engagements confirmed him in this pleasing delusion; but he soon discovered his mistake, and assured the King that it was hopeless to contend with an enemy, who were defeated one day, and rose up with renewed energy the next. As a last resource he suggested the policy of conciliation, which Henry appears to have adopted, as he empowered him to confer the honour of knighthood on any of the Irish chieftains to whom he considered it desirable to offer the compliment, and he sent a collar of gold to O'Neill. About the same time Surrey wrote to inform Wolsey, that Cormac Oge MacCarthy and MacCarthy Reagh were " two wise men, and more conformable to order than some English were;" but he was still careful to keep up the old policy of fomenting discord among the native princes, for he wrote to the King that " it would be dangerful to have them

---

[6] *Letter.*—The deposition accusing Kildare is printed in the " State Papers," part iii. p. 45. The following is an extract from the translation which it gives of his letter to O'Carroll. The original was written in Irish: " Desiring you to kepe good peas to English men tyll an English Deputie come there; and when any English Deputie shall come thydder, doo your beste to make warre upon English men there, except suche as bee towardes mee, whom you know well your silf."

both agreed and joined together, as the longer they continue in war, the better it should be for your Grace's poor subjects here."

Surrey became weary at last of the hopeless conflict, and at his own request he was permitted to return to England and resign his office, which was conferred on his friend, Pierse Butler,[7] of Carrick, subsequently Earl of Ormonde. The Scotch had begun to immigrate to Ulster in considerable numbers, and acquired large territories there; the Pale was almost unprotected; and the Irish Privy Council applied to Wolsey for six ships-of-war, to defend the northern coasts, A.D. 1522. The dissensions between the O'Neills and O'Donnells had broken out into sanguinary warfare.

The Earl of Kildare left Ireland for the third and last time, in February, 1534. Before his departure he summoned a Council at Drogheda, and appointed his son, Thomas, to act as Deputy in his absence. On the Earl's arrival in London, he was at once seized and imprisoned in the Tower. A false report was carefully circulated in Ireland that he had been beheaded, and that the destruction of the whole family was even then impending. Nor was there anything very improbable in this statement. The English King had already inaugurated his sanguinary career. One of the most eminent English laymen, Sir Thomas More, and one of her best ecclesiastics, Bishop Fisher, had been accused and beheaded, to satisfy the royal caprice. When the King's tutor and his chancellor had been sacrificed, who could hope to escape?

The unfortunate Earl had advised his son to pursue a cautious and gentle policy; but Lord Thomas' fiery temper could ill brook such precaution, and he was but too easily roused by the artful enemies who incited him to rebellion. The reports of his father's execution were confirmed. His proud blood was up, and he rushed madly on the career of self-destruction. On the 11th of June, 1534, he flung down the sword of state on the table of the council-

---

[7] *Pierse Butler.*—Called by the Irish, Red Pierse. Leland gives a curious story about him. He was at war with MacGillapatrick, who sent an ambassador to Henry VIII. to complain of the Earl's proceedings. The messenger met the English King as he was about to enter the royal chapel, and addressed him thus: "Stop, Sir King! my master, Gillapatrick, has sent me to thee to say, that if thou wilt not punish the Red Earl he will make war on thee." Pierse resigned his title in favour of Sir Thomas Boleyn, in 1527, and was created Earl of Ossory; but after the death of the former he again took up the old title, and resigned the new.

hall at St. Mary's Abbey, and openly renounced his allegiance to
the English monarch. Archbishop Cromer implored him with tears
to reconsider his purpose, but all entreaties were vain. Even had
he been touched by this disinterested counsel, it would probably
have failed of its effect; for an Irish bard commenced chanting his
praises and his father's wrongs, and thus his doom was sealed. An
attempt was made to arrest him, but it failed. Archbishop Allen,
his father's bitterest enemy, fled to the Castle, with several other
nobles, and here they were besieged by FitzGerald and his followers.
The Archbishop soon contrived to effect his escape. He embarked
at night in a vessel which was then lying at Dame's Gate; but the ship
was stranded near Clontarf, either through accident or design, and
the unfortunate prelate was seized by Lord Thomas' people, who
instantly put him to death. The young nobleman is said by some
authorities to have been present at the murder, as well as his two
uncles : there is at least no doubt of his complicity in the crime.
The sentence of excommunication was pronounced against him, and
those who assisted him, in its most terrible form.

Ecclesiastical intervention was not necessary to complete his ruin.
He had commenced his wild career of lawless violence with but few
followers, and without any influential companions. The Castle of
Maynooth, the great stronghold of the Geraldines, was besieged
and captured by his father's old enemy, Sir William Skeffington.
In the meanwhile the intelligence of his son's insurrection had
been communicated to the Earl, and the news of his excommunication followed quickly. The unfortunate nobleman succumbed
beneath the twofold blow, and died in a few weeks. Lord Thomas
surrendered himself in August, 1535, on the guarantee of Lord
Leonard and Lord Butler, under a solemn promise that his life
should be spared.[8] But his fate was in the hands of one who had
no pity, even where the tenderest ties were concerned. Soon after
the surrender of "Silken Thomas," his five uncles were seized
treacherously at a banquet; and although three of them had no part
in the rebellion, the nephew and the uncles were all executed

[8] *Spared.*—It is quite evident from the letter of the Council to Henry VIII.
(State Papers, ciii.), that a promise was made. Henry admits it, and regrets
it in his letter to Skeffington (S. P. cvi.): "The doyng whereof [FitzGerald's
capture], albeit we accept it thankfully, yet, if he had been apprehended after
such sorte as was convenable to his deservynges, the same had been muche more
thankfull and better to our contentacion."

together at Tyburn, on the 3rd of February, 1537. If the King
had hoped by this cruel injustice to rid himself of the powerful
family, he was mistaken.   Two children of the late Earl's still
existed.   They were sons by his second wife, Lady Elizabeth Grey.
The younger, still an infant, was conveyed to his mother in England;
the elder, a youth of twelve years of age, was concealed by his
aunts, who were married to the chieftains of Offaly and Donegal,
and was soon conveyed to France, out of the reach of the enemies
who eagerly sought his destruction.   It is not a little curious to find
the native princes, who had been so cruelly oppressed by his forefathers, protecting and helping the hapless youth, even at the risk
of their lives.   It is one of many evidences that the antipathy of
Celt to Saxon is not so much an antipathy of race or person, as
the natural enmity which the oppressed entertains towards the
oppressor.

Henry made his first appearance at establishing his spiritual supremacy in the year 1534, by appointing an Augustinian friar, who
had already[9] become a Protestant, to the see of Dublin.   He was
consecrated by Cranmer, always the servile instrument of the royal
pleasure.   The previous events in England, which resulted in the
national schism, are too well known to require much observation.
It must be admitted as one of the most patent facts of history, that
the English King never so much as thought of asserting his supremacy in spiritual matters, until he found that submission to Papal
supremacy interfered with his sinful inclinations.   If Pope Clement
VII. had dissolved the marriage between Queen Catherine and
Henry VIII. in 1528, Parliament would not have been asked to
legalize the national schism in 1534.   Yet it would appear as if
Henry had hesitated for a moment before he committed the final
act of apostacy.   It was Cromwell who suggested the plan which
he eventually followed.   With many expressions of humility he
pointed out the course which might be pursued.   The approbation
of the Holy See, he said, was the one thing still wanting.   It was
plain now that neither bribes nor threats could procure that favour.
But was it so necessary as the King had hitherto supposed ?   It
might be useful to avert the resentment of the German Emperor ;
but if it could not be obtained, why should the King's pleasure

---

[9] *Already.*—Mant describes him as a man " whose mind was happily freed
from the thraldom of Popery," before his appointment.—*History of the Church
of Ireland*, vol. i. p. 111.

depend on the will of another? Several of the German princes had thrown off their allegiance to the Holy See : why, then, should not the English King? The law could legalize the King's inclination, and who dare gainsay its enactments? Let the law declare Henry the head of the Church, and he could, as such, give himself the dispensations for which he sought. The law which could frame articles of faith and sanction canons, could regulate morals as easily as it could enact a creed.

Such counsel was but too acceptable to a monarch resolved to gratify his passions at all hazards, temporal or spiritual. Cromwell was at once appointed a member of the Privy Council. He received a patent for life of the Chancellorship of the Exchequer, and he was authorized to frame the necessary bills, and conduct them through the two houses.[1] Parliament complied without hesitation; the clergy in convocation made a show of opposition, which just sufficed to enhance their moral turpitude, since their brief resistance intimated that they acted contrary to their consciences in giving their final assent. The royal supremacy in matters ecclesiastical, was declared to be the will of God and the law of the land.

The King's mistress was now made his wife, by the same authority which had made the King head of the Church; and it was evident that the immediate cause of the separation of the English nation from the Catholic Church was the desire of the monarch, that his profligacy should obtain some kind of sanction. But this commencement of the Anglican Establishment, however true, is so utterly disreputable, that English historians have been fain to conceal, as far as might be, the real cause, and to justify the schism by bringing grave charges[2] against the Church. This, after all, is a mere

---

[1] *Houses.*—Lingard, vol. vi. p. 203.

[2] *Charges.*—Mr. Froude has adopted this line with considerable ability, in his *History of England.* He has collected certain statements, which he finds in the books of the Consistory Courts, and gives details from these cases which certainly must "shock his readers" considerably, as he expects. He leaves it to be implied that, as a rule, ecclesiastics lived in open immorality. He gives names and facts concerning the punishment of priests for vicious lives (*History of England*, vol. i. pp. 178–180) ; and asserts that their offences were punished lightly, while another measure was dealt out to seculars. He might as well select the cases of scandal given by Protestant clergymen in modern times from the law books, and hold them up as specimens of the lives of all their brethren. The cases were exceptions ; and though they do prove, what is generally admitted, that the moral condition of the clergy was not all that

petitio principii. It has been already remarked that England was demoralized socially to an extraordinary degree, as a nation always has been by a continuance of civil war. The clergy suffered from the same causes which affected the laity, and the moral condition of the ecclesiastical body was not all that could be desired. These were remote causes, which acted powerfully as they rolled along the stream of time, and which broke the barriers of faith like an overwhelming torrent, when an additional impetus was given. But it should be distinctly remembered (1) that the direct act of schism was committed when Henry required Parliament and Convocation to exalt him to the spiritual supremacy ; and (2) that the sins of churchmen and the faith of the Church are two distinct questions. There may have been more corruption of life and morals, both in the laity and the priesthood of the Catholic Church at the Reformation, than at any other period of the Church's history ; but the Jews had been commanded to obey the Scribes and Pharisees, because they sat in Moses' seat, at the very time when the Lamb of God could find no milder term to describe their hypocrisy and iniquity than that of a generation of vipers.

If schism is admitted to be a sin, it is difficult to see how any amount of crime with which other individuals can be charged, even justly, lessens the guilt of the schismatic. There can be little doubt that the members of the Church are most fervent and edifying in their lives, when suffering from persecution. Ambition has less food when there are no glittering prizes within its reach. Faith is more sincere when there are no motives for a false profession, and every natural motive to conceal religious belief. The Irish clergy were never charged with the gross crimes which have been mentioned in connexion with some few of their brethren in England. Those who ministered outside the Pale, lived in poverty and simplicity. The monasteries were not so richly endowed as the English conventual houses ; and, perhaps, this freedom from the world's

could be desired in individual cases, they also prove that such cases were exceptional, and that they were condemned by the Church, or they would not have been punished. With regard to the punishment, we can scarcely call it a light penance for a *priest* to be compelled to go round the church barefoot, to kneel at each altar and recite certain prayers, and this while High Mass was singing. It was a moral disgrace, and keener than a corporal punishment. The writer also evidently misunderstands the Catholic doctrine of absolution, when he says that a fine of six-and-eightpence was held sufficient penalty for a mortal sin.

goods, served to nerve them for the coming trial; and that their purer and more fervent lives saved the Irish Church and people from national apostacy.

Soon after Dr. Browne's arrival in Ireland, he received an official letter from Cromwell, containing directions for his conduct there. He is informed it is " the royal will and pleasure of his Majesty, that his subjects in Ireland, even as those in England, should obey his commands in spiritual matters as in temporal, and renounce their allegiance to the See of Rome." This language was sufficiently plain.. They are required to renounce their allegiance to the See of Rome, simply because " the King wills it." The affair is spoken of as if it were some political matter, which could easily be arranged. But the source of this prelate's authority was simply political; for Henry writes to him thus: " Let it sink into your remembrance, that we be as able, for the not doing thereof, to re-move you again, and put another man of more virtue and honesty into your place, as we were at the beginning to prefer you." Browne could certainly be in no doubt from whom he had received his commission to teach and preach to the people of Ireland; but that nation had received the faith many centuries before, from one who came to them with very different credentials; and years of oppres-sion and most cruel persecution have failed in inducing them to obey human authority rather than divine.

Dr. Browne soon found that it was incomparably easier for Henry to issue commands in England, than for him to enforce them in Ireland. He therefore wrote to Cromwell, from Dublin, on " the 4th of the kal. of December, 1535," and informed him that he " had endeavoured, almost to the danger and hazard of my temporal life, to procure the nobility and gentry of this nation to due obe-dience in owning of his Highness their supreme head, as well spiritual as temporal; and do find much oppugning therein, especially by my brother Armagh, who hath been the main oppugner, and so hath withdrawn most of his suffragans and clergy within his see and diocese. He made a speech to them, laying a curse on the people whosoever should own his Highness' supremacy, saying, that isle— as it is in their Irish chronicles, *insula sacra*—belongs to none but the Bishop of Rome, and that it was the Bishop of Rome that gave it to the King's ancestors."[3]   Dr. Browne then proceeds to inform

---

[3] *Ancestors.*—See the *Phœnix,* a collection of valuable papers, published in London, 1707; and the *Harleian Miscellany,* &c.

his correspondent that the Irish clergy had sent two messengers to Rome.[4] He states "that the common people of this isle are more zealous in their blindness, than the saints and martyrs were in truth ;" and he advises that a Parliament should at once be summoned, " to pass the supremacy by Act ; for they do not much matter his Highness' commission, which your lordship sent us over." Truly, the nation which had been so recently enlightened in so marvellous a manner, might have had a little patience with the people who could not so easily discern the new light ; and, assuredly, if the term " Church by law established " be applicable to the Protestant religion in England, it is, if possible, still more applicable to the Protestant Establishment in Ireland, since the person delegated to found the new religion in that country, has himself stated it could only be established there by Act of Parliament.

The Parliament was summoned in 1536 ; but, as a remote preparation, the Lord Deputy made a "martial circuit" of Ireland, hoping thereby to overawe the native septs, and compel their submission to the royal will and pleasure. " This preparation being made," *i.e.*, the "martial circuit"—I am quoting from Sir John Davies;[5] I request the reader's special attention to the statement—"he first propounded and passed in Parliament these Lawes, which made the great alteration in the State Ecclesiastical, namely, the Act which declared King Henry VIII. to be Supreme Head of the Church of Ireland ; the Act prohibiting Apeales to the Church of Rome ; the Act for first fruites and twentieth part to be paid to the King ; and lastly, the Act that did utterly abolish the usurped Authoritie of the Pope. Next, for the increase of the King's Revenew. By one Act he suppressed sundry Abbayes and Religious Houses, and by another Act resumed the Lands of the Absentees."

The royal process of conversion to the royal opinions, had at least the merits of simplicity. There is an old rhyme—one of those old rhymes which are often more effectual in moving the hearts of the multitude than the most eloquent sermons, and truer exponents of popular feeling than Acts of Parliament—which describes the fate of Forrest, the Franciscan friar, confessor of the King's only lawful

---

[4] *Rome.*—This was the invariable practice of the Irish Church. It will be remembered how letters and expostulations had been sent to the Holy See in regard to the temporal oppressions of the English settlers.

[5] *Davies.*—*Cause why Ireland was never Subdued.*—Thom's Reprints, vol. i. p. 694.

wife, and the consequences of his temerity in denying the King's supremacy :—

> "Forrest, the fryar,
> That obstinate lyar,
> That wilfully will be dead ;
> Incontinently
> The Gospel doth deny,
> The King to be supreme head."

There is a grand and simple irony in this not easily surpassed. Some very evident proofs had been given in England, that to deny the King's spiritual supremacy was " wilfully to be dead," although neither the King nor the Parliament had vouchsafed to inform the victims in what part of the Gospel the keys of the kingdom of heaven had been given to a temporal prince. Still, as I have observed, the royal process was extremely simple—if you believed, you were saved ; if you doubted, you died.

With the example of Sir Thomas More[6] before their eyes, the Anglo-Norman nobles and gentlemen, assembled in Parliament by the royal command, were easily persuaded to do the royal bidding. But the ecclesiastics were by no means so pliable. Every diocese had the privilege of sending two proctors to Parliament ; and these proctors proved so serious an obstacle, that Lords Grey and Brabazon wrote to Cromwell, that they had prorogued the Parlia-

---

[6] *More.*—Sir Thomas More's son-in-law, Roper, gives the following account of his condemnation : " Mr. Rich, pretending friendly talk with him, among other things of a set course, said this unto him : ' Admit there were, sir, an Act of Parliament that the realm should take me for king ; would not you, Master More, take me for King ?' ' Yes, sir,' quoth Sir Thomas More, ' that I would.' ' I put the case further,' quoth Mr. Rich, ' that there were an Act of Parliament that all the realm should take me for Pope ; would not you then, Master More, take me for Pope ?' ' For answer, sir,' quoth Sir Thomas More, ' to your first case, the Parliament may well, Master Rich, meddle with the state of temporal princes ; but to make answer to your other case, I will put you this case. Suppose the Parliament should make a law that God should not be God, would you then, Master Rich, say that God were not God ?' ' No, sir,' quoth he, ' that I would not, sith no Parliament may make any such law.' ' No more,' quoth Sir Thomas More, ' could the Parliament make the King supreme head of the Church.' Upon whose only report was Sir Thomas indicted for high treason on the statute to deny the King to be supreme head of the Church, into which indictment were put these heinous words—maliciously, traitorously, and diabolically."

ment in consequence of the " forwardness and obstinacy of the
proctors, of the clergy, and of the bishops and abbots ;" and they
suggest that " some means should be devised, whereby they should
be brought to remember their duty better," or that " means may be
found which shall put these proctors from a voice in Parliament."[7]
The means were easily found—the proctors were forbidden to
vote.[8] The Act was passed. Every one who objected to it having
been forbidden to vote, Henry's agents on the Continent proclaimed triumphantly that the Irish nation had renounced the
supremacy of Rome. A triumph obtained at the expense of truth,
is but poor compensation for the heavy retribution which shall
assuredly be demanded of those who have thus borne false witness
against their neighbour. Men forget too often, in the headlong
eagerness of controversy, that truth is eternal and immutable, and
that no amount of self-deceit or successful deception of others can
alter its purity and integrity in the eyes of the Eternal Verity.

The Irish Parliament, or, we should say more correctly, the men
permitted to vote in Ireland according to royal directions, had
already imitated their English brethren by declaring the marriage
of Henry and Catherine of Arragon null and void, and limiting the
succession to the crown to the children of Anna Boleyn. When
this lady had fallen a victim to her husband's caprice, they attainted
her and her posterity with equal facility. A modern historian has
attempted to excuse Henry's repudiation of his lawful wife, on the
ground of his sincere anxiety to prevent disputes about the succession.[9] But the King's subsequent conduct ought surely to have
deterred any one from attempting so rash an apology. To doubt
the royal supremacy, or the right of the lady, who for the time
being held a place in Henry's affections, to royal honours, was an
evidence of insincerity in devotion to himself which he could not
easily pardon.

As it was now ascertained that the Irish people would not apos-

---

[7] *Parliament.*—State Papers, vol. ii. p. 437.

[8] *Vote.*—Irish Statutes, 28th Henry VIII. c. xii.

[9] *Succession.*—Froude, vol. i. p. 94. He also quotes Hall to the effect that
" all indifferent and discreet persons judged that it was right and necessary."
Persons who were " indifferent" enough to think that any reason could make
a sin necessary, or " discreet" enough to mind losing their heads or their property, were generally of that opinion. But Henry's difficulties in divorcing
his wife are a matter of history.

tatize as a nation, an expedient was prepared for their utter extirpation. It would be impossible to believe that the human heart could be guilty of such cruelty, if we had not evidence of the fact in the State Papers. By this diabolical scheme it was arranged to kill or carry away their cattle, and to destroy their corn while it was green. "The very living of the Irishry," observes the writer, "doth clearly consist in two things; and take away the same from them, and they are past power to recover, or yet to annoy any subject in Ireland. Take first from them their corn—burn and destroy the same; and then have their cattle and beasts, which shall be most hardest to come by, and yet, with guides and policy, they be often had and taken." Such was the arrangement; and it was from no want of inclination that it was not entirely carried out, and the "Irishry" starved to death in their own land.

The title of King of Ireland had not as yet been given to English monarchs, but the ever-subservient Parliament of this reign granted Henry this addition to his privileges, such as it was. We have already seen the style in which the "supreme head of the Church" addressed the bishops whom he had appointed; we shall now give a specimen of their subserviency to their master, and the fashion in which they executed his commands, before returning to secular history.

Henry's letter to Dr. Browne is dated July 7th, 1537; the Bishop's reply is given on the 27th September, 1537. He commences by informing his most excellent Highness that he had received his most gracious letter on the 7th September, and that " it made him tremble in body for fear of incurring his Majesty's displeasure," which was doubtless the most truthful statement in his epistle. He mentions all his zeal and efforts against Popery, which, he adds, "is a thing not little rooted among the inhabitants here." He assures the King of his activity in securing the twentieth part and first-fruits for the royal use (what had been given to God was now given to Cæsar), and states what, indeed, could not be denied, that he was the " first spiritual man who moved" for this to be done. He concludes with the fearful profanity of " desiring of God, that the ground should open and swallow him up the hour or minute that he should declare the Gospel of Christ after any sort than he had done heretofore, in rebuking the Papistical power, *or in any other point concerning the advancement of his Grace's affairs.*"

Such a tissue of profanity and absurdity was seldom penned;

but men who could write and act thus were fitting instruments for a man, who made it a point of conscience to commit immoral crimes that he might preserve the succession ; who kept his mistress in the same palace with his queen; and only went through the form of marriage when he found his real or pretended wishes about the same succession on the point of being realized in a manner that even he could not fail to see would scarcely be admitted as legal or legitimate by public opinion, whatever an obsequious Parliament might do. It is at least certain that such letters never were addressed by Catholic prelates to the Holy See, and that those who speak of its tyranny and priestcraft, and the absolute submission it requires from its subjects, would do well to remember the trite motto, *Audi alteram partem*, and to inquire whether a similar charge might not be made more justly against the founders of the Protestant Establishment.

Dr. Browne and the Lord Deputy now rivalled each other in their efforts to obtain the royal approbation, by destroying all that the Irish people held most sacred, determined to have as little cause as possible for " the trembling in body" which the King's displeasure would effect. They traversed the land from end to end, destroying cathedrals, plundering abbeys, and burning relics—all in the name of a religion which proclaimed liberty of conscience to worship God according to individual conviction, as the great boon which it was to confer on the nation. However full of painful interest these details may be, as details they belong to the province of the ecclesiastical historian. The Four Masters record the work of desecration in touching and mournful strains. They tell of the heresy which broke out in England, and graphically characterize it as " the effect of pride, vain-glory, avarice, and sensual desire." They mention how " the King and Council enacted new laws and statutes after their own will." They observe that all the property of the religious orders was seized for the King; and they conclude thus : " They also made archbishops and bishops for themselves ; and although great was the persecution of the Roman emperors against the Church, it is not probable that so great a persecution as this ever came upon the world ; so that it is impossible to tell or narrate its description, unless it should be told by him who saw it."[1]

---

[1] *Saw it.*—Four Masters, vol. v. p. 1445.

The era of religious persecution was thus inaugurated; and if Ireland had made no martyrs of the men who came to teach her the faith, she was not slow to give her best and noblest sons as victims to the fury of those who attempted to deprive her of that priceless deposit.   Under the year 1540, the Four Masters record the massacre of the Guardian and friars of the Convent at Monaghan, for refusing to acknowledge the spiritual supremacy of the King. Cornelius, Bishop of Down, a Franciscan friar, and Father Thomas FitzGerald, a member of the noble family of the Geraldines, and a famous preacher, were both killed in the convent of that Order in Dublin.   Father Dominic Lopez has given a detailed account of the sufferings of the religious orders in Ireland during the reign of Henry VIII., in a rare and valuable work, entitled, *Noticias Historicas de las tres florentissimas Provincias del celeste Ordem de la Ssma. Trinidad.*[2] I shall give two instances from this history, as a sample of the fashion in which the new doctrine of the royal supremacy was propagated.   In 1539 the Prior and religious of the Convent of Atharee were commanded to take the oath of supremacy, and to surrender their property to the crown.   The Superior, Father Robert, at once assembled his spiritual children, and informed them of the royal mandate.   Their resolution was unanimous; after the example of the early Christians, when threatened with martyrdom and spoliation by heathen emperors, they at once distributed their provisions, clothing, and any money they had in hand amongst the poor, and concealed the sacred vessels and ornaments, so that not so much as a single emblem of our redemption was left to be desecrated by men professing to believe that they had been redeemed by the cross of Christ.   Father Robert was summoned thrice to recognize the new authority.   Thrice he declined; declaring that " none had ever sought to propagate their religious tenets by the sword, except the pagan emperors in early ages, and Mahomet in later times.   As for himself and his community, they were resolved that no violence should move them from the principles of truth : they recognized no head of the Catholic Church save the Vicar of Jesus Christ; and as for the King of England, they regarded him not even as a member of that holy Church, but as head of the synagogue of Satan."   The conclusion of his reply was a signal for massacre.   An officer instantly struck off his head with one blow.

[2] *Trinidad.*—Madrid, 1714.

As the prisons were already full of "recusants," the friars were placed in confinement in private houses, some were secretly murdered, and others were publicly hanged in the market-place. These events occurred on the 12th and 13th of February, 1539.

An almost similar tragedy was enacted in the Trinitarian Convent of Limerick, where the Prior was coadjutor to the Bishop of that city. He also assembled the brethren, exhorted them to perseverance, distributed their few poor possessions, and concealed the sacred vessels. On the feast of St. John Baptist, 24th June, in the year of grace 1539, he preached in his cathedral against the new heresy, and exhorted his flock to persevere in the faith. The emissaries of Government were afraid to attack him openly; but that evening they visited him at his private residence, and offered him his choice between death and apostacy. For all reply the venerable prelate knelt down, and exclaimed: "O Lord, on this morning I offered to Thee on the altar the unbloody sacrifice of the body of my Saviour; grant that I may now offer, to Thy greater honour and glory, the sacrifice of my own life." Then he turned towards a picture of the most holy Trinity, which was suspended in his room, and scarce had time to pronounce the aspiration of his Order, "*Sancta Trinitas, unus Deus, miserere nobis,*" ere his head was severed from his body, and he entered upon the beatific vision of the Three in One, for Whom he had so gladly sacrificed his life.

The Protestant Archbishop, Dr. Browne, the Lord Chancellor, and some other members of the Council, set out on a "visitation" of the four counties of Carlow, Wexford, Waterford, and Tipperary, in which the church militant was for the nonce represented by the church military. They transmitted an account of their expedition, and the novel fashion in which they attempted to propagate the Gospel, to England, on the 18th January, 1539. One brief extract must suffice as a specimen of their proceedings. "The day following we kept the sessions there [at Wexford]. There was put to execution four felons, accompanied with another, a friar, whom we commanded to be hanged in his habit, and so to remain upon the gallows for a mirror to all his brethren to live truly."[3]

There was One, whom from reverence I name not here, who said, when about to die, that, when "lifted up, He should draw all men unto Him." Centuries have rolled by since those most blessed

---

[3] *Truly.*—State Papers, vol. iii. p. 108.

words were uttered, but they have been verified in the disciples as well as in the Master. The "lifting up" of a friar upon the gallows, or of a bishop upon the block, has but served to draw men after them ; and the reformations they failed to effect during their lives, by their preaching and example, have been accomplished after and because of their martyrdoms.

The reformers now began to upbraid each other with the very crimes of which they had accused the clergy in England. When mention is made of the immense sums of money which were obtained by the confiscation of religious houses at this period, it has been commonly and naturally supposed, that the religious were possessors of immense wealth, which they hoarded up for their own benefit ; and although each person made a vow of poverty, it is thought that what was possessed collectively, was enjoyed individually. But this false impression arises (1) from a mistaken idea of monastic life, and (2) from a misapprehension as to the kind of property possessed by the religious.

A brief account of some of the property forfeited in Ireland, will explain this important matter. We do not find in any instance that religious communities had large funds of money. If they had extensive tracts of land, they were rather the property of the poor, who farmed them, than of the friars, who held them in trust. Any profit they produced made no addition to the fare or the clothing of the religious, for both fare and clothing were regulated by certain rules framed by the original founders, and which could not be altered. These rules invariably required the use of the plainest diet and of the coarsest habits. A considerable portion—indeed, by far the most considerable portion—of conventual wealth, consisted in the sacred vessels and ornaments. These had been bestowed on the monastic churches by benefactors, who considered that what was used in the service of God should be the best which man could offer. The monk was none the richer if he offered the sacrifice to the Eternal Majesty each morning in a chalice of gold, encrusted with the most precious jewels ; but if it were right and fitting to present that chalice to God for the service of His Divine Majesty, who shall estimate the guilt of those who presumed to take the gift from Him to whom it had been given ? We know how terrible was the judgment which came upon a heathen monarch who dared to use the vessels which had belonged to the Jewish Temple, and we may well believe that a still more terrible judgment is prepared for those who desecrate Christian churches, and that it will be none the less sure, because, under the new dispensation of mercy, it comes less swiftly.

All the gold and silver plate, jewels, ornaments, lead, bells, &c., were reserved by special command for the King's use.[4] The church-lands were sold to the highest bidder, or bestowed as a reward on those who had helped to enrich the royal coffers by sacrilege. Amongst the records of the sums thus obtained, we find £326 2s. 11d., the price of divers pieces of gold and silver, of precious stones, silver ornaments, &c.; also £20, the price of 1,000 ℔s. of wax. The sum of £1,710 2s. was realized from the sale of sacred vessels belonging to thirty-nine monasteries. The profits on the spoliation of St. Mary's, Dublin, realized £385. The destruction of the Collegiate Church of St. Patrick must have procured an enormous profit, as we find that Cromwell received £60 for his pains in effecting the same. It should also be remembered that the value of a penny then was equal to the value of a shilling now, so that we should multiply these sums at least by ten to obtain an approximate idea of the extent of this wholesale robbery.

The spoilers now began to quarrel over the spoils. The most active or the most favoured received the largest share; and Dr. Browne grumbled loudly at not obtaining all he asked for. But we have not space to pursue the disedifying history of their quarrels. The next step was to accuse each other. In the report of the Commissioners appointed in 1538 to examine into the state of the country, we find complaints made of the exaction of undue fees, extortions for baptisms and marriages, &c. They also (though this was not made an accusation by the Commissioners) received the fruits of benefices in which they did not officiate, and they were accused of taking wives and dispensing with the sacrament of matrimony. The King, whatever personal views he might have on this subject, expected his clergy to live virtuously; and in 1542 he wrote to the Lord Deputy, requiring an Act to be passed " for the continency of the clergy," and some " reasonable plan to be devised

---

[4] *Use.*—28th Henry VIII. cap. xvi. In Shirley's *Original Letters*, p. 31, we find the following order from the Lord Protector, Somerset, to the Dean of St. Patrick's : " Being advertised that one thousand ounces of plate of crosses and such like things remaineth in the hands of you, we require you to deliver the same to be employed to his Majesty's use," &c. He adds that the Dean is to receive " £20 in ready money " for the safe keeping of the same.

for the avoiding of sin." However, neither the Act nor the reasonable
plan appear to have succeeded.   In 1545, Dr. Browne writes: "Here
reigneth insatiable ambition ; here reigneth continually coigne and
livery, and callid extortion." Five years later, Sir Anthony St.
Leger, after piteous complaints of the decay of piety and the
increase of immorality, epitomizes the state of the country thus :
" I never saw the land so far out of good order."[5] Pages might be
filled with such details ; but the subject shall be dismissed with a
brief notice of the three props of the Reformation and the King's
supremacy in Ireland.   These were Dr. Browne of Dublin, Dr. Staples of Meath, and Dr. Bale of Ossory.   The latter writing of the
former in 1553, excuses the corruption of his own reformed clergy,
by stating that "they would at no hand obey ; alleging for their
vain and idle excuse, the lewd example of the Archbishop of Dublin,
who was always slack in things pertaining to God's glory." He
calls him "an epicurious archbishop, a brockish swine, and a dissem-
bling proselyte," and accuses him in plain terms of " drunkenness
and gluttony." Dr. Browne accuses Dr. Staples of having preached
in such a manner, " as I think the three-mouthed Cerberus of hell
could not have uttered it more viperously." And Dr. Mant, the
Protestant panegyrist of the Reformation and the Reformers, admits
that Dr. Bale was guilty of "uncommon warmth of temperament "—
a polite appellation for a most violent temper ; and of " unbecoming
coarseness"—a delicate definement of a profligate life.   His antecedents were not very creditable.   After flying from his convent in
England, he was imprisoned for preaching sedition in York and
London.   He obtained his release by professing conformity to the
new creed.   He eventually retired to Canterbury, after his expulsion
from Kilkenny by the Catholics, and there he died, in 1563.

[5] *Order.*—The original letter may be seen in Shirley, pp. 41, 42.

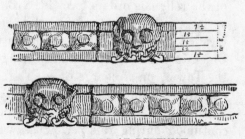

SCULPTURES AT DEVENISH.

ROSS ISLAND.

CHAPTER XXV.

Creation of the Earls of Thomond and Clanrickarde—How the King procured Money—Prayers in English—Opposition of Dr. Dowdall—Accession of Queen Mary—Joy of the Irish—The Catholic Service restored Publicly—Accession of Queen Elizabeth—Shane O'Neill obtains his Dominions—Parliament assembled—Unfair Dealing—Martyrs in the Reign of Elizabeth—The Protestant Archbishop advises Persecution—Cruelties enacted by English Officers—Shane O'Neill—The Deputy tries to get him Poisoned or Assassinated, with the Queen's Concurrence—His Visit to England—He refuses to Dress in the English Fashion.

[A.D. 1540—1567.]

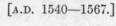

EVERY official was now required to take the oath of supremacy, and the consequences of refusal were too well known to be estimated lightly. It has been asserted by several historians, that no Irish clergyman suffered death during this reign; but this statement is quite incorrect. A careful examination of the State Papers and of the private records of the religious orders, prove the contrary. In the spring of the year 1540, Lord Leonard Grey was recalled, and Sir William Brereton was appointed Chief Justice. Grey was soon after committed to the Tower, on a charge of high treason, and was executed in the following year. The usual feuds between the Irish chieftains and the settlers were continued during this period, as well as the usual feuds between the chiefs of each party. Sir Anthony St. Leger, who was appointed Deputy at the close of the year 1540, tried to reconcile the Ormondes and the Desmonds, and describes the latter as "undoubtedly a very wise and discreet gentleman"—a character which must be taken with some qualifications.

On the 1st of July, 1543, Murrough O'Brien was created Earl of Thomond and Baron of Inchiquin; and De Burgo, known by the soubriquet of Ulich-na-gceann ("of the heads"), from the number of persons whom he decapitated in his wars, was created Earl of Clanrickarde and Baron of Dunkellin. These titles were conferred by the King, with great pomp, at Greenwich; but the Irish chieftains paid for the honour, if honour it could be called where honour was forfeited, by acknowledging the royal supremacy.

The Four Masters record the following events under the year 1545 :—A dispute between the Earl of Ormonde and the Lord Justice. Both repaired to the King of England to decide the quarrel, and both swore that only one of them should return to Ireland. "And so it fell out; for the Earl died in England, and the Lord Justice returned to Ireland." Sir Richard Cox asserts that the Earl and thirty-five of his servants were poisoned, at a feast at Ely House, Holborn, and that he and sixteen of them died; but he does not mention any cause for this tragedy. It was probably accidental, as the Earl was a favourer of the reformed religion, and not likely to meet with treachery in England. The Irish annalists do not even allude to the catastrophe; the Four Masters merely observe, that " he would have been lamented, were it not that he had greatly injured the Church by advice of the heretics."[6]

Great dearth prevailed this year, so that sixpence of the old money was given for a cake of bread in Connaught, or six white pence in Meath.

In 1546 they mention a rising of the Geraldines, "which did indescribable damages;" and two invasions of the Lord Justice in Offaly, who plundered and spoiled, burning churches and monasteries, crops and corn. They also mention the introduction of a new copper coin into Ireland, which the men of Ireland were obliged to use as silver.

The immense sums which Henry had accumulated by the plunder of religious houses, appear to have melted away, like snow-wreaths in sunshine, long before the conclusion of his reign. His French

---

[6] *Heretics.*—Annals, vol. v. p. 1493.

and Scotch wars undoubtedly exhausted large supplies ; his mistresses made large demands for their pleasures and their needy friends ; yet there should have been enough, and to spare, for all these claims. When the monasteries were destroyed, the English clergy trembled for their own existence. The King could easily have dispensed with their services, and deprived them of their revenues. They were quite aware of their precarious tenure of office, and willingly agreed, in 1543, to give Henry ten per cent. on their incomes for three years, after the deduction of the tenths already vested in the crown. Their incomes were thus ascertained, and a loan was demanded, which, when granted, was made a gift by the ever-servile Parliament.

In 1545 a benevolence was demanded, though benevolences had been declared illegal by Act of Parliament. This method of raising money had been attempted at an early period of his reign ; but the proposal met with such spirited opposition from the people, that even royalty was compelled to yield. A few years later, when the fatal result of opposition to the monarch's will and pleasure had become apparent, he had only to ask and obtain. Yet neither percentage, nor tenths, nor sacrilegious spoils, sufficed to meet his expenses ; and, as a last expedient, the coin was debased, and irreparable injury inflicted on the country.

On the 28th of January, 1547, Edward VI. was crowned King of England. The Council of Regency appointed by Henry was set aside, and Seymour, Duke of Somerset, appointed himself Protector. St. Leger was continued in the office of Lord Deputy in Ireland ; but Sir Edward Bellingham was sent over as Captain-General, with a considerable force, to quell the ever-recurring disturbances. His energetic character bore down all opposition, as much by the sheer strength of a strong will as by force of arms. In 1549 the Earl of Desmond refused to attend a Council in Dublin, on the plea that he wished to keep Christmas in his own castle. Bellingham, who had now replaced St. Leger as Lord Deputy, set out at once, with a small party of horse, for the residence of the refractory noble, seized him as he sat by his own fireside, and carried him off in triumph to Dublin.

In 1548 O'Connor and O'More were expelled from Offaly and Leix, and their territory usurped by an Englishman, named Francis Bryan. Cahir Roe O'Connor, one of the sept, was executed in Dublin, and a number of the tribe were sent to assist in the Scotch wars. The political cabals in England consequent on the youth of the King, who nominally governed the country, occasioned frequent changes in the Irish administration.

In 1551 the Lord Deputy Crofts succeeded Sir Thomas Cusack, and led an army into Ulster against the Scotch settlers, who had long been regarded with a jealous eye by the English Government; but he was defeated both at this time and on a subsequent occasion. No Parliament was convened during this short reign, and the affairs of the country were administered by the Privy Council. Dr. Browne and Dr. Staples were leading members. The Chancellor, Read, and the Treasurer, Brabazon, were both English. The Irish members were Aylmer, Luttrell, Bath, Howth, and Cusack, who had all recently conformed, at least exteriorly, to the new religion.

The most important native chieftain of the age was Shane O'Neill. His father, Con, surnamed Baccagh ("the lame"), had procured the title of Baron of Dungannon, and the entail of the earldom of Tyrone, from Henry VII., for his illegitimate son, Ferdoragh. He now wished to alter this arrangement; but the ungrateful youth made such charges against the old man, that he was seized and imprisoned by the Deputy. After his death Shane contended bravely for his rights. The French appear to have made some attempt about this period to obtain allies in Ireland, but the peace which ensued between that country and England soon terminated such intrigues.

All efforts to establish the new religion during this reign was equally unsuccessful. On Easter Sunday, A.D. 1551, the liturgy was read for the first time in the English tongue, in Christ Church Cathedral. As a reward for his energy in introducing the reform in general, and the liturgy in particular, Edward VI. annexed the primacy of all Ireland to the see of Dublin by Act of Parliament. There was one insuperable obstacle, however, in the way of using the English tongue, which was simply that the people did not understand it. Even the descendants of the Anglo-Norman were more familiar with the Celtic dialect, and some attempt was made at this time to procure a Latin translation of the Protestant communion service.[7]

[7] Service.—Shirley's Original Letters, p. 47. Dr. Browne gives an account of his signal failures in attempting to introduce the Protestant form of prayer

Dr. Dowdall had been appointed, in 1543, to the primatial see of Armagh, by Henry VIII., who naturally hoped he would prove a ready instrument in his service ; but, to the surprise of the court, he put himself at the head of the orthodox party, and was one of the most faithful opposers of the introduction of the Protestant form of prayer. In 1552 he was obliged to seek refuge on the Continent. On the death of Dr. Wauchop, petitions were sent to Rome, requesting his appointment to the see of Armagh. He was proposed in Consistory on the 1st of March, 1553.

Mary succeeded to the crown in 1553. A Protestant writer explains the difference between the religious persecutions of her reign, and those which occurred during the reign of Henry VIII., with admirable discrimination and impartiality : " The religious persecutions which prevailed in this reign, proceeded altogether from a different cause from that which stands as an everlasting blot on the memory of Henry VIII. In Henry's instance, people were tortured and murdered in the name of religion, but the real cause was their opposition to the will of an arbitrary tyrant ; whereas those who suffered under Mary, were martyred because the Queen conscientiously believed in those principles to which she clung with such pertinacity."[8] One of the principal of these victims was Archbishop Cranmer, who had already caused several persons to suffer in the flames for differing from his opinions, and thus almost merited his fate. It is a curious fact that several Protestants came to Ireland during this reign, and settled in Dublin ; they were subsequently the founders of respectable mercantile families.

Although the English people had adopted the reformed religion nationally, there were still a few persons whom neither favour nor indifference could induce to renounce the ancient faith ; and this brief respite from persecution tended to confirm and strengthen those who wavered. In Ireland, always Catholic, the joy was unbounded. Archbishop Dowdall immediately prepared to hold a provincial synod at Drogheda, where enactments were made for depriving the conforming prelates and priests. Happily their number was so few that there was but little difficulty in making the

in his letters to Cromwell. He says one prebendary of St. Patrick's " thought scorn to read them." He adds : "They be in a manner all the same point with me. There are twenty-eight of them, and yet scarce one that favoureth God's Word."—State Papers, vol. iii. p. 6.

[8] Pertinacity.—The Victoria History of England, p. 256.

necessary arrangements. The only prelates that were removed were Browne, of Dublin ; Staples, of Meath; Lancaster, of Kildare ; and Travers, of Leighlin. Goodacre died a few months after his intrusion into the see of Armagh ; Bale, of Ossory, fled beyond the seas ; Casey, of Limerick, followed his example. All were English except the latter, and all, except Staples, were professing Protestants at the time of their appointment to their respective sees. Bale, who owed the Kilkenny people a grudge, for the indignant and rather warm reception with which they treated him on his intrusion into the see, gives a graphic account of the joy with which the news of Edward's death was received. The people " flung up their caps to the battlements of the great temple ;" set the bells ringing ; brought out incense and holy water, and formed once more a Catholic procession, chanting the *Sancta Maria, ora pro nobis*, as of old. In fact, " on the accession of Mary to the throne, so little had been done in the interest of the Reformation, that there was little or nothing to undo. She issued a licence for the celebration of Mass in Ireland, where no other service was or had been celebrated worth mentioning, and where no other supreme head had been ever in earnest acknowledged but the Pope."[9]

But the Irish obtained no temporal advantages during this reign— an illustration of the truth of what I have before remarked, that the nation has suffered almost as much from political as from religious causes. The work of extermination still went on. The boundaries of the Pale were increased thereby. Leix was designated the Queen's county, and the fort of Campa obtained the name of Maryborough, in compliment to the Queen. Offaly was named the King's county, and the fortress of Daingèan, Philipstown, in compliment to her Spanish consort.

In the year 1553 Gerald and Edward, the sons of the late Earl of Kildare, returned from exile, and were restored to the family honours and possessions. The Four Masters say that " there was great rejoicing because of their arrival, for it was thought that not one of the descendants of the Earls of Kildare or of the O'Connors Faly would ever again come to Ireland." They also mention that Margaret, a daughter of O'Connor Faly, went to England, " relying on the number of her friends and relatives there, and her knowledge of the English language, to request Queen Mary to restore

[9] *Pope.—Lib. Mun. Hib.* part i. p. 37.

her father to her." Her petition was granted, but he was soon after seized again by the English officials, and cast into prison.

Shane O'Neill made an unsuccessful attempt to recover his paternal dominions, in 1557. The following year his father died in captivity,[1] in Dublin, and he procured the murder of Ferdoragh, so that he was able to obtain his wishes without opposition. Elizabeth had now ascended the English throne (A.D. 1558), and, as usual, those in power, who wished to retain office, made their religion suit the views of the new ruler. The Earl of Sussex still continued Viceroy, and merely reversed his previous acts. Sir Henry Sidney also made his worldly interests and his religious views coincide. A Parliament was held in Dublin, in 1560, on the 12th of January. It was composed of seventy-six members, the representatives of ten counties, the remainder being citizens and burgesses of those towns in which the royal authority was predominant. " It is little wonder," observes Leland, " that, in despite of clamour and opposition, in a session of a few weeks, the whole ecclesiastical system of Queen Mary was entirely reversed." Every subject connected with this assembly and its enactments, demands the most careful consideration, as it has been asserted by some writers—who, however, have failed to give the proofs of their assertion—that the Irish Church and nation conformed at this time to the Protestant religion. This certainly was not the opinion of the Government officials, who were appointed by royal authority to enforce the Act, and who would have been only too happy could they have reported success to their mistress.

A recent writer, whose love of justice has led him to take a position in regard to Irish ecclesiastical history which has evoked unpleasant remarks from those who are less honest, writes thus: " There was not even the show of free action in the ordering of that Parliament, nor the least pretence that liberty of choice was

---

[1] *Captivity.*—Lord Chancellor Cusack addressed a very curious " Book on the State of Ireland" to the Duke of Northumberland, in 1552, in which he mentions the fearful condition of the northern counties. He states that "the cause why the Earl was detained [in Dublin Castle] was for the wasting and destroying of his county." This Sir Thomas Cusack, who took a prominent part in public affairs during the reign of Queen Elizabeth, was a son of Thomas Cusack, of Cassington, in Meath, an ancient Norman-Irish family, who were hereditary seneschals and sheriffs of that county.—*Ulster Arch. Jour.* vol. iii. p. 51.

to be given to it. The instructions given to Sussex, on the 10th of May, 1559, for making Ireland Protestant by Act of Parliament, were peremptory, and left no room for the least deliberation. Sussex had also other instructions (says Cox) to him and the Council, to set up the worship of God as it is in England, and make such statutes next Parliament as were lately made in England, *mutatis mutandis.* [Hist. Angl. Part I. p. 313.] It is plain that her Majesty's command is not sufficient warrant for a national change of faith, and that a convocation of bishops only is not the proper or legal representative assembly of the Church. It is also plain that the acts of an unwilling Parliament, and that Parliament one which does not deserve the name of a Parliament, cannot be justly considered as the acts of either the Irish Church or the Irish people."[2]

The official list of the members summoned to this Parliament, has been recently published by the Irish Archæological Society. More than two-thirds of the upper house were persons of whose devotion to the Catholic faith there has been no question; there were but few members in the lower house. No county in Ulster was allowed a representative, and only one of its borough towns, Carrickfergus, was permitted to elect a member. Munster furnished twenty members. No county members were allowed in Connaught, and it had only two boroughs, Galway and Athenry, from which it could send a voice to represent its wishes. The remaining fifty members were chosen from a part of Leinster. In fact, the Parliament was constituted on the plan before-mentioned. Those who were considered likely to agree with the Government, were allowed to vote; those of whose dissent there could be no doubt, were not allowed a voice in the affairs of the nation.

It might be supposed that, with the exception of a few members of the upper house, such a Parliament would at once comply with the Queen's wishes; but the majority made no secret of their intention to oppose the change of religion, and the penal code which should be enacted to enforce it. The Deputy was in an unpleasant position. Elizabeth would not easily brook the slightest opposition to her wishes. The Deputy did not feel prepared to encounter her anger, and he determined to avoid the difficulty, by having recourse

[2] *People.—The Irish Reformation,* by the Rev. W. Maziere Brady, D.D., fifth edition, pp. 32, 33.

to a most unworthy stratagem. First, he prorogued the house from the 11th of January to the 1st of February, 1560; and then took advantage of the first day of meeting, when but few members were present, to get the Act passed; secondly, he solemnly swore that the law should never be carried into execution, and by this false oath procured the compliance of those who still hesitated. I shall give authority for these statements.

The letter of Elizabeth, with her positive instructions to have the law passed, was dated October 18, 1559, and may be seen *in extenso* in the *Liber Munerum Hibernia,* vol. i. p. 113. There are several authorities for the dishonest course pursued by the Lord Deputy. The author of *Cambrensis Eversus* says: "The Deputy is said to have used force, and the Speaker treachery. I heard that it had been previously announced in the house that Parliament would not sit on that very day on which the laws against religion were enacted; but, in the meantime, a private summons was sent to those who were well known to be favourable to the old creed."[3] Father George Dillon, who died in 1650, a martyr to his charity in assisting the plague-stricken people of Waterford, gives the following account of the transaction: " James Stanihurst, Lord of Corduff, who was Speaker of the lower house, by sending private summons to some, without any intimation to the more respectable Irish who had a right to attend, succeeded in carrying that law by surprise. As soon as the matter was discovered, in the next full meeting of Parliament, there was a general protest against the fraud, injustice, and *deliberate treachery* of the proceeding; but the Lord Justice, having solemnly sworn that the law would never be carried into execution, the remonstrants were caught in the dexterous snare, and consented that the enactment should remain on the statute-book."[4] Dr. Rothe corroborates these statements, and records the misfortunes which followed the Speaker's family from that date.[5] Dr. Moran[6] has very acutely observed, that the day appointed for the opening of Parliament was the festival of St. Brigid, which was always kept with special solemnity in Ireland; therefore, the orthodox members would probably have absented themselves,

---

[3] *Creed.—Cambrensis Eversus,* vol. iii. p. 19.

[4] *Book.—Orationes et Motiva,* p. 87.

[5] *Date.—Analecta,* p. 387.

[6] *Dr. Moran.—Archbishops of Dublin,* p. 68. Further information may be obtained also in Curry's *Historical Review.*

unless informed of some business which absolutely required their attendance.

The Loftus MS., in Marsh's Library, and Sir James Ware, both mention the positive opposition of the Parliament to pass this law, and the mission of the Earl of Sussex to consult her Majesty as to what should be done with the refractory members. If he then proposed the treachery which he subsequently carried out, there is no reason to suppose her Majesty would have been squeamish about it, as we find she was quite willing to allow even more questionable methods to be employed on other occasions.

The Loftus MS. mentions a convocation of bishops which assembled this year, " by the Queen's command, for establishing the Protestant religion." The convocation was, if possible, a greater failure than the Parliament. If the bishops had obeyed the royal command, there would have been some record of their proceedings; but until the last few years, when the *ipse dixit* of certain writers was put forward as an argument—for proof it cannot be called—that the Irish Catholic bishops had conformed to the Protestant religion, so wild a theory was not even hazarded. It would be impossible here to go into details and proofs of the nonconformity of each bishop. The work has been already undertaken, with admirable success, by an Anglican clergyman.[7] I shall, however, give some of the impediments offered to the progress of the Reformation in the time of Queen Elizabeth, and of the cruel persecutions which were inflicted on those who dared to wish for liberty to worship God according to their conscience.

Notwithstanding the solemn promise of the Lord Deputy, the penal statutes against Catholics were carried out. In 1563 the Earl of Essex issued a proclamation, by which all priests, secular and

---

[7] *Clergyman.*—The Rev. W. Maziere Brady, D.D.   Mr. Froude remarks, in his *History of England*, vol. x. p. 480 : "There is no evidence that any of the bishops in Ireland who were in office at Queen Mary's death, with the exception of Curwin, either accepted the Reformed Prayer-Book, or abjured the authority of the Pope." He adds, in a foot-note : "I cannot express my astonishment at a proposition maintained by Bishop Mant and others, that the whole hierarchy of Ireland went over to the Reformation with the Government. In a survey of the country supplied to Cecil in 1571, after death and deprivation had enabled the Government to fill several sees, the Archbishops of Armagh, Tuam, and Cashel, with almost every one of the Bishops of the respective provinces, are described as *Catholici et Confederati*. The Archbishop of Dublin, with the Bishops of Kildare, Ossory, and Ferns, are alone returned as ' Protestantes.' "

regular, were forbidden to officiate, or even to reside in Dublin. Fines and penalties were strictly enforced for absence from the Protestant service; before long, torture and death were inflicted. Priests and religious were, as might be expected, the first victims. They were hunted into mountains and caves; and the parish churches and few monastic chapels which had escaped the rapacity of Henry VIII., were sacrificed to the sacrilegious emissaries of Elizabeth. Curry gives some account of those who suffered for the faith in this reign. He says: "Among many other Roman Catholic bishops and priests, there were put to death for the exercise of their function in Ireland, Globy O'Boyle, Abbot of Boyle, and Owen O'Mulkeran, Abbot of the Monastery of the Holy Trinity, hanged and quartered by Lord Grey, in 1580. John Stephens suffered the same punishment from Lord Burroughs, for saying Mass, in 1597; Thady O'Boyle was slain in his own monastery at Donegal; six friars were slain at Moynihigan; John O'Calyhor and Bryan O'Freeor were killed at their monastery in Ulster, with Felimy O'Hara, a lay brother. Eneus Penny was massacred at the altar of his own parish church, Killagh. Fourteen other priests died in Dublin Castle, either from hard usage, or the violence of torture.

Dr. Adam Loftus, the Protestant Archbishop of Armagh, was one of the most violent persecutors of the Catholics. In his first report to the Queen, dated May 17th, 1565, he describes the nobility of the Pale as all devoted to the ancient creed; and he recommends that they should be fined "in a good round sum," which should be paid to her Majesty's use, and "sharply dealt withal."[8] An original method of conversion, certainly! But it did not succeed. On the 22nd of September, 1590, after twenty-five years had been spent in the fruitless attempt to convert the Irish, he writes to Lord Burleigh, detailing the causes of the general decay of the Protestant religion in Ireland, and suggesting "how the same may be remedied." He advises that the ecclesiastical commission should be put in force, "for the people are poor, and fear to be fined." He requests that he and such commissioners as are "well affected in religion, may be permitted to imprison and fine all such as are obstinate and disobedient;" and he has no doubt, that "within a short time they will be reduced to good conformity." He concludes: "And *this*

---

[8] *Withal.*—Shirley, *Original Letters,* p. 194.

course of reformation, the sooner it is begun the better it will prosper; and the longer it is deferred, the more dangerous it will be." When Catholics remember that such words were written, and such deeds were enacted, by the head of the Protestant Church in Ireland, and sanctioned by the head of the Protestant Church in England, they may surely be content to allow modern controversialists the benefit of their pleasant dream that Catholic bishops conformed. If they had conformed to such doctrines and such practice, it can scarcely be seen what advantage the Anglican Establishment could gain from their parentage.

Seven years later, when the same prelate found that the more the Church was persecuted the more she increased, he wrote to advise pacification : " The rebels are increased, and grown insolent. I see no other cure for this cursed country but pacification, [he could not help continuing] until, hereafter, when the fury is passed, her Majesty may, with more convenience, correct the heads of those traitors."[9] The prelate was ably seconded by the Lord Deputy. Even Sir John Perrot, who has the name of being one of the most humane of these Governors, could not refrain from acts of cruelty where Catholics were concerned. On one occasion he killed fifty persons, and brought their heads home in triumph to Kilmallock, where he arranged them as a trophy round the cross in the public square. In 1582 he advised her Majesty "that friars, monks, Jesuits, priests, nuns, and such like vermin, who openly uphold the Papacy, should be executed by martial law."[1] The English officers seem to have rivalled each other in acts of cruelty. One is said to have tied his victim to a maypole, and then punched out his eyes with his thumbs.[2] Others amused themselves with flinging up infants into the air, and catching them on the points of their swords.[3] Francis Crosby, the deputy of Leix, used to hang men, women, and children on an immense tree which grew before his door, without any crime being imputed to them except their faith, and then to watch with delight how the unhappy infants hung by the long hair of their martyred mothers.[4]

---

[9] *Traitors.*—Letter of October 18, 1597.—State Paper Office.

[1] *Law.*—Letter to the Queen, in *Government of Ireland under Sir John Perrot*, p. 4.

[2] *Thumbs.*—Despatch of Castlerosse, in State Paper Office, London.

[3] *Swords.*—O'Sullivan Beare, *Hist. Cath.* p. 238.

[4] *Mothers.*—*Ibid.* p. 99.

Father Dominic à Rosario, the author of *The Geraldines*, scarcely exceeded truth when he wrote these memorable words : "This far-famed English Queen has grown drunk on the blood of Christ's martyrs ; and, like a tigress, she has hunted down our Irish Catholics, exceeding in ferocity and wanton cruelty the emperors of pagan Rome." We shall conclude this painful subject for the present with an extract from O'Sullivan Beare : "All alarm from the Irish chieftains being ceased, the persecution was renewed with all its horrors. A royal order was promulgated, that all should renounce the Catholic faith, yield up the priests, receive from the heretical minister the morality and tenets of the Gospel. Threats, penalties, and force were to be employed to enforce compliance. Every effort of the Queen and her emissaries was directed to despoil the Irish Catholics of their property, and exterminate them. More than once did they attempt this, for they knew that not otherwise could the Catholic religion be suppressed in our island, *unless by the extermination of those in whose hearts it was implanted ;* nor could their heretical teachings be propagated, while the natives were alive to detest and execrate them."[5]

In 1561 Sussex returned from England with reinforcements for his army, and marched to Armagh, where he established himself in the Cathedral. From thence he sent out a large body of troops to plunder in Tyrone, but they were intercepted by the redoubtable Shane O'Neill, and suffered so serious a defeat as to alarm the inhabitants of the Pale, and even the English nation. Fresh supplies of men and arms were hastily despatched from England, and the Earls of Desmond, Ormonde, Kildare, Thomond, and Clanrickarde assembled round the Viceregal standard to assist in suppressing the formidable foe. And well might they fear the lion-hearted chieftain ! A few years later, Sidney describes him as the only strong man in Ireland. The Queen was warned, that unless he were speedily put down, she would lose Ireland, as her sister had lost Calais. He had gained all Ulster by his sword, and ruled therein with a far stronger hand, and on a far firmer foundation, than ever any English monarch had obtained in any part of Ireland. Ulster was his *terra clausa ;* and he would be a bold, or, perhaps I should rather say, a rash man, who dare intrude in these dominions. He could muster seven thousand men in the field ; and

---

[5] *Them.—Hist. Cath.* p. 133.

though he seldom hazarded a general engagement, he "slew in divers conflicts 3,500 soldiers and 300 Scots of Sidney's army."[6] The English chronicler, Hooker, who lived in times when the blaze and smoke of houses and haggards, set on fire by Shane, could be seen even from Dublin Castle, declares that it was feared he intended to make a conquest over the whole land.

Even his letters are signed, if not written, in royal style.[7] He dates one *Ex finibus de Tirconail*, when about to wage war with the neighbouring sept of O'Donnell; he dates another, *Ex silvis meis*, when, in pursuance of his Celtic mode of warfare, he hastened into his woods to avoid an engagement with the English soldiers; he signs himself *Misi O'Neill*—Me, the O'Neill. As this man was too clever to be captured, and too brave to be conquered, a plan was arranged, with the full concurrence of the Queen, by which he might be got rid of by poison or assassination. Had such an assertion been made by the Irish annalists, it would have been scouted as a calumny on the character of "good Queen Bess;" but the evidence of her complicity is preserved in the records of the State Paper Office. I shall show presently that attempts at assassination were a common arrangement for the disposal of refractory Irish chieftains during this reign.

The proposal for this diabolical treachery, and the arrangements made for carrying it out, were related by Sussex to the Queen. He writes thus: "In fine, I brake with him to kill Shane, and bound myself by my oath to see him have a hundred marks of land to him and to his heirs for reward. He seemed desirous to serve your Highness, and to have the land, but fearful to do it, doubting his own escape after. I told him the ways he might do it, and how to escape after with safety; which he offered and promised to do." The Earl adds a piece of information, which, no doubt, he communicated to the intended murderer, and which, probably, decided him on making the attempt: "I assure your Highness he may do it without danger if he will; and if he will not do what he may in your service, there will be done to him what others may."[8]

Her Majesty, however, had a character to support; and whatever

---

[6] *Army.*—See Dr. Stuart's *History of Armagh*, p. 261.

[7] *Style.*—In one of the communications from Sussex to O'Neill, he complains of the chieftain's letters as being "*nimis superbe scriptæ.*"—State Papers for 1561.

[8] *May.*—Moore's *History of Ireland*, vol. iv. p. 33.

she may have privately wished and commanded, she was obliged to disavow complicity publicly. In two despatches from court she expresses her "displeasure at John Smith's horrible attempt to poison Shane O'Neill in his wine." In the following spring John Smith was committed to prison, and "closely examined by Lord Chancellor Cusake." What became of John is not recorded, but it is recorded that "Lord Chancellor Cusake persuaded O'Neill to forget the poisoning." His clan, however, were not so easily persuaded, and strongly objected to his meeting the Viceroy in person, or affording him an opportunity which he might not live to forget. About this time O'Neill despatched a document to the Viceroy for his consideration, containing a list of "other evill practices devised to other of the Irish nation within ix or tenn yeares past." The first item mentions that Donill O'Breyne and Morghe O'Breyne, his son, "required the benefit of her Majesty's laws, by which they required to be tried, and thereof was denied;"[9] and that when they came to Limerick under the protection of the Lord Deputy, they were proclaimed traitors, and their lands and possessions taken from them. Several other violations of protection are then enumerated, and several treacherous murders are recorded, particularly the murder of Art Boy Cavanagh, at Captain Hearn's house, after he had dined with him, and of Randall Boye's two sons, who were murdered, one after supper, and the other in the tower, by Brereton, "who escaped without punishment."

In October, 1562, Shane was invited to England, and was received by Elizabeth with marked courtesy. His appearance at court is thus described by Camden, A.D. 1562 : "From Ireland came Shane O'Neill, who had promised to come the year before, with a guard of axe-bearing galloglasses, their heads bare, their long curling hair flowing on their shoulders, their linen garments dyed with saffron, with long open sleeves, with short tunics, and furry cloaks, whom the English wondered at as much as they do now at the Chinese or American aborigines." Shane's visit to London was considered of such importance, that we find a memorandum in the State Paper Office, by "Secretary Sir W. Cecil, March, 1562," of the means to be used with Shane O'Neill, in which the first item is, that "he be procured to change his gar-

---

9 *Denied.*—This document has been printed in the *Ulster Arch. Jour.* vol. ii. p. 221, but the editor does not mention where the original was procured.

ments, and go like an Englishman."[1] But this was precisely what O'Neill had no idea of doing. Sussex appears to have been O'Neill's declared and open enemy. There is more than one letter extant from the northern chief to the Deputy. In one of these he says : "I wonder very much for what purpose your Lordship strives to destroy me." In another, he declares that his delay in visiting the Queen had been caused by the "amount of obstruction which Sussex had thrown in his way, by sending a force of occupation into his territory without cause ; for as long as there shall be one son of a Saxon in my territory against my will, from that time forth I will not send you either settlement or message, but will send my complaint through some other medium to the Queen." In writing to the Baron of Slane, he says that "nothing will please him [the Deputy] but to plant himself in my lands and my native territory, as I am told every day that he desires to be styled Earl of Ulster."

The Lord Chancellor Cusack appears, on the contrary, to have constantly befriended him. On 12th January, 1568, he writes of O'Neill's "dutifulness and most commendable dealing with the Scots ;" and soon after three English members of the Dublin Government complain that Cusack[2] had entrapped them into signing a letter to the unruly chieftain. There is one dark blot upon the escutcheon of this remarkable man. He had married the daughter of O'Donnell, Lord of one of the Hebrides. After a time he and his father-in-law quarrelled, and Shane contrived to capture O'Donnell and his second wife. He kept this lady for several years as his mistress ; and his own wife is said to have died of shame and horror at his conduct, and at his cruel treatment of her

[1] *Englishman.*—Moore, vol. iv. p. 37, has "like a gentleman," but the above is the correct reading. In 1584 Sir J. Perrot tried to get the Irish chieftains to attend Parliament clothed in the English fashion, and even offered them robes and cloaks of velvet and satin. The chieftains objected ; the Lord Deputy insisted. At last one of them, with exquisite humour, suggested that if he were obliged to wear English robes, a Protestant minister should accompany him attired in Irish garments, so that the mirth and amazement of the people should be fairly divided between them.—*Sir J. Perrot's Life*, p. 198.

[2] *Cusack.*—One reason, perhaps, was that the Chancellor always treated O'Neill with the respect due from one gentleman to another. Flemyng mentions, in a letter to Cecil, November 29, 1563, that O'Neill told him, when about to take the oaths of his people to an agreement with the Queen, that "Cusack did not give them their oath so, *but let me give them their oath.*"

father. English writers have naturally tried to blacken his character as deeply as possible, and have represented him as a drunkard
and a profligate; but there appears no foundation for the former
accusation. The foundation for the latter is simply what we
have mentioned, which, however evil in itself, would scarcely
appear so very startling to a court over which Henry VIII. had so
long presided.

After many attempts at assassination, *Shane-an-Diomais* [John
the Ambitious] fell a victim to English treachery. Sir William
Piers, the Governor of Carrickfergus, invited some Scotch soldiers
over to Ireland, and then persuaded them to quarrel with him, and
kill him. They accomplished their purpose, by raising a disturbance at a feast, when they rushed on the northern chieftain, and
despatched him with their swords. His head was sent to Dublin,
and his old enemies took the poor revenge of impaling it on the
Castle walls.

The Earl of Sussex was recalled from Ireland in 1564, and Sir
Henry Sidney was appointed Viceroy. The Earls of Ormonde and
Desmond had again quarrelled, and, in 1562, both Earls were summoned to court by the Queen. Elizabeth was related to the Butlers
through her mother's family, and used to boast of the loyalty of
the house of Ormonde. The Geraldines adhered to the ancient
faith, and suffered for it. A battle was fought at Affane, near
Cappoquin, between the two parties, in which Desmond was
wounded and made prisoner. The man who bore him from the
field asked, tauntingly: "Where is now the proud Earl of Desmond?" He replied, with equal pride and wit: "Where he should
be; upon the necks of the Butlers!"

GOLD EAR-RING, TORQUE PATTERN, FROM THE COLLECTION OF THE
R.I.A., FOUND AT CASTLEREA, CO. ROSCOMMON.

KILCOLMAN CASTLE.

CHAPTER XXVI.

Spenser's Castle—Sidney's Official Account of Ireland—Miserable State of the
Protestant Church—The Catholic Church and its Persecuted Rulers—The
Viceroy's Administration—A Packed Parliament and its Enactments—Claim
of Sir P. Carew—An Attempt to plant in Ulster—Smith's Settlement in the
Ards—His Description of the Native Irish—He tries to induce Englishmen
to join him—Smith is killed, and the attempt to plant fails—Essex next
tries to colonize Ulster—He dies in Dublin—Sidney returns to Ireland—
His Interview with Granuaile—Massacre at Mullamast—Spenser's Account
of the State of Ireland.

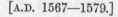
[A.D. 1567—1579.]

ILCOLMAN CASTLE, with its fair domains, were
bestowed on the poet Spenser, who had accompanied
Lord Grey to Ireland in 1579. He has left a fearful
description of the miseries of the country; but it
scarcely exceeds the official report of Sir Henry
Sidney, which must first be noticed. At the close
of the month of January, 1567, the Lord Deputy set
out on a visitation of Munster and Connaught. In
his official account he writes thus of Munster:
"Like as I never was in a more pleasant country
in all my life, so never saw I a more waste and
desolate land. Such horrible and lamentable spec-
tacles are there to behold—as the burning of villages,
the ruin of churches, the wasting of such as have
been good towns and castles ; yea, the view of the
bones and skulls of the dead subjects, who, partly by murder, partly

by famine, have died in the fields—as, in truth, hardly any Christian
with dry eyes could behold." He declares that, in the territory
subject to the Earl of Ormonde, he witnessed "a want of justice and
judgment." He describes the Earl of Desmond as "a man devoid
of judgment to govern, and will be to be ruled." The Earl of
Thomond, he says, "had neither wit of himself to govern, nor
grace or capacity to learn of others." The Earl of Clanrickarde he
describes as "so overruled by a putative wife, as ofttimes, when he
best intendeth, she forceth him to do the worst;" and it would
appear that neither he nor his lady could govern their own family,
for their sons were so turbulent they kept the whole country in
disturbance. In Galway he found the people trying to protect
themselves, as best they might, from their dangerous neighbours;
and at Athenry there were but four respectable householders, who
presented him with the rusty keys of their town—"a pitiful and
lamentable present;" and they requested him to keep those keys,
for "they were so impoverished by the extortions of the lords
about them, as they were no longer able to keep that town."

Well might he designate the policy by which the country had
been hitherto governed as "cowardly," and contemn the practice
of promoting division between the native princes, which was still
practised. He adds: "So far hath that policy, or rather lack of
policy, in keeping dissensions among them, prevailed, as now, albeit
all that are alive would become honest and live in quiet, yet there
are not left alive, in those two provinces, the twentieth person necessary to inhabit the same." Sidney at once proceeded to remedy
the evils under which the unfortunate country groaned, by enacting
other evils. We shall leave him to give his own account of his
proceedings. He writes thus, in one of his official despatches:
"I write not the names of each particular varlet that hath died
since I arrived, as well by the ordinary course of the law, as of the
martial law, as flat fighting with them, when they would take food
without the good will of the giver, for I think it no stuff worthy
the loading of my letters with; but I do assure you the number of
them is great, and some of the best, and the rest tremble. For most
part they fight for their dinner, and many of them lose their heads
before they be served with supper. Down they go in every corner,
and down they shall go, God willing."[3]

---

[3] *Willing.*—Sidney's Despatches, British Museum, MSS. Cat. Titus B. x.

When we remember Sidney's own description of the desolation of the country, and read of the fashion in which he remedied that desolation, we cannot wonder at the piteous account given a few years later by the English poet; for who could escape the threefold danger of " ordinary law, martial law, and flat fighting." Nor was the state of religious affairs at all more promising. The Deputy describes the kingdom as " overwhelmed by the most deplorable immorality and irreligion ;"[4] the Privy Council, in their deliberations, gives a similar account. " As for religion, there was but small appearance of it ; the churches uncovered, and the clergy scattered."[5] An Act of Parliament was then passed to remedy the evils which Acts of Parliament had created. In the preamble (11th Elizabeth, sess. iii. cap. 6) it mentions the disorders which Sidney had found, and complains of " the great abuse of the clergy in getting into the said dignities by force, simony, friendship, and other corrupt means, to the great overthrow of God's holy Church ;" and for remedy, the Act authorizes the *Lord Deputy* to appoint, for ten years, to all the ecclesiastical benefices of these provinces, with the exception of the cathedral churches of Waterford, Limerick, Cork, and Cashel.

But it was soon evident that Acts of Parliament could not effect ecclesiastical reform, though they might enforce exterior conformity to a new creed. In 1576, Sidney again complains of the state of the Irish Church, and addresses himself, with almost blasphemous flattery to the head of that body, " as to the only sovereign salve-giver to this your sore and sick realm, the lamentable state of the most noble and principal limb thereof—the Church I mean— as foul, deformed, and as cruelly crushed as any other part thereof, only by your gracious order to be cured, or at least amended. I would not have believed, had I not, for a greater part, viewed the same throughout the whole realm." He then gives a detailed account of the state of the diocese of Meath, which he declares to be the best governed and best peopled diocese in the realm ; and from his official report of the state of religion there, he thinks her Majesty may easily judge of the spiritual condition of less favoured districts. He says there are no resident parsons or vicars, and only a very simple or sorry curate appointed to serve them ; of them, only eighteen could speak English, the rest being " Irish ministers, or rather Irish rogues, having very little Latin, and less

[4] *Irreligion.*—Mant, vol. i. p. 287.   [5] *Scattered.*—Cox, vol. i. p. 319.

learning or civility."[6]　In many places he found the walls of the churches thrown down, the chancels uncovered, and the windows and doors ruined or spoiled—fruits of the iconoclastic zeal of the original reformers and of the rapacity of the nobles, who made religion an excuse for plunder.　He complains that the sacrament of baptism was not used amongst them, and he accuses the " prelates themselves" of despoiling their sees, declaring that if he told all he should make " too long a libel of his letter.　But your Majesty may believe it, that, upon the face of the earth where Christ is professed, there is not a Church in so miserable a case."

A Protestant nobleman, after citing some extracts from this document, concludes thus : " Such was the condition of a Church which was, half a century ago, rich and flourishing, an object of reverence, and a source of consolation to the people.　It was now despoiled of its revenues ; the sacred edifices were in ruins ; the clergy were either ignorant of the language of their flocks, or illiterate and uncivilized intruders ; and the only ritual permitted by the laws was one of which the people neither comprehended the language nor believed the doctrines.　And this was called establishing the Reformation !"[7]

It should be observed, however, that Sir Henry Sidney's remarks apply exclusively to the Protestant clergy.　Of the state of the Catholic Church and clergy he had no knowledge, neither had he any interest in obtaining information.　His account of the Protestant clergy who had been intruded into the Catholic parishes, and of the Protestant bishops who had been placed in the Catholic dioceses, we may presume to be correct, as he had no interest or object in misrepresentation ; but his observation concerning the neglect of the sacrament of baptism, may be taken with some limitation.　When a religious revolution takes place in a Catholic country, there is always a large class who conform exteriorly to whatever opinions may be enforced by the sword.　They have not the generosity to become confessors, nor the courage to become martyrs.　But these persons rarely renounce the faith in their hearts ; and sacrifice their conscience to their worldly interest, though not

[6] *Civility.*—Sidney's *Letters and Memorials*, vol. i. p. 112.　Sidney's memoir has been published *in extenso* in the *Ulster Arch. Journal*, with most interesting notes by Mr. Hore of Wexford.

[7] *Reformation.*—*Past and Present Policy of England towards Ireland*, p. 27. London, 1845.

without considerable uneasiness. In such cases, these apparently conforming Protestants would never think of bringing their children to be baptized by a minister of the new religion ; they would make no nice distinctions between the validity of one sacrament and another ; and would either believe that sacraments were a matter of indifference, as the new creed implied, or if they were of any value, that they should be administered by those who respected them, and that their number should remain intact. In recent famine years, the men who risked their spiritual life to save their temporal existence, which the tempter would only consent to preserve on his own terms, were wont to visit the church, and bid Almighty God a solemn farewell until better times should come. They could not make up their minds to die of starvation, when food might be had for formal apostacy ; they knew that they were denying their God when they appeared to deny their religion. It is more than probable that a similar feeling actuated thousands at the period of which we are writing ; and that the poor Celt, who conformed from fear of the sword, took his children by night to the priest of the old religion, that he might admit them, by the sacrament of baptism, into the fold of the only Church in which he believed.

It is also a matter of fact, that though the Protestant services were not attended, and the lives of the Protestant ministers were not edifying, that the sacraments were administered constantly by the Catholic clergy. It is true they date their letters "from the place of refuge" (e loco refugii nostri), which might be the wood nearest to their old and ruined parish-church, or the barn or stable of some friend, who dared not shelter them in his house ; yet this was no hindrance to their ministrations ; for we find Dr. Loftus complaining to Sir William Cecil that the persecuted Bishop of Meath, Dr. Walsh, was " one of great credit amongst his countrymen, and upon whom (as touching cause of religion) they wholly depend."[8] Sir Henry Sidney's efforts to effect reformation of conduct in the clergy and laity, do not seem to have been so acceptable at court as he might have supposed. His strong measures were followed by tumults ; and the way in which he obtained possession

[8] Depend.—Shirley, p. 219. An admirable History of the Diocese of Meath, in two volumes, has been published lately by the Rev. A. Cogan, Catholic priest of Navan. It is very much to be wished that this rev. author would extend his charitable labours to other dioceses throughout Ireland.

of the persons of some of the nobles, was not calculated to enhance his popularity. He was particularly severe towards the Earl of Desmond, whom he seized in Kilmallock, after requiring his attendance, on pretence of wishing him to assist in his visitation of Munster. In October, 1567, the Deputy proceeded to England to explain his conduct, taking with him the Earl of Desmond and his brother, John, whom he also arrested on false pretences. Sidney was, however, permitted to return, in September, 1568. He landed at Carrickfergus, where he received the submission of Turlough O'Neill, who had been elected to the chieftaincy on the death of Shane the Proud.

The first public act of the Lord Deputy was to assemble a Parliament, in which all constitutional rules were simply set at defiance (January 17th, 1569). Mayors and sheriffs returned themselves; members were sent up for towns not incorporated, and several Englishmen were elected as burgesses for places they had never seen. One of these men, Hooker, who was returned for Athenry, has left a chronicle of the age. He had to be protected by a guard in going to his residence. Popular feeling was so strongly manifested against this gross injustice, that the judges were consulted as to the legality of proceedings of whose iniquity there could be no doubt. The elections for non-corporate towns, and the election of individuals by themselves, were pronounced invalid; but a decision was given in favour of non-resident Englishmen, which still gave the court a large majority.[9] In this Parliament—if, indeed, it could be called such—Acts were passed for attainting Shane O'Neill, for suppressing the name, and for annexing Tyrone to the royal possessions. Charter schools were to be founded, of which the teachers should be English and Protestants; and the law before-mentioned, for permitting the Lord Deputy to appoint persons to ecclesiastical benefices for ten years, was passed.

Sir Philip Carew came to Ireland about this time, and renewed the claim of his family to possessions in Ireland. This plea had been rejected in the reign of Edward III.; but he now produced a forged roll, which the corrupt administration of the day readily admitted as genuine. His claim was made in right of Robert Fitz-Stephen, one of the first adventurers; his demand included one-half of the "kingdom of Cork," and the barony of Idrone, in Carlow. Several engagements ensued, in one of which Carew boasted of

[9] *Majority.*—Leland, vol. ii. p. 241.

having slain 400 Irish, and lost only one man. If his statement be true, it is probable the engagement was simply a massacre. The war became so formidable, that the MacCarthys, FitzGeralds, Cavanaghs, and FitzMaurices united against the "common enemy," and at last despatched emissaries to the Pope to implore his assistance. It is strange to find native Irish chieftains uniting with Anglo-Norman lords to resist an English settler.

Sidney now began to put his plan of local governments into execution; but this arrangement simply multiplied the number of licensed oppressors. Sir Edward Fitton was appointed President of Connaught, and Sir John Perrot, of Munster. Both of these gentlemen distinguished themselves by "strong measures," of which cruelty to the unfortunate natives was the predominant feature. Perrot boasted that he would "hunt the fox out of his hole," and devoted himself to the destruction of the Geraldines. Fitton arrested the Earl of Clanrickarde, and excited a general disturbance. In 1570 the Queen determined to lay claim to the possessions in Ulster, graciously conceded to her by the gentlemen who had been permitted to vote according to her royal pleasure in the so-called Parliament of 1569. She bestowed the district of Ards, in Down, upon her secretary, Sir Thomas Smith. It was described as "divers parts and parcels of her Highness' Earldom of Ulster that lay waste, or else was inhabited with a wicked, barbarous, and uncivil people." There were, however, two grievous misstatements in this document. Ulster did not belong to her Highness, unless, indeed, the Act of a packed Parliament could be considered legal; and the people who inhabited it were neither "wicked, barbarous, nor uncivil." The tract of country thus unceremoniously bestowed on an English adventurer, was in the possession of Sir Rowland Savage. His first ancestor was one of the most distinguished of the Anglo-Norman settlers who had accompanied De Courcy to Ireland. Thus, although he could not claim the prescriptive right of several thousand years for his possessions, he certainly had the right of possession for several centuries. An attempt had been made about ten years before to drive him out of part of his territory, and he had written a letter to "The Right Hon. the Earl of Sussex, Lieutenant-General of Ireland," asking for "justice," which justice he had not obtained. He was permitted to hold the Southern Ards, because he could not be expelled from it without considerable difficulty, and because it was the least valuable part of his property.

Smith confided the conduct of the enterprise to his natural son,
who has already been mentioned as the person who attempted to
poison Shane O'Neill.   The first State Paper notice of this enterprise is in a letter, dated February, 8, 1572, from Captain Piers to
the Lord Deputy, stating that the country is in an uproar "at Mr.
Smith coming over to plant in the north."   There is a rare black
letter still extant, entitled, "𝔏etter by 𝔍. 𝔅. on t𝔥e 𝔓eopling of t𝔥e 𝔄rdes,"
which Smith wrote to induce English adventurers to join him in
his speculation.   It is composed with considerable ability.   He con-
demns severely the degeneracy of the early English settlers, "who
allied and fostered themselves with the Irish."   He says that " England was never fuller of people than it is at this day," and attributes this to " the dissolution of abbeys, which hath doubled the
number of gentlemen and marriages."   He says the younger sons
who cannot " maintain themselves in the emulation of the world,"
as the elder and richer do, should emigrate ; and then he gives
glowing accounts of the advantages of this emigration.

Strange to say, one of the principal inducements he offers is that
the " churle of Ireland is very simple and toylsomme man, desiring
nothing but that he may not be eaten out with ceasse [rent], coyne,
and liverie."   He passes over the subject of rent without any comment, but he explains very fully how " the churle is eaten up" with
the exactions of " coyne and liverie."   He says these laborious Irish
will gladly come " to live under us, and to farm our ground ;" but
he does not say anything about the kind of treatment they were to
receive in return for their labour.   His next inducement is the immense sale (and profit) they might expect by growing corn ; and he
concludes by relieving their fears as to any objections which the
inhabitants of this country might make to being dispossessed from
their homes and lands, or any resistance they might offer.   He considers it immaterial, "for the country of Lecale [which had been
taken in a similar manner from Savage] was some time kept by
Brereton with a hundred horses, and Lieutenant Burrows kept *Castle
Rean* [Castlereagh], and went daily one quarter of a mile to fetch
his water, against five hundred Irish that lay again him."

Smith concludes with " an offer and order" for those who wished
to join in the enterprise.   Each footman to have a pike,[1] or hal-

---

[1] *Pike.*—This was probably the *Morris pike* or Moorish pike, much used in
the reign of Henry VIII. and Elizabeth.   The common pike was used very

berd, or caliver, and a convenient livery cloak, of red colour or carnation, with black facings. Each horseman to have a staffe[2] and a case of dagges,[3] and his livery[4] to be of the colour aforesaid.

Strype wrote a life of Sir Thomas Smith, Bart., Oxford, 1620. He mentions this attempt at colonizing Ulster, having this good design therein : " that those half-barbarous people might be taught some civility." He speaks of " the hopeful gentleman," Sir Thomas Smith's son, and concludes with stating how the expedition terminated : " But when matters went on thus fairly, Mr. Smith was intercepted and slain by a wild Irishman."

Before his assassination Smith had written an account of his proceedings to his father, in which he says that " envy had hindered him more than the enemy," and that he had been ill-handled by some of his own soldiers, ten of whom he had punished. He also expresses some fear of the native Irish, whom he had tried to drive out of their lands, as he says they sometimes " lay wait to intrap and murther the maister himself."

I have given details of this attempted plantation in Ulster, because it illustrates the subject ; and each plantation which will be recorded afterwards, was carried out on the same plan. The object of the Englishman was to obtain a home and a fortune; to do this he was obliged to drive the natives out of their homes, and to deprive them of their wealth, whether greater or less. The object of the Irishman was to keep out the intruder ; and, if he could not be kept out, to get rid of him by fair means or foul.

It is probable that the attempt of Smith was intended by Govern-

generally by foot soldiers until the reign of George II. The halberd was introduced during the reign of Henry VIII. It was peculiar to the royal guard, and is still carried by them. In Shirley's comedy, *A Bird in a Cage* (1633), one of the characters is asked, " You are one of the guard ?" and replies, " A poor halberd man, sir." The caliver was quite recently introduced. It was a light kind of musket, fired without a rest. It derived its name from the *calibre* or width of its bore.

[2] *Staffe.*—This was probably a cane staff. We read in *Piers Plowman's Vision* of " hermits on a heap with hookyd staves."

[3] *Dagges.*—" Pistols."—" My *dagge* was levelled at his heart."

[4] *Livery.*—It was usual for all retainers of a noble house to wear a uniform-coloured cloth in dress. Thus, in the old play of *Sir Thomas More*, we find :

> " That no man whatsoever
> Do walk without the *livery* of his lord,
> Either in cloak or any other garment."

ment principally as an experiment to ascertain whether the plantation could be carried out on a larger scale. The next attempt was
made by Walter Devereux, Earl of Essex, who received part of the
signories of Clannaboy and Ferney, provided he could expel the
" rebels " who dwelt there. Essex mortgaged his estates to the
Queen to obtain funds for the enterprise. He was accompanied by
Sir Henry Kenlis, Lord Dacres, and Lord Norris' three sons.

Sir William FitzGerald, the then Lord Deputy, complained loudly
of the extraordinary powers granted to Essex; and some show of
deference to his authority was made by requiring the Earl to receive
his commission from him. Essex landed in Ireland in 1573, and
the usual career of tyranny and treachery was enacted. The native
chieftains resisted the invasion of their territories, and endeavoured
to drive out the men whom they could only consider as robbers.
The invaders, when they could not conquer, stooped to acts of treachery. Essex soon found that the conquest of Ulster was not
quite so easy a task as he had anticipated. Many of the adventurers who had assumed his livery, and joined his followers, deserted
him; and Brian O'Neill, Hugh O'Neill, and Turlough O'Neill rose
up against him. Essex then invited Conn O'Donnell to his camp ;
but, as soon as he secured him, he seized his Castle of Lifford, and
sent the unfortunate chieftain a prisoner to Dublin.

In 1574 the Earl and Brian O'Neill made peace. A feast was
prepared by the latter, to which Essex and his principal followers
were invited; but after this entertainment had lasted for three
days and nights, "as they were agreeably drinking and making
merry, Brian, his brother, and his wife were seized upon by the
Earl, and all his people put unsparingly to the sword—men, women,
youths, and maidens—in Brian's own presence. Brian was afterwards sent to Dublin, together with his wife and brother, where
they were cut in quarters. Such was the end of their feast. This
wicked and treacherous murder of the lord of the race of Hugh
Boy O'Neill, the head and the senior of the race of Eoghan, son of
Nial of the Nine Hostages, and of all the Gaels, a few only
excepted, was a sufficient cause of hatred and dispute to the English
by the Irish."[5]

---

[5] *Irish.*—Four Masters, vol. v. pp. 1678-9. Camden mentions the capture
of O'Neill, and says Essex slew 200 of his men; but he does not mention the
treachery with which this massacre was accomplished.

Essex visited England in 1575, and tried to induce the Queen to give him further assistance in his enterprise. On her refusal, he retired to Ireland, and died in Dublin, on the 22nd September, 1576. It was rumoured he had died of poison, and that the poison was administered at the desire of the Earl of Leicester, who soon after divorced his own wife, and married the widow of his late rival Essex complained bitterly, in his letter to Sir Henry Sidney, of the way in which he had been treated in his projected plantation of Clannaboy, and protested against the injustice which had been done through him on O'Donnell, MacMahon, and others, who were always peaceable and loyal, but "whom he had, on the pledged word of the Queen, undone with fair promises." Probably, only for his own " undoing," he would have had but scant pity for others.

Yet Essex could be generous and knightly with his friends, kind and courtly, at least to his English dependents. There are some curious accounts of his expenses while he was " *Lord-General of Ulster*," in a State Paper, from which it will appear that he could be liberal, either from natural benevolence or from policy. The entries of expenditure indicate a love of music, which he could easily gratify in Ireland, still famous for the skill of its bards. He gave ten shillings to the singing men of Mellifont, then inhabited by Edward Moore, to whom it had been granted at the suppression of monasteries. A harper at Sir John Bellew's received three shillings; "Crues, my Lord of Ormonde's harper," received the large sum of forty shillings, but whether in compliment to the bard or the bard's master is doubtful. The Earl of Ormonde's "musicians" also got twenty shillings. But there are other disbursements, indicating that presents were gratefully received and vails expected. "A boy that brought your lordship a pair of greyhounds" had a small donation; but "M'Genis, that brought your lordship two stags," had 13s. 4d., a sum equivalent to £7 of our money. Nor were the fair sex forgotten, for Mrs. Fagan, wife of the Lord Mayor of Dublin, was presented with a piece of taffeta " for good entertainment."

Sir Henry Sidney returned to Ireland in 1575. He tells us himself how he took on him, "the third time, that thanklesse charge; and so taking leave of her Majesty, kissed her sacred hands, with most gracious and comfortable wordes, departed from her at Dudley Castell, passed the seas, and arrived the xiii of September, 1575, as nere the city of Dublin as I could saufly; for at that tyme the city was greevously infested with the contagion of the pestilence."[6]   He proceeded thence to Tredagh (Drogheda), where he received the sword of the then Deputy.   He next marched northward, and attacked Sorley Boy and the Scotch, who were besieging Carrickfergus; and after he had conquered them, he received the submission of Turlough O'Neill and other Ulster chieftains.   Turlough's wife, the Lady Agnes O'Neill, *née* M'Donnell, was aunt to the Earl of Argyle, and appears to have been very much in favour with the Lord Deputy.

In the " depe of wynter" he went to Cork, were he remained from Christmas to Candlemas.   He mentions his entertainment at Barry's Court with evident zest, and says " there never was such a Christmas kept in the same."   In February he visited Thomond, and subdued " a wicked generation, some of whom he killed, and some he hanged by order of law."   A nice distinction, which could hardly have been appreciated by the victims.   The Earl of Clanrickarde caused his " two most bade and rebellious sonnes" to make submission, "whom I would to God I had then hanged."   However, he kept them close prisoners, and " had a sermon made of them and their wickedness in the chief church in the town."   John seems to have been the principal delinquent.   Some time after, when they had been set at liberty, they rebelled again; and he records the first " memorable act" which one of them had done, adding, " which I am sure was John."[7]

Sidney then marched into the west, and had an interview with the famous Grace O'Malley, or Granuaile, which he describes thus : " There came to me also a most famous femynyne sea captain, called Granuge I'Mally, and offered her services unto me wheresoever I would command her, with three galleys and two hundred fighting men.   She brought with her her husband, for she was as well by sea as by land more than master's-mate with him.   He was of the nether Burkes, and called by nickname Richard in Iron.   This was a notorious woman in all the coasts of Ireland.   This woman did Philip Sidney

---

[6] *Pestilence.*—Memoir or Narrative addressed to Sir Francis Walsingham, 1583. Ware says he wrote "Miscellanies of the Affairs of Ireland," but the MS. has not yet been discovered.   The Four Masters notice the pestilence, which made fearful ravages.

[7] *John.*—He was called *Shane Seamar Oge*, or John of the Shamrocks, from having threatened to live on shamrocks sooner than submit to the English. John was the younger of the two De Burgos or Burkes.

see, and speak with ; he can more at large inform you of her."
Grana, or Grace O'Malley, was the daughter of a chieftain of the
same patronymic. Her paternal clan were strong in galleys and
ships. They owned a large territory on the sea-coast, besides the
islands of Arran. Her first husband was Donnell O'Flaherty. His
belligerent propensities could scarcely have been less than hers, for
he is termed *Aith Chogaid*, or "of the wars." Her second husband,
Sir Richard Burke, or Richard *an Iarainn*, is described by the Four
Masters as a "plundering, warlike, unjust, and rebellious man."
He obtained his soubriquet from the circumstance of constantly ap-

CARRIG-A-HOOLY—GRACE O'MALLEY'S CASTLE.

pearing in armour. It would appear from this account that Sidney's
statement of the Lady Grana being "more than master's-mate with
him," must be taken with some limitations, unless, indeed, he who
ruled his foes abroad, failed to rule his wife at home, which is quite
possible. The subjoined illustration represents the remains of one
of her castles. It is situated near the lake of Borrishoole, in the
county Mayo. The ruins are very striking, and evince its having
once been an erection of considerable strength.

Sir William Drury was made Lord President of Munster, 1576,
in place of Sir John Perrot. Sir Nicholas Malby was installed in the

same office in Connaught ; but the barbarities enacted by his predecessor, Fitton, made the very name of president so odious, that
Sidney gave the new Governor the title of Colonel of Connaught.
The Earl of Desmond and Drury were soon at variance. Sidney
says, in his *Memoir*, that the Earl " was still repyning at the government of Drury." After causing great apprehension to the governors, the Lord Deputy sent the whole party to Kilkenny, and found
the " Earl hot, wilful, and stubborn ; but not long after, as you
know, he and his two brothers, Sir John and Sir James, fell into
actual rebellion, in which the good knight, Sir William Drury, the
Lord Justice, died, and he, as a malicious and unnatural rebel, still
persisteth and liveth."

In 1577 serious complications were threatened, in consequence of
the pecuniary difficulties of the crown. An occasional subsidy had
been granted hitherto for the support of the Government and the
army ; an attempt was now made to convert this subsidy into a
tax. On previous occasions there had been some show of justice,
however little reality, by permitting the Parliament to pass the
grant; a scheme was now proposed to empower the Lord Deputy
to levy assessments by royal authority, without any reference to
Parliament. For the first time the Pale opposed the Government,
and resisted the innovation. But their opposition was speedily
and effectually silenced. The deputies whom they sent to London
to remonstrate were committed to the Tower, and orders were
despatched to Ireland that all who had signed the remonstrance
should be consigned to Dublin Castle.

It is said that Elizabeth was not without some misgivings as
to the injustice with which her Irish subjects were treated, and that
she was once so touched by the picture presented to her of their
sufferings under such exactions, that she exclaimed : " Ah, how I
fear lest it be objected to us, as it was to Tiberius by Bato, concerning the Dalmatian commotions ! You it is that are in fault,
who have committed your flocks, not to shepherds, but to wolves."
Nevertheless, the " wolves" were still permitted to plunder; and any
impression made on the royal feelings probably evaporated under
the fascinating influence of her next interview with Leicester, and
the indignation excited by a " rebel " who refused to resign his
ancestral home quietly to some penniless adventurer. There had
been serious difficulties in England in 1462, in consequence of the
shameful state of the current coin ; and the Queen has received

considerable praise for having accomplished a reform. But the idea, and the execution of the idea, originated with her incomparable minister, Cecil, whose master-mind applied itself with equal facility to every state subject, however trifling or however important; and the loss and expenditure which the undertaking involved, was borne by the country to the last penny. Mr. Froude says it was proposed that the "worst money might be sent to Ireland, as the general dust-heap for the outcasting of England's vileness."[8] The standard for Ireland had always been under that of England, but the base proposal above-mentioned was happily not carried into execution. Still there were enough causes of misery in Ireland apart from its normal grievances. The Earl of Desmond wrote an elaborate and well-digested appeal to Lord Burleigh, complaining of military abuses, and assuring his Lordship that if he had " sene them [the poor who were burdened with cess], he would rather give them charitable alms than burden them with any kind of chardge." He mentions specially the cruelty of compelling a poor man to carry for five, eight, or ten miles, on his back, as many sheaves as the " horseboies" choose to demand of him ; and if he goes not a "good pace, though the poor soule be overburdened, he is all the waye beaten outt of all measure."

Cess was also commanded to be delivered at the " Queen's price," which was considerably lower than the market price. Even Sidney was supposed to be too lenient in his exactions ; but eventually a composition of seven years' purveyance, payable by instalments, was agreed upon, and the question was set at rest. The Queen and the English Council naturally feared to alienate the few nobles who were friendly to them, as well as the inhabitants of the Pale, who were as a majority in their interest.

The Pale was kept in considerable alarm at this period, by the exploits of the famous outlaw, Rory Oge O'More. In 1577 he stole into Naas with his followers, and set the town on fire ; after this exploit he retired, without taking any lives. He continued these depredations for eighteen years. In 1571 he was killed by one of MacGillapatrick's men, and the Pale was relieved from a most formidable source of annoyance. But the same year in which this brave outlaw terminated his career, is signalized by one of the most fearful acts of bloodshed and treachery on record. The heads of the

---

[8] *Vileness.—Reign of Elizabeth*, vol. i. p. 458.

Irish families of Offaly and Leix, whose extirpation had long been attempted unsuccessfully, were invited in the Queen's name, and under the Queen's protection, to attend a conference at the great rath on the hill of Mullach-Maistean (Mullamast). As soon as they had all assembled, they were surrounded by a treble line of the Queen's garrison soldiers, and butchered to a man in cold blood.

This massacre was performed with the knowledge and approval of the Deputy, Sir Henry Sidney. The soldiers who accomplished the bloody work were commanded by Captain Francis Crosby, to whom the chief command of all the kerne in the Queen's pay was committed. We have already related some incidents in his career, which show how completely destitute he was of the slightest spark of humanity.[9]

Sir Henry Sidney retired from office finally on the 26th of May, 1578. He dates his *Memoir* from " Ludlow Castell, with more payne than harte, the 1st of March, 1582." In this document he complains bitterly of the neglect of his services by Government, and bemoans his losses in piteous strains. He describes himself as " fifty-four yeres of age, toothlesse and trembling, being five thousand pounds in debt." He says he shall leave his sons £20,000 worse off than his father left him. In one place he complains that he had not as much ground as would " feede a mutton," and he evidently considers his services were worth an ampler remuneration ; for he declares : " I would to God the country was yet as well as I lefte it almost fyve yeres agoe." If he did not succeed in obtaining a large grant for his services, it certainly was not for want of asking it ; and if he did not succeed in pacifying the country, it was not for lack of summary measures. Even in his postscript he mentions how he hanged a captain of Scots, and he thinks " véry nere twenty of his men."

It seems almost needless to add anything to the official descriptions of Ireland, which have already been given . in such detail ;

---

[9] *Humanity.*—Dr. O'Donovan, with his usual conscientious accuracy, has given a long and most interesting note on the subject of this massacre, in the *Annals of the Four Masters*, vol. v. p. 1695. Dowling is the oldest writer who mentions the subject, and he expressly mentions Crosby and Walpole as the principal agents in effecting it. Dr. O'Donovan gives a curious traditional account of the occurrence, in which several Catholic families are accused of having taken part.

but as any remark from the poet Spenser has a special interest, I shall give some brief account of his *View of Ireland*. The work which bears this name is written with considerable prejudice, and abounds in misstatements. Like all settlers, he was utterly disgusted with the hardships he endured, though the poet's eye could not refuse its meed of admiration to the country in which they were suffered. His description of the miseries of the native Irish can scarcely be surpassed, and his description of the poverty of the country is epitomized in the well-known lines :—

> " Was never so great waste in any place,
> Nor so foul outrage done by living men ;
>   For all the cities they shall sack and raze,
> And the green grass that groweth they shall burn,
> That even the wild beast shall die in starved den."[1]

Yet this misery never touched his heart ; for the remedy he proposes for Irish sufferings is to increase them, if possible, a thousandfold ; and he would have troops employed to " tread down all before them, and lay on the ground all the stiff-necked people of the land." And this he would have done in winter, with a refinement of cruelty, that the bitter air may freeze up the half-naked peasant, that he may have no shelter from the bare trees, and that he may be deprived of all sustenance by the chasing and driving of his cows.

It is probable that Spenser's " view" of Irish affairs was considerably embittered by his own sufferings there. He received his property on the condition of residence, and settled himself at Kilcolman Castle. Here he spent four years, and wrote the three first books of the *Faerie Queene*. He went to London with Sir Walter Raleigh to get them published. On his return he married a country girl, named Elizabeth—an act which was a disgrace to himself, if the Irish were what he described them to be. In 1598, during Tyrone's insurrection, his estate was plundered, his castle burned, and his youngest child perished in the flames. He then fled to London, where he died a year after in extreme indigence.

His description of the condition of the Protestant Church coincides with the official account of Sidney. He describes the clergy as "generally bad, licentious, and most disordered;" and he adds: " Whatever

---

[1] *Den.—Faerie Queene*, book iii. c. 3.

disorders[2] you see in the Church of England, you may find in Ireland, and many more, namely, gross simony, greedy covetousness,
incontinence, and careless sloth." And then he contrasts the zeal of
the Catholic clergy with the indifference of "the ministers of the
Gospel," who, he says, only take the tithes and offerings, and
gather what fruit else they may of their livings.

[2] *Disorders.*—"In many dioceses in England (A.D. 1561), a third of the
parishes were left without a clergyman, resident or non-resident. . . . . The
children grew up unbaptized; the dead buried their dead." Elizabeth had to
remonstrate with Parliament upon the "open decays and ruins" of the
churches. "They were not even kept commonly clean, and nothing was done
to make them known to be places provided for divine service." "The cathedral plate adorned the prebendal sideboards and dinner-tables. The organ
pipes were melted into dishes for their kitchens. The organ frames were
carved into bedsteads, where the wives reposed beside their reverend lords.
The copes and vestments were slit into gowns and bodices. Having children
to provide for, the chapters cut down their woods, and worked their fines . . . .
for the benefit of their own generation." "The priests' wives were known by
their dress in the street, and their proud gait, from a hundred other women."—
Froude, *Reign of Elizabeth,* vol. i. pp. 465-467.

THE HOUSE WHERE SIR WALTER RALEIGH LIVED.

SALTEE ISLANDS, WEXFORD.

CHAPTER XXVII.

FitzMaurice obtains Help from Spain and from Rome—The Martyrs of Kil-
mallock—Death of FitzMaurice—Drury's Cruelties and Death—Arrival of
San José—His Treachery—Massacre at the Fort del Ore—O'Neill shows
Symptoms of Disaffection—Treacherous Capture of O'Donnell—Injustice to
Tenants—O'Donnell attempts to Escape—O'Neill's Marriage with Mabel
Bagnal—O'Donnell Escapes from Dublin Castle—Causes of Discontent—
Cruel Massacre of Three Priests—Tortures and Death inflicted in Dublin on
Bishop O'Hurley—O'Neill's Insurrection—His Interview with Essex—He
marches to the South—His Fatal Reverse at Kinsale—The Siege of Dun-
boy—O'Neill's Submission—Foundation of Trinity College, Dublin, on the
Site and with the Funds of a Catholic Abbey.

[A.D. 1579–1605.]

EXAGGERATED rumours were now spread throughout Munster, of the probability of help from
foreign sources—A.D. 1579. James FitzMaurice
had been actively employed on the Continent
in collecting troops and assistance for the Irish
Catholics. In France his requests were politely
refused, for Henry III. wished to continue on
good terms with Elizabeth. Philip II. of Spain
referred him to the Pope. In Rome he met with
more encouragement; and at the solicitation of the
Franciscan Bishop of Killaloe, Cornelius O'Mull-
rain, Dr. Allen, and Dr. Saunders, he obtained a
Bull, encouraging the Irish to fight for the recovery
of religious freedom, and for the liberation of their
country. An expedition was fitted out at the

expense of the Holy See, and maintained eventually by Philip of Spain. At the earnest request of FitzMaurice, an English adventurer, named Stukeley, was appointed admiral. The military command was bestowed on Hercules Pisano, a soldier of some experience.

Stukeley was reported to be an illegitimate son of Henry VIII. He was a wild and lawless adventurer, and entirely unfitted for such a command. At Lisbon he forsook his squadron, and joined the expedition which Sebastian, the romantic King of Portugal, was preparing to send to Morocco. FitzMaurice had travelled through France to Spain, from whence he proceeded to Ireland, with a few troops. He had three small vessels besides his own, and on his way he captured two English ships. He was accompanied by Dr. Saunders,[3] as Legate, the Bishop of Killaloe, and Dr. Allen.[4] They were entirely ignorant of Stukeley's desertion until their arrival in Ireland. The squadron reached Dingle on the 17th of July, 1579. Eventually they landed at Smerwick Harbour, and threw themselves into the Fort del Ore, which they fortified as best they could. If the Earl of Desmond had joined his brother at once, the expedition might have ended differently; but he stood aloof, fearing to involve himself in a struggle, the issue of which could scarcely be doubtful.

A short time before the arrival of this little expedition, three persons had landed in disguise at Dingle, whom Desmond, anxious to show his zeal towards the ruling powers, consigned to the authorities in Limerick. They were discovered to be Dr. Patrick O'Haly, a Franciscan, and Bishop of Mayo, and Father Cornelius O'Rourke; the name of the third person has not been ascertained. On Sir William Drury's arrival at Kilmallock, they were brought before him, and condemned to torture and death. The torture was executed with unusual barbarity, for Drury was a man who knew no mercy. The confessors were first placed upon the rack, and then, as if the agony of that torment was not sufficient, their hands and feet were broken with large hammers, and other torments were added. When life was nearly extinct, they were released, and their martyrdom was finally accomplished by hanging. For fourteen

---

[3] *Dr. Saunders.*—He has given a full and most interesting account of this expedition, in a letter to the Roman court. The original has been printed by Monsignor Moran, in his *Archbishops*, a work which every reader should possess.

[4] *Dr. Allen.*—He was a medical man, and was killed in an engagement immediately after the arrival of the expedition.

days their bodies remained suspended in chains, and the soldiers used them as targets in their shooting exercises.

The Earl of Desmond, however, soon joined his brother. John Geraldine allied himself with the movement from its commencement. A second expedition was fitted out in Spain, which reached Ireland on the 13th of September, 1580. It was commanded by Colonel Sebastian San José, who proved eventually so fearful a traitor to the cause he had volunteered to defend. Father Mathew de Oviedo, a member of the Franciscan Order, was the principal promoter of this undertaking. He was a native of Spain, and had been educated in the College of Salamanca, then famous for the learning and piety of its *alumni*. The celebrated Florence Conry, subsequently Archbishop of Tuam, was one of his companions; and when he entered the Franciscan novitiate, he had the society of eleven brethren who were afterwards elevated to the episcopate. Oviedo was the bearer of a letter from the Roman Pontiff, Gregory XIII., granting indulgences to those who joined the army.

On the 18th of August, scarcely a month after he had landed in Ireland, James FitzMaurice was killed by Theobald and Ulick Burke, his own kinsmen. Their father, Sir William Burke, was largely rewarded for his loyalty in opposing the Geraldines; and, if Camden is to be believed, he died of joy in consequence of the favours heaped upon him. The death of FitzMaurice was a fatal blow to the cause. John Geraldine, however, took the command of the force; but the Earl hastened to Kilmallock to exculpate himself, as best he could, with the Lord Deputy. His apologies were accepted, and he was permitted to go free on leaving his only son, James, then a mere child, as hostage with Drury. The Geraldines were successful soon after in an engagement with the English; and Drury died in Waterford at the end of September. Ecclesiastical historians say that he had been cited by the martyrs of Kilmallock to meet them at Christ's judgment, and answer for his cruelties.

Sir Nicholas Malby was left in command of the army, and Sir William Pelham was elected Lord Deputy in Dublin. The usual career of burning and plundering was enacted—"the country was left one levelled plain, without corn or edifices." Youghal was burned to the ground, and the Mayor was hanged at his own door. James Desmond was hanged and quartered, by St. Leger and Raleigh, in Cork. Pelham signalized himself by cruelties, and executed a gentleman who had been blind from his birth, and another who was over a hundred years of age.

But the crowning tragedy was at hand. The expedition commanded by San José now arrived in Ireland. The Fort del Ore was once more occupied and strengthened; the courage of the insurgents was revived. Meanwhile Lord Grey was marching southward with all possible haste. He soon reached the fort, and, at the same time, Admirals Winter and Bingham prepared to attack the place by sea. In a few days the courage of the Spanish commander failed, and he entered into treaty with the Lord Deputy. A bargain was made that he should receive a large share of the spoils. He had obtained a personal interview in the Viceroy's camp,[5] and the only persons for whom he made conditions were the Spaniards who had accompanied him on the expedition. The English were admitted to the fortress on the following day, and a feast was prepared for them. All arms and ammunition were consigned to the care of the English soldiers, and, this accomplished, the signal for massacre was given; and, according to Lord Grey's official[6] account, 600 men were slain in cold blood. So universal was the reprobation of this fearful tragedy, that Sir Richard Bingham tried to make it appear that it had not been premeditated. Grey's official despatch places the matter beyond question, and Dr. Saunders' letter supplies the details on authority which cannot be disputed.

Three persons who had been treacherously given up to the Viceroy, were spared for special torments; those were—a priest named Law-

[5] *Camp.*—Dr. Saunders' letter, Moran's *Archbishops*, p. 202.

[6] *Official.*—Lord Grey says, in his official despatch to the Queen, dated "From the camp before Smerwick, November 12, 1580:" "I sent streighte certeyne gentlemen to see their weapons and armouries laid down, and to guard the munition and victual, then left, from spoil; *then put in certeyne bandes, who streighte fell to execution. There were* 600 *slayn.*" After this exploit, "Grey's faith"—*Graia fides*—became proverbial even on the Continent. Grey appears to have a touch of the Puritan (by anticipation) in his composition, for we find him using very unctuous language about one John Cheeke, who "so wrought in him God's Spirit, plainlie declairing him a child of His elected;" and he calls the Pope "a detestable shaveling." Raleigh is said to have had the execution of this butchery; his friend, Spenser, was "not far off," according to his own account. He has attempted to excuse his patron, Lord Grey, but his excuse simply shows that the massacre was reprobated by all persons not destitute of common humanity.

rence, an Englishman named William Willick, and Oliver Plunket. They were offered liberty if they would renounce the faith ; but on their resolute refusal, their legs and arms were broken in three places, and after they had been allowed to pass that night and the next day in torment, they were hanged and quartered. The State Papers confirm the account given by Saunders of these barbarities. The English officers now endeavoured to rival each other in acts of cruelty, to obtain official commendation and royal favour. Sir Walter Raleigh was especially active in Cork, and brought a charge of treason against the Barrys and Roches, old English settlers; but Barry set fire to his castle, and took to the woods, where he joined Lord Desmond. Lord Roche was taken prisoner, but eventually escaped from his persecutors. Pretended plots were rumoured in all directions, and numbers of innocent persons were executed. William Burke was hanged in Galway, and forty-five persons were executed. The Geraldine cause was reduced to the lowest ebb by the treachery of José. The Earl of Desmond and his sons were fugitives in their own country. The latter was offered pardon if he would surrender Dr. Saunders, the Papal Legate, but this he resolutely refused. Saunders continued his spiritual ministrations until he was entirely worn out with fatigue, and he died, at the close of the year 1581, in a miserable hovel in the woods of Claenglass. He was attended by the Bishop of Killaloe, from whom he received the last rites of the Church.

Immense rewards were now offered for the capture of the Geraldine leaders, but their faithful followers would not be bribed. John was at length seized, through the intervention of a stranger. He was wounded in the struggle, and died immediately after ; but his enemies wreaked their vengeance on his remains, which were gibbeted at Cork. The Earl of Desmond was assassinated on the 11th of November, 1583, and the hopeless struggle terminated with his death. He had been hunted from place to place like a wild beast, and, according to Hooker, obliged to dress his meat in one place, to eat it in another, and to sleep in a third. He was surprised, on one occasion, while his soldiers were cooking their mid-day meal, and five-and-twenty of his followers were put to the sword ; but he escaped, and fled to Kerry, where he was apprehended and slain. His head was sent to Elizabeth, and impaled on London-bridge, according to the barbarous practice of the time. His body was interred in the little chapel of Kilnamaseagh, near

Castleisland. Complaints of the extreme severity of Lord Grey's administration had been sent to the English court. Even English subjects declared that he had " left her Majesty little to reign over but carcasses and ashes." He was therefore recalled. The administration was confided to Loftus, the Protestant Archbishop of Dublin, and Sir Henry Wallope, and an amnesty was proclaimed. Sir Thomas Norreys was appointed Governor of Munster, and Sir Richard Bingham, Governor of Connaught. In 1584 Sir John Perrot was made Deputy, and commenced his career by executing Beg O'Brien, who had taken an active part in the late insurrections, at Limerick, with a refinement of cruelty, as " a warning to future evil-doers."

In 1585 Perrot held a Parliament in Dublin, from which, however, no very important enactments proceeded. Its principal object appears to have been the confiscation of Desmond's estates. This was opposed by many of the members ; but the crown was determined to have them, and the crown obtained them. Thus lands to the extent of 574,628 acres were ready for new adventurers. The most tempting offers were made to induce Englishmen to plant ; estates were given for twopence an acre ; rent was only to commence after three years. No Irish families were to be admitted as tenants, though their labours might be accepted or compelled. English families were to be substituted in certain proportions ; and on these conditions, Raleigh, Hatton, Norris, St. Leger, and others, obtained large grants. The Irish question was to be settled finally, but somehow it was not settled, though no one seemed exactly prepared to say why.

Meanwhile Sir Richard Bingham was opposing the conciliatory policy of the Deputy, and hanged seventy persons at one session in Galway, in January, A.D. 1586. Perrot interfered ; but the Burkes, who had been maddened by Bingham's cruelties, broke out into open rebellion ; and he pointed to the revolt which he had himself occasioned, as a justification of his former conduct. The Scotch now joined the Burkes, but were eventually defeated by the President, the Irish annalists say, with the loss of 2,000 men. Another bloody assize was held in Galway, where young and old alike were victims.

The state of Ulster was now giving considerable anxiety to the English Government. Hugh O'Neill was just commencing his famous career ; and although he had fought under the English standard in the Geraldine war, it was thought quite possible that he might set up a standard of his own. He had taken his seat in Parliament as Baron of Dungannon. He had obtained the title of Earl of Tyrone. He had visited Elizabeth, and by a judicious mixture of flattery and deference, which she was never able to resist, he obtained letters-patent under the Great Seal restoring his inheritance and his rank. He was even permitted, on his return, to keep up a standing army of six companies, " to preserve the peace of the north."

In 1586 a thousand soldiers were withdrawn from Ireland to serve in the Netherlands; and as the country was always governed by force, it could scarcely be expected not to rebel when the restraint was withdrawn. O'Neill manifested alarming symptoms of independence. He had married a daughter of Sir Hugh O'Donnell, and Sir Hugh refused to admit an English sheriff into his territory. The Government had, therefore, no resource but war or treachery. War was impossible, when so large a contingent had been withdrawn; treachery was always possible; and even Sir John Perrot stooped to this base means of attaining his end. The object was to get possession of Hugh Roe O'Donnell, a noble youth, and to keep him as hostage. The treachery was accomplished thus : a vessel, laden with Spanish wine, was sent to Donegal on pretence of traffic. It anchored at Rathmullen, where it had been ascertained that Hugh Roe O'Donnell was staying with his foster-father, Mac-Sweeny. The wine was distributed plentifully to the country people; and when MacSweeny sent to make purchases, the men declared there was none left for sale, but if the gentlemen came on board, they should have what was left. Hugh and his companions easily fell into the snare. They were hospitably entertained, but their arms were carefully removed, the hatches were shut down, the cable cut, and the ship stood off to sea. The guests who were not wanted were put ashore, but the unfortunate youth was taken to Dublin, and confined in the Castle.[7]

In 1588 Sir John Perrot was succeeded by Sir William FitzWilliam, a nobleman of the most opposite character and disposition. Perrot

---

[7] *Castle.*—The Four Masters give a detailed account of this treachery, taken from the life of Hugh Roe O'Donnell, which was written by one of themselves. A copy of this work, in the handwriting of Edward O'Reilly, is still preserved in the Library of the Royal Irish Academy.

was generally regretted by the native Irish, as he was considered one of the most humane of the Lord Deputies.   The wreck of the Spanish Armada occurred during this year, and was made at once an excuse for increased severity towards the Catholics, and for acts of grievous injustice.   Even loyal persons were accused of harbouring the shipwrecked men, as it was supposed they might have obtained some treasure in return for their hospitality.   FitzWilliam, according to Ware, wished to "finger some of it himself," and invaded the territories of several Irish chieftains.   A complete history of FitzWilliam's acts of injustice, and the consummate cruelty with which they were perpetrated, would be so painful to relate, that they can scarcely be recorded in detail.   He farmed out the country to the highest bidders, who practised every possible extortion on the unfortunate natives.   The favourite method of compelling them to yield up their lands without resistance, was to fry the soles of their feet in boiling brimstone and grease.   When torture did not succeed, some unjust accusation was brought forward, and they were hanged.   A tract preserved in Trinity College, Dublin, gives details of these atrocities, from which I shall only select one instance.   A landlord was anxious to obtain the property of one of his tenants, an Irishman, who had lived "peaceably and quietly, as a good subject," for many years.   He agreed with the sheriff to divide the spoil with him, if he would assist in the plot.   The man and his servant were seized; the latter was hanged, and the former was sent to Dublin Castle, to be imprisoned on some pretence.   The gentleman and the sheriff at once seized the tenant's property, and turned his wife and children out to beg.   After a short time, "they, by their credit and countenance, being both English gentlemen, informed the Lord Deputy so hardly of him, as that, without indictment or trial, they executed him."[8]

It was considered a grave reproach, and an evidence of barbarism, when Maguire sent word to the Lord Deputy, who wished to send a sheriff to Fermanagh: "Your sheriff will be welcome, but let me know his eric [the fine which would be levied on the district if he were killed], that if my people cut off his head, I may levy it on the country."   One other instance from another source will sufficiently prove that the dread of an English sheriff was well founded.   The

[8] *Him.*—This document was written by Captain Lee, and presented to the Queen in 1594. It is printed in *Desiderata Curiosa Hibernica*, vol. ii. p. 91.

chieftain of Oriel, Hugh MacMahon, had given a present of 600 cows to the Lord Deputy to recognize his rights. Sir Henry Bagnal, the Marshal of Ireland, had his head-quarters at Newry, where his property had been principally acquired by deeds of blood, and he wished for a share of the spoil. A charge of treason was made against MacMahon after the cows had been accepted; a jury of common soldiers was empannelled to try the case. A few were Irish, and they were locked up without food until they agreed to give the required verdict of guilty, while the English jurors were permitted to go in and out as they pleased. The unfortunate chieftain was hanged, in two days after his arrest, at his own door; his property was divided amongst those whom we must call his murderers. The MacMahon sept were, however, permitted to retain a portion on payment of a " good fine, underhand," to the Lord Deputy.[9]

In 1590, Hugh of the Fetters, an illegitimate son of the famous Shane O'Neill, was hanged by the Earl of Tyrone, for having made false charges against him to the Lord Deputy. This exercise of authority excited considerable fear, and the Earl was obliged to clear himself of blame before Elizabeth. After a brief detention in London, he was permitted to return to Ireland, but not until he had signed certain articles in the English interest, which he observed precisely as long as it suited his convenience. About this time his nephew, Hugh O'Donnell, made an ineffectual attempt to escape from Dublin Castle, but he was recaptured, and more closely guarded. This again attracted the attention of Government to the family; but a more important event was about to follow. O'Neill's wife was dead, and the chieftain was captivated by the beauty of Sir Henry Bagnal's sister. How they contrived to meet and to plight their vows is not known, though State Papers have sometimes revealed as romantic particulars. It has been discovered, however, from that invaluable source of information, that Sir Henry was furious, and cursed himself and his fate that his " bloude, which had so often been spilled in reppressinge this rebellious race, should nowe be mingled with so traitorous a stocke and kindred." He removed the lady from Newry to her sister's house, near Dublin, who was the wife of Sir Patrick Barnwell. The Earl followed Miss Bagnal

---

[9] *Deputy.*—Four Masters, vol. vi. p. 1878. The State Papers clearly prove the Deputy's guilt.

thither. Her brother-in-law received him courteously ; and while
the O'Neill engaged the family in conversation, a confidential friend
rode off with the lady, who was married to O'Neill immediately
after.

But a crisis was approaching; and while this event tended to
embitter the English officials against the Earl, a recurrence of outrages against the northern chieftains prepared them for revolt. One
of their leading men, O'Rourke, was executed this year (A.D. 1591)
in London. He had taken refuge in Scotland some time before,
from those who wished to take his life, as the easiest method of securing his property, but the Scots had given him up to the English
Government. He was said to be one of the handsomest and bravest
men of his times, and his execution excited universal pity. The
apostate, Miler Magrath, attempted to tamper with his faith in his
last moments, but the chieftain bade him rather to repent himself,
and to return to the faith of his fathers.

Hugh O'Donnell made another attempt to escape from confinement at Christmas, A.D. 1592. He succeeded on this occasion,
though his life was nearly lost in the attempt. Turlough Roe
O'Hagan, his father's faithful friend, was the principal agent in
effecting his release. Henry and Art O'Neill, sons of Shane the
Proud, were companions in his flight. They both fell exhausted
on their homeward journey. Art died soon after, from the effects
of fatigue and exposure, and Hugh recovered but slowly. He continued ill during the remainder of the winter, and was obliged to
have his toes amputated. As soon as he was sufficiently recovered,
a general meeting of his sept was convened, when he was elected to
the chieftaincy, and inaugurated in the usual manner. He then commenced incursions on the territories occupied by the English ; but
as the Earl of Tyrone was anxious to prevent a premature rebellion,
he induced the Lord Deputy to meet him at Dundalk, where he
obtained a full pardon for his escape from Dublin Castle, and a temporary pacification was arranged.

In 1593 he collected another army; Turlough Luineach resigned
his chieftaincy to the Earl of Tyrone ; and Ulster became wholly
the possession of its old chieftains—the O'Neill and O'Donnell. An
open rebellion broke out soon after, in consequence of the exactions
of two English officers on the territories of Oge O'Rourke and
Maguire. Several trifling engagements took place. The Earl of
Tyrone was placed in a difficult position. He was obliged to join

the English side, while his heart and inclination were with his own people; but he contrived to send a messenger to Hugh Roe, who had joined Maguire's party, requesting him not to fight against him. He was placed in a still greater difficulty at the siege of Enniskillen, which took place the following year; but he compromised matters by sending his brother, Cormac O'Neill, with a contingent, to fight on the national side. Cormac met the English soldiers, who had been sent to throw provisions into the town, almost five miles from their destination, and routed them with great slaughter. The site of the engagement was called the "Ford of the Biscuits," from the quantity of that provision which he obtained there. An Irish garrison was left at Enniskillen, and the victorious party, after retaliating the cruelties which had been inflicted on the natives, marched into northern Connaught to attack Sir Richard Bingham.

On the 11th of August, in this year, 1594, Sir William Russell was appointed Deputy in place of FitzWilliam. Tyrone appeared at the Castle soon after, and complained of the suspicions which were entertained of his loyalty, not, it is to be supposed, without a very clear personal conviction that they were well founded. The Viceroy would have received him favourably, but his old enemy, Bagnal, charged him with high treason. O'Neill's object was to gain time. He was unwilling to revolt openly, till he could do so with some prospect of success; and if his discretion was somewhat in advance of the average amount of that qualification as manifested by Irish chieftains hitherto, his valour redeemed him from all possible imputation of having made it an excuse for cowardice, or any conciliation with the "English enemy," which was not warranted by motives of prudence.

Tyrone now offered to clear himself by the ordeal of single combat with his adversary, but Bagnal declined the offer. The following year (A.D. 1595), the new Deputy took O'Byrne's Castle, at Glenmalure. One of the Kildare Geraldines revenged the injuries done to this chieftain, by making nocturnal attacks in the neighbourhood of Dublin; but he was soon captured, and hanged in Dublin. These and similar outrages excited popular feeling to an unwonted degree; but there were other wrongs besides the robberies of chieftains' estates, and their subsequent murder if they resisted oppression. The men whose lives the Irish nation have always held even more sacred than those of their most ancient chiefs, were daily slaughtered before their eyes, and the slaughter was perpetrated with cruelties which were so utterly uncalled-for, so barbarously inhuman, that they might well have excited the burning indignation of a heathen or a Turk.

These men were the priests of the old faith which the Irish had received so many hundred years before, and which neither death nor torments could induce them to forsake. I shall mention but two of these outrages, premising that there were few places in Ireland where similar scenes had not been enacted. In the year 1588 three Franciscan fathers were martyred, who had devoted themselves for some years previously to the spiritual necessities of the people. Many Catholic families from Carlow, Wexford, and Wicklow had been obliged to fly into the mountainous districts of Leinster, to escape further persecution. The three fathers, John Molloy, Cornelius Dogherty, and Wilfred Ferral, were unwearied in their ministrations. They spoke to these poor creatures of the true Home, where all their sufferings should be rewarded with eternal joy—of how wise it was to exchange the passing things of time for the enduring goods of eternity; they visited the sick, they consoled the dying; above all, they administered those life-giving sacraments so precious to the Catholic Christian; and if, like the holy martyrs, persecuted by heathen emperors, they were obliged to offer the adorable sacrifice on a rock or in a poor hut, it was none the less acceptable to God, and none the less efficacious to the worshippers. These shepherds of the flock were specially obnoxious to the Government. They preached patience, but they were accused of preaching rebellion; they confirmed their people in their faith, but this was supposed to be equivalent to exciting them to resist their oppressors. The three fathers were at last seized by a party of cavalry, in a remote district of the Queen's county. They were tied hand and foot, and conducted with every species of ignominy to the garrison of Abbeyleix. Here they were first flogged, then racked, and finally hanged,[1] drawn, and quartered. The soldiers, brutalized as man can be brutalized by familiarity with scenes of blood, scoffed at the agonies they inflicted, and hardened themselves for fresh barbarities. But there were men who stood by to weep and pray; and though they were obliged to conceal their tears, and to breathe their prayers softly into the eternal and ever-open

---

[1] *Hanged.*—It was usual to hang the Franciscans by their own cord, or to tie them together with their cords, and hurl them from the summit of a tower or from a high rock into the sea

ear of God, the lash which mangled the bodies of the men they revered lacerated their souls yet more deeply; and as they told to others the tale of patient suffering endured for Christ and His Church, the hearts of the people were bound yet closer to their faithful pastors, and they clung yet more ardently to the religion which produced such glorious examples.

The other execution is, if possible, more barbarous. If the duty of an historian did not oblige me to give such details, I would but too gladly spare you the pain of reading and myself the pain of writing them. The name of Dermod O'Hurley has ever stood prominent in the roll of Irish martyrs. He was a man of more than ordinary learning, and of refined and cultivated tastes; but he renounced even the pure pleasures of intellectual enjoyments for the poor of Christ, and received for his reward the martyr's crown. After he had taught philosophy in Louvain and rhetoric at Rheims, he went to Rome, where his merit soon attracted the attention of Gregory XIII., who appointed him to the see of Cashel. O'Sullivan describes his personal appearance as noble and imposing, and says that "none more mild had ever held the crozier of St. Cormac." His position was not an enviable one to flesh and blood; but to one who had renounced all worldly ties, and who only desired to suffer like his Lord, it was full of promise. His mission was soon discovered; and though he complied with the apostolic precept of flying, when he was persecuted, from one city to another, he was at last captured, and then the long-desired moment had arrived when he could openly announce his mission and his faith.

When he had informed his persecutors that he was a priest and an archbishop, they at once consigned him to "a dark and loathsome prison, and kept him there bound in chains till the Holy Thursday of the following year (1584)." He was then summoned before the Protestant Archbishop Loftus and Wallop. They tempted him with promises of pardon, honour, and preferment; they reasoned with him, and urged all the usual arguments of heretics against his faith; but when all had failed, they declared their determination to use "other means to change his purpose." They did use them—they failed. But these were the means: the Archbishop was again heavily ironed. He was remanded to prison. His persecutors hastened after him; and on the evening of Thursday, May 5, 1584, they commenced their cruel work. They tied him firmly to a tree, as his Lord had once been tied. His hands were bound, his body chained, and then his feet and legs were thrust into long boots, filled with oil, turpentine, and pitch, and stretched upon an iron grate, under which a slow fire was kindled. The spectacle which was exhibited when the instruments of torture were withdrawn has been described, but I cannot write the description. What sufferings he must have endured during that long night, no words could tell. Again he was tempted with the offer of earthly honours, and threatened with the vengeance of prolonged tortures. Through all his agony he uttered no word of complaint, and his countenance preserved its usual serene and tranquil expression. His sister was sent to him, as a last resource, to tempt him to apostatize, but he only bade her ask God's forgiveness for the crime she had committed. Meanwhile, the cruelties which had been executed on him became known; public feeling, as far as it was Catholic, was excited; and it was determined to get rid of the sufferer quietly. At early dawn of Friday, May 6, 1584, he was carried out to the place now called Stephen's-green, where what remained of human life was quickly extinguished, first by putting him again to torture, and then by hanging.

O'Neill had hitherto acted merely on the defensive; but the memory of the events just related was still fresh in the minds of thousands, and it was generally felt that some effort must be made for freedom of conscience, if not for deliverance from political oppression. A conference was held at Dundalk. Wallop, the Treasurer, whose name has been so recently recorded in connexion with the torture of the Archbishop, and Gardiner, the Chief Justice, received the representatives of the northern chieftains, but no important results followed.

In 1598 another conference was held, the intervening years having been spent in mutual hostilities, in which, on the whole, the Irish had the advantage. O'Neill's tone was proud and independent; he expected assistance from Spain, and he scorned to accept a pardon for what he did not consider a crime. The Government was placed in a difficult position. The prestige of O'Neill and O'Donnell was becoming every day greater. On the 7th of June, 1598, the Earl laid siege to the fort of the Blackwater, then commanded by Captain Williams, and strongly fortified. Reinforcements were sent to the besieged from England, but they were attacked *en route* by the Irish, and lost 400 men at Dungannon. At last the Earl of Ormonde and Bagnal determined to take up arms—the former marching against the Leinster insurgents; the latter, probably but too willing, set out to encounter his old enemy and brother-in-law. He commanded a fine body of men, and had but little doubt on which side victory should declare itself.

The contingent set out for Armagh on the 14th of August, and soon reached the Yellow Ford, about two miles from that city, where the main body of the Irish had encamped. They were at once attacked on either flank by skirmishers from the hostile camp; but the vanguard of the English army advanced gallantly to the charge, and were soon in possession of the first entrenchments of the enemy. Although Bagnal's personal valour is unquestionable, he was a bad tactician. His leading regiment was cut to pieces before a support could come up; his divisions were too far apart to assist each other. Bagnal raised the visor of his helmet for one moment, to judge more effectually of the scene of combat, and that moment proved his last. A musket ball pierced his forehead, and he fell lifeless to the ground. Almost at the same moment an ammunition waggon exploded in his ranks—confusion ensued. O'Neill took advantage of the panic; he charged boldly; and before one o'clock the rout had become general.

The English officers and their men fled to Armagh, and shut themselves up in the Cathedral; but they had left twenty-three officers and 1,700 rank and file dead or dying on the field. " It was a glorious victory for the rebels," says Camden, " and of special advantage; for thereby they got both arms and provisions, and Tyrone's name was cried up all over Ireland. Ormonde thought that the " devil had bewitched Bagnal," to leave his men unsupported; the Irish annalists thought that Providence had interfered wonderfully on their behalf.[2] O'Neill retired for a time to recruit his forces, and to rest his men; and a revolt was organized under his auspices in Munster, with immense success. O'Donnell was making rapid strides; but a new Viceroy was on his way to Ireland, and it was hoped by the royalist party that he would change the aspect of affairs.

Essex arrived on the 15th of April, 1599. He had an army of 20,000 foot and 2,000 horse—the most powerful, if not the best

[2] *Behalf.*—The Four Masters give copious details of this important engagement, which O'Donovan has supplemented with copious notes, vol. vi. pp. 2061-2075.

equipped force ever sent into the country. He at once issued a proclamation, offering pardon to all the insurgents who should submit, and he despatched reinforcements to the northern garrison towns, and to Wicklow and Naas. He then marched southward, not without encountering a sharp defeat from Rory O'More. He attacked the Geraldines, without much success, in Fermoy and Lismore, having, on the whole, lost more than he had accomplished by the expedition. An engagement took place between O'Donnell and Sir Conyers Clifford, in the pass of Balloghboy, on the 16th of August, in which Conyers was killed, and his army defeated. His body was recognized by the Irish, towards whom he had always acted honorably, and they interred the remains of their brave and noble enemy with the respect which was justly due to him.

Essex wrote to England for more troops, and his enemies were not slow to represent his incapacity, and to demand his recall : but he had not yet lost grace with his royal mistress, and his request was granted. The Viceroy now marched into the northern provinces. When he arrived at the Lagan, where it bounds Louth and Monaghan, O'Neill appeared on the opposite hill with his army, and sent the O'Hagan, his faithful friend and attendant, to demand a conference. The interview took place on the following day; and O'Neill, with chivalrous courtesy, dashed into the river on his charger, and there conversed with the English Earl, while he remained on the opposite bank. It was supposed that the Irish chieftain had made a favourable impression on Essex, and that he was disposed to conciliate the Catholics. He was obliged to go to Englan d to clear himself of these charges ; and his subsequent arrest and execution would excite more sympathy, had he been as amiable in his domestic relations as he is said to have been in his public life.

Ulster enjoyed a brief period of rest under the government of its native princes. In 1600 O'Neill proceeded southward, laying waste the lands of the English settlers, but promoting the restoration of churches and abbeys, and assisting the clergy and the native Irish in every possible way. Having lost Hugh Maguire, one of his best warriors, in an accidental engagement with St. Leger, the President of Munster, he determined to return to Ulster. A new Viceroy had just arrived in Ireland, and he attempted to cut off his retreat ineffectually.

O'Neill had now obtained a position of considerable importance, and one which he appears to have used invariably for the general

Interview between Essex and O'Neill.

good. The fame of his victories [3] had spread throughout the Continent. It was well known now that the Irish had not accepted the Protestant Reformation, and it appeared as if there was at last some hope of permanent peace in Ireland.

Sir George Carew was sent over as President of Munster. He has left an account of his exploits in the *Pacata Hibernia*, which are not very much to the credit of his humanity, but which he was pleased to consider refined strokes of policy. The English Government not only countenanced his acts, but gave the example of a similar line of conduct. James, son of Gerald, Earl of Desmond, who had long been imprisoned in London, was now sent to Ireland, and a patent, restoring his title and estates, was forwarded to Carew, with private instructions that it should be used or not, as might be found expedient. The people flocked with joy to meet the heir of the ancient house, but their enthusiasm was soon turned into contempt. He arrived on a Saturday, and on Sunday went to the Protestant service, for he had been educated in the new religion in London. His people were amazed; they fell on their knees, and implored him not to desert the faith of his fathers; but he was ignorant of their language as well as of their creed. Once this was understood, they showed how much dearer that was to them than even the old ties of kindred, so revered in their island; and his return from prayers was hailed by groans and revilings. The hapless youth was found to be useless to his employers; he was therefore taken back to London, where he died soon after of a broken heart.

Attempts were made to assassinate O'Neill in 1601. £2,000 was offered to any one who would capture him alive; £1,000 was offered for his head; but none of his own people could be found to play the traitor even for so high a stake. The "Sugane Earl" was treacherously captured about the end of August, and was sent to London in chains, with Florence MacCarthy. But the long-expected aid from Spain had at last arrived. The fleet conveyed a force of 3,000 infantry, and entered the harbour of Kinsale on the 23rd of September, under the command of Don Juan d'Aquila. It would appear

---

[3] *Victories.*—The victory of the Blackwater was hailed with salvos of artillery from S. Angelo. The Pope and Philip III. of Spain corresponded with O'Neill constantly, the one about the affairs of the Church, the other with generous offers of assistance. At one time the Emperor sent him 22,000 crowns of gold.

as if Spanish expeditions were not destined to succeed on Irish soil, for only part of the expedition arrived safely, and they had the misfortune to land in the worst situation, and to arrive after the war had ceased. The northern chieftains set out at once to meet their allies when informed of their arrival; and O'Donnell, with characteristic impetuosity, was the first on the road. Carew attempted to intercept him, but despaired of coming up with " so swift-footed a general," and left him to pursue his way unmolested.

The Lord Deputy was besieging Kinsale, and Carew joined him there. The siege was continued through the month of November, during which time fresh reinforcements came from Spain; and on the 21st of December, O'Neill arrived with all his force. Unfortunately, the Spanish general had become thoroughly disgusted with the enterprise; and, although the position of the English was such that the Lord Deputy had serious thoughts of raising the siege, he insisted on decisive measures; and O'Neill was obliged to surrender his opinion, which was entirely against this line of action. A sortie was agreed upon for a certain night; but a youth in the Irish camp, who had been in the President's service formerly, warned him of the intended attack. This was sufficient in itself to cause the disaster which ensued. But there were other misfortunes. O'Neill and O'Donnell lost their way; and when they reached the English camp at dawn, found the soldiers under arms, and prepared for an attack. Their cavalry at once charged, and the new comers in vain struggled to maintain their ground, and a retreat which they attempted was turned into a total rout.

A thousand Irish were slain, and the prisoners were hanged without mercy. The loss on the English side was but trifling. It was a fatal blow to the Irish cause. Heavy were the hearts and bitter the thoughts of the brave chieftains on that sad night. O'Neill no longer hoped for the deliverance of his country; but the more sanguine O'Donnell proposed to proceed at once to Spain, to explain their position to King Philip. He left Ireland in a Spanish vessel three days after the battle—if battle it can be called; and O'Neill marched rapidly back to Ulster with Rory O'Donnell, to whom Hugh Roe had delegated the chieftaincy of Tir-Connell.

D'Aquila, whose haughty manners had rendered him very unpopular, now surrendered to Mountjoy, who received his submission with respect, and treated his army honorably. According to one account, the Spaniard had touched some English gold, and had thus been induced to desert the Irish cause ; according to other authorities, he challenged the Lord Deputy to single combat, and wished them to decide the question at issue. In the meantime, O'Sullivan Beare contrived to get possession of his own Castle of Dunboy, by breaking into the wall at the dead of night, while the Spanish garrison were asleep, and then declaring that he held the fortress for the King of Spain, to whom he transferred his allegiance. Don Juan offered to recover it for the English by force of arms ; but the Deputy, whose only anxiety was to get him quietly out of the country, urged his immediate departure. He left Ireland on the 20th of February ; and the suspicions of his treachery must have had some foundation, for he was placed under arrest as soon as he arrived in Spain.

The siege of Dunboy is one of the most famous and interesting episodes in Irish history. The castle was deemed almost impregnable from its situation ; and every argument was used with Sir George Carew to induce him to desist from attacking it. It was then, indeed—

"Dunboy, the proud, the strong,
The Saxon's hate and trouble long."[4]

But the Lord Deputy had resolved that it should be captured. The Lord President considered the enterprise would be by no means difficult, for " he declared that he would plant the ordnance without the losse of a man; and within seven dayes after the battery was begun, bee master of all that place."[5] There was considerable delay in the arrival of the shipping which conveyed the ordnance, and operations did not commence until the 6th of June. The defence of the castle was intrusted by O'Sullivan to Richard MacGeoghegan. The chief himself was encamped with Tyrrell in the interior of the country. The soldiers were tempted, and the governor was tempted, but neither flinched for an instant from their duty. The garrison only consisted of 143 fighting men, with a few pieces of cannon. The besieging army was about 3,000 strong, and they were amply supplied with ammunition. On the 17th of June, when the castle was nearly shattered to pieces, its brave defenders offered to surrender if they were allowed to depart with their arms; but the only reply vouchsafed was to hang their messenger, and to commence an assault.

[4] *Long.—Dunboy and other Poems,* by T. D. Sullivan, Esq.
[5] *Place.—Hibernia Pacata,* vol. ii. p. 559.

The storming party were resisted for an entire day with undaunted bravery. Their leader was mortally wounded, and Taylor
took the command. The garrison at last retreated into a cellar,
into which the only access was a narrow flight of stone steps, and
where nine barrels of gunpowder were stored. Taylor declared he
would blow up the place if life were not promised to those who surrendered. Carew refused, and retired for the night, after placing a
strong guard over the unfortunate men. The following morning
he sent cannon-ball in amongst them, and Taylor was forced by his
companions to yield without conditions. As the English soldiers
descended the steps, the wounded MacGeoghegan staggered towards
the gunpowder with a lighted candle, and was in the act of throwing it in, when he was seized by Captain Power, and in another
moment he was massacred. Fifty-eight of those who had surrendered were hanged immediately ; a few were reserved to see if they
could be induced to betray their old companions, or to renounce
their faith ; but as they " would not endeavour to merit life,"[6] they
were executed without mercy. One of these prisoners was a Father
Dominic Collins.   He was executed in Youghal, his native town—
a most unwise proceeding; for his fate was sure to excite double
sympathy in the place where he was known, and, consequently, to
promote double disaffection.[7]   O'Sullivan Beare assigns the 31st of
October as the day of his martyrdom.

The fall of Dunboy was a fatal blow to the national cause.   The
news soon reached Spain.   Hugh O'Donnell had been warmly received there ; but the burst of grief which his people uttered when
they saw him departing from his native land, was his death-keen,
for he did not long survive his voluntary expatriation.   The war
might now be considered over—at least, until the victims recovered courage to fight once more for their own ; but the victims
had to be taught how dearly they should pay for each attempt at
national independence. Captain Harvey was sent to Carberry, " to
purge the country of rebels "[8] by martial law. Wilmot was sent to
Kerry, with orders to extirpate whole districts, which arrangement

---

[6] *Life.—Hib. Pac.* vol. ii. p. 578.

[7] *Disaffection.*— Dr. Moran quotes a letter from Dublin, written 26th Feb.,
1603, which says that he imparted great edification to the faithful by his constancy, and that the whole city of Cork accompanied him with its tears.

[8] *Rebels.*—Commission from the Lord Deputy to Harvey.—See the document
in extenso, Hib. Pac. vol. ii. p. 447.

is called "settling the country," in the official document from which I quote. On one occasion a number of wounded Irish soldiers were found, who are described as "hurt and sick men;" they were at once massacred, and this is called putting them out of pain.[9]

Donnell O'Sullivan now found his position hopeless, and commenced his famous retreat to Leitrim. He set out with about 1,000 people, of whom only 400 were fighting men; the rest were servants, women, and children. He fought all the way, and arrived at his destination with only thirty-five followers.[1]

O'Neill now stood merely on the defensive. The land was devastated by famine; Docwra, Governor of Derry, had planted garrisons at every available point; and Mountjoy plundered Ulster. In August he prepared to attack O'Neill with a large army, and, as he informs Cecil, "by the grace of God, as near as he could, utterly to waste the country of Tyrone." O'Neill had now retired to a fastness at the extremity of Lough Erne, attended by his brother, Cormac Art O'Neill, and MacMahon. Mountjoy followed him, but could not approach nearer than twelve miles; he therefore returned to Newry. In describing this march to Cecil, he says: "O'Hagan protested to us, that between Tullaghoge and Toome there lay unburied 1,000 dead."

The news of O'Donnell's death had reached Ireland; and his brother submitted to the Deputy. In 1603 Sir Garret More entered into negotiations with O'Neill, which ended in his submitting also. The ceremony took place at Mellifont, on the 31st of March. Queen Elizabeth had expired, more miserably than many of the victims who had been executed in her reign, on the 24th of March; but the news was carefully concealed until O'Neill had made terms with the Viceroy.

Trinity College, Dublin, was founded during this reign. Sir John Perrot had proposed to convert St. Patrick's Cathedral into an university; but Loftus, the Protestant Archbishop, would not allow it, because, according to Leland, " he was particularly interested in

---

[9] *Pain.—Hib. Pac.* p. 659.

[1] *Followers.*—The father and mother of the celebrated historian, O'Sullivan Beare, were amongst the number of those who reached Leitrim in safety. Philip, the author, had been sent to Spain while a boy, in 1602, for his education : the whole family joined him there soon after. Dr. O'Donovan is not correct in his genealogy. It is well known that the real representative of the family is Murtough O'Sullivan, Esq., of Clohina, co. Cork.

the livings of this church, by leases and estates, which he had procured for himself and his kinsmen." When the Deputy, whom he cordially hated, had been withdrawn, he proposed a plan which gave him the credit of the undertaking without any expenditure on his part. The site he selected was in what was then called Hoggesgreen, now College-green; and the place was the "scite, ambit, and presinct"[2] of the Augustinian Monastery of All Saints, which had been founded by Dermod MacMurrough, King of Leinster, A.D. 1166. Dr. Loftus, after obtaining this grant, and such rents as still belonged to the old Catholic monastery, endeavoured to raise a subscription to supply the further funds still necessary to complete the work. In this he signally failed; for those to whom he applied excused themselves on the plea of poverty. Other funds were therefore sought for, and easily obtained; and the revenues of some suppressed Catholic houses in Kerry, Mayo, and Ulster, were taken to endow and erect the Protestant University.

[2] *Presinct.—History of the University of Dublin*, by W. B. S. Taylor. London, 1845.

RUIN—BLACKWATER.

TULLY CASTLE, COUNTY FERMANAGH.

CHAPTER XXVIII.

Accession of King James—Joy of the Irish Catholics—Their Disappointment—
Bishops, Priests, and Laity imprisoned for the Faith—Paul V. encourages
the Catholics to Constancy—Plot to entrap O'Neill and O'Donnell—Flight
of the Earls—Ulster is left to the Mercy of the English Nation—The Plantation commences—Chichester's Parliament, and how he obtained Members—Death of James I., and Accession of Charles—The Hopes of the
Catholics are raised again—They offer a large sum of Money to obtain
"Graces"—It is accepted, and the "Graces" are treacherously refused—
The Plantation of Connaught—How Obedience was enforced and Resistance
punished—Conspiracy to seize Dublin—Sir Phelim O'Neill—Massacre of
Island Magee.

[A.D. 1605—1642.]

REAT was the joy of the Irish nation when James
the First of England and the Sixth of Scotland
ascended the throne. The people supposed him
to be a Catholic in heart, and a prince in feeling.
They should have judged less favourably of one
who could see his mother sacrificed without making one real effort to avert her doom. His weakness, obstinacy, and duplicity, helped to prepare
the way for the terrible convulsion of English
society, whose origin was the great religious
schism, which, by lessening national respect for
the altar, undermined national respect for the
throne.

The Irish Catholics, only too ready to rejoice in
the faintest gleam of hope, took possession of their

own churches, and hoped they might practise their religion openly. The Cathedral of Limerick was re-dedicated by Richard Arthur, the Cathedral of Cork and Cloyne by Robert Urigh, the Metropolitan Church of Cashel by Thomas Rachtar, the churches of Wexford by John Coppinger. Dr. White restored himself the churches of Clonmel, Kilkenny, and Ross, and other clergymen acted in like manner in other places. But the most open and remarkable manifestation of devotion to the old faith was in Cork, always famous for its Catholicity, for the generosity of its people, and their special devotion to literature and religion. All the Protestant Bibles and Prayer-books were publicly and solemnly burned, the churches were hallowed, and Smith says: "They had a person named a Legate from the Pope [Dr. Moran, who quotes this passage, supposes him to have been a Vicar-Apostolic], who went about in procession with a cross, and forced people to reverence it. They buried the dead with the Catholic ceremonies; and numbers took the sacrament to defend that religion with their lives and fortunes."[3]

But the Catholics were soon undeceived. King James drank "to the eternal damnation of the Papists"[4] solemnly at a public dinner, no doubt to convince the sceptical of his Protestantism; and he divided his time very equally between persecuting the Puritans and the Catholics, when not occupied with his pleasures or quarrelling with his Parliament. The Puritans, however, had the advantage; popular opinion in England was on their side; they were sufficiently wealthy to emigrate if they pleased: while the Catholics were not only unpopular, but hated, and utterly impoverished by repeated fines and exactions.

James' conduct on his accession was sufficiently plain. He was proclaimed in Dublin on the 28th September, 1605. A part of his proclamation ran thus: " We hereby make known to our subjects in Ireland, that no toleration shall ever be granted by us. This we do for the purpose of cutting off all hope that any other religion shall be allowed, save that which is consonant to the laws and statutes of this realm." The penal statutes were renewed, and enforced with increased severity. Several members of the Corporation and some of the principal citizens of Dublin were sent to prison; similar outrages on religious liberty were perpetrated at Waterford, Ross, and

---

[3] *Fortunes.*—Smith's *History of Kerry*, vol. ii. p. 97.
[4] *Papists.*—Oliver's *Collections*, quoted by Dr. Moran, p. 250.

Limerick. In some cases these gentlemen were only asked to attend the Protestant church once, but they nobly refused to act against their conscience even once, though it should procure them freedom from imprisonment, or even from death. The Vicar-Apostolic of Waterford and Lismore wrote a detailed account of the sufferings of the Irish nation for the faith at this period to Cardinal Baronius. His letter is dated " Waterford, 1st of May, 1606." He says : " There is scarcely a spot where Catholics can find a safe retreat. The impious soldiery, by day and night, pursue the defenceless priests, and mercilessly persecute them. Up to the present they have only succeeded in seizing three : one is detained in Dublin prison, another in Cork, and the third, in my opinion, is the happiest of all, triumphing in heaven with Christ our Lord ; for in the excess of the fury of the soldiery, without any further trial or accusation, having expressed himself to be a priest, he was hanged upon the spot."

He then narrates the sufferings of the Catholic laity, many of whom he says are reduced to " extreme poverty and misery ;" " if they have any property, they are doubly persecuted by the avaricious courtiers." But so many have given a glorious testimony of their faith, he thinks their enemies and persecutors have gained but little. Thus, while one party was rejoicing in their temporal gain, the other was rejoicing in temporal loss; and while the former were preaching liberty of conscience as their creed, the latter were martyrs to it.

Another letter to Rome says: " 2,000 florins are offered for the discovery of a Jesuit, and 1,000 for the discovery of any other priest, or even of the house where he lives. Whenever the servants of any of the clergy are arrested, they are cruelly scourged with whips, until they disclose all that they know about them. Bodies of soldiers are dispersed throughout the country in pursuit of bandits and priests ; and all that they seize on, they have the power, by martial law, of hanging without further trial. They enter private houses, and execute whom they please, vieing with each other in cruelty. It is difficult to define the precise number of those who are thus put to death. All who are greedy and spendthrifts, seek to make a prey of the property of Catholics. No doors, no walls, no enclosures can stop them in their course. Whatever is for profane use they profess to regard as sacred, and bear it off; and whatever is sacred they seize on to desecrate. Silver cups are called chalices, and gems are designated as *Agnus Deis;* and all are, therefore, carried away. There are already in prison one bishop, one vicar-general, some religious, very many priests, and an immense number of the laity of every class and condition. In one city alone five of the aldermen were thrown into prison successively, for refusing to take the nefarious oath of allegiance, on their being nominated to the mayoralty; in another city, no less than thirty were likewise thrust into prison at Easter last, for having approached the holy communion in the Catholic Church."

The Catholics protested against this treatment in vain. A petition was considered an offence, and the petitioners were sent to gaol for their pains.

In 1611 the Bishop of Down and Connor was executed in Dublin. He had been seized, in 1587, by Perrot, and thrown into prison. He was released in 1593, and, according to Dr. Loftus, he took the oath of supremacy. This statement, however, is utterly incredible, for he devoted himself to his flock immediately after his release, and continued to administer the sacraments to them at the risk of his life, until June, 1611, when he was again arrested in the act of administering the sacrament of confirmation to a Catholic family. Father O'Luorchain was imprisoned with him, and they were both sentenced and executed together. At the trial the Bishop declared that the oath of spiritual supremacy was impious, and said that his enemies could not thirst more eagerly for his blood than he himself was desirous to shed it for Christ his Redeemer. This venerable prelate had attained his eightieth year, but he was full of the vigour of saintly heroism. When on the scaffold he asked the executioner to allow him to be the last victim, as he wished to spare Father O'Luorchain the terrible spectacle of his sufferings. But the good priest was not behind the Franciscan bishop in his zeal, and he exclaimed, with a touching grace of courtesy, which the occasion made sublime, that "it was not fitting for a bishop to be without a priest to attend him, and he would follow him without fear." And he did follow him, for the Bishop went first to his crown.

There was great difficulty in procuring any one who would carry out the sentence. The executioner fled, and could not be found, when he learned on whom he was to do his office. At last an English culprit, under sentence of death, undertook the bloody work, on a promise that his own life should be granted as his reward.

Communications with Rome were still as frequent and as intimate as they had ever been since Ireland received the faith at the hands of the great Apostle. To be children of Patrick and children of Rome were convertible terms ; and the Holy See watched still more tenderly over this portion of the Church while it was suffering and persecuted. Paul V. wrote a special letter to the Irish Catholics, dated from " St. Mark's, 22nd of September, 1606," in which he mourns over their afflictions, commends their marvellous constancy, which he says can only be compared to that of the early Christians, and exhorts them specially to avoid the sin of attending Protestant places of worship—a compliance to which they were strongly tempted, when even one such act might procure exemption, for a time at least, from severe persecution or death.

On another occasion the same Pontiff writes thus : " You glory in that faith by which your fathers procured for their country the distinguished appellation of the Island of Saints. Nor have the sufferings which you have endured been allowed to remain unpublished ; your fidelity and Christian fortitude have become the subject of universal admiration; and the praise of your name has long since been loudly celebrated in every portion of the Christian world.[5]

O'Neill and O'Donnell may be justly considered the last of the independent native chieftains. When the latter died in exile, and the former accepted the coronet of an English earl, the glories of the olden days of princes, who held almost regal power, had passed away for ever. The proud title of " the O'Neill" became extinct ; his country was made shire ground; he accepted patents, and held his broad acres " in fee ;" sheriffs were admitted ; judges made circuits ; king's commissioners took careful note of place, person, and property ; and such a system of espionage was established, that Davies boasts, " it was not only known how people lived and what they do, but it is foreseen what they purpose and intend to do ;" which latter species of clairvoyance seems to have been largely practised by those who were waiting until all suspicions were lulled to rest, that they might seize on the property, and imprison the persons of those whose estates they coveted.

In May, 1603, O'Neill had visited London, in company with Lord Mountjoy and Rory O'Donnell. The northern chieftains

[5] *World.*—Dr. Rothe, quoted by Monsignor Moran, p. 251.

were graciously received; and it was on this occasion that O'Neill renounced his ancient name for his new titles. O'Donnell was made Earl of Tyrconnel at the same time. The first sheriffs appointed for Ulster were Sir Edward Pelham and Sir John Davies. The latter has left it on record, as his deliberate opinion, after many years' experience, " that there is no nation of people under the sun that doth love equal and indifferent justice better than the Irish, or will rest better satisfied with the execution thereof, *although it be against themselves, so that they may have the protection and benefits of the law, when, upon just cause, they do desire it.*"

A plot was now got up to entrap O'Neill and O'Donnell. Their complicity in it has long been questioned, though Dr. O'Donovan appears to think that Moore has almost decided the question against them. Moore's evidence, however, is hardly complete, while there is unquestionable authority which favours the opinion that "artful Cecil" was intriguing to accomplish their destruction. Curry says, in his *Historical Review:* " The great possessions of these two devoted Irish princes, proved the cause of their ruin. After the successful issue of the plot-contriving Cecil's gunpowder adventure in England, he turned his inventive thoughts towards this country. A plot to implicate the great northern chieftains was soon set on foot, and finally proved successful. The conspiracy is thus related by a learned English divine, Dr. Anderson, in his *Royal Genealogies*, printed in London, 1736 : ' Artful Cecil employed one St. Lawrence to entrap the Earls of Tyrone and Tyrconnel, the Lord Delvin, and other Irish chiefs, into a sham plot, which had no evidence but his.' "

The next movement was to drop an anonymous letter at the door of the council-chamber, mentioning a design, as then in contemplation, for seizing the Castle of Dublin, and murdering the Lord Deputy. No names were mentioned, but it was publicly stated that Government had information in their possession which fixed the guilt of the conspiracy on the Earl of Tyrone. His flight, which took place immediately after, was naturally considered as an acknowledgment of his guilt. It is more probable that the expatriation was prompted by his despair.

The Four Masters give a touching account of their departure, and exclaim : " Woe to the heart that meditated, woe to the mind that conceived, woe to the council that decided on the project of their setting out on the voyage !" The exiles left Rathmullen on the

14th of September, 1607.   O'Neill had been with the Lord Deputy shortly before ; and one cannot but suppose that he had then obtained some surmise of premeditated treachery, for he arranged his flight secretly and swiftly, pretending that he was about to visit London.   O'Neill was accompanied by his Countess, his three sons, O'Donnell, and other relatives.   They first sailed to Normandy, where an attempt was made by the English Government to arrest them, but Henry IV. would not give them up.   In Rome they were received as confessors exiled for the faith, and were liberally supported by the Pope and the King of Spain.   They all died in a few years after their arrival, and their ashes rest in the Franciscan Church of St. Peter-in-Montorio.   Rome was indeed dear to them, but Ireland was still dearer ; and the exiled Celt, whether expatriated through force or stern necessity, lives only to long for the old home, or dies weeping for it.

The Red Hand of the O'Neills had hitherto been a powerful protection to Ulster.   The attempts " to plant " there had turned out failures ; but now that the chiefs were removed, the people became an easy prey.   O'Dogherty, Chief of Innishowen, was insulted by Sir George Paulett, in a manner which no gentleman could be expected to bear without calling his insulter to account ; and the young chieftain took fearful vengeance for the rude blow which he had received from the English sheriff.   He got into Culmore Fort at night by stratagem, and then marched to Derry, killed Paulett, massacred the garrison, and burned the town.   Some other chieftains joined him, and kept up the war until July ; when O'Dogherty was killed, and his companions-in-arms imprisoned.   Sir Arthur Chichester received his property in return for his suggestions for the plantation of Ulster, of which we must now make brief mention.

There can be little doubt, from Sir Henry Docwra's own account, that O'Dogherty was purposely insulted, and goaded into rebellion.   He was the last obstacle to the grand scheme, and he was disposed of.   Ulster was now at the mercy of those who chose to accept grants of land ; and the grants were made to the highest bidders, or to those who had paid for the favour by previous services.   Sir Arthur Chichester evidently considered that he belonged to the latter class, for we find him writing[6] at considerable length

---

[6] *Writing.*—The original is in the Cot. Col. British Museum.

to the Earl of Northampton, then a ruling member of King James'
cabinet, to request that he may be appointed President of Ulster.
He commences his epistle by stating how deeply he is indebted to
his Lordship for his comfortable and kind letters, and the praise he
has given him in public and private.   He then bestows an abundant
meed of commendation on his justice in return.   He next explains
his hopes and desires.   He declares that he wishes for the Presidency
of Ulster, "more for the service he might there do his Majesty, than
for the profit he expects,"—a statement which the Earl no doubt
read exactly as it was intended; and he says that he only mentions

CASTLE MONEA, CO. FERMANAGH.

his case because " charitie beginnes with myeselfe," which, indeed,
appears to have been the view of that virtue generally taken by all
planters and adventurers.   He concludes with delicately informing
his correspondent, that if he can advance any friend of his in any
way he will be most happy to do so.   This letter is dated from the
" Castle of Dublin, 7th of February, 1607."   The date should read,
according to the change of style, 1608.   The Lord Deputy knew
well what he was asking for.   During the summer of the preceding year, he had made a careful journey through Ulster, with Sir
John Davies; and Carte has well observed, that " nobody knew the
territories better to be planted ;" and he might have added, that

few persons had a clearer eye to their own advantage in the arrangements he made.

The plan of the plantation was agreed upon in 1609. It was the old plan which had been attempted before, though with less show of legal arrangement, but with quite the same proportion of legal iniquity. The simple object was to expel the natives, and to extirpate the Catholic religion. The six counties to be planted were Tyrone, Derry, Donegal, Armagh, Fermanagh, and Cavan. These were parcelled out into portions varying from 2,000 to 4,000 acres, and the planters were obliged to build bawns and castles, such as that of Castle Monea, county Fermanagh, of which we subjoin an illustration. Tully Castle[7] was built by Sir John Hume, on his plantation. Both these castles afford good examples of the structures erected at this period. The great desiderata were proximity to water and rising ground—the beauty of the surrounding scenery, which was superadded at least at Tully Castle, was probably but little valued.

Chichester now proposed to call a Parliament. The plantation of Ulster had removed some difficulties in the way of its accomplishment. The Protestant University of Dublin had obtained 3,000 acres there, and 400,000 acres of tillage land had been partitioned out between English and Scotch proprietors. It was expressly stipulated that their tenants should be English or Scotch, and Protestants; the Catholic owners of the land were, in some cases, as a special favour, permitted to remain, if they took the oath of supremacy, if they worked well for their masters, and if they paid double the rent fixed for the others. Sixty thousand acres in Dublin and Waterford, and 385,000 acres in Westmeath, Longford, King's county, Queen's county, and Leitrim, had been portioned out in a similar manner. A Presbyterian minister, whose father was one of the planters, thus describes the men who came to establish English rule, and root out Popery : "From Scotland came many, and from England not a few ; yet all of them generally the scum of both nations, who, from debt, or making and fleeing from justice, or seeking shelter, came hither, hoping to be without fear of man's justice, in a land where there was nothing or but little as yet of the fear of God. . . . . . Most of the people were all void of godliness. . . . . . On all hands atheism increased, and disregard

---

[7] *Tully Castle.*—See heading of this chapter.

of God; iniquity abounds, with contention, fighting, murder, and adultery."[8]

It was with such persons as these the lower house was filled. The upper house was composed of the Protestant bishops and English aristocracy, who were of course unanimous in their views. Chichester obtained ample powers to arrange the lower house. Forty new boroughs were formed, many of them consisting merely of a few scattered houses ; some of them were not incorporated until after the writs were issued. The Catholics were taken by surprise, as no notice had been given, either of the Parliament or the laws intended to be enacted. Six Catholic lords of the Pale remonstrated with the King, but he treated them with the utmost contempt. The house assembled ; there was a struggle for the Speaker's chair. The Catholic party proposed Sir John Everard, who had just resigned his position as Justice of the King's Bench sooner than take the oath of supremacy ; the court party insisted on having Sir John Davies. The Catholics protested, and sent a deputation to James, who first lectured[9] them to show his learning, and them imprisoned them to show his power. Some kind of compromise was eventually effected. A severe penal law was withdrawn ; a large subsidy was voted. In truth, the Irish party acted boldly, considering their peculiar circumstances, for one and all refused to enter the old cathedral, which their forefathers had erected, when Protestant service was read therein on the day of the opening of Parliament ; and even Lord Barry retired when he laid the sword of state before the Lord Deputy. We may excuse them for submitting to the attainder of O'Neill and O'Donnell, for there were few national members who had not withdrawn before the vote was passed.

Chichester retired from the government of Ireland in 1616. In 1617 a proclamation was issued for the expulsion of the Catholic clergy, and the city of Waterford was deprived of its charter in consequence of the spirited opposition which its corporation offered to the oath of spiritual supremacy. In 1622 Viscount Falkland

[8] *Adultery.*—MS. History, by Rev. A. Stuart, quoted in Reid's *History of the Presbyterian Church*, vol. i. p. 96.

[9] *Lectured.*—The address of the Irish party to James is given in O'Sullivan Beare's *History*, p. 316, and also the King's reply, p. 323. A collection was made throughout Ireland to defray the expenses of the delegates.

came over as Lord Deputy, and Usher, who was at heart a Puritan,[1] preached a violent sermon on the occasion, in which he suggested a very literal application of his text, " He beareth not the sword in vain." If a similar application of the text had been made by a Catholic divine, it would have been called intolerance, persecution, and a hint that the Inquisition was at hand ; as used by him, it was supposed to mean putting down Popery by the sword.

James I. died on the 27th March, 1625, and left his successor no very pleasant prospects in any part of his kingdom. He was pronounced by Sully to be " the wisest fool in Europe ;" Henry IV. styled him " Captain of Arts and Clerk of Arms ;" and a favourite epigram of the age is thus translated :—

> " When Elizabeth was England's King,
> That dreadful name thro' Spain did ring·
> How altered is the case, ah sa' me !
> The juggling days of good Queen Jamie."

On the accession of Charles I., in 1625, it was so generally supposed he would favour the Catholic cause, that the earliest act of the new Parliament in London was to vote a petition, begging the King to enforce the laws against recusants and Popish priests. The Viceroy, Lord Falkland, advised the Irish Catholics to propitiate him with a voluntary subsidy. They offered the enormous sum of £120,000, to be paid in three annual instalments, and in return he promised them certain " graces." The contract was ratified by royal proclamation, in which the concessions were accompanied by a promise that a Parliament should be held to confirm them. The first instalment of the money was paid, and the Irish agents returned home to find themselves cruelly deceived and basely cheated. Falkland was recalled by the Puritan party, on suspicion of favouring the Catholics ; Viscount Ely and the Earl of Cork were appointed Lords Justices ; and a reign of terror was at once commenced.

The Protestant Archbishop of Dublin, Dr. Bulkely, was fore-

---

[1] *Puritan.*—Plowden's *History of Ireland*, vol. i. p. 338. "By his management and contrivance, he provided the whole doctrine of Calvin to be received as the public belief of the Protestant Church of Ireland, and ratified by Chichester in the King's name." Chichester himself was a thorough Puritan, and a disciple of Cartwright, who used to pray, "O Lord, give us grace and power as one man to set ourselves against them" (the bishops).

most in commencing the persecution.   He marched, with the Mayor
and a file of soldiers, to the Franciscan[2] church in Cook-street, on St.
Stephen's Day, 1629, dispersed the congregation, seized the friars,
profaned the church, and broke the statue of St. Francis.   The
friars were rescued by the people, and the Archbishop had " to take
to his heels and cry out for help," to save himself.   Eventually the
Franciscans established their novitiates on the Continent, but still
continued their devoted ministrations to the people, at the risk
of life and liberty.   Their house in Cook-street was pulled down
by royal order, and three other chapels and a Catholic seminary
were seized and converted to the King's use.   Wentworth assembled a Parliament in July, 1634, the year after his arrival in Ireland.
Its subserviency was provided for by having a number of persons
elected who were in the pay of the crown as military officers.
The " graces" were asked for, and the Lord Deputy declared they
should be granted, if the supply was readily voted.   " Surely," he
said, " so great a meanness cannot enter your hearts as once to
suspect his Majesty's gracious regards of you, and performance with
you, when you affix yourself upon his grace."   This speech so
took the hearts of the people, that all were ready to grant all that
might be demanded; and six subsidies of £50,000 each were voted,
though Wentworth only expected £30,000.   In the meanwhile
neither Wentworth nor the King had the slightest idea of granting
the " graces ;" and the atrocious duplicity and incomparable " meanness" of the King is placed eternally on record, in his own letter to
his favourite, in which he thanks him " for keeping off the envy
[odium] of a necessary negative from me, of those unreasonable
graces that people expected from me."[3]   Wentworth describes
himself how two judges and Sir John Radcliffe assisted him in the
plan, and how a positive refusal was made to recommend the
passing of the " graces" into law at the next session.

    " Charles' faith" might now safely rank with Grey's ; and the

---

    [2] *Franciscan.*—An account of the sufferings of the Franciscans will be found
in *St. Francis and the Franciscans.*   The Poor Clares, who are the Second
Order of St. Francis, were refounded and established in Ireland, by Sir John
Dillon's sister, about this time, and suffered severe persecutions.   Miss Dillon,
the Abbess, was brought before the Lord Deputy ; but her quiet dignity made
such impression on the court, that she was dismissed without molestation for
the time.

    [3] *From me.*—Strafford's State Letters, vol. i. p. 331.

poor impoverished Irishman, who would willingly have given his last penny, as well as the last drop of his blood, to save his faith, was again cruelly betrayed where he most certainly might have expected that he could have confided and trusted. One of the "graces" was to make sixty years of undisputed possession of property a bar to the claims of the crown; and certainly if there ever were a country where such a demand was necessary and reasonable, it was surely Ireland. There had been so many plantations, it was hard for anything to grow; and so many settlements, it was hard for anything to be settled. Each new monarch, since the first invasion of the country by Henry II., had his favourites to provide for and his friends to oblige. The island across the sea was considered "no man's land," as the original inhabitants were never taken into account, and were simply ignored, unless, indeed, when they made their presence very evident by open resistance to this wholesale robbery. It was no wonder, then, that this "grace" should be specially solicited. It was one in which the last English settler in Ulster had quite as great an interest as the oldest Celt in Connemara. The Burkes and the Geraldines had suffered almost as much from the rapacity of their own countrymen as the natives, on whom their ancestors had inflicted such cruel wrongs. No man's property was safe in Ireland, for the tenure was depending on the royal will; and the caprices of the Tudors were supplemented by the necessities of the Stuarts.

But the "grace" was refused, although, probably, there was many a recent colonist who would have willingly given one-half of his plantation to have secured the other to his descendants. The reason of the refusal was soon apparent. As soon as Parliament was dissolved, a Commission of "Defective Titles" was issued for Connaught. Ulster had been settled, Leinster had been settled, Munster had been settled; there remained only Connaught, hitherto so inaccessible, now, with advancing knowledge of the art of war, and new means of carrying out that art, doomed to the scourge of desolation.

The process was extremely simple. The lawyers were set to work to hunt out old claims for the crown; and as Wentworth had determined to invalidate the title to every estate in Connaught, they had abundant occupation. Roscommon was selected for a commencement. The sheriffs were directed to select jurors who would find for the crown. The jurors were made clearly to understand what was expected from them, and what the consequences would be if they were "contumacious." The object of the crown was, of course, the general good of the country. The people of Connaught were to be civilized and enriched; but, in order to carry out this very desirable arrangement, the present proprietors were to be replaced by new landlords, and the country was to be placed entirely at the disposal of the Sovereign.[4]

It was now discovered that the lands and lordships of De Burgo, adjacent to the Castle of Athlone, and, in fact, the whole remaining province, belonged to the crown. It would be useless here to give details of the special pleading on which this statement was founded; it is an illustration of what I have observed before, that the tenure of the English settler was quite as uncertain as the tenure of the Celt. The jury found for the King; and as a reward, the foreman, Sir Lucas Dillon, was graciously permitted to retain a portion of his own lands. Lowther, Chief Justice of the Common Pleas, got four shillings in the pound of the first year's rent raised under the Commission of "Defective Titles." The juries of Mayo and Sligo were equally complacent; but there was stern resistance made in Galway, and stern reprisals were made for the resistance. The jurors were fined £4,000 each and were imprisoned, and their estates seized until that sum was paid. The sheriff was fined £1,000, and, being unable to pay that sum, he died in prison. And all this was done with the full knowledge and the entire sanction of the "royal martyr."

The country was discontented, and the Lord Deputy demanded more troops, "until the intended plantation should be settled." He could not see why the people should object to what was so very much for their own good, and never allowed himself to think that the disturbance had anything to do with the land question. The new proprietors were of the same opinion. Those who were or who feared to be dispossessed, and those who felt that their homes, whether humble or noble, could not be called their own, felt differently; but their opinion was as little regarded as their sufferings.

The Earl of Ormonde's property was next attacked, but he made a prudent compromise, and his party was too powerful to permit of its refusal. A Court of Wards was also established about this time, for the purpose of having all heirs to estates brought up in the

---

[4] *Sovereign.*—Strafford's Letters, vol. ii. p. 241.

Protestant religion; and a High Commission Court was instituted, which rivalled the exactions of the Star Chamber in England.

In 1640 another appeal was made by the King for assistance, and Wentworth headed the contribution with £20,000. He had devoted himself with considerable ability to increasing the Irish revenue, and the trade of the country had improved, although the Irish woollen manufacture had been completely crushed, as it threatened to interfere with English commerce. The Lord Deputy now saw the advantage of procuring a standing army in Ireland, and he proceeded to embody a force of 10,000 foot and 1,000 horse. These men were principally Irish and Catholics, as he knew they would be most likely to stand by the King in an hour of trial, notwithstanding the cruel persecutions to which they had been subjected. But the Deputy's own career was nearer its termination than he had anticipated. When he forsook the popular side in England, Pym had remarked significantly: "Though you have left us, I will not leave you while your head is on your shoulders." The Puritan faction never lost sight of a quarry when once they had it in sight, and it scarcely needed Strafford's haughtiness and devotion to the King to seal his doom. The unhappy King was compelled to sign his death-warrant; and the victim was executed on the 12th of May, 1641, redeeming in some manner, by the nobleness of his death, the cruelties, injustices, and duplicity of which he had been guilty during his life.

The kingdom of England was never in a more critical state than at this period. The King was such only in name, and the ruling powers were the Puritan party, who already looked to Cromwell as their head. The resistance, which had begun in opposition to tyrannical enactments, and to the arbitrary exercise of authority by the King and his High Church prelates, was fast merging into, what it soon became, an open revolt against the crown, and all religion which did not square with the very peculiar and ill-defined tenets of the rebellious party. In 1641 the Queen's confessor was sent to the Tower, and a resolution was passed by both houses never to consent to the toleration of the Catholic worship in Ireland, or in any other part of his Majesty's dominions. The country party had determined to possess themselves of the command of the army; and whatever struggles the King might make, to secure the only support of his throne, it was clear that the question was likely to be decided in their favour. The conduct of Holles, Pym,

Hampden, and Stroud was well known even in Ireland; and in Ireland fearful apprehensions were entertained that still more cruel sufferings were preparing for that unfortunate country.

An insurrection was organized, and its main supports were some of the best and bravest of the old race, who had been driven by political and religious persecution to other lands, where their bravery had made them respected, and their honorable dealings had made them esteemed. Spain had received a considerable number of these exiles. In June, 1635, an Irish regiment in the Spanish service, commanded by Colonel Preston, had immortalized themselves by their heroic defence of Louvain. Wherever they went they were faithful to the sovereign under whom they served; and French and Spanish generals marvelled how the English nation could be so infatuated as to drive their noblest and bravest officers and men into foreign service. An important official document still exists in the State Paper Office, which was prepared by a Government spy, and which details the names, rank, and qualifications of many of these gentlemen. They were serving in Spain, Italy, France, Germany, Poland, and the Low Countries. Don Richard Burke—strange that the first on the list of Irish exiles should be of Anglo-Norman descent—was Governor of Leghorn, and had seen great service in Italy and in the West Indies; "Phellemy O'Neill, nephew to old Tyrone," lived with great respect in Milan. There were one hundred able to command companies, and twenty fit to be made colonels under the Archduchess alone. The list of the names would fill several pages, and those, it should be remembered, were leading men. There were, besides, to be considered, an immense number of Irish of the lower classes, who had accompanied their chiefs abroad, and served in their regiments. The report says: "They have long been providing of arms for any attempt against Ireland, and had in readiness five or six thousand arms laid up in Antwerp for that purpose, *bought out of the deduction of their monthly pay, as will be proved; and it is thought now they have doubled that proportion by those means.*"[5]

The reason of the increased sacrifice they made for their country, was probably the report that the moment was at hand when it might be available. The movement in Ireland was commenced by Roger O'More, a member of the ancient family of that name, who

---

[5] *Means.*—This curious document was first published in the *Nation* of February 5th, 1859.

had been so unjustly expelled from their ancestral home in Leix; by Lord Maguire, who had been deprived of nearly all his ancient patrimony at Fermanagh, and his brother Roger; by Sir Phelim O'Neill, of Kinnare, the elder branch of whose family had been expatriated; by Turlough O'Neill, his brother, and by several other gentlemen similarly situated. O'More was the chief promoter of the projected insurrection. He was eminently suited to become a popular leader, for he was a man of great courage, fascinating address, and imbued with all the high honour of the old Celtic race. In May, 1641, Nial O'Neill arrived in Ireland with a promise of assistance from Cardinal Richelieu; and the confederates arranged that the rising should take place a few days before or after All Hallows, according to circumstances. In the meanwhile the exiled Earl of Tyrone was killed; but his successor, Colonel Owen Roe O'Neill, then serving in Flanders, entered warmly into all their plans.

The King was now obliged to disband his Irish forces, and their commanders were sent orders for that purpose. They had instructions, however, to keep the men at home and together, so that they might easily be collected again if they could be made available, as, strange to say, the so-called "Irish rebels" were the only real hope which Charles had to rely on in his conflict with his disloyal English subjects. An understanding was soon entered into between these officers and the Irish party. They agreed to act in concert; and one of the former, Colonel Plunket, suggested the seizure of Dublin Castle. The 23rd of October was fixed on for the enterprise; but, though attempted, the attempt was frustrated by a betrayal of the plot, in consequence of an indiscretion of one of the leaders.

The rage of the Protestant party knew no limits. The Castle was put in a state of defence, troops were ordered in all directions, and proclamations were issued. In the meantime the conspirators at a distance had succeeded better, but unfortunately they were not aware of the failure in Dublin until it was too late. Sir Phelim O'Neill was at the head of 30,000 men. He issued a proclamation, stating that he intended "no hurt to the King, or hurt of any of his subjects, English or Scotch;" but that his only object was the defence of Irish liberty. He added that whatever hurt was done to any one, should be personally repaired. This proclamation was dated from "Dungannon, the 23rd of October, 1641," and signed "Phelim O'Neill."

A few days after he produced a commission, which he pretended he had received from the King, authorizing his proceedings; but he amply atoned for this *ruse de guerre* afterwards, by declaring openly and honorably that the document was forged. The Irish were treated with barbarous severity, especially by Sir Charles Coote; while they were most careful to avoid any bloodshed, except what was justifiable and unavoidable in war. Dr. Bedell, the good and gentle Protestant Bishop of Kilmore, and all his people, were protected; and he drew up a remonstrance, from the tenor of which he appears to have given some sanction to the proceedings of the northern chieftains. The massacre of Island Magee took place about this period; and though the exact date is disputed, and the exact number of victims has been questioned, it cannot be disproved that the English and Scotch settlers at Carrickfergus sallied forth at night, and murdered a number of defenceless men, women, and children. That there was no regular or indiscriminate massacre of Protestants by the Catholics at this period, appears to be proved beyond question by the fact, that no mention of such an outrage was made in any of the letters of the Lords Justices to the Privy Council. It is probable, however, that the Catholics did rise up in different places, to attack those by whom they had been so severely and cruelly oppressed; and although there was no concerted plan of massacre, many victims, who may have been personally innocent, paid the penalty of the guilty. In such evidence as is still on record, ghost stories predominate; and even the Puritans seem to have believed the wildest tales of the apparition of Protestants, who demanded the immolation of the Catholics who had murdered them.

ANCIENT DRINKING VESSEL OR METHER, FROM THE
COLLECTION OF THE R.I.A.

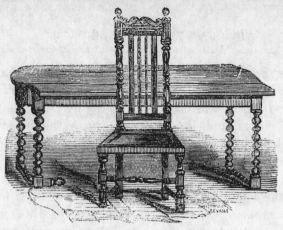

TABLE AND CHAIR USED AT THE CONFEDERATION OF KILKENNY.

CHAPTER XXIX.

English Adventurers speculate on Irish Disaffection—Coote's Cruelties—Meeting of Irish Noblemen and Gentlemen—Discontent of the People—The Catholic Priests try to save Protestants from their fury—A National Synod to deliberate on the State of Irish Affairs—The General Assembly is convened at Kilkenny—A Mint is established—A Printing-Press set up—Relations are entered into with Foreign States, and a Method of Government is organized—Differences of Opinion between the Old Irish and Anglo-Irish—A Year's Treaty is made—Arrival of Rinuccini—He lands at Kenmare—His Account of the Irish People—His Reception at Kilkenny—His Opinion of the State of Affairs—Divisions of the Confederates—Ormonde's Intrigues—The Battle of Benburb—Divisions and Discord in Camp and Senate—A Treaty signed and published by the Representatives of the English King—Rinuccini returns to Italy.

[A.D. 1642—1649.]

'NEILL now took the title of " Lord-General of the Catholic army in Ulster." A proclamation was issued by the Irish Government, declaring he had received no authority from the King; and the ruling powers were often heard to say, " that the more were in rebellion, the more lands should be forfeited to them."[6] A company of adventurers were already formed in London on speculation, and a rich harvest was anticipated. Several engagements took place, in which the insurgents were on the whole successful. It was now confidently stated that a general massacre of the Catholics was intended; and, indeed, the conduct of those engaged in putting down the rising, was very suggestive of such a purpose. In Wicklow, Sir Charles Coote put many

[6] *Them.*—Castlehaven's *Memoirs*, p. 28.

innocent persons to the sword, without distinction of age or sex.
On one occasion, when he met a soldier carrying an infant on the
point of his pike, he was charged with saying that "he liked such
frolics."[7]   Carte admits that his temper was rather "sour;" but he
relates incidents in his career which should make one think "barbarous" would be the more appropriate term.   The Lords Justices
approved of his proceedings; and Lord Castlehaven gives a fearful
account of the conduct of troops sent out by these gentlemen, who
"killed men, women, and children promiscuously; which procedure,"
he says, "not only exasperated the rebels, and *induced them to commit the like cruelties upon the English*, but frightened the nobility and
gentry about; who, seeing the harmless country people, without
respect of age or sex, thus barbarously murdered, and themselves
then openly threatened as favourers of the rebellion, for paying the
contributions they could not possibly refuse, resolved to stand upon
their guard."[8]

Before taking an open step, even in self-defence, the Irish noblemen and gentlemen sent another address to the King; but their
unfortunate messenger, Sir John Read, was captured, and cruelly
racked by the party in power—their main object being to obtain
something from his confessions which should implicate the King and
Queen. Patrick Barnwell, an aged man, was also racked for a similar
purpose. The Lords Justices now endeavoured to get several gentlemen into their possession, on pretence of holding a conference.
Their design was suspected, and the intended victims escaped; but
they wrote a courteous letter, stating the ground of their refusal.
A meeting of the principal Irish noblemen and gentlemen was now
held on the Hill of Crofty, in Meath. Amongst those present were
the Earl of Fingall, Lords Gormanstown, Slane, Louth, Dunsany,
Trimbleston, and Netterville, Sir Patrick Barnwell and Sir Christopher Bellew; and of the leading country gentlemen, Barnwell,
Darcy, Bath, Aylmer, Cusack, Malone, Segrave, &c. After they

---

[7] *Frolics.*—Carte's *Ormonde*, vol. i. p. 245, folio edition.

[8] *Guard.*—Castlehaven's *Memoirs*, p. 30. Coote's cruelties are admitted on
all sides to have been most fearful. Leland speaks of "his ruthless and indiscriminate carnage."—*History of Ireland*, vol. iii. p. 146. Warner says "he
was a stranger to mercy."—*History of the Irish Rebellion*, p. 135. "And yet
this was the man," says Lord Castlehaven, "whom the Lords Justices picked
out to entrust with a commission of martial-law, which he performed with
delight, and with a wanton kind of cruelty."

had been a few hours on the ground, the leaders of the insurgent party came up, and were accosted by Lord Gormanstown, who inquired why they came armed into the Pale.   O'More replied that they had "taken up arms for the freedom and liberty of their consciences, the maintenance of his Majesty's prerogative, in which they understood he was abridged, and the making the subjects of this kingdom as free as those of England."   Lord Gormanstown answered : "Seeing these be your true ends, we will likewise join with you therein."

On the 1st of January, 1642, Charles issued a proclamation against the Irish rebels, and wished to take the command against them in person; but his Parliament was his master, and the members were glad enough of the excuse afforded by the troubles in Ireland to increase the army, and to obtain a more direct personal control over its movements.   They voted away Irish estates, and uttered loud threats of exterminating Popery ; but they had a more important and interesting game in hand at home, which occupied their attention, and made them comparatively indifferent to Irish affairs.

Sir Phelim O'Neill was not succeeding in the north.   He had been obliged to raise the siege of Drogheda, and the English had obtained possession of Dundalk.   £1,000 was offered for his head, and £600 for the heads of some of his associates.   Ormonde and Tichburne were in command of the Government forces, but Ormonde was considered to be too lenient ; and two priests, Father Higgins and Father White, were executed by Coote, the one without trial, and the other without even the forms of justice, although they were under the Earl's protection.   Carte says that Father Higgins' case excited special interest, for he had saved many Protestants from the fury of the Irish, and afforded them relief and protection afterwards.   Indeed, at this period, the Catholic clergy were unwearied in their efforts to protect the Protestants.   They must have been actuated by the purest motives of religion, which were none the less sacred to them because they could neither be understood nor appreciated by those whose whole conduct had been so different. Father Saul, a Jesuit, sheltered Dr. Pullen, the Protestant Dean of Clonfert, and his family ; Father Everard and Father English, Franciscan friars, concealed many Protestants in their chapels, and even under their altars.   Many similar instances are on record in the depositions concerning the murders and massacres of the times, at present in Trinity College, Dublin ; though those depositions were taken with the avowed object of making out a case against the Catholics of having intended a general massacre. In Galway the Jesuits were especially active in charity to their enemies, and went through the town exhorting the people, for Christ's sake, our Lady's, and St. Patrick's, to shed no blood. But although the Catholic hierarchy were most anxious to prevent outrages against humanity, they were by no means insensible to the outrages against justice, from which the Irish nation had so long suffered. They were far from preaching passive submission to tyranny, or passive acceptance of heresy. The Church had long since not only sanctioned, but even warmly encouraged, a crusade against the infidels, and the deliverance, by force of arms, of the holy places from desecration; it had also granted[9] similar encouragements and similar indulgences to all who should fight for " liberties and rights" in Ireland, and had " exhorted, urged, and solicited" the people to do so with "all possible affection." The Irish clergy could have no doubt that the Holy See would sanction a national effort for national liberty. The Archbishop of Armagh, therefore, convened a provincial synod, which was held at Kells, on the 22nd of March, 1641, which pronounced the war undertaken by the Catholics of Ireland lawful and pious, but denounced murders and usurpations, and took steps for assembling a national synod at Kilkenny during the following year.

The Catholic cause, meanwhile, was not advancing through the country. The Irish were defeated in nearly every engagement with the English troops. The want of a competent leader and of unanimity of purpose was felt again, as it had so often been felt before; but the Church attempted to supply the deficiency, and, if it did not altogether succeed, it was at least a national credit to have done something in the cause of freedom.

The synod met at Kilkenny, on the 10th of May, 1642. It was attended by the Archbishops of Armagh, Cashel, and Tuam, and the Bishops of Ossory, Elphin, Waterford and Lismore, Kildare, Clonfert, and Down and Connor. Proctors attended for the Arch-

---

[9] *Granted.*—This most important and interesting document may be seen in O'Sullivan's *Hist. Cath.* p. 121. It is headed : " Gregory XIII., to the Archbishops, Bishops, and other prelates, as also to the Catholic Princes, Earls, Barons, Clergy, Nobles, and People of Ireland, health and apostolic benediction." It is dated : " Given at Rome, the 13th day of May, 1580, the eighth of our pontificate."

bishop of Dublin, and for the Bishops of Limerick, Emly, and Killaloe. There were present, also, sixteen other dignitaries and heads of religious orders. They issued a manifesto explaining their conduct, and, forming a Provisional Government, concluded their labours, after three days spent in careful deliberation.

Owen Roe O'Neill and Colonel Preston arrived in Ireland in July, 1642, accompanied by a hundred officers, and well supplied with arms and ammunition. Sir Phelim O'Neill went at once to meet O'Neill, and resigned the command of the army ; and all promised fairly for the national cause. The Scots, who had kept up a war of their own for some time, against both the King and the Catholics, were wasting Down and Antrim ; and O'Neill was likely to need all his military skill and all his political wisdom in the position in which he was placed.

Preston had landed in Wexford, and brought a still larger force; while all the brave expatriated Irishmen in foreign service, hastened home the moment there appeared a hope that they could strike a blow with some effect for the freedom of their native land.

The General Assembly projected by the national synod in Kilkenny, held its first meeting on October 14, 1642,—eleven spiritual and fourteen temporal peers, with 226 commoners, representing the Catholic population of Ireland. It was, in truth, a proud and glorious day for the nation. For once, at least, she could speak through channels chosen by her own free will ; and for once there dawned a hope of legislative freedom of action for the long-enslaved people. The old house is still shown where that Assembly deliberated—a Parliament all but in name. The table then used, and the chair occupied by the Speaker, are still preserved, as sad mementos of freedom's blighted cause.[1] The house used was in the market-place. The peers and commoners sat together; but a private room was allotted for the lords to consult in. Dr. Patrick Darcy, an eminent lawyer, represented the Chancellor and the judges. Mr. Nicholas Plunket was chosen as Speaker; the Rev. Thomas O'Quirk, a learned Dominican friar, was appointed Chaplain to both houses.

The Assembly at once declared that they met as a provisional government, and not as a parliament. The preliminary arrangements occupied them until the 1st of November. From the 1st

---

[1] *Cause.*—See illustration at head of this chapter.

until the 4th, the committee was engaged in drawing up a form for the Confederate Government ; on the 4th it was sanctioned by the two houses. Magna Charta, and the common and statute law of England, in all points not contrary to the Catholic religion, or inconsistent with the liberty of Ireland, were made the basis of the new Government. The administrative authority was vested in a Supreme Council, which was then chosen, and of which Lord Mountgarret was elected President.

There were six members elected for each province. For Leinster, the Archbishop of Dublin, Lords Gormanstown and Mountgarret, Nicholas Plunket, Richard Belling, and James Cusack. For Ulster,

PARLIAMENT HOUSE, KILKENNY.

the Archbishop of Armagh, the Bishop of Down, Philip O'Reilly, Colonel MacMahon, Heber Magennis, and Turlough O'Neill. For Munster, Viscount Roche, Sir Daniel O'Brien, Edmund Fitz-Maurice, Dr. Fennell, Robert Lambert, and George Comyn. For Connaught, the Archbishop of Tuam, Viscount Mayo, the Bishop of Clonfert, Sir Lucas Dillon, Geoffrey Browne, and Patrick Darcy. The Earl of Castlehaven, who had just escaped from his imprisonment in Dublin, was added as a twenty-fifth member. Generals were appointed to take the command of the forces—Owen Roe O'Neill, for Ulster; Preston, for Leinster; Barry, for Munster; and Burke, for Connaught. A seal was made, a printing-press set up, and a mint established. Money was coined and levied for the necessary expenses; and a levy of 31,700 men was prepared to be drilled by the new officers. Envoys were sent to solicit assistance from the Catholic courts of Europe; and the famous and learned Franciscan, Father Luke Wadding, applied himself to the cause with unremitting earnestness. Father John Talbot was employed in a similar manner in Spain.

The Assembly broke up on the 9th of January, 1643, after sending a remonstrance to the King, declaring their loyalty, and explaining their grievances. The complicated state of English politics proved the ruin of this noble undertaking, so auspiciously commenced. Charles was anxious to make terms with men whom he knew would probably be the only subjects on whose loyalty he could thoroughly depend. His enemies—and the most cursory glance at English history during this period proves how many and how powerful they were—desired to keep open the rupture, and, if possible, to bring it down, from the high stand of dignified remonstrance, to the more perilous and lower position of a general and ill-organized insurrection. The Lords Justices Borlase and Parsons were on the look-out for plunder; but Charles had as yet sufficient power to form a commission of his own, and he sent the Marquis of Ormonde and some other noblemen to treat with the Confederates. Ormonde was a cold, calculating, and, if we must judge him by his acts, a cruel man; for, to give only one specimen of his dealings, immediately after his appointment, he butchered the brave garrison of Timolin, who had surrendered on promise of quarter.

The Confederates were even then divided into two parties. The section of their body principally belonging to the old English settlers, were willing to have peace on almost any terms; the ancient Irish had their memories burdened with so many centuries of wrong, that they demanded something like certainty of redress before they would yield. Ormonde was well aware of the men with whom, and the opinions with which, he had to deal, and he acted accordingly. In the various engagements which occurred, the Irish were on the whole successful. They had gained an important victory near Fermoy, principally through the headlong valour of a troop of mere boys, who dashed down with wild impetuosity on the English, and showed what mettle there was still left in the country. Envoys were arriving from foreign courts, and Urban VIII. had sent Father Scarampi with indulgences and a purse of 30,000 dollars, collected by

Father Wadding. It was, therefore, most important that the movement should be checked in some way ; and, as it could not be suppressed by force, it was suppressed by diplomacy.

On the 15th of September, 1643, a cessation of arms for one year was agreed upon ; and the tide, which had set in so gloriously for Irish independence, rolled back its sobbing waves slowly and sadly towards the English coast, and never returned again with the same hopeful freedom and overpowering strength.

The Irish, even those whose wisdom or whose ardour made them most dissatisfied with the treaty, observed it honorably. The Puritan party professed to regard the cessation as a crime, and therefore did not consider themselves bound to observe it. As they were in fact the ruling powers, the unfortunate Irish were, as usual, the victims. The troops, who had been trained and collected for the defence of their native land, were now sent to Scotland, to shed their blood in the royal cause. As honorable men, having undertaken the duty, they fulfilled it gloriously, and won the admiration even of their enemies by their undaunted valour.

The unhappy English monarch was now besieged by petitions and counter-petitions. The Confederates asked for liberty of conscience ; the Puritans demanded a stern enforcement of the penal laws. Complaints were made on both sides of the infringement of the cessation ; but Munroe was the chief offender ; and Owen O'Neill was summoned to consult with the Supreme Council in Kilkenny. Lord Castlehaven, who was utterly incompetent for such an appointment, was given the command of the army; and O'Neill, though he felt hurt at the unjust preference, submitted generously.

In August, 1644, the cessation was again renewed by the General Assembly until December, and subsequently for a longer period. Thus precious time, and what was still more precious, the fresh energies and interests of the Confederates, were hopelessly lost. The King's generals, or rather it should be said the Parliamentary officers, observed or held these engagements at their convenience, and made treaties of their own—Inchiquin and Purcell making a truce between themselves in the south. As the King's affairs became daily more complicated, and his position more perilous, he saw the necessity for peace with his Irish subjects, and for allying himself with them, if possible. Had he treated them with more consideration, or rather with common justice and humanity, at the commencement of his reign, England might have been saved the guilt of regicide and Cromwell's iron rule. Ormonde had received ample powers from Charles to grant the Catholics every justice now; but Ormonde could not resist the inclination to practise a little subtle diplomacy, even at the risk of his master's kingdom and his master's head. The Confederate commissioners rejected his temporizing measures with contempt, though a few of their members, anxious for peace, were inclined to yield.

When Inchiquin set out to destroy the growing crops early in summer, Castlehaven was sent against him, and obliged him to retire into Cork. At the same time Coote was overrunning Connaught, and took possession of Sligo. The Irish forces again recovered the town; but, in the attempt, the Archbishop and two friars fell into the hands of the enemy,.and were cruelly murdered. Charles now made another attempt to obtain the assistance of the Catholic party, and sent over Lord Herbert to Ireland on a secret mission for that purpose. This nobleman and his father-in-law, the Earl of Thomond, were almost romantically attached to the King, and had already advanced £200,000 for the support of the royal cause. He proceeded to Kilkenny, after a brief interview with Ormonde. England's difficulty proved Ireland's opportunity. Everything that could be desired was granted; and all that was asked was the liberty to worship God according to each man's conscience, and the liberty of action and employment, which is the right of every member of civil society who has not violated the rules of moral conduct which governors are bound to enforce. In return for the promise that they should enjoy the rights of subjects, the Irish Confederates promised to do the duty of subjects. They had already assisted more than one English King to rule his Scotch dominions; they were now to assist Charles to rule his English subjects; and they promised to send him 10,000 armed men, under the command of Lord Herbert. It was a great risk to trust a Stuart; and he made it a condition that the agreement should remain secret until the troops had landed in England.

In the meantime Belling, the Secretary of the Supreme Council, was sent to Rome, and presented to Innocent X., by Father Wadding, as the envoy of the Confederate Catholics, in February, 1645. On hearing his report, the Pope sent John Baptist Rinuccini,[2] Arch-

---

[2] *Rinuccini.*—A work was published in Florence, 1844, entitled *Nunziatura in Irlanda,* di M. Gio. Battista Rinuccini, &c. This work, which only forms

bishop of Fermo, to Ireland, as Nuncio-Extraordinary. This prelate set out immediately ; and, after some detention at St. Germains, for the purpose of conferring with the English Queen, who had taken refuge there, he purchased the frigate *San Pietro* at Rochelle, stored it with arms and ammunition; and, after some escapes from the Parliamentary cruisers, landed safely in Kenmare Bay, on the 21st of October, 1645. He was soon surrounded and welcomed by the peasantry ; and after celebrating Mass in a poor hut,[3] he at once proceeded to Limerick. Here he celebrated the obsequies of the Archbishop of Tuam, and then passed on to Kilkenny. He entered the old city in state, attended by the clergy. At the entrance to the Cathedral he was met by the Bishop of Ossory, who was

a portion of the Rinuccini MS., throws much valuable light upon the history of the period. It is supposed to have been written by the Dean of Fermo, who attended the Nuncio during his official visit to Ireland. This volume also contains, in the original Italian, the report presented by Rinuccini to the Pope on his return from Ireland. Burke has given some extracts from the MS. in his *Hibernia Dominicana*, and Carte mentions it also ; but otherwise these very important documents appear to have been quite overlooked.

Since the publication of the first edition of this work, I have obtained a copy of a translation of the Nuncio's narrative, which appeared in the *Catholic Miscellany* for 1829. This translation was made by a Protestant clergyman, from a Latin translation of the original, in the possession of Mr. Coke, of Holham, Norfolk. The Nuncio's account is one of great importance, but it would demand considerable space if treated of in detail. There was a very able article on the subject in the *Dublin Review* for March, 1845.

[3] *Hut.*—Some extracts from a curious and interesting letter, describing the voyage from France and the landing in Ireland of Rinuccini and his party, were published in the *Dublin Review* for March, 1845. It is addressed to Count Thomas Rinuccini, but the writer is supposed to have been the Dean of Fermo. He gives a graphic description of their arrival at Kenmare—"al porto di Kilmar"—and of the warm reception they met from the poor, and their courtesy— "La cortesia di quei poveri popoli dove Monsignor capitò, fu incomparabile." He also says : "Gran cosa, nelle montagne e luoghi rozzi, e gente povera per le devastazioni fatte dei nemici eretici, trovai però la nobilta della S. fede Catolica, giaché auro vi fu uomo, o donna, o ragazzo, ancor che piccolo, che non me sapesse recitar il Pater, Ave, Credo, e i commandamenti della Santa Chiesa." "It is most wonderful that in this wild and mountainous place, and a people so impoverished by the heretical enemy, I found, nevertheless, the noble influence of the holy Catholic faith ; for there was not a man or woman, or a child however young, who could not repeat the Our Father, Hail Mary, Creed, and the commands of Holy Church." We believe the same might be said at the present day of this part of Ireland. It is still as poor, and the people are still as well instructed in and as devoted to their faith now as in that century.

unable to walk in the procession. When the *Te Deum* had been sung, he was received in the Castle by the General Assembly, and addressed them in Latin.   After this he returned to the residence prepared for him.

In a Catholic country, and with a Catholic people, the influence of a Papal Nuncio was necessarily preponderant, and he appears to have seen at a glance the difficulties and advantages of the position of Irish affairs and the Confederate movement.   "He had set his mind," says the author of the *Confederation of Kilkenny*, " on one grand object—the freedom of the Church, in possession of all her rights and dignities, and the emancipation of the Catholic people from the degradation to which English imperialism had condemned them.   The churches which the piety of Catholic lords and chieftains had erected, he determined to secure to the rightful inheritors. His mind and feelings recoiled from the idea of worshipping in crypts and catacombs ; he abhorred the notion of a priest or bishop performing a sacred rite as though it were a felony ; and despite the wily artifices of Ormonde and his faction, he resolved to teach the people of Ireland that they were not to remain mere dependents on English bounty, when a stern resolve might win for them the privileges of freemen."[4]

The following extract from Rinuccini's own report, will show how thoroughly he was master of the situation in a diplomatic point of view : " From time immemorial two adverse parties have always existed among the Catholics of Ireland.   The first are called the ' old Irish.'   They are most numerous in Ulster, where they seem to have their head-quarters ; for even the Earl of Tyrone placed himself at their head, and maintained a protracted war against Elizabeth. The second may be called the ' old English,'—a race introduced into Ireland in the reign of Henry II., the fifth king in succession from William the Conqueror ; so called to distinguish them from the ' new English,' who have come into the kingdom along with the modern heresy.   These parties are opposed to each other principally on the following grounds: the old Irish, entertaining a great aversion for heresy, are also averse to the dominion of England, and have refused, generally speaking, to accept the investiture of Church property offered to them since the apostacy of the Kings of England from the Church.   The others, on the contrary, enriched with the

<hr>

[4] *Freemen.—Confederation of Kilkenny*, p. 117,

spoils of the monasteries, and thus bound to the King by obligation, no less than by interest, neither seek nor desire anything but the exaltation of the crown, esteem no laws but those of the realm, are thoroughly English in their feelings, and, from their constant familiarity with heretics, are less jealous of differences of religion."

The Nuncio then goes on to state how even the military command was divided between these two parties,—O'Neill belonging to the old Irish interest, and Preston to the new. He also mentions the manner in which this difference of feeling extended to the lower classes, and particularly to those who served in the army.[5]

I have given this lengthened extract from Rinuccini's report, because, with all the advantages of looking back upon the times and events, it would be impossible to explain more clearly the position of the different parties. It remains only to show how these unfortunate differences led to the ruin of the common cause.

The Confederates now began to be distinguished into two parties, as Nuncionists and Ormondists. Two sets of negotiations were carried on, openly with Ormonde, and secretly with Glamorgan. The Nuncio, from the first, apprehended the treachery of Charles, and events proved the correctness of his forebodings. Glamorgan produced his credentials, dated April 30th, 1645, in which the King promised to ratify whatever terms he might make ; and he further promised, that the Irish soldiers, whose assistance he demanded, should be brought back to their own shores, if these arrangements were not complied with by his master. Meanwhile a copy of this secret treaty was discovered on the Archbishop of Tuam, who had been killed at Sligo. It was used as an accusation against the King. Glamorgan was arrested in Dublin, and the whole scheme was defeated.

The General Assembly met in Kilkenny, in January, 1646, and demanded the release of Glamorgan. He was bailed out; but the King disowned the commission, as Rinuccini had expected, and proved himself thereby equally a traitor to his Catholic and Protestant subjects. Ormonde took care to foment the division between the Confederate party, and succeeded so well that a middle party was formed, who signed a treaty consisting of thirty articles. This document only provided for the religious part of the question, that

[5] *Army.—Nunziatura in Irlanda,* p. 391.

Roman Catholics should not be bound to take the oath of supremacy. An Act of oblivion was passed, and the Catholics were to continue to hold their possessions until a settlement could be made by Act of Parliament. Even in a political point of view, this treaty was a failure; and one should have thought that Irish chieftains and Anglo-Irish nobles had known enough of Acts of Parliament to have prevented them from confiding their hopes to such an uncertain future.

The division of the command in the Confederate army had been productive of most disastrous consequences. The rivalry between O'Neill, Preston, and Owen Roe, increased the complication; but the Nuncio managed to reconcile the two O'Neills, and active preparations were made by Owen Roe for his famous northern campaign. The Irish troops intended for Charles had remained in their own country; the unfortunate monarch had committed his last fatal error by confiding himself to his Scotch subjects, who sold him to his own people for £400,000. Ormonde now refused to publish the treaty which had been just concluded, or even to enforce its observance by Monroe, although the Confederates had given him £3,000 to get up an expedition for that purpose.

In the beginning of June, A.D. 1646, Owen Roe O'Neill marched against Monroe, with 5,000 foot and 500 horse. Monroe received notice of his approach; and although his force was far superior to O'Neill's, he sent for reinforcements of cavalry from his brother, Colonel George Monroe, who was stationed at Coleraine. But the Irish forces advanced more quickly than he expected; and on the 4th of June they had crossed the Blackwater, and encamped at Benburb. O'Neill selected his position admirably. He encamped between two small hills, with a wood in his rear. The river Blackwater protected him on the right, and an impassable bog on the left. Some brushwood in the front enabled him to conceal a party of musketeers; he was also well-informed of Monroe's movements, and took precautions to prevent the advance of his brother's forces. Monroe crossed the river at Kinard, at a considerable distance in the rear of his opponent, and then advanced, by a circuitous march, from the east and north. The approach was anticipated; and, on the 5th of June, 1646, the most magnificent victory ever recorded in the annals of Irish history was won. The Irish army prepared for the great day with solemn religious observances. The whole army approached the sacraments of penance and holy communion, and thus were prepared alike for death or victory. The chaplain deputed by the Nuncio addressed them briefly, and appealed to their religious feelings; their General, Owen Roe, appealed to their nationality. How deeply outraged they had been, both in their religion and in their national feelings, has been already mentioned; how they fought for their altars and their domestic hearths will now be recorded. O'Neill's skill as a military tactician is beyond all praise. For four long hours he engaged the attention of the enemy, until the glare of the burning summer sun had passed away, and until he had intercepted the reinforcements which Monroe expected. At last the decisive moment had arrived. Monroe thought he saw his brother's contingent in the distance; O'Neill knew that they were some of his own men who had beaten that very contingent. When the Scotch general was undeceived, he resolved to retire. O'Neill saw his advantage, and gave the command to charge. With one loud cry of vengeance for desecrated altars and desolated homes, the Irish soldiers dashed to the charge, and Monroe's ranks were broken, and his men driven to flight. Even the General himself fled so precipitately, that he left his hat, sword, and cloak after him, and never halted until he reached Lisburn. Lord Montgomery was taken prisoner, and 3,000 of the Scotch were left on the field. Of the Irish only seventy men were killed, and 200 wounded. It was a great victory; and it was something more—it was a glorious victory; although Ireland remained, both as to political and religious freedom, much as it had been before. The standards captured on that bloody field were sent to the Nuncio at Limerick, and carried in procession to the Cathedral, where a solemn *Te Deum* was chanted—and that was all the result that came of it. Confusion thrice confounded followed in the rear. The King issued orders, under the compulsion of the Scotch, which Lord Digby declared to be just the contrary of what he really wished; and Ormonde proclaimed and ratified the treaty he had formerly declined to fulfil, while the "old Irish" everywhere indignantly rejected it. In Waterford, Clonmel, and Limerick, the people would not permit it even to be proclaimed. The Nuncio summoned a national synod in Waterford, at which it was condemned; and a decree was issued, on the 12th of August, declaring that all who adhered to such terms should be declared perjurers. Even Preston declared for the Nuncio; and the clergy and the nobles who led the unpopular cause, were obliged to ask

Ormonde's assistance to help them out of their difficulty. The Earl arrived at Kilkenny with an armed force; but fled precipitately when he heard that O'Neill and Preston were advancing towards him.

Rinuccini now took a high hand. He entered Kilkenny in state, on the 18th of September, and committed the members of the Supreme Council as prisoners to the Castle, except Darcy and Plunket. A new Council was appointed, or self-appointed, on the 20th, of which the Nuncio was chosen President. The imprisonment of the old Council was undoubtedly a harsh and unwise proceeding, which can scarcely be justified; but the times were such that prompt action was demanded, and the result alone, which could not be foreseen, could justify or condemn it.

The Generals were again at variance; and although the new Council had decided on attacking Dublin, their plans could not be carried out. Preston was unquestionably playing fast and loose; and when the Confederate troops did march towards Dublin, his duplicity ruined the cause which might even then have been gained. A disgraceful retreat was the result. An Assembly was again convened at Kilkenny; the old Council was released; the Generals promised to forget their animosities: but three weeks had been lost in angry discussion; and although the Confederates bound themselves by oath not to lay down their arms until their demands were granted, their position was weakened to a degree which the selfishness of the contending parties made them quite incapable of estimating.

The fact was, the Puritan faction in England was every day gaining an increase of power; while every hour that the Confederate Catholics wasted in discussion or division, was weakening their moral strength. Even Ormonde found himself a victim to the party who had long made him their tool, and was ordered out of Dublin unceremoniously, and obliged eventually to take refuge in France. Colonel Jones took possession of Dublin Castle for the rebel forces, and defeated Preston in a serious engagement at Dungan Hill, soon after his arrival in Ireland. O'Neill now came to the rescue; and even the Ormondists, having lost their leader, admitted that he was their only resource. His admirable knowledge of military tactics enabled him to drive Jones into Dublin Castle, and keep him there for a time almost in a state of siege.

In the meantime Inchiquin was distinguishing himself by his

cruel victories in the south of Ireland. The massacre of Cashel followed. When the walls were battered down, the hapless garrison surrendered without resistance, and were butchered without mercy. The people fled to the Cathedral, hoping there, at least, to escape; but the savage General poured volleys of musket-balls through the doors and windows, and his soldiers rushing in afterwards, piked those who were not yet dead. Twenty priests were dragged out as objects of special vengeance; and the total number of those who were thus massacred amounted to 3,000.

An engagement took place in November between Inchiquin and Lord Taaffe, in which the Confederates were again beaten and cruelly massacred. Thus two of their generals had lost both their men and their *prestige*, and O'Neill alone remained as the prop of a falling cause. The Irish now looked for help from foreign sources, and despatched Plunket and French to Rome, and Muskerry and Browne to France; but Ormonde had already commenced negotiations on his own account, and he alone was accredited at the court of St. Germains. Even at this moment Inchiquin had been treating with the Supreme Council for a truce; but Rinuccini, who detested his duplicity, could never be induced to listen to his proposals. A man who had so mercilessly massacred his own countrymen, could scarcely be trusted by them on so sudden a conversion to their cause; but, unhappily, there were individuals who, in the uncertain state of public affairs, were anxious to steer their barks free of the thousand breakers ahead, and in their eagerness forgot that, when the whole coast-line was deluged with storms, their best chance of escape was the bold resolution of true moral courage. The cautious politicians, therefore, made a treaty with Inchiquin, which was signed at Dungarvan, on the 20th of May. On the 27th of that month the Nuncio promulgated a sentence of excommunication against all cities and villages where it should be received, and, at the same time, he withdrew to the camp of Owen Roe O'Neill, against whom Inchiquin and Preston were prepared to march. It was a last and desperate resource, and, as might be expected, it failed signally of its intended effects. Various attempts to obtain a settlement of the question at issue by force of arms, were made by the contending parties; but O'Neill baffled his enemies, and the Nuncio withdrew to Galway.

Ormonde arrived in Ireland soon after, and was received at Cork, on the 27th of September, 1648, by Inchiquin. He then proceeded to Kilkenny, where he was received in great state by the Confederates. On the 17th of January, 1649, he signed a treaty of peace, which concluded the seven years' war. This treaty afforded the most ample indulgences to the Catholics, and guaranteed fairly that civil and religious liberty for which alone they had contended; but the ink upon the deed was scarcely dry, ere the execution of Charles I., on the 30th of January, washed out its enactments in royal blood; and civil war, with more than ordinary complications, was added to the many miseries of our unfortunate country.

Rinuccini embarked in the *San Pietro* once more, and returned to Italy, February 23, 1649. Had his counsels been followed, the result might have justified him, even in his severest measures; as it is, we read only failure in his career; but it should be remembered, that there are circumstances under which failure is more noble than success.

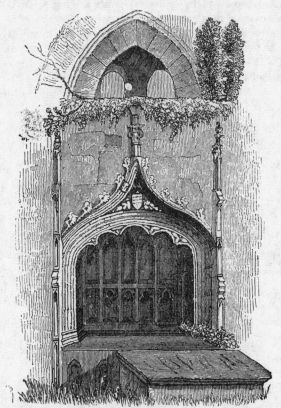

THOMAS FLEMYNG'S TOMB, COLLEGIATE CHURCH, YOUGHAL.

ST. LAWRENCE GATE, DROGHEDA.

CHAPTER XXX.

Cromwell arrives in Ireland—He marches to Drogheda—Cruel Massacre of the Inhabitants after promise of Quarter—Account of an Eyewitness—Brutality of the Cromwellian Soldiers—Ladies are not spared—Cromwell's Letters—He boasts of his Cruelties—Massacre and Treachery at Drogheda—Brave Resistance at Clonmel—Charles II. arrives in Scotland—The Duplicity of his Conduct towards the Irish—Siege of Limerick—Ireton's Cruelties and Miserable Death—The Banishment to Connaught—The Irish are sold as Slaves to Barbadoes—General Desolation and Misery of the People.

[A.D. 1649—1655.]

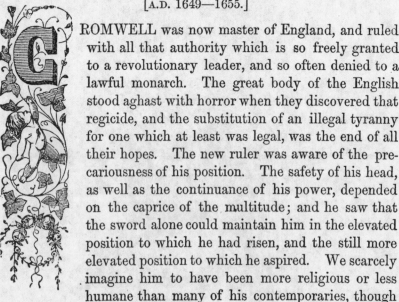

ROMWELL was now master of England, and ruled with all that authority which is so freely granted to a revolutionary leader, and so often denied to a lawful monarch. The great body of the English stood aghast with horror when they discovered that regicide, and the substitution of an illegal tyranny for one which at least was legal, was the end of all their hopes. The new ruler was aware of the precariousness of his position. The safety of his head, as well as the continuance of his power, depended on the caprice of the multitude; and he saw that the sword alone could maintain him in the elevated position to which he had risen, and the still more elevated position to which he aspired. We scarcely imagine him to have been more religious or less humane than many of his contemporaries, though it is evident that he required a great show of the kind of religion then fashionable to support his character as a reformer, and that he considered himself obliged to exercise wholesale cruelties to consolidate his power.

The rightful heir to the English throne was then at the Hague, uncertain how to act and whither he should turn his steps. He wished to visit Ireland, where he would have been received with enthusiastic loyalty by the Catholics; but Ormonde persuaded him, from sinister motives, to defer his intention. Ormonde and Inchiquin now took the field together. The former advanced to Dublin, and the latter to Drogheda. This town was held by a Parliamentary garrison, who capitulated on honorable terms. Monck and Owen O'Neill, in the meantime, were acting in concert, and Inchiquin captured supplies which the English General was sending to the Irish chief. Newry, Dundalk, and the often-disputed and famous Castle of Trim[6] surrendered to him, and he marched back to Ormonde in triumph. As there appeared no hope of reducing Dublin except by famine, it was regularly blockaded; and the Earl wrote to Charles to inform him that his men were so loyal, he could "persuade half his army to starve outright for his Majesty."

Ormonde now moved his camp from Finglas to Rathmines, and at the same time reinforcements arrived for the garrison, under the command of Colonels Reynolds and Venables. The besiegers made an attempt to guard the river, and for this purpose, Major-General Purcell was sent to take possession of the ruined Castle of Bagotrath, about a mile from the camp. Ormonde professed to have expected an attack during the night, and kept his men under arms; but just as he had retired to rest, an alarm was given. Colonel Jones had made a sortie from the city; the sortie became for a brief moment an engagement, and ended in a total rout. The Earl was suspected; and whether he had been guilty of treachery or of carelessness, he lost his credit, and soon after left the kingdom.

Cromwell had been made Lieutenant-General of the English army in Ireland, but as yet he had been unable to take the command in person. His position was precarious; and he wished to secure his influence still more firmly in his own country, before he attempted the conquest of another. He had succeeded so far in the accomplishment of his plans, that his departure and his journey to Bristol were undertaken in royal style. He left the metropolis early in June,

---

[6] *Trim.*—For an illustration of this castle, see p. 560.

in a coach drawn by six gallant Flanders' mares, and concluded his
progress at Milford Haven, where he embarked, reaching Ireland on
the 14th of August, 1649. He was attended by some of the most
famous of the Parliamentary Generals—his son, Henry, the
future Lord Deputy; Monk, Blake, Ireton, Waller, Ludlow, and
others. He brought with him, for the propagation of the Gospel
and the Commonwealth, £200,000 in money, eight regiments of
foot, six of horse, several troops of dragoons, a large supply of
Bibles,[7] and a corresponding provision of ammunition and scythes.
The Bibles were to be distributed amongst his soldiers, and to
be given to the poor unfortunate natives, who could not understand a word of their contents. The scythes and sickles were to
deprive them of all means of living, and to preach a ghastly com-
mentary on the conduct of the men who wished to convert them to
the new Gospel, which certainly was not one of peace. Cromwell
now issued two proclamations: one against intemperance, for he
knew well the work that was before him, and he could not afford
to have a single drunken soldier in his camp. The other proclamation prohibited plundering the country people: it was scarcely less
prudent. His soldiers might any day become his masters, if they
were not kept under strict control; and there are few things which
so effectually lessen military discipline as permission to plunder: he
also wished to encourage the country people to bring in provisions.
His arrangements all succeeded.

Ormonde had garrisoned Drogheda with 3,000 of his choicest troops.
They were partly English, and were commanded by a brave loyalist,
Sir Arthur Aston. This was really the most important town in
Ireland; and Cromwell, whose skill as a military general cannot be
disputed, at once determined to lay siege to it. He encamped before
the devoted city on the 2nd of September, and in a few days had
his siege guns posted on the hill shown in the accompanying illustration, and still known as Cromwell's Fort. Two breaches were
made on the 10th, and he sent in his storming parties about five
o'clock in the evening. Earthworks had been thrown up inside,
and the garrison resisted with undiminished bravery. The besieged

---

[7] *Bibles.*—See *The Cromwellian Settlement of Ireland*, by John P. Prendergast, Esq.—a most important work, and one which merits the careful consideration of all who wish to understand this period of Irish history, and one of the
many causes of Irish disaffection. The scythes and sickles were to cut down
the corn, that the Irish might be starved if they could not be conquered.

Massacre at Drogheda.

at last wavered; quarter[8] was promised to them, and they yielded; but the promise came from men who knew neither how to keep faith or to show mercy. The brave Governor, Sir Arthur Aston, retired with his staff to an old mill on an eminence, but they were disarmed and slain in cold blood. The officers and soldiers were first exterminated, and then men, women, and children were put to the sword. The butchery occupied five entire days: Cromwell has himself described the scene, and glories in his cruelty. Another eyewitness, an officer in his army, has described it also, but with some faint touch of remorse.

CROMWELL'S FORT, DROGHEDA.

A number of the townspeople fled for safety to St. Peter's Church, on the north side of the city, but every one of them was murdered, all defenceless and unarmed as they were; others took refuge in the church steeple, but it was of wood, and Cromwell himself gave orders that it should be set on fire, and those who attempted to escape the flames were piked. The principal ladies of the city had sheltered themselves in the crypts. It might have been supposed

[8] *Quarter.*—Cromwell says, in his letters, that quarter was not promised; Leland and Carte say that it was.

that this precaution should be unnecessary, or, at least, that English officers would respect their sex; but, alas for common humanity ! it was not so.   When the slaughter had been accomplished above, it was continued below.   Neither youth nor beauty was spared. Thomas Wood, who was one of these officers, and brother to Anthony Wood, the Oxford historian, says he found in these vaults "the flower and choicest of the women and ladies belonging to the town; amongst whom, a most handsome virgin, arrayed in costly and gorgeous apparel, kneeled down to him with tears and prayers to save her life."   Touched by her beauty and her entreaties, he attempted to save her, and took her out of the church; but even his protection could not save her.   A soldier thrust his sword into her body; and the officer, recovering from his momentary fit of compassion, "flung her down over the rocks," according to his own account, but first took care to possess himself of her money and jewels.   This officer also mentions that the soldiers were in the habit of taking up a child, and using it as a buckler, when they wished to ascend the lofts and galleries of the church, to save themselves from being shot or brained.   It is an evidence that they knew their victims to be less cruel than themselves, or the expedient would not have been found to answer.

Cromwell wrote an account of this massacre to the "Council of State."   His letters, as his admiring editor observes, "tell their own tale;"[9] and unquestionably that tale plainly intimates that whether the Republican General were hypocrite or fanatic—and it is probable he was a compound of both—he certainly, on his own showing, was little less than a demon of cruelty.   Cromwell writes thus : "It hath pleased God to bless our endeavours at Drogheda. After battery we stormed it.   The enemy were about 3,000 strong in the town.   They made a stout resistance.   I believe we put to the sword the whole number of defendants.   I do not think thirty of the whole number escaped with their lives.   Those that did are in safe custody for the Barbadoes.   This hath been a marvellous

---

[9] Tale.—Cromwell's Letters and Speeches, vol. i. p. 456.   The simplicity with which Carlyle attempts to avert the just indignation of the Irish, by saying that the garrison "consisted mostly of Englishmen," coupled with his complacent impression that eccentric phrases can excuse crime, would be almost amusing were it not that he admits himself to be as cruel as his hero.—vol. i. p. 453. A man who can write thus is past criticism.   If the garrison did consist mainly of Englishmen, what becomes of the plea, that this barbarity was a just vengeance upon the Irish for the "massacre."

great mercy." In another letter he says that this "great thing" was done "by the Spirit of God."

These savage butcheries had the intended effect. The inhabitants of all the smaller towns fled at his approach, and the garrisons capitulated. Trim, Dundalk, Carlingford, and Newry, had yielded; but Wexford still held out. The garrison amounted to about 3,000 men, under the command of Colonel Sinnot, a brave loyalist. After some correspondence on both sides, a conference took place between four of the royalists and Cromwell, at which he contrived to bribe Captain Stafford, the Governor of the Castle. The conditions asked, preparatory to surrender, were liberty of conscience, and permission to withdraw in safety and with military honours. Cromwell's idea of liberty of conscience was as peculiar as his idea of honour. He wrote to the Governor of Ross to say that he would not "meddle with any man's conscience;" but adds: "If by liberty of conscience you mean a liberty to exercise the Mass, I judge it best to use plain dealing, and to tell you now, where the Parliament of England have power, that will not be allowed of;"[1] which, in plain English, meant that he professed liberty of conscience, but allowed it only to such as agreed with himself. Of his estimation of honour, his dealings at Wexford afford a fair sample. As soon as he had found that Stafford could be bribed, he denounced the proposals of the garrison as abominable and impudent. The traitor opened the castle-gates, and the Parliamentary troops marched in. The besieged were amazed and panic-struck; yet, to their eternal credit, they made what even Cromwell admits to have been a "stiff resistance." The massacre of Drogheda was renewed with all its horrors, and the treacherous General held in his hand all the time the formal offer of surrender which had been made by the townspeople and his own reply. He informs the Parliament that he did not intend to destroy the town, but his own letter reveals his treachery; and he congratulates his correspondents on the "unexpected providence" which had befallen them. He excuses the massacre on the plea of some outrages which had been offered to the "poor Protestants," forgetting what incomparably greater cruelties had been inflicted by the Protestants on the Catholics, both for their loyalty and for their religion.

MacGeoghegan mentions the massacre of two hundred women,

---

[1] *Allowed of.—Letters and Speeches,* vol. i. p. 477.

who clung round the market-cross for protection.[2] His statement
is not corroborated by contemporary authority; but there appears
no reason to doubt that it may have taken place, from what has
already been recorded at Drogheda on unquestionable authority.
Owen Roe and Ormonde now leagued together for the royal cause,
but their union was of short duration, for the Irish chieftain died
almost immediately, and it was said, not without suspicion of
having been poisoned by wearing a "pair of russet boots," sent to
him by one Plunket, of Louth, who afterwards boasted of his
exploit. His death was an irreparable loss to the Irish cause; for
his noble and upright conduct had won him universal esteem, while
his military prowess had secured him the respect even of his enemies. New Ross surrendered to Cromwell on the 18th of October,
and Luke Taaffe, the Commander, joined Ormonde at Kilkenny.
The garrisons of Cork, Youghal, Kinsale, and Bandon, revolted to
Cromwell, through the intervention of Lord Broghill, son of the Earl
of Cork, who became one of the leading Parliamentary officers. On
the 24th of November, Cromwell attempted to take Waterford; but
finding the place too strong for him, he marched on to Dungarvan.
Here the garrison surrendered at discretion, and his troops proceeded to Cork through Youghal.

The Irish had now begun to distrust Ormonde thorougly; even
the citizens of Waterford refused to admit his soldiers into their
town. Indeed, the distrust was so general, that he had considerable
difficulty in providing winter quarters for his troops, and he wrote
to ask permission from the exiled King to leave the country.
The month of January, 1650, was spent by Cromwell in continuing his victorious march. He set out from Youghal on the
29th, and approached as near Limerick as he dared, taking such
castles as lay in his way, and accepting the keys of Cashel and
other towns, where the authorities surrendered immediately. On
the 22nd of March he arrived before Kilkenny, to meet a resistance
as hopeless as it was heroic. A fearful pestilence had reduced the
garrison from 1,200 men to about 400, yet they absolutely refused

[2] *Protection.*—Dr. French, the Catholic Bishop of Ferns, has given an
account of the storming of Wexford, in a letter to the Papal Nuncio, in which
he states that the soldiers were not content with simply murdering their victims, but used "divers sorts of torture." As he was then in the immediate
neighbourhood, he had every opportunity of being correctly informed. Cromwell must have sanctioned this, if he did not encourage it.

to obey the summons to surrender, but, after a brave resistance, they were obliged to yield; and Cromwell hastened on to Clonmel, where he had to encounter the most formidable resistance he experienced in his Irish campaigns. The garrison was commanded by Hugh Dubh O'Neill. The Bishop of Ross attempted to raise the siege, but was taken and hanged by Broghill, because he would not desire the defenders of Carrigadrohid to surrender. The first attack on Clonmel took place on the 9th of May, and O'Neill determined to resist with the energy of despair, and the full knowledge of the demon vengeance with which the Puritans repaid such deeds of valour. When the place was no longer tenable, he withdrew his troops under cover of darkness; and the English General found next morning that he had been outwitted, and that nothing remained for his vengeance but the unfortunate townspeople.

Pressing demands were now made by the Parliament for his return to England, where the royalists had also to be crushed and subdued; and after committing the command of his army to Ireton, he sailed from Youghal, on the 20th of May, leaving, as a legacy to Ireland, a name which was only repeated to be cursed, and an increase of miseries which already had seemed incapable of multiplication. In the meantime the Irish clergy held frequent conferences, and made every effort in their power to obtain peace for their unfortunate country. Ormonde became daily more and more distrusted; the people of Limerick and of Galway had both refused to receive him; and on the 6th of August the clergy met in synod at Jamestown, in the county Leitrim, and sent him a formal message, requesting his withdrawal from the kingdom, and asking for the appointment of some one in whom the people might have confidence. His pride was wounded, and he refused to retire until he should be compelled to do so; but the bishops published a declaration, denouncing his government, and threatening to impeach him before the King. They were yet to learn that the King, whom they served so faithfully, and in whom, despite all past disappointments, they confided so loyally, could be guilty of the greatest duplicity and the basest subterfuge.

Charles II. landed in Scotland on the 28th of June, 1650, and soon after signed the Covenant, and a declaration in which he stated the peace with Ireland to be null and void, adding, with equal untruthfulness and meanness, that "he was convinced in his conscience of the sinfulness and unlawfulness of it, and of allowing them [the Catholics] the liberty of the Popish religion; for which he did from his heart desire to be deeply humbled before the Lord." Ormonde declared, what was probably true, that the King had been obliged to make these statements, and that they meant nothing; but neither his protestations nor his diplomacy could save him from general contempt; and having appointed the Marquis of Clanrickarde to administer the Government of Ireland for the King, he left the country, accompanied by some of the leading royalists, and, after a stormy passage, arrived at St. Malo, in Brittany, early in the year 1651. The Irish again sacrificed their interests to their loyalty, and refused favourable terms offered to them by the Parliamentary party; they even attempted to mortgage the town of Galway, to obtain money for the royal cause, and an agreement was entered into with the Duke of Lorraine for this purpose; but the disasters of the battle of Worcester, and the triumphs of the republican faction, soon deprived them of every hope.

It will be remembered that Cromwell had passed by Limerick at a respectful distance; but the possession of that city was none the less coveted. Ireton now prepared to lay siege to it. To effect this, Coote made a feint of attacking Sligo; and when he had drawn off Clanrickarde's forces to oppose him, marched back hastily, and took Athlone. By securing this fortress he opened a road into Connaught; and Ireton, at the same time, forced the passage of the river at O'Briensbridge, and thus was enabled to invest Limerick. Lord Muskerry marched to its relief; but he was intercepted by Lord Broghill, and his men were routed with great slaughter. The castle at the salmon weir was first attacked; and the men who defended it were butchered in cold blood, although they had surrendered on a promise of quarter. At length treachery accomplished what valour might have prevented. The plague was raging in the city, and many tried to escape; but were either beaten back into the town, or killed on the spot by Ireton's troopers. The corporation and magistrates were in favour of a capitulation; but the gallant Governor, Hugh O'Neill, opposed it earnestly. Colonel Fennell, who had already betrayed the pass at Killaloe, completed his perfidy by seizing St. John's Gate and Tower, and admitting Ireton's men by night. On the following day the invader was able to dictate his own terms. 2,500 soldiers laid down their arms in St. Mary's Church, and marched out of the city, many dropping dead on their road of the fearful pestilence. Twenty-four persons were exempted

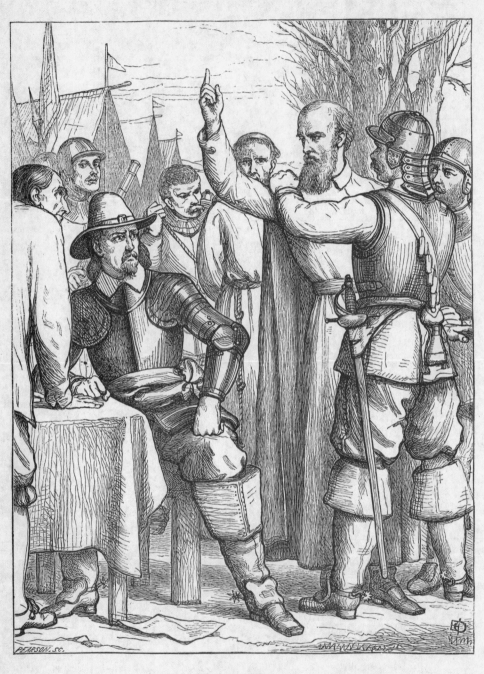

Ireton condemning the Bishop of Limerick.

from quarter. Amongst the number were a Dominican prelate, Dr. Terence O'Brien, Bishop of Emly, and a Franciscan, Father Wolfe. Ireton had special vengeance for the former, who had long encouraged the people to fight for their country and their faith, and had refused a large bribe[3] which the Cromwellian General had offered him if he would leave the city. The ecclesiastics were soon condemned; but, ere the Bishop was dragged to the gibbet, he turned to the dark and cruel man who had sacrificed so many lives, and poured such torrents of blood over the land, summoning him, in stern and prophetic tones, to answer at God's judgment-seat for the evils he had done. The Bishop and his companion were martyred on the Eve of All Saints, October 31st, 1651. On the 26th of November Ireton was a corpse. He caught the plague eight days after he had been summoned to the tribunal of eternal justice; and he died raving wildly of the men whom he had murdered, and accusing everyone but himself of the crime he had committed.

Several of the leading gentry of Limerick were also executed; and the traitor Fennell met the reward of his treachery, and was also hanged. Hugh O'Neill was saved through the remonstrances of some of the Parliamentary officers, who had the spirit to appreciate his valour and his honorable dealing.

Ludlow now took the command, and marched to assist Coote, who was besieging Galway. This town surrendered on the 12th of May, 1652. The few Irish officers who still held out against the Parliament, made the best terms they could for themselves individually; and there was a brief peace, the precursor of yet more terrible storms.

I have already given such fearful accounts of the miseries to which the Irish were reduced by confiscations, fines, and war, that it seems useless to add fresh details; yet, fearful as are the records given by Spenser of 1580, when neither the lowing of a cow nor the voice of a herdsman could be heard from Dunquin, in Kerry, to Cashel, in Munster, there seems to have been a deeper depth of misery after Cromwell's massacres. In 1653 the English themselves were nearly starving, even in Dublin; and cattle had to be imported from Wales. There was no tillage, and a licence was required to kill lamb.[4] The Irish had fled into the mountains, the only refuge

---

[3] *Bribe.*—40,000 golden crowns, and free leave to emigrate where he chose.— *Hib. Dom.* p. 448.

[4] *Lamb.*—*Cromwellian Settlement*, p. 16. See also Petty's *Political Anatomy of Ireland.*

left to them now; and the Parliamentary officers were obliged to issue proclamations inviting their return, and promising them safety and protection. But the grand object of the revolutionary party was still to carry out the wild scheme of unpeopling Ireland of the Irish, and planting it anew with English—a scheme which had been so often attempted, and had so signally failed, that one marvels how it could again have been brought forward. Still there were always adventurers ready to fight for other men's lands, and subjects who might be troublesome at home, whom it was found desirable to occupy in some way abroad. But a grand effort was made now to get rid of as many Irishmen as possible in a peaceable manner. The valour of the Irish soldier was well known abroad;[5] and agents from the King of Spain, the King of Poland, and the Prince de Condé, were contending for those brave fellows, who were treated like slaves in their native land; and then, if they dared resist, branded with the foul name of rebels. If a keen had rung out loud and long when O'Donnell left his native land never to return, well might it ring out now yet more wildly. In May, 1652, Don Ricardo White shipped 7,000 men for the King of Spain; in September, Colonel Mayo collected 3,000 more; Lord Muskerry took 5,000 to Poland; and, in 1654, Colonel Dwyer went to serve the Prince de Condé with 3,500 men. Other officers looked up the men who had served under them, and expatriated themselves in smaller parties; so that, between 1651 and 1654, 34,000 Irishmen had left their native land; and few, indeed, ever returned to its desolate shores.

But their lot was merciful compared with the fate of those who still remained. In 1653 Ireland was considered sufficiently depopulated by war and emigration to admit of a commencement of the grand planting. The country was again portioned out; again the ruling powers selected the best portion of the land for themselves and their favourites; again the religion of the country was reformed, and Protestant prelates were condemned as loudly, though they were not hunted as unmercifully, as Popish priests; again the wild and lawless adventurer was sent to eject the old proprietor, who

[5] *Abroad.*—The Prince of Orange declared they were born soldiers. Sir John Norris said that he "never beheld so few of any country as of Irish that were idiots or cowards." Henry IV. of France said that Hugh O'Neill was the third soldier of the age; and declared that no nation had such resolute, martial men.—*Cromwellian Settlement*, p. 22.

might starve or beg while the intruder held his lands, and sheltered himself in his mansion, while a new cruelty was enacted, a new terror devised, a new iniquity framed, and this by rulers who talked so loudly of political and religious liberty. It was not convenient, or, more probably, it was not possible, to massacre all the native population who still survived; so they were to be banished—banished to a corner of their own land, imprisoned there safely by their ruthless conquerors, and there, without hope or help, it was supposed they must soon die out quietly.

This is the official proclamation which was issued on the subject: "The Parliament of the Commonwealth of England, having, by an Act lately passed (entitled an Act for the Settling of Ireland), declared that it is not their intention to extirpate this whole nation . . . . it is ordered that the Governor and Commissioners of Revenue . . . . . do cause the said Act of Parliament, with this present declaration, to be published and proclaimed in their respective precincts, by beat of drum and sound of trumpet, on some market-day within ten days after the same shall come unto them within their respective precincts."

We may imagine the dismay and anguish which this announcement caused. The old Irish chieftain and the Anglo-Irish lord still had some kind of home and shelter on their own estate—it might be but an outhouse or a barn; it was certainly on the worst and least cultivated portion of their land, for the old castle had long since been taken from them, and their broad acres transferred to others. Yet, though they tilled the soil of which they so lately had been the lords, this little spot was home: there the wife and mother loved her little ones as tenderly as in the stately halls which her husband or his fathers had so lately possessed. It was home, and if not the dear old home, it was, perhaps, loved all the more for its sorrowful proximity to the ancestral castle—for the faint hope that the rightful owner might still be restored. But the trumpet had sounded the nation's doom. Confiscation and banishment, wholesale plunder and untold iniquity, reigned supreme. The name of the God of justice was invoked to sanction[6] the grossest outrages upon justice; and men who professed to have freed their own nation from

---

[6] *Sanction.*—See *Cromwellian Settlement*, p. 61, for a specimen of the "Bible stuff with which they crammed their heads and hardened their hearts."

the tyranny of kingcraft and of Popery, perpetrated a tyranny on another nation, which has made the name of their leader a byword and a curse.

The majority of the Catholic nobility and gentry were banished; the remainder of the nation, thus more than decimated, were sent to Connaught. On the 26th of September, 1653, all the property of the Irish people was declared to belong to the English army and adventurers, "and it was announced that the Parliament had assigned Connaught [America was not then accessible] for the habitation of the Irish nation, whither they must transplant, with their wives, and daughters, and children, before 1st May following, under the penalty of death, if found on this side of the Shannon after that day."[7] It must not be supposed that this death penalty was a mere threat; I shall give instances to prove the contrary. Any man, woman, or child who had disobeyed this order, no matter from what cause, could be instantly executed in any way, by any of these soldiers or adventurers, without judge, jury, or trial. It was in fact constituting a special commission for the new comers to murder[8] all the old inhabitants.

Connaught was selected for two reasons: first, because it was the most wasted province of Ireland; and secondly, because it could be, and in fact was, most easily converted into a national prison, by erecting a *cordon militaire* across the country, from sea to sea. To make the imprisonment more complete, a belt four miles wide, commencing one mile to the west of Sligo, and thence running along the coast and the Shannon, was to be given to the soldiery to plant. Thus, any Irishman who attempted to escape, would be sure of instant capture and execution.

The Government, as it has been already remarked, reserved the best part of the land for themselves. They secured the towns, church-lands, and tithes, and abolished the Protestant Church, with all its officers, which had been so recently declared the religion of the country. A "Church of Christ" was now the established religion, and a Mr. Thomas Hicks was approved by the "Church of Christ" meeting at Chichester House, as one fully qualified to preach and dispense the Gospel as often as the Lord

---

[7] *Day.—Cromwellian Setilement*, p. 163.

[8] *Murder.*—"Whenever any unwary person chanced to pass these limits, he was knocked on the head by the first officer or soldier who met him. Colonel Astell killed *six women* in this way."—*Ibid.* p. 164.

should enable him, and in such places as the Lord should make his ministry most effectual. The Parliament also reserved for themselves the counties of Dublin, Kildare, Carlow, and Cork; and from these lands and the church property they were to enrich themselves, and, with what they could spare, to reward the leading regicides and rebels. The adventurers were next provided for. They claimed £960,000. This was divided into three lots, to be paid in lands in Munster, Leinster, and Ulster. All these were to be drawn by lot; and a lottery was held at Grocers' Hall, London, which commenced at eight o'clock in the morning, on the 20th of July, 1653, at which time and place men who professed the advancement of the Christian religion to be the business of their lives, openly and flagrantly violated the most solemn and explicit commands of that very belief which they declared themselves so zealous in upholding. The soldiers and officers were to obtain whatever was left after the adventurers had been satisfied.

A book was written by a Franciscan father, called *Threnodia Hiberno-Catholica, sive Planctus Universalis totius Cleri et Populi Regni Hiberniæ*,[9] in which the writer states he had heard a great Protestant statesman give three reasons why this transplantation was confined to the gentry, and why the poor, who had not been either transported or hanged, were allowed to remain: (1) because the English wanted them to till the ground; (2) they hoped they would become Protestants when deprived of their priests; (3) because the settlers required servants, or else they should have worked for themselves.

But the fatal day at length arrived, and those who had dared to linger, or to hope that so cruel a sentence would not be finally executed, were at once undeceived. The commissioners had been in trouble all the winter: the people who were to be driven out of their farms refused to sow for those who were to succeed them; and the very plotters of the iniquity began to tremble for the consequences which

---

[9] *Hiberniæ.—The Wail of the Irish Catholics; or, Groans of the Whole Clergy and People*, &c. By Father Maurice Morison, of the Minors of Strict Observance, an eyewitness of these cruelties. Insbruck, A.D. 1659. This religious had remained in Ireland, like many of his brethren, in such complete disguise, that their existence was not even suspected. In order to minister the more safely to their afflicted people, they often hired as menials in Protestant families, and thus, in a double sense, became the servants of all men. Father Maurice was in the household of Colonel Ingolsby, the Parliamentary Governor of Limerick.

might accrue to themselves. They fasted, they prayed, and they wrote pages of their peculiar cant, which would be ludicrous were it not profane. They talked loudly of their unworthiness for so great a service, but expressed no contrition for wholesale robbery. Meanwhile, however, despite cant, fasts, and fears, the work went on. The heads of each family were required to proceed to Loughrea before the 31st of January, 1654, to receive such allotments as the commissioners pleased to give them, and that they might erect some kind of huts on these allotments, to shelter their wives and daughters when they arrived. The allotment of land was proportioned to the stock which each family should bring; but they were informed that, at a future day, other commissioners were to sit at Athlone, and regulate even these regulations, according to their real or supposed affection or disaffection to the Parliament. All this was skilfully put forward, that the unfortunate people might transplant the more quietly, in the hope of procuring thereby the good-will of their tyrants; but the tyrants were quite aware that the stock would probably die from the fatigue of transportation and the want of food ; then the land could be taken from the victim, and, as a last favour, he might be allowed to remain in the poor hut he had erected, until misery and disease had terminated his life also.

Remonstrances and complaints were sent to the faction who governed England, but all was in vain. The principal petitioners were the descendants of the English nobles; they were now, by a just retribution, suffering themselves the very miseries which they had so ruthlessly inflicted on the native Irish. The petitioners, says Mr. Prendergast,[1] were the noble and the wealthy, men of ancient English blood, descendants of the invaders—the FitzGeralds, the Butlers, the Plunkets, the Barnwalls, Dillons, Cheevers, Cusacks, names found appended to various schemes for extirpating or transplanting the Irish, after the subduing of Lord Thomas FitzGerald's rebellion in 1535—who were now to transplant as Irish. The

---

[1] *Prendergast.—Cromwellian Settlement*, p. 34. We can only recommend this volume to the consideration of our readers. It would be impossible, in anything less than a volume, to give the different details which Mr. Prendergast has brought together with so much judgment, and at the expense of years of research. We might have selected some cases from his work, but, on the whole, we think it will be more satisfactory to the reader to peruse it in its entirety. It may be obtained from our publishers, Messrs. Longmans and Co., Paternoster-row, London.

native Irish were too poor to pay scriveners and messengers to the Council, and their sorrows were unheard; though under their rough coats beat hearts that felt as great pangs at being driven from their native homes as the highest in the land.

One of these English families demands special mention. Edmund Spenser's grandson was now commanded to transplant, as though he too had been "mere Irish;" and the very estate near Fermoy, which had been confiscated from the FitzGeralds seventy years before, and which the poet had obtained thus fraudulently, was now confiscated anew, and granted to Cromwell's soldiers. William Spenser protested; he pleaded his grandfather's name, he pleaded his grandfather's services, especially the odium he had incurred amongst the Irish by the way in which he had written of them; and lastly, William Spenser declares of himself that he had utterly renounced Popery since he came to years of discretion. But even Cromwell's interference could not save him; the soldiers were determined to have his lands, and they had them.

The commissioners appointed to conduct the transplanting had a busy time. They were overwhelmed with petitions: the heads of families demanding permission to return and save their crops; the women requesting to remain a few months longer for a similar purpose, when the men were not permitted to return. Hundreds of petitions were sent from aged and bedridden persons, to obtain leave to die in peace where they were. Then there were complaints from the officers who had charge of driving the people into the plantation; and above all, there was a charge, a grave charge, against the Irish people—they were as stiff-necked, wicked, and rebellious[2] as ever, and could not be brought to see that they were created for no other end than to be sacrificed for the benefit of English adventurers; and, moreover, they were declared to be a most treacherous race, for, years after, they might revenge all this kindness, by murdering the men who had taken possession of their lands and farms; and some had absolutely refused to transplant, and preferred death.

---

[2] *Rebellious.*—If the subject were not so serious, the way in which the officials write about the feelings of the Irish would almost provoke a smile. They say: "It is the nature of this people to be rebellious; and they have been so much the more disposed to it, having been highly exasperated by the transplanting work." Surely they could not be expected to be anything else but rebellious and exasperated!

The manner in which these difficulties were met is thus recorded in a letter which was written for publication in London :—

"*Athy, March* 4, 1664-5.

"I have only to acquaint you that the time prescribed for the transplantation of the Irish proprietors, and those that have been in arms and abettors of the rebellion, being near at hand, the officers are resolved to fill the gaols and to seize them; by which this bloody people will know that they [the officers] are not degenerated from English principles ; though I presume we shall be very tender of hanging any except leading men ; yet we shall make no scruple of sending them to the West Indies, where they will serve for planters, and help to plant the plantation that General Venables, it is hoped, hath reduced."

So examples were made. Mr. Edward Hetherington was hanged in Dublin, on the 3rd of April, 1655, with placards on his breast and back, on which were written, " For not transplanting;" and at the summer assizes of 1658, hundreds were condemned to death for the same cause, but were eventually sent as slaves to Barbadoes. The miseries of those who did transplant was scarcely less than those of the persons who were condemned to slavery. Some committed suicide, some went mad, all were reduced to the direst distress. The nobles of the land were as cruelly treated and as much distrusted as the poorest peasant. The very men who had laid down their arms and signed articles of peace at Kilkenny, were not spared; and the excuse offered was, that the Act of Parliament overrode the articles. One of the gentlemen thus betrayed was Lord Trimbleston, and his tomb may still be seen in the ruined Abbey of Kilconnell, with the epitaph :—

"HERE LIES MATHEW, LORD BARON OF TRIMBLESTON,
ONE OF THE TRANSPLANTED."

SCULPTURES AT DEVENISH.

CHAPTER XXXI.

The Irish transported as Slaves to Barbadoes—The Three Beasts who were to be hunted : the Wolf, the Priest, and the Tory—Origin and Causes of Agrarian Outrages—Cases of Individual Wrongs—Lord Roche—Mr. Luttrel—Accession of Charles II.—His Base Conduct towards the Irish Loyalists—Gross Injustice towards the Irish Catholic Landowners—The Remonstrance opposed by the Clergy—A Quarrel in the House of Lords—The Popish Plot—Ormonde's Difficulties—Seizure and Imprisonment of the Archbishop of Dublin—Imprisonment and Execution of the Most Rev. Dr. Plunkett, Archbishop of Armagh.

[A.D.—1655—1681.]

MANY of the Irish soldiers who had entered into the service of foreign princes, were obliged to leave their wives and families behind. When we recall the number of those who were thus expatriated, it will not seem surprising that thousands of young children were left utterly destitute. These boys and girls, however, were easily disposed of by the Government; and Sir William Petty states, that 6,000 were sent out as slaves to the West Indies. The Bristol sugar merchants traded in these human lives, as if they had been so much merchandize; and merchandize, in truth, they were, for they could be had for a trifle, and they fetched a high price in the slave-market. Even girls of noble birth were subjected to this cruel fate. Morison mentions an instance of this kind which came to his own knowledge. He was present when Daniel Connery, a gentleman of Clare, was sentenced to banishment, by Colonel Ingoldsby, for harbouring a priest. Mrs. Connery died of destitution, and three of his daughters, young and beautiful girls, were transported as slaves to Barbadoes. [3]

A court was established for the punishment of "rebels and malignants;" the former consisting of persons who refused to surrender their houses and lands, and the latter being those who would not act contrary to their conscientious convictions in religious matters. These courts were called "Cromwell's Slaughter-houses." Donnellan, who had acted as solicitor to the regicides, at the trial of Charles I., held the first court at Kilkenny, October 4, 1652. Lord Louther held a court in Dublin, in February, 1653, for the special purpose of trying "all massacres and murders committed since the 1st day of October, 1641." The inquiries, however, were solely confined to the accused Catholics; and the result proved the falsehood of all the idle tales which had been circulated of their having intended a great massacre of Protestants, for convictions could only be obtained against 200 persons, and even these were supported by forged and corrupt evidence.[4] Sir Phelim O'Neill was the only person convicted in Ulster, and he was offered his life again and again, and even on the very steps of the scaffold, if he would consent to criminate Charles I.

As the majority of the nation had now been disposed of, either by banishment, transportation, or hanging, the Government had time to turn their attention to other affairs. The desolation of the country was such, that the smoke of a fire, or the sign of a habitation, was considered a rare phenomenon. In consequence of this depopulation, wild beasts had multiplied on the lands, and three "beasts" were especially noted for destruction. In the Parliament held at Westminster in 1657, Major Morgan, member for the county Wicklow, enumerated these beasts thus : "We have three beasts to destroy that lay burdens upon us. The first is the wolf, on whom we lay £5 a head if a dog, and £10 if a bitch. The second beast is a priest, on whose head we lay £10; if he be eminent, more.

---

[3] *Barbadoes.—Threnodia Hib.* p. 287.

[4] *Evidence.*—In a work written expressly to excite feeling in England against the Irish, it is stated that they [the Irish] failed in the massacre.— See *Cromwellian Settlement*, p. 5, for further evidence.

The third beast is a Tory, on whose head, if he be a public Tory, we lay £20 ; and forty shillings on a private Tory."[5]

Wolves had increased so rapidly, that the officers who left Ireland for Spain, in 1652, were forbidden to take their dogs with them, and were thus deprived of the pleasure and the pride (for Irish dogs were famous) of this consolation in their exile. Public hunts were ordered, and every effort made to keep down beasts of prey. But the whole blame was thrown on the second beast. It was declared solemnly that if there had been no priests there would have been no wolves.[6] The syllogism ran somewhat in this fashion :—

The Popish priests are the cause of every misery in Ireland ;

The wolves are a misery :

Therefore the priests are to blame for the existence of the wolves.

"By a similar process of reasoning," observes Mr. Prendergast, "it is proved that the Irish have caused the ruin, the plundering, and the desolation of the country, from the first invasion, for so many ages." And this is undoubtedly true ; for if there had been no Irish, no Irish could have been plundered ; and if there had been no plunder, there could not have been the misery of the plundered. The number of wolves to be destroyed may be estimated from the fact, that some lands valued at a high rate were let for a stipulated number of wolves' heads in lieu of rent. But the wolves were more easily got rid of than the priests. The priests were accustomed to be persecuted, and accustomed to be hunted. They came to Ireland, as a general rule, with the full knowledge that this would be their fate, and that if they ended their lives, after a few years' ministration, by hanging, without any extra torture, it was the best they could hope for, as far as this world was concerned. Some, however, would have preferred the torture, expecting an additional recompense for it in the next. But there were parts of the country where it was incomparably more difficult to hunt out a priest than a wolf; so the Government gave notice, on the 6th of January, 1653, that all priests and friars who were willing to transport themselves, should have liberty to do so for twenty days. But the priests and friars had no idea of leaving the country. They had gone abroad, at the risk of their lives, to fit themselves in some of the splendid

---

[5] *Tory.—Cromwellian Settlement*, p. 150.
[6] *No wolves*—Declaration printed at Cork, 1650.

continental colleges for their duties, and to obtain authority to administer the sacraments ; they returned, at the risk of their lives, to
fulfil their mission ; and they remained, at the risk of their lives, to
devote them to their own people, for whose sakes they had renounced, not only earthly pleasures and joys, but even that quiet
and peaceful life, which, as Christian priests, they might have had
in foreign lands.   The people for whom they suffered were not ungrateful.   Poor as they were, none could be found to take the proffered bribe.   Long lists may be found of priests who were captured
and executed, and of the men who received the rewards for their
capture; but you will not see a real Irish name amongst them ; you
will perceive that the priest-catchers were principally English
soldiers ; and you will remark that the man in whose house the
priest was discovered generally shared his fate.   But it was useless.
They were hung, they were tortured, they were transported to
Barbadoes, and, finally, such numbers were captured, that it was
feared they would contaminate the very slaves, and they were
confined on the island of Innisboffin, off the coast of Connemara.
Yet more priests came to take the place of those who were thus
removed, and the " hunt " was still continued.

The number of secular priests who were victims to this persecution cannot be correctly estimated.   The religious orders, who were
in the habit of keeping an accurate chronicle of the entrance and
decease of each member, furnish fuller details.   An official record,
drawn up in 1656, gives the names of thirty Franciscans who had
suffered for the faith ; and this was before the more severe search
had commenced.   The martyrdom of a similar number of Dominicans is recorded almost under the same date ; and Dr. Burgat[7]
states that more than three hundred of the clergy were put to death
by the sword or on the scaffold, while more than 1,000 were sent
into exile.

The third " beast " was the Tory.   The Tory was the originator
of agrarian outrages in Ireland, or we should rather say, the English
planters were the originators, and the Tories the first perpetrators
of the crime.   The Irish could scarcely be expected to have very
exalted ideas of the sanctity and inviolable rights of property, from

___

[7] *Dr. Burgat.*—*Brevis Relatio.*   Presented to the Sacred Congregation in
1667.   Dr. Moran's little work, *Persecution of the Irish Catholics*, gives ample
details on this subject; and every statement is carefully verified, and the
authority given for it.

the way in which they saw it treated. The English made their will law, and force their title-deed. The Anglo-Normans dispossessed the native Irish, the followers of the Tudors dispossessed the Anglo-Normans, and the men of the Commonwealth dispossessed them all. Still, the Celt, peculiarly tenacious of his traditions, had a very clear memory of his ancient rights, and could tell you the family who even then represented the original proprietor, though that proprietor had been dispossessed five or six hundred years. The ejectments from family holdings had been carried out on so large a scale, that it can scarcely be a matter of surprise if some of the ejected resented this treatment. There were young men who preferred starving in the woods to starving in Connaught ; and after a time they formed into bands in those vast tracts of land which had been wholly depopulated. The men were desperate. It is difficult to see how they could have been anything else, when driven to desperation. They were called robbers ; but there was a general confusion about *meum* and *tuum* which they could not understand. Strangers had taken possession of their cattle, and they did not comprehend why they should not try to obtain it again in any possible way. Young men, whose fathers had landed estates of £2,000 a-year, which were quietly divided amongst Cromwell's Life-Guards, while the proprietor was sent out to beg, and his daughters compelled to take in washing or do needlework, could scarcely be expected to take such a change in their circumstances very calmly. A man who had been transplanted from an estate worth £2,500 a year near Dublin, which his family had owned for four hundred years, and whose daughters were given the munificent gratuity of £10 a-piece by the Council Board, and forbidden for the future to ask for any further assistance, might certainly plead extenuating circumstances[8] if he took to highway robbery. Such circumstances as these were common at this period ; and it should be borne in mind that the man whose holding was worth but £40 a-year felt the injustice, and resented the inhumanity of his expulsion, quite as much as the noble-

[8] *Circumstances.*—Lord Roche and his daughters were compelled to go on foot to Connaught, and his property was divided amongst the English soldiers. His wife, the Viscountess Roche, was hanged without a shadow of evidence that she had committed the crime of which she was accused. Alderman Roche's daughters had nothing to live on but their own earnings by washing and needlework ; and Mr. Luttrell, the last case mentioned above, was allowed as a favour to occupy his *own stables* while preparing to transplant.

man with £4,000. So the Tories plundered their own property; and, if they could be captured, paid the penalty with their lives; but, when they were not caught, the whole district suffered, and some one was made a scapegoat for their crime, though it did not seem much to matter whether the victim could be charged with complicity or not. After some years, when even the sons of the proprietors had become old inhabitants, and the dispossessed generation had passed away, their children were still called Tories. They wandered from village to village, or rather from hovel to hovel, and received hospitality and respect from the descendants of those who had been tenants on the estates of their forefathers, and who still called them gentlemen and treated them as such, though they possessed nothing but the native dignity, which could not be thrown off, and the old title-deeds, which were utterly worthless, yet not the less carefully treasured. Yet, these men were condemned by their oppressors because they did not work for their living, and because they still remembered their ancient dignity, and resented their ancient wrongs. To have worked and to have forgotten might have been wiser; but those who are accustomed to ease are slow to learn labour, even with the best intentions; and those who had inflicted the wrongs were scarcely the persons who should have taunted the sufferers with the miseries they had caused.

Charles II. commenced his reign *de facto* in 1660, under the most favourable auspices. People were weary of a Commonwealth which had promised so much and performed so little; of the name of liberty without the reality; of the exercise of kingly power without the appurtenances or right of majesty. But the new monarch had been educated in a bad school. Surrounded with all the prestige of royalty without its responsibilities, and courted most ardently by followers whose only object was their own future advancement, which they hoped to secure by present flattery, it is scarcely a matter of surprise that Charles should have disappointed the hopes of the nation. In England public affairs were easily settled. Those who had been expelled from their estates by the Cromwellian faction, drove out[9] by the new proprietors; but in Ireland the case was very different. Even the faithful loyalists, who had sacrificed everything for the King, and had so freely assisted his necessities out of their poverty, were now treated with contempt, and their

[5] *Drove out.*—Carte's *Ormonde*, vol. ii. p. 398.

claims silenced by proclamation; while the men who had been most opposed to the royal interest, and most cruel in their oppression of the natives, were rewarded and admitted into favour. Coote and Broghill were of this class. Each tried to lessen the other in the opinion of their royal master as they ran the race for favour, and each boasted of services never accomplished, and of loyalty which never existed. The two enemies of each other and of the nation were now appointed Lord Justices of Ireland; and a Parliament was assembled on the 8th of May, 1661, the first meeting of the kind which had been held for twenty years.

The Catholic, or national interest, was certainly not represented; for there were present seventy-two Protestant peers, and only twenty-one Catholics; while the House of Commons comprised two hundred and sixty members, all of whom were burgesses except sixty-four, and the towns had been so entirely peopled by Cromwell's Puritan followers, that there could be no doubt what course they would pursue. An attempt was now made to expel the few Catholics who were present, by requiring them to take the oath of supremacy. The obsequious Parliament voted £30,000 to the Duke of Ormonde, whose career of duplicity was crowned with success. It is almost amusing to read his biographer's account[1] of the favours bestowed on him, and the laudations he bestows on his master for his condescension in accepting them. Carte would have us believe that Ormonde was a victim to his king and his country, and that the immense sums of money he received did not nearly compensate him for his outlays. Posterity will scarcely confirm the partiality of the biographer.

The Bill of Settlement was opposed by the Irish Catholics through their counsel, but their claims were rejected and treated with contempt. Charles had told his Parliament, on his restoration, that he expected they would have a care of his honour and of the promise he had made. This promise had been explicitly renewed by Ormonde for the King, before he left for Breda; but the most solemn engagements were so regularly violated when Irish affairs were concerned, that nothing else could have been expected. A Court of Claims was at length established, to try the cases of ejectment which had occurred during the Commonwealth; but this

---

[1] *Accounts.*—Carte's *Ormonde*, vol. ii. pp. 398, 399. He considers all "bounties" granted to him as mere acts of justice.

excited so much indignation and alarm amongst the Protestants, that all hope of justice was quickly at an end, and the time-serving Ormonde closed the court. The grand occupation of each new reign, for the last few centuries, appears to have been to undo what had been done in the preceding reigns. An Act of Explanation was now passed, and a Protestant militia raised, to satisfy that party. It was provided by the new Act that the Protestants were, in the first place, and especially, to be settled; that any doubt which arose should be decided in their favour ; and that no Papist, who, by the qualifications of the former Act, had not been adjudged innocent, should at any future time be reputed innocent, or entitled to claim any lands or settlements. It will be remembered that Ormonde had cut short the sittings of the court to satisfy Protestant clamour; in consequence of this, more than 3,000 Catholic claimants were condemned to forfeit their estates, without even the shadow of an inquiry, but with the pretence of having justice done to them, or, as Leland has expressed it, "without the justice granted to the vilest criminal—that of a fair and equal trial."[2]

Although it would seem to the ordinary observer that the Catholics had been dealt with severely, the dominant faction were still dissatisfied; and Ormonde was obliged to threaten a dissolution, and to expel some members for complicity in a plot to overthrow the English Government, which had just been discovered, and of which the ringleader was a man named Blood. It was now ascertained that the Cromwellian distribution of lands had been carried out with the most shameful injustice towards the very Government which had sanctioned it; and that the soldiers, who went with texts of Scripture on their lips, and swords in their hands, to destroy Popery, had cheated[3] their officers and self-elected rulers with shameless audacity.

The famous Remonstrance was drawn up about this time. It was prepared by Peter Walsh, a Franciscan friar, who was a pro-

[2] *Trial.*—Chief Justice Nugent, afterwards Lord Riverston, in a letter, dated Dublin, June 23rd, 1686, and preserved in the State Paper Office, London, says: "There are 5,000 in this kingdom who were never outlawed."

[3] *Cheated.*—Books were found in the office of the surveyor for the county Tipperary alone, in which only 50,000 acres were returned as unprofitable, and the adventurers had returned 245,207.—Carte's *Ormonde*, vol. ii. p. 307. "These soldiers," says Carte, " were for the most part Anabaptists, Independents, and Levellers." Equal roguery was discovered in other places.

tégé of Ormonde's, and who devoted more attention to politics than to his religious duties. The Remonstrance contained expressions which were by no means consonant with that pure Catholic feeling for which the Irish had been always remarkable; but it suited the Duke's purpose all the better, and he induced a considerable number of the nobility, and some of the clergy, to affix their signatures to it. They were little aware, in giving expression to the loyalty they so sincerely felt, that they were supposed to countenance disrespect to the Church which they so deeply revered. A synod of the Irish bishops and clergy was therefore held in Dublin, to consider the document, June 11th, 1666. Although ecclesiastics were then under the penal laws, and liable to suffer at any moment, Ormonde connived at the meeting, hoping that his ends would be thereby attained. He has himself left his object on record. It was to "sow divisions among the clergy;" and Lord Orrery had written to him, being well aware of his plans, suggesting that this was a fitting time for their accomplishment. But the clergy were not so easily deceived; and even the miserable friar has left it on record, that out of 1,850 ecclesiastics, regular and secular, only sixty-nine signed the Remonstrance. The synod now prepared another document; and if the expression of loyalty was all that Ormonde required, he should have been fully satisfied; but, unfortunately, this was not the case, and he bided his time to avenge himself bitterly on the men who refused to sacrifice their conscience to his will.

During the same year (1660), the Irish sent over a contribution of 15,000 bullocks, to relieve the distress which occurred in London after the Great Fire. In return for their charity, they were assured that this was a mere pretence to keep up the cattle trade with England; and accordingly an Act was passed in which the importation of Irish cattle was forbidden, and termed a "nuisance," and language was used which, in the present day, would be considered something like a breach of privilege. The Duke of Buckingham, whose farming interests were in England, declared "that none could oppose the Bill, except such as had Irish estates or Irish understandings." Lord Ossory protested that "such virulence became none but one of Cromwell's counsellors;" and he being the eldest son of the Duke of Ormonde, and having Irish interests, opposed it. Several noble lords attempted to draw their swords. Ossory challenged Buckingham; Buckingham declined the challenge. Ossory was sent to the Tower; the word "nuisance" remained; some mem-

bers of the " Cabal" said it should have been " felony;" and the Irish
trade was crushed.   Even the Puritan settlers in Ireland began to
rebel at this, for they, too, had begun to have " Irish interests," and
could not quite see matters relative to that country in the same
light as they had done when at the other side of the Channel.   At
last they became openly rebellious.   Some soldiers mutinied for
arrears of pay, and seized Carrickfergus Castle—ten of them were
executed, and peace was restored; but the old Cromwellians, both in
England and Ireland, gave considerable anxiety to the Government;
and, indeed, it seems marvellous that they should not have revolted
more openly and in greater force.

So many complaints were made of Ormonde's administration, that
he was now removed for a time.   He was succeeded by Lord
Berkeley, in May, 1670, a nobleman whose honest and impartial
government earned him the respect of all who were not interested
in upholding a contrary line of conduct.   The Catholics offered
him an address, which was signed by two prelates, who held a prominent position, not only in their Church, but also in the history
of the period; these were Dr. Plunkett, Archbishop of Armagh,
and Dr. Talbot, Archbishop of Dublin.   Colonel Richard Talbot,
who was afterwards created Earl of Tyrconnel by James II., had
been, for some time, the accredited agent of the Irish Catholics at
the English court; he now (A.D. 1671) attempted to obtain some
examination into the claims of those who had been ejected from
their estates during the Commonwealth.   After some delay and
much opposition, a commission was appointed; but although the
" Popish Plot" had not yet made its appearance, a wild " no
Popery " cry was raised, and the King was obliged to recall Lord
Berkeley, and substitute the Earl of Essex.   Even this did not
quiet the storm.   On the 9th of March, 1673, an address was presented to the King by the Commons in England, demanding the
persecution of Papists in Ireland; and the weak monarch, all the
more afraid of appearing to show partiality, because of his apprehension that Popery might be the true religion, and his still more
serious apprehensions that his people might find out his opinion, at
once complied, and even recalled the Commission of Enquiry.

In 1677 Ormonde was again appointed Viceroy, and he held the
office during the ensuing seven years, at an advanced age, and at a
period of extraordinary political excitement.   The " Popish treason" was the first and the most fearful of these panics.   Ormonde

was at Kilkenny when he received the first intimation of the conspiracy, October 3, 1678 ; but he had too much knowledge of the world to credit it for a moment. Like other politicians of that, and indeed of other ages, he was obliged to keep up his reputation by appearing to believe it in public, while in private[4] he treated the whole affair with the contempt it merited. It was soon reported that the plot had extended to Ireland, and Archbishop Talbot was selected as the first victim. The prelate then resided with his brother, Colonel Talbot, at Carton, near Maynooth. He was in a dying state ; but although his enemies might well have waited for his end, he was taken out of his bed, carried to Dublin, and confined a prisoner in the Castle. He died two years later. "He was the last distinguished captive destined to end his days in that celebrated state prison, which has since been generally dedicated to the peaceful purposes of a reflected royalty."[5] His brother was arrested, but allowed to go beyond the seas ; and a Colonel Peppard was denounced in England as one of the leading Irish traitors. But the Colonel was quite as imaginary as the plot. No such person existed, and a *non est inventis* was all the return that could be made to the most active inquiries. There was one illustrious victim, however, who was found, who was executed, and who was not guilty, even in thought, of the crime of which he was accused.

Oliver Plunkett had been Archbishop of Armagh since the death of Dr. O'Reilly, in 1669. He belonged to the noble family of Fingall ; but he was more respected for his virtues and his office than even for his rank. He was now accused of being in correspondence with the French ; it was a favourite charge against Catholics at that time, and one which could be easily brought forward by men who did not mind swearing to a lie, and not easily disproved by men who could only assert their innocence. Lord Shaftesbury was the great patron of Titus Oates, the concocter of the plot, and the perjured murderer of scores of innocent men. It was a serious disappointment to find that no evidence of a conspiracy could be found in Ireland.

---

[4] *Private.*—For full information on this subject, see Carte's *Ormonde*, vol. ii. pp. 476-482. I will give one extract to verify the statement above. "The Duke of Ormonde had, in truth, difficulties enough to struggle with in the government of Ireland, to preserve that kingdom in peace, and yet to give those who wished to imbroil it no handle of exception to the measures he took for that end."—vol. ii. p. 477.

[5] *Royalty.*—D'Arcy M'Gee's *History of Ireland,* vol. ii. p. 560.

Carte, who certainly cannot be suspected of the faintest shadow of preference for an Irishman or a Catholic, says that every effort was made to drive the people into rebellion. He gives the reason for this, which, from former experience, one fears must be true. "There were," he says, "too many Protestants in Ireland who wanted another rebellion, that they might increase their estates by new forfeitures." "It was proposed to introduce the Test Act and all the English penal laws into Ireland; and that a proclamation should be forthwith issued for encouraging all persons that could make any further discoveries of the horrid Popish plot, to come in and declare the same."

Unfortunately for the credit of our common humanity, persons can always be found who are ready to denounce their fellow-creatures, even when guiltless, from mere malice. When, to the pleasure of gratifying a passion, there is added the prospect of a reward, the temptation becomes irresistible; and if the desire of revenge for an injury, real or imaginary, be superadded, the temptation becomes overwhelming. In order to satisfy the clamours of the "no Popery" faction, an order had been issued, on the 16th of October, 1677, for the expulsion of all ecclesiastics from Ireland; and a further proclamation was made, forbidding Papists to enter into the Castle of Dublin, or any fort or citadel; and so far, indeed, did this childish panic exceed others of its kind, that orders were sent to the great market-towns, commanding the markets to be held outside the walls, to prevent the obnoxious Catholics from entering into the interior. Rewards were offered of £10 for an officer, £5 for a trooper, and £4 for a soldier, if it could be proved that he attended Mass; and how many were sworn away by this bribery it would be difficult to estimate. On the 2nd of December, a strict search was ordered for the Catholic ecclesiastics who had not yet transported themselves. Dr. Plunkett had not left the country. At the first notice of the storm he withdrew, according to the apostolic example, to a retired situation, where he remained concealed, more in hope of martyrdom than in fear of apprehension.

The prelate had never relaxed in his duties towards his flock, and he continued to fulfil those duties now with equal vigilance. One of the most important functions of a chief shepherd is to oversee the conduct of those who govern the flock of Christ under him. There was a Judas in the college of the Apostles, and many Judases have been found since then. The Archbishop had been obliged to

excommunicate two of his priests and two friars, who had been denounced by their superiors for their unworthy lives. The unhappy
men resented the degradation, without repenting of the crimes which
had brought it upon them. They were ready for perjury, for they
had renounced truth; and the gratification of their malice was probably a far stronger motive than the bribe for the capture of a
bishop. The holy prelate was seized on the 6th December, 1679.
Even Ormonde wished to have spared him, so inoffensive and peaceful had been his life. He was arraigned at the Dundalk assizes;
but although every man on the grand jury was a Protestant, from
whom, at least, less partiality might be expected towards him
than from members of his own Church, the perjured witnesses
refused to come forward. Indeed, the prelate himself had such
confidence in his innocence, and in the honorable dealing of his
Protestant fellow-countrymen, when their better judgment was not
bewildered by fanaticism, that he declared in London he would put
himself on trial in Ireland before any Protestant jury who knew
him, and who knew the men who swore against him, without the
slightest doubt of the result.

Jones, the Protestant Bishop of Meath, was, unfortunately for himself, influenced by fanaticism. He had served in Cromwell's army,[6]
and had all that rancorous hatred of the Catholic Church so characteristic of the low class from whom the Puritan soldiery were
drawn. He was determined that the Archbishop should be condemned; and as men could not be found to condemn him in Ireland,
he induced Lord Shaftesbury to have him taken to London. The
Archbishop was removed to Newgate, about the close of October,
1680, and so closely confined, that none of his friends could have
access to him. He spent his time in prayer, and his gaolers were
amazed at his cheerfulness and resignation. His trial took place on
the 8th of June, 1681; but he was not allowed time to procure the
necessary witnesses, and the court would not allow certain records
to be put in, which would have proved the character of his accusers.
Six of the most eminent English lawyers were arrayed against
him. The legal arrangements of the times deprived him of the
assistance of counsel, but they did not require the judges to help
out the men who swore against him: this, however, they did do.

[6] *Army.*—Carte says " he was Scout-Master-General."—*Ormonde*, vol. ii.
p. 478.

The prelate was condemned to die. The speech of the judge who pronounced sentence was not distinguished by any very special forensic acumen. Dr. Plunkett had been charged by the witnesses with political crimes; the judge sentenced[7] him for his religious convictions; and, by a process of reasoning not altogether peculiar to himself, insisted that his supposed treason was a necessary result of the faith he professed. The Archbishop suffered at Tyburn, on Friday, July 11, 1681. He went to his death rejoicing, as men go to a bridal. His dying declaration convinced his hearers of his innocence; and, perhaps, the deep regret for his martyrdom, which was felt by all but the wretches who had procured his doom, tended to still the wild storm of religious persecution, or, at least, to make men see that where conscience was dearer than life, conscientious convictions should be respected. It is at least certain that his name was the last on the long roll of sufferers who had been executed at Tyburn for the faith. Blood was no longer exacted there as the price which men should pay for liberty of belief. It were well had that liberty been allowed by men to their fellow-men in after years, without fines or confiscations—without those social penalties, which, to a refined and sensitive mind, have in them the bitterness of death, without the consolations of martyrdom.

[7] *Sentenced.*—See Dr. Moran's *Memoir of the Most Rev. Dr. Plunkett.* This interesting work affords full details of the character of the witnesses, the nature of the trial, and the Bishop's saintly end.

ANCIENT PITCHER, FROM THE COLLECTION OF THE R.I.A., FOUND IN A CRANNOGE, AT LOUGH TAUGHAN, LECALE, CO. DOWN.

OLDERFLEET CASTLE, LARNE.

CHAPTER XXXII.

Glimpses of Social Life in the Seventeenth Century—Literature and Literary Men—Keating—the Four Masters—Colgan—Ward—Usher—Ware—Lynch—Trade—Commerce depressed by the English—Fairs—Waterford Rugs—Exportation of Cattle forbidden—State of Trade in the Principal Towns—Population—Numbers employed in different Trades—Learned Professions—Physicians—Establishment of their College in Dublin—Shopkeepers—Booksellers—Coffee-houses—Clubs—Newspapers—Fashionable Churches—Post-houses and Post-offices established—Custom-house—Exchange—Amusements—Plays at the Castle—The First Theatre set up in Werburgh-street—Domestics Manners and Dress—Food—A Country Dinner Party in Ulster.

[A.D. 1600—1700.]

NOTWITHSTANDING the persecutions to which the Irish had been subjected for so many centuries, they preserved their love of literature, and the cultivated tastes for which the Celt has been distinguished in all ages. Indeed, if this taste had not existed, the people would have sunk into the most degraded barbarism; for education was absolutely forbidden, and the object of the governing powers seems to have been to reduce the nation, both intellectually and morally, as thoroughly as possible. In such times, and under such circumstances, it is not a little remarkable to find men devoting themselves to literature with all the zest of a freshman anticipating collegiate distinctions, while surrounded by difficulties which would certainly have dismayed, if they did not altogether crush, the intellects of the present age. I have already spoken of the mass of untranslated national literature existing in this country and in continental libraries. These treasures of mental labour are by no means confined to one period of our history ; but it could scarcely be expected that metaphysical studies or the fine arts could flourish at a period when men's minds were more occupied with the philosophy of war than with the science of Descartes, and were more inclined to patronize a new invention in the art of gunnery, than the *chef d'œuvre* of a limner or sculptor. The Irish language was the general medium of conversation in this century. No amount of Acts of Parliament had been able to repress its use, and even the higher classes of English settlers appear to have adopted it by preference. Military proclamations were issued in this language ;[8] or if the Saxon tongue were used, it was translated for the general benefit into the vernacular. During the Commonwealth, however, the English tongue made some way ; and it is remarkable that the English-speaking Irish of the lower classes, in the present day, have preserved the idioms and the accentuation used about this period. Many of the expressions which provoke the mirth of the modern Englishman, and which he considers an evidence of the vulgarity of the uneducated Irish, may be found in the works of his countrymen, of which he is most justly proud.

The language of Cromwell's officers and men, from whom the Celt had such abundant opportunities of learning English, was (less the cant of Puritanism) the language of Shakspeare, of Raleigh, and of Spenser. The conservative tendencies of the Hibernian preserved the dialect intact, while causes, too numerous for present detail, so modified it across the Channel, that each succeeding century condemned as vulgarism what had been the highest fashion with their predecessors. Even as Homeric expressions lingered for centuries after the blind bard's obit had been on record, so the expressions of Chaucer, Spenser, and Shakspeare, may still be discovered in provincial dialects in many parts of the British Isles. I do not intend to quote *Tate and Brady* as models of versification and of syntax ; but if the best poets of the age did not receive the commission to translate the Psalms into verse, it was a poor compliment to reli-

---

[8] *Language.*—A proclamation in Irish, issued by Tyrone in 1601, is still extant, with a contemporary English translation.—*See Ulster Arch. Jour.* vol. vi. p. 57.

gion. We find the pronunciation of their rhymes corresponding with the very pronunciation which is now condemned as peculiarly Irish. Newton also rhymes *way* and *sea*, while one can scarcely read a page of Pope[9] without finding examples of pronunciation now supposed to be pure Hibernicism. In the Authorized Protestant version of the Bible, *learn* is used in the sense of *to teach*, precisely as it is used in Ireland at the present day : "If thy children shall keep my covenant and my testimonies that I shall *learn* them" and their use of the term *forninst* is undoubtedly derived from an English source, for we find it in Fairfax's *Tasso*.[1]

History and theology were the two great studies of the middle ages, and to these subjects we find the *literati* of Ireland directing special attention. The importance and value of Latin as a medium of literary intercommunication, had been perceived from an early period : hence that language was most frequently employed by Irish writers after it had become known in the country. It is unquestionably a national credit, that no amount of suffering, whether inflicted for religious or political opinions, deprived the Irish of historians.[2] Some of their works were certainly compiled under the most disadvantageous circumstances.

None of the writers whom we shall presently enumerate, worked for hope of gain, or from any other motive save that of the purest patriotism. Keating, whose merits are becoming more and more recognized since modern research has removed Celtic traditions from the region of fable to the tableland of possibility, wrote his *History* principally in the Galtee Mountains, where he had taken refuge from the vengeance of Carew,[3] Lord President of Munster. Although he had received a high education in the famous College

[9] *Pope.*—He rhymes spirit and merit ; fit and yet; civil and devil; obey and tea.

[1] *Tasso.*—

"The land fornenst the Greekish shore he held."

Chaucer, too, uses *faute* for *fault* in the *Canterbury Tales*.

[2] *Historians.*—Max Müller—*Lectures on the Science of Language*, p. 271—states, that labourers in country parishes in England do not use more than 300 words. A friend of mine, who is an excellent Irish scholar, assures me the most illiterate Irish-speaking peasant would use at least 500.

[3] *Carew.*—The tradition of the country says that this vengeance was excited by the complaints of a lady, with whom the Lord President had some gallantries, and whose conduct Keating had reproved publicly.

of Salamanca, for the sake of his people he preferred suffering persecution, and, if God willed it, death, to the peaceful life of literary quiet which he might have enjoyed there. He wrote in his mother-tongue, although master of many languages; and in consequence of this choice his work remained in MS. for many years. When it came to light, those who were ignorant of the MS. materials of ancient Irish history, were pleased to suppose that he had invented a considerable portion, and supplied the remainder from the *viva voce* traditions of the country people. Unfortunately, he was not sufficiently master of the science of criticism to give the authorities

TUBRID CHURCHYARD—BURIAL-PLACE OF THE HISTORIAN KEATING.

which he had used so carefully, and to prove their value and authenticity. But truth has at length triumphed. Several of the works from which he has quoted have been discovered ; and it has been shown that, wild as some of his legends may read in the garb in which he has given them, there is proof that important facts underlie the structure, though it has been somewhat overembellished by a redundant fancy.

Keating was also a poet.   Many of his pieces are still well known and highly popular in Munster, and copies of nearly all of them are preserved by the Royal Irish Academy.   One of his ballads has been " coaxed " into verse by D'Arcy M'Gee, in his *Gallery of Irish Writers.*   It is entitled " Thoughts on Innisfail."   I shall give one verse as a specimen, and as an illustration of the popular feelings of the time :

> " And the mighty of Naas are mighty no more,
>   Like the thunders that boomed 'mid the banners of yore ;
>   And the wrath-ripened fields, 'twas they who could reap them ;
>   Till they trusted the forsworn, no foe could defeat them."

INSCRIPTION IN HONOUR OF KEATING.

The poet-priest must have died at an advanced age, though the precise date of his demise has not been ascertained.   He has also left some religious works ; and his " Shaft of Death" is well known and much admired both by divines and Celtic scholars.[4]

[4] *Scholars.*—We have been favoured with an accurate photograph of this inscription, by William Williams, Esq., of Dungarvan, from which the engraving given above has been made.   The view of Tubrid Churchyard is

O'Sullivan Beare's history is too well known to require more than a passing mention. It was said that he wrote as fiercely as he fought. Archbishop Usher, with whom he had many a literary feud, appears to have been of this opinion; for, after having described O'Sullivan as an "egregious liar," he was so sensitive to any counter abuse he might receive in return, that he carefully cut out every disparaging epithet which the historian used from the copy of his reply, which at present lies, with Usher's other works, in the Library of Trinity College, Dublin.

The Four Masters are included amongst the Irish writers of this century, but I have already given ample details of their labours. The *Acta Sanctorum* of Colgan, and Ward's literary efforts in a foreign land for his country, are beyond all praise. Usher and Ware were also amongst the giants of these days; and, considering the state of political and religious excitement amongst which they lived and wrote, it is incomparably marvellous that they should not have dipped their pens still deeper into the gall of controversy and prejudice. Usher was one of the *Hibernis ipsis Hiberniores*, for his family came to Ireland with King John; but he admired and wrote Celtic history with the enthusiasm of a Celt, and he gathered materials for other men's work with patient industry, however he may have allowed party spirit to influence and warp his own judgment in their use. Usher was Ware's most ardent patron. Habits of indefatigable research did for him, in some degree, what natural genius has done for others. Nor was he slow to recognize or avail himself of native talent; and there can be no doubt, if he had lived a few years longer after his acquaintance with MacFirbis, that Irish literature would have benefited considerably by the united efforts of the man of power, who was devoted to learning, and the man of gifts, who had the abilities which neither position nor wealth can purchase. John Lynch, the Bishop of Killala, and the indefatigable and successful impugner of Cambrensis, was another literary luminary of the age. His career is a fair sample of the extraordi-

also engraved from a sketch with which he has favoured us. It is hoped that many Irishmen in distant lands will look with no little interest on these beautifully executed engravings, and breathe a blessing on the memory of the good and gifted priest. A Keating Society was established a few years ago, principally through the exertions of Mr. Williams and the Rev. P. Meany, C.C. A Catechism in Irish has already appeared, and other works will follow in due time.

nary difficulties experienced by the Irish in their attempts to cultivate intellectual pursuits, and of their undaunted courage in attaining
their end.   Usher has himself recorded his visit to Galway, where
he found Lynch, then a mere youth, teaching a school of humanity
(A.D. 1622).   "We had proofe," he says, " during our continuance
in that citie, how his schollars profitted under him, by the verses
and orations which they brought us."[5]   Usher then relates how he
seriously advised the young schoolmaster to conform to the popular
religion ; but, as Lynch declined to comply with his wishes, he was
bound over, under sureties of £400 sterling, to "forbear teaching."
The tree of knowledge was, in truth, forbidden fruit, and guarded
sedulously by the fiery sword of the law.   I cannot do more than
name a few of the other distinguished men of this century.   There
was Florence Conry, Archbishop of Tuam, and founder of the Irish
College of Louvain.   He was one of the first to suggest and to carry
out the idea of supplying Irish youth with the means of education
on the Continent, which they were denied at home.   It is a fact,
unexampled in the history of nations, that a whole race should have
been thus denied the means of acquiring even the elements of learning, and equally unexampled is the zeal with which the nation
sought to procure abroad the advantages from which they were so
cruelly debarred at home.   At Louvain some of the most distinguished
Irish scholars were educated.   An Irish press was established within
its halls, which was kept constantly employed, and whence proceeded some of the most valuable works of the age, as well as a
scarcely less important literature for the people, in the form of short
treatises on religion or history.   Colleges were also established at
Douay, Lisle, Antwerp, Tournay, and St. Omers, principally through
the exertions of Christopher Cusack, a learned priest of the diocese
of Meath.   Cardinal Ximenes founded an Irish College at Lisbon,
and Cardinal Henriquez founded a similar establishment at Evora.
It is a remarkable evidence of the value which has always been set
on learning by the Catholic Church, that even in times of persecution, when literary culture demanded such sacrifices, she would not
admit uneducated persons to the priesthood. The position which the
proscribed Catholic priesthood held in Ireland at this period, compared with that which the favoured clergy of the Established Church

[5] *Brought us.*—Regal Visitation Book, A.D. 1622, MS., Marsh's Library,
Dublin.

held in England, is curious and significant. Macaulay says of the latter : " A young levite—such was the phrase then in use—might be had for his board, a small garret, and ten pounds a year ; and might not only perform his own professional functions, but might also save the expenses of a gardener or a groom. Sometimes the reverend man nailed up the apricots, and sometimes he curried the coach-horses. He cast up the farrier's bills. He walked ten miles with a message or a parcel. He was permitted to dine with the family, but he was expected to content himself with the plainest fare—till he was summoned to return thanks for the repast, from a great part of which he had been excluded."[6]

In Ireland there were few learned men in the Established Church, and even Usher seems to have been painfully indifferent to the necessity of superior education, as well as regular ordination, for his clergy. In 1623 Dr. Blair was invited to Ireland by Lord Clannaboy, to take the living of Bangor, vacated by the death of the Rev. John Gibson, " sence Reformacione from Popary the first Deane of Down." Dr. Blair objected both to episcopal government and to use the English Liturgy; yet he " procured a free and safe entry to the holy ministry," which, according to his own account, was accomplished thus. His patron, Lord Clannaboy, informed " the Bishop Echlin how opposite I was to episcopacy and their liturgy, and had the influence to procure my admission on easy and honorable terms." At his interview with the Bishop, it was arranged that Dr. Blair was to receive ordination from Mr. Cunningham and the neighbouring clergy, and the Bishop was "to come in among them in no other relation than a presbyter." These are the Bishop's own words; and his reason for ordaining at all was : " I must ordain you, else neither I nor you can answer the law nor brook the land." In 1627 Blair had an interview with Archbishop Usher, and he says " they were not so far from agreeing as he feared." "He admitted that all those things [episcopacy and a form of prayer] ought to have been removed, but the constitution and laws of the place and time would not permit that to be done." A few years later Mr. John Livingstone thus relates his experience on similar subjects. He had been appointed also by Lord Clannaboy to the parish of Killinchy; and, " because it was needful that he should be ordained to the ministry, and the Bishop of Down, in whose diocese Killinchy was, being a corrupt

---

[6] *Excluded.—History of England*, People's Edition, part ii. p. 156.

and timorous man, and would require some engagement, therefore my Lord Clannaboy sent some with me, and wrote to Mr. Andrew Knox, Bishop of Raphoe, who told me he knew my errand, and that I came to him because I had scruples against episcopacy and ceremonies, according as Mr. Josiah Welsh and some others had done before ; and that he thought his old age was prolonged for little other purpose than to perform such ceremonies." It was then arranged that he should be ordained as Dr. Blair and others had been. The Bishop gave him the book of ordination, and said, "though he durst not answer it to the State," that he might draw a line over anything he did not approve of, and that it should not be read. "But," concludes Mr. Livingstone, "I found that it had been so marked by some others before, that I needed not mark anything ; so the Lord was pleased to carry that business far beyond anything that I have thought, or almost ever desired."[7]

Such facts as these were well known to the people ; and we can scarcely be surprised that they increased their reverence for the old clergy, who made such sacrifices for the attainment of the learning necessary for their ministry, and who could not minister, even if they would, without having received the office and authority of a priest by the sacrament of orders.

But literary efforts in Ireland were not confined to the clergy ; O'Flaherty and MacFirbis devoted themselves with equal zeal to the dissemination and preservation of knowledge ; and we envy not the man who can read without emotion the gentle complaint of the former, in his *Ogygia:* "I live a banished man within the bounds of my native soil—a spectator of others enriched by my birthright." And again : "The Lord hath wonderfully recalled the royal heir to his kingdom, with the applause of all good men ; but He hath not found me worthy to be restored to the kingdom of my cottage. Against Thee, O Lord, have I sinned : may the Lord be blessed for ever !"

The customs and dress of the upper classes in Ireland were probably much the same as those of a similar rank in England.[8] Com-

---

[7] *Desired.*—See the Hamilton Manuscripts, *Ulster Arch. Jour.* vol. iii. pp. 145-147. Blair complains also that his patron "would receive the sacrament kneeling."

[8] *England.*—"The diet, housing, and clothing of the 16,000 families abovementioned [those were the middle class] is much the same as in England ;

merce was so constantly restricted by English jealousy, that it had
few opportunities of development.　In a curious old poem, called
the *Libel of English Policie*, the object of which was to impress on
the English the necessity of keeping all trade and commerce in their
own hands, we find Irish exports thus enumerated :—

> "Hides and fish, salmon, hake, herring,
> 　Irish wool and linen cloth, falding
> 　And masternés good be her marchandie ;
> 　Hertes, birds, and others of venerie,
> 　Skins of otter, squirrel and Irish hare,
> 　Of sheep, lambe, and fore is her chaffere,
> 　Felles of kids, and conies great plentie."

It will be observed that this list contains only the natural produce of the country ; and had any attempt been made to introduce
or encourage manufactures, some mention would have been made
of them.　The silver and gold mines of the country are alluded to
further on, and the writer very sensibly observes, that if "we [the
English] had the peace and good-will of the wild Irish, the metal
might be worked to our advantage."　In the sixteenth century the
Irish sent raw and tanned hides, furs, and woollens to Antwerp,[9]
taking in exchange sugar, spices, and mercery.　The trade with
France and Spain for wines was very considerable ; fish was the
commodity exchanged for this luxury ; and even in 1553, Philip II.
of Spain paid[1] £1,000 yearly—a large sum for that period—to
obtain liberty for his subjects to fish upon the north coast of Ireland.
Stafford, in speaking of the capture of Dunboy Castle, says that
O'Sullivan made £500 a-year by the duties which were paid to him
by foreign fishermen, "although the duties they paid were very
little."[2]

Stanihurst has described a fair in Dublin, and another in Waterford, where he says the wares were "dog-cheap."　These fairs
continued for six days, and merchants came to them from Flanders
and France, as well as from England.　He gives the Waterford people

nor is the French elegance unknown in many of them, nor the French and
Latin tongues.　The latter whereof is very frequent among the poorest Irish,
and chiefly in Kerry, most remote from Dublin."—*Political Anatomy of Ireland*, Petty, p. 58.

[9] *Antwerp.—Descrittione dei Paesi Bassi:* Anvers, 1567.

[1] *Paid.—The Sovereignty of the British Seas:* London, 1651.

[2] *Little.—Hib. Pac.*

the palm for commerce, declares they are " addicted to thieving," that they distil the best *aqua vitæ*, and spin the choicest rugs in Ireland. A friend of his, who took a fancy to one of these " choice rugs," being " demurrant in London, and the weather, by reason of a hard hoar frost, being somewhat nipping, repaired to Paris Garden, clad in one of the Waterford rugs. The mastiffs had no sooner espied him, but deeming he had been a bear, would fain have baited him ; and were it not that the dogs were partly muzzled and partly chained, he doubted not he should have been well tugged in this Irish rug."

After the plantation of Ulster, Irish commerce was allowed to flourish for a while ; the revenue of the crown doubled ; and statesmen should have been convinced that an unselfish policy was the best for both countries. But there will always be persons whose private interests clash with the public good, and who have influence enough to secure their own advantage at the expense of the multitude. Curiously enough, the temporary prosperity of Ireland was made a reason for forbidding the exports which had produced it. A declaration was issued by the English Government in 1637, which expressly states this, and places every possible bar to its continuance. The Cromwellian settlement, however, acted more effectually than any amount of prohibitions or Acts of Parliament, and trade was entirely ruined by it for a time. When it again revived, and live cattle began to be exported in quantities to England, the exportation was strictly forbidden. The Duke of Ormonde, who possessed immense tracts of land in Ireland, presented a petition, with his own hands, against the obnoxious measure, and cleverly concluded it with the very words used by Charles himself, in the declaration for the settlement of Ireland at the Restoration, trusting that his Majesty " would not suffer his good subjects to weep in one kingdom when they rejoiced in another." Charles, however, wanted money ; so Ireland had to wait for justice. A vote, granting him £120,000, settled the matter ; and though for a time cattle were smuggled into England, the Bill introduced after the great fire of London, which we have mentioned in the last chapter, settled the matter definitively. The Irish question eventually merged into an unseemly squabble about prerogative, but Charles was determined " never to kiss the block on which his father lost his head."[3] He

---

[3] *Head.*—The tract entitled *Killing no Murder*, which had disturbed Cromwell's " peace and rest," and obliged him to live almost as a fugitive in

overlooked the affront, and accepted the Bill, "nuisance" and all. One favour, however, was granted to the Irish; they were graciously permitted to send contributions of cattle to the distressed Londoners in the form of salted beef. The importation of mutton, lamb, butter, and cheese, were forbidden by subsequent Acts, and salted beef, mutton, and pork were not allowed to be exported from Ireland to England until the general dearth of 1757.

The commercial status of the principal Irish towns at this period (A.D. 1669), is thus given by Mr. Bonnell, the head collector of Irish customs in Dublin : " Comparing together the proceeds of the duties for the six years ending December, 1669, received from the several ports of Ireland, they may be thus ranked according to their worth respectively, expressed in whole numbers, without fractions, for more clearness of apprehension :—

Rate.	Ports.	Proportion per cent.	Rate.	Ports.	Proportion per cent.
1	Dublin - - -	40		Drogheda - -	3
2	Cork - - -	10	5	Londonderry -	3
3	Waterford - -	7		Carrickfergus	3
	Galway - - -	7		Ross - - - -	1
	Limerick - -	5		Wexford - -	1
4	Kinsale - -	5	6	Dundalk - -	1
	Youghal - -	5		Baltimore - -	1
				Sligo - - - -	1 "

Killybeg, Dungarvan, Donaghadee, Strangford, Coleraine, and Dingle, are mentioned as " under rate."

The linen trade had been encouraged, and, indeed, mainly established in Ireland, by the Duke of Ormonde. An English writer [4] says that 200,000 pounds of yarn were sent annually to Manchester, a supply which seemed immense in that age ; and yet, in the present day, would hardly keep the hands employed for forty-eight hours. A political economist of the age gives the " unsettledness of the country " as the first of a series of reasons why trade did not flourish in Ireland, and, amongst other remedies, suggests sumptuary laws and a tax upon celibacy, the latter to weigh quite

the country over which he had hoped to reign as a sovereign, still left its impression on English society. The miserable example of a royal execution was a precedent which no amount of provocation should have permitted.

[4] *Writer.—Merchant's Map of Commerce:* London, 1677.

equally on each sex.[5] Sir William Petty does not mention the linen trade, but he does mention the enormous amount of tobacco [6] consumed by the natives. It is still a disputed question whether the so-called "Danes' pipes," of which I give an illustration, were made before the introduction of tobacco by Sir Walter Raleigh, or whether any other narcotizing indigenous plant may have been used. Until one, at least, of these pipes shall have been found in a position which will indicate that they must have been left there at an earlier period than the Elizabethan age, the presumption remains in favour of their modern use.

I shall now give some brief account of the domestic life of our ancestors 200 years ago, and of the general state of society, both

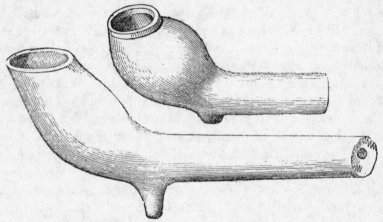

"DANES' PIPES," FROM THE COLLECTION OF THE R.I.A.

in the upper and lower classes. Petty estimates the population of Ireland at 1,100,000, or 200,000 families. Of the latter he states that 160,000 have no fixed hearths; these, of course, were the very poorest class, who lived then, as now, in those mud hovels, which are the astonishment and reprobation of foreign tourists. There were 24,000 families who had "one chimney," and 16,000 who had

[5] *Sex.—The Interest of Ireland in its Trade and Wealth*, by Colonel Lawrence: Dublin, 1682.

[6] *Tobacco.*—A Table of the Belfast Exports and Imports for the year 1683, has been published in the *Ulster Arch. Jour.* vol. iii. p. 194, which fully bears out this statement, and is of immense value in determining the general state of Irish commerce at this period. There are, however, some mistakes in the quotations of statistics, probably misprints.

more than one. The average number appears to be four. Dublin Castle had 125, and the Earl of Meath's house, twenty-seven. There were, however, 164 houses in Dublin which had more than ten.

Rearing and tending cattle was the principal employment of the people, as, indeed, it always has been. There were, he estimates, 150,000 employed in this way, and 100,000 in agriculture. "Tailors and their wives" are the next highest figure—45,000. Smiths and apprentices, shoemakers and apprentices, are given at the same figure—22,500. Millers and their wives only numbered 1,000, and the fishery trade the same. The woolworkers and their wives, 30,000 ; but the number of alehouse-keepers is almost incredible. In Dublin, where there were only 4,000 families, there was, at one time, 1,180 alehouses and ninety-one public brew-houses. The proportion was equally great throughout the country; and if we may judge from the Table of Exports from Belfast before-mentioned, the manufacture was principally for home consumption, as the returns only mention three barrels of beer to Scotland, 124 ditto to the Colonies, 147 to France and Flanders, nineteen to Holland, and forty-five to Spain and the Mediterranean. There are considerable imports of brandy and wines, but no imports of beer. We find, however, that "Chester ale" was appreciated by the faculty as a medicament, for Sir Patrick Dun, who was physician to the army during the wars of 1688, sent two dozen bottles of Chester ale, as part of his prescription, to General Ginkles, Secretary-at-War, in the camp at Connaught, in 1691. He added two dozen of the best claret, and at the same time sent a "lesser box," in which there was a dozen and a-half potted chickens in an earthen pot, and in another pot "foure green geese." "This," writes the doctor, "is the physic I advise you to take ; I hope it will not be nauseous or disagreeable to your stomach—a little of it upon a march."[7] It is to be supposed such prescriptions did not diminish the doctor's fame, and that they were appreciated as they deserved.

A century previous (A.D. 1566), Thomas Smyth seems to have been the principal, if not the only English practitioner in Dublin ; and although he sold his drugs with his advice, his business did not pay. However, Thomas was "consoled" and "comforted," and "induced to remain in the country," by the united persuasions of

[7] March.—Gilbert's Dublin, vol. i. p. 178.

the Lord Deputy, the Counsellors of State, and the whole army. The consolation was administered in the form of a concordat, dated April 25th, 1566, by which an annual stipend was settled on him, the whole army agreeing to give him one day's pay, and every Counsellor of State twenty shillings, " by reason of his long contynuance here, and his often and chardgeable provision of druggs and other apothecarie wares, which have, from tyme to tyme, layen and remained in manner for the most part unuttered ; for the greater part of this contray folke ar wonted to use the mynisterie of their leeches and such lyke, and neglecting the apothecarie's science, the said Thomas thereby hath been greatly hyndered, and in manner enforced to abandon that his faculty."[8]   It was only natural that the English settler should distrust the *leeche* who gathered his medicines on the hillside by moonlight, " who invoked the fairies and consulted witches ;" and it was equally natural that the native should distrust the Saxon, who could kill or cure with those magical little powders and pills, so suspiciously small, so entirely unlike the traditionary medicants of the country.   In a list still preserved of the medicines supplied for the use of Cromwell's army, we may judge of the " medicants " used in the seventeenth century.   They must have been very agreeable, for the allowance of sugar, powder and loaf, of " candie," white and brown, of sweet almonds and almond cakes, preponderates wonderfully over the " rubarcke, sarsaparill, and aloes."[9]   Mr. Richard Chatham was Apothecary-General, and had his drugs duty free by an order, dated at " ye new Customs' House, Dublin, ye 24th of June, 1659."

Dr. William Bedell was the first who suggested the foundation of a College of Physicians.   On the 15th of April, 1628, he wrote to Usher thus : " I suppose it hath been an error all this while to neglect the faculties of law and physic, and attend only to the ordering of one poor college of divines."   In 1637 a Regius Professor of Physic was nominated.   In 1654 Dr. John Stearne was appointed President of Trinity Hall, which was at this time set apart " for the sole and proper use of physicians ;" and, in 1667, the physicians received their first charter from Charles II.   The new corporation obtained the title of " The President and College of

---

[8] *Faculty.*—Document in the State Paper Office, Dublin, entitled *Smyth's Information for Ireland.*

[9] *Aloes.*— *Ulster Arch. Jour.* vol. iii. p. 163.

Physicians."[4] It consisted of fourteen Fellows, including the President, Dr. Stearne. Stearne was a grand-nephew of Archbishop Usher, and was born in his house at Ardbraccan, county Meath. He was a man of profound learning; and although he appears to have been more devoted to scholastic studies than to physic, the medical profession in Ireland may well claim him as an ornament and a benefactor to their faculty. The College of Physicians was without a President from 1657 until 1690, when Sir Patrick Dun was elected. The cause of this was the unfortunate illiberality of the Provost and Fellows of Trinity College, who refused to confirm the election of Dr. Crosby, simply because he was a Roman Catholic. In 1692 the College received a new charter and more extended privileges; and these, with certain Acts of Parliament, form its present constitution.

In medieval cities the castle was the centre round which the town extended itself. Dublin was no exception to this rule, and in this century we find High-street and Castle-street the fashionable resorts. The nobility came thither for society, the tradesmen for protection. Castle-street appears to have been the favourite haunt of the bookselling fraternity, and Eliphud Dobson (his name speaks for his religious views) was the most wealthy bookseller and publisher of his day. His house was called the Stationers' Arms, which flourished in the reign of James II. The Commonwealth was arbitrary in its requirements, and commanded that the printer (there was then only one) should submit any works he printed to the Clerk of the Council, to receive his *imprimatur* before publishing the same. The Williamites were equally tyrannical, for Malone was dismissed by them from the office of State Printer, and tried in the Queen's Bench, with John Dowling, in 1707, for publishing "A Manuall of Devout Prayers," for the use of Roman Catholics.[1]

There were also a great number of taverns and coffee-houses in this street; the most noted was the Rose Tavern, which stood

---

[1] *Roman Catholics.*—The noisy and violent opposition which was made to a Catholic if he attempted to enter either a trade or a profession, would scarcely be credited at the present day; yet it should be known and remembered by those who wish to estimate the social state of this country accurately and fairly. After the Revolution, the Protestant portion of the Guild of Tailors petitioned William III. to make their corporation exclusively Protestant, and their request was granted.

nearly opposite to the present Castle steps. Swift alludes to this in the verses which he wrote on his own death, in 1731 :—

> "Suppose me dead ; and then suppose
> A club assembled at the *Rose*."

Political clubs, lawyers' clubs, and benevolent clubs, all assembled here ; and the Friendly Brothers of St. Patrick had their annual dinner at the *Rose*, at the primitive hour of four o'clock, annually, on the 17th of March, having first transacted business and heard a sermon at St. Patrick's.

The first Dublin newspaper was published in this century, by Robert Thornton, bookseller, at the sign of the Leather Bottle, in Skinner's-row, A.D. 1685. It consisted of a single leaf of small folio size, printed on both sides, and written in the form of a letter, each number being dated, and commencing with the word " sir." The fashionable church was St. Michael's in High-street. It is described, in 1630, as " in good reparacion ; and although most of the parishioners were recusants, it was commonly full of Protestants, who resorted thither every Sunday to hear divine service and sermon." This church had been erected originally for Catholic worship. Meanwhile the priests were obliged to say Mass wherever they could best conceal themselves ; and in the reign of James I. their services were solemnized in certain back rooms in the houses of Nicholas Quietrot, Carye, and the Widow O'Hagan, in High-street.[2] Amongst the fashionables who lived in this locality we find the Countess of Roscommon, Sir P. Wemys, Sir Thady Duff, and Mark Quin, the Lord Mayor of Dublin in 1667. Here, too, was established the first Dublin post-house, for which the nation appears to have been indebted indirectly to Shane O'Neill, of whose proceedings her Majesty Queen Elizabeth was anxious to be cognizant with as little delay as possible. In 1656, it having been found that the horses of the military, to whom postal communications had been confided previously, were "much wearied, and his Highness' affayres much prejudiced for want of a post-office to carry publique letters," Evan Vaughan was employed to arrange postal communications, and was made Deputy Postmaster. Major Swift was the Postmaster at Holyhead, and he was allowed £100 a-year for the maintenance of four boatmen, added to the packet boats, at the rate of 8*d*. per diem and 18*s*. per month for wages. Post-houses were established

---

[2] *High-street.*—Gilbert's *Dublin*, vol. i. p. 220.

in the principal towns in Ireland about the year 1670, by means of which, for 8*d.* or 12*d.*, letters could be conveyed, twice a week, to the "remotest parts of Ireland," and which afforded "the conveniency of keeping good correspondence."

The Dublin Philosophical Society held their first meetings on Cork-hill, at the close of this century, and it is evident that there were many men in that age who had more than ordinary zeal for scientific research. Dr. Mullen has left a detailed account of the difficulties under which he dissected an elephant, which had been burned to death in the booth where it was kept for exhibition, on the 17th June, 1682. According to Haller, oculists are indebted to him for some important discoveries connected with the organs of vision.[3]

The old Custom-house stood on the site of houses now comprised in that part of Dublin known as Wellington-quay. Here a locality was selected, in the reign of James I., for the purpose of " erecting cranes and making wharves." This street, now so busy and populous, was then in the suburbs, and is described in the lease, A.D. 1620, as "a certain parcel of ground, lying in or near Dame-street, in the suburbs of the city of Dublin." A new Custom-house was erected about the period of the Restoration, with the addition of a council-chamber, where the Privy Council and Committees of the House of Commons were accustomed to assemble. By an order of the Privy Council, 19th September, 1662, the Custom-house-quay was appointed the sole place for landing and lading the exports and imports of the city of Dublin. In 1683 the public Exchange of Dublin was transferred from Cork House to the Tholsel, a building erected early in the reign of Edward II., and described by Camden as built of hewn stone. Here the Mayor was elected on Michaelmas Day, and the citizens held their public meetings. A clock was set up in 1560, no doubt very much to the admiration of the citizens. A new Tholsel or City Hall was erected in 1683, on the same site, and there was a " 'Change," where merchants met every day, as in the Royal Exchange in London. Public dinners were given here also with great magnificence ; but from the marshy nature of the ground on which the building had been set up, it fell to decay in 1797, and a new Sessions-house was erected in Green-street.

[3] *Vision.*—Gilbert's *Dublin*, vol. ii. p. 149.

Nor did the good people of Dublin neglect to provide for their amusements. Private theatricals were performed in the Castle at the latter end of the reign of Queen Elizabeth, if not earlier. The sum of one-and-twenty shillings and two groats was expended on wax tapers for the play of "Gorbodne," "done at the Castle," in September, 1601. Miracle and mystery plays were enacted as early as 1528, when the Lord Deputy was "invited to a new play every day in Christmas;" where the Tailors acted the part of Adam and Eve, it is to be supposed because they initiated the trade by introducing the necessity for garments; the Shoemakers, the story of Crispin and Crispianus; the Vintners, Bacchus and his story; the Carpenters, Mary and Joseph; the Smiths represented Vulcan; and the Bakers played the comedy of Ceres, the goddess of corn. The stage was erected on Hogges-green, now College-green; and probably the entertainment was carried out *al fresco*. The first playhouse established in Dublin was in Werburgh-street, in 1633. Shirley's plays were performed here soon after, and also those of "rare Ben Jonson." Ogilvy, Shirley's friend, and the promoter of this enterprise, was appointed Master of the Revels in Ireland in 1661; and as his first theatre was ruined during the civil war, he erected a "noble theatre," at a cost of £2,000, immediately after his new appointment, on a portion of the Blind-quay. Dunton describes the theatres, in 1698, as more frequented than the churches, and the actors as "no way inferior to those in London." The Viceroys appear to have been very regular in their patronage of this amusement; and on one occasion, when the news reached Dublin of the marriage of William of Orange and Mary, the Duke of Ormonde, after "meeting the nobility and gentry in great splendour at the play, passed a general invitation to all the company to spend that evening at the Castle."[4]

The inventory of the household effects of Lord Grey, taken in 1540, affords us ample information on the subject of dress and household effects. The list commences with "eight tun and a

---

[4] *Castle.*—Gilbert's *Dublin*, vol. ii. p. 69. There is a curious account in the *Quarterly Journal of the Kilkenny Archæological Society*, July, 1862, p. 165, of a comic playbill, issued for a Kilkenny theatre, in May, 1793. The value of the tickets was to be taken, if required, in candles, bacon, soap, butter, and cheese, and no one was to be admitted into the boxes without shoes and stockings; which leads one to conclude that the form of admission and style of attire were not uncommon, or there would have been no joke in the announcement.

pype of Gaskoyne wine," and the "long board in the hall." A great advance had been made since we described the social life of the eleventh century ; and the refinements practised at meals was not the least of many improvements. A *bord-clothe* was spread on the table, though forks were not used until the reign of James I. They came from Italy, to which country we owe many of the new fashions introduced in the seventeenth century. In *The Boke of Curtosye* there are directions given not to "foule the *bord-clothe* wyth the knyfe ;" and Ben Jonson, in his comedy of "The Devil is an Ass," alludes to the introduction of forks, and the consequent disuse of napkins :

> "The laudable use of forks,
> Brought into custom here as they are in Italy,
> To th' sparing o' napkins."

The English edition of the *Janua Linguarum* of Comenius, represents the fashion of dining in England during the Commonwealth. The table was simply a board placed on a frame or trestles, which was removed after the meal to leave room for the dancers. Old Capulet's hall was prepared thus :

> "A hall ! a hall ! give room, and foot it, girls !
> More light, ye knaves, and turn the table up."

The head of the table, where the principal person sat, was called the "board-end ;" and as one long table was now used instead of several smaller ones, the guests of higher and lower degree were divided by the massive saltcellar, placed in the centre of the table. Thus, in Ben Jonson, it is said of a man who treats his inferiors with scorn, "He never drinks below the salt." The waiters, after settling the cloth, placed the spoons, knives, forks, bread, and napkins beside the trenchers. The butler served out the drink from the cupboard, the origin of our modern sideboard. The "cobbord," erroneously supposed to have been like our modern cupboard, is specially mentioned amongst Lord Grey's effects. Lord Fairfax, in his directions to his servants, written about the middle of the seventeenth century, says : "No man must fill beer or wine but the cupboard keeper," and he should know which of his "cups be for beer and which for wine, for it were a foul thing to mix them together." There was another reason, however, for this arrangement—much "idle tippling" was cut off thereby ; for as the draught of beer or wine had to be asked for when it was needed, the demand was not likely to be so quick as if it were always at hand. There were also cups of " assaye," from which the cupbearer was obliged to drink before his master, to prove that there was no poison in the liquor which he used. The cupboard was covered with a carpet, of which Lord Grey had two. These carpets, or tablecovers, were more or less costly, according to the rank and state of the owner. His Lordship had also " two chares, two fformes, and two stooles." Chairs were decidedly a luxury at that day. Although the name is of Anglo-Norman origin, they did not come into general use until a late period ; and it was considered a mark of disrespect to superiors, for young persons to sit in their presence on anything but hard benches or stools. The Anglo-Saxons called their seats *sett* and *stol*, a name which we still preserve in the modern stool. The hall was ornamented with rich hangings, and there was generally a *traves*, which could be used as a curtain or screen to form a temporary partition. The floor was strewn with rushes, which were not removed quite so frequently as would have been desirable, considering that they were made the repository of the refuse of the table. Perfumes were consequently much used, and we are not surprised to find " a casting bottel, dooble gilte, for rose-water," in the effects of a Viceroy of the sixteenth century. Such things were more matters of necessity than of luxury at even a later period. Meat and pudding were the staple diet of the upper classes in 1698. Wright[5] gives a long and amusing extract from a work published by a foreigner who had been much in England at this period, and who appears to have marvelled equally at the amount of solid meat consumed, the love of pudding, and the neglect of fruit at dessert.

We are able, fortunately, to give a description of the fare used during the same period in Ireland, at least by the upper classes, who could afford to procure it. Captain Bodley, a younger brother of the founder of the famous Bodleian Library in Oxford, has left an account of a journey into Lecale, in Ulster, in 1603, and of the proceedings of his companions-in-arms, and the entertainment they met with. His " tour " is full of that gossiping, chatty, general

---

[5] *Wright.—Domestic Manners*, pp. 465, 466 : " Oh ! what an excellent thing is an English pudding ! Make a pudding for an Englishman, and you will regale him, be he where he will."

information, which gives an admirable idea of the state of society. This is his description of a dinner: " There was a large and beautiful collar of brawn, with its accompaniments, to wit, mustard and Muscatel wine; there were well-stuffed geese (such as the Lord Bishop is wont to eat at Ardbraccan), the legs of which Captain Caulfield always laid hold of for himself; there were pies of venison, and various kinds of game; pasties also, some of marrow, with innumerable plums; others of it with coagulated milk, such as the Lord Mayor and Aldermen of London almost always have at their feasts; others, which they call tarts, of divers shapes, materials, and colours, made of beef, mutton, and veal." Then he relates the amusements. After dinner they rode, and in the evening they played cards, and had, " amongst other things, that Indian tobacco, of which I shall never be able to make sufficient mention." Later in the evening " maskers " came to entertain them; and on one occasion, their host gave them up his own " good and soft bed, and threw himself upon a pallet in the same chamber."[6]

The large stand-bed, or four-post, was then coming into use, and was, probably, the " good and soft bed " which the host resigned to the use of the officers, and which, if we may judge by the illustration of this piece of furniture, would conveniently hold a considerable number of persons. The pallet was placed on the truckle-bed, which rolled under the large bed, and was generally used by a servant, who slept in his master's room. The reader will remember the speech of Mine Host of the Garter, in the " Merry Wives of Windsor," who says of Falstaff's room : " There's his chamber, his house, his castle, his standing-bed and truckle-bed."

However interesting the subject may be, there is not space to go into further details. The inventory of Lord Grey's personal effects can scarcely be given as a picture of costume in this century, for even a few years produced as considerable changes in fashion then as now. Dekker, in his *Seven Deadly Sinnes of London*, describes an Englishman's suit as being like a traitor's body that had been hanged, drawn, and quartered, and set up in several places; and says : " We that mock every nation for keeping one fashion, yet steal patches from every one of them to piece out our pride, and are now

---

[6] *Chamber.*—This most interesting and amusing journal is published in the *Ulster Arch. Jour.* vol. iii. p. 73, with a translation and notes. The original is in Latin.

laughing-stocks to them. The block for his head alters faster than the feltmaker can fit him, and hereupon we are called in scorn block-heads." The courtiers of Charles II. compensated themselves for the stern restraints of Puritanism, by giving way to the wildest excesses in dress and manners. Enormous periwigs were introduced, and it became the fashion for a man of *ton* to be seen combing them on the Mall or at the theatre. The hat was worn with a broad brim, ornamented with feathers; a falling band of the richest lace adorned the neck; the short cloak was edged deeply with gold lace; the doublet was ornamented in a similar manner—it was long, and swelled out from the waist; but the "petticoat breeches" were the glory of the outer man, and sums of money were spent on ribbon and lace to add to their attractions.

The ladies' costume was more simple, at least at this period; they compensated themselves, however, for any plainness in dress, by additional extravagances in their head-dresses, and wore "heart-breakers," or artificial curls, which were set out on wires at the sides of the face. Patching and painting soon became common, and many a nonconformist divine lifted up his voice in vain against these vanities. Pepys has left ample details of the dress in this century; and, if we may judge from the entry under the 30th of October, 1663, either he was very liberal in his own expenditure, and very parsimonious towards his wife, or ladies' attire was much less costly than gentlemen's, for he murmurs over his outlay of about £12 for Mrs. Pepys and £55 for himself. The country people, however, were attired more plainly and less expensively, while many, probably—

"Shook their heads at folks in London,"

and wondered at the follies of their superiors.

The arms and military accoutrements of the period have already been mentioned incidentally, and are illustrated by the different costumes in our engravings, which Mr. Doyle has rendered with the minutest accuracy of detail. This subject, if treated at all, would require space which we cannot afford to give it. The Life Guards were embodied by Charles II., in 1681, in imitation of the French "Gardes des Corps." The Coldstream were embodied by General Monk, in 1660, at the town from whence they obtained their name.

From an account in the Hamilton MSS., published in the *Ulster*

Archæological Journal, it would appear that it was usual, or, at least, not uncommon, for young men of rank to go abroad for some time, attended by a tutor, to perfect themselves in continental languages. It need scarcely be said that travelling was equally tedious and expensive. A journey from Dublin to Cork occupied several days; postchaises are a comparatively modern invention; and Sir William Petty astonished the good people of Dublin, in the

seventeenth century, by inventing some kind of carriage which could be drawn by horses. With his description of the condition of the lower classes in Ireland at this period, I shall conclude this chapter. The accompanying figure represents the costume of the Irish peasant about the fifteenth century. The dress was found on the body of a male skeleton, in the year 1824, which was preserved so perfectly, that a coroner was called to hold an inquest on it. The remains were taken from a bog in the parish of Killery, co. Sligo. The cloak was composed of soft brown cloth; the coat of the same material, but of finer texture. The buttons are ingeniously formed of the cloth. The trowsers consists of two distinct parts, of different colours and textures; the upper part is thick, coarse, yellowish-brown cloth; the lower, a brown and yellow plaid.

" The diet of these people is milk, sweet and sour, thick and thin; but tobacco, taken in short pipes seldom burned, seems the pleasure of their lives. Their food is bread in cakes, whereof a penny serves a week for each; potatoes from August till May; muscles, cockles, and oysters, near the sea; eggs and butter, made very rancid by keeping in bogs. As for flesh they seldom eat it. Their fuel is turf in most places." The potatoe, which has brought so many national calamities on the country, had been then some years in the country, but its use was not yet as general as it has become since, as we find from the mention of "bread in cakes" being an edible during a considerable part of the year.

CASTLE CAULFIELD, COUNTY TYRONE.

SCENE OF THE BATTLE OF THE BOYNE.

CHAPTER XXXIII.

Accession of James II.—Position of Public Affairs—Birth of an Heir—Landing of William of Orange—Arrival of King James in Ireland—The Siege of Derry—Cruelties of the Enniskilleners—Disease in Schomberg's Camp—The Battle of the Boyne—James' Defeat and Disgraceful Flight—The Siege of Athlone—The Siege of Limerick—Marlborough appears before Cork—William raises the Siege of Limerick and returns to England—The Siege of Athlone, Heroic Valour of its Defenders—The Battle of Aughrim—Surrender of Limerick.

[A.D. 1688—1691.]

KING JAMES' accession again raised the hopes of the Catholics, and again they were doomed to disappointment; while the Protestants, who had their fears also, soon learned that policy would bend itself to popularity. Colonel Richard Talbot was now raised to the peerage as Earl of Tyrconnel, and appointed Commander-in-Chief of the forces, with an authority independent of the Lord Lieutenant. His character, as well as that of his royal master, has been judged rather by his political opinions than by facts, and both have suffered considerably at the hands of a modern historian, who has offered more than one holocaust to the manes of his hero, William of Orange.

The moderate and cautious Clarendon was appointed Viceroy, and did his best to appease the fears of the Protestants; but he was soon succeeded by Tyrconnel, whose zeal for Irish interests was not always tempered by sufficient moderation to conciliate English politicians. He had fought against O'Neill; he had opposed Rinuccini; he had served in the Duke of Ormonde's army; he had helped to defend Drogheda against the Republicans, and had lain there apparently dead, and thus escaped any further suffering; he was of the Anglo-Irish party, who were so faithfully loyal to the crown, and whose loyalty was repaid with such cold indifference; yet his virtues have been ignored, and Macaulay accuses him of having "adhered to the old religion, like the Celts," which was true, and of "having taken part with them in the rebellion of 1641," which was not true.

James commenced his reign by proclaiming his desire for religious liberty. Individually he may not have been much beyond the age in opinion on this subject, but liberty of conscience was necessary for himself. He was a Catholic, and he made no secret of his religion; he was, therefore, obliged from this motive, if from no other, to accord the same boon to his subjects. The Quakers were set free in England, and the Catholics were set free in Ireland. But the Puritan faction, who had commenced by fighting for liberty of conscience for themselves, and who ended by fighting to deny liberty of conscience to others, were quite determined that neither Quakers nor Catholics should worship God as they believed themselves bound to do. Such intolerance, unhappily, was not altogether confined to the illiterate. Coke, in a previous generation, had declared that it was felony even to counsel the King to tolerate Catholics; and Usher, that it was a deadly sin. The King had neither the good sense nor the delicacy of feeling to guide him through these perils. His difficulties, and the complications which ensued, belong to the province of the English historian, but they were not the less felt in Ireland.

The Protestants professed to be afraid of being massacred by the Catholics; the Catholics apprehended a massacre from the Protestants. Catholics were now admitted to the army, to the bar, and to the senate. Protestants declared this an infringement of their rights, and forgot how recently they had expelled their Catholic fellow-subjects, not merely from honours and emoluments, but even from their altars and their homes.

An event now occurred which brought affairs to a crisis. The King's second wife, Mary of Modena, gave him an heir, and the heir appeared likely to live (A.D. 1688). William of Orange, who had long flattered himself that he should one day wear the crown of England, saw that no time should be lost if he intended to secure the prize, and commenced his preparations with all the ability and with all the duplicity for which his career has been admired by one party, and denounced by the other, according as political and religious opinions viewed the deceit under the strong light of the ability, or the ability under the glare of the deceit. The Protestant party could not but see all that was to be apprehended if a Catholic heir should succeed to the throne, and they sacrificed their loyalty to their interests, if not to their principles.

William arrived in England on the 5th of November, 1688. He professed to have come for the purpose of investigating the rumours which had been so industriously circulated respecting the birth of the heir who had barred his pretensions, and to induce the King to join the league which had been just formed against France; but he took care to come provided with an armament, which gave the lie to his diplomatic pretensions; and as soon as he had been joined by English troops, of whose disaffection he was well aware, his real motive was no longer concealed. James fled to France, whither he had already sent his Queen and heir. Still there was a large party in England who had not yet declared openly for the usurper; and had not James entirely alienated the affection of his subjects by his tyrannical treatment of the Protestant bishops, his conduct towards the University of Oxford, and the permission, if not the sanction, which he gave to Jeffreys in his bloody career, there can be little doubt that William should have fought for the crown on English ground as he did on Irish.

Ulster was principally peopled by Protestant Presbyterians, from the north of Scotland. They were not likely to be very loyal even to a Stuart, for the Irish had been called over to Scotland before now to defend royal rights; they had not very defined religious opinions, except on the subject of hatred of Popery and Prelacy. It cannot be a matter of surprise, therefore, that these men hailed the prospect of a new sovereign, whose opinions, both religious and political, coincided with their own. If he, too, had very general views as to the rights of kings, and no very particular view as to rights of conscience being granted to any who did not agree with him, he was none the less acceptable.

Tyrconnel had neither men, money, nor arms, to meet the emergency. He had to withdraw the garrison from Derry to make up the contingent of 3,000 men, which he sent to assist the King in England ; but they were immediately disarmed, and the young men of Derry closed their gates, and thus were the first to revolt openly against their lawful King. The native Irish had been loyal when loyalty cost them their lives, without obtaining for them any increased liberty to exercise their religion ; they were, therefore, not less likely to be loyal now, when both civil and religious liberty might depend upon their fealty to the crown. The Enniskilleners revolted ; and the whole of Ulster, except Charlemont and Carrick-fergus, declared for William of Orange.

James determined to make an effort to regain his throne ; and by this act rendered the attempt of his son-in-law simply a rebellion. Had the King declined the contest, had he violated the rules of government so grossly as no longer to merit the confidence of his people, or had there been no lawful heir to the throne, William's attempt might have been legitimate ; under the circumstances, it was simply a successful rebellion. The King landed at Kinsale, on the 12th of March, 1689, attended by some Irish troops and French officers. He met Tyrconnel in Cork, created him a duke, and then proceeded to Bandon, where he received the submission of the people who had joined the rebellion. On his arrival in Dublin, he summoned a Parliament and issued proclamations, after which he proceeded to Derry, according to the advice of Tyrconnel. Useless negotiations followed ; and James returned to Dublin, after having confided the conduct of the siege to General Hamilton. If that officer had not been incomparably more humane than the men with whom he had to deal, it is probable that the 'Prentice Boys of Derry would not have been able to join in their yearly commemoration of victory. The town was strongly fortified, and well supplied with artillery and ammunition ; the besiegers were badly clad, badly provisioned, and destitute of almost every thing necessary to storm a town. Their only resource was to starve out the garrison ; but of this resource they were partly deprived by the humanity of General Hamilton, who allowed a considerable number of men, women, and children to leave Derry, and thus enabled its defenders to hold out longer. Lundy, who urged them to capitulate to King James, was obliged to escape in disguise ; and Major Baker, assisted by the Rev. George Walker, a Protestant clergyman, then took the command. According to the statements of the latter, the garrison amounted to 7,500 men, and they had twenty-two cannon, which alone gave them an immense advantage over the royal army. So much has been already said, and written, and sung of the bravery of the Derry men, that nothing more remains to say. That they were brave, and that they bravely defended the cause which they had adopted, there is no doubt; but if polemics had not mingled with politics in the encounter, it is quite possible that we should have heard no more of their exploits than of those other men, equally gallant and equally brave. The Enniskilleners, who have obtained an unenviable notoriety for their merciless cruelty in war, occupied the King's troops so as to prevent them from assisting the besiegers. Several encounters took place between the Derry men and the royalists, but with no other result than loss of lives on each side. On the 13th of June, a fleet of thirty ships arrived from England with men and provisions; but the Irish had obtained the command of the river Foyle, and possession of Culmore Fort at the entrance, so that they were unable to enter. De Rosen was now sent by James to assist Hamilton. He proposed and carried out the barbarous expedition of driving all the Protestants whom he could find before the walls, and threatening to let them starve there to death unless the garrison surrendered. His plan was strongly disapproved by the King, it disgusted the Irish, and exasperated the besieged. The next day they erected a gallows on the ramparts, and threatened to hang their prisoners then and there if the unfortunate people were not removed. It is to the credit of the Derry men that they shared their provisions to the last with their prisoners, even while they were dying themselves of starvation. Perhaps the example of humanity set to them by General Hamilton was not without its effect, for kindness and cruelty seem equally contagious in time of war. Kirke's squadrons at last passed the forts, broke the boom, and relieved the garrison, who could not have held out forty-eight hours longer. It was suspected that English gold had procured their admittance, and that the officers who commanded the forts were bribed to let them pass unscathed. The siege was at once raised; the royal army withdrew on the 5th of August; and thus terminated the world-famed siege of Derry.

James now held his Parliament in Dublin, repealed the Act of Settlement, passed the Act of Attainder, and issued an immense quantity of base coin. He has been loudly condemned by some historians for these proceedings; but it should be remembered (1) that the Act of Settlement was a gross injustice, and, as such, it was but justice that it should be repealed. Had the measure been carried out, however severely it might have been felt by the Protestant party, they could not have suffered from the repeal as severely as the Catholics had suffered from the enactment. (2) The Act of Attainder simply proclaimed that the revolutionists were rebels against their lawful King, and that they should be treated as such. (3) The utterance of base coin had already been performed by several Governments, and James only availed himself of the prerogatives exercised by his predecessors.

The day on which the siege of Derry was raised, the royalists met with a severe reverse at Newtownbutler. They were under the command of Lord Mountcashel, when attacked by the Enniskilleners. The dragoons had already been dispirited by a reverse at Lisnaskea; and a word of command[7] which was given incorrectly, threw the old corps into confusion, from which their brave leader in vain endeavoured to rally them. Colonel Wolseley, an English officer, commanded the Enniskilleners; and the cruelties with which they hunted down the unfortunate fugitives, has made the name almost a byword of reproach. Five hundred men plunged into Lough Erne to escape their fury, but of these only one was saved. Lord Mountcashel was taken prisoner, but he escaped eventually, and fled to France. Sarsfield, who commanded at Sligo, was obliged to retire to Athlone; and the victorious Williamites remained masters of that part of the country.

Schomberg arrived[8] at Bangor, in Down, on the 13th of August, 1689, with a large army, composed of Dutch, French Huguenots, and new levies from England. On the 17th he marched to Belfast, where he met with no resistance; and on the 27th Carrickfergus surrendered to him on honorable terms, after a siege of eight days, but not until its Governor, Colonel Charles MacCarthy More, was

[7] *Command.*—Mountcashel gave the word "right face;" it was repeated "right about face." Colonel Hamilton and Captain Lavallin were tried in Dublin by court-martial for the mistake, and the latter was shot.

[8] *Arrived.*—The journals of two officers of the Williamite army have been published in the *Ulster Arch. Jour.*, and furnish some interesting details of the subsequent campaign. One of the writers is called Bonnivert, and was probably a French refugee; the other was Dr. Davis, a Protestant clergyman, who obtained a captaincy in William's army, and seemed to enjoy preaching and fighting with equal zest.

reduced to his last barrel of powder. Schomberg pitched on Dundalk for his winter quarters, and entrenched himself there strongly; but disease soon broke out in his camp, and it has been estimated that 10,000 men, fully one-half of the force, perished of want and dysentery. James challenged him to battle several times, but Schomberg was too prudent to risk an encounter in the state of his troops; and the King had not the moral courage to make the first attack. Complaints soon reached England of the condition to which the revolutionary army was reduced. If there were not "own correspondents" then in camp, it is quite clear there were

THE CASTLE OF TRIM.

very sharp eyes and very nimble pens. Dr. Walker, whose military experience at Derry appears to have given him a taste for campaigning, was one of the complainants. William sent over a commission to inquire into the matter, who, as usual in such cases, arrived too late to do any good. The men wanted food, the horses wanted provender, the surgeons and apothecaries wanted medicines for the sick. [9] In fact, if we take a report of Crimean mismanage-

[9] *Sick.*—Harris' *Life of King William*, p. 254, 1719. Macaulay's account of the social state of the camp, where there were so many divines preaching, is

ment, we shall have all the details, minus the statement that several of the officers drank themselves to death, and that some who were in power were charged with going shares in the embezzlement of the contractor, Mr. John Shales, who, whether guilty or not, was made the scapegoat on the occasion, and was accused, moreover, of having caused all this evil from partiality to King James, in whose service he had been previously. Mr. John Shales was therefore taken prisoner, and sent under a strong guard to Belfast, and from thence to London. As nothing more is heard of him, it is probable the matter was hushed up, or that he had powerful accomplices in his frauds.

Abundant supplies arrived from England, which, if they could not restore the dead, served at least to renovate the living ; and Schomberg was ready to take the field early in the year 1690, not-withstanding the loss of about 10,000 men. James, with the con-stitutional fatuity of the Stuarts, had lost his opportunity. If he had attacked the motley army of the revolutionary party while the men were suffering from want and disease, and while his own troops were fresh and courageous, he might have conquered ; the most sanguine now could scarcely see any other prospect for him than defeat. He was in want of everything ; and he had no Eng-lishmen who hoped for plunder, no French refugees who looked for a new home, no brave Dutchmen who loved fighting for its own sake, to fall back upon in the hour of calamity. His French coun-sellors only agreed to disagree with him. There was the ordinary amount of jealousy amongst the Irish officers—the inevitable result of the want of a competent leader in whom all could confide. The King was urged by one party (the French) to retire to Connaught, and entrench himself there until he should receive succours from France; he was urged by another party (the Irish) to attack Schom-

a proof that their ministrations were not very successful, and that the lower order of Irish were not at all below the English of the same class in education or refinement. "The moans of the sick were drowned by the blasphemy and ribaldry of their companions. Sometimes, seated on the body of a wretch who had died in the morning, might be seen a wretch destined to die before night, cursing, singing loose songs, and swallowing usquebaugh to the health of the devil. When the corpses were taken away to be buried, the survivors grum-bled. A dead man, they said, was a good screen and a good stool. Why, when there was so abundant a supply of such useful articles of furniture, were people to be exposed to the cold air, and forced to crouch on the moist ground?" —Macaulay's *History of England*, People's Ed. part viii. p. 88.

berg without delay. Louvais, the French Minister of War, divided his hatred with tolerable impartiality between James and William: therefore, though quite prepared to oppose the latter, he was by no means so willing to assist the former ; and when he did send men to Ireland, under the command of the Count de Lauzan, he took care that their clothing and arms should be of the worst description. He received in exchange a reinforcement of the best-equipped and best-trained soldiers of the Irish army. Avaux and De Rosen were both sent back to France by James ; and thus, with but few officers, badly-equipped troops, and his own miserable and vacillating counsel, he commenced the war which ended so gloriously or so disastrously, according to the different opinions of the actors in the fatal drama. In July, 1690, some of James' party were defeated by the Williamites at Cavan, and several of his best officers were killed or made prisoners. Another engagement took place at Charlemont; the Governor, Teigue O'Regan, only yielded to starvation. He surrendered on honorable terms ; and Schomberg, with equal humanity and courtesy, desired that each of his starving men should receive a loaf of bread at Armagh.

William had intended for some time to conduct the Irish campaign in person. He embarked near Chester on the 11th of June, and landed at Carrickfergus on the 14th, attended by Prince George of Denmark, the Duke of Wurtemburg, the Prince of Hesse Darmstadt, the Duke of Ormonde, and the Earls of Oxford, Portland, Scarborough, and Manchester, with other persons of distinction. Schomberg met him half-way between Carrickfergus and Belfast. William, who had ridden so far, now entered the General's carriage, and drove to Belfast, where he was received with acclamations, and loud shouts of " God bless the Protestant King !" There were bonfires and discharges of cannon at the various camps of the Williamites. The officers of several regiments paid their respects to him in state. On the 22nd the whole army encamped at Loughbrickland, near Newry. In the afternoon William came up and reviewed the troops, pitching his tent on a neighbouring eminence.[1] The army comprised a strange medley of nationalities. More than half were foreigners; and on these William placed his principal reliance, for at any moment a reaction might take place in favour of the lawful King.

---

[1] *Eminence.*—Journal of Captain Davis, published in the *Ulster Archæological Journal*, vol. iv.

The Williamite army was well supplied, well trained, admirably commanded, accustomed to war, and amounted to between forty and fifty thousand. The Jacobite force only consisted of twenty thousand,[2] and of these a large proportion were raw recruits. The officers, however, were brave and skilful; but they had only twelve field-pieces, which had been recently received from France. On the 22nd, news came that James had encamped near Dundalk; on the 23rd he marched towards Drogheda. On the same day William went to Newry; he was thoroughly aware of the movements of his hapless father-in-law, for deserters came into his camp from time to time. James obtained his information from an English officer, Captain Farlow, and some soldiers whom he made prisoners at a trifling engagement which took place between Newry and Dundalk.

James now determined on a retreat to the Boyne through Ardee. His design was to protract the campaign as much as possible,—an arrangement which suited his irresolute habits; but where a kingdom was to be lost or won, it only served to discourage the troops and to defer the decisive moment.

The hostile forces confronted each other for the first time on the banks of the Boyne, June 30, 1689. The Jacobite army was posted on the declivity of the Hill of Dunore—its right wing towards Drogheda, its left extending up the river. The centre was at the small hamlet of Oldbridge. Entrenchments were hastily thrown up to defend the fords, and James took up his position at a ruined church on the top of the Hill of Dunore. The Williamite army approached from the north, their brave leader directing every movement, and inspiring his men with courage and confidence. He obtained a favourable position, and was completely screened from view until he appeared on the brow of the hill, where his forces debouched slowly and steadily into the ravines below. After planting his batteries on the heights, he kept up an incessant fire on the Irish lines during the afternoon of the 30th. But James' officers were on the alert, even if their King were indifferent. William was recognized as he approached near their lines to reconnoitre. Guns were brought up to bear on him quietly and stealthily; " six shots were fired at him, one whereof fell and struck off the top of the Duke Wurtemberg's pistol and the whiskers of his horse, and another tore the King's coat on his shoulder."[3]

[2] *Twenty thousand.*—Captain Davis' Journal.
[3] *Shoulder.*—Davis' Journal. The coat was exhibited at the meeting of the

William, like a wise general as he was, took care that the news of his accident should not dispirit his men.   He showed himself everywhere, rode through the camp, was as agreeable as it was in his nature to be ; and thus made capital of what might have been a cause of disaster.   In the meantime James did all that was possible to secure a defeat.   At one moment he decided to retreat, at the next he would risk a battle; then he sent off his baggage and six of his field-pieces to Dublin, for his own special protection ; and while thus so remarkably careful of himself, he could not be persuaded to allow the most necessary precaution to be taken for the safety of his army.   Hence the real marvel to posterity is, not that the battle of the Boyne should have been lost by the Irish, but that they should ever have attempted to fight at all.   Perhaps nothing but the inherent loyalty of the Irish, which neither treachery nor pusillanimity could destroy, and the vivid remembrance of the cruel wrongs always inflicted by Protestants when in power, prevented them from rushing over *en masse* to William's side of the Boyne. Perhaps, in the history of nations, there never was so brave a resistance made for love of royal right and religious freedom, as that of the Irish officers and men who then fought on the Jacobite side.

The first attack of William's men was made at Slane.   This was precisely what the Jacobite officers had anticipated, and what James had obstinately refused to see.   When it was too late, he allowed Lauzan to defend the ford, but even Sir Nial O'Neill's gallantry was unavailing.   The enemy had the advance, and Portland's artillery and infantry crossed at Slane.   William now felt certain of victory, if, indeed, he had ever doubted it.   It was low water at ten o'clock ; the fords at Oldbridge were passable ; a tremendous battery was opened on the Irish lines ; they had not a single gun to reply, and yet they waited steadily for the attack. The Dutch Blue Guards dashed into the stream ten abreast, commanded by the Count de Solmes ; the Londonderry and Enniskillen Dragoons followed, supported by the French Huguenots.   The English infantry came next, under the command of Sir John Hanmer and the Count Nassau.   William crossed at the fifth ford, where the water was deepest, with the cavalry of his left wing.   It was a

British Association in Belfast, in 1852.   It had descended as an heirloom through Colonel Wetherall, William's aide-de-camp, who took it off him after the accident.

grand and terrible sight. The men in the water fought for William and Protestantism; the men on land fought for their King and their Faith. The men were equally gallant. Of the leaders I shall say nothing, lest I should be tempted to say too much. James had followed Lauzan's forces towards Slane. Tyrconnel's valour could not save the day for Ireland against fearful odds. Sarsfield's horse had accompanied the King. The Huguenots were so warmly received by the Irish at the fords that they recoiled, and their commander, Caillemont, was mortally wounded. Schomberg forgot his age, and the affront he had received from William in the morning; and the man of eighty-two dashed into the river with the impetuosity of eighteen. He was killed immediately, and so was Dr. Walker, who headed the Ulster Protestants. William may have regretted the brave old General, but he certainly did not regret the Protestant divine. He had no fancy for churchmen meddling in secular affairs, and a rough "What brought him there?" was all the reply vouchsafed to the news of his demise. The tide now began to flow, and the battle raged with increased fury. The valour displayed by the Irish was a marvel even to their enemies. Hamilton was wounded and taken prisoner. William headed the Enniskilleners, who were put to flight soon after by the Irish horse, at Platten, and were now rallied again by himself. When the enemy had crossed the ford at Oldbridge, James ordered Lauzan to march in a parallel direction with Douglas and young Schomberg to Duleek. Tyrconnel followed. The French infantry covered the retreat in admirable order, with the Irish cavalry. When the defile of Duleek had been passed, the royalist forces again presented a front to the enemy. William's horse halted. The retreat was again resumed; and at the deep defile of Naul the last stand was made. The shades of a summer evening closed over the belligerent camps. The Williamites returned to Duleek; and eternal shadows clouded over the destinies of the unfortunate Stuarts—a race admired more from sympathy with their miseries, than from admiration of their virtues.

Thus ended the famous battle of the Boyne. England obtained thereby a new governor and a national debt; Ireland, fresh oppression, and an intensification of religious and political animosity, unparalleled in the history of nations.

James contrived to be first in the retreat which he had anticipated, and for which he had so carefully prepared. He arrived in

Dublin in the evening, and insulted Lady Tyrconnel by a rude remark about the fleetness of her husband's countrymen in running away from the battle ; to which she retorted, with equal wit and truth, that his Majesty had set them the example. He left Dublin the next morning, having first insulted the civil and military authorities, by throwing the blame of the defeat on the brave men who had risked everything in his cause. Having carefully provided for his own safety by leaving two troops of horse at Bray to defend the bridge, should the enemy come up, he hastened towards Duncannon, where he arrived at sunrise. Here he embarked in a small French vessel for Kinsale, and from thence he sailed to France, and was himself the bearer of the news of his defeat. The command in Ireland was intrusted to Tyrconnel, who gave orders that the Irish soldiery should march at once to Limerick, each under the command of his own officer. William entered Dublin on Sunday, July 7th. He was received with acclamations by the Protestants, who were now relieved from all fear lest the Catholics should inflict on them the sufferings they had so remorselessly inflicted on the Catholics. Drogheda, Kilkenny, Duncannon, and Waterford, capitulated to the victorious army, the garrisons marching to Limerick, towards which place William now directed his course. Douglas was sent to besiege Athlone ; but the Governor, Colonel Grace, made such brave resistance there, he was obliged to withdraw, and join William near Limerick.

The French officers, who had long since seen the hopelessness of the conflict, determined to leave the country. Lauzan, after having surveyed Limerick, and declared that it might be taken with " roasted apples," ordered all the French troops to Galway, where they could await an opportunity to embark for France. But the brave defenders of the devoted city were not deterred. The Governor consulted with Sarsfield, Tyrconnel, and the other officers ; and the result was a message to William, in reply to his demand for a surrender, to the effect, that they hoped to merit his good opinion better by a vigorous defence of the fortress, which had been committed to them by their master, than by a shameful capitulation. By a skilfully executed and rapid march, Sarsfield contrived to intercept William's artillery on the Keeper Mountains, and after killing the escort, bursting the guns, and blowing up the ammunition, he returned in triumph to Limerick. His success animated the besieged, and infuriated the besiegers. But the walls of Limerick were not as stout as the brave hearts of its defenders.   William sent for more artillery to Waterford; and it was found that two of the guns which Sarsfield had attempted to destroy, were still available.

The trenches were opened on the 17th of August.   On the 20th the garrison made a vigorous sortie, and retarded the enemy's progress; but on the 24th the batteries were completed, and a murderous fire of red-hot shot and shells was poured into the devoted city. The trenches were carried within a few feet of the palisades, on the 27th; and a breach having been made in the wall near St. John's Gate, William ordered the assault to commence.   The storming party were supported by ten thousand men.   For three hours a deadly struggle was maintained.   The result seemed doubtful, so determined was the bravery evinced on each side.   Boisseleau, the Governor, had not been unprepared, although he was taken by surprise, and had opened a murderous cross-fire on the assailants when first they attempted the storm.   The conflict lasted for nearly three hours.   The Brandenburg regiment had gained the Black Battery, when the Irish sprung a mine, and men, faggots, and stones were blown up in a moment.   A council of war was held; William, whose temper was not the most amiable at any time, was unusually morose.   He had lost 2,000 men between the killed and the wounded, and he had not taken the city, which a French General had pronounced attainable with "roasted apples."   On Sunday, the 31st of August, the siege was raised.   William returned to England, where his presence was imperatively demanded.   The military command was confided to the Count de Solmes, who was afterwards succeeded by De Ginkell; the civil government was intrusted to Lord Sidney, Sir Charles Porter, and Mr. Coningsby.

Lauzan returned to France with Tyrconnel, and the Irish forces were confided to the care of the Duke of Berwick, a youth of twenty, with a council of regency and a council of war to advise him. Under these circumstances it was little wonder that there should have been considerable division of opinion, and no little jealousy, in the royal camp; and even then the seeds were sowing of what eventually proved the cause of such serious misfortune to the country.

The famous Marlborough appeared before Cork with an army of 1,500 men, on the 22nd of September, and the garrison were made prisoners of war after a brief and brave resistance; but the conditions on which they surrendered were shamefully violated.   Kinsale was next attacked; but with these exceptions, and some occasional skirmishes with the "Rapparees," the winter passed over without any important military operations.

Tyrconnel returned to Ireland in January, with a small supply of money and some provisions, notwithstanding the plots made against him by Luttrell and Purcell. He brought a patent from James, creating Sarsfield Earl of Lucan. A French fleet arrived in May, with provisions, clothing, and ammunition. It had neither men nor money; but it brought what was supposed to be a fair equivalent, in the person of St. Ruth, a distinguished French officer, who was sent to take the command of the Irish army. In the meantime Ginkell was organizing the most effective force ever seen in Ireland: neither men nor money was spared by the English Parliament. And this was the army which the impoverished and ill-provisioned troops of the royalists were doomed to encounter.

Hostilities commenced on 7th June, with the siege of Ballymore Castle, in Westmeath. The Governor surrendered, and Athlone was next attacked. This town is situated on the river Shannon. Its position must be thoroughly understood, to comprehend the heroic bravery with which it was defended. It will be remembered that Athlone was one of the towns which the English of the Pale had fortified at the very commencement of their invasion of Ireland. That portion of the city which lay on the Leinster or Pale side of the river, had never been strongly fortified, and a breach was made at once in the wall. Ginkell assaulted it with 4,000 men, and the defenders at once withdrew to the other side; but they held the bridge with heroic bravery, until they had broken down two of the arches, and placed the broad and rapid Shannon between themselves and their enemies. St. Ruth had arrived in the meantime, and posted his army, amounting to about 15,000 horse and foot, at the Irish side of the river. The English had now raised the works so high on their side, that they were able to keep up an incessant fire upon the town. According to their own historian, Story, they threw in 12,000 cannon balls and 600 bombs, and the siege cost them "nigh fifty tons of powder." The walls opposite to the batteries were soon broken down, and the town itself reduced to ruins. The besiegers next attempted to cross in a bridge of boats, but the defenders turned their few field-pieces on them. They then tried to mend the broken bridge; huge beams were flung across, and they had every hope of success. But they knew not yet what Irish valour could dare. Eight or ten devoted men dashed into the water, and tore down the planks, under a galling fire; and, as they fell dead or dying into the river, others rushed to take the places of their fallen comrades, and to complete the work.

St. Ruth now ordered preparations to be made for an assault, and desired the ramparts on the Connaught side of the town to be levelled, that a whole battalion might enter abreast to relieve the garrison when it was assailed. But the Governor, D'Usson, opposed the plan, and neglected the order. All was now confusion in the camp. There never had been any real head to the royalist party in Ireland; and to insure victory in battle, or success in any important enterprise where multitudes are concerned, it is absolutely essential that all should act with union of purpose. Such union, where there are many men, and, consequently, many minds, can only be attained by the most absolute submission to one leader; and this leader, to obtain submission, should be either a lawfully constituted authority, or, in cases of emergency, one of those master-spirits to whom men bow with unquestioning submission, because of the majesty of intellect within them. There were brave men and true men in that camp at Athlone, but there was not one who possessed these essential requisites.

According to the Williamite historian, Ginkell was informed by traitors of what was passing, and that the defences on the river side were guarded by two of the "most indifferent Irish regiments." He immediately chose 2,000 men for the assault, distributed a gratuity of guineas amongst them, and at a signal from the church bell, at six in the evening, on the 30th of June, the assault was made, and carried with such rapidity, that St. Ruth, who was with the cavalry at a distance, was not aware of what had happened until all was over. St. Ruth at once removed his army to Ballinasloe, twelve miles from his former post, and subsequently to Aughrim. Tyrconnel was obliged to leave the camp, the outcry against him became so general.

St. Ruth's ground was well chosen. He had placed his men upon an eminence, and each wing was protected by a morass or bog. The Williamites came up on Sunday, July 11th, while the Irish were hearing Mass. In this instance, as in so many others, it is impossible to ascertain correctly the numerical force of each army. The historians on either side were naturally anxious to magnify the numbers of their opponents, and to lessen their own. It is at least certain, that on this, as on other occasions, the Irish were miserably deficient in all the appliances of the art of war, while the English were admirably supplied. The most probable estimate of the Irish force appears to be 15,000 horse and foot; and of the English, 20,000. Ginkell opened fire on the enemy as soon as his guns were planted. Some trifling skirmishes followed. A council of war was held, and the deliberation lasted until half-past four in the evening, at which time a general engagement was decided on. A cannonade had been kept up on both sides, in which the English had immensely the advantage, St. Ruth's excellently chosen position being almost useless for want of sufficient artillery. At half-past six Ginkell ordered an advance on the Irish right centre, having previously ascertained that the bog was passable. The defenders, after discharging their fire, gradually drew the Williamites after them by an almost imperceptible retreat, until they had them face to face with their main line. Then the Irish cavalry charged with irresistible valour, and the English were thrown into total disorder. St. Ruth, proud of the success of his strategies and the valour of his men, exclaimed, "Le jour est a nous, mes enfans." But St. Ruth's weak point was his left wing, and this was at once perceived and taken advantage of by the Dutch General. Some of his infantry made good their passage across the morass, which St. Ruth had supposed impassable; and the men, who commanded this position from a ruined castle, found that the balls with which they had been served did not suit their fire-arms, so that they were unable to defend the passage. St. Ruth at once perceived his error. He hastened to support them with a brigade of horse; but even as he exclaimed, "They are beaten; let us beat them to the purpose," a cannon-ball carried off his head, and all was lost. Another death, which occurred almost immediately after, completed the misfortunes of the Irish. The infantry had been attended and encouraged by Dr. Aloysius Stafford, chaplain to the forces; but when "death interrupted his glorious career,"[4] they were panic-struck; and three hours after the death of the general and the priest, there was not a man of the Irish army left upon the field. But the real cause of the failure was the fatal misunderstanding which existed between the leaders. Sarsfield, who was thoroughly able to have taken St. Ruth's position, and to have retrieved the fortunes of the day, had

---

4 Career.—*History of the King's Inns*, p. 239.

been placed in the rear by the jealousy of the latter, and kept in entire ignorance of the plan of battle. He was now obliged to withdraw without striking a single blow. The cavalry retreated along the highroad to Loughrea; the infantry fled to a bog, where numbers were massacred, unarmed and in cold blood.

The loss on both sides was immense, and can never be exactly estimated. Harris says that "had not St. Ruth been taken off, it would have been hard to say what the consequences of this day would have been."[5] Many of the dead remained unburied, and their bones were left to bleach in the storms of winter and the sun of summer. There was one exception to the general neglect. An Irish officer, who had been slain, was followed by his faithful dog. The poor animal lay beside his master's body day and night; and though he fed upon other corpses with the rest of the dogs, he would not permit them to touch the treasured remains. He continued his watch until January, when he flew at a soldier, who he feared was about to remove the bones, which were all that remained to him of the being by whom he had been caressed and fed. The soldier in his fright unslung his piece and fired, and the faithful wolf-dog laid down and died by his charge.[6]

Ginkell laid siege to Galway a week after the battle of Aughrim. The inhabitants relied principally upon the arrival of Balldearg O'Donnell for their defence; but, as he did not appear in time, they capitulated on favourable terms, and the Dutch General marched to Limerick.

Tyrconnel died at Limerick, of apoplexy, while he was preparing to put the city into a state of defence. He was a faithful and zealous supporter of the royal cause, and devoted to the Irish nation. His loyalty has induced one party to blacken his character; his haughty and unconciliatory manner prevented his good qualities from being fully appreciated by the other.

The real command now devolved on M. D'Usson, the Governor of Limerick. Active preparations for the siege were made on both sides. Ginkell contrived to communicate with Henry Luttrell, but his perfidy was discovered, and he was tried by court-martial and imprisoned. Sixty cannon and nineteen mortars were planted against

[5] *Been.—Life of William III.* p. 327.
[6] *Charge.*—See the *Green Book*, p. 231, for some curious stories about this engagement, and for a detailed account of St. Ruth's death.

the devoted city, and on the 30th the bombardment commenced.
The Irish horse had been quartered on the Clare side of the Shannon;
but, through the treachery or indifference of Brigadier Clifford, who
had been posted, with a strong body of dragoons, to prevent such
an attempt, Ginkell threw across a pontoon-bridge, and sent over
a large detachment of horse and foot, on the morning of the 16th,
which effectually cut off communication between the citizens and
their camp.   On the 22nd he made a feint of raising the siege, but
his real object was to lull suspicion, while he attacked the works at
the Clare end of Thomond-bridge.   The position was bravely defended by Colonel Lacy, but he was obliged to yield to overpowering numbers; and the Town-Major, fearing that the enemy would
enter in the *mêlee* with the Irish, drew up the bridge.   The English
gave no quarter, and, according to their own account, 600 men
were slaughtered on the spot.   This was the last engagement.
Sarsfield recommended a surrender.   Resistance was equally hopeless and useless; it could only end in a fearful sacrifice of life on
both sides.   A parley took place on the 23rd, and on the 24th a
three days' truce was arranged.   Hostages were exchanged, and a
friendly intercourse was established.   On the 3rd of October, 1691,
the Treaty was signed.   The large stone is still shown which was
used as a table on the occasion.   What that Treaty contained, and
how it was violated, are matters which demand a careful and impartial consideration.

THE TREATY STONE, LIMERICK.

This stone was placed on a handsome pedestal a few years since, by the then
Mayor of Limerick.

SITE OF THE BATTLE OF AUGHRIM.

CHAPTER XXXIV.

Formation of the Irish Brigade—Violation of the Treaty of Limerick—Enactment of the Penal Laws—Restrictions on Trade—The Embargo Laws—The
Sacramental Test introduced—The Palatines—The Irish forbidden to enlist
in the Army—Dean Swift and the Drapier's Letters—Attempts to form a
Catholic Association—Irish Emigrants defeat the English in France, Spain,
and America—The Whiteboys—An Account of the Cause of these Outrages,
by an English Tourist—Mr. Young's Remedy for Irish Disaffection—The
Peculiar Position and Difficulties of Irish Priests—The Judicial Murder of
Father Nicholas Sheehy—Grattan's Demand for Irish Independence—The
Volunteers—A Glimpse of Freedom.

[A.D. 1691—1783.]

ST. JOHN'S GATE and the Irish outworks were surrendered to the English; the English town was left
for the Irish troops to occupy until their departure
for France. The men were to have their choice
whether they would serve under William III. or
under the French. A few days after they were mustered on the Clare side of the Shannon, to declare
which alternative they preferred. An Ulster battalion, and a few men in each regiment, in all about
1,000, entered the service of Government; 2,000
received passes to return home; 11,000, with all
the cavalry, volunteered for France, and embarked
for that country in different detachments, under
their respective officers. They were warmly re-

ceived in the land of their adoption; and all Irish Catholics going to France were granted the privileges of French citizens, without the formality of naturalization. And thus was formed the famous "Irish Brigade," which has become a household word for bravery and the glory of the Irish nation.

The Treaty, as I have said, was signed on the 3rd of October, 1691. The preamble states that the contracting parties were Sir Charles Porter and Thomas Coningsby, Lords Justices, with the Baron de Ginkell as Commander-in-Chief, on the part of William and Mary; Sarsfield, Earl of Lucan, Viscount Galmoy, Colonel Purcell, Colonel Cusack, Sir J. Butler, Colonel Dillon, and Colonel Brown, on the part of the Irish nation. The articles were fifty-two in number. They guaranteed to the Catholics (1) the free exercise of their religion; (2) the privilege of sitting in Parliament; (3) freedom of trade; (4) the safety of the estates of those who had taken up arms for King James; (5) a general amnesty; (6) all th᷎ honours of war to the troops, and a free choice for their future destination. The articles run to considerable length, and cannot, therefore, be inserted here; but they may be seen *in extenso* in Mac-Geoghegan's *History of Ireland*, and several other works. So little doubt had the Irish that this Treaty would be solemnly observed, that when the accidental omission of two lines was discovered in the clean copy, they refused to carry out the arrangements until those lines had been inserted. The Treaty was confirmed by William and Mary, who pledged "the honour of England" that it should be kept inviolably, saying : "We do, for us, our heirs and successors, as far as in us lies, ratify and confirm the same, and every clause, matter, and thing therein contained." Two days after the signing of the Treaty, a French fleet arrived in the Shannon, with 3,000 soldiers, 200 officers, and 10,000 stand of arms. Sarsfield was strongly urged to break faith with the English; but he nobly rejected the temptation. How little did he foresee how cruelly that nation would break faith with him !

Two months had scarcely elapsed after the departure of the Irish troops, when an English historian was obliged to write thus of the open violation of the articles : "The justices of the peace, sheriffs, and other magistrates, presuming on their power in the country, dispossessed several of their Majesties' Catholic subjects, not only of their goods and chattels, but also of their lands and tenements, to the great reproach of their Majesties' Government."[7] These complaints were so general, that the Lords Justices were at last obliged to issue a proclamation on the subject (November 19, 1691), in which they state that they had " received complaints from all parts of Ireland of the ill-treatment of the Irish who had submitted ; and that they [the Irish] were so extremely terrified with apprehensions of the continuance of that usage, that some of those who had quitted the Irish army and went home, with the resolution not to go to France, were then come back again, and pressed earnestly to go thither, rather than stay in Ireland, where, contrary to the public faith, as well as law and justice, they were robbed in their persons and abused in their substance." Let it be remembered that this was an official document, and that it emanated from the last persons who were likely to listen to such complaints, or relieve them if they could possibly have been denied.

The men who had hoped for confiscations that they might share the plunder, now began to clamour loudly. It was necessary to get up a popular cry against Papists, as the surest means of attaining their end. Individuals who had as little personal hatred to the Pope as they had to the Grand Turk, and as little real knowledge of the Catholic Faith as of Mahometanism, uttered wild cries of " No Popery !" and " No Surrender !" William, whose morals, if not his professions, proclaimed that he was not troubled with any strong religious convictions, was obliged to yield to the faction who had set him on the throne. Probably, he yielded willingly ; and was thus able, in some measure, to make a pretence of doing under pressure what he really wished to do of his own will.

On the 28th of October, 1692, the Parliament in Dublin rejected a Bill which had been sent from England, containing restrictions on certain duties, solely to proclaim their independence. A few days after they were taught a lesson of obedience. Lord Sidney came down to the House unexpectedly, and prorogued Parliament, with a severe rebuke, ordering the Clerk to enter his protest against the proceedings of the Commons on the journals of the House of Lords. The hopes of the English were raised, and the Parliament brought forward the subject of the Limerick articles, with torrents of complaints against the Irish in general, and the Irish Catholics in particular. William received their remonstrance coolly, and the

[7] *Government.*—Harris' *Life of William III.* p. 357.

matter was allowed to rest for a time. In 1695 Lord Capel was appointed Viceroy. He at once summoned a Parliament, which sat for several sessions, and in which some of the penal laws against Catholics were enacted. As I believe the generality even of educated persons, both in England and Ireland, are entirely ignorant of what these laws really were, I shall give a brief account of their enactments, premising first, that seven lay peers and seven Protestant bishops had the honorable humanity to sign a protest against them.

(1) The Catholic peers were deprived of their right to sit in Parliament. (2) Catholic gentlemen were forbidden to be elected as members of Parliament. (3) It denied all Catholics the liberty of voting, and it excluded them from all offices of trust, and indeed from *all remunerative* employment, however insignificant.[8] (4) They were fined £60 a-month for absence from the Protestant form of worship. (5) They were forbidden to travel five miles from their houses, to keep arms, to maintain suits at law, or to be guardians or executors. (6) Any four justices of the peace could, without further trial, banish any man for life if he refused to attend the Protestant service. (7) Any two justices of the peace could call any man over sixteen before them, and if he refused to abjure the Catholic religion, they could bestow his property on the next of kin. (8) No Catholic could employ a Catholic schoolmaster to educate his children; and if he sent his child abroad for education, he was subject to a fine of £100, and the child could not inherit any property either in England or Ireland. (9) Any Catholic priest who came to the country should be hanged. (10) Any Protestant suspecting any other Protestant of holding property[9] in trust for any Catholic, might file a bill against the suspected trustee, and take the estate or property from him. (11) Any Protestant seeing

---

[8] *Insignificant.*—A petition was sent in to Parliament by the Protestant porters of Dublin, complaining of Darby Ryan for employing Catholic porters. The petition was respectfully received, and referred to a "Committee of Grievances."—*Com. Jour.* vol. ii. f. 699. Such an instance, and it is only one of many, is the best indication of the motive for enacting the penal laws, and the cruelty of them.

[9] *Property.*—It will be remembered that at this time Catholics were in a majority of at least five to one over Protestants. Hence intermarriages took place, and circumstances occurred, in which Protestants found it their interest to hold property for Catholics, to prevent it from being seized by others. A gentleman of considerable property in the county Kerry, has informed me that his property was held in this way for several generations.

a Catholic tenant-at-will on a farm, which, in his opinion, yielded one-third more than the yearly rent, might enter on that farm, and, by simply swearing to the fact, take possession. (12) Any Protestant might take away the horse of a Catholic, no matter how valuable, by simply paying him £5. (13) Horses and wagons belonging to Catholics, were in all cases to be seized for the use of the militia. (14) Any Catholic gentleman's child who became a Protestant, could at once take possession of his father's property.

I have only enumerated some of the enactments of this code, and I believe there are few persons who will not be shocked at their atrocity. Even if the rights of Catholics had not been secured to them by the Treaty of Limerick, they had the rights of men; and whatever excuse, on the ground of hatred of Popery as a religion, may be offered for depriving men of liberty of conscience, and of a share in the government of their country, there can be no excuse for the gross injustice of defrauding them of their property, and placing life and estate at the mercy of every ruffian who had an interest in depriving them of either or of both. Although the seventeenth century has not yet been included in the dark ages, it is possible that posterity, reading these enactments, may reverse present opinion on this subject.

But though the Parliament which sat in Dublin, and was misnamed Irish, was quite willing to put down Popery and to take the property of Catholics, it was not so willing to submit to English rule in other matters. In 1698 Mr. Molyneux, one of the members for the University of Dublin, published a work, entitled *The Case of Ireland's being bound by Acts of Parliament in England, stated.* But Mr. Molyneux's book was condemned by the English Parliament; and after a faint show of resistance, the Irish members succumbed. The next attention which the English Houses paid to this country, was to suppress the woollen trade. In 1698 they passed a law for the prevention of the exportation of wool and of woollen manufactures from Ireland, "under the forfeiture of goods and ship, and a penalty of £500 for every such offence." The penal laws had made it "an offence" for a man to practise his religion, or to educate his children either in Ireland or abroad; the trade laws made it "an offence" for a man to earn[1] his bread in an honest

[1] *Earn.*—One of the articles of the "violated Treaty" expressly provided that the poor Catholics should be allowed to exercise their trade. An

calling. The lower class of Protestants were the principal sufferers by the destruction of the woollen trade ; it had been carried on by them almost exclusively; and it is said that 40,000 persons were reduced to utter destitution by this one enactment. In addition to this, navigation laws were passed, which prohibited Irish merchants from trading beyond seas in any ships except those which were built in England. The embargo laws followed, of which twenty-two were passed at different periods during forty years. They forbade Irish merchants, whether Protestant or Catholic, to trade with any foreign nation, or with any British colony, direct—to export or import *any article*, except to or from British merchants resident in England. Ireland, however, was allowed one consolation, and this was the permission to import rum duty free. I am certain that none of the honorable members who voted such laws had the deliberate intention of making the Irish a nation of beggars and drunkards ; but if the Irish did not become such, it certainly was not the fault of those who legislated for their own benefit, and, as far as they had the power to do so, for her ruin, politically and socially.

William had exercised his royal prerogative by disposing, according to his own inclination, cf the estates forfeited by those who had fought for the royal cause. His favourite, Mrs. Villiers, obtained property worth £25,000 per annum. In 1799 the English Parliament began to inquire into this matter, and the Commons voted that "the advising and passing of the said grants was highly reflecting upon the King's honour." William had already began to see on what shifting sands the poor fabric of his popularity was erected. He probably thought of another case in which his honour had been really pledged, and in which he had been obliged to sacrifice it to the clamours of these very men. He had failed in the attempt to keep his Dutch Guards ; his last days were embittered ; and had not his death occurred soon after, it is just possible that even posterity might have read his life in a different fashion.

Anne succeeded to the throne in 1702 ; and the following year the Duke of Ormonde was sent to Ireland as Lord Lieutenant. The

Act to prevent the further growth of Popery was passed afterwards, which made it forfeiture of goods and imprisonment for any Catholic to exercise a trade in Limerick or Galway, except seamen, fishermen, and day labourers, and they were to be licensed by the Governor, and not to exceed twenty.—*Com. Jour.* vol. iii. f. 133.

House of Commons waited on him with a Bill "to prevent the further growth of Popery." A few members, who had protested against this Act, resigned their seats, but others were easily found to take their places, whose opinions coincided with those of the majority. The Queen's Tory advisers objected to these strong measures, and attempted to nullify them, by introducing the clause known as the "Sacramental Test," which excludes from public offices all who refused to receive the sacrament according to the forms of the Established Church. As dissenters from that Church had great influence in the Irish Parliament, and as it was well known that their abhorrence of the Church which had been established by law was little short of their hatred of the Church which had been suppressed by law, it was hoped that they would reject the bill ; but they were assured that they would not be required to take the test, and with this assurance they passed the Act. It seems to those who look back on such proceedings, almost a marvel, how men, whose conscience forbade them to receive the sacrament according to certain rites, and who, in many cases, certainly would have resigned property, if not life, sooner than act contrary to their religious convictions, should have been so blindly infatuated as to compel other men, as far as they had power to do so, to violate their conscientious convictions. The whole history of the persecutions which Catholics have endured at the hands of Protestants of all and every denomination, is certainly one of the most curious phases of human perversity which the philosopher can find to study.

Two of the gentlemen, Sir Toby Butler and Colonel Cusack, who had signed the Treaty of Limerick, petitioned to be heard by counsel against the Bill. But appeals to honour and to justice were alike in vain, when addressed to men who were destitute of both. The petitioners were dismissed with the insulting remark, that if they suffered from the Act it was their own fault, since, if they complied with its requirements, honours and wealth were at their command. But these were men who would not violate the dictates of conscience for all that the world could bestow on them, and of this one should think they had already given sufficient proof. The Bill was passed without a dissentient voice ; and men who would themselves have rebelled openly and violently if the Sacramental Test had been imposed on them, and who would have talked loudly of liberty of conscience, and the blasphemy of interfering with any one's religious convictions, now, without a shadow of hesitation, imposed this burden upon their fellow-men, and were guilty of the very crime of persecution, with which they so frequently charged their Catholic fellow-subjects.

One Act followed another, each adding some new restriction to the last, or some fresh incentive for persecution. In 1709 an attempt was made to plant some Protestant families from Germany in various parts of the country. These settlements obtained the name of Palatines. But it was labour lost. Sir John Chichester once observed, that it was useless to endeavour to root Popery out of Ireland, for it was impregnated in the very air. A few of the Palatines, like other settlers, still kept to their own religion; but the majority, as well as the majority of other settlers, learned to understand and then to believe the Catholic faith—learned to admire, and then to love, and eventually to amalgamate with the long-suffering and noble race amongst whom they had been established.

It would appear that Queen Anne wished her brother to succeed her on the throne; but he had been educated a Catholic, and he resolutely rejected all temptations to renounce his faith. Her short and troubled reign ended on the 1st of August, 1714. Before her death the Parliament had chosen her successor. Her brother was proscribed, and a reward of £50,000 offered for his apprehension. The rebellion in favour of James III., as he was called on the Continent, or the Pretender, as he was called by those who had no resource but to deny his legitimacy, was confined entirely to Scotland; but the Irish obtained no additional grace by their loyalty to the reigning monarch. A new proclamation was issued, which not only forbid them to enlist in the army, but offered rewards for the discovery of any Papist who had presumed to enlist, in order that " he might be turned out, and punished with the utmost severity of the law." In the next reign we shall see how the suicidal effect of this policy was visited on the heads of its promoters.

The Irish Parliament now came into collision with the English on a case of appellate jurisdiction, but they were soon taught their true position, and with becoming submission deferred to their fate. The Irish Parliament had long been such merely in name; and the only power they were allowed to exercise freely, was that of making oppressive and unjust enactments against their Catholic fellow-subjects. It is a poor consolation, but one which is not unfrequently indulged, when those who are oppressed by others become themselves in turn the oppressors of those who are unfortunate enough to be in their power.

A new phase in Irish history was inaugurated by the versatile talents, and strong will in their exercise, which characterized the famous Dr. Jonathan Swift. The quarrels between Whigs and Tories were at their height. Swift is said to have been a Whig in politics and a Tory in religion. He now began to write as a patriot; and in his famous "Drapier's Letters" told the Government of the day some truths which were more plain than palatable.[2] An Englishman named Wood had obtained a patent under the Broad Seal, in 1723, for the coinage of copper halfpence. Even the servile Parliament was indignant, and protested against a scheme[3] which promised to flood Ireland with bad coin, and thus to add still more to its already impoverished condition. There was reason for anxiety. The South Sea Bubble had lately ruined thousands in England, and France was still suffering from the Mississippi Scheme. Speculations of all kinds were afloat, and a temporary mania seemed to have deprived the soberest people of their ordinary judgment. Dr. Hugh Boulter, an Englishman, was made Archbishop of Armagh, and sent over mainly to attend to the English interests in Ireland. But he was unable to control popular feeling; and Swift's letters accomplished what the Irish Parliament was powerless to effect. Although it was well known that he was the author of these letters, and though a reward of £300 was offered for the discovery of the secret, he escaped unpunished. In 1725 the patent was withdrawn, and Wood received £3,000 a-year for twelve years as an indemnification—an evidence that he must have given a very large bribe for the original permission, and that he expected to

[2] *Palatable.*—In his fourth letter he says: "Our ancestors reduced this kingdom to the obedience of England, in return for which we have been rewarded with a worse climate, the privilege of being governed by laws to which we do not consent, a ruined trade, a house of peers without jurisdiction, almost an incapacity for all employments, and the dread of Wood's halfpence."

[3] *Scheme.*—The very bills of some of the companies were so absurd, that it is marvellous how any rational person could have been deceived by them. One was "for an undertaking which shall be in due time revealed." The undertaker was as good as his word. He got £2,000 paid in on shares one morning, and in the afternoon the "undertaking" was revealed, for he had decamped with the money. Some wag advertised a company "for the invention of melting down sawdust and chips, and casting them into clean deal boards, without cracks or knots."

make more by it than could have been made honestly.   One of the
subjects on which Swift wrote most pointedly and effectively, was
that of absentees.   He employed both facts and ridicule ; but each
were equally in vain.   He describes the wretched state of the
country; but his eloquence was unheeded.   He gave ludicrous
illustrations of the extreme ignorance of those who governed in
regard to those whom they governed.   Unfortunately the state of
things which he described and denounced has continued, with few
modifications, to the present day ; but on this subject I have said
sufficient elsewhere.

George I. died at Osnaburg, in Germany, on the 10th of June,
1727.   On the accession of his successor, the Catholics offered an
address expressing their loyalty, but the Lords Justices took care
that it should never reach England.   The next events of importance
were the efforts made by Dr. Boulter, the Protestant Primate, to
establish Charter Schools, where Catholic children might be educated ; and his equally zealous efforts to prevent Catholics, who had
conformed exteriorly to the State religion, from being admitted to
practise at the Bar.   It may be observed in passing, that these
men could scarcely have been as degraded in habits and intellect as
some historians have been pleased to represent them, when they
could at once become fit for forensic honours, and evinced such
ability as to excite the fears of the Protestant party.   It should be
remarked that their " conversion " was manifestly insincere, otherwise there would have been no cause for apprehension.

The country was suffering at this period from the most fearful
distress.   There were many causes for this state of destitution,
which were quite obvious to all but those who were interested
in maintaining it.   The poorer classes, being almost exclusively
Catholics, had been deprived of every means of support.   Trade was
crushed, so that they could not become traders ; agriculture was not
permitted, so that they could not become agriculturists.   There was,
in fact, no resource for the majority but to emigrate, to steal, or to
starve.   To a people whose religion always had a preponderating
influence on their moral conduct, the last alternative only was available, as there was not the same facilities for emigration then as
now.   The cultivation of the potato had already become general ;
it was, indeed, the only way of obtaining food left to these un-
fortunates.   They were easily planted, easily reared ; and to men
liable at any moment to be driven from their miserable holdings, if

they attempted to effect " improvements," or to plant such crops as might attract the rapacity of their landlords, they were an invaluable resource.   The man might live who eat nothing but potatoes all the year round, but he could scarcely be envied or ejected for his wealth.   In 1739 a severe frost destroyed the entire crop, and a frightful famine ensued, in which it was estimated that 400,000 persons perished of starvation.

In 1747 George Stone succeeded Dr. Hoadley as Primate of Ireland.   His appointment was made evidently more in view of temporals than spirituals, and he acted accordingly.   Another undignified squabble took place in 1751 and 1753, between the English and Irish Parliaments, on the question of privilege.   For a time the " patriot " or Irish party prevailed ; but eventually they yielded to the temptation of bribery and place.   Henry Boyle, the Speaker, was silenced by being made Earl of Shannon ; Anthony Malone was made Chancellor of the Exchequer ; and the opposition party was quietly broken up.

An attempt was now made to form a Catholic Association, and to obtain by combination and quiet pressure what had been so long denied to resistance and military force.   Dr. Curry, a physician practising in Dublin, and the author of the well-known *Historical and Critical Review of the Civil Wars of Ireland;* Charles O'Connor, of Belanagar, the Irish antiquary, and Mr. Wyse, of Waterford, were the projectors and promoters of this scheme.   The clergy stood aloof from it, fearing to lose any liberty they still possessed if they demanded more ; the aristocracy held back, fearing to forfeit what little property yet remained to them, if they gave the least excuse for fresh "settlements" or plunderings.   A few Catholic merchants, however, joined the three friends ; and in conjunction they prepared an address to the Duke of Bedford, who was appointed Lord Lieutenant in 1757.   The address was favourably received, and an answer returned after some time.   The Government already had apprehensions of the French invasion, and it was deemed politic to give the Catholics some encouragement, however faint.   It is at least certain that the reply declared, "the zeal and attachment which they [the Catholics] professed, would never be more seasonably manifested than at the present juncture."

Charles Lucas now began his career of patriotism ; for at last Irish Protestants were beginning to see, that if Irish Catholics suffered, Irish interests would suffer also ; and if Irish interests suffered, they should have their share in the trial. A union between England and Ireland, such as has since been carried out, was now proposed, and violent excitement followed. A mob, principally composed of Protestants, broke into the House of Lords; but the affair soon passed over, and the matter was dropped.

George II. died suddenly at Kensington, and was succeeded by his grandson, George III. But I shall request the attention of the reader to some remarks of considerable importance with regard to foreign events, before continuing the regular course of history. The predilections of the late King for his German connexions, had led him into war both with France and Spain; the imprudence of ministers, if not the unwise and unjust policy of colonial government, involved the country soon after in a conflict with the American dependencies. In each of these cases expatriated Irishmen turned the scale against the country from which they had been so rashly and cruelly ejected. In France, the battle of Fontenoy was won mainly by the Irish Brigade, who were commanded by Colonel Dillon; and the defeat of England by the Irish drew from George II. the well-known exclamation : " Cursed be the laws that deprive me of such subjects !" In Spain, where the Irish officers and soldiers had emigrated by thousands, there was scarcely an engagement in which they did not take a prominent and decisive part. In Canada, the agitation against British exactions was commenced by Charles Thompson, an Irish emigrant, and subsequently the Secretary of Congress ; Montgomery, another Irishman, captured Montreal and Quebec; O'Brien and Barry, whose names sufficiently indicate their nationality, were the first to command in the naval engagements; and startled England began to recover slowly and sadly from her long infatuation, to discover what had, indeed, been discovered by the sharp-sighted Schomberg[4] and his master long before, that Irishmen, from their habits of endurance and undaunted courage, were the best soldiers she could find, and that, Celts and Papists

---

[4] *Schomberg.*—He wrote to William of Orange, from before Dundalk, that the English nation made the worst soldiers he had ever seen, because they could not bear hardships ; " yet," he adds, " the Parliament and people have a prejudice, that an English new-raised soldier can beat above six of his enemies."—Dalrymple's *Memoirs*, vol. ii. p. 178. According to the records of the War Office in France, 450,000 Irishmen died in the service of that country from 1691 to 1745, and, in round numbers, as many more from 1745 to the Revolution.

as they were, her very existence as a nation might depend upon their co-operation.

The agrarian outrages, the perpetrators of which were known at first by the name of Levellers, and eventually by the appellation of Whiteboys, commenced immediately after the accession of George III. An English traveller, who carefully studied the subject, and who certainly could have been in no way interested in misrepresentation, has thus described the cause and the motive of the atrocities they practised. The first cause was the rapacity of the landlords, who, having let their lands far above their value, on condition of allowing the tenants the use of certain commons, now enclosed the commons, but did not lessen the rent. The bricks were to be made, but the straw was not provided ; and the people were told that they were idle. The second cause was the exactions of the tithemongers, who were described by this English writer as " harpies who squeezed out the very vitals of the people, and by process, citation, and sequestration, dragged from them the little which the landlord had left them." It was hard for those who had been once owners of the soil, to be obliged to support the intruders into their property in affluence ; while they, with even the most strenuous efforts, could barely obtain what would keep them from starvation. It was still harder that men, who had sacrificed their position in society, and their worldly prospects, for the sake of their religion, should be obliged to support clergymen and their families, some of whom never resided in the parishes from which they obtained tithes, and many of whom could not count above half-a-dozen persons as regular members of their congregation.

Mr. Young thus suggests a remedy for these crimes, which, he says, were punished with a " severity which seemed calculated for the meridian of Barbary, while others remain yet the law of the land, which would, if executed, tend more to raise than to quell an insurrection. From all which it is manifest, that the gentlemen of Ireland never thought of a radical cure, from overlooking the real cause of disease, which, in fact, lay in themselves, and not in the wretches they doomed to the gallows. Let them change their own conduct entirely, and the poor will not long riot. Treat them like men, who ought to be as free as yourselves ; put an end to that system of religious persecution, which, for seventy years, has divided the kingdom against itself—in these two circumstances lies the cure of insurrection ; perform them completely, and you will have an affectionate poor, instead of oppressed and discontented vassals."[5]

How purely these outrages were the deeds of desperate men, who had been made desperate by cruel oppression, and insensible to cruelty by cruel wrongs, is evident from the dying declaration of five Whiteboys, who were executed, in 1762, at Waterford, and who publicly declared, and took God to witness, " that in all these tumults it never did enter into their thoughts to do anything against the King or Government."[6]

It could not be expected that the Irish priest would see the people exposed to all this misery—and what to them was far more painful, to all this temptation to commit deadly sin—without making some effort in their behalf. There may have been some few priests, who, in their zeal for their country, have sacrificed the sacredness of their office to their indignation at the injury done to their people—who have mixed themselves up with feats of arms, or interfered with more ardour than discretion in the arena of politics; but such instances have been rare, and circumstances have generally made them in some degree excusable. The position of the Irish priest in regard to his flock is so anomalous, that some explanation of it seems necessary in order to understand the accusations made against Father Nicholas Sheehy, and the animosity with which he was hunted to death by his persecutors. While the priest was driven from cave to mountain and from mountain to cave, he was the consoler of his equally persecuted people. The deep reverence which Catholics feel for the office of the priesthood, can scarcely be understood by those who have abolished that office, as far as the law of the land could do so ; but a man of ordinary intellectual attainments ought to be able to form some idea of the feelings of others, though he may not have experienced them personally ; and a man of ordinary humanity should be able to respect those feelings, however unwise they may seem to him. When education was forbidden to the Irish, the priest obtained education in continental colleges ; and there is sufficient evidence to show that many Irish priests of

---

[5] *Vassals.*—Young's *Tour*, vol. ii. pp. 41, 42. It should be remembered that Mr. Young was an Englishman and a Protestant, and that he had no property in Ireland to blind him to the truth.

[6] *Government.*—Curry's *Historical Review*, vol. ii. p. 274, edition of 1786. This work affords a very valuable and accurate account of the times, written from personal knowledge.

that and of preceding centuries were men of more than ordinary abilities. The Irish, always fond of learning, are ever ready to pay that deference to its possessors which is the best indication of a superior mind, however uncultivated. Thus, the priesthood were respected both for their office and for their erudition. The land-lord, the Protestant clergyman, the nearest magistrate, and, perhaps, the tithe-proctor, were the only educated persons in the neighbour-hood; but they were leagued against the poor peasant; they de-manded rent and tithes, which he had no means of paying; they refused justice, which he had no means of obtaining. The priest, then, was the only friend the peasant had. His friendship was disinterested—he gained nothing by his ministration but poor fare and poor lodging; his friendship was self-sacrificing, for he risked his liberty and his life for his flock. He it was—

> "Who, in the winter's night,
> When the cold blast did bite,
> Came to my cabin door,
> And, on the earthen floor,
> Knelt by me, sick and poor;"

and he, too, when the poor man was made still poorer by his sickness,

> "Gave, while his eyes did brim,
> What I should give to him."[7]

But a time came when the priest was able to do more. Men had seen, in some measure, the absurdity, if not the wickedness, of persecuting the religion of a nation; and at this time priests were tolerated in Ireland. Still, though they risked their lives by it, they could not see their people treated unjustly without a protest. The priest was independent of the landlord; for, if he suffered from his vengeance, he suffered alone, and his own sufferings weighed lightly in the balance compared with the general good. The priest was a gentleman by education, and often by birth; and this gave him a social status which his uneducated people could not

---

[7] *Him.*—The ballad of *Soggarth Aroon* (priest, dear) was written by John Banim, in 1831. It is a most true and vivid expression of the feelings of the Irish towards their priests.

possess.[8]   Such was the position of Father Nicholas Sheehy, the parish priest of Clogheen.   He had interfered in the vain hope of protecting his unfortunate parishioners from injustice; and, in return, he was himself made the victim of injustice.   He was accused of encouraging a French invasion—a fear which was always present to the minds of the rulers, as they could not but know that the Irish had every reason to seek for foreign aid to free them from domestic wrongs.   He was accused of encouraging the Whiteboys, because, while he denounced their crimes, he accused those who had driven them to these crimes as the real culprits.   He was accused of treason, and a reward of £300 was offered for his apprehension.   Conscious of his innocence, he gave himself up at once to justice, though he might easily have fled the country.   He was tried in Dublin and acquitted.   But his persecutors were not satisfied.   A charge of murder was got up against him; and although the body of the man could never be found, although it was sworn that he had left the country, although an *alibi* was proved for the priest, he was condemned and executed.   A gentleman of property and position came forward at the trial to prove that Father Sheehy had slept in his house the very night on which he was

---

[8] *Possess.*—While these pages were passing through the press, a circumstance has occurred which so clearly illustrates the position of the Irish priest, that I cannot avoid mentioning it.   A gentleman has purchased some property, and his first act is to give his three tenants notice to quit.   The unfortunate men have no resource but to obey the cruel mandate, and to turn out upon the world homeless and penniless.   They cannot go to law, for the law would be against them.   They are not in a position to appeal to public opinion, for they are only farmers.   The parish priest is their only resource and their only friend.   He appeals to the feelings of their new landlord in a most courteous letter, in which he represents the cruel sufferings these three families must endure.   The landlord replies that he has bought the land as a "commercial speculation," and of course he has a right to do whatever he considers most for his advantage; but offers to allow the tenants to remain if they consent to pay double their former rent—a rent which would be double the real value of the land.   Such cases are constantly occurring, and are constantly exposed by priests; and we have known more than one instance in which fear of such exposure has obtained justice.   A few of them are mentioned from time to time in the Irish local papers.   The majority of cases are entirely unknown, except to the persons concerned; but they are remembered by the poor sufferers and their friends.   I believe, if the people of England were aware of one-half of these ejectments, and the sufferings they cause, they would rise up as a body and demand justice for Ireland and the Irish; they would marvel at the patience with which what to them would be so intolerable has been borne so long.

accused of having committed the murder; but the moment he appeared in court, a clergyman who sat on the bench had him taken into custody, on pretence of having killed a corporal and a sergeant in a riot. The pretence answered the purpose. After Father Sheehy's execution Mr. Keating was tried; and, as there was not even a shadow of proof, he was acquitted. But it was too late to save the victim.

At the place of execution, Father Sheehy most solemnly declared, on the word of a dying man, that he was not guilty either of murder or of treason; that he never had any intercourse, either directly or indirectly, with the French; and that he had never known of any such intercourse being practised by others. Notwithstanding this solemn declaration of a dying man, a recent writer of Irish history says, "there can be no doubt" that he was deeply implicated in treasonable practices, and "he seems to have been" a principal in the plot to murder Lord Carrick. The "no doubt" and "seems to have been" of an individual are not proofs, but they tend to perpetuate false impressions, and do grievous injustice to the memory of the dead. The writer has also omitted all the facts which tended to prove Father Sheehy's innocence.

In 1771 a grace was granted to the Catholics, by which they were allowed to take a lease of fifty acres of bog, and half an acre of arable land for a house; but this holding should not be within a mile of any town. In 1773 an attempt was made to tax absentees; but as they were the principal landowners, they easily defeated the measure. A pamphlet was published in 1769, containing a list of the absentees, which is in itself sufficient to account for any amount of misery and disaffection in Ireland. There can be no doubt of the correctness of the statement, because the names of the individuals and the amount of their property are given in full. Property to the amount of £73,375 belonged to persons who *never* visited Ireland. Pensions to the amount of £371,900 were paid to persons who lived out of Ireland. Property to the amount of £117,800 was possessed by persons who visited Ireland occasionally, but lived abroad. Incomes to the amount of £72,200 were possessed by officials and bishops, who generally lived out of Ireland. The state of trade is also treated in the same work, in which the injustice the country has suffered is fully and clearly explained.

The American war commenced in 1775, and the English Parliament at once resolved to relieve Ireland of some of her commercial disabilities.   Some trifling concessions were granted, just enough to show the Irish that they need not expect justice except under the compulsion of fear, and not enough to benefit the country.   Irish soldiers were now asked for and granted; but exportation of Irish commodities to America was forbidden, and in consequence the country was reduced to a state of fearful distress.   The Irish debt rose to £994,890, but the pension list was still continued and paid to absentees.   When the independence of the American States was acknowledged by France, a Bill for the partial relief of the Catholics passed unanimously through the English Parliament.   Catholics were now allowed a few of the rights of citizens.   They were permitted to take and dispose of leases, and priests and schoolmasters were no longer liable to prosecution.

Grattan had entered Parliament in the year 1775.   In 1779 he addressed the House on the subject of a free trade[9] for Ireland; and on the 19th of April, 1780, he made his famous demand for Irish independence.   His address, his subject, and his eloquence were irresistible.   "I wish for nothing," he exclaimed, "but to breathe in this our land, in common with my fellow-subjects, the air of liberty.   I have no ambition, unless it be the ambition to break your chain and to contemplate your glory.   I never will be satisfied as long as the meanest cottager in Ireland has a link of the British chain clinging to his rags; he may be naked, but he shall not be in irons.   And I do see the time is at hand, the spirit is gone forth, the declaration is planted; and though great men should apostatize, yet the cause will live; and though the public speaker should die, yet the immortal fire shall outlast the organ which conveyed it; and the breath of liberty, like the word of the holy man, will not die with the prophet, but survive him."

The country was agitated to the very core.   A few links of the chain had been broken.   A mighty reaction set in after long bondage. The newly-freed members of the body politic were enjoying all the delicious sensations of a return from a state of disease to a state of partial health.   The Celt was not one to be stupefied or numbed by long confinement; and if the restraint were loosened a little more,

---

[9] *Free trade.*—A very important work was published in 1779, called *The Commercial Restraints of Ireland Considered.*   It is a calm and temperate statement of facts and figures.   The writer shows that the agrarian outrages of the Whiteboys were caused by distress, and quotes a speech of Lord Northumberland to the same effect.—*Com. Res.* p. 59.

Grattan demanding Irish Independence.

he was ready to bound into the race of life, joyous and free, too happy to mistrust, and too generous not to forgive his captors. But, alas! the freedom was not yet granted, and the joy was more in prospect of what might be, than in thankfulness of what was.

The Volunteer Corps, which had been formed in Belfast in 1779, when the coast was threatened by privateers, had now risen to be a body of national importance. They were reviewed in public, and complimented by Parliament. But they were patriots. On the 28th of December, 1781, a few of the leading members of the Ulster regiments met at Charlemont, and convened a meeting of delegates from all the Volunteer Associations, at Dungannon, on the 15th of February, 1782. The delegates assembled on the appointed day, and Government dared not prevent or interrupt their proceedings. Colonel William Irvine presided, and twenty-one resolutions were adopted, demanding civil rights, and the removal of commercial restraints. One resolution expresses their pleasure, as Irishmen, as Christians, and as Protestants, at the relaxation of the penal laws. This resolution was suggested by Grattan to Mr. Dobbs, as he was leaving Dublin to join the assembly. It was passed with only two dissentient votes.

The effect of this combined, powerful, yet determined agitation, was decisive. On the 27th of May, 1782, when the Irish Houses met, after an adjournment of three weeks, the Duke of Portland announced the unconditional concessions which had been made to Ireland by the English Parliament. Mr. Grattan interpreted the concession in the fullest sense, and moved an address, " breathing the generous sentiments of his noble and confiding nature." Mr. Flood and a few other members took a different and more cautious view of the case. They wished for something more than a simple repeal of the Act of 6 George I., and they demanded an express declaration that England would not interfere with Irish affairs. But his address was carried by a division of 211 to 2 ; and the House, to show its gratitude, voted that 20,000 Irish seamen should be raised for the British navy, at a cost of £100,000, and that £50,000 should be given to purchase an estate and build a house for Mr. Grattan, whose eloquence had contributed so powerfully to obtain what they hoped would prove justice to Ireland.

GOLDSMITH'S WELL.

CHAPTER XXXV.

Celebrated Irishmen of the Eighteenth Century—BURKE—His School and College Life—Early Hatred of Oppression—Johnson's Estimate of Burke—*Essay on the Sublime and Beautiful*—Commencement of his Political Career—Opinions on the American Question—English Infatuation and Injustice—Irishmen Prominent Actors in the American Revolution—Its Causes and Effects—Burke on Religious Toleration—Catholic Emancipation—His Indian Policy—MOORE—His Poetry and Patriotism—CURRAN—SWIFT—LUCAS—FLOOD—GRATTAN—EARL OF CHARLEMONT—Irish Artists, Authors, and Actors—SHERIDAN—Scene in the House of Lords during the Impeachment of Warren Hastings—GOLDSMITH.

[A.D. 1700—1800.]

EACH century of Irish history would require a volume of its own, if the lives of its eminent men were recorded as they should be; but the eighteenth century may boast of a host of noble Irishmen, whose fame is known even to those who are most indifferent to the history of that country. It was in this century that Burke, coming forth from the Quaker school of Ballitore, his mind strengthened by its calm discipline, his intellect cultivated by its gifted master, preached political wisdom to the Saxons, who were politically wise as far as they followed his teaching, and politically unfortunate when they failed to do so. His public career demands the most careful consideration from every statesman who may have any higher object in view than the mere fact of having a seat in the cabinet; nor should it be of less interest or value to those whose intellectual capacities are such as to enable them to grasp any higher subject than the plot of a sensational novel. It was in this century also that Moore began to write his world-famed songs, to amaze the learned by his descriptions of a country which he had never seen, and to fling out those poetical hand grenades, those pasquinades and squibs, whose rich humour and keenly-pointed satire had so much influence on the politics of the day. It was in this century that Sheridan, who was the first to introduce Moore to London society, distinguished himself at once as dramatist, orator, and statesman, and left in his life and death a terrible lesson to his nation of the miseries and degradations consequent on indulgence in their besetting sin. In was in this century that Steele, the bosom friend of Addison, and his literary equal, contributed largely to the success and popularity of the *Spectator*, the *Guardian*, and the *Tatler*, though, as usual, English literature takes the credit to itself of what has been accomplished for it by Irish writers.[1]

Burke is, however, unquestionably both the prominent man of his age and of his nation in that age ; and happily we have abundant material for forming a correct estimate of his character and his works. Burke was born in Dublin, on the 1st of January, 1730. His father was an attorney in good business, and of course a Protestant, as at that period none, except those who professed the religion of a small minority, were permitted to govern the vast majority, or to avail themselves of any kind of temporal advancement. The mother of the future statesman was a Miss Nagle, of Mallow, a descendant of whose family became afterwards very famous as the foundress of a religious order.[2] The family estate was at Castletown-Roche, in the vicinity of Doneraile ; this property descended to Garrett, Edmund's elder brother. A famous school had been

[1] *Writers.*—As a general rule, when Irishmen succeed either in literature, politics, or war, the credit of their performances is usually debited to the English : when they fail, we hear terrible clamours of Irish incapacity. Thackeray commences his " *English* Humourists of the Eighteenth Century " with Swift, and ends them with Goldsmith ! I do not suppose he had any intention of defrauding the Celtic race ; he simply followed the usual course. Irishmen are, perhaps, themselves most to blame, for much of this is caused by their suicidal deference to a dominant race.

[2] *Order.*—The Presentation Order was founded by Miss Nano Nagle, of Cork.

founded by a member of the Society of Friends at Ballitore, and thither young Burke and his brother were sent for their education. The boys arrived there on the 26th May, 1741. A warm friendship soon sprang up between Edmund and Richard Shackleton, the son of his master, a friendship which only terminated with death. We have happily the most ample details of Burke's school-days in the *Annals of Ballitore*, a work of more than ordinary interest, written by Mrs. Leadbeater, the daughter of Burke's special friend. His native talent was soon developed under the care of his excellent master, and there can be little doubt that the tolerant ideas of his after life were learned, or at least cultivated, at the Quaker school.

One instance of the early development of his talent for humour, and another of his keen sense of injustice, must find record here. The entrance of the judges to the county town of Athy was a spectacle which had naturally special attraction for the boys. All were permitted to go, but on condition that each of the senior pupils should write a description of what he had seen in Latin verse. Burke's task was soon accomplished—not so that of another hapless youth, whose ideas and Latinity were probably on a par. When he had implored the help of his more gifted companion, Edmund determined at least that he should contribute an idea for his theme, but for all reply as to what he had noticed in particular on the festal occasion, he only answered, "A fat piper in a brown coat." However Burke's ideas of "the sublime" may have predominated, his idea of the ludicrous was at this time uppermost; and in a few moments a poem was composed, the first line of which only has been preserved—

"Piper erat fattus, qui brownum tegmen habebat."

"He loved humour," writes Mrs. Leadbeater,[3] "and my father was very witty. The two friends sharpened their intellect and sported their wit till peals of laughter in the schoolroom often caused the reverend and grave master to implore them, with suppressed smiles, to desist, or he should have to turn them out, as their example might be followed, where folly and uproar would take the place of humour and wisdom."

---

[3] *Leadbeater.—Annals of Ballitore*, vol. i. p. 50, second edition, 1862. I shall refer to this interesting work again.

His hatred of oppression and injustice was also manifested about this time. A poor man was compelled to pull down his cabin, because the surveyor of roads considered that it stood too near the highway. The boy watched him performing his melancholy task, and declared that, if he were in authority, such scenes should never be enacted. How well he kept his word, and how true he was in manhood to the good and holy impulses of his youth, his future career amply manifests.

Burke entered Trinity College, Dublin, in 1744; Goldsmith entered college the following year, and Flood was a fellow-commoner ; but these distinguished men knew little of each other in early life, and none of them were in any way remarkable during their academic career. In 1753 Burke arrived in London, and occupied himself in legal studies and the pursuit of literature. His colloquial gifts and his attractive manner won all hearts, while his mental superiority commanded the respect of the learned. Even Johnson, who was too proud to praise others, much as he loved flattery himself, was fain to give his most earnest word of commendation to the young Irishman, and even admitted that he envied Burke for being " continually the same," though he could not refrain from having a fling at him for not being a " good listener"— a deadly sin in the estimation of one who seldom wished to hear any other voice but his own. Burke, sir, he exclaimed to the obsequious Boswell—Burke is such a man, that if you met him for the first time in the street, and conversed with him for not five minutes, he'd talk to you in such a manner, that, when you parted, you would say that is an extraordinary man.[4]

Some essays in imitation of Dr. Charles Lucas, and a translation of part of the second Georgic of Virgil, which, in finish of style, is, at least, not inferior to Dryden, were among the earliest efforts of his gifted pen ; and, no doubt, these and other literary occupations gave him a faculty of expressing thought in cultivated language, which was still further developed by constant intercourse with Johnson, ever ready for argument, and his club, who were all equally desirous to listen when either spoke. His *Essay on the Sublime and Beautiful*,

[4] *Man.*—The exact words are : " If a man were to go by chance at the same time with Burke, under a shed to shun a shower, he would say : ' This is an extraordinary man.' "—*Boswell's Johnson*, vol. iv. p. 245. Foster's version is as above.

unfortunately better known in the present day by its title than by its contents, at once attracted immense attention, and brought considerable pecuniary help to the author.   But the constant pressure of intellectual labour soon began to tell upon a constitution always delicate.   His health gave way entirely, and he appeared likely to sink into a state of physical debility, entirely incompatible with any mental exertion.   He applied for advice to Dr. Nugent; the skilful physician saw at once that something more was required than medicine or advice.   It was one of those cases of suffering to which the most refined and cultivated minds are especially subjected—one of those instances which prove, perhaps, more than any others, that poor humanity has fallen low indeed.   The master-mind was there, the brilliant gems of thought, the acute power of reasoning, that exquisitely delicate sense of feeling, which has never yet been accurately defined, and which probably never can be—which waits for some unseen mystic sympathy to touch it, and decide whether the chord shall be in minor or major key—which produces a tone of thought, now sublime, and now brimming over with coruscations of wit from almost the same incidents ; and yet all those faculties of the soul, though not destroyed, are held in abeyance, because the body casts the dull shadow of its own inability and degradation over the spirit—because the spirit is still allied to the flesh, and must suffer with it.

There was something more than perfect rest required in such a case.   Rest would, indeed, recruit the body, worn out by the mind's overaction, but the mind also needed some healing process.   Some gentle hand should soothe the overstrained chords of thought, and touch them just sufficiently to stimulate their action with gentlest suasion, while it carefully avoided all that might irritate or weary. And such help and healing was found for Burke, or, haply, from bodily debility, mental weakness might have developed itself into mental malady ; and the irritability of weakness, to which cultivated minds are often most subjected, might have ended, even for a time, if not wisely treated, in the violence of lunacy.   It was natural that the doctor's daughter should assist in the doctor's work ; and, perhaps, not less natural that the patient should be fascinated by her.   In a short time the cure was perfected, and Burke obtained the greatest earthly blessing for which any man can crave—a devoted wife, a loving companion, a wise adviser, and, above all, a sympathizing friend, to whom all which interested her husband, either in public or private, was her interest as much as, and, if possible, even more than his.   Burke's public career certainly opened with happy auspices.   He was introduced by the Earl of Charlemont to Mr. Hamilton in 1759, and in 1761 he returned to Ireland in the capacity of private secretary to that gentleman. Mr. Hamilton has acquired, as is well known, the appellation of " single speech," and it is thought he employed Burke to compose his oration ; it is probable that he required his assistance in more important ways.   But the connexion was soon dissolved, not without some angry words on both sides.   Hamilton taunted Burke with having taken him out of a garret, which was not true, for Burke's social position was scarcely inferior to his own ; Burke replied with ready wit that he regretted having *descended* to know him.

In the year 1765, when Lord Grenville was driven from office by the "American Question," the Marquis of Rockingham succeeded him, appointed Burke his private secretary, and had him returned for the English borough of Wendover.   His political career commenced at this period.   Then, as now, Reform, Ireland, and America were the subjects of the day ; and when one considers and compares the politics of the eighteenth and the nineteenth centuries, the progress of parliamentary intellectual development is not very encouraging.   The speeches of honorable members, with some few very honorable exceptions, seem to run in the same groove, with the same utter incapacity of realizing a new idea, or a broad and cosmopolitan policy.   There were men then, as there are men now, who talked of toleration in one breath, and proclaimed their wooden determination to enforce class ascendency of creed and of station in the next.   There were men who would tax fresh air, and give unfortunate wretches poisonous drinks on the cheapest terms.   There were men whose foreign policy consisted in wringing all that could be wrung out of dependencies, and then, when the danger was pointed out, when it was shown that those dependencies were not only likely to resist, but were in a position to resist— in a position in which neither shooting nor flogging could silence, if it did not convince—they hid their heads, with ostrich-like fatuity, in the blinding sands of their own ignorance, and declared there could be no danger, for *they* could not discern it.

I have said that there were three great political questions which occupied the attention of statesmen at that day.   I shall briefly glance at each, as they form a most important standpoint in our national history, and are subjects of the first interest to Irishmen and to Irish history ; and as Burke's maiden speech in the House of Commons was made in favour of conciliating America, I shall treat that question first. The facts are brief and significant, but by no means as thoroughly known or as well considered as they should be, when we remember their all-important results—results which as yet are by no means fully developed.[5] The actual contest between the English nation and her American colonies commenced soon after the accession of George III.; but, as early as the middle of the eighteenth century, Thomas Pownal, Governor and Commander-in-Chief of Massachusetts, South Carolina, and New Jersey, came to England, and published a work on the administration of the colonies. He seems even then to have had a clear view of the whole case. There is an old proverb about the last grain of rice breaking the back of the camel, but we must remember that the load was made up of many preceding grains. The Stamp Act and Tea Duty were unquestionably the last links of an attempted chain of slavery with which England ventured to fetter the noblest of her colonies, but there were many preceding links. Pownal's work affords evidence of the existence of many. The crown, he said, *in theory* considered the lands and plantations of the colonists its own, and attempted a far greater control over the personal liberty of the subject than it dared to claim in England. The people, on the other hand, felt that they had by no means forfeited the rights of Englishmen because they had left England ; and that, if they submitted to its laws, they should at least have some share in making them. A series of petty collisions, which kept up a state

---

[5] *Developed.*—Since this sentence was penned, I find, with great satisfaction, that a similar view has been taken by a recent writer. See *Secularia ; or, Surveys on the Main Stream of History*, by S. Lucas, p. 250. He opens a chapter on the revolt of the American States thus : " The relations of Great Britain to its colonies, past and present, are an important part of the history of the world ; and the form which these relations *may hereafter take, will be no small element in the political future.* Even our Professors of History . . . abstain from noticing their system of government, or *the predisposing motives to their subsequent revolt.*" The italics are our own. Neglect of the study of Irish history is, I believe, also, one of the causes why Irish grievances are not remedied by the English Government. But grievances may get settled in a way not always satisfactory to the neglecters of them, while they are waiting their leisure to investigate their cause.

of constant irritation, prepared the way for the final declaration, which flung aside the bonds of allegiance, and freed the people from the galling chains by which that allegiance was sought to be maintained. A wise policy at home might have averted the fatal disruption for a time, but it is doubtful that it could have been averted for many years, even if the utter incapacity of an obstinate sovereign, and the childish vindictiveness of a minister, had not precipitated the conclusion.

The master intellect of Burke at once grasped the whole question, and his innate sense of justice suggested the remedy. Unfortunately for England, but happily for America, Burke was beyond his age in breadth of policy and in height of honour. Englishmen of the nineteenth century have very freely abused Englishmen of the eighteenth century for their conduct on this occasion; and more than one writer has set down the whole question as one in which "right" was on the side of England, but he argues that there are circumstances under which right should be sacrificed to policy. I cannot agree with this very able writer.[6] The question was not one of right, but of justice; and the English nation, in the reign of George III., failed to see that to do justice was both morally and politically the wisest course. The question of right too often develops itself into the question of might. A man easily persuades himself that he has a right to do what he has the power and the inclination to do; and when his inclination and his opportunities are on the same side, his moral consciousness becomes too frequently blinded, and the question of justice is altogether overlooked.

It was in vain that Burke thundered forth denunciations of the childish policy of the Treasury benches, and asked men to look to first principles, who could hardly be made comprehend what first principles were. He altogether abandoned the question of right, in which men had so puzzled themselves as almost to lose sight of the question of policy. The King would tax the colony, because his nature was obstinate, and what he had determined to do he would do. To such natures reasoning is much like hammering on iron—it

---

[6] *Writer.*—Morley. *Edmund Burke, an Historical Study:* Macmillan and Co., 1867. A masterly work, and one which every statesman and every thinker would do well to peruse carefully. He says: "The question to be asked by every statesman, and by every citizen, with reference to a measure that is recommended to him as the enforcement of a public right, is whether the right is one which it is to the public advantage to enforce."—p. 146.

only hardens the metal.   The minister would tax the colony because the King wished it ; and he had neither the strength of mind nor the conscientiousness to resist his sovereign.   The Lords stood on their dignity, and would impose the tax if only to show their power.   The people considered the whole affair one of pounds, shillings, and pence, and could not at all see why they should not wring out the last farthing from a distant colony—could not be taught to discern that the sacrifice of a few pounds at the present moment, might result in the acquisition of a few millions at a future day.

Burke addressed himself directly to the point on all these questions.   He laid aside the much-abused question of right; he did not even attempt to show that right and justice should not be separated, and that men who had no share in the government of a country, could not be expected in common justice to assist in the support of that country.   He had to address those who could only understand reasons which appealed to their self-interest, and he lowered himself to his audience.   The question he said was, "not whether you have a right to render your people miserable, but whether it is not your interest to make them happy.   It is not what a lawyer tells me I *may* do, but what humanity, reason, and justice, tell me I *ought* to do."

The common idea about the separation of the States from England, is simply that they resisted a stamp duty and a tax on tea; the fact is, as I have before hinted, that this was simply the last drop in the cup.   Previous to this period, the American colonies were simply considered as objects of English aggrandizement.   They were treated as states who only existed for the purpose of benefiting England.   The case was in fact parallel to the case of Ireland, and the results would probably have been similar, had Ireland been a little nearer to America, or a little further from England.   For many years the trade of America had been kept under the most vexatious restrictions.   The iron found there must be sent to England to be manufactured ; the ships fitted out there must be at least partly built in England ; no saw-mills could be erected, no colony could trade directly with another colony, nor with any nation except England.   This selfish, miserable policy met with a well-deserved fate.   Even Pitt exclaimed indignantly, in the House of Commons: "We are told that America is obstinate—that America is almost in open rebellion.   I rejoice that she has resisted.   Three millions of people, so dead to all sentiments of liberty as voluntarily to become slaves, would have been fit instruments to enslave their fellow-subjects."

In 1765 an agitation was commenced in Philadelphia, by Mr. Charles Thompson, an Irishman, who, after ten years devoted to the cause of his adopted country, was appointed the Secretary of Congress. It has been well remarked, that the Irish, and especially the Irish Catholics, were, of the three nationalities, the most devoted to forwarding the Revolution ; and we cannot wonder that it was so, since the Government which had driven them from their native land, ceased not to persecute them in the land of their exile.[7] The first naval engagement was fought under the command of Jeremiah O'Brien, an Irishman.[8] John Barry, also an Irishman, took the command of one of the first American-built ships of war. The first Continental Regiment was composed almost exclusively of Irish-born officers and men, and was the first Rifle Regiment ever organized in the world. Thompson, its first, and Hand, its second colonel, were natives of Ireland. At the siege of Boston the regiment was particularly dreaded by the British.

In 1764 Franklin came to England[9] for the second time, and was

---

[7] *Exile.*—Maguire's *Irish in America*, p. 355: "It would seem as if they instinctively arrayed themselves in hostility to the British power ; a fact to be explained alike by their love of liberty, and *their vivid remembrance of recent or past misgovernment.*" The italics are our own. The penal laws were enacted with the utmost rigour against Catholics in the colonies, and the only place of refuge was Maryland, founded by the Catholic Lord Baltimore. Here there was liberty of conscience for all, but here only. The sects who had fled to America to obtain "freedom to worship God," soon manifested their determination that no one should have liberty of conscience except themselves, and gave the lie to their own principles, by persecuting each other for the most trifling differences of opinion on religious questions, in the cruelest manner. Cutting off ears, whipping, and maiming were in constant practice. See Maguire's *Irish in America*, p. 349; Lucas' *Secularia*, pp. 220-246.

[8] *Irishman.*—See Cooper's *Naval History*.

[9] *England.*—He wrote to Thompson, from London, saying that he could effect nothing : "The sun of liberty is set; we must now light up the candles of industry." The Secretary replied, with Celtic vehemence : "Be assured we shall light up torches of a very different kind." When the Catholics of the United States sent up their celebrated Address to Washington, in 1790, he alludes in one part of his reply to the immense assistance obtained from them in effecting the Revolution : "I presume that your fellow-citizens will not

examined before the House of Commons on the subject of the Stamp Act. He was treated with a contemptuous indifference, which he never forgot; but he kept his court suit, not without an object; and in 1783, when he signed the treaty of peace, which compelled England to grant humbly what she had refused haughtily, he wore the self-same attire. Well might the immortal Washington say to Governor Trumbull : "There was a day, sir, when this step from our then acknowledged parent state, would have been accepted with gratitude ; but that day is irrevocably past."

In 1774, Burke was called upon by the citizens of Bristol to represent them in Parliament, and he presented a petition from them to the House in favour of American independence ; but, with the singular inconsistency of their nation, they refused to re-elect him in 1780, because he advocated Catholic Emancipation.

The same principle of justice which made Burke take the side of America against England, or rather made him see that it would be the real advantage of England to conciliate America, made him also take the side of liberty on the Catholic question. The short-sighted and narrow-minded politicians who resisted the reasonable demands of a colony until it was too late to yield, were enabled, unfortunately, to resist more effectually the just demands of several millions of their own people.

It is unquestionably one of the strangest of mental phenomena, that persons who make liberty of conscience their boast and their watchword, should be the first to violate their own principles, and should be utterly unable to see the conclusion of their own favourite premises. If liberty of conscience mean anything, it must surely mean perfect freedom of religious belief for all; and such freedom is certainly incompatible with the slightest restraint, with the most trifling penalty for difference of opinion on such subjects. Again, Burke had recourse to the *argumentum ad hominum*, the only argument which those with whom he had to deal seemed capable of comprehending.

"After the suppression of the great rebellion of Tyrconnel by William of Orange," writes Mr. Morley,[1] "ascendency began in all

forget the patriotic part which you took in the accomplishment of their revolution and the establishment of their government, or the important assistance they received from a nation in which the Roman Catholic religion is professed."

[1] *Morley.—Edmund Burke, an Historical Study*, p. 181.

its vileness and completeness.   The Revolution brought about in Ireland just the reverse of what it effected in England.   Here it delivered the body of the nation from the attempted supremacy of a small sect ; there it made a small sect supreme over the body of the nation."   This is in fact an epitome of Irish history since the so-called Reformation in England, and this was the state of affairs which Burke was called to combat.   On all grounds the more power-ful party was entirely against him.   The merchants of Manchester and Bristol, for whose supposed benefit Irish trade had been ruined, wished to keep up the ascendency, conceiving it to be the surest way of replenishing their coffers.   The majority of Irish landlords, who looked always to their own immediate interest, and had none of the far-sighted policy which would enable them to see that the pros-perity of the tenant would, in the end, most effectively secure the prosperity of the landlord, were also in favour of ascendency, which promised to satisfy their land hunger, and their miserable greed of gain.   The Protestant Church was in favour of ascendency : why should it not be, since its ministers could only derive support from a people who hated them alike for their creed and their oppressions, at the point of the sword and by the " brotherly agency of the tithe-procter," who, if he did not assist in spreading the Gospel, at least took care that its so-called ministers should lack no luxury which could be wrung from a starving and indignant people ?[2]

There were but two acts of common justice required on the part of England to make Ireland prosperous and free.   It is glorious to say, that Burke was the first to see this, and inaugurate the reign of concession ; it is pitiful, it is utterly contemptible, to be obliged to add, that what was then inaugurated is not yet fully accomplished. Burke demanded for Ireland political and religious freedom.   Slowly some small concessions of both have been made when England has feared to refuse them.   Had the grant been made once for all with manly generosity, some painful chapters of Irish history might have

[2] *People.* — Chesterfield said, in 1764, that the poor people in Ireland were used "worse than negroes."   "Aristocracy," said Adam Smith, "was not founded in the natural and respectable distinctions of birth and fortune, but in the most odious of all distinctions, those of religious and political prejudices—distinctions which, more than any other, animate both the in-solence of the oppressors, and the hatred and indignation of the oppressed."— Morley's *Edmund Burke*, p. 183.

been omitted from this volume—some moments, let us hope, of honest shame might have been spared to those true-hearted Englishmen who deplore the fatuity and the folly of their countrymen. In 1782 the Irish Volunteers obtained from the fears of England what had been vainly asked from her justice. Burke's one idea of good government may be summed up in the words, "Be just, and fear not." In his famous *Letter to Sir Hercules Langrishe*, written in 1792, upon the question of admitting the Catholics to the elective franchise, he asks: "Is your government likely to be more secure by continuing causes of grounded discontent to two-thirds of its subjects? Will the constitution be made more solid by depriving this large part of the people of all concern or share in the representation?"

His Indian policy was equally just. "Our dealings with India," says an English writer, "originally and until Burke's time, so far from being marked with virtue and wisdom, were stained with every vice which can lower and deprave human character. How long will it take only to extirpate these traditions from the recollections of the natives? The more effectually their understandings are awakened by English efforts, the more vividly will they recognize, and the more bitterly resent, the iniquities of our first connexion with them." The Indian policy of England and her Irish policy might be written with advantage in parallel columns. It would, at least, have the advantage of showing Irishmen that they had been by no means worse governed than other dependencies of that professedly law and justice loving nation.

I have treated, briefly indeed, and by no means as I should wish, of two of the questions of the day, and of Burke's policy thereon; of the third question a few words only can be said. Burke's idea of Reform consisted in amending the administration of the constitution, rather than in amending the constitution itself. Unquestionably a bad constitution well administered, may be incomparably more beneficial to the subject than a good constitution administered corruptly. Burke's great leading principle was: Be just—and can a man have a nobler end? To suppress an insurrection cruelly, to tax a people unjustly, or to extort money from a nation on false pretences, was to him deeply abhorrent. His first object was to secure the incorruptibility of ministers and of members of parliament. When the post of royal scullion could be confided to a member of parliament, and a favourable vote secured by appointing a representative of the people to the lucrative post of turnspit in the king's kitchen, administration was hopelessly corrupt. There were useless treasurers for useless offices. Burke gave the example of what he taught; and having fixed the Paymaster's salary at four thousand pounds a year, was himself the first person to accept the diminished income.

He has been accused of forsaking his liberal principles in his latter days, simply and solely from his denunciations of the terrible excesses of the French Revolution. Such reprobation was rather a proof that he understood the difference between liberty and licentiousness, and that his accusers had neither the intellect nor the true nobility to discriminate between the frantic deeds of men, whose bad passions, long indulged, had led them on to commit the crimes of demons, and those noble but long-suffering patriots, who endured until endurance became a fault, and only resisted for the benefit of mankind as well as for their own.

So much space has been given to Burke, that it only remains to add a few brief words of the other brilliant stars, who fled across the Channel in the vain pursuit of English patronage— in the vain hope of finding in a free country the liberty to ascend higher than the rulers of that free country permitted in their own.

Moore was born in the year 1780, in the city of Dublin. His father was in trade, a fact which he had the manliness to acknowledge whenever such acknowledgment was necessary. He was educated for the bar, which was just then opened for the first time to the majority of the nation, so long governed, or misgoverned, by laws which they were neither permitted to make or to administer. His poetical talents were early manifested, and his first attempts were in the service of those who are termed patriots or rebels, as the speaker's opinion varies. That he loved liberty and admired liberators can scarcely be doubted, since even later in life he used to boast of his introduction to Thomas Jefferson, while in America, exclaiming : " I had the honour of shaking hands with the man who drew up the Declaration of American Independence." His countryman, Sheridan introduced him to the Prince of Wales. His Royal Highness inquired courteously if he was the son of a certain baronet of the same name. " No, your Royal Highness," replied Moore ; " I am the son of a Dublin grocer." He commenced writing his immortal *Melodies* in 1807, soon after his marriage. But he by no means confined himself to such subjects. With that keen sense of humour, almost inseparable from, and generally proportionate to, the most exquisite sensibility of feeling, he caught the salient points of controversy in his day, and no doubt contributed not a little to the obtaining of Catholic Emancipation by the telling satires which he poured forth on its opposers. His reflections, addressed to the *Quarterly Review*, who recommended an increase of the Church Establishment as the grand panacea of Irish ills, might not be an inappropriate subject of consideration at the present moment. It commences thus :

" I'm quite of your mind : though these Pats cry aloud,
    That they've got too much Church, tis all nonsense and stuff ;
For Church is like love, of which Figaro vowed,
    That even *too much* of it's not quite enough."

Nor was his letter to the Duke of Newcastle, who was an obstinate opposer of Catholic Emancipation, less witty, or less in point at the present time, for the Lords would not emancipate, whatever the Commons might do :

" While intellect, 'mongst high and low,
    Is hastening on, they say,
Give me the dukes and lords, who go,
    Like crabs, the other way."

Curran had been called to the bar a few years earlier. He was the son of a poor farmer in the county of Cork, and won his way to fame solely by the exercise of his extraordinary talent. Curran was a Protestant; but he did not think it necessary, because he belonged to a religion which professed liberty of conscience, to deny its exercise to every one but those of his own sect. He first distinguished himself at a contested election. Of his magnificent powers of oratory I shall say nothing, partly because their fame is European, and partly because it would be impossible to do justice to the subject in our limited space. His terrible denunciations of the horrible crimes and cruelties of the soldiers, who were sent to govern Ireland by force, for those who were not wise enough or

humane enough to govern it by justice—his scathing denunciations of crown witnesses and informers, should be read at length
to be appreciated fully.[3]

Swift's career is also scarcely less known. He, too, was born in
Dublin of poor parents, in 1667. Although he became a minister
of the Protestant Church, and held considerable emoluments therein,
he had the honesty to see, and the courage to acknowledge, its many
corruptions. The great lesson which he preached to Irishmen was
the lesson of nationality ; and, perhaps, they have yet to learn it in
the sense in which he intended to teach it. No doubt, Swift, in
some way, prepared the path of Burke ; for, different as were their
respective careers and their respective talents, they had each the
same end in view. The " Drapier " was long the idol of his countrymen, and there can be little doubt that the spirit of his
writings did much to animate the patriots who followed him—
Lucas, Flood, and Grattan. Lucas was undoubtedly one of
the purest patriots of his time. His parents were poor farmers in
the county Clare, who settled in Dublin, where Lucas was born, in
1713; and in truth patriotism seldom develops itself out of purple
and fine linen. Flood, however, may be taken in exception to
this inference ; his father was a Chief Justice of the Irish King's
Bench. When elected a member of the Irish House, his first
public effort was for the freedom of his country from the atrocious
imposition of Poyning's Law. Unfortunately, he and Grattan
quarrelled, and their country was deprived of the immense benefits
which might have accrued to it from the cordial political union of
two such men.

But a list of the great men of the eighteenth century, however
brief, would be certainly most imperfect if I omitted the name of the
Earl of Charlemont, who, had his courage been equal to his honesty
of purpose, might have been enrolled not merely as an ardent, but
even as a successful patriot. He was one of the *Hibernis ipsis
Hiberniores*,—one of those who came to plunder, and who learned to
respect their victims, and to repent their oppressions. It is probable
that the nine years which the young Earl spent in travelling on the
Continent, contributed not a little to his mental enlargement. On
his return from countries where freedom exists with boasting, to a

---

[3] *Fully.*—See *Curran's Letters and Speeches :* Dublin, 1865.

country where boasting exists without a corresponding amount of freedom, he was amazed and shocked at the first exhibition of its detestable tyranny of class. A grand procession of peers and peeresses was appointed to receive the unfortunate Princess Caroline ; but, before the Princess landed, the Duchess of Bedford was commanded to inform the Irish peeresses that they were not to walk, or to take any part in the ceremonial. The young Earl could not restrain his indignation at this utterly uncalled-for insult. He obtained a royal audience, and exerted himself with so much energy, that the obnoxious order was rescinded. The Earl's rank, as well as his patriotism, naturally placed him at the head of his party ; and he resolutely opposed those laws which Burke had designated as a " disgrace to the statute-books of any nation, and so odious in their principles, that one might think they were passed in hell, and that demons were the legislators." In 1766, his Lordship brought a bill into the House of Lords to enable a poor Catholic peasant to take a lease of a cabin and a potato-garden ; but, at the third reading, the Lords rushed in tumultuously, voted Lord Charlemont out of the chair, and taunted him with being little better than a Papist. The failure and the taunt bewildered an intellect never very clear ; and, perhaps, hopelessness quenched the spirit of patriotism, which had once, at least, burned brightly. In fear of being taunted as a Papist, like many a wiser man, he rushed into the extreme of Protestant loyalty, and joined in the contemptible outcry for Protestant ascendency.

The eighteenth century was also rife in Irishmen whose intellects were devoted to literature. It claims its painters in Barrett, who was actually the founder of the Royal Academy in England, and in Barry, the most eminent historical painter of his age ; its poets in Parnell, Goldsmith, Wade, O'Keeffe, Moore, and many others ; its musician in Kelly, a full list of whose operatic music would fill several pages ; its authors in Steele, Swift, Young, O'Leary, Malone, Congreve, Sheridan, and Goldsmith ; and its actors in Macklin, Milliken, Barry, Willis, and Woffington.

Sheridan was born in Dublin, in the year 1757. He commenced his career as author by writing for the stage ; but his acquaintance with Fox, who soon discerned his amazing abilities, led him in another direction. In 1786 he was employed with Burke in the impeachment of Warren Hastings. The galleries of the House of Lords were filled to overflowing; peers and peeresses secured seats early in the day; actresses came to learn declamation, authors to learn style. Mrs. Siddons, accustomed as she was to the simulation of passion in herself and others, shrieked and swooned while he denounced the atrocities of which Hastings had been guilty. Fox, Pitt, and Byron, were unanimous in their praise. And on the very same night, and at the very same time, when the gifted Celt was thundering justice to India into the ears of Englishmen, his *School for Scandal*, one of the best comedies on the British stage, was being acted in one theatre, and his *Duenna*, one of its best operas, was being performed in another.

Sheridan died in 1816, a victim to intemperance, for which he had not even the excuse of misfortune. Had not his besetting sin degraded and incapacitated him, it is probable he would have been prime-minister on the death of Fox. At the early age of forty he was a confirmed drunkard. The master mind which had led a senate, was clouded over by the fumes of an accursed spirit; the brilliant eyes that had captivated a million hearts, were dimmed and bloodshot; the once noble brain, which had used its hundred gifts with equal success and ability, was deprived of all power of acting; the tongue, whose potent spell had entranced thousands, was scarcely able to articulate. Alas, and a thousand times alas! that man can thus mar his Maker's work, and stamp ruin and wretchedness where a wealth of mental power had been given to reign supreme.

Goldsmith's father was a Protestant clergyman. The poet was born at Pallas, in the county Longford. After a series of adventures, not always to his credit, and sundry wanderings on the Continent in the most extreme poverty, he settled in London. Here he met with considerable success as an author, and enjoyed the society of the first literary men of the day. After the first and inevitable struggles of a poor author, had he possessed even half as much talent for business as capacity for intellectual effort, he might soon have obtained a competency by his pen; but, unfortunately, though he was not seriously addicted to intemperance, his convivial habits, and his attraction for the gaming table, soon scattered his hard-won earnings. His "knack of hoping," however, helped him through life. He died on the 4th April, 1774. His last words were sad indeed, in whatever sense they may be taken.   He was suffering from fever, but his devoted medical attendant, Doctor Norton, perceiving his pulse to be unusually high even under such circumstances, asked, "Is your mind at ease?"   "No, it is not," was Goldsmith's sad reply; and these were the last words he uttered.

GOLDSMITH'S MILL AT AUBURN.

BANTRY BAY—SCENE OF THE LANDING OF THE FRENCH.

CHAPTER XXXVI.

The Volunteers deserted by their Leaders—Agrarian Outrages and their Cause
—Foundation of the United Irishmen—Cruelties of the Orangemen—Government Spies and Informers—Lord Moira exposes the Cruelty of the Yeomanry in Parliament—Mr. Orr's Trial and Death—Details of the Atrocities
enacted by the Military from a Protestant History—Tom the Devil—
Cruelties practised by Men of Rank—Licentiousness of the Army—Death of
Lord Edward FitzGerald—The Rising—Martial Law in Dublin—The Insurrection in Wexford—Massacres at Scullabogue House and Wexford-bridge
by the Insurgents—How the Priests were rewarded for saving Lives and
Property—The Insurrection in Ulster—The State Prisoners—The Union.

[A.D. 1783—1800.]

PARLIAMENT was dissolved on the 15th of July, 1783,
and summoned to meet in October. The Volunteers
now began to agitate on the important question of
parliamentary reform, which, indeed, was necessary,
for there were few members who really represented
the nation. The close boroughs were bought and sold
openly and shamelessly, and many members who were
returned for counties were not proof against place or
bribes. But the Volunteers had committed the fatal
mistake of not obtaining the exercise of the elective
franchise for their Catholic fellow-subjects : hence the
Irish Parliament obtained only a nominal freedom, as
its acts were entirely in the hands of the Government
through the venality of the members. On the 10th of
November, one hundred and sixty delegates assembled

at the Royal Exchange, Dublin. They were headed by Lord Charlemont, and marched in procession to the Rotundo. The Earl of Bristol, an eccentric, but kind and warm-hearted character, who was also the Protestant Bishop of Derry, took a leading part in the deliberations. Sir Boyle Roche, an equally eccentric gentleman, brought a message from Lord Kenmare to the meeting, assuring them that the Catholics were satisfied with what had been granted to them. He had acted under a misapprehension; and the Bishop of Derry, who was in fact the only really liberal member of the corps, informed the delegates that the Catholics had held a meeting, with Sir Patrick Bellew in the chair, in which they repudiated this assertion. Several plans of reform were now proposed; and a Bill was introduced into the House by Mr. Flood, on the 29th of November, and warmly opposed by Mr. Yelverton, who was now Attorney-General, and had formerly been a Volunteer. A stormy scene ensued, but bribery and corruption prevailed. The fate of the Volunteers was sealed. Through motives of prudence or of policy, Lord Charlemont adjourned the convention *sine die;* and the flame, which had shot up with sudden brilliancy, died out even more rapidly than it had been kindled. The Volunteers were now deserted by their leaders, and assumed the infinitely dangerous form of a democratic movement. Such a movement can rarely succeed, and seldom ends without inflicting worse injuries on the nation than those which it has sought to avert.

The delegates were again convened in Dublin, by Flood and Napper Tandy. They met in October, 1784, and their discussions were carried on in secret. Everywhere the men began to arm themselves, and to train others to military exercises. But the Government had gained a victory over them in the withdrawal of their leaders, and the Attorney-General attempted to intimidate them still further by a prosecution. In 1785 a Bill was introduced for removing some of the commercial restraints of the Irish nation; it passed the Irish House, but, to satisfy popular clamours in England, it was returned with such additions as effectually marred its usefulness. Grattan now saw how grievously he had been mistaken in his estimate of the results of all that was promised in 1782, and he denounced the measure with more than ordinary eloquence. It was rejected by a small majority, after a debate which lasted till eight o'clock in the morning; and the nationality of the small majority purchased the undying hatred of the English minister,

William Pitt. The people were still suffering from the cruel exactions of landlords and tithe-proctors. Their poverty and misery were treated with contempt and indifference, and they were driven to open acts of violence, which could not be repressed either by the fear of the consequences, or the earnest exhortations of the Catholic bishops and clergy.[4]

In the north some disturbances had originated as early as 1775, amongst the Protestant weavers, who suffered severely from the general depression of trade, and the avariciousness of commercial speculators. Their association was called "Hearts of Steel." The author of the *United Irishmen* mentions one instance as a sample of many others, in which the ruling elder of a Presbyterian congregation had raised the rents on a number of small farms, and excited in consequence severe acts of retaliation from them.[5] In 1784 two parties commenced agrarian outrages in Ulster, called respectively Peep-o'-Day Boys and Defenders. As the Catholics sided with one party, and the Protestants with another, it merged eventually into a religious feud. The former faction assumed the appellation of Protestant Boys, and at last became the Orange Society, whose atrocities, and the rancorous party-spirit which they so carefully fomented, was one of the principal causes of the rebellion of 1798. The Catholics had assumed the name of Defenders, from being obliged to band in self-defence ; but when once a number of uneducated persons are leagued together, personal feeling and strong passions will lead to acts of violence, which the original associates would have shrunk from committing.

Pitt was again thwarted by the Irish Parliament on the Regency question, when the insanity of George III. required the appointment of his heir as governor of England. The Marquis of Buckingham, who was then Lord Lieutenant, refused to forward their address ; but the members sent a deputation of their own. This nobleman was open and shameless in his acts of bribery, and added £13,000 a-year to the pension list, already so fatally oppressive to the country. In 1790 he was succeeded by the Earl of Westmoreland, and various clubs were formed ; but the Catholics were still

---

[4] *Clergy.*—Barrington says, in his *Rise and Fall of the Irish Nation*, p. 67, the Catholic clergy had every inclination to restrain their flocks within proper limits, and found no difficulty in effecting that object. The first statement is unquestionably true ; the second statement is unfortunately disproved by many painful facts.

[5] *Them.*—Vol. ii. p. 93.

excluded from them all. Still the Catholics were an immense majority nationally ; the French Revolution had manifested what the people could do ; and the rulers of the land, with such terrible examples before their eyes, could not for their own sakes afford to ignore Catholic interests altogether. But the very cause which gave hope was itself the means of taking hope away. The action of the Irish Catholics was paralyzed through fear of the demonlike cruelties which even a successful revolution might induce ; and the general fear which the aristocratic party had of giving freedom to the uneducated classes, influenced them to a fatal silence. Again the middle classes were left without leaders, who might have tempered a praiseworthy nationality with a not less praiseworthy prudence, and which might have saved both the nation and some of its best and bravest sons from fearful suffering. A Catholic meeting was held in Dublin, on the 11th of February, 1791, and a resolution was passed to apply to Parliament for relief from their disabilities. This was in truth the origin of the United Irishmen. For the first time Catholics and Protestants agreed cordially and worked together harmoniously. The leading men on the Catholic committee were Keogh, M'Cormic, Sweetman, Byrne, and Branghall ; the Protestant leaders were Theobald Wolfe Tone and the Hon. Simon Butler. Tone visited Belfast in October, 1791, and formed the first club of the Society of United Irishmen. He was joined there by Neilson, Simms, Russell, and many others. A club was then formed in Dublin, of which Napper Tandy became a leading member. The fundamental resolutions of the Society were admirable. They stated : " 1. That the weight of English influence in the government of this country is so great, as to require a cordial union among all the people of Ireland, to maintain that balance which is essential to the preservation of our liberties and the extension of our commerce. 2. That the sole constitutional mode by which this influence can be opposed, is by a complete and radical reform of the representation of the people in Parliament. 3. That no reform is just which does not include every Irishman of every religious persuasion."

Tone had already obtained considerable influence by his political pamphlets, which had an immense circulation. There can be no doubt that he was tinctured with republican sentiments ; but it was impossible for an Irish Protestant, who had any real sympathy with his country, to feel otherwise : it had endured nothing but misery from the monarchical form of government. The Catholics, probably, were only prevented from adopting similar opinions by their inherent belief in the divine right of kings. In 1791 the fears of those who thought the movement had a democratic tendency, were confirmed by the celebration of the anniversary of the French Revolution in Belfast, July, 1791; and in consequence of this, sixty-four Catholics of the upper classes presented a loyal address to the throne. The Catholic delegates met in Dublin in December, 1792, and prepared a petition to the King representing their grievances. It was signed by Dr. Troy, the Catholic Archbishop of Dublin, and Dr. Moylan, on behalf of the clergy. Amongst the laity present were Lords Kenmare, Fingall, Trimbleston, Gormanstown, and French. Five delegates were appointed to present the petition, and they were provided with a very large sum of money, which induced those in power to obtain them an audience. They were introduced to George III. by Edmund Burke. His Majesty sent a message to the Irish Parliament, requesting them to remove some of the disabilities; but the Parliament treated the message with contempt, and Lord Chancellor FitzGibbon brought in a Bill to prevent any bodies from meeting by delegation for the future.

In 1793 a Relief Bill was passed, in consequence of the war with France; a Militia Bill, and the Gunpowder and Convention Bills, were also passed, the latter being an attempt to suppress the Volunteers and the United Irishmen. A meeting of the latter was held in February, 1793, and the chairman and secretary were brought before the House of Lords, and sentenced to six months' imprisonment and a fine of £500 each. The following year, January, 1794, Mr. Rowan was prosecuted for an address to the Volunteers, made two years before. Even Curran's eloquence, and the fact that the principal witness was perjured, failed to obtain his acquittal. He was sentenced to two years' imprisonment and a fine of £500. His conviction only served to increase the popular excitement, as he was considered a martyr to his patriotism. An address was presented to him in Newgate by the United Irishmen, but he escaped on the 1st of May, and got safely to America, though £1,000 was offered for his apprehension.

The English minister now appears to have tried the old game of driving the people into a rebellion, which could be crushed at once by the sword, and would spare the necessity of making concessions; or of entangling the leaders in some act of overt treason, and quashing the movement by depriving it of its heads. An opportunity for the latter manœuvre now presented itself. A Protestant clergyman, who had resided many years in France, came to the country for the purpose of opening communications between the French Government and the United Irishmen. This gentleman, the Rev. William Jackson, confided his secret to his solicitor, a man named Cockayne. The solicitor informed Mr. Pitt, and by his desire continued to watch his victim, and trade on his open-hearted candour, until he had led him to his doom. The end of the unfortunate clergyman was very miserable. He took poison when brought up for judgment, and died in the dock. His object in committing this crime was to save his property for his wife and children, as it would have been confiscated had his sentence been pronounced.

The Viceroyalty of Earl FitzWilliam once more gave the Irish nation some hope that England would grant them justice. But he was soon recalled; Lord Camden was sent in his stead; and the country was given up to the Beresford faction, who were quite willing to co-operate in Mr. Pitt's plan of setting Protestants and Catholics against each other, of exciting open rebellion, and of profiting by the miseries of the nation to forge new chains for it, by its parliamentary union with England. Everything was done now that could be done to excite the Catholics to rebellion. The Orangemen, if their own statement on oath[6] is to be trusted, were actually bribed to persecute the Catholics; sermons[7] were preached by Protestant ministers to excite their feelings; and when the Catholics resisted, or offered reprisals, they were punished with the utmost

---

[6] *Oath.*—I give authority for these details. In the spring of 1796, three Orangemen swore before a magistrate of Down and Armagh, that the Orangemen frequently met in committees, amongst whom were some members of Parliament, who gave them money, and promised that they should not suffer for any act they might commit, and pledged themselves that they should be provided for by Government. The magistrate informed the Secretary of State, and asked how he should act; but he never received any answer. For further details on this head, see Plowden's *History of the Insurrection.*

[7] *Sermons.*—On the 1st of July, 1795, the Rev. Mr. Monsell, a Protestant clergyman of Portadown, invited his flock to celebrate the anniversary of the battle of the Boyne by attending church, and preached such a sermon against the Papists that his congregation fell on every Catholic they met going home, beat them cruelly, and finished the day by murdering two farmer's sons, who were quietly at work in a bog.—Mooney's *History of Ireland,* p. 876.

severity, while their persecutors always escaped. Lord Carhampton, a grandson of the worthless Henry Luttrell, who had betrayed the Irish at the siege of Limerick, commanded the army, and his cruelty is beyond description. An Insurrection Act was passed in 1796 ; magistrates were allowed to proclaim counties ; suspected persons were to be banished the country or pressed into the fleet, without the shadow of trial ; and Acts of Indemnity[8] were passed, to shield the magistrates and the military from the consequences of any unlawful cruelties which fanaticism or barbarity might induce them to commit.

Grattan appealed boldly and loudly against these atrocities. "These insurgents," he said, " call themselves Protestant Boys— that is, a banditti of murderers, committing massacre in the name of God, and exercising despotic power in the name of liberty." The published declaration of Lord Gosford and of thirty magistrates, who attempted to obtain some justice for the unfortunate subjects of these wrongs, is scarcely less emphatic. It is dated December 28, 1795 : " It is no secret that a persecution, accompanied with all the circumstances of ferocious cruelty which have in all ages distinguished this calamity, is now raging in this country ; neither age, nor sex, nor even acknowledged innocence, is sufficient to excite mercy or afford protection. The only crime which the unfortunate objects of this persecution are charged with, is a crime of easy proof indeed ; it is simply a profession of the Roman Catholic faith. A lawless banditti have constituted themselves judges of this species of delinquency, and the sentence they pronounce is equally concise and terrible ; it is nothing less than a confiscation of all property and immediate banishment—a prescription that has been carried into effect, and exceeds, in the number of those it consigns to ruin and misery, every example that ancient or modern history can supply. These horrors are now acting with impunity. The spirit of justice has disappeared from the country ; and the supineness of the magistracy of Armagh has become a common topic of conversation in every corner of the kingdom."

One should have supposed that an official declaration from such an authority, signed by the Governor of Armagh and thirty magistrates,

---

[8] *Indemnity.*—Lord Carhampton sent 1,300 men on board the fleet, on mere suspicion. They demanded a trial in vain. An Act of Indemnity was at once passed, to free his Lordship from any unpleasant consequences.

would have produced some effect on the Government of the day ; but the sequel proved that such honorable exposure was as ineffective as the rejected petition of millions of Catholics. The formation of the yeomanry corps filled up the cup of bitterness. The United Irishmen, seeing no hope of constitutional redress, formed themselves into a military organization. But, though the utmost precautions were used to conceal the names of members and the plans of the association, their movements were well known to Government from an early period. Tone, in the meantime, came to France from America, and induced Carnot to send an expedition to Ireland, under the command of General Hoche. It ended disastrously. A few vessels cruised for a week in the harbour of Bantry Bay ; but, as the remainder of the fleet, which was separated by a fog, did not arrive, Grouchy, the second in command, returned to France.

Meanwhile, the Society of United Irishmen spread rapidly, and especially in those places where the Orangemen exercised their cruelties. Lord Edward FitzGerald now joined the movement ; and even those who cannot commend the cause, are obliged to admire the perfection of his devoted self-sacrifice to what he believed to be the interests of his country. His leadership seemed all that was needed to secure success. His gay and frank manner made him popular ; his military bearing demanded respect ; his superior attainments gave him power to command ; his generous disinterestedness was patent to all. But already a paid system of espionage had been established by Government. A set of miscreants were found who could lure their victims to their doom—who could eat and drink, and talk and live with them as their bosom friends, and then sign their death-warrant with the kiss of Judas. There was a regular gang of informers of a low class, like the infamous Jemmy O'Brien, who were under the control of the Town-Majors, Sirr and Swan. But there were gentlemen informers also, who, in many cases, were never so much as suspected by their dupes. MacNally, the advocate of the United Irishmen, and Mr. Graham, their solicitor, were both of that class. Thomas Reynolds, of Killeen Castle, entered their body on purpose to betray them. Captain Armstrong did the same. John Hughes, a Belfast bookseller, had himself arrested several times, to allay their suspicions. John Edward Nevill was equally base and treacherous. However necessary it may be for the ends of government to employ spies and informers, there is no necessity for men to commit crimes of the basest treachery.   Such men and such crimes will ever be handed down to posterity with the reprobation they deserve.

Attempts were now made to get assistance from France.   Mr. O'Connor and Lord Edward FitzGerald proceeded thither for that purpose ; but their mission was not productive of any great result. The people were goaded to madness by the cruelties which were committed on them every day ; and it was in vain that persons above all suspicion of countenancing either rebels or Papists, protested against these enormities in the name of common humanity. In 1797 a part of Ulster was proclaimed by General Lalor, and Lord Moira described thus, in the English House of Lords, the sufferings of the unhappy people : " When a man was taken up on suspicion, he was put to the torture ; nay, if he were merely accused of concealing the guilt of another, the punishment of picketing, which had for some years been abolished as too inhuman even in the dragoon service, was practised.   I have known a man, in order to extort confession of a supposed crime, or of that of some of his neighbours, picketed until he actually fainted ; picketed a second time, until he fainted again ; picketed a third time, until he once more fainted ; and all upon mere suspicion.   Nor was this the only species of torture ; many had been taken and hung up until they were half dead, and then threatened with a repetition of this cruel treatment unless they made confession of the imputed guilt.   These," continued his Lordship, " were not particular acts of cruelty, exercised by men abusing the power committed to them, *but they formed part of a system*.   They were notorious ; and no person could say who would be the next victim of this oppression and cruelty."   As redress was hopeless, and Parliament equally indifferent to cruelties and to remonstrances, Mr. Grattan and his colleagues left the Irish House to its inhumanity and its fate.

In the autumn of this year, 1797, Mr. Orr, of Antrim, was tried and executed, on a charge of administering the oath of the United Irishmen to a soldier.   This gentleman was a person of high character and respectability.   He solemnly protested his innocence ; the soldier, stung with remorse, swore before a magistrate that the testimony he gave at the trial was false.   Petitions were at once sent in, praying for the release of the prisoner, but in vain ; he was executed on the 14th of October, though no one doubted his innocence ; and " Orr's fate" became a watchword of and an incitement to rebellion. Several of the jury made a solemn oath after the trial, that, when locked up for the night to "consider" their verdict, they were supplied abundantly with intoxicating drinks, and informed, one and all, that, if they did not give the required verdict of guilty, they should themselves be prosecuted as United Irishmen. Mr. Orr was offered his life and liberty again and again if he would admit his guilt; his wife and four young children added their tears and entreaties to the persuasions of his friends; but he preferred truth and honour to life and freedom. His end was worthy of his resolution. On the scaffold he turned to his faithful attendant, and asked him to remove his watch, as he should need it no more. Mr. Orr was a sincere Protestant; his servant was a Catholic. His last words are happily still on record. He showed the world how a Protestant patriot could die; and that the more sincere and deep his piety, the less likely he would be to indulge in fanatical hatred of those who differed from him. " You, my friend," he said to his weeping and devoted servant—"you, my friend, and I must now part. Our stations here on earth have been a little different, and our mode of worshipping the Almighty Being that we both adore. Before His presence we shall stand equal. Farewell! Remember Orr!"[9]

Alas! there was more to remember than the fate of this noble victim to legal injustice. I have before alluded to that strange phenomenon of human nature, by which men, who, at least, appear to be educated and refined, can, under certain circumstances, become bloodthirsty and cruel. The demon enters into the man, and make him tenfold more demoniacal than himself. But fearful as the deeds of officers and men have been in India, where the unhappy natives were shattered to atoms from the cannons' mouths; or, in more recent times, when men, and even women, have all but expired under the lash; no deeds of savage vengeance have ever exceeded those which were perpetrated daily and hourly in Ireland, before the rebellion of 1798. For the sake of our common humanity I would that they could be passed over unrecorded; for the sake of our common humanity I shall record them in detail, for it may be that the terror of what men can become when they give way to unrestrained passions, may deter some of my fellow-creatures from

[9] *Remember Orr.—Lives and Times of the United Irishmen*, second series, vol. ii. p. 380.

allowing themselves to participate in or to enact such deeds of blood. Historical justice, too, demands that they should be related. Englishmen have heard much of the cruelties of Irish rebels at Wexford, which I shall neither palliate nor excuse. Englishmen have heard but little of the inhuman atrocities which excited that insurrection, and prompted these reprisals. And let it be remembered, that there are men still living who saw these cruelties enacted in their childhood, and men whose fathers and nearest relations were themselves subjected to these tortures. To the Celt, so warm of heart and so tenacious of memory, what food this is for the tempter, who bids him recall, and bids him revenge, even now, these wrongs! What wonder if passion should take the place of reason, and if religion, which commands him to suffer patiently the memory of injuries inflicted on others, often harder to bear than one's own pain, should sometimes fail to assert its sway![1]

I shall give the account of these atrocities in the words of a Protestant historian first. The Rev. Mr. Gordon writes thus, in his narrative of these fearful times : " The fears of the people became

---

[1] *Sway.*—An important instance of how the memory or tradition of past wrongs excites men to seize the first opportunity of revenge, if not of redress, has occurred in our own times. It is a circumstance which should be very carefully pondered by statesmen who have the real interest of the whole nation at heart. It is a circumstance, as a sample of many other similar cases, which should be known to every Englishman who wishes to understand the cause of "Irish disturbances." One of the men who was shot by the police during the late Fenian outbreak in Ireland, was a respectable farmer named Peter Crowley. His history tells the motive for which he risked and lost his life. His grandfather had been outlawed in the rebellion of '98. His uncle, Father Peter O'Neill, had been imprisoned and *flogged most barbarously, with circumstances of peculiar cruelty*, in Cork, in the year 1798. The memory of the insult and injury done to a priest, who was entirely guiltless of the crimes with which he was charged, left a legacy of bitterness and hatred of Saxon rule in the whole family, which, unhappily, religion failed to eradicate. Peter Crowley was a sober, industrious, steady man, and his parish priest, who attended his deathbed, pronounced his end "most happy and edifying." Three clergymen and a procession of young men, women, and children, scattering flowers before the coffin, and bearing green boughs, attended his remains to the grave. He was mourned as a patriot, who had loved his country, not wisely, but too well ; and it was believed that his motive for joining the Fenian ranks was less from a desire of revenge, which would have been sinful, than from a mistaken idea of freeing his country from a repetition of the cruelties of '98, and from her present grievances.

so great at length, that they forsook their houses in the night, and slept (if, under such circumstances, they could sleep) in the ditches, and the women were even delivered in that exposed condition. *These facts were notorious at the time.* . . . . Some abandoned their house from fear of being whipped; and this infliction many persons appeared to fear *more than death itself.* Many unfortunate men were strung up as it were to be hanged, but were let down now and then, to try if strangulation would oblige them to become informers." He then goes on to relate at length how the magistrates tortured smiths and carpenters at once, because it was supposed from their trade they must have made pikes; and how they, at last, professed to know a United Irishman by his face, and "never suffered any person whom they deigned to honour with this distinction, to pass off without convincing proof of their attention." He also mentions the case of a hermit named Driscoll, whose name and the same details of his sufferings are given in Clancy's account of the insurrection. This man was strangled three times, and flogged four times, because a Catholic prayer-book was found in his possession, on which it was *supposed* that he used to administer oaths of disloyalty.

I shall now give the account of another historian. Plowden writes thus: "These military savages [the yeomanry corps—it will be remembered what Lord Moira said of them in Parliament] were permitted, both by magistrates and officers, in open day, to seize every man they wished or chose to suspect as a *Croppy*, and drag him to the guardhouse, where they constantly kept a supply of coarse linen caps, besmeared inside with pitch; and when the pitch was well heated, they forced the cap on his head; and sometimes the melted pitch, running into the eyes of the unfortunate victim, superadded blindness to his other tortures. They generally detained him till the pitch had so cooled, that the cap could not be detached from the head without carrying with it the hair and blistered skin; they then turned him adrift, disfigured, often blind, and writhing with pain. They enjoyed with loud bursts of laughter the fiendlike sport—the agonies of their victim. At other times, they rubbed moistened gunpowder into the hair, in the form of a cross, and set fire to it; and not unfrequently sheared off the ears and nose of the unfortunate Croppy." Plowden then details the atrocities of a sergeant of the Cork Militia, who was called *Tom the Devil.* He concludes: "It would be uncandid to detail only instances of the brutality of the lower orders, whilst evidence is forthcoming of persons of fortune and education being still more brutalized by its deleterious spirit." He then mentions an instance, on the authority of both an eyewitness and the victim, in which Lord Kingsborough, Mr. Beresford, and an officer whose name he did not know, tortured two respectable Dublin tradesmen, one named John Fleming, a ferryman, the other Francis Gough, a coachmaker. The nobleman superintended the flagellation of Gough, and at every stroke insulted him with taunts and inquiries how he liked it. The unfortunate man was confined to his bed in consequence, for six months after the infliction. On Whit-Sunday, 1798, these men were again tortured with pitchcaps by the gentlemen. Other instances might be added, but these will suffice to show the feeling which actuated the rulers who permitted, and the men who perpetrated, these deeds of blood. " With difficulty," says Mr. Plowden, " does the mind yield reluctant consent to such debasement of the human species. The spirit which degrades it to that abandonment is of no ordinary depravity. The same spirit of Orangeism moved the colonel in Dublin, and his sergeant at Wexford. The effect of that spirit can only be faintly illustrated by facts. Those have been verified to the author by the spectator and the sufferer."[2]

From a letter of Lady Napier's, never intended for publication, and above all suspicion of any sympathy with the lower order of Irish, it will be seen how the tenantry of the Duke of Leinster were driven to revolt. It is dated Castletown, 27th June, 1798, and addressed to the Duke of Richmond. " The cruel hardships put on his tenants preferably to all others, has driven them to despair, and they join the insurgents, saying: ' It is better to die with a pike in my hand, than be shot like a dog at my work, or to see my children faint for want of food before my eyes.' "

Sir Ralph Abercrombie was appointed to command the army in Ireland, in 1797 ; but he threw up his charge, disgusted with atrocities which he could not control, and which he was too humane even to appear to sanction.[3] He declared the army to be in a state

---

[2] *Sufferer.*—Plowden, *Hist.* p. 102.

[3] *Sanction.*—His son says : " His estimate of the people led him to appreciate justly the liveliness of their parts. But while he knew their vices, and the origin of them, he knew that there was in their character much of the generosity and warmth of feeling which made them acutely sensitive when they were treated considerately and kindly. His judgment of the upper classes of

of licentiousness, which made it formidable to every one but the enemy. General Lake, a fitting instrument for any cruelty, was appointed to take his place; and Lord Castlereagh informs us that "measures were taken by Government to cause a premature explosion." It would have been more Christian in the first place, and more politic in the second place, if Government had taken measures to prevent any explosion at all.[4]

On the 12th of March, 1798, the Leinster delegates, who had been long since betrayed, were seized by Major Swan, in Dublin. Fifteen persons were present, the greater number of whom were Protestants. Emmet, MacNevin, Jackson, and Sweetman, were seized the same day. Arthur O'Connor had already been arrested on his way to France, with Father Coigley. The latter was convicted on May 22, at Maidstone, and hanged on evidence so inconclusive, that Lord Chancellor Thurlow said : " If ever a poor man was murdered, it was Coigley !" The arrest of Lord Edward FitzGerald occurred soon after. The room in which he was arrested and the bed on which he lay is still shown, for the brave young noble had won for himself the heart's love of every true Irishman. The story of his life would occupy more space than can be given to it. To abridge it would be to destroy more than half of its real interest. A severe wound which he received in the struggle with his captors, combined with the effects of excitement and a cruel imprisonment, caused his death. He was a chevalier *sans peur et sans reproche*. Even his enemies, and the enemies of his country, could find no word to say against him. With him died the best hopes of the United Irishmen, and with his expiring breath they lost their best prospect of success.[5]

society, and of the purity and wisdom of the government, was less favorable. He saw that the gentry were imperfectly educated ; that they were devoted to the pursuits of pleasure and political intrigue ; and that they were ignorant or neglectful of the duties imposed on them as landlords, and as the friends and protectors of those who depended on them for their existence."—*Memoir of Sir Ralph Abercrombie*, p. 72.

[4] *All.*—Lord Holland says, in his *Memoirs of the Whig Party :* " The fact is incontestable that the people of Ireland were driven to resistance, which, *possibly*, they meditated before, by the free quarters and excesses of the soldiery, which are not permitted in civilized warfare, even in an enemy's country." The state prisoners declared the immediate cause of the rising was " the free quarters, the house-burnings, the tortures, and the military executions."

[5] *Success.*—The real betrayer of this brave but unfortunate nobleman has

Lord Edward died on the 4th of June. The 23rd of May had been fixed for the rising; but informations were in the hands of the Government. Captain Armstrong had betrayed the Sheares, two brothers who had devoted themselves to the cause of their country with more affection than prudence. The base traitor had wound himself into their confidence, had dined with them, and was on the most intimate social relations with their family. On the 12th of July he swore their lives away; and two days after they were executed, holding each other's hands as they passed into eternity.

The rising did take place, but it was only partial. The leaders were gone, dead, or imprisoned; and nothing but the wild desperation, which suggested that it was better to die fighting than to die inch by inch, under inhuman torture, could have induced the people to rise at all. The ferocity with which the insurrection was put down, may be estimated by the cruelties enacted before it commenced. Lord Cornwallis, in his Government report to the Duke of Portland, declared that "murder was the favourite pastime" of the militia. He declared that the principal persons in the country and the members of Parliament were averse to all conciliation, and " too much heated to see the effects which their violence must produce." To General Ross he writes : " The violence of our friends, and their folly in endeavouring to make it a religious war, added to the ferocity of our troops, who delight in murder, must powerfully counteract all plans of conciliation ; and the conversation, even at my table, where you will suppose I do all I can to prevent it, always turns on hanging, shooting, burning, &c.; and if a priest

only been discovered of late years. Dr. Madden was the first to throw light upon the subject. He discovered the item of £1,000 entered in the *Secret Service Money-book*, as paid to F. H. for the discovery of L. E. F. The F. H. was undoubtedly Francis Higgins, better known as the Sham Squire, whose infamous career has been fully exposed by Mr. Fitzpatrick. In the fourth volume of the *United Irishmen*, p. 579, Dr. Madden still expresses his doubt as to who was the person employed by Higgins as " setter." It evidently was some one in the secrets of Lord Edward's party. The infamous betrayer has been at last discovered, in the person of Counsellor Magan, who received at various times large sums of money from Government for his perfidy. See the *Sham Squire*, p. 114. Higgins was buried at Kilbarrack, near Clontarf. In consequence of the revelations of his vileness, which have been lately brought before the public, the tomb was smashed to pieces, and the inscription destroyed. See Mr. Fitzpatrick's *Ireland before the Union*, p. 152.

has been put to death, the greatest joy is expressed by the whole company."

On the 23rd of May, Dublin was placed under martial law; the citizens were armed, the guard was trebled, the barristers pleaded with regimentals and swords, and several of the lamplighters were hung from their own lamp-posts for neglecting to light the lamps. The country people were prepared to march on the city, but Lord Roden and his Foxhunters soon put down their attempt. The next morning the dead were exhibited in the Castle-yard, and the prisoners were hanged at Carlisle-bridge. Sir Watkins Wynn and his Ancient Britons distinguished themselves by their cruelties. The Homsperg Dragoons and the Orange Yeomanry equalled them in deeds of blood. The fighting commenced in Kildare, on the 24th, by an attack on Naas, which was repelled by Lord Gosport. Two of his officers and thirty men were killed, and the people were shot down and hanged indiscriminately. "Such was the brutal ferocity of some of the King's troops," says Plowden, "that they half roasted and eat the flesh of one man, named Walsh, who had not been in arms." At Prosperous the insurgents attacked and burned the barracks, and piked any of the soldiers who attempted to escape from the flames. This regiment, the North Cork Militia, had been specially cruel in their treatment of the people, who were only too willing to retaliate. A troop of dragoons, commanded by Captain Erskine, was almost annihilated at Old Kilcullen. But reverses soon followed. At Carlow the insurgents met with a severe defeat; and the defenceless and innocent inhabitants, who fled into their houses for shelter from the fire, were cruelly and ruthlessly burned to death in their own habitations by the military.

A body of 2,000 men, under a leader named Perkins, encamped on the Hill of Allan, and agreed with General Douglas to lay down their arms. The General was honorable and humane, but his subordinates were not so. Major-General Duff, to whom the arms were to have been delivered up, ordered his troops to fire on the people, when they had assembled for that purpose. Lord Roden's cavalry cut them down, and an immense number were slaughtered in cold blood. Another attack took place at Tara, where the Irish were again defeated. The insurrection now broke out in Wexford. The people in this part of the country had not joined the movement in any way, until the arrival of the North

Cork Militia, commanded by Lord Kingsborough. The men paraded in orange ribbons, fired at the peaceful country people, and employed pitchcaps and torture, until their victims were driven to desperation. The county was proclaimed on the 27th of April, by the magistrates; and before any riot had taken place, Mr. Hunter Gowan paraded through Gorey at the head of his yeomanry, with a human finger on the point of his sword, which was subsequently used to stir their punch in the evening.

On Whit-Sunday, the 27th of May, the yeomen burned the Catholic Chapel of Boulavogue. Father John Murphy, the parish priest, who had hitherto tried to suppress the insurrection, placed himself at the head of the insurgents. The men now rose in numbers, and marched to Enniscorthy, which they took after some fighting. Vinegar Hill, a lofty eminence overlooking the town, was chosen for their camp. Some of the leading Protestant gentlemen of the county had either favoured or joined the movement; and several of them had been arrested on suspicion, and were imprisoned at Wexford. The garrison of this place, however, fled in a panic, caused by some successes of the Irish troops, and probably from a very clear idea of the kind of retaliation they might expect for their cruelties. Mr. Harvey, one of the prisoners mentioned above, was now released, and headed the insurgents; but a powerful body of troops, under General Loftus, was sent into the district, and eventually obtained possession of New Ross, which the Irish had taken with great bravery, but which they had not been able to hold for want of proper military discipline and command. They owed their defeat to insubordination and drunkenness. A number of prisoners had been left at Scullabogue House, near Carrickburne Hill. Some fugitives from the Irish camp came up in the afternoon, and pretended that Mr. Harvey had given orders for their execution, alleging, as a reason, what, indeed, was true, that the royalists massacred indiscriminately. The guard resisted, but were overpowered by the mob, who were impatient to revenge without justice the cruelties which had been inflicted on them without justice. A hundred were burned in a barn, and thirty-seven were shot or piked. This massacre has been held up as a horrible example of Irish treachery and cruelty. It was horrible, no doubt, and cannot be defended or palliated; but, amid these contending horrors of cruel war, the question still recurs: Upon whom is the original guilt of causing them to be charged?

Father Murphy[6] was killed in an attack on Carlow, and his death threw the balance strongly in favour of the Government troops, who eventually proved victorious. After the battle of Ross, the Wexford men chose the Rev. Philip Roche as their leader, in place of Mr. Bagenal Harvey, who had resigned the command. The insurgents were now guilty of following the example of their persecutors, if not with equal cruelty, at least with a barbarity which their leaders in vain reprobated. The prisoners whom they had taken were confined in the jail, and every effort was made to save them from the infuriated people. But one savage, named Dixon, would not be content without their blood; and while the army and their leaders were encamped on Vinegar Hill, he and some other villains as wicked as himself found their way into the jail, and marched the prisoners to the bridge, held a mock trial, and then piked thirty-five of their victims, and flung them into the water. At this moment a priest, who had heard of the bloody deed, hastened to the spot; and after in vain commanding them to desist, succeeded at last in making them kneel down, when he dictated a prayer that God might show them the same mercy which they would show to the surviving prisoners. This had its effect; and the men who waited in terror to receive the doom they had so often and so mercilessly inflicted on others, were marched back to prison.

The camp on Vinegar Hill was now beset on all sides by the royal troops. An attack was planned by General Lake, with 20,000 men and a large train of artillery. General Needham did not arrive in time to occupy the position appointed for him; and after an hour and a-half of hard fighting, the Irish gave way, principally from want of gunpowder. The soldiers now indulged in the most wanton deeds of cruelty. The hospital at Enniscorthy was set on fire, and the wounded men shot in their beds. At Wexford, General Moore prevented his troops from committing such outrages; but when the rest of the army arrived, they acted as they had done at Enniscorthy. Courts-martial were held, in which the officers were not even sworn, and victims were consigned to execution with reckless atrocity. The bridge of Wexford, where a Catholic priest had

[6] *Murphy.*—Rev. Mr. Gordon says: "Some of the soldiers of the Ancient British regiment cut open the dead body of Father Michael Murphy, after the battle of Arklow, took out his heart, roasted his body, and oiled their boots with the grease which dropped from it."—*History of the Rebellion,* p. 212.

saved so many Protestant lives, was now chosen for the scene of slaughter ; and all this in spite of a promise of amnesty. Father Roche and Mr. Keogh were the first victims of the higher classes ; Messrs. Grogan, Harvey, and Colclough were hanged the following day. A mixed commission was now formed of the magistrates, who were principally Orangemen, and the military, whose virulence was equally great. The Rev. Mr. Gordon, the Protestant clergyman whose account I have principally followed, as above all suspicion, declares that " whoever could be proved to have saved an Orangeman or royalist from assassination, his house from burning, or his property from plunder, was considered as having influence amongst the revolters, and consequently as a rebel commander." The reward for their charity now was instant execution. The Rev. John Redmond, the Catholic priest of Newtownbarry, had saved Lord Mountmorris and other gentlemen from the fury of the exasperated people, and had preserved his house and property from plunder. He was now sent for by this nobleman ; and, conscious of his innocence, and the benefits he had rendered him, he at once obeyed the summons. On his arrival, he was seized, brought before the court, and executed on the pretence of having been a commander in the rebel army. He had, indeed, commanded, but the only commands he ever uttered were commands of mercy. Well might Mr. Gordon sorrowfully declare, that he had " heard of hundreds of United Irishmen, during the insurrection, who have, at the risk of their lives, saved Orangemen ; but I have not heard of a single Orangeman who encountered any danger to save the life of a United Irishman." With equal sorrow he remarks the difference in the treatment of females by each party. The Irish were never once accused of having offered the slightest insult to a woman ; the military, besides shooting them indiscriminately with the men, treated them in a way which cannot be described, and under circumstances which added a more than savage inhumanity to their crime.

The next act of the fatal drama was the execution of the State prisoners. The rising in Ulster had been rendered ineffective, happily for the people, by the withdrawal of some of the leaders at the last moment. The command in Antrim was taken by Henry M'Cracken, who was at last captured by the royalists, and executed at Belfast, on the 17th of June. At Saintfield, in Down, they were commanded by Henry Monroe, who had been a Volunteer, and had some knowledge of military tactics. In an engagement at

Ballinahinch, he showed considerable ability in the disposal of his forces, but they were eventually defeated, and he also paid the forfeit of his life. A remnant of the Wexford insurrection was all that remained to be crushed. On the 21st of June, Lord Cornwallis was sent to Ireland, with the command both of the military forces and the civil power. On the 17th of July an amnesty was proclaimed; and the majority of the State prisoners were permitted eventually to leave the country, having purchased their pardon by an account of the plans of the United Irishmen, which were so entirely broken up that their honour was in no way compromised by the disclosure.

Several men, however, were executed, in whose fate the country had, for many reasons, more than ordinary interest. To have pardoned them would have been more humane and better policy. These were the two Sheares, M'Cann, and Mr. William Byrne. Their history will be found in the *Lives of the United Irishmen*, by Dr. Madden, a work of many volumes, whose contents could not possibly be compressed into the brief space which the limits of this work demands.

Some painfully interesting details of this fearful period may be found in the *Annals of Ballitore*, a work already referred to in this volume. The writer being a member of the Society of Friends, must be beyond all suspicion of partiality for rebels or Papists; yet, happily, like many members of that Society, was distinguished for humanity and toleration for the opinions of others. Her account of '98, being the annals of a family and a village, is, perhaps, almost better calculated to give an exact idea of the state of the times than a work comprising a more extended range of observation; and yet what was suffered in Ballitore was comparatively trifling when compared with the sufferings of other villages and towns. The first trial was the quartering of the yeomen, "from whose bosom," writes this gentle lady, " pity seemed banished." The Suffolk Fencibles and the Ancient Britons were next quartered on the unfortunate inhabitants. Then commenced the cruel torturing, for which the yeomen and militia obtained an eternal reprobation; the public floggings, of which she writes thus—" the torture was excessive, and the victims were long in recovering, and in almost every case it was applied fruitlessly;" yet these demons in human form never relaxed their cruelty. " The village, once so peaceful, exhibited a scene of tumult and dismay; and the air rang with the shrieks or the sufferers, and the lamentations of those who beheld them suffer."[7] Then follow fearful details, which cannot be given here, but which prove how completely the people were driven into rebellion, and how cruelly they were punished. Reprisals, of course, were made by the unfortunate victims; and on one occasion, Mrs. Leadbeater relates how Priest Cullen begged the life of a young man on his knees, and, as a reward of his humanity, was apprehended soon after, and condemned to death. The most cruel scene of all was the murder of the village doctor, a man who had devoted himself unweariedly to healing the wounds of both parties; but because he attended the " rebels," and showed them any acts of common humanity, he was taken before a court-martial, and " hacked to death" by the yeomen with their swords. " He was alone and unarmed when seized," writes Mrs. Leadbeater, " and I believe had never raised his hand to injure any one."

The French allies of Irish insurgents appear to have a fatality for arriving precisely when their services are worse than useless. On the 22nd of August, 1798, Humbert landed at Killala with a small French force, who, after a number of engagements, were eventually obliged to surrender at discretion.

Ireland having been reduced to the lowest state of misery and servitude, the scheme for which much of this suffering had been enacted was now proposed and carried out. The first parliamentary intimation was given in a speech from the throne, on the 22nd of January, 1799; a pamphlet was published on the subject by Mr. Cooke, the Under-Secretary; but it required more cogent arguments than either speeches from the throne or pamphlets to effect the object of Government. Mr. Pitt had set his heart upon the Union, and Mr. Pitt had determined that the Union should be carried out at any expense of honour. The majority of the Irish lawyers protested against it. The Irish people, as far as they dared do so, opposed it. At a meeting of the Irish bar, on the 9th of December, there were 166 votes against the Union and only thirty-two in favour of it. The published correspondence of Lord Cornwallis and Lord Castlereagh has revealed an amount of nefarious corruption and treachery at which posterity stands aghast. " These noblemen," writes Sir Jonah Barrington, " seemed to have been created for such a crisis, and for each other. An unremitting perseverance,

an absence of all political compunctions, an unqualified contempt
of public opinion, and a disregard of every constitutional principle,
were common to both." But Lord Cornwallis had some compunctions ; for he wrote to General Ross, describing his office as " the
most cursed of all situations," and expressing, in language more
forcible than gentlemanly, his ardent desire to "kick those whom
his public duty obliged him to court."

The immediate arrangements made for carrying out the Union
were extremely simple. A scale of "compensation" was arranged—
a word which could, by a slight perversion of the ordinary
meaning of the English language, be used as a new form of expressing what was formerly called bribery. Every one was promised everything that he wished for, if he would only consent
to the measure. The Catholics were to have emancipation, the
Protestants ascendency, the bar promotion, the people higher
wages, the boroughmongers magnificent compensation. Fitz-
Gibbon, who had been made Lord Clare, and was then Chancellor, bribed, threatened, and cajoled the Upper House ; Mr. Secretary Cooke employed himself with equal ability in the Lower
House. Grattan had left Ireland ; Flood was in retirement ; the
members of the bar who had voted against the Union were dismissed from office, and the Prime Serjeant, Mr. FitzGerald, was the
first victim. The thirty-two who formed the minority were at
once removed. I have not space for the details of the various attempts which were made to pass the unpopular measure. Barrington has given a list of the members for the Union, and the rewards
they received. His description of the last night of the Irish Parliament is too graphic to be omitted :—

" The Commons' House of Parliament, on the last evening, afforded the most melancholy example of a fine, independent people,
betrayed, divided, sold, and, as a State, annihilated. British clerks
and officers were smuggled into her Parliament, to vote away the
constitution of a country to which they were strangers, and in which
they had neither interest nor connexion. They were employed to
cancel the royal charter of the Irish nation, guaranteed by the
British Government, sanctioned by the British Legislature, and un-
equivocally confirmed by the words, the signature, and the Great
Seal of their monarch.

" The situation of the Speaker on that night was of the most distressing nature. A sincere and ardent enemy of the measure, he headed its opponents ; he resisted with all the power of his mind, the resources of his experience, his influence, and his eloquence. It was, however, through his voice that it was to be proclaimed and consummated. His only alternative (resignation) would have been unavailing, and could have added nothing to his character. His expressive countenance bespoke the inquietude of his feeling; solicitude was perceptible in every glance, and his embarrassment was obvious in every word he uttered.

"The galleries were full, but the change was lamentable ; they were no longer crowded with those who had been accustomed to witness the eloquence and to animate the debates of that devoted assembly. A monotonous and melancholy murmur ran through benches, scarcely a word was exchanged amongst the members, nobody seemed at ease, no cheerfulness was apparent, and the ordinary business, for a short time, proceeded in the usual manner.

" At length the expected moment arrived. The order of the day for the third reading of the Bill for a ' Legislative Union between Great Britain and Ireland,' was moved by Lord Castlereagh. Unvaried, tame, coldblooded, the words seemed frozen as they issued from his lips ; and, as a simple citizen of the world, he seemed to have no sensation on the subject.

" At that moment he had no country, no God but his ambition : he made his motion, and resumed his seat with the utmost composure and indifference.

" Confused murmurs again ran through the House ; it was visibly affected. Every character in a moment seemed involuntary rushing to its index—some pale, some flushed, some agitated ; there were few countenances to which the heart did not despatch some messenger. Several members withdrew before the question could be repeated, and an awful momentary silence succeeded their departure. The Speaker rose slowly from that chair which had been the proud source of his honours and of his high character ; for a moment he resumed his seat, but the strength of his mind sustained him in his duty, though his struggle was apparent. With that dignity which never failed to signalize his official actions, he held up the Bill for a moment in silence; he looked steadily around him on the last agony of the expiring Parliament. He at length repeated, in an emphatic tone, ' As many as are of opinion that *this Bill* do pass, say aye.' The affirmative was languid but indisputable; another momentary pause ensued; again his lips seemed to decline their office; at length, with an eye averted from the object which he hated, he proclaimed, with a subdued voice, 'The Ayes have it.' The fatal sentence was now pronounced; for an instant he stood statue-like; then indignantly, and with disgust, flung the Bill upon the table, and sunk into his chair with an exhausted spirit.

"An independent country was thus degraded into a province—Ireland, as a nation, was extinguished."

LYNCH'S HOUSE, GALWAY.

SWORDS' CASTLE, COUNTY DUBLIN.

CHAPTER XXXVII.

The State of Ireland before and after the Union—Advancement of Trade before the Union—Depression after it—Lord Clare and Lord Castlereagh in the English Parliament—The Catholic Question becomes a Ministerial Difficulty —The Veto—The O'Connell Sept—Early Life of Daniel O'Connell—The Doneraile Conspiracy—O'Connell as Leader of the Catholic Party—The Clare Election—O'Connell in the English House of Parliament—Sir Robert Peel—George IV. visits Ireland—Disturbances in Ireland from the Union to the year 1834, and their Causes—Parliamentary Evidence—The "Second Reformation"—Catholic Emancipation—Emigration, its Causes and Effects —Colonial Policy of England—Statistics of American Trade and Population —Importance of the Irish and Catholic Element in America—Conclusion.

[A.D. 1800—1868.]

T is both a mistake and an injustice to suppose that the page of Irish history closed with the dawn of that summer morning, in the year of grace 1800, when the parliamentary union of Great Britain and Ireland was enacted. I have quoted Sir Jonah Barrington's description of the closing night of the Irish Parliament, because he writes as an eyewitness, and because few could describe its "last agony" with more touching eloquence and more vivid truthfulness; but I beg leave, in the name of my country, to protest against his conclusion, that "Ireland, as a nation, was extinguished." There never was, and we must almost fear there never will be, a moment in the history of our nation, in which her independence was proclaimed more triumphantly or gloriously, than when O'Connell; the noblest and the best of her sons, obtained Catholic Emancipation.

The immediate effects of the dissolution of the Irish Parliament were certainly appalling. The measure was carried on the 7th of June, 1800. On the 16th of April, 1782, another measure had been carried, to which I must briefly call your attention. That measure was the independence of the Irish Parliament. When it passed, Grattan rose once more in the House, and exclaimed: "Ireland is now a nation! In that new character I hail her, and bowing to her august presence, I say, *Esto perpetua!*" A period of unexampled prosperity followed. The very effects of a reaction from conditions under which commerce was purposely restricted and trade paralyzed by law, to one of comparative freedom, could not fail to produce such a result. If the Parliament had been reformed when it was freed, it is probable that Ireland at this moment would be the most prosperous of nations. But the Parliament was not reformed. The prosperity which followed was rather the effect of reaction, than of any real settlement of the Irish question. The land laws, which unquestionably are *the* grievance of Ireland, were left untouched, an alien Church was allowed to continue its unjust exactions; and though Ireland was delivered, her chains were not all broken; and those which were, still hung loosely round her, ready for the hand of traitor or of foe. Though nominally freed from English control, the Irish Parliament was not less enslaved by English influence. Perhaps there had never been a period in the history of that nation when bribery was more freely used, when corruption was more predominant. A considerable number of the peers in the Irish House were English by interest and by education; a majority of the members of the Lower House were their creatures. A man who ambitioned a place in Parliament, should conform to the opinions of his patron; the patron was willing to receive a "compensation" for making his opinions, if he had any, coincide with those of the Government. Many of the members were anxious for preferment for themselves or their friends; the price of preferment was a vote for ministers. The solemn fact of individual responsibility for each individual act, had yet to be understood. Perhaps the lesson has yet to be learned.

One of the first acts of the Irish independent Parliament, was to order the appointment of a committee to inquire into the state of the manufactures of the kingdom, and to ascertain what might be necessary for their improvement. The hearts of the poor, always praying for employment, which had been so long and so cruelly withheld from them, bounded with joy. Petitions poured in on every side. David Bosquet had erected mills in Dublin for the manufacture of metals; he prayed for help. John and Henry Allen had woollen manufactories in the county Dublin; they prayed for help. Thomas Reilly, iron merchant, of the town of Wicklow, wished to introduce improvements in iron works. James Smith, an Englishman, had cotton manufactories at Balbriggan; he wished to extend them. Anthony Dawson, of Dundrum, near Dublin, had water mills for making tools for all kinds of artisans; this, above all, should be encouraged, now that there was some chance of men having some use for tools. Then there were requests for aid to establish carpet manufactories, linen manufactories, glass manufactories, &c.; and Robert Burke, Esq., of the county Kildare, prayed for the loan of £40,000 for seven years, that he might establish manufactories at Prosperous. These few samples of petitions, taken at random from many others, will enable the reader to form some faint idea of the state of depression in which Ireland was kept by the English nation—of the eagerness of the Irish to work if they were only permitted to do so.

The Irish revenue for the year 1783 was, in round numbers, £900,000, which amounted to a tax of about six shillings per annum on each person. It was distributed thus:

For the interest of the National Debt, - - -	£120,000
Army and Ordnance, Civil Government, and other funds, - - - - - - - - - - - -	450,000
Pensions, grants, bounties, and aids to manufacturers, - - - - - - - - - - - -	250,000
Surplus unappropriated, - - - - - - - -	80,000
Total, - - - - - - - - -	£900,000

More than £200,000 was spent during that year in erecting forts, batteries, and other public buildings, which gave employment to the people in certain districts. Large sums were granted to the poor of Cork and Dublin for coals; and large grants were made to encourage manufactures. I have observed, however, in carefully examining these grants, which are by far too numerous for insertion, that they were principally, and, indeed, I might say exclusively, made to persons in Dublin and its neighbourhood, in the north of Ireland, and in the *cities* of Cork and Limerick.   Hence, the prosperity of Ireland was only partial, and was confined exclusively, though, probably, not intentionally, to certain districts.   This will explain why the misery and starvation of the poor, in the less favoured parts of the country, were a principal cause of the fearful insurrection which occurred within a few short years.

Lord Clare proclaimed, in the House of Parliament, that "no nation on the habitable globe had advanced in cultivation, commerce, and manufactures, with the same rapidity as Ireland, from 1782 to 1800." *The population increased from three millions to five.* There were 5,000 carpenters fully employed in Dublin ; there were 15,000 silk-weavers.   Nor should we be surprised at this ; for Dublin possesses at the present day substantial remains of her former prosperity, which are even now the admiration of Europe. All her great public buildings were erected at this period.   The Custom-house was commenced, and completed in ten years, at a cost of a quarter of a million sterling.   The Rotundo was commenced in 1784.   The Law Courts, the most elegant and extensive in the British Empire, were begun in 1786.   In 1788 there were 14,327 dwelling-houses in Dublin, and 110,000 inhabitants.   Two hundred and twenty peers and three hundred commoners had separate residences.   Dublin was fashionable, and Dublin prospered.[8]

I have already said that corruption soon did its fatal work.   It sanctioned, nay, it compelled, the persecution of the majority of the nation for their religious creed ; and with this persecution the last flame of national prosperity expired, and the persecutors and the persecuted shared alike in the common ruin.   In 1792 Lord Edward FitzGerald denounced the conduct of the House in these ever-memorable words : "I do think, sir, that the Lord Lieutenant and the majority of this House are the worst subjects the King has ;" and when a storm arose, the more violent from consciousness that his words were but too true, for all retraction he would only say :

---

[8] *Prospered.*—This gives an average of about eight persons to each house. There were 22,276 inhabited houses in Dublin in 1861, and the population was 254,480.   This would leave an average of eleven persons to each house.   There are only seventy-five carpenters in *Thom's Directory*, and sixty-four cabinet-makers : if we give them an average of ten men each in their employment, it would not give more than 680 at the trade in all.

" I am accused of having said that I think the Lord Lieutenant and the majority of this House are the worst subjects the King has. I said so; 'tis true; and I am sorry for it."

On the 1st of January, 1801, a new imperial standard was exhibited on London Tower, and on the Castles of Dublin and Edinburgh. It was formed of the three crosses of St. George, St. Patrick, and St. Andrew, and is popularly known as the Union Jack. The *fleur de lis* and the word France were omitted from royal prerogatives and titles; and a proclamation was issued appointing the words *Dei Gratia, Britaniarum Rex, Fidei Defensor.* The *Dublin Gazette* of July, 1800, contained the significant announcement of the creation of sixteen new peerages. The same publication for the last week of the year contained a fresh list of twenty-six others. Forty-two creations in six months were rather an extensive stretch of prerogative; and we cannot be surprised if the majority of the nation had more respect for the great untitled, whose ancestry were known, and were quite above accepting the miserable bribe of a modern peerage.

Strangely enough, from the very day on which the Union was proclaimed, the Catholic question became a ministerial difficulty. Pitt's administration failed on this very point, although it had seemed invincible a few weeks before. The obstinacy of the King, which, indeed, almost amounted to a monomania, was the principal cause. He made it a personal matter, declared it the "most jacobinical thing he had ever heard of;" and he informed the world at large that he would consider any man who proposed it his personal enemy. Pitt resigned. Opinions varied as to his motives. He returned to office in 1804, having promised that he would not again press the subject; and he adhered to his determination until his death. The Irish nobles, who had worked hardest to carry the Union, were somewhat disappointed as to the result. Lord Clare was told by the Duke of Bedford, that the Union had not transferred his dictatorial powers to the Imperial Parliament. He retired to Ireland deeply chagrined, and was soon borne to his grave, amid the revilings of the people whom he had betrayed. Lord Castlereagh, who had been less accustomed to command, and had less difficulty in stooping to conquer, succeeded better with his English friends, and in a few years he ruled the cabinets of Europe; while the Iron Duke, another Irishman, dictated to their armies.

In 1803 the flame of insurrection again broke out, and again

French aid was expected, and the expedition ended in disappoint-ment. Napoleon himself regretted that he had turned his armies towards Egypt, instead of towards Ireland. Emmet's career was brief, and would probably have been almost forgotten, but for his famous speech at the moment of receiving sentence, and for the history of his love and her devoted attachment to his memory.

In 1805 Grattan entered the Imperial Parliament, at the request of Fox. An English constituency was found for him. At the same time, Plunket was brought into the house by Pitt ; and thus these two famous men, the one so full of the brilliant, and the other so full of the powerful, gifts of mental science, again pleaded their country's cause together, and in perfect harmony, though differing on some political points. When Grattan first rose to address the British Senate, there was a hushed attention to his every word ; as his eloquence kindled with his subject, there were suppressed murmurs of approbation ; when he had concluded, there were thunders of applause. His subject was a petition from the Irish Catholics, which was presented to both Houses in 1805. The division gave 339 to 124 against going into committee ; still it was something gained, when Englishmen even listened to Irish grievances, or made some effort to understand them.

The *Veto* was now suggested. The object of this was to allow the crown a passive voice, if not an active one, in the nomination of Catholic bishops. Happily for the Catholic Church in Ireland, the proposal was steadily rejected, though with a determination which brought even members of the same Church into collision. Connexion with the State might have procured temporal advan-tages, but they would have been in truth a poor compensation for the loss of that perfect freedom of action so essential to the spiritual advancement of the Church.

The Duke of Richmond came to Ireland in 1807, with Sir Arthur Wellesley as Chief Secretary. The young man, whose fame was yet unattained, showed himself as clearheaded in the cabinet as in the camp. He made every attempt to suppress the party demonstrations which have been the curse of Ireland, and in-duced the Wexford people to discontinue their annual celebration of the battle of Vinegar Hill. If he could have suppressed a few other anniversaries in the north, it would have been a blessing to the United Kingdom. In 1806 Mr. Grattan was returned for

Dublin, and generously refused the sum of £4,000, which his constituents had collected to pay his expenses. The Catholic question was now constantly coming up, and more than one cabinet was formed and dissolved according to the views of the different members on that matter. A new element of vitality had been introduced by the relaxation of the penal laws. Men were no longer afraid to ask for a grace which they wanted, lest they should lose a grace which they had. The people found that they might speak their real opinions without apprehensions of attempts at conversion in the shape of pitchcaps and half-hangings ; and when the people were ready for a leader, the leader was ready for the people ; and Daniel O'Connell took the place in the guidance of the Irish nation, which he will never lose in their memory and in their affections.

The history of Ireland and the life of O'Connell are convertible terms for five-and-forty years. O'Connell represented Ireland, and Ireland was represented by O'Connell. We have had our great men and our good men, our brave men and our true men ; but, to my poor thinking, the greatest of our men was O'Connell—for who ever approached him in his mighty power of ruling a nation by moral suasion only? the best of our men was O'Connell, for who dare assert that he was ever unfaithful to his country or to his country's faith? the bravest of our men was O'Connell, equally fearless in every danger, moral or physical ; and the truest of our men was O'Connell, dying of a broken heart in a faraway land, because he saw his country's cause all but ruined—because he knew that with his failing breath one of his country's surest helpers would pass from her for ever. A *thoughtfully* written " History of the Life and Times of O'Connell," by some one really competent to do justice to the subject, is much wanted. I believe that posterity will do justice to his memory as one of the best and noblest patriots which the world has ever seen—a justice which as yet has been scarcely accorded to him as fully as he has merited. Had O'Connell accomplished no other work for Ireland than this—the giving of a tone of nationality and manliness to the people—he had accomplished a most glorious work. He taught Irishmen that chains do not make the slave, but rather the spirit in which the chains are worn. He awoke, in the hearts of his countrymen, that love of freedom, which is the first step towards making a successful effort to obtain it. He showed them how

they might intimidate their oppressors without injuring themselves—a lesson eminently necessary where the oppressors are
incomparably more powerful than the oppressed.

The sept of O'Connell, from which this noble man was descended,
held a prominent position among the early Milesian clans. Pure
Celtic blood ran in his veins ; the fire of Celtic wit sparkled in his
utterances ; the lighthearted happiness of a Celtic spirit guided his
actions ; and the undaunted bravery of a Celtic warrior's courage
looked out of his clear beaming eye. A nobleman, in truth, was
Daniel O'Connell—a nobleman of whom any nation might justly
be proud—a nobleman to whom we must hope that Ireland will
yet raise some monument of enduring fame. The O'Connell sept
were driven from their ancestral homes, in 1172, by Raymond,
Strongbow's son-in-law. Their territory lay along the Shannon.
They were now compelled to take refuge in a wild and desolate
part of Kerry, too wild and too desolate to attract English cupidity.
A MS. is still preserved in the British Museum, written by one of
the O'Connell family ; it is in the Irish language, and bears date
1245. In this document mention is made of a Daniel O'Connell,
who proceeded to the north of Ireland, at the head of a large body
of men, to resist an invading force. The Celts were successful ; and
when they had won the day, the chieftain and his vanquished foes
feasted together. In 1586 Richard O'Connell was High Sheriff of
Kerry ; but, from the accession of William III., until the illustrious
Liberator obtained some degree of freedom for his country, all the
O'Connells were prescribed from positions of emolument, for having
held with unswerving fidelity to the old faith.

O'Connell was born on the 6th of August, 1775, "the very
year," as he himself says, in a letter to the *Dublin Evening Post*, "in
which the stupid obstinacy of British oppression *forced* the reluctant people of America to seek for security in arms, and to
commence that bloody struggle for national independence, which
has been in its results beneficial to England, whilst it has shed
glory, and conferred liberty, pure and sublime, on America." He
was educated at St. Omers, and it is said manifested some inclination for the priesthood ; but there can be no doubt that his
vocation lay in another direction, as he was incomparably too
deeply religious and too thoroughly honest not to have obeyed
the call of God at any cost, had such a favour been vouchsafed to
him. It is said, whatever his dislike of physical force may have

been in after-life, that he unquestionably knew how to use the *argumentum baculinum* in his early days; and that more than one student was made to feel the effects thereof, when attempting ill-natured jokes on the herculean Celt. During his residence abroad he had some opportunities of witnessing the fearful effects of the French Revolution; and it is probable that a remembrance of these scenes, added to his own admirably keen common sense, saved him from leading his countrymen on to deeds of open violence. He was called to the Irish bar in the memorable year of 1798. For some time he failed to obtain practice; for who would confide their case to a young Catholic lawyer, when the fact of his creed alone would be sufficient to condemn his client in the eyes of Protestant juries, judges, and attorneys? His maiden speech was made in opposition to the Union, even as his life was spent in the most strenuous efforts to obtain the reversal of that most fatal measure. A meeting was held in the Royal Exchange, Dublin, at the close of the year 1799, to petition against it; but even as O'Connell was denouncing, in his most eloquent language, the new attempt at national degradation, Major Sirr and his file of military rushed into the apartment, and separated the assembly. O'Connell now retired into private life, and, with the marvellous foresight of true genius, devoted himself to storing up that forensic knowledge which he felt sure he should one day use for the benefit of his countrymen.

One of the most important instances in which O'Connell's legal acumen saved the lives of his countrymen, is known as the "Doneraile Conspiracy;" and as all the facts are eminently illustrative of the history of Ireland at that period, and of the character and abilities of one of her most distinguished sons, I shall relate the circumstances. Several Protestant gentlemen in the neighbourhood of Doneraile, had been making those abortive efforts to "convert" their tenants from Popery, which usually end in no small amount of ill-feeling on both sides; another of these gentlemen, with equal zeal and equal want of common sense and common humanity, had devoted himself to hunting out real or supposed rebels. This gentleman had at last brought on himself an armed attack, for which he deserved little pity. He contrived, however, to capture one of his assailants, who, of course, was hung. The gentlemen having thus excited the unfortunate peasantry, pointed to the results of their own folly as though these results had been the cause of it; and an informer came forward, who, with the usual recklessness of his atrocious class, accused some of the most respectable farmers of the district of having entered into a conspiracy to murder the Protestant gentlemen,—a cruel return certainly, had it been true, for their earnest efforts to convert the natives from "the errors of Popery to those of the Protestant Church." A special commission was sent down; the wildest excitement prevailed on all sides; and, as was usual in such cases, the bitterest prejudice against the unfortunate accused. The Solicitor-General led for the crown: the defence was a simple denial. In such cases the examination of the approvers is the great point for the accused, and should be confided to the ablest counsel. One of the unfortunate prisoners was a respectable farmer, aged seventy, of whom the highest character was given. But it was all in vain ; after five minutes' deliberation, the jury gave in the verdict of guilty. As the men were to be made an " example of," they were sentenced to be hanged in six days. This was on Saturday. The next lot of prisoners was to be tried at nine o'clock on Monday morning. There was one universal cry for " O'Connell," from the great multitude who knew these poor victims were perfectly innocent. On Saturday night a farmer mounted the best horse that could be found in Cork, and, after a night of incessant riding, he reached Derrynane Abbey on Sunday morning at nine o'clock. His name was William Burke : let it be transmitted with all honour to posterity! He told his errand to one who never listened unmoved to the tale of his country's sorrows and wrongs ; and he assured O'Connell that, unless he were in Cork by nine next morning, the unfortunate prisoners, "though innocent as the child unborn," would all be hanged. The great man at once prepared for his journey ; and so wild was the joy of Burke, so sure was he that there would now be a hope, if not a certainty, of justice, that only the earnest entreaties of O'Connell could induce him to remain a few hours to rest his weary horse. On the same good horse he set out again, and reached Cork at eight o'clock on Monday morning, having travelled 180 miles in thirty-eight hours. Scouts had been posted all along the road to watch the man's return : even as he passed through each little village, there was an anxious crowd waiting the word of life or death. "O'Connell's coming, boys !" was enough; and a wild cheer, which rent the very mountains, told how keenly an act of justice could be appreciated by the most justice-loving people upon earth. And O'Connell did come. He has himself described the sensations of that midnight journey, through all the autumn beauties of the most beautiful scenery in the United Kingdom. And then he exclaims: "After that glorious feast of soul, I found myself settled down amid all the rascalities of an Irish court of justice."

The Solicitor-General was actually addressing the jury, when the shouts of the excited crowd announced the arrival of one who, by this act of his life alone, deserves, *par excellence*, the proud and glorious title of the LIBERATOR. He entered the courthouse, apologized for his unprofessional attire; and as he had no refreshment, and there was no time to lose, he requested permission of the judges to have a bowl of milk and some sandwiches sent to him. The Solicitor-General resumed his address, but had not proceeded far before the stentorian voice of O'Connell was heard exclaiming: "That's not law." The bench decided in his favour. He was rapidly swallowing as much food as was necessary to sustain nature, and once more, with his mouth full, he exclaims: "That's no longer law; the Act is repealed." Again the mortified counsel proceeded with his case, and once more O'Connell's knowledge of law served him in good stead. "The learned Solicitor," he exclaimed, "has *no right* to make such a statement; the crown cannot give such matters in evidence." For the third time the ruling was in favour of the Liberator. Then came the all-important cross-examination of the approvers; and the men who had lied so well and so boldly on Saturday, prevaricated, cursed, and howled under the searching questions of their new examiner; Nowlan, the vilest of the lot, exclaiming at last: "It's little I thought I'd have to meet you, Counsellor O'Connell." Alas! thrice-wretched man, who thought still less of another Court and another Judgment. O'Connell won the day. He threatened the very Solicitor-General with impeachment before the House of Commons, for the way he conducted the case. He taunted him, bewildered him, scolded him, laughed at him, as he only could do; and when at last the unfortunate man came out with some observation about "false *facts*," O'Connell threw the whole court into a roar of laughter by directing attention to the bull, and by his inimitable imitation of his English accent. The jury could not agree, and the men were acquitted. Another trial came on next day, and it was then discovered that one of the approvers differed in most important matters from his statements on oath before the magistrates of Doneraile, and in what he now stated. This was enough; and the jury brought in a verdict of not guilty, though, on the very same evidence, a verdict of guilty had been given on Saturday. As an act, however, of great clemency, the men who had been sentenced to be hanged in six days, were now *only* transported.

During the time of O'Connell's retirement and study, he had but too many opportunities of knowing how little justice was likely to be meted out to Irishmen accused, justly or unjustly, of political crimes; and, doubtless, he directed his studies to those special points most likely to be helpful hereafter. Robert Emmet's execution took place in October, 1803; and from that hour, until the accession of the Whigs to office, in 1806, Ireland was ruled by martial law. The Habeas Corpus Act and trial by jury were suspended, and the jails and transport ships were crowded with the victims of military ferocity and magisterial vengeance. In the debate of 1805, when the Catholic petition was brought into the House of Commons by Mr. Fox, and treacherously opposed by Pitt, Mr. Ponsonby exclaimed, speaking of the Irish Catholics: " I know them well; and I know, at the same time, that whatever is good in them, they owe to themselves; whatever is bad in them, they owe to you, and to your bad government." Mr. Grattan accused the English Tories of " running about like old women in search of old prejudices; *preferring to buy foreign allies by subsidies, rather than to subsidize fellow-subjects by privileges.*" He might have said by justice, for the Irish have never asked for privileges; they ask simply for the same justice as is shown to English subjects. Mr. Foster, the last Speaker of the Irish House of Commons, declared that, " under the Union Act, by compact, the Protestant boroughs were suppressed, and a compensation of £1,400,000 paid to Protestant owners, and not one shilling to the Catholics."

O'Connell came prominently forward as a leader of the Catholic party in 1810. A meeting was held in the Royal Exchange, Dublin, to petition for Repeal of the Union, at which the High Sheriff of that city presided, and many distinguished men were present—a proof that, however corrupted Irish Parliaments may have been by English gold, there was still some advantage to be gained to the country by possessing even a partial independence. O'Connell's speech was published, and circulated widely. To give the full details of his career as a leader of the people, would require a volume the size of the present work; to give even a sufficiently comprehensive outline, would require several chapters : I can but hope that some able hand

O'Connell refusing to take the Oath.

will take up the subject, and with equal earnestness do I hope that it may be some one really capable of doing justice to it. One who would write the "Life and Times of O'Connell" as such a work should be written, would require to bring more than ordinary abilities to the task, and would deserve, at the hands of his countrymen, the highest expression of gratitude which they could give. Such a work would be incomparably the noblest monument which could be dedicated to his memory.

The Clare election is undoubtedly the culminating point in O'Connell's career. Men stood aghast in amazement at the boldness of the man who presumed to make such an attempt. Even his friends could scarcely believe that he was in earnest, or that he was wise. His success was a splendid example of what the energy and determination of one single man could accomplish. Well might the Lord Chancellor declare that "this business must bring the Roman Catholic question to a crisis and a conclusion." The words were prophetic; the prophecy was realized. On the 5th of March, 1829, Mr. Peel moved a committee of the whole House, "to go into the consideration of the civil disabilities of his Majesty's Roman Catholic subjects." The motion was carried by a majority of 188. On the 15th of May, 1829, O'Connell appeared in the House to take his seat. He was introduced by Lords Ebrington and Dungannon. The House was thronged. The very peeresses came to gaze upon the arch-agitator, expecting to see a demagogue, and to hear an Irish brogue. There were whispers of surprise when they saw a gentleman, and a man who could speak, with the versatility of true talent, to suit his audience. The card containing the oath was handed to O'Connell; he read a portion of it over in an audible voice—the portion which required him to say that "the sacrifice of the Mass, and the invocation of the Blessed Virgin Mary and other saints, as now practised in the Church of Rome, are impious and idolatrous;" and to deny the dispensing power of the Pope, which never existed, except in the imagination of its framers. With a courteous bow he said, in a voice to be heard throughout the House: "I decline, Mr. Clerk, to take this oath: part of it I know to be false; another part I believe not to be true."

Again he sought the votes of the electors of Clare, and again he was returned by them. On the 13th of April, 1829, the royal signature was affixed to the Act of Emancipation, and Irishmen were no longer refused the rights of citizens because they respected the rights of conscience.

In the year 1812, the late Sir Robert Peel came to Ireland as Chief Secretary, unfortunately destitute of the enlargement of mind and the native genius of his predecessor, Sir Arthur Wellesley. His abilities, however great, were not such as to enable him to understand a nationality distinct from his own ; and hence he could not deal with the Irish, either to his credit, or for their advantage. From the year 1815 to 1817 the conduct of the English Parliament towards Ireland was regulated with the nicest attention to the movements of the General who ruled the Continent. In 1817 an Act was passed, which, with admirable policy, excused Catholic officers, naval and military, from forswearing transubstantiation. In 1821 George IV. visited Ireland. It was the first time that an English King had come to Ireland as the acknowledged sovereign of the people. Their hopes were high ; and the deference for royalty, so eminently characteristic of the Celt, had at last found an opportunity of expressing itself. All that loyalty could do was done ; all that the warmest heart could say was said. The King appeared impressed by demonstrations so entirely new to him ; he wore a large bunch of shamrocks constantly during his brief stay ; but before the shamrocks were faded, Irish wants and Irish loyalty were alike forgotten.

In the year 1824 the subject of Irish disturbances was carefully inquired into by Select Committees of both Houses of Parliament. Some extracts from their reports will give the best and most correct idea of the state of the country from the Union to the year 1834, when another investigation was made. In 1807 the county Limerick was alarmingly disturbed. In 1812 the counties of Tipperary, Waterford, Kilkenny, Limerick, Westmeath, Roscommon, and the King's county, were the theatre of the same sanguinary tumults. Limerick and Tipperary remained under the Insurrection Act until 1818. In 1820 there were serious disturbances in Galway, and in 1821, in Limerick.

These disturbances are thus accounted for Maxwell Blacker, Esq., Barrister, who was appointed to administer the Insurrection Act, in 1822, in the counties of Cork and Tipperary : " The immediate cause of the disturbance I consider to be the great increase of population, and the fall in the price of produce after the war ; the consequence of which was, that it was impossible to pay the rent or the tithes that had been paid when the country was prosperous." Sir Matthew Barrington, Crown Solicitor of the Munster Circuit for seventeen years, was asked : " Do you attribute the inflammable state of the population to the state of misery in which they generally are ?" " I do, to a great extent ;. I seldom knew any instance when there was sufficient employment for the people that they were inclined to be disturbed ; if they had plenty of work and employment, they are generally peaceable." John Leslie Foster, Esq., M.P., in his examination, states : " I think the proximate cause [of the disturbances] is the extreme physical misery of the peasantry, coupled with their liability to be called upon for the payment of different charges, which it is often perfectly impossible for them to meet." Matthew Singleton, Esq., Chief Magistrate of Police in the Queen's county, said, on his examination : "I have seen, and I know land to be set one-third above its value."

It would be useless to give more of this evidence, for the details are always the same. The people were almost starving. They could scarcely get a sufficiency of the poorest food, yet they were compelled to pay rent and tithes far above the value of their land. If they were unable, they were thrown out upon the wayside to die like dogs.

There can be no doubt that the outrages thus perpetrated were very fearful. Every man's hand was against them, and their hand was against every man. They shot their landlords, and they " carded " the tithe-proctors. Gentlemen's houses were barricaded, even in the daytime. Many families of the higher classes lived in a state of siege. The windows were made bullet-proof ; the doors were never opened after nightfall. It was a fearful state of society for a Christian country, and the guilt and disgrace of it was surely on those who had caused it. Yet we do not find that the knowledge of these facts produced any effect upon the men who heard them, and who alone had it in their power to apply the remedy. Still something was done ; and although it is one of the stern facts of history, one can scarcely choose but smile at the simplicity of those who planned and carried out such a scheme for the improvement of Ireland.

The " second reformation " was commenced in 1827. The Catholic priests were challenged to controversy ; even laymen interfered. Theology and theological differences became the town and table-talk of Ireland. Bibles and tracts were distributed in all directions amongst the starving poor, food and clothing were occasionally added; yet, notwithstanding these powerful inducements, the people starved and remained Catholics. Writs of ejectment were then tried; and the Irish poor had their choice between the Bible and beggary—but they chose beggary.

So far did the Bible craze go, that it almost amounted to a monomania. One noble lord, to show his reverence for that book, and to convince his tenantry of the estimation in which he held it, flung every volume of his library into the lake of his demesne, and with the Bible in his hand, which commanded him to feed the hungry, refused to feed them unless they complied with his commands. Moore's satires were, unquestionably, the best weapons against such fanaticism. Sheil wrote in the *Gazette de France*, and hundreds of pens wrote in the American papers. A loud cry of "Shame!" arose in every quarter of the world; the echo reached the ears of the promoters of the movement; and the force of public opinion succeeded in suppressing the futile attempt.

The influence of Irish emigrants in America was already beginning to be felt. Large sums of money poured in from that country to swell the Catholic rent, and a considerable portion of the funds were employed by O'Connell in providing for men who had been ejected by their landlords, for refusing either to believe a creed, or to give a vote contrary to their conscience. He even threatened to buy up the incumbrances on some of these gentlemen's estates, to foreclose their mortgages, and to sell them out. His threat, added to his well-known determination, was not without its effect.

The whole subject of Irish emigration may be safely predicted to be the key which will unlock the future fate of Great Britain. It is true that, at this moment, every effort is being made by the English nation to conciliate America; it remains to be seen how Americans will be disposed to accept present flattery as a compensation for past injustice, and scarcely past contempt. A better knowledge of Irish history might prevent some fatal mistakes on both sides of the Atlantic. I have, therefore, felt it a duty to devote the concluding pages of this *History* to this important subject.

The great tide of western emigration was undoubtedly caused, in part, by the sufferings of the famine year; but these sufferings were in themselves an effect, rather than a cause; and we must look to more remote history for the origin of the momentous exodus. It has, indeed, been well observed, that " when a man leaves his country for one subject to foreign rule, it must, in general, be that he does not care for it, or that it does not care for him; it must either be that he is so little attached to the institutions of his own country, that he is willing to submit to those of another; or that he despises the latter sufficiently to look forward to replacing them by those of his own."[9] No unprejudiced person can for a moment doubt which of these causes has been most active in producing Irish emigration. The Irishman's love of home and of his native land, is a fact beyond all dispute : his emigration, then, can have no other cause than this, that his country, or the country which governs his native land, does not care for him; and when we find noble lords and honorable members suggesting " the more emigration the better," we cannot doubt that he is the victim to indifference, if not to absolute dislike. Undoubtedly, if the Irishman did not care for his country, and if the Englishman, when planted in Ireland, did not become equally discontented and rather more indignant than his predecessors under English rule in Ireland, the arrangement might be a very admirable one ; but Irishmen, to the third and fourth generation, do not forget their country, neither do they forget why they have been compelled to leave it. A work has been published lately on the subject of the Irish in America. It is much to be regretted, that the very able writer did not give statistics and facts, as well as inferences and anecdotes. A history of the Irish in America, should include statistics which could not be disputed, and facts which could not be denied. The facts in the work alluded to are abundant, and most important ; but they should have been prefaced by an account of the causes which have led to emigration, and as accurate statistics as possible of its results.

Some few English writers have had the honesty to admit that their colonial policy has not been the most admirable; "nor should we forget," says the author of the *History of the United States*, " that the spirit in which these colonies were ruled from England was one, in the main, of intense selfishness. The answer of Seymour, an English Attorney-General under William and Mary, or towards

---

[9] *Own.—History of the United States*, p. 3. Ludlow and Hughes; Macmillan, London, 1862. The title of this work is singularly infelicitous, for it is merely a sketchy and not very clear account of the late war in America.

the close of the seventeenth century, to the request of Virginia, for a college, when her delegate begged him to consider that the people of Virginia had souls to be saved as well as the people of England: "Souls! damn your souls! plant tobacco!" is scarcely an unfair exponent of that spirit.[2] Another writer says: "Historians, in treating of the American rebellion, have confined their arguments too exclusively to the question of internal taxation, and the right or policy of exercising this prerogative. The true source of the rebellion lay deeper—in our traditional colonial policy."[3] One more quotation must suffice: "The legal rights of those colonies have been perpetually violated. Those which were strong enough were driven to separation; those which adhered to us in that great contest, or which we have subsequently acquired or founded, are either denied constitutions, or, if the local authorities oppose the will of the Imperial Parliament, find their constitutions changed, suspended, or annulled."[4] It will be remembered that the original colonists of America were principally Englishmen, who were driven from their own country by religious intolerance; yet no sooner had they established themselves in their new home, than they commenced to practise even more fearful persecutions on others than those from which they had fled. There was one honorable exception; the Roman Catholics who fled from persecution in England, never, even in the plenitude of their power, attempted the slightest persecution, religious, social, or legal.

It will be seen, then, that the first emigrants to America from the British dominions, could not have had any special attachment to the country they had left; that, on the contrary, their feelings were embittered against the mother country before their departure from her shores; and after that departure she did nothing to allay the irritation, but much to increase it. For several centuries after the arrival of the "May Flower," the number of emigrants from England and Ireland were, probably, tolerably equal, and by no means numerous. It was not an age of statistics, and no accurate statistics can be given.

The disruption between the States and England, or rather the

---

[2] *Spirit.—History of the United States,* p. 7.
[3] *Policy.—*Morley's *Burke,* p. 153.
[4] *Annulled.—Historical and Philosophical Essays,* Senior, vol. i. p. 197.

causes which led to it, re-opened whatever feelings there may have been against the mother country, and at the same time increased its bitterness a hundredfold. The tide of Irish emigration had set in even then—slowly, indeed, but surely; and it will be remembered that the Irish in America, few though they were, became the foremost to fan the flame of rebellion, and were amongst the first to raise the standard of revolt. The States obtained a glorious freedom—a freedom which, on the whole, they have used wisely and well ; and even their bitterest enemies cannot deny that they have formed a powerful nation—a nation which may yet rule the destinies of the world. Let us endeavour now to estimate in some degree the influence of Irish emigration on American society. If the history of Ireland were written in detail up to the present day, fully one-fourth the detail should comprise a history of the Irish in America. Never in the world's history has an emigration been so continuous or so excessive ; never in the world's history have emigrants continued so inseparably united, politically and socially, to the country which they have left. The cry of "Ireland for the Irish," is uttered as loudly on the shores of the Mississippi as on the shores of the Shannon. It is almost impossible to arrive at accurate statistics of the number of Irish in America, but a fair approximation may be obtained. The population of America, according to a recent writer, was, in 1840, 17,063,353 ; in 1850, it had risen to 23,191,876 ; it is now [1868], 35,000,000. In 1842, the imports were in value, $100,162,087 ; the exports, $104,691,534 ; and the tonnage was 2,092,391. In 1859, the imports were $383,768,130 ; the exports were $356,789,462 ; and the tonnage was 5,146,037. This increase is beyond all historical precedence, and a future historian, who found such amazing statistics of increase, and knew nothing of emigration, would be strangely puzzled to account for it. But if he searched the files of an old English or Irish newspaper office, whatever might have been the creed or politics of its proprietors, he would soon arrive at a satisfactory solution. In the *Irish Times*, the leading Irish paper of the day, he would find the following reference to the present history of Ireland : "The Emigration Commissioners notice with some surprise the fact, that, during the past year [1867], the emigrants from Ireland were better clothed, and carried with them better furnished kits, than either the English or foreign emigrants. During the past year, 51,000 Irish emigrants left Liverpool alone—

a regiment nearly one thousand strong every week. The loss of 100,000 persons annually, chiefly of the labouring classes, and generally strong, active, well-built men, affords matter for serious consideration. If the Government be contented that 100,000 yearly of the Irish population *should increase the power of America* [the italics are our own], they have but to refuse those generous and considerate measures which alone can keep our people at home, by giving them a chance of progressing as they do in America."

This is the honestly avowed opinion of a Protestant paper, whose editors are beyond all suspicion of writing to encourage "Popery," or preach Fenianism. An admirable parliamentary comment has just occurred in the rejection of the Protestant Church Suspension Bill by the House of Lords, though there is no doubt that the good sense and the native justice of the English nation will at length compel its acceptance.

The fact is, that at this moment nearly one-half the population of America are Irish and Catholics. The writer lately quoted, cannot refrain from a sneer at the "low Irish" in America, to whom he attributes the "insult and injury" which ne is pleased to consider that Americans manifest to foreign nations, and especially to England ; he forgets the old sources of injury, which no American can forget ; and he forgets, also, how easily the same "low Irish" might have been prevented from exhibiting the feeling which he attributes to them.

Let those who wish to understand the present history of Ireland, read Mr. Maguire's *Irish in America*, carefully and thoughtfully. If they do so, and if they are not blinded by wilful prejudices, they must admit that the oft-repeated charges against Irishmen of being improvident and idle are utterly groundless, unless, indeed, they can imagine that the magic influence of a voyage across the Atlantic can change a man's nature completely. Let them learn what the Irishman can do, and does do, when freed from the chains of slavery, and when he is permitted to reap some reward for his labour. Let him learn that Irishmen do not forget wrongs ; and if they do not always avenge them, that is rather from motives of prudence, than from lack of will. Let him learn that the Catholic priesthood are the true fathers of their people, and the true protectors of their best interests, social and spiritual. Let him read how the good pastor gives his life for his sheep, and counts no

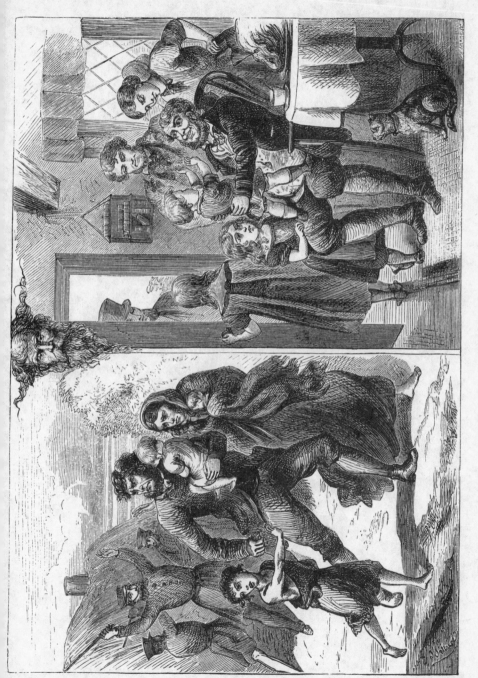

Irland and Amerika.

journey too long or too dangerous, when even a single soul may be concerned. Let him judge for himself of the prudence of the same priests, even as regards the temporal affairs of their flocks, and see how, where they are free to do so, they are the foremost to help them, even in the attainment of worldly prosperity. Let him send for Sadlier's *Catholic Directory for the United States and Canada*, and count over the Catholic population of each diocese ; read the names of priests and nuns, and see how strong the Irish element is there. Nay, let him send for one of the most popular and best written of the Protestant American serials, and he will find an account of Catholics and the Catholic religion, which is to be feared few English Protestants would have the honesty to write, and few English Protestant serials the courage to publish, however strong their convictions. The magazine to which I refer, is the *Atlantic Monthly;* the articles were published in the numbers for April and May, 1868, and are entitled " Our Roman Catholic Brethren." Perhaps a careful perusal of them would, to a thoughtful mind, be the best solution of the Irish question. The writer, though avowing himself a Protestant, and declaring that under no circumstances whatever would he be induced to believe in miracles, has shown, with equal candour and attractiveness, what the Catholic Church is, and what it can do, when free and unfettered. He shows it to be the truest and best friend of humanity ; he shows it to care most tenderly for the poor and the afflicted ; and he shows, above all, how the despised, exiled Irish are its best and truest supports ; how the " kitchen often puts the parlour to the blush ;" and the self-denial of the poor Irish girl assists not a little in erecting the stately temples to the Almighty, which are springing up in that vast continent from shore to shore, and are only lessened by the demands made on the same willing workers for the poor father and mother, the young brother or sister, who are supported in their poverty by the alms sent them freely, generously, and constantly by the Irish servant-girl.

Nor have the Catholics of America overlooked the importance of literary culture. A host of cheap books and serials are in circulation, and are distributed largely and freely in convent schools, collegiate establishments, and country parishes; and with a keen appreciation of the religious necessities of the great mass of non-Catholics, of which, unfortunately, English Catholics are oblivious, tracts are published in thousands for general reading, and given to travellers in the railcars, and steamboats. Nor has a higher class of literature been overlooked. The gifted superior of the Congregation of St. Paul has been mainly instrumental in getting up and superintending the labours of the *Catholic Publication Society*, which, in addition to the multitude of valuable works it has published, sends forth its monthly magazine, well entitled *The Catholic World*, which is unquestionably the best serial of its kind, and may vie with those conducted by the most gifted Protestant writers of the day, while it is far superior to anything which has as yet been published by the Catholics of this country.

Such is a brief outline, and scarcely even an outline, of the *present* history of Ireland, in which the hearts of so many of our people are in one country, while their bodies are in another. There is another phase of this present history on which I could have wished to have dwelt much longer; I mean the political union between America and Ireland. So long as Irish emigration continues—I should rather say, so long as real Irish grievances are permitted to continue—so long will this state of things be dangerous to England. Justice to Ireland may be refused with impunity just so long as there is peace between England and America; but who shall dare predict how long that peace will continue, when, as must assuredly happen in a few short years, the Irish in America, or their direct descendants, shall form the preponderating class, and therefore guide the political affairs of that mighty people?

The maps which are appended to this edition of the *Illustrated History of Ireland*, will, it is hoped, be found not only interesting, but important. Irishmen in America will see, by a glance at the map of family names, the territories in Ireland formerly held by their ancestors. Statistics showing the fearful depopulation of the country, which, notwithstanding all the boasts of those who advocated it, has not benefited those who remain, will be found in another map. The third map is not less important; by that will be seen the immense preponderance of Catholics to Protestants; and it will suggest, no doubt, to thoughtful minds, the injustice of sacrificing the multitude to the individual few.

A few words must also be said about the two full-page illustrations which have been added to this Edition. One of the most important events in the life of O'Connell has been chosen for the one; and, alas! one of the most frequent occurrences in Irish history, from the first English invasion to the present day, has been chosen for the other. In the engraving of O'Connell, it was impossible to preserve the likeness, as the expression demanded by the incident could not be produced from any of the portraits extant; with regard to the eviction scene, it is unfortunately true to the life. Those who have read Mr. Maguire's *Irish in America*, will recognize the special subject represented. Those who read the Irish local papers of the day, may continually peruse accounts of evictions; but only an eyewitness can describe the misery and despair of the unfortunate victims. When shall the picture be reversed? When will Irishmen return from America, finding it possible to be as free and as prosperous here? Finding that a man who is willing to toil may obtain a fair remuneration for his labour, and that a man may have the rights of men ;—then, and not till then, may we hope that Irish history will, for the future, be a record of past injustice, amply compensated for by present equity.

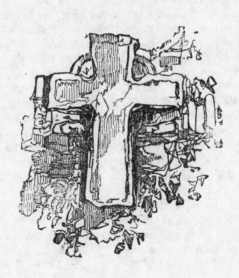

APPENDIX.

THE letter given below, which is from the pen of a distinguished Protestant clergyman, appears to me of such importance, that I place it here to be a permanent record for the future historian of Ireland, as an important opinion on the present history of this country, but too well supported by facts.

TO ISAAC BUTT, ESQ., LL.D.

MY DEAR BUTT,—If every other man in the world entertained doubts of my sincerity, you, at least, would give me credit for honesty and just intentions. I write to you accordingly, because my mind has been stirred to its inmost depths by the perusal of your address in my native city of Limerick. I do not regard the subject of your address as a political one. It ought to be regarded solely as a question of humanity, justice, common sense, and common honesty. I wish my lot had never been cast in rural places. As a clergyman, I hear what neither landlords nor agents ever heard. I see the depression of the people; their sighs and groans are before me. They are brought so low as often to praise and glorify those whom, in their secret hearts, are the objects of abhorrence. All this came out gradually before me. Nor did I feel as I ought to have felt in their behalf, until, in my own person and purse, I became the victim of a system of tyranny which cries from earth to heaven for relief. Were I to narrate my own story, it would startle many of the Protestants of Ireland. There are good landlords—never a better than the late Lord Downshire, or the living and beloved Lord Roden. But there are too many of another state of feeling and action. There are estates in the north where the screw is never withdrawn from its circuitous and oppressive work. Tenant-right is an unfortunate and delusive affair, simply because it is invariably used to the landlord's advantage. Here we have an election in prospect, and in many counties no farmer will be permitted to think or act for himself. What right any one man has to demand the surrender of another's vote I never could see. It is an act of sheer felony—a perfect "stand-and-deliver" affair. To hear a man slavishly and timorously, say, "I must give my vote as the landlord wishes," is an admission that the Legislature, which bestowed the right of voting on the tenant, should not see him robbed of his right, or subsequently scourged or banished from house and land, because he disregarded a landlord's nod, or the menace of a land-agent. At no little hazard of losing the friendship of some who are high, and good, and kind, I write as I now do.

Yours, my dear Butt, very sincerely,

THOMAS DREW.

Dundrum, Clough, co. Down, Sept. 7, 1868.

INDEX.

———

A.

Abbey, the Black, Kilkenny, 318.
  of Mellifont, 231.
  of St. Mary, 317.
  of Holy Cross, 317.
  of Dunbrody, 289.
  of Tintern, 317.
  of St. Saviour's, Dublin, 318.
  of St. Thomas the Martyr, 287.
  of Boyle, 316.
Abercrombie, Sir Ralph, 623.
Act of Emancipation passed, 647.
Adamnan, St., 172.
Adrian's Bull, 274.
Aedh, St., 221.
Aengus, St., 179—his Festology, 180—
  his Chronicle, 41.
Aengus Grove, Synod at, 227.
Aengus, King, baptism of, 123—his
  death, 130 — ancestor of the
  O'Keeffes, O'Sullivans, O'Cal-
  lahans, and MacCarthys, 130.
Africa, Phœnician circumnavigation
  of, 69.
Agrarian outrages and their causes,
  613.
Agricola, 95.
Aideadh Chonchobair, legend of, 127.
Ailbhé, Princess, 105.
Ainmire, Hugh, 167.
All Hallows Eve, 88n.
Altan, St., 177.
Amalgaidh, King, and his seven sons,
  123.
Amato, prelate who consecrated St.
  Patrick, 115.
Amlaff the Dane, 195—in Dublin, 191.
Ancient pitcher, 240.
  fireplaces, 240.
  shoes, 252.
  brooch, 270.
  boot, 251.

Andrew, St., Church of, in Henry II.'s
  time, 272.
Anglo-Irish and old Irish, their differences at Kilkenny, 487.
Annals of Ulster, 39—compiled by
  Four Masters, 51—accounts in,
  confirmed ab extra, 68—poetry
  from, 198—kept with great care,
  233—dedication of, 53—quotations
  from, 58, 59, 75, 88, 90, 94, 132,
  144, 198, 199, 218, 232n, 265, 283,
  388, 307, 312n, 313.
  of Tighernach, 48.
  of Iuis MacNerinn, 39.
  of Innisfallen, 39.
  of Boyle, 39.
  of Clonmacnois, 60n.
  of Loch Cé, 115.
  of Ballitore, 630.
  preserved by Celtic Race, 67.
Anselm, St., commends the Irish
  prelates, 229.
Antiquities of pre-Christian Erinn,
  148.
Antwerp, Irish soldiers in, 478.
Aqua vini and aqua vitæ, 245.
Architecture of Tara, 167.
Ardmore round tower, 237.
Armagh, See of, 114—founded, 126—
  streets of, 187n.
Arnold on pedigree, 85n—on history
  taught by verse, 86n.
Athlone, siege of, 568—castle of, 314
  —bridge built, 308n.
Attacotti, revolt of the, 96.
Augustinians, Order of, 316.

B.

Bachall Isu, St. Patrick's, 114—its
  wanton destruction, 115.
Ballitore, sufferings in, 630.
Balor of the Evil Eye, 64.

Banbha, the Lady, 43.
Banqueting hall at Tara, 166.
Baptism, ceremonies at, 229.
Baraid, a Scandinavian chief, 195.
Barbadoes, the Irish sent as slaves to, 515.
Bards of Erinn, or filés, 40.
Barretts, feud between Cusacks and, 332.
Barrington, Sir Jonah, on the last night of Irish Parliament, 639.
Barry, an Irishman, 601.
Barrys and Roches, 445.
Battle of Magh Tuireadh, 61.
  of Sliabh Mis, 75.
  at Taillten, 75.
  between the Firbolgs and Tuatha Dé Dananns, 62.
  Connor, 343.
  of Géisill, 78n.
  of Bealagh Mughna (Ballaghmoon), Kildare, 193.
  of Dundalk, 201.
  of Sulcoit, near Tipperary, 205.
  of Belach-Lechta, near Macroom, co. Cork, 207.
  of Glen-Mama (Glen of the Gap), near Dunlavin, 208.
  of Clontarf, 214.
  of Downpatrick, 325.
  of Benburb, 493.
  of the Boyne, 563.
  of Aughrim, 570.
  of the Ford of Comar, Westmeath, 160.
  of Magh-Rath, 171.
  of Almhain (near Kildare), 186.
  of Desertcreaght, 332.
  of St. Callixtus' day, 352.
  of Ford of the Biscuits, 451.
Beare, O'Sullivan, his History, 534.
Beasts, the three, to be hunted, 517.
Bede's account of Ireland, 79—on Irish saints, 173.
Belgium, MSS. preserved in, 46.
Beltinne, or fire of Baal, 119—origin of, 164.
Benignus, St., St. Patrick's successor in the See of Armagh, 116.
Berchan, St., 162.
Beresford faction, 616.
Bill, curious, of a play, 547n.
Bishops, Protestant, indifferent about regular ordination, 536.
Black Death, 86.
Blefed or pestilence, 162.
Bog butter and cheese, 246.

Bohun, Humphrey de, 270.
Bonnell, his statistics, 540.
Book, a, given for a ransom, 377.
Books preserved, list of, 39, 44—list of lost, 39, 40.
Book of Chronicum Scotorum, 39.
  of Laws, 40.
  of Ballymote, 37.
  of Leinster, 40.
  of Lecain, 37—when written, 50n.
  Annals of Ulster, 39.
    of Innisfallen, 39.
    of Boyle, 39.
    of Four Masters, 51.
    of Tighernach, 39.
    of Inis MacNerinn, 39.
    of Clonmacnois, 60n.
  Speckled, 37.
  Cuilmenn, 40.
  Saltair of Tara, 39—when written 40.
    of Uachongbhail, 39.
  Cin Droma Snechta, 39—when compiled, 43.
  Saltair of Cashel, 39—when compiled, 44.
  Saltair of Cormac, 41.
    of St. Mochta, 44.
    of Cuana, 44.
    of Dubhdaleithe, 44.
  Saltair of Temair, 43.
  Saltair-na-Rann, 41.
    of Leabhar buidhe Sláine, 44.
    of Leabhar na h-Uidhre, 44.
    of Eochaidh O'Flannagain, 44.
    of Inis an Duin, 44.
  Short, of St. Buithe's Monastery, 44.
    of Flann of St. Buithe's Monastery, 44.
    of Flann of Dungeimhin (Dungiven, co. Derry), 44.
    of Dun da Leth Ghlas (Downpatrick), 44.
    of Doiré (Derry), 44.
    of Sabhall Phatraic (co. Down), 44.
    of Uachongbhail (Navan), 44.
  Leabhar dubh Molaga, 44.
  Leabhar buidhe Moling, 44.
  Leabhar buidhe Mhic Murchadha, 44.
  Leabhar Arda Macha, 44.
  Leabhar ruadh Mhic Aedhagain, 44.
  Leabhar breac Mhic Aedhagain, 44.
    of O'Scoba of Cluain Mhic Nois (or Clonmacnois), 44.
    of Leabhar fada Leithghlinne, 44.

Book of Invasions, 54.
of Duil Droma Ceata, 44.
of Clonsost, (Queen's county), 44.
of Trias Thaumaturgas, 52.
of Hispania Illustrata, 70.
of Acaill, 104.
of Armagh, 109.
of Rights, 253n.
Boromean Tribute, the origin of, 98—remitted, 185.
Boulter, Dr., 581.
Bran Dubh, bravery and stratagem of, 168.
Bravery of the Dalcassians, 218.
Breas, the warrior, 62.
Brehon laws, 147—by whom compiled, 144.
Brendan, St., and his voyages, 169.
Brian Boroimhé, 205—avenges the death of Mahoun, 207—deposes Malachy, 209—his wife, 211—his death, 217—romantic ballad of the lady, 209—originator of surnames, 210n.
Brigid, St., her birthplace, 131.
Briton, origin of name, 60.
Brodir, the apostate Dane, 212—kills Brian Boroimhé, 217.
Browne, Dr., 395.
Bruce, invasion of, 350.
Bruce's, Edward, campaign, 342—his death, 345.
Brunehalt, Queen, 173.
Burke, MacWilliam, 299—head of the Burke family in Ireland, 299.
Burke, MacWilliam, 326 — wars of, with the FitzGeralds, 326—defeat of, by O'Connor, 328.
Burke, celebrated statesman of 18th century, 593—his school days, 594—his hatred of oppression, 595—his marriage, 596—becomes secretary, 597—his maiden speech, 598—on Indian policy, 604.
Burkes and Geraldines, 333.
Burgat, Dr., his Brevis Relatio, 518n.
Burgo, Richard de, 309.
Burnt Njal, quotations from, 217.
Butlers, the, their history, 354.

C.

Cæsar, his accounts of the Druids, 138.
Cairbré, Satire of, 63.
Cairbré, Cinn-Cait, 97.
Cairbrés, the three, 102.
Caligraphy, Irish skilled in, 185.

Callaghan of Cashel, 196.
Cambridge, treatise on origin of, 71.
Camden on Ogygia, 72.
Cannibalism, charge of, refuted, 74.
Cannon-balls first used, 381n.
Canons, St. Patrick's, 117.
Carew's, Sir P., claim, 428.
Carhampton, Lord, cruelties of, 617n.
Carmelite monasteries, 323.
Cashel, the Saltair of, 44.
the Synod of, 275.
massacre at, 496.
Castlehaven Memoirs, 482n.
Casts for celts, 246.
Cataldus, St., 178.
Catalogue of lost books, 44.
Cathair Crofinn, a circular fort, 165.
Cathal Carragh, 296.
Cathal Crovderg, 296.
Catholic Emancipation, 647.
worship publicly restored, 411.
Association, 583.
priests, their peculiar position and difficulties, 586.
question, a ministerial difficulty, 639.
delegates met in Dublin, 615.
Catholics, Orangemen bribed to persecute, 616n—penal laws against, 576.
Cauldrons as tribute, 241.
Cavalry, 309n.
Ceann Cruach, great ancient idol of the Irish, 121.
Ceasair, taking of Erinn by, 54—landing in Ireland of, 57.
Celedabhaill, his quatrains, 198.
Celestine, Pope, sends St. Patrick to Ireland, 115.
Celsus, St., 227—when buried, 227.
Celtic language, antiquity of, 147—remains of, 46.
Celtic literature, 37.
Celtic and Roman history, 81.
Celts, description of, 160.
Chariots used in Ireland, 167.
Charlemont, Earl of, his life, 607.
Charles I., reign of, 473—his "faith," 475.
Charles II., reign of, 520—his treatment of the loyalists, 521.
Chesterfield and Adam Smith on Ireland, 603.
Chichester, Sir John, 580.
Chichester's Parliament, 471.
Chieftains, Irish, 303.
Child, interment of a, 157n.

Christ, the age of, 94.
Christian missions, 108.
Christianity, introduction of, 112.
Chronicle of Cormac MacCullinan, 41.
    of Aengus Ceilé Dé, 41.
    of Richard of Cirencester, 139.
Chronicum Scotorum, 58—compiled
    by, 50—account in, 57—on Par-
    tholan's landing in Ireland, 58.
Chronology, difficulties of, 44—Irish,
    80.
Cin Droma Snechta, 39—quotations
    from, 43—on Irish immigration,
    58.
Circular forts, 165.
Cistercians, Order of, 316.
Cities and Cemeteries of Etruria, 155.
Clanrickarde, Earl of, 356.
Clare, Lord, on Irish cultivation, 638.
Clare election, the, 649.
Clarence, Duke of, 371.
Clergy, state of the Catholic, in the
    reign of Elizabeth, 426.
Clonmacnois, the Annals of, 60n.
Clubs in the seventeenth century, 545
Clynn, the annalist, 319.
Cobhthach Cael, 90.
Codex, containing Venerable Bede's
    works, 47.
Coigley, Father, arrested and hanged,
    624.
Colgan, his labours, 52—mention of,
    534.
College of Physicians, establishment
    of, in Dublin, 543.
Colleges, continental, established for
    Irish students, 535.
Colonists—Scythians, Greeks, 68.
Colonization, proofs of our early, 55—
    the last, 75.
Columba, St., and the Bards, 168.
Columbanus, St., his rule, 173—on
    papal supremacy, 176.
Commercial status of Irish towns, 540.
Comyn, John, Archbishop of Dublin,
    291—his imprisonment, 295.
Conchessa, 112.
Confessions, St. Patrick's, 113.
Conairé II., 103—collects laws, 104.
Conn of the Hundred Battles, 101.
Conn's half of Ireland, 102.
Connaught, ancient, 64—massacre in,
    297—three claimants for, 307—
    rising of the men, 323—plantation
    of, 475.
Conor Mac Nessa, legend of, 127—
    death of, 128.

Controversy, theological, of the
    "Three Chapters," 175.
Cooke, Mr., publishes a pamphlet, 631.
Coote's cruelties, 482.
Cork Militia, cruelties of the, 626.
Cormac, author of Saltair of Tara, 104.
Council at Tara, 172.
Courcy, John de, in Ulster, 286—his
    valour, 286—his defeat in An-
    trim, 288—his death, 298.
Craftiné, the poet, 91.
Crannoges, 159.
Cranmer, Archbishop, 410.
Cremation not usual in Erinn, 155.
Crom Chonaill, the, 162.
Cromlechs, 155—in the Phœnix Park,
    161.
Cromwell arrives in Ireland, 500—
    marches to Drogheda, 500—mas-
    sacre at Drogheda, 501—letters,
    502—his cruelties, 503—brutality
    of his soldiers, 503—his massacre
    at Wexford, 503.
Cromwellian settlement in Ireland,
    512n.
Crovderg, Hugh, 307—his death, 308.
Cruelties of English officers, 417.
Crystède, his account of Ireland, 363.
Cuilmenn, the, 40.
Culdees, the, 182—question on the,
    179n.
Curia Regis, held at Lismore, 273.
Curragh of Kildare, 255.
Curran, his life, 606.
Cusack, Sir Thomas, 409—favours
    O'Neill, 421.
Custom-house built, 638.

                        D.

Dá Derga, destruction of the court of,
    91.
Dagges, 413n.
Dalriada, the Irish, 131.
Danes, Malachy's exploits against the,
    207—in Ireland, 204—cruelties of
    the, 190—divided into Black and
    White Gentiles, 191—found sea-
    port towns, 200—supposed con-
    version of, 204—pipes, 241—the
    Dalcassians fight the, 205.
Danish fortress in Dublin, 278n—the
    first invasion, 188—attempted
    second invasion, 224—pirates,
    first raid of the, 188—valour,
    battle of Clontarf, 215.
Dante, 385.

D'Alton on the Round Towers, 153—
  on History, Religion, &c., of An-
  cient Ireland, 68n.
Dathi, 107.
Defective Titles, Commission of, 475.
Derry, siege of, 558.
Dervorgil, the Lady, 234.
Desmond, Earls of, their ancestors
  and descendants, 282n.
  Castle, 221.
  Earl of, his witty reply, 384.
Destruction of the idols, 121.
Details of the atrocities of the military,
  621.
Diarmaid, Princess, pursuit of, 106.
Diarmaid's reign, misfortunes of, 167.
Dicho, St. Patrick's first convert, 116.
Dinnseanchus, a topographical work,
  164.
Dog, story of a faithful, 571.
Domhnach, Gaedhilic term for Sunday,
  121.
Domhnach Airgid, 134n.
Dominican Order in Ireland, 318.
Donatus, St., 178.
Doneraile Conspiracy, 643.
Dowdall, Dr., opposition of, 410.
Downpatrick, battle of, 325.
Drapier's Letters, the, 581.
Dress of the poorer classes in Ireland
  in seventeenth century, 552.
Drink of the ancient Irish, 243.
Drinking vessels of different kinds,
  243.
Druids and their teaching, 137.
Drumceat, first convention held at,
  167.
Drury, his cruelties, 443—his death,
  443.
Dubhdaleithe, Book of, 44.
Dublin in the seventeenth century,
  544.
Dublin, fashionable and prosperous,
  638.
Dubtach salutes St. Patrick at Tara,
  121.
Duke of Clarence, Viceroy, 371.
Duke of York, viceroyalty of, 375.
Dunboy, siege of, 460.
Duncheadh, St., 221.
Dundalk, battle of, 201.

E.

Early missionaries, 108.
Eber, 84.
Ecclesiastics, cruelties practised on, 452.

Ecclesiastical property, confiscation of,
  403.
Edward I., reign of, 329.
Elizabeth, Queen, accession of, 412—
  martyrs in the reign of, 416.
Emania, Palace of, 89.
Embargo laws, 578.
Emmet's career, 640.
Enda, St., 169.
English, invasion of the, 257.
  come to Ireland for instruction,
    178.
  quarrels of, barons, 300.
  law refused to Ireland, 362.
  writers, mistakes of, 361.
  schism, real cause of, 394.
  Irish emigrants defeat the, 584.
Enniskilleners, cruelties of the, 559.
Eras, three, in Irish history, 387.
Eremon, reign of, 77—his death, 78—
  families descended from, 84.
Eric, or compensation for murder,
  · 146.
Erinn, St. Patrick's mission to, 112.
  ancient chronicles of, 48n.
  pre-Noahacian colonization of, 55.
  takings of, 57.
  early geographical accounts of, 72.
  social accounts of, 73.
  ancient laws of, 144.
  religion of, 137.
  customs of, 139.
  language of, 147.
  antiquities of, 153.
  five great roads of ancient, 101.
Essex, Earl of, tries to colonize Ulster, 432—his interview with
  O'Neill, 456—his death, 433.
Ethnea, Princess, 123.
Eva, her marriage with Strongbow,
  264.
Exchequer of the King of England in
  Dublin, fourteenth century, 339.
Exiled Irishmen, 478.

F.

Fairs, Irish, seventeenth century, 538.
Falkland, Lord, suspected of favour-
  ing the Catholics, 473.
Fauna, description of, 253.
Fené-men, the, 42n.
Fenian poems and tales, 87—ascribed
  to, 105.
Fes, or triennial assembly, 163.
Fethlimia, Princess, 122.
Fiacc's Hymn, Scholiast on, 111.

Fidh Aengussa, the Synod of, 227.
Fifth taking of Ireland, 62.
Fiacre, St., 177.
Finnachta Fleadhach, the Hospitable, 171.
Finnen, St., 162.
Fintan, son of Bochra, the Irish historian, 40.
Firbolg chiefs, division of Ireland by, 60—battles of, 62.
Fish in Ireland, 80n—anecdote on, 72n.
FitzAldelm, his viceroyalty, 285—his death, 299.
FitzGerald, war between De Burgo and, 326.
FitzGerald, war between De Vesci and, 333.
FitzGerald, Lord Edward, joins the United Irishmen, 618—arrest of, 624—his death, 624.
Fithil, the poet, 40.
FitzMaurice obtains foreign aid, 441—his death, 443.
FitzStephen, 260.
FitzWilliam, Earl, viceroyalty, of 616.
Flahertach, Abbot, and King of Munster, 194.
Flann, his Synchronisms, 49—synchronizes the chiefs and monarchs with the kings of Erinn, 50.
Flann, King, his reign, 192.
Flint used to make weapons of defence, 160.
Flood, his life, 607.
Flora, description of, 253.
Foillan, St., 177.
Fomorians, the, 60-64.
Food of the ancient Irish, 241—of poorer classes in seventeenth century, 553.
Ford of the Biscuits, battle of, 451.
Fothadh of the Canons, 180.
Franciscan Order in Ireland, 319—their patriotism, 344—their convents, 312—remarkable spring, 319—persecution of, 474.
Friars Preachers, Order of, 318.
Fridolin, St., 178.
Froude's History of England, quotations from his account of the English clergy, 440.
Fursey, St., 177.

G.

Gall, St., 177.
Galls, description of, 187n.

Gallic Church, labours of the Irish in, 177.
Gaul, the Celts of, 73.
Irish saints venerated in, 183.
Géisill, battle of, 78n.
Genealogies, differences between, and pedigrees, 80-82.
Milesian, 79.
peculiar historical value of, 80.
and pedigrees, 51.
General Assembly at Kilkenny, 485.
Geographical accounts of Ireland, 72.
George I., 582.
Geraldines, rising of, 1534, 390—ancestor of the, 333 — their wars, 334—defeated at Kenmare, 325.
Germanus, St., his Canons, 117.
Gertrude, St., daughter of King Pepin, 177.
Gherardini, letter from the, 384.
Gilla Caemhain, an Irish writer, 49—gives annals of all times, 49.
Ginkell, General, 568.
Glundubh, Nial, lamentation for, 196.
Gold ornaments, 157.
Goldsmith, his life, 609.
Gordon's, Mr., account of the atrocities of the military, 628, 629.
Gormgal, St., 221.
Gormflaith, Brian Boroimhé's wife, 210.
Gospels, the, used by St. Patrick, 134.
Graces, the, 474.
Grammatica Celtica, 46.
Granard and Staigue, 237.
Grattan's demand for Irish independence, 590—his life, 607—entrance into the Imperial Parliament, 640.
Grainné, pursuit of, and Diarmaid, 106.
Greeks said to have visited Ireland, 139.
Grey, Lord, desecrates churches, 133.
Grey, John de, 301.
Guaire, his hostility to St. Columba, 167.

H.

Harp, when first used as an emblem, 249.
Haverty's History of Ireland, 221n.
Henry II. lands in Ireland, 270—produces the Bull, 274—makes his son Lord of Ireland, 287—holds a synod at Cashel, 273—his palace, 272.

Henry IV., his reign, 368—his death, 294.
Henry V., 369.
Henry VI., Wars of the Roses, 371.
Henry VII., 379.
Henry VIII., 387—persecutions during the reign of, 401—Dr. Browne's letter to, 399.
Herodotus, quotations from, 69.
Hibernia, the first buried in, 57.
Himantiliginos, game of, 141.
Himerus and Iberus, 70.
Hispania Illustrata, 70.
Historians of Erinn, 40.
Historians of the seventeenth century, 531.
Historic Tales, 86.
Historical value of genealogies, 80, 87.
History, Ecclesiastical, 227.
History of the Exile, 91.
Hoggen's Butt, and Le Hogges, 272.
Holy wells not superstitious, 143.
Honorius III., 305.
Howth family founded, 298n.
Hua Alta, race of, 125.
Hy-Figeinte (Munster), 125.
Hy-Kinsallagh (co. Carlow), 125.
Hymn of St. Fiacc, 117.
  of St. Patrick, 120.
Hy-Nials, contention between the, 223 —palace of, 224—the northern, 192—divided into two clans, 204.

I

Idols, worship of, 88.
Immoralities of the reformed clergy, 404.
Imperial standard, 639.
Inchiquin, 488—massacre at Cashel by, 496.
Innocent I., 100.
Innocent X., 490.
Insult to the Irish peeresses, 608.
Insurrection in Wexford, 626.
  in Ulster, 629.
Ireland, climate of, 80.
  colonization of, 57.
  article on, in Rees' Cyclopædia, 67.
  last colonization of, 75.
  ancient laws of, 144.
  antiquarian remains in, 153.
  first mill in, 165.
  fauna and flora of, 253.
  literary ladies in, 374.
  persecutions in, 388.

Ireland, ecclesiastical property forfeited in, 403.
  plantations attempted in, 429, 432.
  social life in, seventeenth century, 529.
  before the Union, and after, 637.
  early geographical account of, 72.
  early social account of, 73.
  Bede's account of, 79.
  the Romans feared to invade, 95.
  Saxon invasion of, 185.
  first Danish invasion of, 188—second invasion, 224.
  the circuit of, 197.
  Murtough's circuit of, 224.
  Spenser's account of, 439.
  division of, by the Firbolg chiefs, 60.
  receives the faith generously, 111.
  given the name of Hibernia, 70.
  the first writer who names, 71.
  called Iernis, 71.
Ireton's cruelties and miserable death, 507.
Irish genealogies, their rise, 85.
  keen, 141.
  painters, 608.
  musicians, 608.
  MSS., 45.
  authors, 608.
  actors, 608.
  missionaries, 173.
  missionary saints, 178.
  poetry, 180.
  poets, 605.
  bishops at the Council of Lateran, 289.
  war-cries forbidden, 383.
  pedigrees, their importance, 81.
  people transplanted as slaves to Barbadoes, 514.
  chronology compared with Roman, 81.
  schools and scholars, 183.
  alphabet, 152.
  butter and cheese, 246.
  fireplace, 247.
  clothing, 250.
  priests, their devotion to the people, 587.
  communications with Rome, 490.
  old, the, and the new English, 491.
  priests, their peculiar position, 586.
  history, materials for, 39.
  martyr, the first, 125.
  saints, 167.
  religious, 221.

Irish king sent to the Isle of Man, 225.
Rinuccini's account of the, 491.
Catholic landowners, injustice towards, 509.
Brigade, formation of, 574.
Irishmen, celebrated, of the eighteenth century, 592.
Iron Duke, 639.
Island Magee, massacre of, 481.
Ita, St., 169.

J.

Jackson, Rev. William, his miserable death, 616.
James I., his reign, 463.
James II., his reign, 555—arrival in Ireland, 557.
Japhet, Milesians descended from, 84.
Jerome's, St., statement on Ireland, 74.
John of the Shamrocks, 434.
John, Prince, receives title of King of Ireland, 287—his visit to Ireland, 292—second visit to Ireland, 302—succeeds to the English crown, 296—starves a bishop to death, 301—letter of Innocent III. to, 295—death, 304.
Josephus, 68.
Judgment of a king, 103.

K.

Kadlubeck, historian of Poland, 48.
Keating, the historian, 531.
  on Erinn, 43n.
  quotations from, on the division of Ireland, 60.
  on descent from the Scythians, 68.
  on the battle of Bealagh Mughna, 193.
  books referred to by, 45.
  on colour, as a distinction of rank, 89n.
  on battle of Dundalk, 203.
  burial-place, 532.
  inscription in honour of, 533.
Kennedy, Prince of Munster, 202.
Kildare, Earl of, and Henry VII., 384.
  accused of treason, 384.
  last Catholic Earl of, 387.
  letter of, 388.
Kildare, Monastery of, 132.
Kilian, St., 177.
Kincora, Brian's "Happy Family" at, 209—destruction of, 226.
Knights of the Royal Branch, 125.
Kunrann the poet, 187.

L.

Lacy, De, made Viceroy of Ireland, 289—endeavours to become King of Ireland, 291—cruel death, 293—family become extinct, 311.
Lady physicians, 66.
Laeghairé, King, holds a pagan festival, 119—receives St. Patrick at Tara, 120—his oath, 129—his death, 129—his burial, 129n.
Lammas-day, 164.
Landing of the Picts, 79.
  of Partholan, 58.
  of Ceasair, 57.
Lanfranc, Archbishop of Canterbury, 228.
Langton, Stephen, Archbishop of Canterbury, 301.
Language of ancient Erinn, 147—writing in pre-Christian Erinn, 148—Ogham writing, 150.
Laws, the Brehon code of, 144—its peculiarities, 145.
  of the Innocents, 172.
  of succession, 146.
  of ancient Erinn, 144.
Leix, St. Patrick's visit to, 124—cruelties of the deputy of, 417.
Lewis, Sir G. C., 85n.
Lhind, quotations from, 95n.
Lia Fail, 76—or Stone of Destiny, 165—mention of, 165.
Life, social, previous to the English invasion, 237.
Limerick, siege of, by Ireton, 506—by William of Orange, 566—by Ginkell, 571.
Linen trade, 251, 540.
Literary ladies in Ireland, 374
Literary men of the seventeenth century, 531.
Livin, St., 178.
Londres, Henry de, made Governor of Ireland, 306—surnamed Scorch Villain, 306.
Louvain collection, 46—friars, 52.
Loyola, St. Ignatius, 120n.
Lucas, his life, 607.

M.

Macaille, St., 131.
MacArt's, Cormac, Saltair, 40—his reign, 103—his death, 105.
Macaulay, Lays of Ancient Rome, 247n.

Maccallin, St., 221.

MacCarthy, King of Desmond, 229.

MacCarthy More murdered at Tralee, 357.

MacCullinan, Cormac, priest and king, 192—his reign, 193—his death, 193n.

MacCumhaill, Finn, 105—his courtship with the Princess Ailbhe, 105.

MacFirbis, quotations from, 54, 58—his book on pedigrees, 85—his pedigrees of the ancient Irish and Anglo-Norman families, 50—murdered, 51.

MacGilluire, Coarb of St. Patrick, 315.

MacLiag, the poet, 210n.

MacMurrough, Dermod, King of Leinster, 233—attends synod at Mellifont, 234—his interview with Henry II., 258—Henry grants him letters-patent, 259—his death, 266.

MacMurrough, Art, 367—his death, 370.

MacNally, advocate of the United Irishmen, 618.

Macutenius on St. Patrick's Canons, 118.

Maelmuire, "servant of Mary," 227n.

Maelruain, St., of Tallaght, 179.

Magna Charta, 305.

Magog and his colony, 68—his descendants, 84.

Magrath, Miler, the apostate, 78.

Mahoun, brother to Brian, 204—is murdered, 206.

Mailduf, St., 178.

Malachy, St., 229—visits Rome, 231—death of, 231.

Malachy II., 198—exploits against the Danes, 208—wins his "collar of gold," 208—Brian deposes, 209—his death, 218.

Manners and Customs of Ancient Greece, 141.

Marco Polo, 46.

Marisco, De, his treachery, 311—his death, 312.

Mary, Queen, 410.

Massacre of a prelate, priest, and friars, 402—of a bishop, 466—at Wexford-bridge, 628—at Cashel, 496—at Wexford, 503—of three priests, 445—of three Franciscans, 453—at Drogheda, 501—at Mullamast, 438—at Fort del Ore, 444—at Scullabogue House, 627.

Mellifont, Abbey of, 231—Synod at, 234—founded, 317.

Meloughlin, King of Meath, 191.

Metalogicus, the, of John of Salisbury, 275n.

Milcho, St. Patrick's master in captivity, 116.

Milesian genealogies, 84, 88.

Milesians, landing of the, 75—they conquer, 77.

Milford Haven, 292.

Milidh, fleet of the sons of, entrance into Ireland, 75.

Mississippi Scheme, 584.

Mochta, St., 151.

Moira, Lord, exposes the cruelty of the yeomanry, 619.

Moling, St., 109.

Monastery of Kildare, St. Brigid's, 132.

 Kilcrea, 321.

 of Bobbio, 176.

 of Timoleague, 321.

 of Tallaght, 179.

 of St. Columbkille, 293.

 of Cluain Eidhneach, 179.

 of Donegal, 321—desolation and plunder of, 189.

 of Clonbroney, 188n.

 of St. Columba, 230, 234.

 of Ibrach (Ivragh), Kerry, 230.

 of Lismore, 226.

 of St. Kevin, 235.

 of Dunbrody, 289.

 of St. Peter's of Lemene, near Chambery, 381.

 of Clonfert, 170.

 of Mellifont, 234.

 of Clonmacnois, 221.

 Irrelagh (Muckross), 322.

 Clonmel, 322.

 Drogheda, 322.

 Cill-Achaidh, 374.

Montgomery, 584.

Montmarisco, 237—becomes a monk, 289

Monroe, 493.

Monroe, Henry, 629.

Moore, his History, 37—his partiality for Malachy, 209—on religion, 111—his life, 605.

Morann the good, and his collar of gold, 97.

MSS. preserved in Trinity College, 44.

 of ancient Irish history, 39n.

 Celtic, preserved in Belgium, 45.

 Continental, 45n.

 in British Museum, 46.

 Stowe collection of, 45n.

MSS., Latin, 46.
　Loftus, 415.
　Burgundian, 46.
　legendary and historical, of Irish
　　history, 39.
Muckross Abbey, 322.
Muircheartach, first Christian king of
　Ireland, 131.
Muircheartach, his circuit of Ireland,
　197—killed by Blacaire, 197.
Murphy, Father, killed, 628.
Murrough's game of chess, 211.
Murtough of the Leathern Cloaks, 196.

N.

Neamhnach, the well, 164.
Napier's, Lady, letter respecting the
　tenantry of Duke of Leinster, 623.
Nathi, King, 116.
National joy at the restoration of
　Catholic worship, 464.
Nemedh, arrival of, 59.
Nemenians, emigration of, 60, 62.
Nemthur, St. Patrick's birthplace, 110.
Nennius, 69.
Nesta, her beauty and infamy, 259.
Nestor, 48.
Netterville, John, Archbishop of Ar-
　magh, 318.
Newspapers in seventeenth century,
　545.
Newtownbutler, engagement at, 595.
Nial of the Nine Hostages, 106.
Nial Black Knee, 194.
Nicholas, St., College of, 51.
Niebuhr, his theory of history, 82.
　on the story of Tarpeia, 82n.
　on learning by verse, 86.
Noah, genealogies from, 58.
Normans, their arrival in Ireland, 257.
　their luxurious habits, 272.
　Cambrensis' account of them, 277.
　the, ridicule the Irish nobles, 293.
　feuds of the, in Ireland, 300.
　their treachery, 311.
　Viceroys, 285.
Nuada of the Silver Hand, 61—his
　privy council, 64.
Numa Pompilius, 89.

O.

O'Brien, Turlough, Monarch of Ire-
　land, 222—his death, 223.
O'Brien, Donnell, King of Thomond,
　271.

O'Briens, from whom descended, 84.
O'Clery, Michael, one of the Four
　Masters, 52—his literary labours
　and piety, 54—his first work, Trias
　Thaumaturgas, 52—rewrote the
　Book of Invasions, 54—patronized
　by Fearghal O'Gara, 53.
O'Connell, Daniel, in the House of
　Parliament, 647—obtains Catholic
　Emancipation, 647—represented
　Ireland, 641—his life, 642—his
　maiden speech, 643—Doneraile
　Conspiracy, 643.
O'Curry, when Moore visited, 37—his
　opinion of early Irish civilization,
　104—his labours, 38—on Erinn,
　48n—on Keating's statement of
　Irish descent, 68—on Cormac's
　writings, 104n—on the Bachall
　Isu, 115—on Brehon Laws, 145—
　on Irish saints, 178—on musical
　instruments, 250—on Irish mar-
　tyrs, 416.
O'Connor, Hugh, 308.
　Felim, 309, 313.
　of Offaly, 339.
　Roderic, 235.
　expelled from Offaly, 408—returns
　　to Ireland, 411.
　Margaret, a literary lady, 374.
　Nuala, 321—establishes the monas-
　　tery of Franciscans at Donegal,
　　321—her death, 322.
　Arthur, 624.
O'Connor Faly, Margaret, visits Eng-
　land, 411.
O'Daly, the poet, 303.
O'Donnell, Hugh, entertainment of, at
　Windsor, 387.
O'Donnell, Hugh Roe, his treacherous
　capture, 447—leaves Ireland, 459.
O'Donnell More, died at Assaroe, 313.
O'Donovan, Dr., quotations from, on
　Brehon laws, 144.
Odran, St., 147.
O'Duffy, Catholicus, 304.
O'Duffy, Donnell, 233.
O'Flaherty, his Chronology, 81.
Ogham writing, 149.
Oghma, Danann prince, invented the
　writing called Ogham Craove, 76.
Ogygia of the Greeks, 72.
Ogygia, account in, of ancient writings,
　148n.
O'Hagan, the Abbot Imar, 229.
O'Hartigan, Kenneth, 221.
O'Hurly, Dr., 453.

Ollamh Fodhla, 89.
Ollamh, office and qualifications of a, 83, 86.
O'Loughlin, Donnell, 226.
O'Loughlins of Tyrone, 231.
O'More, Rory Oge, 437
Roger, 480.
O'Neill, Donough, 207
O'Neill, Shane, 409—feared by the English, 418—attempts to poison him, 419—Lord Chancellor Cusack persuades him to forget the poisoning, 420—he is killed treacherously, 422.
O'Neill, Hugh, marriage of, 450—his insurrection, 454—defeats Bagnal, 455—his interview with Essex, 456—attempts to assassinate him, 458—his power decreases, 461—plot to entrap him, 468—his flight and death in Rome, 469.
O'Neill, Sir Phelim, 480—marches against Monroe, 493.
O'Neill, Owen Roe, 480.
O'Neill, Hugh Boy, slain in 1283, 332.
O'Neill, Donnell, 198.
Ormonde, the Duke of, 483—his intrigues, 492.
Orpheus, first writer who mention Ireland, 71.
Orr, Mr., his trial and death, 620.
O'Toole, St. Laurence, Archbishop of Dublin, 234—his genealogy, 235—Abbot of St. Kevin's monastery, at Glendalough, 235—his patriotism, 267—his journey to France, 290—sent as ambassador to Henry II., 281—his death, 290.
Oirdnidhe, Hugh, the legislator, 179.

P.

Palatines, the, 580.
Palladius, St., mission of, 109.
Palliums, 231.
Partholan, landing of, 58.
Partholyan, English traditions of, 71.
Patrick, St., his birthplace, 112—visits Tara, 120—his successful preaching, 123—relic of his hand, 134—his copy of the Gospels, 134—his burial-place, 133—devotion of his servant, 125—his death, 126—his vision, 113—his prayer for Ireland, 135—destruction of the idols, 121—his Hymn, 120—his captivity, 113.

Peep-o'-Day Boys and Defenders, 613.
Pelasgian remains, 158.
Pembroke, Earl of, plots against, 311.
Penal Laws, enactment of, 576.
Perrot, Sir John, 417.
Petrie, Dr., quotations from, on Brehon laws, 115.
Petty, Sir William, 541.
Philosophical Society, the Dublin, 546.
Phœnician colonization of Spain, 70—circumnavigation of Africa, 69.
Physicians, establishment of their college in Dublin, 543.
Picts, landing of the, 79.
Pitt, William, 613.
Plantation of Connaught, 510 — of Ulster, 469.
Plowden's account of the atrocities of the military, 602.
Plunkett, Dr., his trial and execution, 528.
Plunkett, Lord, in parliament, 640.
Poyning's Parliament, 379—law, and its effects, 382.
Presentation Order, 593n.
Priests, cruel massacre of, 496—their efforts to save Protestants, 483.
Protestant Church, state of, 425.

Q.

Quipus used as a register by the Indians, 150.

R.

Ráith Beóthaigh (Rath Beagh), an ancient burial-place, 78.
Raleigh, Sir Walter, 439.
Rath at Leighlin, 200—of the Synods, 165.
Reformation, attempts to introduce the, 415.
Reformed clergy, preaching of, 405.
Religious houses and their founders, 316.
Remonstrance to the Holy See, 341.
Reports on the state of Ireland, 648
Richard I., accession of, 294.
Richard II. visits Ireland, 365.
Rinuccini, 489n—lands at Kenmare, 490—reception in Kilkenny, 491—returns to Italy, 497.
Rock of Cashel, 193.
Rodanus, St., 162.
Romantic Tales, 91.
Rose Tavern, 544.
Rotundo built, 638.

Round Tower controversy, 153.
Rowan, A. Hamilton, 615
Rufus, William, boast of, 257.

S.

Sacramental test, 579.
Saltair of Temair, 41.
　　na-Rann, 41.
　　of Cashel, 44.
　　of Cormac, 41.
San José, arrival of, 443.
Saviour's, St.. Dublin, 318.
Schomberg's camp, disease in, 560.
Scots, 69.
Scraball, 164.
Scythian colonists, 68—Irish claim
　　descent from, 65.
Seanchaidhé, poet, 83n.
Seanchus Mor, language of, 145—
　　translator of, 145.
Sedulus, St., 178.
Segetius, priest, 115.
Senchan Torpéist, 40.
Severe winters and pestilences in Ire-
　　land, 223.
Sheehy, Father Nicholas, judicial mur-
　　der of, 589.
Sheridan, his life, 608.
Shrines of the three saints, 133.
Sidney's official account of Ireland,
　　423—his interview with Granu-
　　aile, 434.
Silken Thomas, his rebellion, 391—his
　　execution, 392.
Silver shields, 89.
Simnel crowned in Dublin, 380.
Simon, Rabbi, 68.
Sitric, arrival of, 195—treachery of, 201.
Smith, Adam, on Ireland, 603.
Smithfield, origin of the name, 241n.
South Sea Bubble, 581.
Spenser's Castle, 423—grandson, 513—
　　description of Irish misery, 439.
Sreng, warrior, 62.
Statements in our annals confirmed by
　　a Jewish writer, 68.
Statute of Kilkenny and its effects, 359.
Stierman, 48.
Sterne, Dr., 544.
Strafford, Earl of, 77.
Strongbow, Earl of Clare, arrives in
　　Ireland, 263—genealogy, 263—
　　marriage of, and Eva. 264—pro-
　　claims himself king of Leinster,
　　266—returns to England. 268—
　　death of, 282—his seal, 284.
Succession, law of. 146.

Superstitions, Irish, 142.
Swan, Major, 624.
Swift, Dean, 581—his writings, 581—
　　his life, 607.
Swords and chariots of ancient Ire-
　　land, 167.

T.

Tacitus, 95.
Táin bó Chuailgné, the expedition of,
　　92—the story of, 93.
Talbot, Archbishop, 525.
Tanaiste, 147.
Tandy, Napper, 612.
Tara, account of ancient, 163—site of,
　　41—cursing of, 162.
Taverns and coffee-houses, 544.
Theatre, the first, in Dublin, 547.
Thomas, St., of Canterbury, 266.
Thompson, Charles, Secretary of Con-
　　gress, 601.
Threnodia Hiberno-Catholica, 511.
Tighernach's Annals, 49—uses the
　　dominical letter, 49—mentions
　　the lunar cycle, 49—quotes his-
　　torical writers, 49—his home, 48.
Tighearnmas, 88.
Timoleague, Monastery of, 321.
Tithes introduced into Ireland, 232.
Tom the Devil, 622.
Tone, Theobald Wolfe, 614.
Tradition, its use in history, 40.
Trias Thaumaturgas, 52.
Trinity College, foundation of, 462.
Tuatha Dé Dananns, fifth taking of
　　Ireland by, 61—their skill as arti-
　　ficers, 61—battles of, 62, 75—
　　dynasty passed away, 76.
Tuathal, reign of, 98.
Tuite, Richard (the great baron), 333.
Turgesius the Dane, 189.
Tussach, St., 126.

U.

Ugainé Môr, reign of, 90.
Ultan, St., 171.
Union, the, 632.
United Irishmen, the, 618.
Usher, Archbishop, 534—his indiffe-
　　rence about orders, 536—on St.
　　Patrick's Canons, 117—as an his-
　　torian, 534.
Usher's Island, 318n.

V.

Veto, the, 643.
Victoricus, 113n.

Vinegar Hill, the battle of, 627.
Volunteers, the, 591.
Virgilius, St., 178.
Vivian, Cardinal, 286—entombs the relics of the three saints anew, 294.

W.

Warbeck's plot, 381.
Ware, 415.
Ward, Father, 52.
Waterford rugs, 539.
Wellesley, Chief Secretary, 640.
Wesley, John, his remark about Moira House, 318n.
Wheat planted early, 243.
White and Black Gentiles, 191.
Whiteboys, the, 584.

Wilde, Sir W., 79n.
Wives purchased in Erinn, 43—exchanged, 229.
Words and Places, 58n.
Wood's halfpence, 581.
Wren, veneration for the, 140.

Y.

Yeomanry, fearful cruelties of the, 630.
York, house of, 371—Duke of, made Viceroy, 375.
Yorkists, popularity in Ireland, 376. insurrection of the, 378.
Youghal, foundation of Convent of, 318 — College of, 378 — burned down, 443.
Young's remedy for Irish disaffection, 585.